Using Microsoft® Word
For Windows

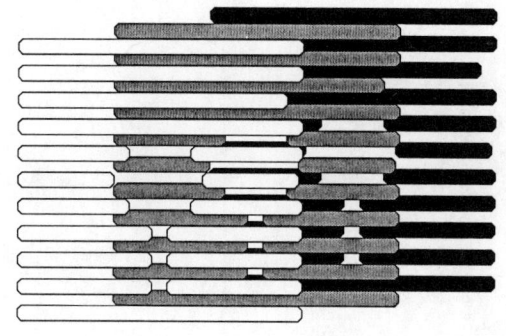

Using Microsoft® Word
For Windows

David Dean

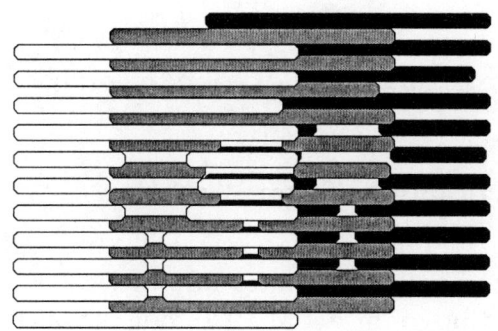

Osborne **McGraw-Hill**

Berkeley   New York   St. Louis   San Francisco
Auckland   Bogotá   Hamburg   London   Madrid
Mexico City   Milan   Montreal   New Delhi   Panama City
Paris   São Paulo   Singapore   Sydney
Tokyo   Toronto

Osborne **McGraw-Hill**
2600 Tenth Street
Berkeley, California 94710
U.S.A.

For information on translations and book distributors outside of
the U.S.A., please write to Osborne **McGraw-Hill** at the above
address.

A complete list of trademarks appears on page 579.

Using Microsoft® Word for Windows

   34567890 DOC 99876543210

ISBN 0-07-881498-7

To my parents, Barbara and Burton, for the love and support
they have given throughout all my endeavors

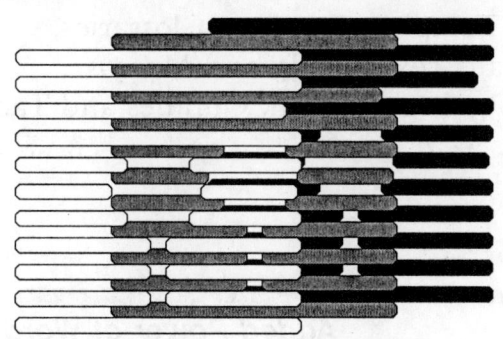

Contents at a Glance

Why This Book Is for You 1

PART I   **3**

Learning Word for Windows

1 Up and Running 5
2 Formatting Text.............................. 59
3 Cut and Paste: Adding Tables and Images 117
4 For the Record: Styles and Templates 163

5 Printing: Picture Perfect Output. 209

6 Advanced Template Features: Glossaries,
Boilerplate Text, Fields, and Macros. 249

7 Time Saving Organization: Outlines and Tables of
Contents. 303

PART II   353

Added Power of Word for Windows

8 Group Productions 355

9 Data Handling: Formulas, Equations, Indexing, and
File Importation. 381

PART III   421

Making the Most of Word for Windows

10 Desktop Publishing with Word for Windows. 423

11 Fine Tuning Windows. 473

PART IV   501

Appendixes

A How Much PC Do I Need? 503

B Peripheral Interests. 511

C Setting Up Word for Windows 519

D Supporting Software and Hardware 533

E Font Character Sets and Sources 549

F Journals, Books, and User Groups 569

Index. 583

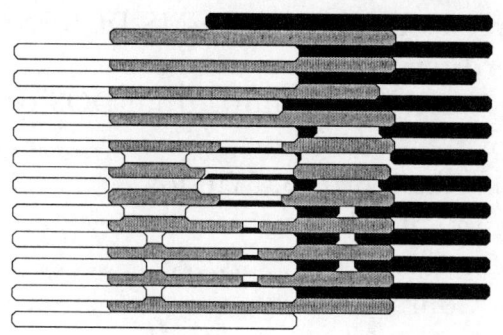

Contents

Introduction . . . . **xxv**
Who Should Use This Book xxvi
How This Book Is Organized xxvii
Conventions Used in This Book xxxi
Additional Help from Osborne/McGraw-Hill xxxii
Learn More About Microsoft Word xxxiv
Why This Book Is for You **1**

Part I
Learning Word
for Windows

1   **Up and Running** **5**
Running Word for Windows 7

Windows: A Graphical Interface   7
   CUA Screen Elements in the MS-DOS Executive . .   8
Opening Word for Windows   17
   Loading Word for Windows from DOS or from
   Windows   17
   The Mouse in Word for Windows   22
   The Document Window   25
Pull-Down Menus   26
   Program Control Menu   27
   Document Control Menu   30
   File Menu   32
   Edit Menu   35
   View Menu   38
   Insert Menu   40
   Format Menu   42
   Utilities Menu   43
   Macro Menu   45
   Window Menu   46
   Help Menu   47
   Overall Hierarchy of Commands   49
Dialog Box Operations   49
   Text Entry Fields   49
   Scroll-down Boxes   52
   Toggle Boxes and Buttons   55

2   **Formatting Text** **59**
When to Format?   60
The Format Command Family   61
   Accessing the Format Commands   62
   Word for Windows' Visual Orientation   63
   Keystroke Combinations   64

Mouse Versus Keyboard Formatting................. 65

Dialog Box Operations............................. 67

    Option Fields................................. 67

    Scroll-down Boxes............................. 69

    Toggle Boxes................................. 71

    Buttons...................................... 72

    An Option Selection Caveat................... 72

Formatting Blocks of Text......................... 74

Format Menu 75

Character Formatting 76

    Fonts.. 78

    Color.. 80

    Emphasis Options 81

    Points 83

    Position..................................... 84

    Character Spacing 85

Speed Character Formatting........................ 86

Paragraph Formatting.............................. 88

    Alignment.................................... 88

    Indents...................................... 90

    Style.. 91

    Keep Paragraph 93

    Spacing...................................... 95

    Border and Pattern 96

    Page Break Before............................ 97

    Line Numbering............................... 98

Speed Formatting................................. 100

Section Formatting............................... 100

    Frames Versus Sections 101

    Multicolumn Heads........................... 102

    Automatic Line Numbering.................... 103

    Layout...................................... 103

Columns. 104

Include Footnotes 105

Line Numbers. 105

Vertical Alignment. 107

Section Start 108

Document Formatting. 109

Paper Size/Tab Default. 109

Format Margins 110

Footnotes 111

Template 114

Widow Control 115

Set Default. 115

Summary 116

3   Cut and Paste: Adding Tables and Images **117**

The Clipboard. 117

Linking Data. 119

Importing Data Using the Clipboard 120

Creating a Table. 120

Format Table Options. 124

Moving Around in Tables 128

Using the Mouse 129

Using the Keyboard. 133

Deleting, Inserting, and Merging Cells. 134

Incorporating Tabular Data into a Table. 138

Importing an Image with the Clipboard 143

Inserting an Image File from Disk. 148

Cropping and Sizing Images. 151

Importing Spreadsheet Data from Microsoft Excel 154

4   For the Record: Styles and Templates **163**

Styles 164

Creating Styles 165

The Format Define Styles Dialog Box 165
Creating Your Own Styles 169
Templates 186
Why Create Document Templates? 186
Creating Document Templates 187
Using Templates 194
Format Styles 194
Using the Style Name Area 196
The Ruler 197
The Ribbon 202
The Ruler and Ribbon with Multiple Document
Windows 205

5   Printing: Picture Perfect Output **209**
Word for Windows Views......................... 211
Normal Editing View 212
Print Preview................................... 213
Page View 220
Draft View 221
Printer Installation and Setup................... 223
Installing More Than One Printer Driver 225
Printing to a File 226
Using the Control Panel....................... 227
Word for Windows Print Commands 235
Printer Setup 235
Print Merge 239
Print 240

**6   Advanced Template Features: Glossaries, Boilerplate
Text, Fields, and Macros** **249**
Glossaries...................................... 251
Creating Glossaries 251
Boilerplate Text 256

Fields.. 258

   Inserting Fields.................................. 259

   Using the Insert Field Dialog Box.............. 265

   Inserting Field Codes Manually 270

   Using the Field Codes Toggle Key 274

   Keeping Fields Up to Date 274

   Nesting Field Codes............................ 275

   Locking Fields................................. 276

Macros 276

   Auto Macros 278

   Macro Recorder 279

   Macro Run Command 281

   Assign to Key.................................. 282

   Assign to Menu................................ 284

   Macro Editor................................... 286

Creating an Interactive Print Merge Macro.......... 290

   Word for Windows Data Documents............ 290

   Interactive Print Merge Macro 293

7   Time Saving Organization: Outlines and Tables of Contents **303**

Outline Processing................................. 305

Outline View Buttons 306

   Promote Button 311

   Demote Button................................. 311

   Vertical Move Up Button....................... 312

   Vertical Move Down Button 312

   Demote to Body Text Button 312

   Expand Button.................................. 314

   Collapse Button 315

   Show Buttons 315

Outline View Tools 317

Moving Heads Manually.......................... 318
Numbering Heads 320
Sorting Text and Heads........................ 326
Alphanumeric, Numeric, and Date Sorting 326
Sorting in the Outline View.................... 330
Adding Footnotes.............................. 331
Line Numbering............................... 335
Generating a Table of Contents 339
Creating a Table of Contents in the
  Outline View................................ 339
Creating a Table of Contents in the Normal
  Editing View 344
Using TC Field Entries with the Insert Table of
  Contents Command.......................... 347
Using TC Field Entries with the TOC Field 348

Part II
Added Power of Word
for Windows

8 Group Productions **355**
Annotations 356
Preparing a Document for Annotation 357
Inserting Bookmarks........................... 357
Using Character, Word, and Page Counts........ 360
Locking a Document........................... 362
Unavailable Features in Locked Documents 363
Entering Annotations 363
Locating Bookmarks 366
Incorporating Annotations........................ 367
Using the Edit Go To Command................ 369

Comparing Revised and Original Documents......... 372
   Using Multiple Document Windows 372
   Using the Utilities Compare Versions Command.. 374
   Using the Utilities Revision Marks Command..... 376
Word for Windows on a Network 379

9   Data Handling: Formulas, Equations, Indexing, and
      File Importation **381**
Formulas and Equations......................... 383
   Using Formulas 383
   Using Equations 389
   Using the Utilities Calculate Command 394
Indices and Glossaries......................... 396
   Creating Index Entries........................ 397
   Using the Insert Index Command............... 400
Long Documents 403
   Spike Glossaries 405
File Importation.............................. 406
   Importing and Exporting Word Processed Files .. 406
   Importing Database and Spreadsheet Files 413
   Print Merge Form Letters 415
   Print Merge Address Labels................... 418
   Missing Fields 420

Part III
Making the Most of
Word for Windows

10   Desktop Publishing with Word for Windows **423**
Copy Preparation Tools 424
   Using the Utilities Spelling Command 424

Using the Utilities Thesaurus Command   430
Using the Utilities Hyphenate Command.   434
Images   438
    Paint: Bitmap Images   439
    Draw: Object Oriented Art.   442
    Importing Images into Word for Windows   444
Desktop Publishing Preformatting   445
    Special Marks   446
    Typeset Quality Printing and Service Bureaus   448
Layout Tools   450
Setting Type   451
    Leading.   451
    Letterspacing.   455
    Setting Off Text   457
Page Layout.   462
    Title Pages   463
    Headers and Footers.   465
    Columns.   469

11   Fine Tuning Windows   473
Editing WIN.INI   474
    WIN.INI Sections.   477
    Windows Print Spooler.   482
    Windows SMARTDrive Disk Cache   483
    Windows Dynamic Link Libraries: Format
        Conversions.   488
    Installing Screen Fonts   491
DDE Paste Link   492
Printing to a File   497
What Happens When Windows Freezes?   498

Part IV
Appendixes

A   **How Much PC Do I Need?** **503**
System CPU: 80286 or 80386? 504
    Software 506
Random Access Memory........................... 507
Floppy and Hard Disk Drives..................... 508

B   **Peripheral Interests** **511**
Monitors.. 512
Printers... 513
Keyboards 515
Mice.. 516
Modems 517

C   **Setting Up Word for Windows** **519**

D   **Supporting Software and Hardware** **533**
Memory and File Management..................... 534
Utilities 538
Paint, Draw, and Presentation Graphics Packages 541
Spreadsheets 543
Databases 544
Specialized Hardware Options 544
    Manual Input Devices........................ 545
    Scanners.................................... 546
    Add-in Boards for LaserJet Printers 547

E   **Font Character Sets and Sources** **549**

Font Sources 550
    Typeface Vendors 558
    Font Editing 564
    Font Management 566
    Special Effects 567

F   **Journals, Books, and User Groups** **569**
Journals 570
Books 574
User Groups 576

Index **583**

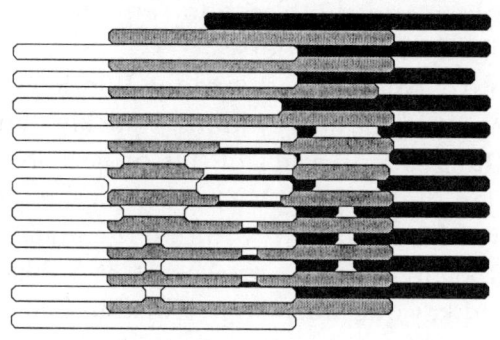

Acknowledgements

This project has been an endurance odyssey that began over a year and a half ago. For me, the entire process of learning Word for Windows has been a look into the future of document production. The result is the product of collaboration between so many parties that it is difficult to know where to begin to offer thanks. Therefore I shall start with my best friend, and wife, Sharon. Her support at critical points throughout this project allowed it to happen on time.

Elizabeth Fisher, my acquisitions editor, offered me the opportunity to write this book, and then carefully monitored each step to see that things were going smoothly for me. Laurie Beaulieu provided editorial support and carefully checked all of the artwork. Thanks also to several anonymous proofreaders whose careful work made my proofreading that much easier.

Harriet Serenkin, my technical editor, attempted all of the descriptive and tutorial exercises in this book. She also read the entire text for accuracy. All credit for the profit you gain from this book goes to her, and the blame for any detours or delays you encounter falls on my shoulders.

Michel Girard, Microsoft's Word for Windows writers' liaison, answered my technical questions quickly and thoroughly throughout the last four-fifth's of this project (Niel Hoopman of Microsoft began the project). Michel also designed and wrote the very useful Word for Windows Print Merge Macro which appears in Chapter 6. Tanya Van Dam, Microsoft Publisher/Press Relations, answered key questions on product timing when they arose. Tanya also made sure that I had up-to-date releases of Word for Windows, Windows, and Excel as they became available. Finally, Microsoft Corp. kindly granted us permission to modify tables from the Beta (pre-release) documentation for inclusion in this book.

All of the equipment used to prepare the manuscript for this book was donated to the project by major computer hardware firms that I approached after a careful product search. I would like to thank each of the firms involved for their support before I thank the human agents involved.

Most of this book was written with Microsoft Word 4.0 running under DESQview 386 (Quarterdeck Office Systems, Santa Monica, CA). Word for Windows was used to prepare the manuscript of the final chapters. Throughout the project, DESQview 386 Windows were used to multitask between writing in Word 4.0 or Word for Windows and making, editing, and printing screen captures of Word for Windows.

The manuscript of this book was produced on an IBM (Armonk, NY) PS/2 Model 80-111. The unit used had a PS/2 microchannel bus, a 20-Megahertz Intel 80386 CPU (Central Processing Unit), an Intel 80387 Coprocessor, 6 Megabytes of RAM, an external 5.25" 360-Kilobyte floppy drive, and an 8514A adapter card and monitor. This machine was the most dependable we have encountered. There were no installation troubles or any down-time at any point during this year-and-a-half project.

All screen captures in this book were done on an 8514 monitor running in the VGA mode with HotShot (SymSoft, Mountain View, CA). They were first converted to black-and-white with HotShot and then converted to *.PCX format. Fine touch editing was done with ZSoft's (Marietta, GA) Publisher's Paintbrush.

The copy was printed on a Texas Instruments (Austin, TX) Omnilaser 2115 laser printer. It has true PostScript, a high-contrast black-writer engine, 2.5 Megabytes of printer memory, and two 250-page-capacity paper trays.

Many image primitives taken from prepared illustrations or line drawings were scanned on a Xerox DataCopy (Mountain View, CA) 830 flatbed desktop scanner. Xerox PC Image software was used to choose dithering patterns, brightness, contrast, and grey scale levels (usually 64 levels).

A Tecmar (Solon, OH) QT-150 internal tape drive was used daily to back up the 110-Megabyte hard disk. The QT operating software recorded the first backup session's commands, and thereafter replayed the backup sequence without a human monitor.

Scott Brooks, of the IBM US Marketing and Services Group, has kept me abreast of the PC industry for three years in my editorial capacity at *PC Publishing*. He also arranged for me to get the IBM PS/2 Model 80-111, 8514 monitor, external 5.25" floppy drive, and PC-DOS, through the IBM Press Program. The speed of this 386 computer and graphics monitor has been essential in the face of endless deadlines. Also assisting me at IBM were Tracey O'Neill and Hal Reinish.

Sylvia Hawkins, Texas Instruments' Merchandising Product Manager, and her colleague Cathy Sang supplied me with the Texas Instruments Omnilaser 2115 printer. All of the text submissions for this book were produced on this printer. Its 15-page-per-minute, high-contrast images were also instrumental in the timely completion of my work. One warning: laser printers often have a high wattage rating; check the wattage rating on your printer, and make sure that your surge protector and the fuse in your office or house that supplies the outlet you are using (fuse amps X outlet volts = available watts). Make sure both are rated as high as the printer. I was reminded of this necessity the first time the Omnilaser 2115 was turned on. Allow your surge protector a healthy wattage rating over your printer and the rest of the components plugged into it. Special thanks to Texas Instruments for replacing my surge protector after the start-up fiasco.

Donna Clenney, of the Xerox Imaging Systems Marketing Department, supplied me with the DataCopy 830 desktop scanner. Line art primitives were scanned, taking advantage of this flatbed scanner's 64 grey level settings. These primitives were then cut and pasted, using the Windows clipboard, into many of the screen captures in this book.

Todd Smith, Division Manager of Evaluation Units for Tecmar, provided me with the QT-150, Tecmar's top-of-the-line internal PS/2 tape drive. It allowed me to back up my hard disk while I slept. Although I never had to use the backup tape in a pinch, I slept a lot easier knowing it was there.

Countless software publishers contributed software that enhanced my use of Word for Windows and Windows in general. Appendix D lists many of these products. One of these software publishers, Bob Fenchel of SoftCraft, Inc. (see the SoftCraft listings in Appendix E, "Font Character Sets and Sources"), deserves special thanks. SoftCraft allowed us to reprint several character sets from their Font Solution Pack manual.

My thanks to all of these people for the time and effort they have spent to make this book the best it could be.

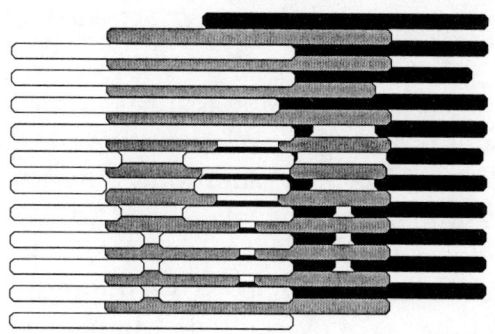

Introduction

Word for Windows is the first release of a new generation of integrated document production software. Because the software is new, everyone stands to benefit from this book. This includes novices who have not seen Word 4.0 or 5.0, all the way up to an MIS executive who is a Word 5.0 power user. This book is meant to complement the dictionary style of many software manuals with hands-on tutorials and example-laden explanation. This book is designed to be read in chapter order. As you become more familiar with Word for Windows, however, it cannot be stressed enough that if you have a specific task in mind you will save time by going to the Index *first,* then to the Table of Contents.

Who Should Use This Book

Using Microsoft Word for Windows assumes no prior knowledge of Word (version 4.0 or 5.0) or Windows. You are expected to be familiar with general PC operation (knowing what a floppy disk drive is, the keyboard arrangement, and so on) and word processing procedures (typing, editing, and so on). The specifics of using Word for Windows and its GUI (Graphical User Interface), Microsoft Windows, are covered here completely. In fact, most of Chapter 1, "Up and Running," and all of Chapter 11, "Fine Tuning Windows," is geared towards helping you learn to get around in Windows.

Even if you are already familiar with Windows, you should read Chapters 1 and 11 carefully. They will introduce you to ways to make Windows work most efficiently with Word for Windows. Earlier versions of Windows (before Windows 2.11) had a reputation for being slow. If you are running Windows on an Intel 80286-based PC, many of these hints will allow you to make the Windows interface, and therefore Word for Windows, run at its fastest.

If you are familiar with Word 4.0 or 5.0, you will be able to get up to speed very quickly. Word 4.0 and 5.0 are mentioned whenever features of these earlier versions are similar to those of Word for Windows. If you have been a user of another word processing program, you will gain just as much from this book as will users of Word 4.0 and 5.0. If your previous word processor was DisplayWrite, Multimate, Wang, WordPerfect, or WordStar, it may be useful for you to look at the "Getting Right to Word" guide supplied by Microsoft. This guide lists direct translations of the commands you are accustomed to using. This way you can compare what you are reading about in this book to what you were used to doing previously.

How This Book Is Organized

This book is divided into four parts: three sections of chapters and a group of appendixes. In Part I, "Learning Word for Windows," Chapters 1 through 7 teach you how Word for Windows is organized and how to get the most basic projects accomplished. In Part II, "Added Power of Word for Windows," Chapters 8 and 9 discuss two specialized applications of Word for Windows—annotations and data handling. In Part III, "Making the Most of Word for Windows," advanced desktop publishing features made possible by the WYSIWYG (What You See—on screen—Is What You Get—from your printer) Windows GUI (Graphical User Interface) and Windows management are discussed. The Appendixes, except for Appendix C, "Setting Up Word for Windows," are intended to provide you with source material on software and hardware applications above and beyond those you need to learn Word for Windows.

Part I: Learning Word for Windows

This section covers the basic Word for Windows commands. The topics are arranged in the order you would normally encounter them while learning to use any document production software.

Chapter 1, "Up and Running," will introduce you to both the Windows GUI and Word for Windows. After you read this chapter you will be able to create, print, and save a simple document. You may need to use Appendix C, "Setting Up Word for Windows," before you begin this chapter.

Chapter 2, "Formatting Text," introduces you to the heart and soul of Word 4.0, 5.0, and Word for Windows, the family of Format commands. It also includes a quick review of Windows dialog boxes, a topic covered in Chapter 1.

Chapter 3, "Cut and Paste: Adding Tables and Images" covers the creation of tables, whether they are newly created or they are data inserts from other applications such as Microsoft Excel. You will also learn how to insert graphic images into a document. Both of these procedures are facilitated by the Windows *clipboard;* the clipboard allows you to effortlessly cut and paste tables, charts, graphic images, and text among all Windows applications.

Chapter 4, "For the Record: Styles and Templates," teaches you how to make styles and save them to a new Word for Windows feature, the *Document Template.* Document Templates are project-specific collections of styles, glossaries (blocks of text and graphics that are saved and can be inserted anywhere in a document), macros (sequences of commands saved for use at any point in the document creation process), and boilerplate text (text, like the letterhead on a memo, that is automatically inserted in a document when you open a Document Template). You will also learn how to set tabs in this chapter. Finally, two special features of Word for Windows, the *Ribbon* and the *Ruler,* are covered in this chapter. Both of these features are used to quickly create and apply styles within a document.

Chapter 5, "Printing: Picture Perfect Output," covers the five Word for Windows document *views.* Views are different presentations of a document used to accomplish various tasks, all of which are aimed at preparing a document entirely on-screen. For example, the Print Preview lets you see what one or two (side-by-side) entire pages will look like when they are printed. With Word for Windows you will not have to actually print out anything other than the final draft.

Chapter 6, "Advanced Template Features: Glossaries, Boiler-plate Text, Fields, and Macros," shows you how to set up a complete, project-specific document template. *Fields* and *macros* are given special attention because of their wide applicability. Fields are codes used to format text or numbers (such as a formula or the result of an equation) as well as to insert file information into a document (such as the file name, author's name, date, or time). Macros are sets of commands saved to a keystroke combination (such as ALT-F1). Chapter 6 includes a Macro example that lets you choose which addresses in a large Print Merge (same as mail merge) database you want to be included in a particular mailing.

Chapter 7, "Time Saving Organization: Outlines and Tables of Contents," shows you how to begin the document creation process within the Word for Windows Outline View. Word for Windows assembles heads into a Table of Contents anywhere within a document and can assemble heads from groups of files (such as chapters in a book) into a central Table of Contents. Footnotes, which can be created while you are in the Outline View, are also discussed in this chapter.

Part II: Added Power of Word for Windows

Part II of *Using Microsoft Word for Windows* discusses two more advanced applications of Word for Windows—annotations and data handling. Annotations are used intensively in the preparation of legal documents; lawyers and anyone else who deals with text that goes through frequent revisions, will be happily surprised to find that Word for Windows supports *redlining*. Redlining is a tool used to mark changes that have been made to different drafts of a document so you can quickly find and approve or delete them. Word for Windows data handling tools facilitate the importation and exportation of various database, spreadsheet, and word processed files.

Chapter 8, "Group Productions," discusses the procedures an author would go through in giving a document to one or more readers for editorial comment. The process of making and incorporating annotations is covered. The use of these features by users linked by a LAN (Local Area Network) or WAN (Wide Area Network) is also discussed.

Chapter 9, "Data Handling: Formulas, Equations, Indexing, and File Importation," covers the importation and exportation of database, spreadsheet, and word processed data. Unlike most document production software, Word for Windows not only imports most major data formats, it also exports data to these formats. This will allow you to move data in to and out of different types of programs, and share data with colleagues who are not yet using Word for Windows.

Part III: Making the Most of Word for Windows

The last chapters of *Using Microsoft Word for Windows* show you how to produce highly polished compound documents (documents containing both text and graphic images). Using Word for Windows as a powerful front end to prepare text for importation into a desktop publishing program is also discussed. The section on fine tuning Windows helps you see how you can adjust the Windows WIN.EXE file (which sets up Windows in the same way that your AUTOEXEC.BAT file sets up your PC when you boot it up) to enhance certain Word for Windows procedures. Advanced uses of the Windows clipboard are also discussed.

Chapter 10, "Desktop Publishing with Word for Windows," shows you how to take full advantage of the character, paragraph, and page formatting features. While these features can be used to produce presentation-quality documents directly from Word for Windows, you will also see how pre-formatting a document within Word for Windows will save you time if you then intend to import the file into a desktop publishing program.

Chapter 11, "Fine Tuning Windows," discusses the WIN.INI file in depth. You can edit this file the same way you would edit the DOS AUTOEXEC.BAT file. You will also learn how to use the DDE (Dynamic Data Exchange) Paste Link function of the Window clipboard. With DDE you can cut and paste, for example, part of a Microsoft Excel spreadsheet into a Word for Windows table. This table would be linked to the original spreadsheet file so that whenever a change was made to this file in Excel it would be reflected in the linked Word for Windows document.

Part IV: Appendixes

The Appendixes offer you information on hardware and software that will support your use of Word for Windows and Windows in general. These appendixes, Appendix A, "How Much PC Do I Need?," Appendix B, "Peripheral Interests," Appendix C, "Setting Up Word for Windows," Appendix D, "Supporting Software and Hardware," Appendix E, "Font Character Sets and Sources," and Appendix F, "Journals, Books, and User Groups," should also provide you with sources to consult for any questions you may have in expanding your use of Word for Windows and other Windows applications.

Conventions Used in This Book

Using Microsoft Word for Windows follows several conventions designed to make the book easier for you to read. These are as follows:

- **Boldface** is used for text that you are instructed to type from the keyboard.
- Defined terms are presented in *italics*.
- The names of keys on the keyboard are presented in small capital letters, such as TAB, UP ARROW and ALT. If the instructions call for you to strike a keystroke combination (several keys held

down at once), then all keys involved are linked by hyphens. If there is a letter to be typed immediately after the keystroke combination, it follows after a comma. For example ALT-t, c instructs you to hold down the ALT key and simultaneously press t, then type c.

Additional Help from Osborne/McGraw-Hill

Osborne/McGraw-Hill provides top-quality books for computer users at every level of computing experience. To help you build your skills, we suggest that you look for the books in the following Osborne series that best address your needs.

The "Teach Yourself" series is perfect for people who have never used a computer before or who want to gain confidence in using program basics. These books provide a simple, slow-paced introduction to the fundamental uses of popular software packages and programming languages. Their "Mastery Skills Check" format ensures that you understand each concept thoroughly before you progress to new material. Plenty of examples and exercises are used throughout the text and the answers are provided at the back of the book.

The "Made Easy" series is also for beginners or for users who need a refresher on the new features of an upgraded product. These in-depth introductions guide users step-by-step from the program basics to intermediate-level usage. Plenty of "hands-on" exercises and examples are used in every chapter.

The "Using" series presents fast-paced guides that cover beginning concepts quickly and move on to intermediate-level techniques and some advanced topics. These books are written for users already familiar with computers and software who want to get up to speed fast with a certain product.

The "Advanced" series assumes that the reader is a user who has reached at least an intermediate skill level and is ready to learn more sophisticated techniques and refinements.

"The Complete Reference" series provides handy desktop references for popular software and programming languages. These books list every command, feature, and function of the product along with brief but detailed descriptions of how they are used. The books are fully indexed and often include tear-out command cards. The "Complete Reference" series is ideal for both beginners and pros.

The "Pocket Reference" series is a pocket-sized, shorter version of "The Complete Reference" series. It provides the essential commands, features, and functions of software and programming languages for users of every level who need a quick reminder.

The "Secrets, Solutions, Shortcuts" series is written for beginning users who are already somewhat familiar with the software and for experienced users at intermediate and advanced levels. This series provides clever tips, points out shortcuts for using the software to greater advantage, and indicates traps to avoid.

Osborne/McGraw-Hill also publishes many fine books that are not included in the series described here. If you have questions about which Osborne books are right for you, ask the salesperson at your local book or computer store, or call us toll-free at 1-800-262-4729.

Other Osborne/McGraw-Hill Books of Interest to You

We hope that *Using Microsoft Word for Windows* will assist you in mastering Microsoft's fine product, and will also pique your interest in learning about other ways to better use your computer.

If you're interested in expanding your skills so you can be even more "computer efficient," be sure to take advantage of

Osborne/McGraw-Hill's large selection of top-quality computer books that cover all varieties of popular hardware, software, programming languages, and operating systems. While we cannot list every title here that may relate to Microsoft Word and to your special computing needs, here are just a few books that complement *Using Microsoft Word for Windows*.

For all PC-DOS and MS-DOS users (from beginners who are somewhat familiar with the program to veteran users) with any DOS version up to 3.3, see *DOS: The Complete Reference, Second Edition* by Kris Jamsa. This book provides comprehensive coverage of every DOS command and feature. Whether you need an overview of the Disk Operating System or a reference for advanced programming and disk management techniques, you'll find it here.

If you're looking for the best way to get started in telecommunications or to get more out of the on-line services available today, see *Dvorak's Guide to PC Telecommunications*. This book/disk package, written by the internationally recognized computer columnist John Dvorak with programming wiz Nick Anis, shows you how to instantly plug into the world of electronic databases, bulletin boards, and on-line services. The package includes an easy-to-read, comprehensive guide plus two diskettes loaded with oustanding free software and is of value to computer users at every skill-level.

Learn More About Microsoft Word

Here is an excellent selection of other Osborne/McGraw-Hill books on Microsoft Word that will help you build your skills and maximize the power of the word processing software you have selected.

If you are a beginning Microsoft Word user with version 5 and an IBM PC, and you're looking for an in-depth guide that leads

you from basics to intermediate-level techniques, see *Microsoft®
Word 5 Made Easy*, by Paul Hoffman. If you are using Microsoft
Word Version 4, look for *Microsoft® Word Made Easy, Third Edition*,
also by Paul Hoffman. For Macintosh users, see *Microsoft® Word
Made Easy for the Macintosh, Version 4, Third Edition*, also by Paul
Hoffman.

For a quick-paced book that covers basics before concentrating
on intermediate-level skills and some advanced topics, see *Using
Microsoft® Word 5*, by Greg Perry.

Microsoft Word®: The Complete Reference, by Eric Alderman, is
ideal for all users, from beginners who are somewhat familiar with
Word to pros. This desktop resource lists every Word version 4
command, feature, and function along with brief yet in-depth
discussions of how they are used, plus plenty of information on
how to make the most of Microsoft Word's capabilities. If you have
Microsoft Word for the Macintosh version 3.01, see *Microsoft
Word® for the Macintosh:The Complete Reference*, by Michael Fischer.
For a quick reference to essential Word version 4 commands, see
Microsoft® Word: The Pocket Reference by Eric Alderman, or, if
applicable, see *Microsoft® Word for the Macintosh: The Pocket Reference* by Paul Hoffman.

Microsoft Word® 5: Secrets, Solutions, Shortcuts, by Tom Sheldon,
contains so many practical ideas that every Word version 5 user,
from novice to pro will keep turning to it again and again. You'll
quickly learn clever techniques that took experts years to develop.

If you're an experienced Word version 4 user looking for
books to help you refine your skills, see *Microsoft Word®: Power
User's Guide*, by John Hedtke.

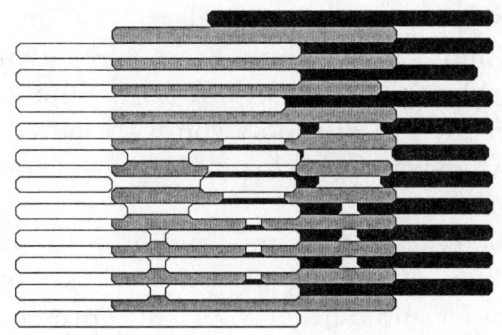

Why This Book Is for You

If you are thinking about buying Word for Windows or already have it, this book is for you. *Using Microsoft Word for Windows* will show you how to gain control of all the features of this cream of a new crop of document production programs called *word publishing programs*. Many of these features are not available in any other product. Programs like Word 5.0, WordPerfect, WordStar 2000, and so on, are often referred to as "high-end word processors." However, in this book they are referred to as word publishing packages because they all include the same group of helpful features not found in either traditional word processing or desktop publishing packages.

This book will also show you how to apply these features so that you will quickly get up to speed with your day-to-day projects. You will learn how to add fonts, format paragraphs and pages, insert graphic images, create tables, use styles and document templates (style sheets), print merge (mail merge), cut-and-paste to and from other Windows applications, make annotations, use redlining, generate tables of contents, indexes, footnotes, and much more. The appendixes will supply you with source information you will need when you decide to purchase supplementary hardware, software, or journals.

By reading this book you will find out how to prepare documents for a desktop publishing program using Word for Windows, making it easier and quicker to produce presentation-quality documents. The final chapter of this book gives you tips on how to fine tune Windows so it will make your work go even more smoothly. You will also learn how to exchange data among Windows applications and use Dynamic Data Exchange, which automatically updates files that are linked.

Along with teaching you the program, this book will show you how easy it is to import all of your old word processed documents into Word for Windows. By using Word for Windows now you will be ready to adopt OS/2, the operating system of the 1990s. Microsoft and IBM have been working together to make Windows a complete and easy stepping stone to OS/2. Windows runs and works the same as the OS/2 Graphical User Interface. Microsoft has announced that Windows 3.0 and OS/2 2.2 will both run multiple Windows applications, including Word for Windows, transparently. This means that you will not skip a beat in bringing work done in Windows applications into OS/2 applications when you make the switch. *Using Microsoft Word for Windows* is just the tool you need to get started using this exciting new product.

PART

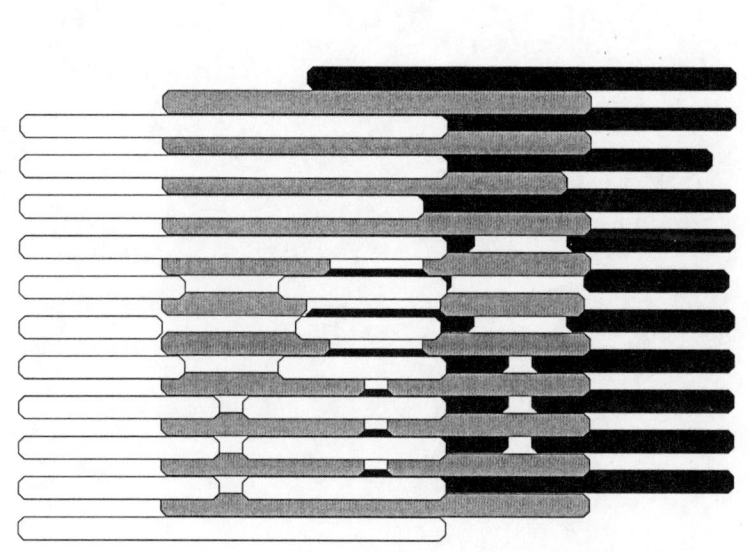

1

Learning Word for Windows

CHAPTER

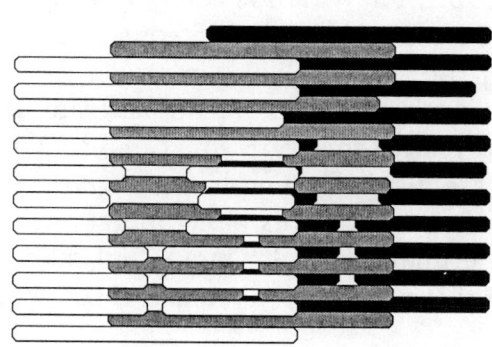

1

Up and
Running

You are about to begin using Word for Windows, a *word publishing program*. Word publishing is a means of producing text using many of the features available now only in desktop publishing programs but at the faster speed of a word processing program. Word publishing is based on combining multiple fonts and graphic images. Documents containing both text and graphics are referred to as *compound documents*. Word for Windows also provides you with the ability to create tables in your compound documents. As you begin to incorporate fonts, images, and tables—many of them generated from data stored in other software applications such as paint, draw, spreadsheet, or database programs—into Word for Windows compound documents, you will be able to expand the scope of your projects. The presentation quality of your work will also improve.

Word for Windows is a large and powerful program. Because the basics are easy to learn, however, you can use Word for Windows even if you are just beginning to produce documents. After you become comfortable with its basic operation, you will want to gradually experiment with the more sophisticated features of Word for Windows that are discussed throughout this book.

Give yourself enough time to learn Word for Windows. You should not expect to master this program as quickly as you might have learned, for example, previous updates to Microsoft Word. Because Word for Windows is a newly released product, you should take time to familiarize yourself with its particular organization.

To help you understand the organization of Word for Windows, this chapter presents the components of both the Microsoft Windows graphical interface and the Word for Windows program. By following the examples presented here, you will become acquainted with all of the menus in Word for Windows. Like all other Windows software, Word for Windows menus contain lists of commands. You can set the parameters of many of these commands, which are called *user-definable* commands. If a command is user-definable, when you select it, a *dialog box* will be displayed in which you enter options that determine the outcome of the command. For example, you enter the page margin settings you want applied to your document in the Format menu's Document dialog box. A brief discussion of how dialog boxes work follows the overview of the Word for Windows menus later in this chapter. After you finish this chapter, you will be able to produce simple documents with Word for Windows.

Running Word for Windows

To run Word for Windows, you must have a fully operational IBM compatible personal computer with a hard disk (preferably with an Intel 80286 or 80386 microprocessor), a graphics monitor, and a mouse. To perform the examples shown in this and subsequent chapters, you must also have set up Word for Windows on your hard disk in a directory of its own named WINWORD. You should also have both the WINDOWS and WINWORD directories listed in the PATH statement in your AUTOEXEC.BAT file in the root directory (C:\) on your hard disk. More detailed information on equipment options that will help you run Word for Windows and other Windows applications are discussed in Appendix A, "How Much PC Do I Need." Installation processes for both Windows and Word for Windows are discussed in Appendix C, "Setting Up Word for Windows."

Once you have installed Word for Windows, you must type **WIN WINWORD** at the DOS prompt "C: > _" to activate the program. Nothing will happen, however, if you have not added both the WINDOWS and the WINWORD directories to the PATH statement in your AUTOEXEC.BAT file in the root directory (C:\) on your hard disk.

Windows: A Graphical Interface

Windows is operated primarily by using a mouse to choose programs, commands, and options that are displayed on the screen. Programs are represented on the screen as *icons* (mnemonic shapes that suggest what program they activate), commands are found in menus listed across a menu bar at the top of the screen, and dialog boxes are activated whenever options must be chosen before a particular command can be executed. Windows is called a *graphical user interface* rather than a *text-based interface* because you activate programs, commands, and options primarily by clicking the mouse on a screen element.

The Microsoft Windows interface has been chosen as the model for the next IBM personal computer interface, Presentation Manager, that will run on a new operating system called OS/2. The current IBM personal computer operating system is called PC-DOS, which is IBM's version of MS-DOS (Microsoft DOS). This operating system is used on both IBM and IBM compatible personal computers.

The program icons, menu bar, and dialog boxes are the screen elements that make up the core of IBM's Common User Access (CUA) interface. Some of the CUA screen elements found in Windows and the OS/2 Presentation Manager are also found in the Apple Macintosh interface. This is because both IBM and Apple, among other software engineering companies, were involved in a cooperative development effort in the late 1970s at the Xerox Palo Alto Research Center (PARC) that produced the PARC interface.

This commonality of menus, screen elements, and organization makes it easier to learn a variety of Windows applications. Because the Windows interface is the same for all Windows-based programs, after you master your first Windows program, you will not need to spend time learning the interface for other Windows applications; rather, you will be able to spend your time learning the particular commands of the new program.

CUA Screen Elements in the MS-DOS Executive

Before beginning to work with Word for Windows, it is important to become familiar with the elements of the Windows opening screen, the MS-DOS Executive, shown in Figure 1-1. Whenever you load Word for Windows, you also load the MS-DOS Executive. You can simultaneously display the MS-DOS Executive and put Word for Windows in the background for now. You do this either by clicking the left mouse button on the boxed down arrow at the upper-right corner of the Word for Windows screen or by pressing the ALT and F9 keys simultaneously. Another way is to load Windows, without loading Word for Windows; type **WIN** at the DOS prompt "C:\WINDOWS > _", and only the MS-DOS Executive will run.

Programs that have you enter commands from the DOS prompt in PC-DOS, or use an all-text screen, utilize what is called

Figure 1-1.

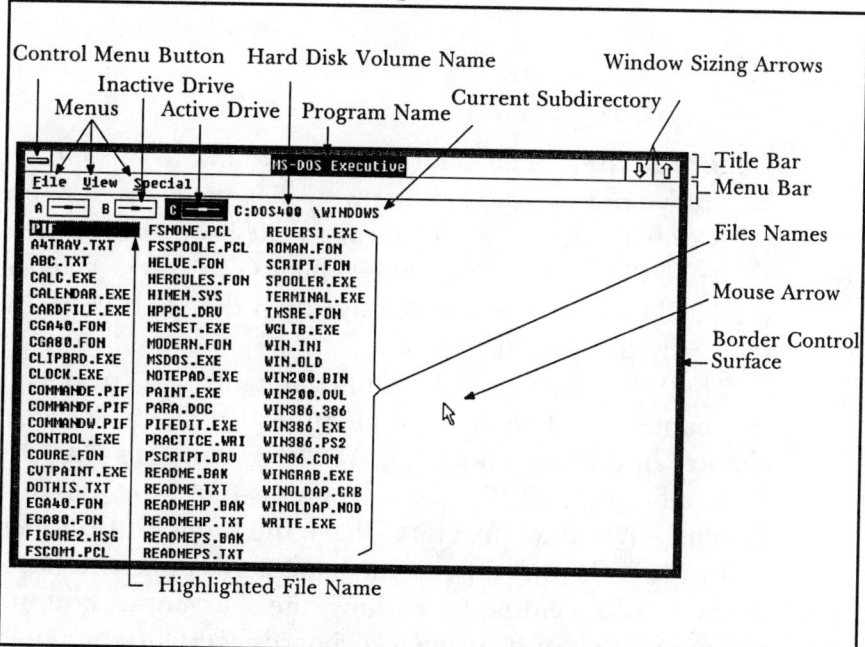

Windows opening screen

a text-based interface. In the MS-DOS Executive, as in all Windows programs, instead of typing commands from the DOS prompt, you find them in menus and activate them with a mouse, or, you use short ALT-*key* keystroke combinations to execute commands. The ALT-*key* keystroke combination notation will appear throughout this book. Written this way, the ALT-*key* keystroke combination means that you press the ALT key and hold it down while pressing the key listed. In this way, with either the mouse menus or keyboard abbreviations, you can perform basic file management or disk operations with the MS-DOS Executive. The next six sections survey the CUA screen elements as seen in the MS-DOS Executive. Additional information on using these screen elements and Windows in general may be found in Chapter 11, "Fine Tuning Windows," and Appendix C, "Setting Up Word for Windows."

Control Button   The *Control button* is found to the left of the title bar shown in Figure 1-1. When you click the left mouse button on the Control button, the Control menu drops down below it, as shown in Figure 1-2. The Control menu can also be activated from the keyboard by pressing ALT and then the SPACEBAR, or by simultaneously pressing ALT-SPACEBAR.

The Windows Control menu commands are covered in detail in Chapter 11. The Control menu is also discussed later in this chapter in the section on the Word for Windows Control menu. Remember that all Windows programs — and the MS-DOS Executive is a Windows program — have the same Control menu.

In general, you can execute commands after you have pulled down a menu either by clicking the left mouse button on the command itself or by using a keyboard macro listed to the right of the command. The pull-down menus allow you to see all of the

Figure 1-2.

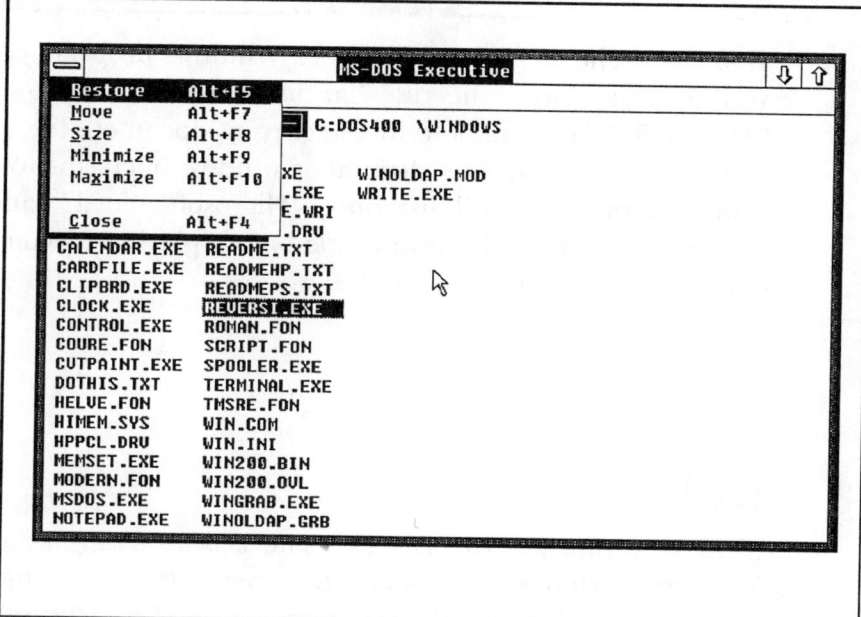

MS-DOS Executive Control command menu

commands; therefore, you do not have to memorize them. To activate a command, you do not need to pull down a menu if you already know the ALT-*key* keystroke combination that corresponds to the command in the menu. In many cases, you will want to execute the command directly from the keyboard. You should not, however, see using the keyboard as an alternative to using a mouse. Windows is a mouse-oriented graphical interface and many operations are greatly eased by using the mouse. The decision on whether to enter commands with the keyboard or the mouse should be based on which method is faster. Even if you know all of the Windows and Word for Windows commands, it is not always faster to perform every function from the keyboard. When to use the mouse or the keyboard is discussed further in Chapter 2, "Formatting Text."

Title Bar   The *title bar* usually lists a Windows program name. As you shall see later, the title bar in Word for Windows reads "Microsoft Word" followed by the current document file name. If you have more than one document window open, the Word for Windows title bar will list only "Microsoft Word," and each document window will have a title bar displaying its constituent document file name.

Window Sizing Arrows Boxes   The *window sizing arrows boxes* found at the right end of the title bar are used to either change the size of the window or collapse the program to an icon. Windows programs can be run in windows of an almost infinite variety of sizes; however, the window sizing arrows boxes only allow you to size the program window to either of two standard sizes or to collapse the program to an icon. In the discussion of mouse border controls later in this chapter, you will see how to make a program window virtually any size.

When a program is collapsed to an icon, the MS-DOS Executive appears on the screen with the program icon below it. An example of the Word for Windows icon under the MS-DOS Executive is shown in Figure 1-3. The collapsed Word for Windows program has not been closed, only taken out of the foreground. Clicking the left mouse button once on the Word for Windows icon activates the Word for Windows Control menu, which appears over the icon. You can now click the left mouse button on either the Restore, Minimize, or Maximize command. These commands perform the same function as the window sizing

Figure 1-3.

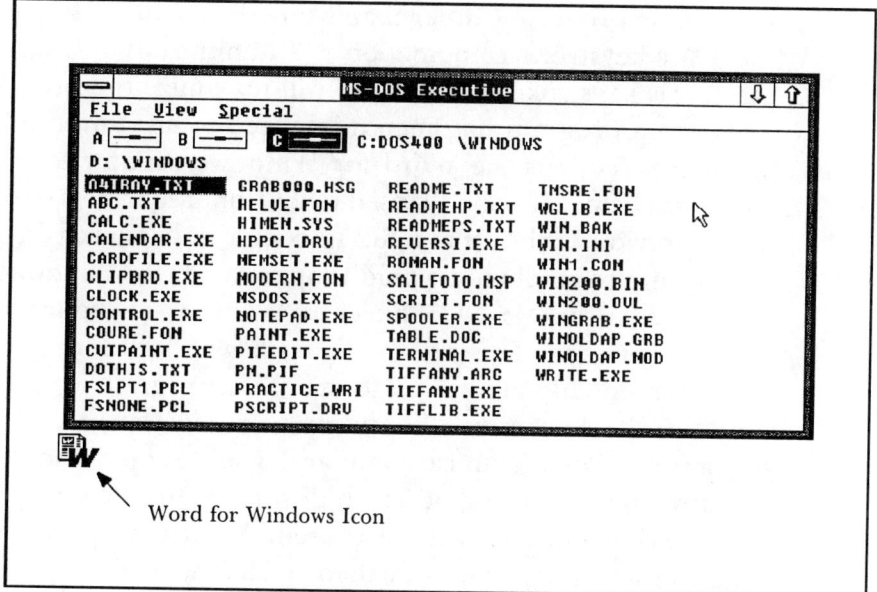

Word for Windows Icon

MS-DOS Executive with Word for Windows icon

arrows boxes when the program is displayed in a fully open window in the foreground. The Minimize and Maximize commands are available when a program is in the foreground or in the background (collapsed to an icon) because the Control menu is always available. However, the window sizing arrows boxes only appear (in the upper-right corner) when a program is in the foreground and its window is open. Remember that you activate the Control menu by clicking the left mouse button on the Control button or by pressing ALT-SPACEBAR when a program is in the foreground, or by clicking the left mouse button once on the program icon when the program has been minimized to an icon.

Look at the Control menu in Figure 1-2. This menu is the same for MS-DOS Executive, Word for Windows, and for all other programs running under Windows. Note that next to the highlighted Restore command you see the keyboard alternative, ALT-F5.

This means that you can use the ALT-F5 keystroke combination to restore the program (rather than using this menu). Also, note that the ALT-F9 keystroke combination will minimize the program and the ALT-F10 keystroke combination will maximize the program.

When a program has been minimized to an icon, the Restore command reopens the Word for Windows window to the same size it was before it was collapsed to an icon, regardless of whether it was previously shown as a full screen or only part of the screen. The Minimize command would reopen Word for Windows to the same size as the MS-DOS Executive window in Figure 1-3, the intermediate size. The intermediate size window does not fill the whole screen, and allows you to see other program icons (such as the MS-DOS Executive's floppy disk-shaped icon) that sit along the bottom. The Maximize command would reopen the Word for Windows program so that its window takes up the entire screen. The intermediate size window is useful because you can see other program icons below it, and then quickly load them by double-clicking the left mouse button on their icons. (Flipping back and forth between different Windows applications is called *task switching*.) If the program window has been maximized, it looks the same but takes up the entire screen. This maximized size is useful with Word for Windows because you can see more text on the screen.

In an intermediate size window, you will see the two window sizing arrows boxes—the right box with an arrow pointing up and the left box with a down arrow. Clicking the left mouse button on the up arrow would maximize the window, and clicking the left mouse button on the down arrow would collapse (minimize) the window back to an icon. Clicking the left mouse button on the box containing both an up and down arrows in the maximized program window reduces the window to the intermediate size where you can see any other program icons that may be at the bottom of the screen.

Program Icons   As was just discussed, a Windows program can always be minimized (the program window is collapsed) to an icon. Each program has a different icon. When you minimize Word for Windows to an icon, the MS-DOS Executive icon, shown below, is displayed on your screen above the Word for Windows icon.

As already mentioned in the section on window sizing arrows boxes, a program collapsed to an icon is only "dormant," not closed. If you are running Windows/386, you can specify that the program keep working while it is collapsed to an icon. For example, with Windows/386 you could print out a document from Word for Windows and simultaneously go into the MS-DOS Executive and open another Word for Windows window and begin work on another document. This concurrent processing of programs is called *multitasking*. Therefore, Windows/386 is a multitasking graphical user interface.

Clicking the left mouse button once on an icon activates the program's Control menu. If you then select the Restore command, the program window will be restored to its previous size. You can restore a Word for Windows icon more quickly if you click the left mouse button twice in rapid succession (called *double-clicking*) on the icon. Using either method to reopen a program brings up the program in the same spot where you left it when you collapsed it to an icon. With Word for Windows, the cursor will be on the same letter of the text and all of your previous command selections will still be in effect.

```
┌─────────────────────────────────────────────────────┐
│ File  View  Special                                   │
└─────────────────────────────────────────────────────┘
```

Menu Bar   The *menu bar* shows you the structure of any Windows program. All Word for Windows commands are listed in the menus accessible from the menu bar. Since the menu bar is always on screen, you do not need to memorize the names of the menus.

The MS-DOS Executive menu bar is shown in Figure 1-1. The menus can be pulled down very quickly with the mouse. You pull down any of the menus listed in the menu bar by clicking the left mouse button on the menu name in the menu bar.

There are two ways to pull down menus with the keyboard. You can bring the cursor into the menu bar by pressing the ALT key once. In the MS-DOS Executive, and in almost every other Windows program including Word for Windows, the cursor will then highlight "File," the menu furthest to the left. You can move the cursor around in the menu bar to another menu heading with both the RIGHT ARROW and LEFT ARROW keys, thus changing the menu heading that is highlighted. Then press ENTER to display the highlighted menu. You can move among the commands within a menu by pressing the UP ARROW and DOWN ARROW keys. Pressing ESC moves the cursor out of the menu bar without making any selections.

You can also cause menus to drop down by entering an ALT-*key* keystroke combination. The second key in the ALT-*key* keystroke combination is the letter underlined in the menu bar choice you want to activate. In the MS-DOS Executive, there are only three command menus; therefore, there are only three ALT-*key* keystroke combinations to use: To activate the File menu use ALT-f, to activate the View menu use ALT-v, or use ALT-s to activate the Special menu (note that f, v, and s are underlined in the menu bar). Once the cursor is in a pull-down menu, the commands can be accessed by typing the underlined letter alone without the ALT key.

Dialog Boxes   If a command has only one option, when the command is selected the option is immediately executed;

examples of this are the Minimize and Maximize commands in the Windows Control menu discussed in the earlier section, "Window Sizing Arrows Boxes." However, if a command has multiple options, the command appears in the menu followed by "..." When it is executed, a dialog box will appear on the screen in which you select the correct option(s) to go with the command by using the mouse or the keyboard.

Dialog boxes often allow you to select among preset options or to type your own definable options. Sample dialog box operations are discussed later in this chapter in the section "Dialog Box Operations;" dialog box operations are also reviewed in Chapter 2.

Opening Word for Windows

The following survey of Word for Windows screen elements and command menus is only preliminary. All of the command menus will be mentioned in later chapters wherever they pertain to specific applications of Word for Windows. This survey is intended as an overview to help you become familiar with Word for Windows.

Loading Word for Windows from DOS or from Windows

To begin this overview of Word for Windows, you must activate the Word for Windows program. If you have just completed the previous demonstration on Windows screen elements using the MS-DOS Executive, you can bring Word for Windows to the foreground by double-clicking the left mouse button on the W shaped Word for Windows icon shown to the left and below the MS-DOS Executive window in Figure 1-3.

If Word for Windows is properly installed, you will be able to call up the program from the root directory by typing **WIN WINWORD** at the DOS prompt and pressing ENTER.

If you have already loaded the MS-DOS Executive, but not Word for Windows, first you must change the display of the Windows subdirectory list of files to the Word for Windows subdirectory list of files. This can be done either with the mouse or the keyboard.

To change subdirectories with the mouse, you would first click the left mouse button on the current subdirectory listing, as shown in Figure 1-4. This action would bring up the MS-DOS Executive Change Directory dialog box. The Change Directory dialog box would appear with the current Windows subdirectory listed in the Change To field; it will display: "\WINDOWS", "\WIN286", or "\WIN386", depending on which version of Windows you are using. You can then use the BACKSPACE key to erase all of the letters except "WIN" from the Windows subdirectory listing and type **WORD** to get the Word for Windows subdirectory path, **\WINWORD**, as has been done in Figure 1-5. Pressing ENTER would cause the files in the Word for Windows subdirectory to appear on screen.

Using the keyboard to change directories is faster than using the mouse in most cases. If you press the BACKSPACE key, the MS-DOS Executive displays the root directory, as shown in Figure 1-6. The boldface listings are subdirectories. You can move the cursor to them with the RIGHT ARROW and DOWN ARROW keys. However, the quickest way to move the cursor to the WINWORD subdirectory listing with the keyboard is to type **w** and then press the DOWN ARROW key. This would move the cursor to the first listing beginning with "w," in this case WINWORD, the Word for Windows subdirectory. You would now press ENTER. You can also change to

Figure 1-4.

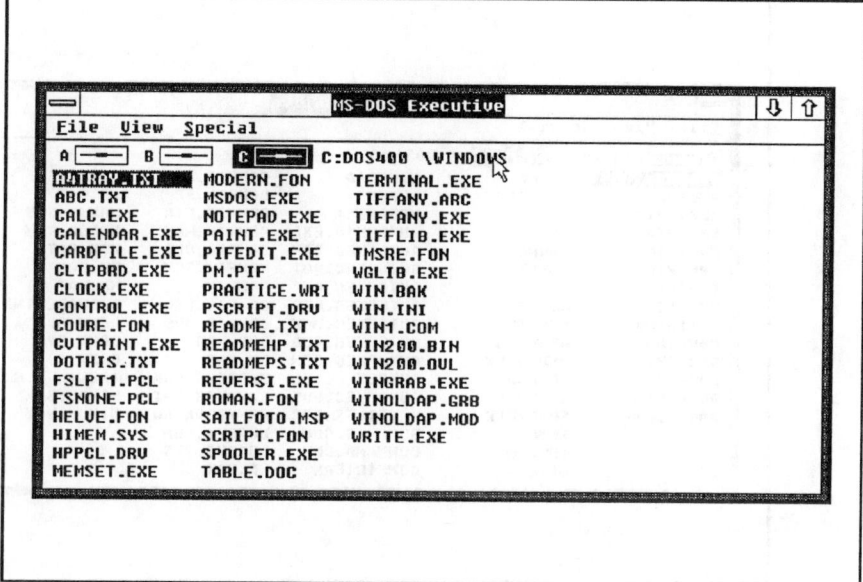

Changing directories using a mouse

Figure 1-5.

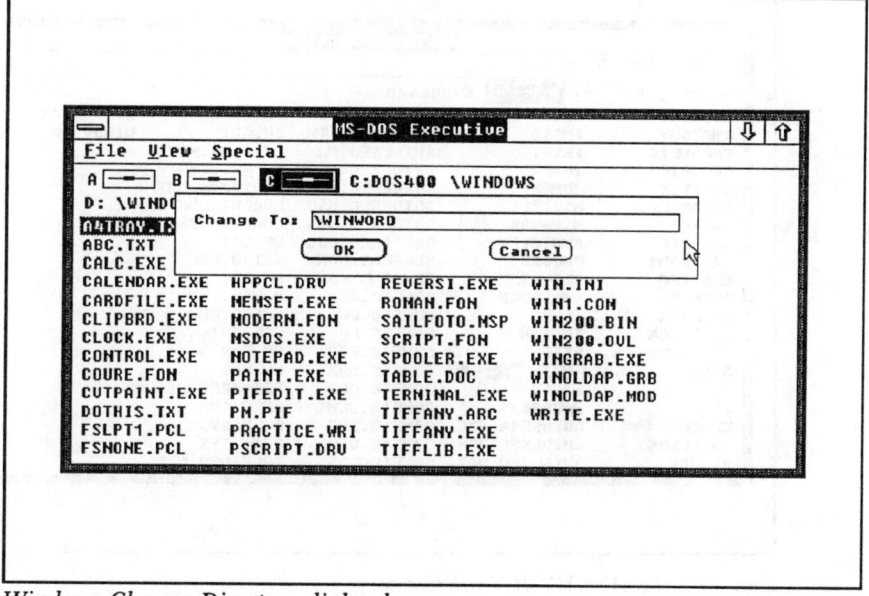

Windows Change Directory dialog box

Figure 1-6.

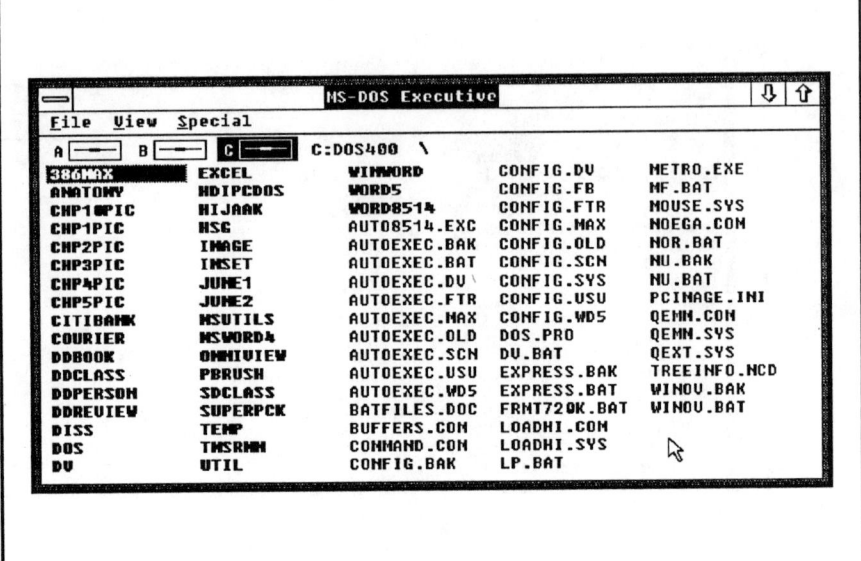

Root directory

Figure 1-7.

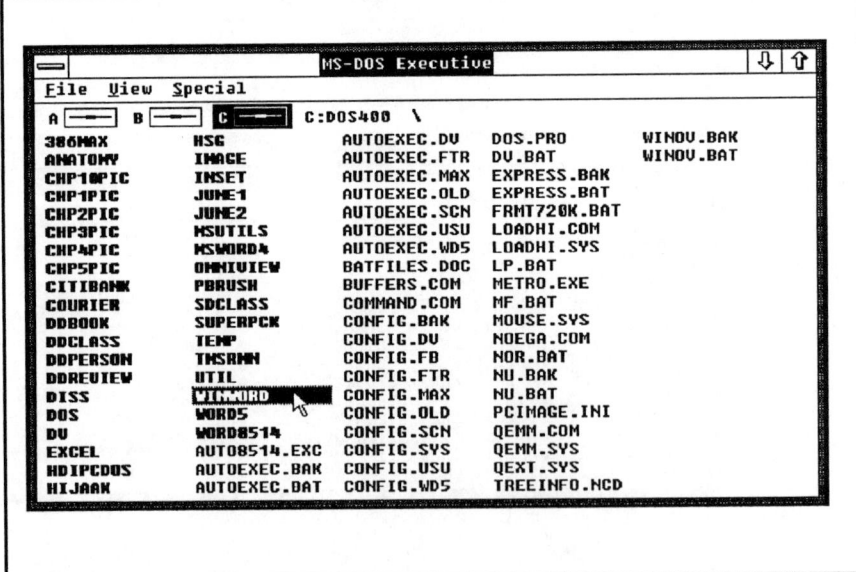

Choosing the WINWORD subdirectory

Figure 1-8.

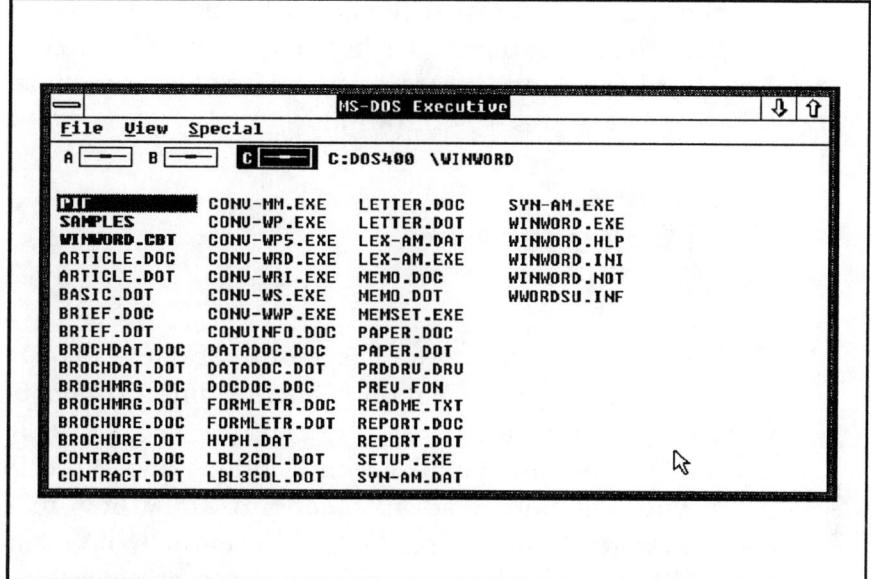

The WINWORD subdirectory

the WINWORD subdirectory by double-clicking the left mouse button (click it twice quickly) on the highlighted WINWORD subdirectory as shown in Figure 1-7; this may seem faster, but remember you have to take your hand off the keyboard to use the mouse.

Whether you used the mouse or the keyboard method to change to the WINWORD subdirectory, your screen should now display the WINWORD subdirectory as shown in Figure 1-8. You see many file names listed. The program file, which you need to execute and load Word for Windows, is the WINWORD.EXE file. Its *.EXE extension stands for "executable file." To move the cursor to WINWORD.EXE with the keyboard, you type a **w**. The cursor moves to the first entry beginning with "w," which is WINWORD.EXE. Then press ENTER and the Word for Windows program window will appear on screen. In this case, the keyboard method is at least as fast as the mouse method of double-clicking the left mouse button on the highlighted WINWORD.EXE file. The Word for Windows program window has now replaced the MS-DOS Executive program window.

The Mouse in Word for Windows

The Windows CUA interface is mouse-oriented. You use the mouse to quickly access Windows' menus, input commands, and move screen elements.

Once you become familiar with Windows and Word for Windows, you will find it advantageous to know how to execute commands with the mouse. You will eventually be comfortable using either the keyboard or the mouse to enter commands, as well as with sequential combinations using both; you will also develop a sense of which method of input accomplishes a task most quickly.

In general, the mouse is the quickest way to highlight blocks of text in Word for Windows. When working with text, the mouse does not have the arrow shape, shown here

that you would see in the MS-DOS Executive or on the Word for Windows title and menu bars. Rather, the mouse has an I-beam shape on the document screen in Word for Windows, as it does on any Windows screen where you can enter text, as shown here.

You block off text by placing the mouse on the first character of the intended block and clicking the left mouse button (if you click twice, the closest word will be highlighted.) This action will instantly move the cursor from its current position to the first character of the new block. Continue to hold down the left mouse button and drag the mouse (up or down) over the text towards the last character of the block; the cursor will extend and all of the text under it will be highlighted. If you want to keep dragging the mouse towards text that is above or below what is shown on the screen, push the mouse against the upper or lower window border. The text will automatically start to scroll up or down. When you reach the last character of the block, let go of the left mouse button. This is the same way that text is blocked off in Word 4.0 and 5.0.

To block text using the keyboard, move the cursor to the first character of the block. Press F8 and press any of the keypad arrows to begin blocking text. If you move the cursor with the keypad arrows, the cursor will extend to highlight a block. (Remember that the F6 key activates the cursor extend function in Word 4.0 and 5.0.) Using the mouse rather than the keyboard to block off text will usually be faster because the mouse can move across the screen diagonally, whereas the arrow keys can only move up or down, right or left.

The mouse takes on a different appearance in the left margin, or *selection bar*, of the document window. As you can see here,

the selection bar mouse is the same shape but points in the opposite direction from the mouse arrow that appears over the menu and title bars.

It does not matter whether you click the left or right button. One click highlights the line horizontally opposite the mouse; two quick clicks, or double-clicking, highlights the paragraph to the right of the selection bar mouse. If you are familiar with Word 4.0 and 5.0, you will note that the mouse arrow for this operation works differently in those programs.

As you have already seen, in almost every instance, Windows programs utilize only the left button of the mouse. This is why throughout this book you are told to "click the left button of the mouse" on various screen elements. Some users may have a mouse with three or more buttons, but Microsoft Windows only accesses one or two of these buttons. When you choose an option in a dialog box, a data file, or a graphic image to load, or when you attempt to run a program file in the MS-DOS Executive (usually these program files have *.COM or *.EXE extensions), you can make your selection by double-clicking the left mouse button on the desired option, file name, or program. Double-clicking the mouse on selections is a standard aspect of the Windows CUA interface. At other times, you will click the left mouse button once on an OK *button* (a button is a small square on the screen surrounding a word) once to make your selection.

NOTE   In Word 4.0 and 5.0, you can use both mouse buttons at any time. Users of these earlier versions of Word may find that their first tendency is to use the right button of the mouse to activate a task rather than to use the standard Windows methods of selecting the OK button or double-clicking the mouse on a desired option.

The mouse takes on a slightly different configuration when you move it to the edge of Windows programs such as the MS-DOS Executive or Word for Windows. The shape, shown here,

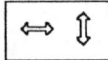

is an arrow pointing to either side of the border. If you click the left mouse button on the border for a program window and hold the left mouse button down, you can then drag that edge of the window inward or outward by rolling the mouse on your desktop. In this way, you can resize a program window to almost any size. You can size windows to display more than one program on your screen at once. Whichever program you click the mouse button on becomes active and the other program is momentarily inactivated.

In this way, you can open different Windows programs and *copy* (block off) data or images from one program and instantly *paste* the information (insert the block) into the other program. In Chapters 3, 9, and 11, you will see that there are many other ways to exchange data between Windows and non-Windows applications. Other standard aspects of Windows mouse use are referred to in Chapter 11.

The Document Window

A few aspects of the Word for Windows screen do not appear in the MS-DOS Executive. Most of these unique elements are in the *document window* within the Word for Windows program window.

The document window has its own borders within the program window. You can separately size the document window with the *border control arrows* (window sizing was discussed previously in the window sizing arrows boxes section in this chapter). Now move the mouse over to the screen borders. You will see that there are separate border control arrows for the program window and for the document window. Remember that when you move the mouse onto a document window border, it changes from an I-beam to a window border control arrow. If you click the left mouse button when you see the border control arrow and hold it down, you can grab the border and drag it to resize the document window. If you click the left mouse button on any of the document or program borders and drag the mouse, however, only one of the two borders follows the mouse. Users of Word 4.0 and 5.0 will remember opening document windows by clicking either mouse button at the top or right border of the screen. Word for Windows lets you move document borders without going into the Window menu. This interactive function is not available in Word 4.0, 5.0, or most other word processing and word publishing software.

The *scroll bar* you see at the left side of the screen allows you to move through a document in much the same way as the scroll bar does in Word 4.0 and 5.0. When the mouse is placed on the white rectangular box at the top of the scroll bar, but below the upward pointing arrow, it changes to an arrow shape. If you click the left mouse button on this rectangle and hold the mouse button down, you can drag the rectangular box down to a part of the document that is off the screen. The entire scroll bar represents 100 percent of the document. If you drag the rectangle halfway down the scroll bar, text from the middle of your document appears in the document window. You can page up or down by clicking the left button of the mouse once on either the up or down boxed scroll bar arrow. These boxed scroll bar arrows function in the same way as the PGUP and PGDN keys on the keyboard. The text shifts one screen at a time, not one printed page at a time. To shift the screen to the top of another page, you have to use the Go To command in the Edit menu (discussed in the "Edit Menu" section later in this chapter).

The document title bar, shown in Figure 1-9, appears above the menu bar and contains the default name of the first document, Document1. The document text page, shown below the document title bar in Figure 1-9, is empty except for the L-shaped text entry cursor at its upper left and the I-beam-shaped mouse. The mouse has an I-beam shape on the text entry portion of the document window, but reverts to the familiar arrow shape when you roll it over the title, scroll, or menu bar.

Pull-Down Menus

The program menu bar is the most important aspect of the Word for Windows screen. You access pull-down command menus in Word for Windows from the program menu bar in the same manner you access the three MS-DOS Executive menus, File, View, and Special. The following survey will familiarize you with the kinds of commands that are found in each of these menus; all

Figure 1-9.

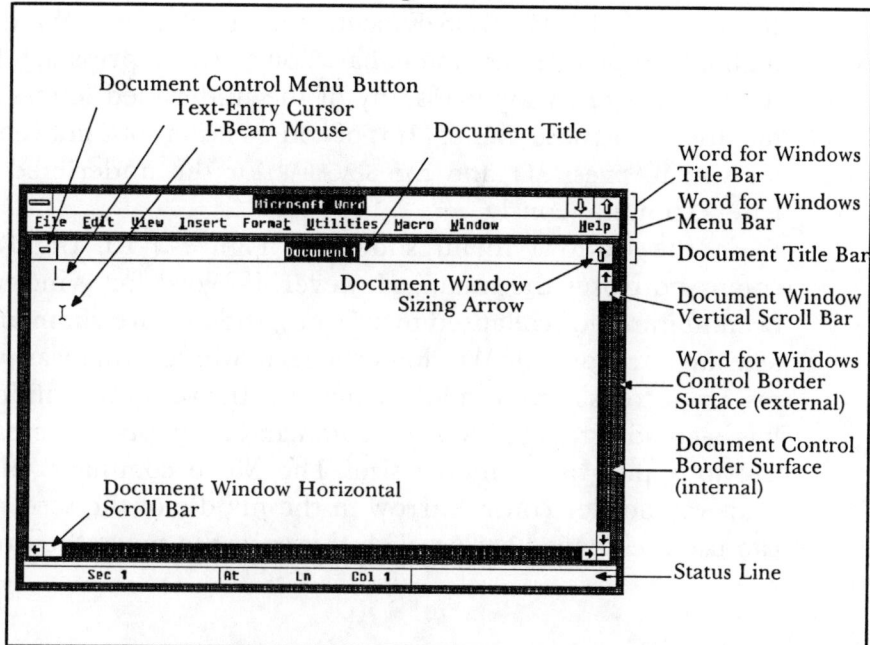

Word For Windows opening screen

of the menus will be discussed in more depth in subsequent chapters. The Control, File, and some of the Edit commands will be covered in more detail here to help you get up and running with Word for Windows.

Program Control Menu

The Word for Windows program Control menu is accessed in the same way as the MS-DOS Executive Control menu. When you click the left mouse button on the Word for Windows program Control button, the Control menu drops down below it, as shown in Figure 1-10. The Control menu can also be activated from the

keyboard by pressing ALT-SPACEBAR. Note that as soon as you press
ALT in either the MS-DOS Executive or in Word for Windows, a
highlight appears in the menu bar. You can then press SPACEBAR for
the Control menu or press any of the underlined letters in the
menu bar for those menus. It is of course faster, but not required,
for you to press ALT and the SPACEBAR, or the underlined menu
letters, simultaneously.

In the Control menu shown in Figure 1-10, the Restore
command closes the menu. However, if Word for Windows has
been minimized (collapsed to an icon), the Restore command will
activate the Word for Windows program window that was present
just prior to its minimization. Whenever the program window size
has been adjusted, the Restore command attempts to recreate the
previous program window size. The Move command places a
four-way border control arrow in the middle of the screen. You
can use the keypad arrows with this arrow to move the program

Figure 1-10.

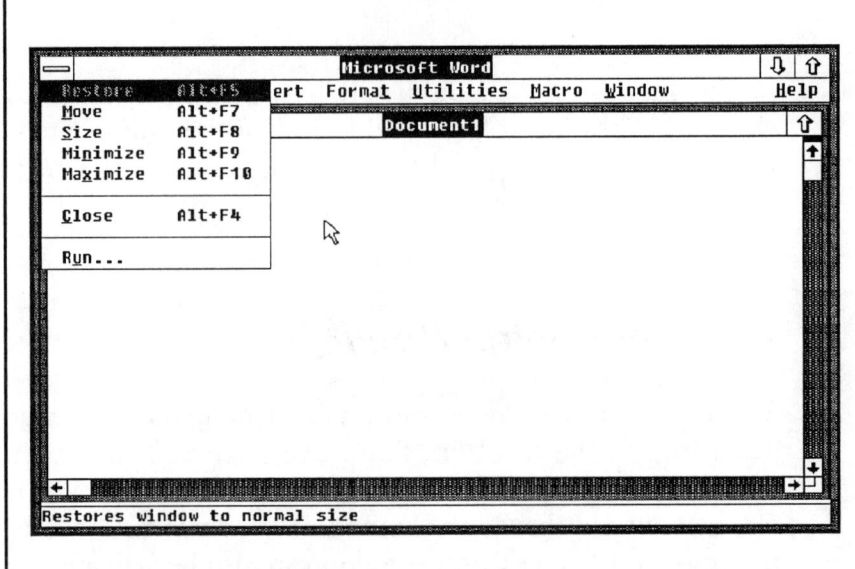

Word for Windows Control menu

window borders. When you press any of these arrows, the border control arrow moves to the appropriate window and continued pressure on the same keypad arrow will drag the border outward. Pressing on the opposite direction arrow at this time drags the border inward. When the border is where you want it to be, release the arrow key and press ENTER. In most cases, it will be faster to use the mouse to resize window borders, as discussed in the previous section. (The Minimize and Maximize commands were discussed earlier in the section on window sizing arrows boxes.) The Close command closes the entire Word for Windows program, but not the Windows MS-DOS Executive.

The "Run. . ." command gives you access to two important features of the Windows MS-DOS Executive, the Clipboard and the Control Panel. Remember that a command followed by ". . ." accesses a dialog box that lists the command's options. When you select the Run command, a dialog box appears offering you either the Clipboard or the Control Panel. The topic of making dialog box selections is explained in detail in a later section on dialog box operations.

Inside the Run dialog box, you can select the Clipboard or the Control Panel by clicking the left button of the mouse on the open circles to the left of either command, or you can type **c** and then press ENTER to choose the Clipboard, or type **p** and press ENTER for the Control Panel. If you select the Clipboard, you can then save blocked off (highlighted) graphics or text temporarily into RAM (Random Access Memory). RAM is the memory where Word for Windows and other programs sit. Any information copied to the Clipboard (into RAM) is not saved to either your hard disk or floppy disk, and disappears when you turn off your computer. Also, graphics or text copied to the Clipboard is dropped out of RAM (disappears) when a different piece of data is copied to the Clipboard. This means that the Clipboard only holds one item of data at a time. You can paste (insert from the Clipboard) graphics or text from the Clipboard into any location in Word for Windows or any other Windows program. Also, within Word for Windows, you can paste text or graphics from document to document. The process of data exchange between different types of Windows applications is discussed in depth in Chapter 11.

The Control Panel lets you adjust the various aspects of the Word for Windows screen, such as the rate at which the cursor blinks. It also lets you set up a communications port for a printer. The Clipboard and Control Panel are actually programs in the MS-DOS Executive, and accessing them with the Run command saves you from exiting Word for Windows and opening the MS-DOS Executive. Their roles in the MS-DOS Executive, which are the same in Word for Windows, are discussed in depth in Chapter 11.

Document Control Menu

The Document Control menu shown in Figure 1-11 is slightly different in appearance from the Word for Windows program

Figure 1-11.

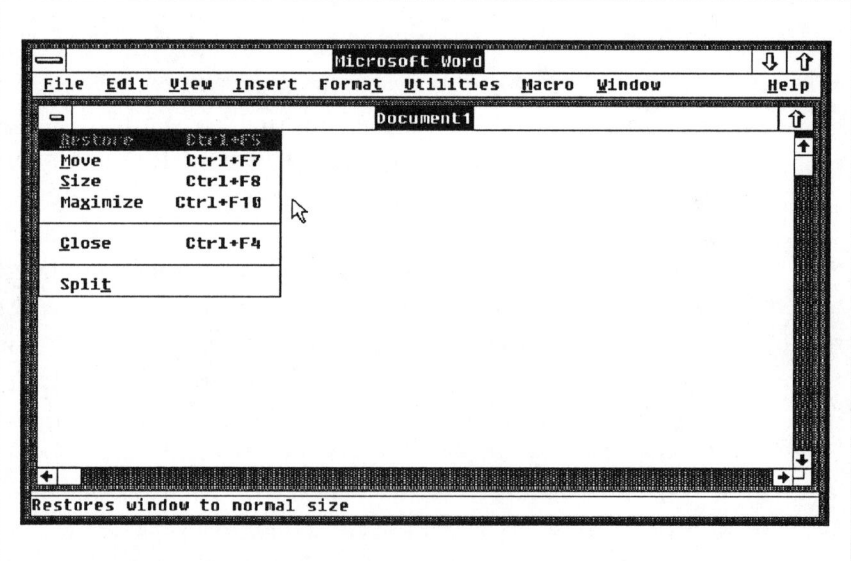

Word for Windows Document Control menu

Control menu. You can access it with the mouse just as you accessed the Windows and Word for Windows Control menu. You do this by clicking the left mouse button on the Document Control button. The Document Control button is slightly smaller than the Word for Windows Control button. To access the Document Control menu via the keyboard, you would type an ALT-HYPHEN keystroke combination. Double-clicking the left mouse button on the Document Control button closes the document window in the same way that double-clicking the left mouse button on the Word for Windows Control button closes Word for Windows.

The commands found in the Document Control menu are also slightly different than those found in the Windows program Control menu. There is no Minimize command because Word for Windows documents, unlike Windows programs, cannot be collapsed to an icon. A document is either open or closed. The Maximize command enlarges the document window to fill the entire space below the Word for Windows menu bar. The document window borders are dropped when you maximize the document window, allowing you to see more text on the screen. However, this also means that if other documents are open in different document windows, they will be covered by the maximized window. To uncover them, you would first have to activate the Restore command in the maximized document's Document Control menu. After you execute this command, the document window borders will return and you could drag them off the other document window either with the border control mouse arrows or with the Document Control menu Move command (as described earlier). The maximized Word for Windows' document screen, without the separate document window borders, appears in the screen views seen in all of the rest of this chapter's figures.

The Split command splits a single document window into two, and no more than two, horizontal panes (panes are separate portions of one window, like the windowpanes in your house). The Split command does not open up a new document window. Instead, the two panes share the same document borders; changes to a part of a document made in the second pane will be saved to the same document file shown in the original pane. Since both panes have their own scroll bars, you can scroll up or down to another part of the same document in the second pane, while maintaining your original place in the first pane. This extra pane is useful when you want to see if you had already discussed a topic at an earlier or later point in a single document. In contrast, Word 4.0 and 5.0 users need to open an entirely new document window with the same document to view two parts of the same document; this requires several extra steps beyond using Word for Windows' Split command.

File Menu

This section contains a brief discussion of the File menu shown in Figure 1-12. The File menu consists of two logically divided parts. They are the two boxes shown above the Exit command in the File menu in Figure 1-12. The upper box contains the commands associated with opening and saving files and the lower box contains commands associated with printing files.

The New dialog box has a document option that can be used to clear the screen and give you a clean text entry page, replacing any document window that may be present. In this way, it functions like the Transfer Clear command of Word 4.0 and 5.0. The New dialog box also has a template option that can be used to assign a new template to a new or existing document. The use of document templates is discussed in depth in Chapter 4, "For the Record," and Chapter 6, "Advanced Templates and Features."

The Open command brings up a dialog box from which you can load pre-existing documents. The Open command is similar to the Transfer Load command of Word 4.0 and 5.0. This command is discussed in depth in the "Dialog Box Operations" section later in this chapter.

The Close command closes all document windows containing the active document. You can load the same document into more

Figure 1-12.

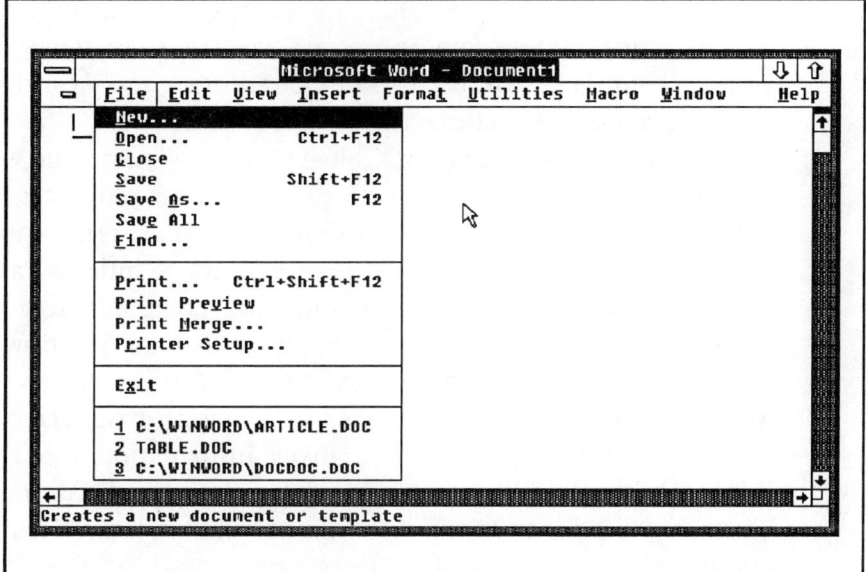

Word for Windows File menu

than one document window, and all changes made to any part of the document are saved to a single document file. As described earlier, the Split command allows you to open only two separate panes within one document window. However, if you need three or four views of the same document, you can open at least two document windows, one or both with two panes. Notice that when you close the Document1 (the only active document file) document window, all the command menus disappear from the menu bar except File. The File menu remains because if there are no files active, the only thing left to do with Word for Windows is to create a new file or open a pre-existing file.

The three Save commands are generally similar to the Transfer Save commands of Word 4.0 and 5.0. If you choose the Save command, the document is saved with the name listed in the document title bar. If you choose the Save As command, you are given a dialog box that allows you to make changes in the way the file is to be saved. The Save All command saves a document file as well as any template, macro, or glossary that you have created with it. Templates are discussed in Chapters 4 and 6, and macros and glossaries will be discussed in Chapter 6.

The Print Preview command lets you see what a page will look like (with correct size fonts, columned text, graphics, and so on) before you print it out. Less developed versions of this option are available when using Word 4.0 if you run the Windows PageView program with it. The Previewing mode of Word 5.0 also gives you some, but not all, of the power of the Word for Windows Print Preview. Print Merge, as in Word 4.0 and 5.0 (as well as in most word processing programs), takes information from records in a data base and inserts each record's information into a form template. Printing form letters and labels is the most common task involving the Print Merge command. The Printer Setup command activates the Setup Printer command in the MS-DOS Executive Control Panel dialog box. The Printer Setup dialog box lets you configure already installed printers or install new ones. Print Preview and Print Merge allow you to select the Print command from within these dialog boxes. You may also select the Print command directly from the File Menu. All of the Print commands are discussed in depth in Chapter 5, "Printing: Picture Perfect Output."

The File menu Exit command does the same thing as the Word for Windows Program Control menu Close command. When you choose Exit, the Word for Windows program window is closed and there is no icon for Word for Windows at the bottom of the screen. The MS-DOS Executive icon at the bottom left of the screen is automatically reopened, and the MS-DOS Executive program window appears.

The files listed as 1, 2, and 3 at the bottom of the File menu are the three most recently opened files. You can open any of these documents by clicking the left mouse button once on their titles.

Edit Menu

The top box of the Edit menu, shown in Figure 1-13, is *ghosted*. Ghosted commands are written in half intensity video to indicate that they are currently unavailable. These Edit commands are unavailable because nothing has been input into the current document file, no text has been entered, and no commands have been executed.

The Undo command negates the effects of the most recently invoked command. It will restore the screen, with the same text, as it appeared before the most recent command was executed. The Undo command cannot be accessed in Figure 1-13 because nothing has been entered, therefore nothing can be undone.

The Repeat command repeats the action of the last command executed. This command is useful if you have to perform the same

Figure 1-13.

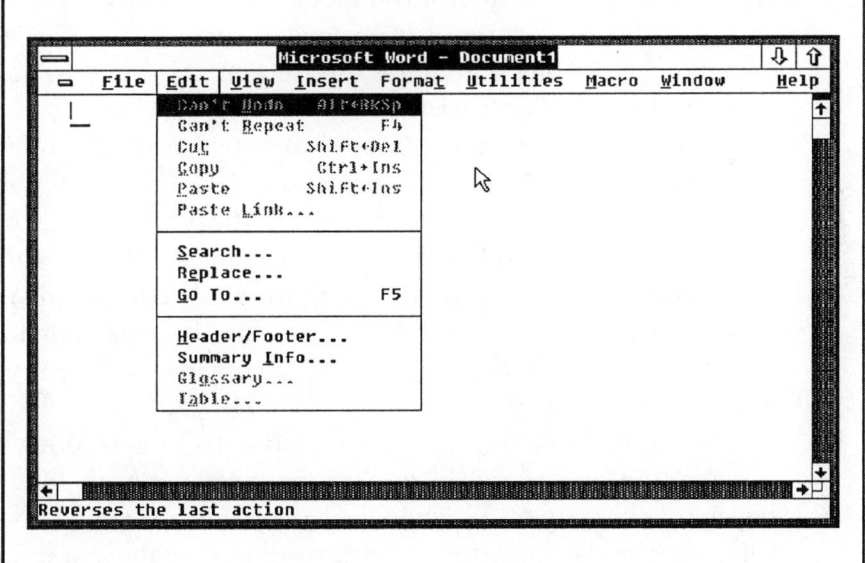

Word for Windows Edit menu

function on several parts of the same manuscript. For example, you may want to use the Search command (discussed later) to find and edit a passage that is repeated throughout a chapter. Instead of activating the Search command and typing in the same characters to search, you can use the Repeat command. If you want to repeat more than one command, or you want Word for Windows to run a search and execute the Repeat command on its own, you would have to create a macro (the Macro menu is discussed later in this chapter).

The next three commands are part of the Clipboard functions that were mentioned earlier in this chapter. Within Word for Windows, the Clipboard functions in the same way that the Scrap works in Word 4.0 and 5.0. Using the Cut command is analogous to deleting text to the Scrap in Word 4.0 and 5.0. Using the Copy command accomplishes the same function as copying text to the Scrap in Word 4.0 or 5.0. Before using the Cut or Copy command, you would first block off a portion of the document. This block may include graphics and tables, as well as text. If you choose the Cut command, the block disappears. It has been cut and transferred to the Clipboard. If you execute the Copy command, the block remains on screen, but it too has been deposited in the Clipboard.

After choosing Cut or Copy, you can paste the block now contained in the Clipboard someplace else in your Word for Windows document or in another Windows program. In Word for Windows, you paste the block by placing the cursor where you wish to insert the block and choosing the Paste command. You can also execute the Paste command repeatedly, inserting multiple copies of a block of text or a graphic image in one or more places within the document.

The Paste Link command allows you to link sections of files copied from one program into another so that both files will be simultaneously updated whenever a change is made in the original source file. An example of this would be a table copied from a

Windows Excel spreadsheet into a Word for Windows document. Linking files is discussed in Chapter 11.

 NOTE   Only the most recently cut or copied block is stored in the Clipboard. Each time you execute either of these commands, anything that was previously held in the Clipboard is dropped out of the Clipboard's memory. Also, since contents of the Clipboard are always held in the same memory space as the program, they are lost when you turn off your computer.

The commands in the second box of the Edit menu are used primarily for finding or moving to a word or phrase in a document. The Search command finds text or formatting in a Word for Windows document. Word 4.0 and 5.0 cannot search for formatting (see Chapter 2, "Formatting Text"). As in Word 4.0 and 5.0, the Replace command is an extension of the Search command. It allows you to search for text and/or formatting and replace it with different text and/or formatting. The Go To command replaces the Jump command in Word 4.0 and 5.0. The Go To command moves the cursor to the top of any page in the document. This is useful as long as you already know what page or bookmark you want to go to. You can leave what are called *bookmarks* (discussed under the section "Insert menu" later in this chapter) at any point in the document and return to these later with the Go To command.

The last box of the Edit menu relates to information that is appended to a document. You may edit headlines and any footnotes with the Header/Footer command. The Summary Info command lets you make notes (that will not be printed) about the document any time you are working on the document. The glossary in Word for Windows works in much the same way as the one in Word 4.0 and 5.0. The glossary lets you save repeatedly used text or graphics to a single key or word. You can then type the key or word alone and have Word for Windows insert the entire passage by pressing ALT-i. (The F3 key accomplished the same function in Word 4.0 and 5.0.) You may also use the mouse to insert glossary entries from the Edit Glossary dialog box which lists glossary names.

Word for Windows has many powerful table editing features, which are for the most part accessed through the Table command. Unlike Word 4.0 and 5.0, Word for Windows allows you to perfectly control the position of columns, rows, and even each cell's entry within a table. The Table command is ghosted in Figure 1-13 because there is no table present in the document. Table input and formatting is discussed in Chapter 3.

View Menu

The commands in the three boxes in the View menu, shown in Figure 1-14, control the appearance of the Word for Windows screen and your document. The uppermost box offers three ways of displaying the document: the Outline, the Draft, and the Page Command.

The Outline command works much as it does in Word 4.0 and 5.0. However, instead of indenting lower level headings, Word for Windows places a number to the left of the heading indicating the heading's importance (1 is the most important section heading in the document). As with Word 4.0 and 5.0, you can easily collapse and move whole sections into one heading and then move just the heading around within the document. Later you can expand the heading and its associated text will reappear. The Draft command activates a screen mode in Word for Windows that is the same as the text mode in Word 4.0 and 5.0. All of Word for Windows' WYSIWYG (What You See Is What You Get) features, such as onscreen typefaces, different size fonts, and graphics, are shown as standard text that is underlined. The Page command causes the screen to show the page exactly as it would look if it were to be printed.

Figure 1-14.

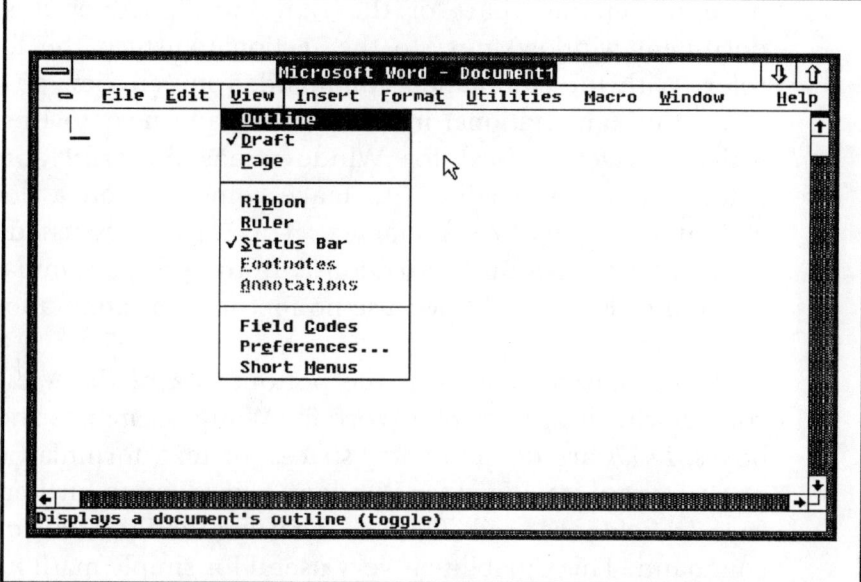

Word for Windows View menu

If you select the Ribbon and Ruler commands, two different screen elements appear, which allow you to quickly implement the Format menu's Character and Paragraph commands discussed in Chapter 2. Both the Ribbon and Ruler take up a large portion of the screen; therefore, they have limited utility (except on a very large monitor). Their use is discussed in Chapter 4.

The *status bar,* located at the bottom of the screen, shows you the page, line, section (section formatting is new to Word for Windows and is discussed in Chapter 2, "Formatting Text"), and column number where the cursor is located. It also indicates whether the Overtype feature (INS key), and CAPS or NUMLOCK keys are active or not. The Status Bar command on the View menu functions like a toggle switch. By default, the status bar is displayed. You can delete the status bar from the bottom of the screen by activating the Status Bar command. You can then redisplay the status bar whenever you want it to show by again selecting the Status Bar command.

The Footnotes command lets you view footnotes in a separate pane (a separate part of the same window, not a separate document window) next to the section to which the footnotes refer. With the Annotation command, you can view an editor's comments (annotations) in a separate pane next to the text to which it refers. Word for Windows has powerful annotation features that allow editors to make comments on a document without changing the original text. This topic is discussed further in Chapter 8, "Group Productions." Both of these commands are ghosted in Figure 1-14 because no footnotes or annotations have been entered.

All of the commands in the bottom box of the View menu control what is displayed in Word for Windows' menus and dialog boxes. *Fields* are defined entry spaces for text, formulas, queries, or even graphics. Word for Windows allows you to further specify the way fields are used. This is done using the Insert Fields Codes command. This capability is very useful for simple math functions or complex mail merge documents, and is discussed in Chapter 6 and Chapter 9. The Preferences command allows you to turn off the display of features such as tabs, paragraph end signs, and graphic images. The program will run faster when these options are turned off. The Short Menus command drops some of the less frequently used commands from the displayed menus. When you choose the Short Menus command, the Full Menus command replaces it in the View menu. Choosing Full Menus puts all the commands back into the menus. You can also change the menus with the Macro Assign to Menu command.

Insert Menu

The commands in the two boxes of the Insert menu shown in Figure 1-15 have obvious functions. Both sets of commands allow the precise insertion of items into a Word for Windows document.

Figure 1-15.

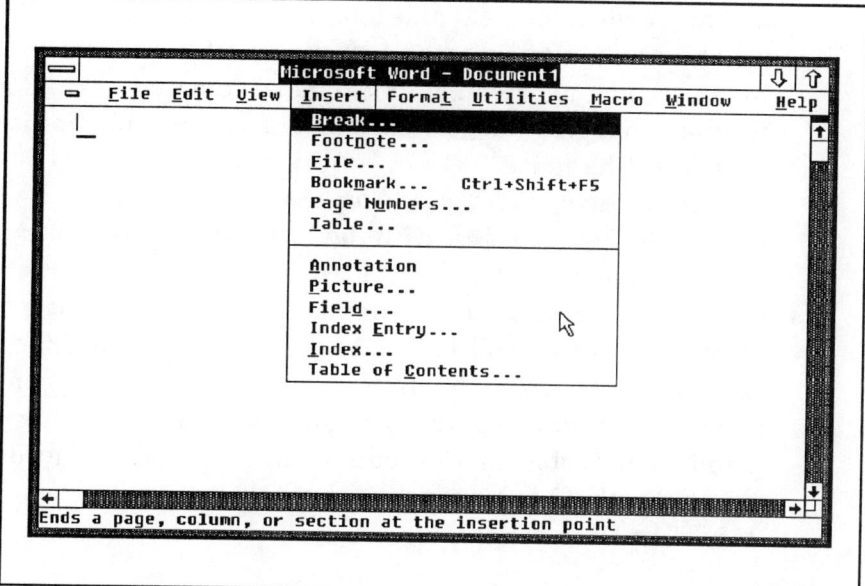

Word for Windows Insert menu

The upper box commands insert simple text related items; the commands in the lower box insert non-text related items.

The Break command inserts a column, page, or section break. A column break causes the next paragraph to begin in a new column and a page break causes text following it to continue on a new page. Sections are a new feature added to Word with the Windows edition; section formatting is discussed in detail in Chapter 2, "Formatting Text." A *section break* causes text following a section to begin a new section that may be on the same page as the first section.

The Footnote, File, Page Numbers, and Table commands allow the precise insertion of all of these document elements within a Word for Windows document. The Bookmark command lets you mark a specific location in the document with a title. Later you can go back to this bookmark by using the Go To command in the Edit menu. Of all these commands, only the ability to insert footnotes is available in Word 4.0 and 5.0.

The Annotation command, as discussed previously in the View menu section, allows an editor to make comments on a document without changing the original text. Editorial functions are discussed in Chapter 8.

The Picture command allows you to precisely insert and position graphic images. With the Field command, you can define fields, as mentioned in the "View Menu" section earlier in this chapter. The Index Entry command allows you to insert a mark (not printed) that will be used later to compile an index to the document. By using the Index command, you can compile an alphabetized index of words marked with the Index Entry command. The Table of Contents command collects headings assigned by the View menu Outline command and assembles a document table of contents.

Format Menu

The Format menu shown in Figure 1-16 is the central text handling feature of Word 4.0, 5.0, and Word for Windows. The formatting and quick editing of text is the essence of word processing. The additional character, section, and formatting features that make up the Format menu are major factors in the elevation of Word for Windows to the word publishing category. These features are the topic of Chapter 2.

Picture (graphic image) and table formatting features are discussed in Chapter 3. The style features of Word for Windows are much improved over Word 4.0 and 5.0. Most notably, you can now incorporate text into a style sheet. This style sheet would act as a template for later documents, preserving repeatedly used document formats such as a standard letter or report.

Figure 1-16.

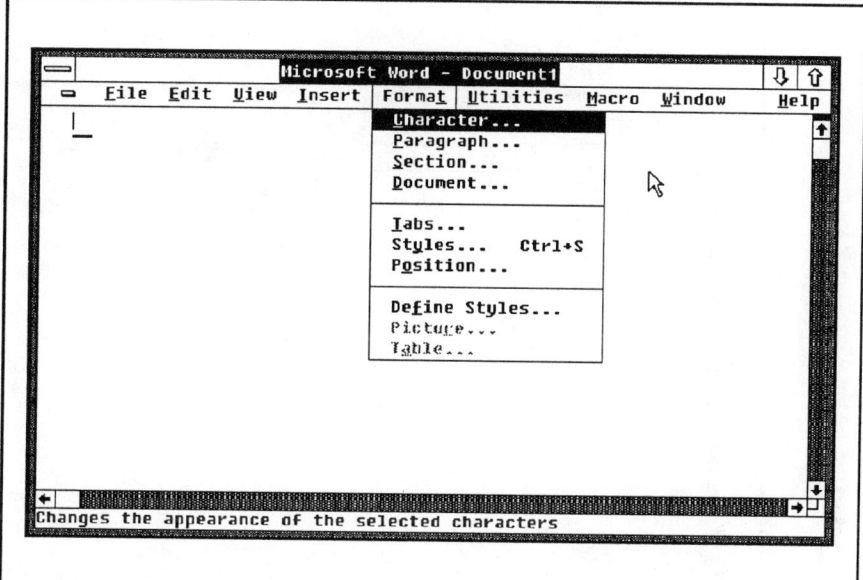

Word for Windows Format menu

Utilities Menu

The Utilities menu commands perform repetitive functions not directly related to document creation. The commands in the Utilities menu are all subprograms of Word for Windows, such as a spelling checker, calculator, and a thesaurus, that can be accessed without leaving Word for Windows. The commands in the upper box and the Renumber command in the lower box of the Utilities menu shown in Figure 1-17 are all similar to commands with the same names found in the Library menu of Word 4.0 and 5.0. The Renumber command numbers or renumbers paragraphs in a highlighted block. Similarly, if you number paragraphs in the order you want them to appear, then highlight them and execute the Sort command, they will be placed in the order you indicated.

Figure 1-17.

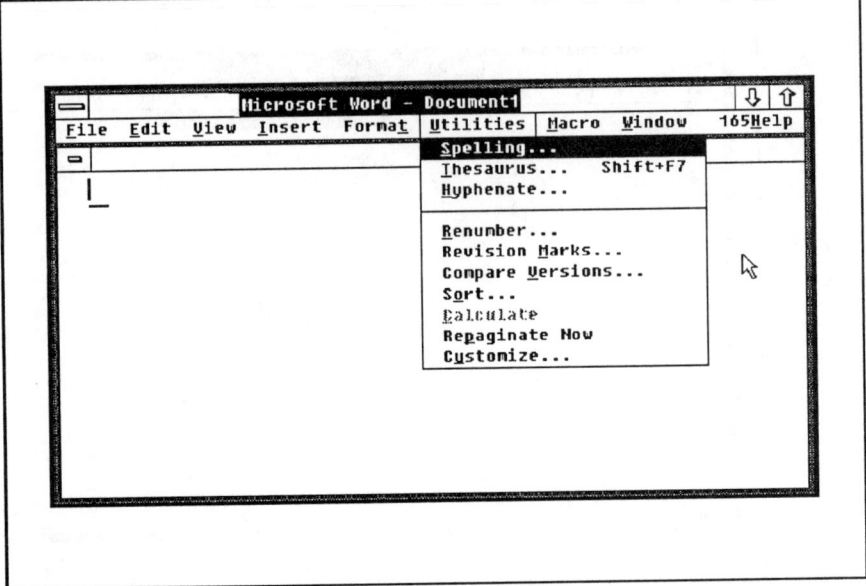

Word for Windows Utilities menu

The Revision Marks and Compare Versions commands are editing commands that are discussed in Chapter 8. The Calculate command solves equations using math functions and is discussed in Chapter 9. The Repaginate Now command repaginates a document when you have turned off background pagination, which makes the program run faster. It will insert page breaks and tell you how many words and pages there are in the document. Because Word 4.0 does not have automatic pagination, whenever you want to know what page you are on as you enter or edit text, you must execute the Print Repaginate command. Word 5.0 has automatic pagination which can be disabled to speed up the program operation.

The Customize command lets you turn automatic pagination on and off, as well as choose the unit of measure (inches, centimeters, points, or picas) to be used by Word for Windows. You can also set the frequency of automatic document saving with the Autosave option. The Autosave option is very useful since it lets you have your computer save your document at standard intervals. If you have ever lost an entire day's work by accidentally kicking out your computer's plug, or from a blown fuse, a black out, or from the screen just freezing, you will be thankful for this feature. It is best to save at least every 20 minutes. Your computer will slow down when it autosaves, but not as much as it would slow you down to have to remember and retype an entire document. The Customize command is discussed in detail in Appendix C.

Macro Menu

Macros are records of a series of operations that are saved to a single key such as FI, or more commonly an ALT-, CTRL- or SHIFT-*key* keystroke combination. For example, you might want to save "Enclosed:" to the ALT-e keystroke combination so that when you need it at the end of a letter, you would merely type ALT-e and Word for Windows would make the insertion. Word for Windows has an all-encompassing keystroke recorder; it can save text, formatting, and program commands. For example, you can type your name and format it in a centered paragraph using 12-point bold Helvetica and have Word for Windows record and save all of this information to ALT-x as you are typing it.

The Macro menu shown in Figure 1-18 includes the Record command which would let you name your ALT-x macro and then record the proper keystrokes as you input them. A Stop Recorder command is inserted in the menu whenever you execute the Record command. (The Stop Recorder command does not show in the Macro menu in Figure 1-18 because the Record command has not been executed.) The Run command lets you select and run a macro from the list of macros you have compiled. The Edit command shows you the keystrokes you have saved to a macro and lets you change them or make additions. The Assign to Key command assigns or reassigns a macro to a key or keystroke

Figure 1-18.

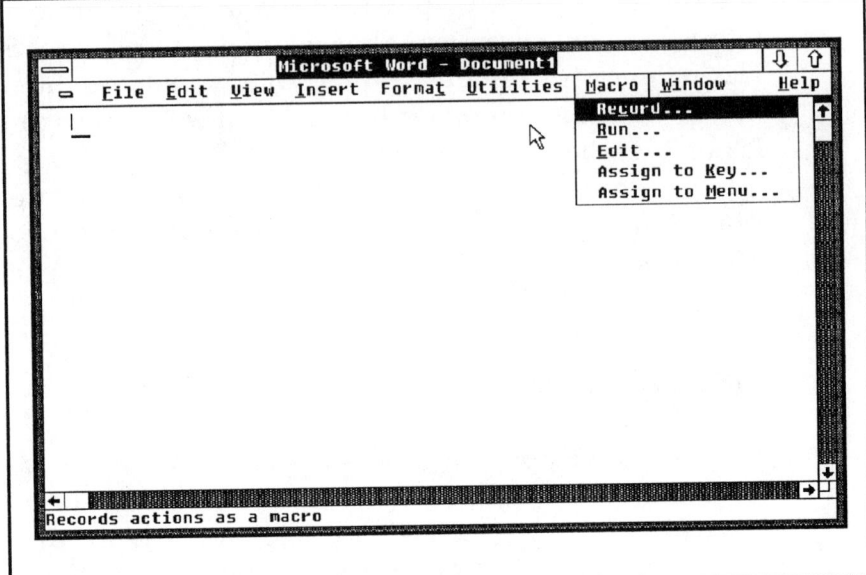

Word for Windows Macro menu

combination. The Assign to Menu command lets you add your own macro to any of Word for Windows' menus. In effect, this function lets you design your own Word for Windows menus. Macro functions are discussed further in Chapter 6.

Window Menu

The commands in the Window menu shown in Figure 1-19 control the document window. The New Window command opens a new window containing the same document as the original window. The Arrange All command arranges all document windows that are open so they do not overlap, which allows you to see all the text in all open document windows. The checked "1 Document1" indicates that DOCUMENT1.DOC in document window number 1 is currently the active document. An

Figure 1-19.

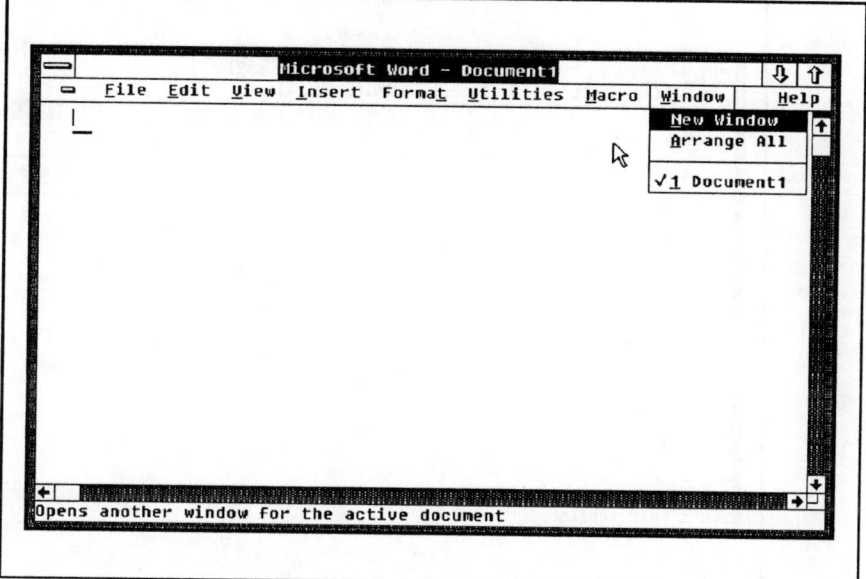

Word for Windows Window menu

active document always has the live, blinking text cursor within it. You can move the cursor to another window by clicking the left mouse button anywhere in the second window (as long as a part of it is exposed), or by clicking the arrow-shaped mouse on the document window numbers listed at the bottom of the Window menu.

Help Menu

Word for Windows has a context sensitive Help menu shown in Figure 1-20. The Index command lists the topics of all of the help modules. The next two commands in the Help menu relate to your computer's screen and keyboard. The Keyboard command shows you the help topics related to using the keyboard and

Figure 1-20.

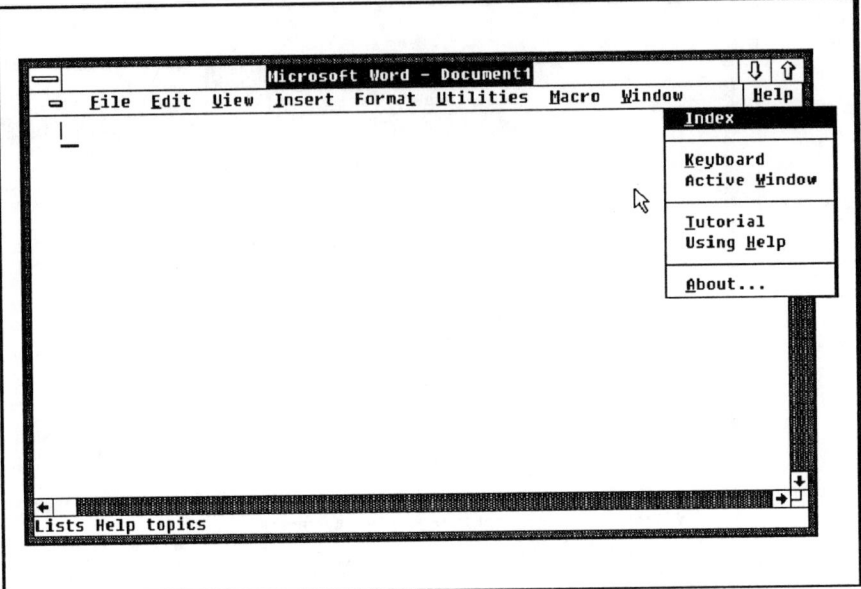

Word for Windows Help menu

keyboard commands. The Active Window command offers information on the View mode of the active window (the document window containing the blinking cursor). The View mode may be the normal editing view, or it may be the Draft view, Outline view, or Page view. These screen modes were discussed in the "View Menu" section earlier in this chapter.

If you want a lesson on Word for Windows in general, or on a specific section of Word for Windows, you can use the Tutorial command. The Using Help command opens a window that will explain how you use the Help menu. The About command tells you what version of Word for Windows you are running and how much conventional, hard disk and expanded memory is currently available for Word for Windows to use.

Overall Hierarchy of Commands

The Word for Windows menus provide an important level of organization for the menus' commands. The menu titles direct you to their contained commands. The hierarchical arrangement of commands and options within menus has been designed so it will be easy for you to find any possible option. A command card showing the menu-command-option hierarchy of Word for Windows can be found at the end of this book. You will want to keep this card close at hand as you go through this book and continue to learn about Word for Windows.

Dialog Box Operations

Dialog boxes were covered briefly in the earlier part of this chapter. Dialog boxes are displayed on your screen whenever you select a command followed by ". . ." Dialog boxes contain options for the command that you want to execute. You select your options in a field, of which there are several types. In this section, you will learn the various ways in which you make these option selections. This discussion centers on the options related to selecting and saving files, commands you need to execute to do at least simple tasks with Word for Windows.

Text Entry Fields

Figure 1-21 shows the File menu with a mouse arrow on the Open command. If you click the left button of the mouse here, the File Open dialog box appears. You also see "Ctrl+F12" next to the

Figure 1-21.

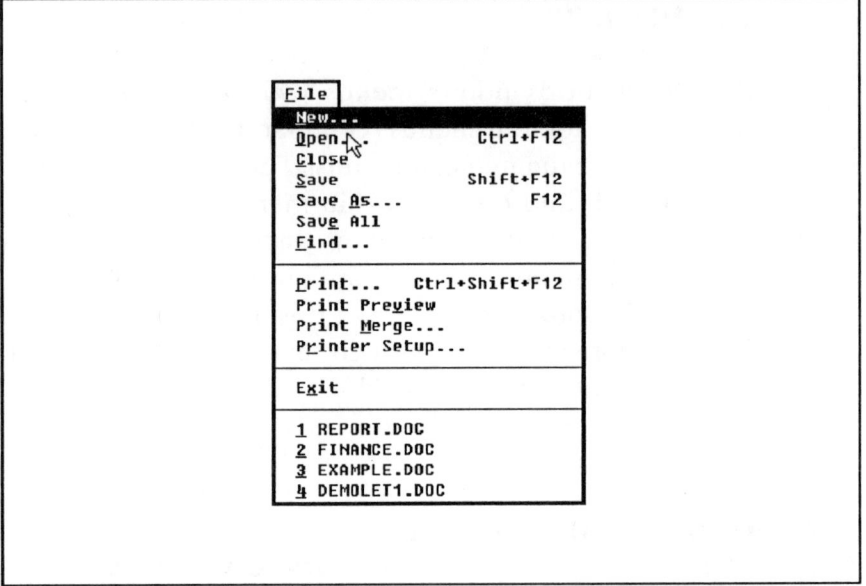

Sample Word for Windows menu

Open command. This means that the File Open dialog box can be accessed from the keyboard by typing the CTRL-F12 keystroke combination.

The File Open dialog box is shown in Figure 1-22. The cursor is in the Open File Name text-entry field which says ∗.DOC. This is the Word for Windows document file default. As in Word 4.0 and 5.0, unless specified otherwise, all Word for Windows documents are appended with the ∗.DOC extension. You see below the Open File Name field, that C:\WINWORD is the current data directory. Other available drives and subdirectories of WIN-WORD are listed to the right of the file listing.

The Open File Name field is a text-entry field which means that you can type information into it. When the mouse is over a text-entry field, it assumes the I-beam shape, shown here.

Figure 1-22.

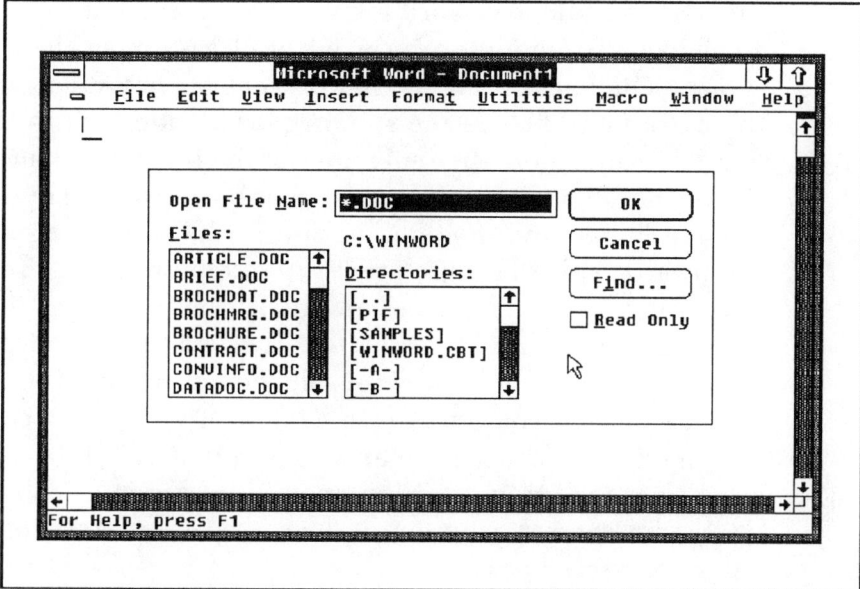

File Open dialog box

Click the left mouse button with the I-beam mouse in this position and a text-entry cursor appears at the end of the text in the Open File Name text-entry field. Backspace all the way to the left of the text-entry field of the Open dialog box and it will become clear, as shown here.

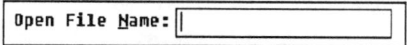

If you Backspace over the default entry, you can then type in the name of any file that you want loaded. Another use of the Open File Name text-entry field is to insert a new subdirectory, as has been done here.

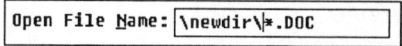

After you are done typing, press ENTER to make the changes. A new list of files, from the new subdirectory, will be exhibited in the Files scroll box.

The Files and Directories scroll boxes work the same way that the scroll bars do in a Word for Windows document window. The scroll bar is present in case the list of files is longer than the box shown. The bar represents 100 percent of the available files. If there are more files in the subdirectory than can fit in the Files box, you can expose the remainder of the files by clicking the left mouse button on the white rectangular box below the up arrow of the scroll bar and holding it down while dragging the box downward. This will cause the list to scroll down past the listings that fit in the box. If you release the left mouse button while the box is halfway down the scroll bar, the middle of the list will be shown. If all the listings fit in the Files box, the white rectangle will not move when you attempt to drag it. Clicking the left mouse button on the up and down arrows at either end of the scroll bar also brings the list up or down one listing at a time. You can also use the PGUP and PGDN buttons if the cursor is in either the Files or Directories scroll box.

When you have found the file name you want in the scroll box, you can click the left mouse button on it once and the name will appear in the Open File Name field. You may then click the left mouse button on the OK box, shown in Figure 1-22, or press ENTER to open this file. Double-clicking the left mouse button on the file name in the Files scroll box will load the file without the need to click the left mouse button on the OK box. The options in the menu's File Save As and Print dialog boxes work in the same way as the File menu's Open dialog box options. If you choose these commands and execute them with their defaults, you can now create, save, and print a simple, unformatted document.

Scroll-down Boxes

There are a few other ways to choose command options in Word for Windows' dialog box. The Format menu's Character dialog

Figure 1-23.

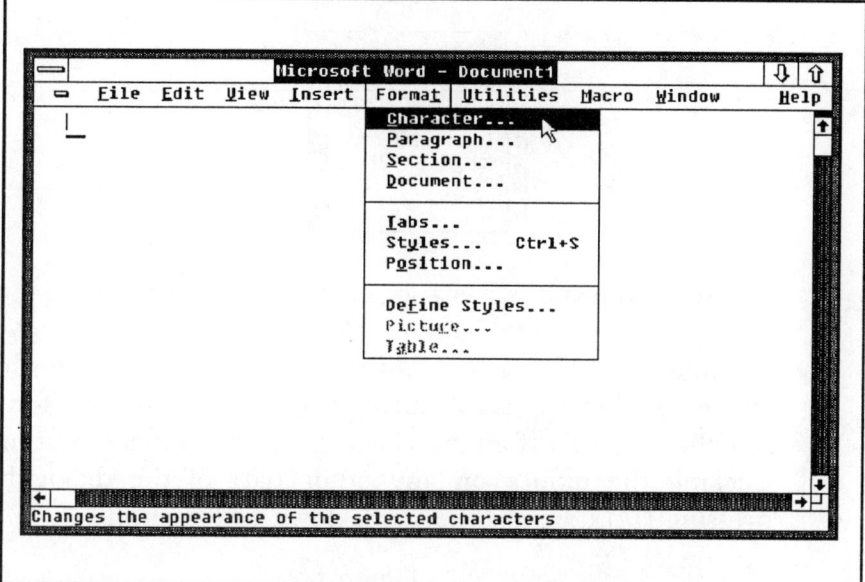

Format menu with the mouse set to activate the Character dialog box

box has all the possible means of entering options. Since the use of the Character dialog box is covered in detail in the next chapter, this discussion will center on the ways in which options are selected, not on the options themselves.

You activate the Format menu's Character dialog box by choosing the Character command as shown in Figure 1-23. The Character dialog box shown in Figure 1-24 will appear. The cursor is highlighting the Font text entry field. Note that at the right of this text entry field there is a boxed downward pointing arrow which activates the Font *scroll-down box*.

The Font scroll-down box comes down when you click the left mouse button on the arrow, as shown here.

The scroll-down box looks like this.

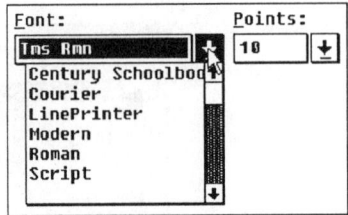

The scroll-down box has a scroll bar which works in the same way as the scroll box in the Open dialog box or the Word for Windows document window. You can use the mouse to drag the white box in the bar down to scroll through the list of available fonts. You can then select a font by clicking the left mouse button on it. Clicking the mouse on any other part of the dialog box, or pressing ENTER, brings the scroll-down box back up.

Figure 1-24.

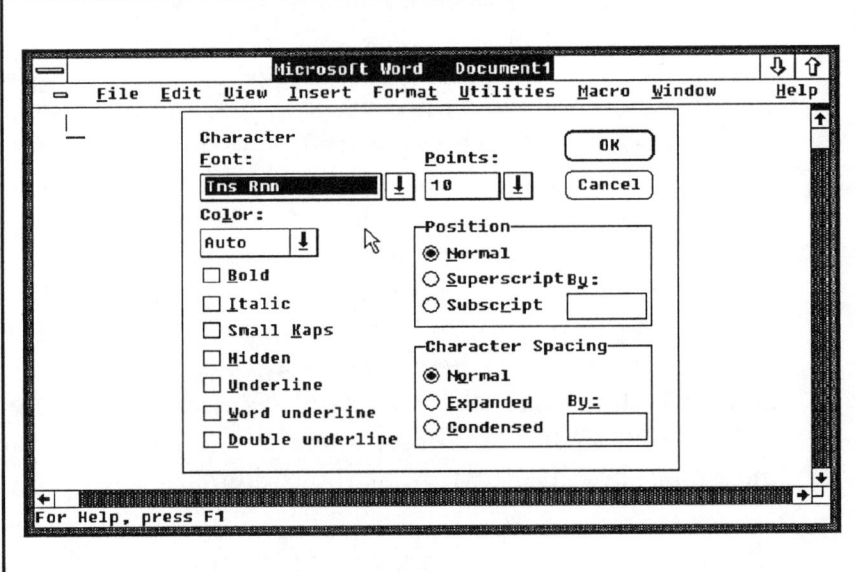

The Character dialog box opening screen

Toggle Boxes and Buttons

Another set of options in the Character dialog box are not user-definable; rather, both *toggle boxes* and buttons are either on or off.

 NOTE Toggle boxes are called "check boxes" in Microsoft's Word for Windows documentation.

Both toggle boxes and buttons "toggle" on and off; the term toggle means that these options will switch on and off, sequentially, as you click the mouse on them. Figure 1-25 shows the mouse arrow positioned over the Bold toggle box. If you click the

Figure 1-25.

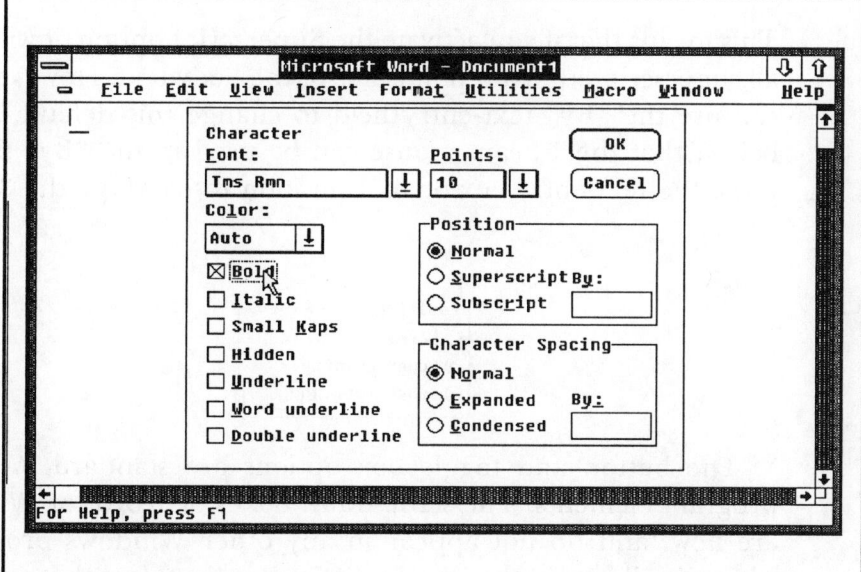

Bold text toggle box activated

left mouse button on this toggle box, it will fill in with an "X." The Bold option is on when there is an "X" in the box. As you will see in Chapter 2, some options have an "on" default.

A button, which is not always round on the screen, works in a way similar to the toggle box. Buttons are either on or off. Some buttons, like the rectangular OK or Cancel buttons, activate commands directly. Buttons often activate sets of options that would not normally be available. When you click the left mouse button on this type of button, the center will fill in; when the center is filled in, it is usually referred to as a *bulleted button*. Notice here that the Superscript button has been bulleted and that its default value is 3 points.

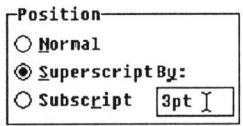

This means that if you activate the Superscript option, it will place all superscripted text 3 points above the body text. However, you can use the "By" text-entry field to change this default. Notice below, that the I-beam mouse can be used in the "By" field to place the text-entry cursor in a position to overtype the 3 point value.

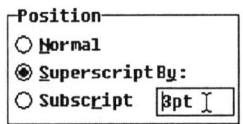

The button and toggle box options are standard Windows program elements. The scroll-down boxes of Word for Windows are new, and do not appear in any other Windows programs. They are all part of the Word for Windows interface that you have just learned.

Word for Windows is an expansive program. You can learn about Word for Windows advanced word publishing features at your own pace and still meet all your daily word processing needs. As you read the subsequent chapters, you will want to take advantage of Word for Windows' ability to bring together multiple fonts, graphic images, and tables.

CHAPTER

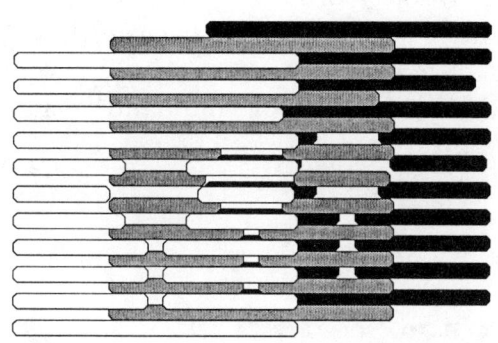

2

Formatting Text

Formatting is the essence of word processing. Word publishing programs, such as Word for Windows, retain the powerful formatting commands found in word processors. More importantly, word publishing programs offer the same formatting speed as word processing programs, while offering additional typographic and graphic functions. Desktop publishing programs have more advanced formatting, typographic, and graphic abilities, but generally do not process text and operate much more slowly than word publishing or even word processing software.

Chapter 1, "Up and Running," introduced you to the appearance and basic operation of Word for Windows. In this chapter, you will take an in-depth look at the structure of the formatting family of commands found in Word for Windows.

59

The information covered in this chapter assumes some familiarity with how formatting commands are generally applied when a word-processed document is created. If you are familiar with previous versions of Microsoft Word, you will already know the basics of *most* of the features covered here. However, the addition to Word for Windows of a new menu system and several new operations (especially the Format Section command) ensures that some of the commands presented here will be new to everyone.

When to Format?

The first question to answer about the Format commands is when to use them. At some stage, formatting is important for every document, but depending on the type of document you are creating, formatting while you write can be an aid or a hindrance. Word for Windows gives you formatting flexibility. You can create a document without setting any format parameters, or you can format your work while you construct it. At times you may want to flow words onto the screen without setting up much of the document's format, especially if you find that adding formatting parameters as you write detracts from the creative process. Constant attention to the final appearance of the printed document requires that you continually adjust format settings. Too much fine tuning can often slow a project past deadline. If you find that paying attention to formatting conventions while you write is distracting, you may decide to make formatting a finishing touch to your document.

On the other hand, formatting choices such as varied typefaces for headers and body text, paragraph indents, and document margins can often provide a structure for organizing ideas that actually aids in the successful and timely completion of your writing task. A document can also become more effective if your writing fits into a well thought out and visually effective text layout. Often the appearance of words and paragraphs can greatly enhance the document's message. In Chapter 4, "For the Record: Styles and Templates," and Chapter 6, "Advanced Template Features," you will see when it is useful to painstakingly format your document.

Recording the formatting as you compose a document can be very useful, especially when you want to create a *template.* A template is a set of standardized character, paragraph, and document formats, created once, which can then be applied to the text in a later document. A template can be as little as a record of a single paragraph format, such as ragged right margin, 1/2" left indent on the first line, and double-spaced type. Or, a template can include every level of formatting detail, from character to document. A template may also include text that must always appear in a particular kind of document, such as a return address in a letter. Templates are especially helpful when you create forms such as memos, questionnaires, or receipts.

Word for Windows offers other organizational tools for recording and manipulating text as well. Word for Windows' composition tools such as macro capabilities, table and index creation aids, and an outlining mode, are discussed in Chapters 3, 4, 6, and 7. Understanding the structure of Word for Windows' formatting capabilities, however, is the first step to deciding the best way to create a particular document.

The Format Command Family

Throughout its evolution, Microsoft Word has by design maintained a cohesive set of formatting commands. As with previous versions of Microsoft Word, choosing Format in Word for Windows displays the Format menu that includes the familiar Format

Character, Paragraph, Section, and Document commands (Document is analogous to Division in earlier versions of Word) as well as the other Format commands. This is a particular strength of Word for Windows since many other word processing and word publishing programs are not menu oriented. Often these other programs do not have logically linked formatting commands, located in one place, as does Word for Windows.

Accessing the Format Commands

The Format menu is activated either by placing the mouse arrow on the word "Format", which appears on the menu bar shown here,

and clicking the left button, or by pressing the ALT and t keys simultaneously. You use the t key in the ALT-t keystroke combination to display the Format menu because in the word "Forma*t*" on the menu bar, the letter "t" is underlined.

When you open the Format menu, you will see *all* of the commands related to formatting a document as shown in Figure 2-1. Thus, without having to memorize any commands, you have accessed the complete family of Format commands. You can choose the Format commands by typing the underlined letter, for example the "c" in Character. You do not need to type in a capital "C" for Character, nor a lowercase "y" for Format Style since Word for Windows' command execution, like DOS, is not case sensitive. To save time, always use the lowercase letter. You may

Figure 2-1.

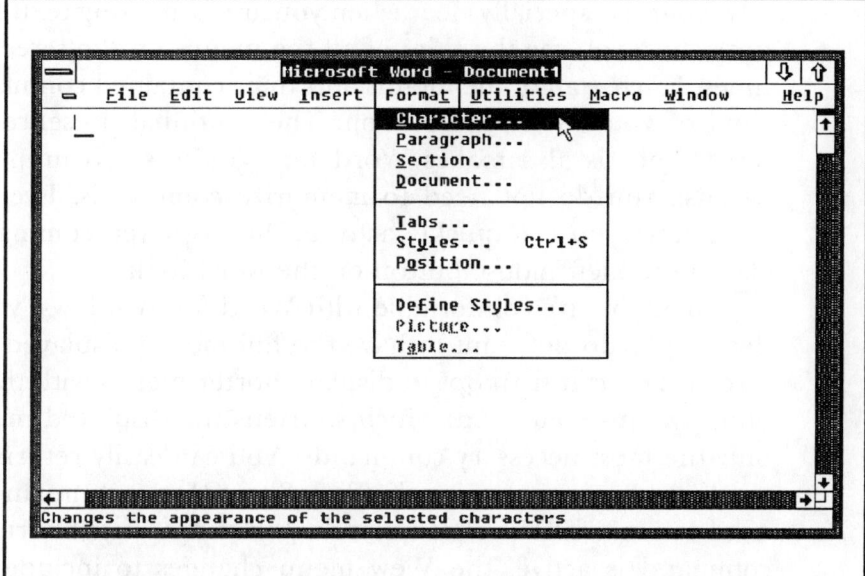

Format menu

also select any of the Format commands by placing the mouse cursor on the menu choice you wish to select and clicking the left mouse button.

Dialog boxes, as discussed in Chapter 1, "Up and Running," illustrate all of the options available for a command. Again, you do not have to memorize either the mouse or keyboard Format menu commands or the command options in a dialog box because Word for Windows displays them all. Selecting options from within dialog boxes will be reviewed later in this chapter.

Word for Windows' Visual Orientation

One of the major advantages of Microsoft Word and Word for Windows is their shared visual orientation as opposed to the mnemonic orientation of many other similar programs. This advantage is especially clear when you are formatting text. In both programs, you see the titles of all the menus on the screen at all times. Having all of the menus and their contained commands in front of you invites exploration. The continual presence of on-screen menus also makes Word for Windows less intimidating because you do not need to memorize commands. Even more important, you can quickly activate the displayed commands by clicking the left mouse button on the word itself.

When you are comfortable with Word for Windows, you may decide you do not want to have the full menus displayed on the screen. You can then opt to display shorter menus with the View Short Menus command, which shortens the displayed menus to only the most necessary commands. You can easily return to full menus when you are using the View Short Menus command if you need to see a full list of commands. When the View Short Menus command is active, the View menu changes to include a Full Menus command. If you activate the View Full Menus command, Word for Windows returns to the default full menus, and the Short Menus command reappears as part of the View menu. Overall, this visual orientation of the common Windows interface found in Word for Windows shortens the time you need to spend learning the program.

Keystroke Combinations

The historical development of word processing software shows that, unlike Microsoft Word and Word for Windows, formatting commands are not commonly shown onscreen; often commands are listed deep within a Help menu or, worse yet, buried in the program manual. Following the lead from early mainframe text editors, many PC word processing and now word publishing applications continue to assign unrelated CTRL-*key* (Control), SHIFT-*key*, or ALT-*key* keystroke combinations to each of the central formatting tasks. The term *keystroke combinations* means that the CTRL, SHIFT, or ALT key is held down while a second key is pressed.

These CTRL-*key*, SHIFT-*key* and ALT-*key* combinations are assigned to commands in many word processing and word publishing packages. Such nonintuitive keystroke combinations have been used primarily because each new formatting feature is added long after the design of the original version's formatting features. In order to not alienate prior users of the program, the commands are not reassigned to new keys, even though they might be easier to learn and remember if they were reassigned (for example, ALT-s to save a file, or ALT-q to quit).

Microsoft has not assigned the ALT-*key* keystroke combinations as an afterthought. Rather, ALT-*key* combinations can be used to open the menu system that is the basis of Word for Windows. For example, the Format menu may be accessed either with the mouse, by clicking the left button of the mouse on the word "Format" in the menu bar, or by using the keystroke combination ALT-t. All of the menus, as well as the commands, can be accessed by similar keystroke combinations. Note that the "*t*" in "Forma*t*" in the menu bar shown in Figure 2-1 is underlined, indicating that t is the key in the ALT-*key* combination, not the intuitive f which is already taken by the File menu. Note that since the underlined letter is not always the first letter, as with the "t" in "Forma*t*," it is not always capitalized. This is different than Word 4.0 and 5.0 in which the letter to choose is always capitalized but not underlined. In both Word for Windows and the earlier versions of Word, you do not have to memorize the program menu structure and its coding to execute commands. Instead of having you memorize nonintuitive ALT-*key* combinations, Word for Windows relates keyboard commands to the menus when possible and visually indicates them by underlining the key in the ALT-*key* combination.

Mouse Versus Keyboard Formatting

Word for Windows lets you use either the mouse or keyboard to format text. If you are about to enter new text and wish to preformat, you will save time by using keyboard commands. Regardless of which selection method you use, all text you type in after you choose a Format command will reflect the choices you have made until you change the formatting. Situations arise, however, when it will be more efficient to use the ALT-*key*, CTRL-*key*, and SHIFT-*key* combinations, or a key that matches the underlined letters of commands and command options. Remember that when you use keyboard formatting, your hand does not have to leave the keyboard to pick up the mouse; you also do not need to roll the mouse to move across the screen to the command you wish to execute.

It will be faster to use the mouse to format text you have already entered, for instance, when you want to perform more than one formatting operation on a single block of text. The mouse helps you block off large sections of text quickly and easily. First, move the I-beam mouse to the character where you want a block to begin. Click the left mouse button once to move the cursor to that location. Hold the left mouse button down and drag the mouse arrow across the screen (vertically, horizontally, or diagonally) to the last character you want included in the block. Finally, let go of the button, and the entire block is highlighted. You can then choose a *series* of Format commands to apply to the blocked text.

You can also block text with the keyboard. To do this, you move the cursor to the first character of the block with the keypad arrows and press F8 to begin blocking. Then, by moving the cursor with any of the keypad arrows or with the PGUP and PGDN keys, you can extend the cursor to highlight the portion of the text you wish to block. Most of the time, however, it is faster to use the mouse to block off text because the mouse can move across the screen diagonally, whereas the arrow keys can only move up or down, right or left.

If you have not entered text that can be formatted with a particular Format command, the command cannot be chosen by mouse or keyboard. These unavailable commands are always *ghosted* (written in grey on a color monitor or half intensity on a monochrome monitor) when displayed in a menu or dialog box. Note that the Format Picture and Format Table commands are ghosted as you can see here.

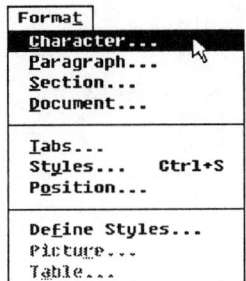

Dialog Box Operations

Dialog boxes were discussed in Chapter 1, "Up and Running," but because they are new to Word for Windows, a brief review of how to use them is provided here. If you skipped the first chapter, this review will enable you to follow the discussion of Format command dialog boxes throughout the rest of the chapter.

Option Fields

Within a dialog box, all option sets have at least a single *option field* (area for data entry) in which you may make a choice. Option fields are the areas within the dialog box where you select or enter settings as shown here.

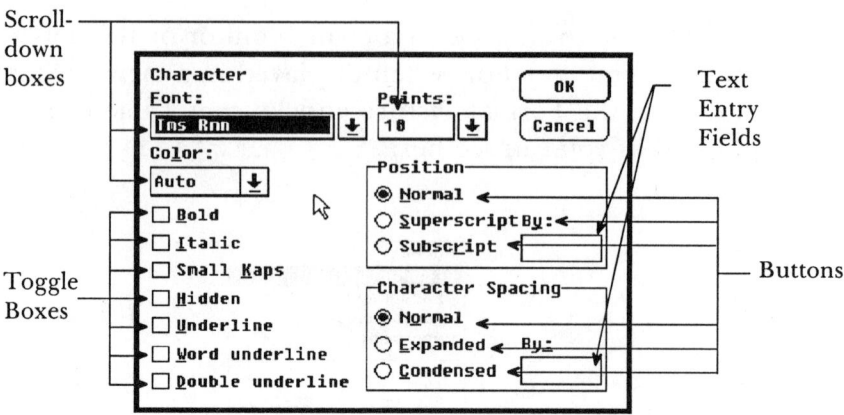

Once you are finished, option field choices and settings will configure the command that opened the dialog box. When you activate any command that causes a dialog box to be displayed, you will see that most of the option fields exhibit a default listing. A few may be ghosted, which means they are unavailable, and others that are inactive may be blank.

Option fields, termed *user-definable option fields,* allow you to define the settings by typing text or numbers over either a default entry or a blank option field. For example, you can supply text to name a style (such as header 1, a default Word for Windows style), or enter any measurement that is within the limits of your printer's output. For example, even though the maximum paper size is 8 1/2" by 11" for most printers, you could use a smaller sheet of paper. You would then change the 8 1/2" by 11" default to, for example, 6" by 9".

You can move the cursor highlight among the various Format command option choices either by clicking the left mouse button on the next option choice or by using the TAB key to move between options one at time. This is also the way you move about in menus in Word 4.0 and 5.0. Tabbing between a group of options that you want to change is often more efficient than taking your hand off the keyboard to use the mouse to move between several options. Once you have positioned the cursor, you are ready to make an option choice selection. Again, the TAB key is usually more efficient because once you have made all your changes, you can simply press ENTER to activate the changes, again keeping both hands on the keyboard.

You can also use the mouse to move the cursor among options by clicking the left mouse button on the option name. This moves the cursor to the option field that you want to select or set. When you finish selecting options in this way, you click the left mouse button on the OK button in the upper right of the dialog box to activate the changes. If you click the left mouse button on the Cancel button, below OK, none of the changes you have made will be incorporated.

Scroll-down Boxes

Scroll-down boxes, such as those associated with the Font, Points, and Color option fields in the Format Character dialog box, can also be used to select options as shown here.

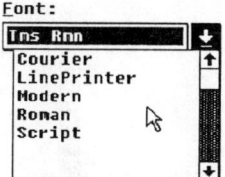

Scroll-down boxes are a new addition to Word for Windows dialog boxes and are not yet found in other Windows applications. Options that have a scroll-down box are identified by the small down arrow in the box to the right of the option field. You can display the list of options in a scroll-down box without pulling down the scroll-down box by using the UP ARROW and DOWN ARROW keys. When the cursor is on a scroll-down box and the keypad UP ARROW or DOWN ARROW is depressed, the available options are listed sequentially, one at a time, in the option field. You can also pull down the scroll-down box to display all of the options in the scroll-down box. You do this by clicking the mouse on the boxed down arrow to the right of the scroll-down box option field. If you pull down the scroll-down box with the mouse, you can change the option by moving the highlight to the option with the keypad arrows or by clicking the left mouse button on an option name in the scroll-down box. After dropping the scroll-down box, if you move the cursor up and down through the dropped scroll-down box with the keypad UP ARROW and DOWN ARROW, the available options appear in the user-definable field above. However, displaying the options in the option field in this way does not mean that the options have been finally chosen. You may continue to scroll up and down with the keypad arrows indefinitely. However, when you choose an option within the scroll-down box by clicking the left mouse button on it, it is immediately inserted into the option field and the scroll-down box is retracted.

If more options exist than can fit in the rolled down scroll-down box, you may use the scroll bar at the right of the scroll-down box shown here,

in the same way that you use the scroll bar in the Word for Windows document window. All of the options are represented by the scroll bar in the dropped scroll-down box. You can expose more options by dragging the white box on the scroll bar down the scroll bar to expose the portion of the list that does not fit in the scroll-down box. Also, clicking the left mouse button on the scroll bar arrows exposes options that do not fit in the scroll-down box one at a time. If you have another option to select, move the cursor away from the scroll-down box with the TAB key or the mouse arrow. The scroll-down box will roll up and the last highlighted option will remain chosen. If you press ENTER, the current option is chosen and the dialog box closes.

As with commands in Word for Windows menus, options listed in a dialog box sometimes have an underlined letter. Such options may be chosen by pressing the underlined letter's key or by clicking the left mouse button on the option name. You can also use the TAB key to move between options and then activate the option by pressing the underlined letter's key.

Toggle Boxes

In some cases, the option field operates like a toggle switch. Toggle switches can be either on or off. A toggle box is a small square where you will see either an "X" inside signaling the option is on (selected), or an open box signaling that the option is off as shown here.

By placing the mouse arrow on the option and clicking the left mouse button, the box alternately fills in with an "X" or clears. You may also tab to a toggle box and press the key of an underlined letter to activate it. An "X" would then appear in the box. Pressing the underlined letter's key again toggles the option to the off state, and the "X" would disappear.

Buttons

Buttons appear as open circles that can be filled in at the center with a dot as shown here.

Like toggle boxes, if you click the left mouse button on a button, it will alternately fill in or clear. Button options are active when they are filled in. A filled-in button is also referred to as a bulleted button. One important difference between toggle boxes and buttons is that toggle boxes are usually tied to a single option while buttons usually activate a further set of options or a user-definable field.

An Option Selection Caveat

You can usually select options by highlighting the option with a mouse or by typing the underlined letter in the option name as it appears in the dialog box. However, one problem can occur when you choose an option by selecting the underlined letter. If the dialog box opens with the highlight positioned on a user-definable field (or if the cursor is on a user-definable field when you decide to activate another option), you must first move the cursor to the option you wish by using the mouse *or* the TAB key before you type the underlined letter representing the option. Otherwise, if you activate an option by pressing the letter that is underlined in the option name, and the cursor is on a user-definable field, the letter you type will appear in the field, replacing the current user-definable option. If this occurs, you can reinstate the current user-definable option by using the mouse to move the cursor to another option or you could press the TAB key until the cursor reaches the desired option.

You can see an example of when this conflict between option field types might occur if you open the Format Character dialog box, partly shown here.

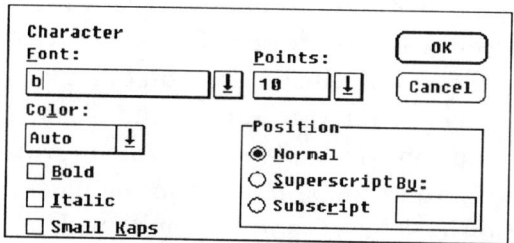

Notice the highlight is automatically positioned on the Font option field because it is the first field in the dialog box. This field is also a user-definable field. If you wish to choose Bold and therefore immediately type **b**, a "b" would appear in the Font field and the cursor would not move to the Bold option. In this example, you must first move the cursor to the Bold field. To do this, you can either click the left mouse button on the word "Bold" or use the TAB key to move the cursor down to the Bold toggle box and then type **b** to activate the Bold option.

In general, you will find moving through the options sets contained in Word for Windows dialog boxes highly intuitive. As you learn Word for Windows, you will have the opportunity to use all of the different types of dialog box option fields.

Formatting Blocks of Text

When you open the Format Character dialog box to set formatting parameters, you may want to change the character formatting of an entire document, or you may want to reformat a passage to make it stand out. If you have already typed in some text, you must first block it off before you can format it. The following is a brief look ahead to Chapter 3, "Cut and Paste: Adding Tables and Images."

If you have already entered your text, only characters that are *highlighted* (blocked-off characters showing in reverse video) are formatted when you open the Format Character dialog box. To block off text with the mouse, you first place the mouse arrow over the first character you want in the block. Then you click the left mouse button *and hold it down* while moving the mouse to the last character you want contained in the block. This is called *dragging* the mouse. The cursor highlight will extend as you drag the mouse. And, if you touch the top or bottom of the document window while you are dragging the mouse, the text and the block will scroll until you push the mouse in the opposite direction (for example, push the mouse down if you want to stop scrolling up). After you have blocked off text, you open the Format Character dialog box to format only the highlighted characters (the block). Highlighting, moving, and importing blocks of text, graphics, and data are topics covered in depth in Chapter 3.

Text can also be blocked off with the keyboard. Using the arrow keys on the keypad, position the cursor on the first character to be blocked off. Press the F8 key, and by using the keypad arrow keys, you will see that the new block (highlighted area) extends from the cursor through the final character to be blocked off. You may then activate formatting commands that will apply to this block. If you use the keypad arrow keys after activating one or more commands affecting this block, the cursor will move away from either end of the block rather than extending the highlighted section. Also, if you move the cursor away from the block by clicking the left mouse button somewhere else, the highlighted block extends to that point. Finally, if you press F8 twice, the nearest word is highlighted; if you press F8 three times, the nearest sentence is highlighted; four times, and the nearest paragraph is highlighted; pressing F8 five times highlights the entire document. "EXT" is shown in reverse video at the bottom of the Word for Windows screen when you press F8, showing that the extend cursor function is activated. You may inactivate the extension function at any time by pressing the ESC key.

If you set parameters using the Format Character dialog box before you enter any text into the document window, every character you type after you set the new parameters will retain the set character parameters. These parameters will be used until you make additional formatting changes with the Format Character dialog box or move the cursor to an area of the document where different formatting features have already been added. If you have already formatted the characters in a passage and then later make changes to that passage, all of the newly entered characters within the passage will be assigned the character formatting that had been previously assigned. This is so even if this format varies from the last Format Character entry you made at a spot elsewhere in the document.

Format Menu

You are now ready to select the Format menu and explore its commands and command options. To display the Format menu shown on the next page, you can either press ALT-t or click the left mouse button on the word "Format" in the menu bar.

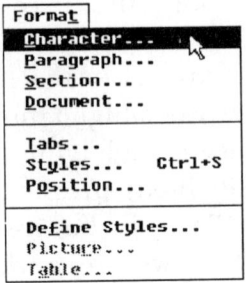

There are three ways to select commands in the Format menu. First, you can place the mouse arrow on a command and click the left mouse button. Second, you can use the keypad DOWN ARROW to move the cursor to the command you want and then press the ENTER key. Finally, you can press the key of the underlined letter of the command. Use either the mouse or the keyboard to choose the Format Character command. The Format Character dialog box containing all of the Format Character options will appear. Leave the Format Character dialog box displayed; you will learn about this dialog box in the next section.

The rest of this chapter will cover the options contained in the Format Character, Paragraph, Section, and Document dialog boxes. After this survey, you will be able to see how these commands and their associated dialog boxes are logically linked by the Format menu.

Character Formatting

When you choose the Format Character command, the Format Character dialog box, as shown in Figure 2-2, appears on screen.

Figure 2-2.

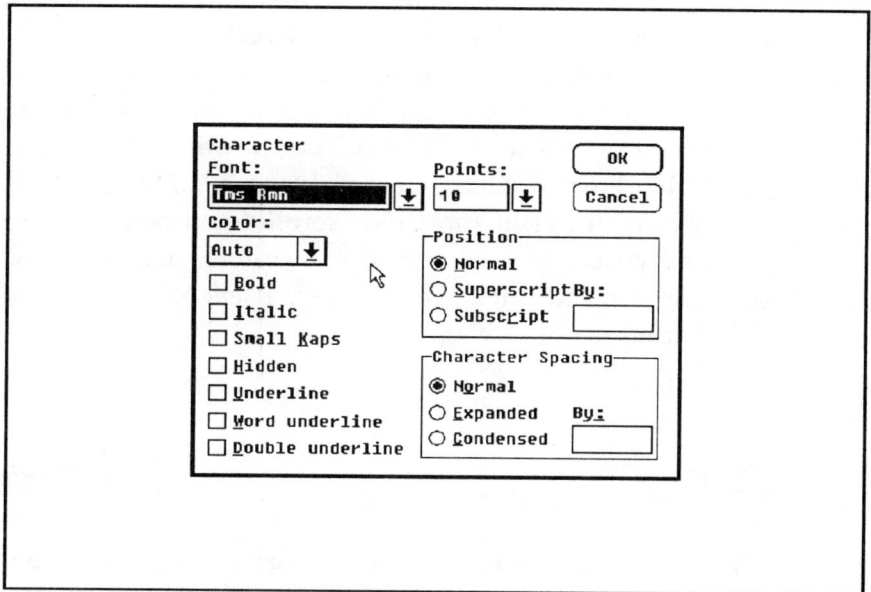

Format Character dialog box

The Format Character dialog box contains six *option sets*—Font, Color, Emphasis options, Points, Position, and Character Spacing—which can be adjusted. The Emphasis options set includes Bold, Italic, Small Kaps, Hidden, Underline, Word underline, and Double underline. Note that unlike the other Format Character option sets, the Emphasis options set is not boxed and labeled as such. There is a full discussion of the Emphasis options set later in this chapter.

Fields are the areas of the dialog box where you enter your option choices. Therefore, the area where you enter your choice is called an option field. These fields use the dialog box devices (toggle boxes, buttons, scroll-down boxes, or text-entry lines) discussed earlier in this chapter. When there is more than one choice available, they are logically tied together by the name of the option set; for example, all of the option choices included in the

Emphasis options set can be used to distinguish characters, words, or phrases within a larger body of text.

Each option set has at least one, but possibly several, fields for you to enter option choices. The Color option set, for example, allows you to choose only one option, or one color, each time you open the Format Character dialog box. The available Color options are listed in the Color scroll-down box (see section on scroll-down boxes earlier in this chapter), but you may choose only one. On the other hand, there are several choices available in the Emphasis options set.

Fonts

The Font field displays the default, or current, font. You can type another font choice over the default as long as you are sure that your choice is one of the fonts available. To see a list of available fonts, click the left mouse arrow on the down arrow next to the field containing the default font name. A list of available fonts will be displayed in the Font scroll-down box, as shown here.

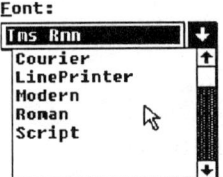

(The fonts listed here are available with a standard PostScript laser printer.) If you click the left mouse button on one of the other available fonts, it will become the default font until you either change it or move the cursor to another section of the document that has been formatted with a different font. In that case, the font that was originally selected for this other portion of the document will override your most recent selection.

Like Word 4.0 and 5.0, Word for Windows does not make the font you choose the system default font; the next document you open will have the original default font. You can change the default font by changing the document template; document templates are discussed in Chapter 4, "For the Record: Styles and Templates." If you change the section default font later in the document, the new font becomes the section default font for any text you add to the document after you made the change. But, if you go back and insert text in the first section of the document (in an area that precedes the one in which you changed to a font different from the system default), the new text will be assigned the system default font.

Once the cursor is on the Font option field, you can scroll through the Font scroll-down box with either the keypad UP ARROW and DOWN ARROW keys or with the mouse. If you use the keypad UP ARROW and DOWN ARROW, you will see the available fonts in the Font option field one at a time. If you click the left mouse button on the boxed down arrow to the right of the scroll-down box, the scroll-down box drops down, exposing the list of available fonts. Clicking the left mouse button on your choice will place it in the Font option field and close the scroll-down box. If all the font names do not fit in the Font scroll-down box, you can scroll through them with the keypad DOWN ARROW or with the scroll bar on the right side of the scroll-down box. The scroll-down box scroll bar works the same way that the document scroll bar works. That is, you click the left mouse button on the open square and drag it down by holding the left mouse button down at the same time as you move the mouse down.

If the only format parameter you want to change is the font selection, after you indicate your selection, close the dialog box with the ENTER key or by clicking the left mouse button on OK. If you wish to set another format parameter, use the TAB key to move to that Format Character option.

Unless you have installed your own printer driver, the fonts listed are resident in your printer and were installed in the menu when you ran the setup program. Remember that the font choices shown on page 78 are for a generic PostScript printer. Your font choices may vary depending on what printer you are using. The topic of fonts and typefaces is covered in Chapter 6, "Advanced Template Features."

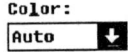

Color

If you use Microsoft Word, recall that in versions 4.0 and 5.0 the color settings are found in the Options menu. In Word for Windows, the Color option is accessed through the Format menu, with the Format Character dialog box.

On most color monitors, text can be displayed in eight colors. This is a limitation of Windows 2.1 and not Word for Windows. As Windows' support for color improves, so will the Word for Windows display. The text colors available for a Postscript printer and a VGA monitor are shown here as they appear onscreen.

To see a complete list of these colors, click the left mouse button on the boxed down arrow at the right side of the Color scroll-down box.

Onscreen colored passages or editorial insertions can be helpful for tracking changes in documents that are edited several times. Editor's annotations in color can be set so they are readable onscreen but not printable. Annotations, and group projects in general, are discussed in Chapter 8, "Group Productions." Remember that text displayed in different colors on your screen will not be printed in color unless you have a color printer or plotter.

☐ B̲old
☐ I̲talic
☐ Small K̲aps
☐ H̲idden
☐ U̲nderline
☐ W̲ord underline
☐ D̲ouble underline

Emphasis Options

Note that the Emphasis options set is not titled or boxed on the screen, but these options are grouped under this name in your Microsoft Word for Windows manual. The Bold, Italic, Underline, Word underline, and Double underline options are all commonly used ways of distinguishing portions of text. Small Kaps provide a specialized typeface also used to distinguish elements of text.

Small Kaps   Superscripts and subscripts, fancy titles, or special words in a passage can be effective when set in Small Kaps. "Kap" refers to uppercase (capital), and is the Word for Windows spelling for "cap." Small Kaps are capital letters in a reduced type size. You press a **k** instead of a c to activate Small Kaps since c is used for Condensed. One way to use Small Kaps is to distinguish a class of specialized terms. Notice that this book uses Small Kaps for key names such as CTRL, SHIFT, ENTER, ALT, etc.

Hidden text Hidden text is useful for editor's comments. It is displayed only when you ask for it to be shown in the View Preferences menu. Even if it is displayed, it is not printed. Hidden text is discussed in more detail in sections on the View menu in Chapter 5, "Printing: Picture Perfect Output."

Underlining The Underline option will underline the entire passage that is highlighted, including the spaces between the words, or any text typed after the option is activated. The Word underline option underlines only the single words in a passage but not the spaces between them.

Unlike Word for Windows, many word processors do not provide the choice between word and complete underlining. This is because the printer driver for each word processing application determines how the printer will be addressed. Virtually all printers are capable of underlining both the words and the spaces between them, or leaving the spaces between words open. Some software developers, however, do not implement and supply these options in their printer drivers.

Another similar problem is moving the underline up or down so it does not cut off the descenders like the tails in the letters "j," "g," and "y." Some printers do not let you do this. The HP LaserJet Series II printer has the capability to do this. A document printed from Word for Windows will not automatically drop the underline below the descenders, and there is no option in Word for Windows to do this. Instead, you could superscript the text above the underline; however, you may prefer to use a desktop publishing program to adjust the vertical position of the underline separate from the text.

Points

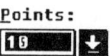

Point size is a unit of measurement applied to type and the space between lines of type. One inch is equivalent to 72 points. For example, most body text is 12 points or 1/6" high. The default point size of the Times Roman font is 10 points. If you click the left mouse button on the scroll-down box arrow to the right of the Points field listing 10 (points), the listing of available point size choices for Times Roman will be displayed, as shown here.

```
Points:
10        ↓
10        ↑
12
14
16   ⇗
18
20
24        ↓
```

Remember that if you are not comfortable using points, Word for Windows will accept inches or centimeters instead of points. You can change units using the Utilities Customize dialog box discussed in Appendix C, "Setting Up Word for Windows."

When you are using scalable fonts, like PostScript, you can position the cursor in the default point size box and type in any size that your printer is capable of producing (usually between 3 and 720 points). With most non-PostScript fonts, you are limited to the sizes listed in the scroll-down box. The difference between scalable and nonscalable fonts is discussed in more detail in Appendix E, "Font Character Sets and Sources."

```
┌Position──────────────────┐
│ ◉ Normal                 │
│ ○ Superscript By:        │
│ ○ Subscript   [        ] │
└──────────────────────────┘
```

Position

The options in the Position option set let you change the *baseline* of superscripted or subscripted text. A baseline is the invisible line on which the characters in each horizontal row of text are positioned. Some characters, such as lower case "g," "j," or "y," have descenders that drop below the baseline. The baseline of superscripted text is above the default body text baseline and the baseline of a subscript is below the default body text baseline.

Word for Windows also gives you the ability to control exactly how far above or below the body text baseline superscripts and subscripts will be placed. The user-definable By option field is the box that appears below the word "By". This box is to the right of the Superscript option, in the lower-right corner of the Position options box as shown at the beginning of this section. The By field entry sets the number of points that the superscripted or subscripted text's baseline will be above or below the baseline of the body text. With body text between 10 and 14 points, the default is 3 points, but you can enter any value between 0 and 63.5 (in increments as small as 0.1). This option is especially important for text that combines two or more font sizes.

Often it is desirable to reduce the point size of a superscript or subscript because a superscript word or exponent printed with the body text point size may cut off the descenders (like the tail on the "g," "j," or "y") above it; also, a standard point size subscript may overwrite the dots of "i"s or the tops of uppercase letters below it. To reduce the point size of superscripted or subscripted text after it has been typed, you highlight the text and change the Points entry in the Format Character dialog box. To reduce the point size of superscripted or subscripted text before you type it, you change the Points entry in the Format Character dialog box at the same time you choose the Superscript or Subscript option.

┌─Character Spacing─┐
◉ **N**ormal
○ **E**xpanded   **By:**
○ **C**ondensed   [   ]

Character Spacing

The Character Spacing option lets you adjust the amount of horizontal space that will be placed between the characters on each line of text. By default, the horizontal character space, also called *letterspacing,* is measured in points.

The default Normal spacing option gives each character a single horizontal character space, a measurement that is defined in the font file. Activating the Expanded spacing option adds a default 3 points to the right side of a character. Note that when you activate the Expanded button, a 3 appears in the By field. However, you can type in any number between 0 and 14 points in 0.25 increments in the By field when you have activated the Expanded spacing option. Expanded spacing is useful for one- or two-word headlines when you want each letter to stand out. This effect calls more attention to the headline, a desired effect for either your company's name or your name at the top of stationery or a memo.

The Condensed spacing option automatically subtracts 1.5 points from the right side of the character. You may also use the By field to set Condensed spacing, but your setting must be in the 0 to 1.75 point range. Condensed spacing is only accurate to within 0.25 point increments. Condensed spacing brings characters together within words, often making it easier to see words as a unit. This feature may also be useful when you are trying to squeeze a word or two onto a page that would have otherwise printed on an entirely new page.

Noticeably missing from Word for Windows is *kerning.* Kerning is a process whereby the letters within a word are printed as close together as possible but still remain legible. In unkerned output, the letter "i" is given as much horizontal space as the letter "m." However, the lowercase letter "i" actually requires much less space than a lowercase "m." *Ligatures,* two letters that are treated as one, such as two lowercase "f"s or two lowercase "t"s sharing a crossbar, are common devices in kerned typefaces. The tighter letterspacing provided by kerning helps the reader see each word as a unit and can be useful when you are justifying text (see discussion of justification in the section on paragraph alignment later in this chapter). As mentioned in Chapter 1, "Up and Running," kerning and frame-setting are two features that are used in professional typesetting and in some desktop publishing programs but are not features of word publishing software like Word for Windows.

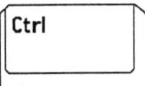

Speed Character Formatting

Word for Windows lets you bypass the Format Character dialog box for all of the Format Character command features in two ways. One way is to use the Word for Windows *ribbon.* The View Ribbon command is found in the View menu. The ribbon lets you format text quickly with a mouse, but it takes up valuable screen space. For a full discussion of the ribbon, see Chapter 4, "For the Record: Styles and Templates." This section will focus on the keyboard method for formatting text without accessing the Format Character dialog box.

In most cases, the fastest way to format text with the options in the Format Character dialog box is to avoid the dialog box and use the keyboard *Speed formatting* CTRL-*key* keystroke combinations instead. Table 2-1 shows how all of the Format Character options discussed in this chapter can be accessed.

Speed formatting allows you to save several mouse clicks or keystrokes; however, you must memorize the appropriate CTRL-*key* combinations since they are not permanently displayed on the screen. Microsoft has tried to make these CTRL-*key* keystroke combinations easy to learn. Consistent use of Word for Windows will help you memorize the speed formatting CTRL-*key* combinations. Remember that you do not have to memorize any Format Character options because the Word for Windows menu bar is always present. However, you may want to photocopy the speed formatting CTRL-*key* combinations shown in Table 2-1; this copy will initially aid your work with the speed formatting CTRL-*key* combinations.

To use these Format Character CTRL-*key* combinations, first highlight the text you wish to format and then press the appropriate CTRL-*key* combination. Either the text will be reformatted or a single option field will be displayed at the bottom of the screen. The Format Character options that display an option field at the bottom of the screen are Color, Font, and Points. Option fields are offered for Color, Font, and Points because these are user-definable options. If you cannot remember what options are

Table 2-1.

Format Character Options	CTRL-*key* Combo
Bold	CTRL-b
Color	CTRL-v
Double Underline	CTRL-d
Font	CTRL-f
Hidden	CTRL-h
Italic	CTRL-i
Undo Character Formatting	CTRL-SPACEBAR
Point Size	CTRL-p
Small Kaps	CTRL-k
$_{Sub}$script	CTRL-=
^{Super}script	CTRL-+
Underline	CTRL-u
Word Underline	CTRL-w

Character Speed Formatting (Adapted with permission from the documentation for Microsoft Word for Windows, Microsoft Corporation, 1990.)

available when the Color, Font, or Points field appears at the bottom of the screen, you can press the option's speed formatting CTRL-*key* combination again and the full Format Character dialog box will appear; all of the options may then be surveyed in the dialog box.

Paragraph Formatting

The Format Paragraph dialog box is accessed from the Format menu as was the Format Character dialog box. To open the Format Paragraph box, either click the left mouse button on Format, then Paragraph, or press ALT-t, and then type **p**. In most cases, the overall operation is faster if you use the mouse.

There are two ways to format paragraphs. First, if you have not entered any text, you can choose your paragraph format. Then, all text you enter will display this formatting until you change the paragraph formatting again. Second, if you have already entered your text and want to format individual paragraphs within the document, you do not need to block off entire paragraphs. Just position the cursor anywhere on the paragraph and the whole paragraph will be assigned whatever paragraph format you choose. You may also extend the cursor over large portions of text and format several paragraphs simultaneously.

The default Format Paragraph dialog box is shown in Figure 2-3. This dialog box will be referred to throughout this section.

Alignment

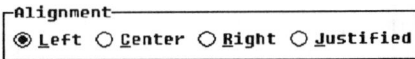

By using the Alignment options, you can *see* paragraphs as units more easily. If you see the paragraph as a unit, it will probably be easier to decide if the paragraph presents a unified theme. For this reason, you will probably want to use some alignment formatting as you write a document.

Figure 2-3.

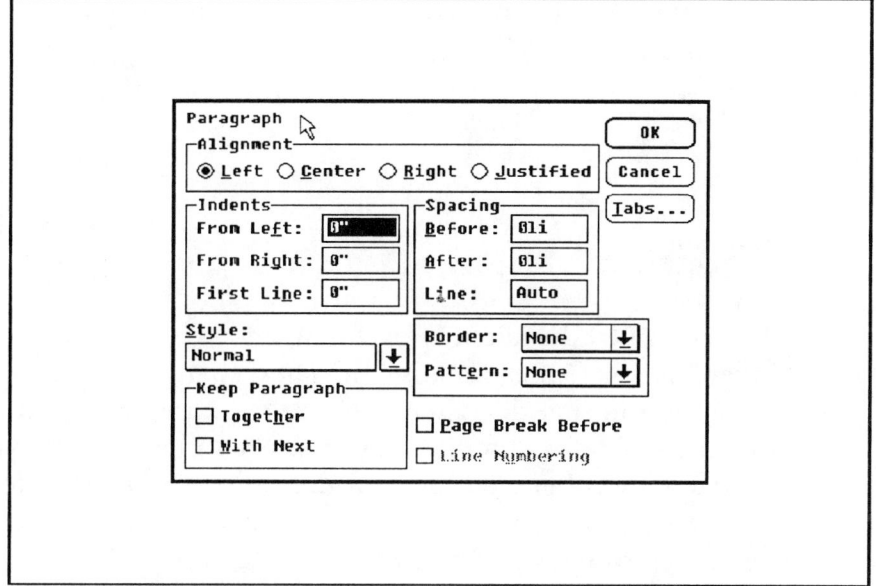

Format Paragraph dialog box

Left-aligned text, the default setting, has a straight left margin and a ragged right margin and is preferred for manuscripts, informal letters, and memos. Centered text is useful for topics, headings, and highlighted passages. Right-aligned text has a flush right margin and a ragged left margin and is useful for headers such as page numbers, dates, return addresses on letters, and so on. Justified text is aligned at both the left and right margins. The default, left-aligned text, is preferred by many over justified text, even for formal documents like newsletters and brochures. To make all the text align at the left and right margins, the Justified option increases the space between words, but not between the characters within words. The space added between words is the space that would remain at the right of the line if the text were left-aligned (ragged right margin). When text is justified, this space is divided evenly and placed between all of the words in the line. If the lines are not very wide (for example, less than 30 characters per line with a 12 point font), justification can over-space the few words that fit on a line, making them appear disconnected.

```
┌Indents────────────┐
│ From Le̲ft:    │0"│ │
│ From R̲ight:   │0"│ │
│ First Li̲ne:   │0"│ │
└───────────────────┘
```

Indents

The From Left default in Word for Windows is 0". If the First Line indent is set to 0.5, unless you later change this field, every paragraph in that document will begin with a 0.5" indent. Note that the default is automatically measured in inches. You do not need to type either a 0 before, or the letters "in" after, .5 to signal 1/2". You can, however, enter a measurement in centimeters or points at any time by adding **cm** or **pt** after your indent entry. The default unit remains inches, and the next time you open the Format Paragraph dialog box, you will see that Word for Windows has converted your entry to inches (for example, your 2.54 cm entry will be changed to 1").

For all paragraphs that are in a section of text directly quoted from another source, called an extract, you may also decide to add 0.5" From Right and From Left margin indents. These indents will set the extract off from the main text. (Also, you might consider changing extracts to single spacing if the body text is double spaced. Using a smaller point size font further isolates an extract or quote from body text.)

Bibliographies often require a left hanging indent, also called an *outdent*. To create an outdent, set the From Left indent to 0.5 and the First Line indent to −0.5. This format might also be useful for lists where the number for each item (each item would be listed in a single paragraph) would be outdented.

If you have used left-aligned text with a ragged right margin, the right margin is not always obvious to the reader. It is an invisible line that the text abuts only with justified or right-aligned paragraph formatting. Therefore, when you have left-aligned (ragged right) text, you can change the right margin until you think it will not cause the reader to miss the end of the line. For example, if you can add a small negative right indent (such as -0.3 or -0.5) in the Format Paragraph dialog box, you may be able to squeeze an extra word onto the last line of a paragraph without changing the right margin for the whole document. Use this trick judiciously. It works best where the last page of a document would have only a few words on an entire page if you did not extend the right margin on all or part of the previous page. If you are just over the page number limit, tricks like moving the right indent, reducing the body text point size, or reducing the line spacing (discussed later in this chapter) can make a big difference.

Style

When you first open Word for Windows, you will see that a default paragraph style has been inserted in the Style option field. However, the Format Paragraph dialog box Style option field is user-definable; therefore, you can overtype the word "Normal." When the cursor is on the Style text-entry field, you may also choose any of the other available paragraph styles. In Figure 2-3, you see that the default Style option is called Normal. The default Normal paragraph style is Times Roman font, 10 point size, flush left (left-aligned) text. The Normal paragraph style is part of the default document template called NORMAL.DOT. You can create a new paragraph style or change the default document template only with the Format Define Styles command; this process will be discussed in detail in Chapter 4.

The other default document template paragraph styles are named *headers* along with numbers explaining their level of priority in the document. Header 1 might be used to format a document title, whereas header 2 might be used to format a section heading, and header 3 might be used to format a subsection heading.

Paragraph Style Scroll-down Box   As with other scroll-down boxes, you may go through the list of Format Paragraph dialog box Style options without dropping the scroll-down box by using the UP ARROW and DOWN ARROW keys. First, place the cursor on Style by using the TAB key to move through the Paragraph Format dialog box. Then press the UP ARROW or DOWN ARROW key to change the entry in the Style option field. When you see the Style option you want, press ENTER or click the left mouse button on OK and you will format your paragraph with that Style option. You may also survey the Style options by dropping the scroll-down box. To do this, click the left mouse button on the down arrow to the right of the Style field. You may then click the left mouse button on any of the displayed paragraph styles. All of the default styles fit in the Style scroll-down box shown here.

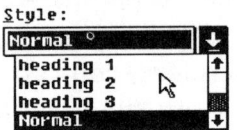

However, if you have added any styles, they may extend beyond the bottom of the box. See the discussion of scroll-down boxes earlier in this chapter to see how you can use the scroll-down box scroll bar to see a long list of paragraph styles that extends beyond the initial four styles.

The default document template, NORMAL.DOT, contains the first four paragraph styles listed in Table 2-2. The last two paragraph styles are not in the default Word for Windows

Table 2-2.

	Margins	**Indents**	**Line Spacing**	**Blank Lines**
Normal	Left	0.5" 1st Line	1 (Single)	0
header 1	Left	0"	1 (Single)	1 Above
header 2	Left	0"	1 (Single)	1 Above
header 3	Left	0.25"	1 (Single)	0
Body Text	Justified	0.5"	2 (Double)	0
Quotation	Justified	Left 0.5" Right 0.5"	1 (Single)	1 Above 1 Below

Paragraph Styles

NORMAL.DOT template, and therefore could be added to the Style scroll-down box by adding them to the NORMAL.DOT template or another template of your own design. The process of creating and naming paragraph styles is discused in Chapter 4. The last two paragraph styles are commonly used in manuscripts and reports where legibility is imperative.

```
┌Keep Paragraph──────────┐
│ ☐ Together             │
│ ☐ With Next            │
└────────────────────────┘
```

Keep Paragraph

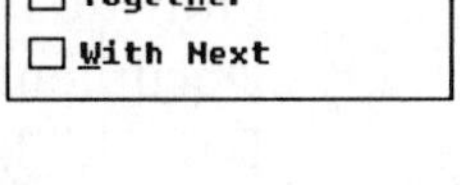

When the last line of a paragraph appears at the top of a new page, it is called a *widow*. When the first line of a paragraph ends a page, it is called an *orphan*. The Keep Paragraph feature allows you to control widows and orphans for each paragraph.

Word for Windows contains automatic widow and orphan control as a default option. This guarantees that the last *two* lines of a paragraph will be carried over to begin a new page (avoiding a widow) and, similarly, that at least the first two lines of a paragraph will be retained at the end of any page (avoiding an orphan). Both widowed and orphaned lines are generally undesirable but sometimes necessary when space is at a premium. For this reason, these functions can be turned off. A more extended discussion of widow and orphan control can be found in the section on the Format Document command later in this chapter.

The Keep Paragraph Together option, shown in Figure 2-3, can be used to ensure that a single paragraph will not be spread over two pages. This option is activated by clicking the left mouse button on the Together toggle box; this will fill in the box with an "X."

The Keep Paragraph With Next option, also shown in Figure 2-3, ensures that a page break will not fall between the paragraph chosen and the one below it. This only works if it is possible to print the last two lines of the chosen paragraph and the first two lines of the next paragraph on one page. This may be impossible with two very long paragraphs. In that case, the command is ignored. The With Next option can also be activated by clicking the left mouse button on the associated toggle box to the left of the option listing.

Both of the Keep Paragraph options duplicate the widows and orphans control defaults of Word for Windows. However, they may be useful if you turn off the widow controls through the Format Document dialog box, but still want to use them for individual paragraphs. This is also discussed in the Format Document command section under "Widow Control" and "Set Default" later in this chapter.

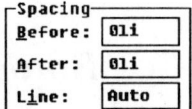

Spacing

The Spacing option lets you precisely set the amount of vertical space between separate lines of text. To set the amount of space that will be left blank between all lines of text within a paragraph, choose the Line option under the Spacing options set shown at the beginning of this section. In most documents, it will only be necessary to set line spacing as single or double by entering **1** or **2**, respectively, in the Line field. The Line field says "Auto" by default. Auto is single spacing; however, if you type **1** in the Line field the next time you go into the Format Paragraph dialog box, you will see "1li" instead of "Auto" ("2li" would appear if you had typed **2**). The "li" unit seen in the Before and After fields in Figure 2-3 (0 extra lines Before and After paragraphs is the default option, that is why "0" appears next to "li" in this figure) is the default unit used for line spacing. However, you can manually overide the default by entering the abbreviations **in, cm, pi,** or **pt** to change the units to inches, centimeters, picas, or points, respectively. Because you can enter units other than lines (li), you can set the vertical line spacing more precisely. The amount of space Before and After options can be used to set paragraph spacing between paragraphs.

There are special terms that refer to spacing between lines of type. The most commonly used is *leading* (pronounced ledding); you might also see linespacing. The Format Paragraph dialog box uses the lone word "Spacing" for this option set that controls a document's vertical spacing. Leading is discussed in depth in Chapter 10, "Desktop Publishing with Word for Windows."

Border and Pattern

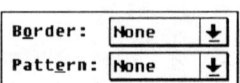

The Border option allows you to underscore, overscore, or box in text. (Underscoring a paragraph is a feature often used to separate articles within a newsletter or a newspaper.) These options can be used from the keyboard. You activate the Border scroll-down box by pressing the TAB key until Border is high-lighted and then, using the keypad UP ARROW or DOWN ARROW, change the options shown in the Border option field. Press ENTER when you have found the selection you wish.

You can also choose the Border options with the mouse. Click the left mouse button on the boxed down arrow to the right of the word "Border." The whole Border scroll-down box is displayed as seen here.

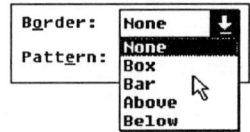

Options are chosen by clicking the left mouse button on the desired word. You can accept the selection either by pressing the ENTER key or by clicking the left mouse button on the OK button. Notice that the Border option, Bar, appears in the option box shown here.

Remember that paragraphs will not be underscored with a bar unless you choose Bar from the scroll-down box because the default Border option is None.

The Pattern scroll-down box is located below the Border option field, as shown here.

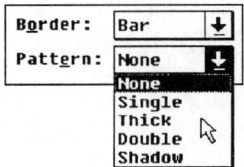

Notice that this shows the Bar option chosen as the type of Border and None for the Border's pattern. Using the Pattern scroll-down box, a Bar border can be set to single or double lines, and this line (or lines) may be thin (default) or thick. There are only two choices for line thickness (thin or thick) in Word for Windows. All of the various Paragraph command Border options are shown here.

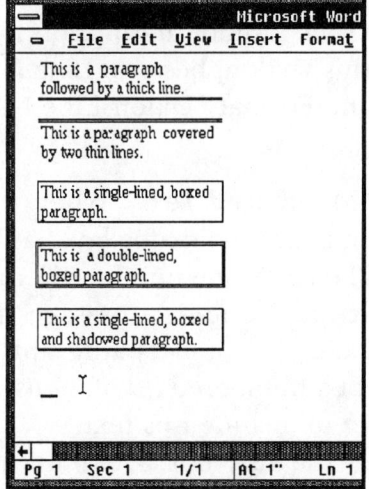

Page Break Before

☐ Page Break Before

The Page Break Before option seen in Figure 2-3 inserts a hard page break before a paragraph, ensuring that the paragraph chosen will appear at the top of a new page. Word for Windows offers even more complete control over page, section, and column breaks in the Insert Break menu covered in Chapter 10. The default for the Page Break Before is off, indicated by the open toggle box to the left of the option.

Line Numbering   ☐ Line Numbering

This option does not activate a feature but rather only acts as an off switch. When line numbering has been activated by the Format Section Line Numbering option (see the "Line Numbers" section later in this chapter), the Format Paragraph Line Numbering option can be used to turn off line numbering. This option is unavailable unless Line Numbering has already been activated (the default is off) in the Format Section Line Numbers option. Note that the Line Numbering option is ghosted, as seen at the beginning of this section, because Line Numbering had not been turned on in the Format Section Line Numbers option set.

Embedded Unnumbered Text   When the Line Numbering option in the Format Section dialog box has been turned on, all lines in a section will display line numbers in the left margin. However, a block of text may contain a passage that you do not wish to number. For example, when a paragraph of explanation is placed in the middle of a numbered *list* of items, you would not want the line numbering to include this text.

To number the list, but avoid numbering the intervening passage, first you must number the list of items including the explanatory passage. This is done by blocking off the entire list including the intervening passage. Then click the left mouse button on the Line Numbering toggle box (or you could tab to it and type **i**) in the Format Section dialog box shown here.

```
┌─────────────────────────────────────────────────┐
│  Section                          ┌─────────────┐│
│  ┌Columns─────────────┐           │     OK      ││
│  │ Number:  1          │    ▷      └─────────────┘│
│  │ Spacing: 0.5"       │          ┌─────────────┐│
│  │ □ Line Between      │          │   Cancel    ││
│  └─────────────────────┘          └─────────────┘│
│                             Section Start:        │
│                             ┌──────────────────┐ │
│  ⊠ Include Footnotes        │New Page         ↓│ │
│  ┌Line Numbers──────────────────────────────────┐│
│  │ □ Line Numbering                             ││
│  │ Start At #: [      ]  ○ Per Page             ││
│  │ From Text:  [      ]  ○ Per Section          ││
│  │ Count By:   [      ]  ○ Continue             ││
│  └──────────────────────────────────────────────┘│
│  ┌Vertical Alignment────────────────────────────┐│
│  │ ◉ Top  ○ Center  ○ Justify                   ││
│  └──────────────────────────────────────────────┘│
└─────────────────────────────────────────────────┘
```

You then press ENTER or click the left mouse button on OK. The entire highlighted section would now be numbered including lines in the intervening passage. You would next block off the intervening passage and open the Format Paragraph dialog box. Note that the Line Numbering toggle box at the lower right corner is no longer ghosted. You would click the left mouse button on the Line Numbering toggle box (or tab to it and type **u**) to turn off the numbers to the left of the lines in the intervening paragraph. The line numbering would then continue sequentially around the inactivated paragraph.

This type of fast line numbering was not possible in earlier versions of Word without using outlining tools that were inaccessible from the text-entry mode. This topic is discussed again in the section entitled "Line Numbers" under the Format Section command later in this chapter. The use of automatic line numbering is discussed in depth in Chapter 7, "Time Saving Organization: Outlines and Tables of Contents."

Speed Formatting

As with the Format Character dialog box, all of the Format Paragraph features can be activated directly (without using the Format Paragraph dialog box) by using CTRL-*key* combinations. Table 2-3 shows how all of the Format Paragraph command options can be accessed. All of these options are also covered in detail in Chapter 6, "Advanced Template Features."

To use these CTRL-*key* combinations, as with the Format Character CTRL-*key* combinations, you must first highlight the text to be modified, then type the CTRL-*key* combination. Either the change is executed or an option field opens at the bottom of the screen. The only Format Paragraph CTRL-*key* combination that requires you to make an entry into an option field is the Apply Style option (CTRL-s). If you select the Apply Style option, you will also have to supply a paragraph style from the default document template or a document template that you had already created. You will learn more about this feature in Chapter 4, "For the Record: Styles and Templates," and Chapter 6.

Section Formatting

Sectional formatting is part of the promise of word publishing. This feature allows you to insert both single and multicolumned text within a single document. It also allows you to place headers over articles or sections within a multicolumned document such as a newsletter or report. You cannot do this with version 4.0 or 5.0

Table 2-3.

Format Paragraph Options	CTRL-*key* Combo
Apply Style	CTRL-s
Centered Text	CTRL-c
Close Space Before	CTRL-e
Double-spaced Text	CTRL-2
Justified Text	CTRL-j
Left-aligned Margins	CTRL-l
One-and-a-half-spaced text	CTRL-5
One Line Open Before Paragraph	CTRL-o
Change the Current Style	CTRL-x
Right-aligned Margins	CTRL-r
Single-spaced text	CTRL-1

Paragraph Speed Formatting (Adapted with permission from the documentation for Microsoft Word for Windows, Microsoft Corporation, 1990.)

of Word. The Format Section dialog box is shown in Figure 2-4. This default dialog box will be referred to throughout the following discussion of section formatting.

Frames Versus Sections

A Word for Windows section is somewhat similar to the desktop publishing *frame*. A frame is an area of a desktop published document page that you define as holding a text file or graphic image. Desktop publishing programs allow you to have text frames begin on one page of a document and continue on any later page, just as an article in a newspaper can begin on page 1 and continue on any page inside. Setting frames, and placing text

Figure 2-4.

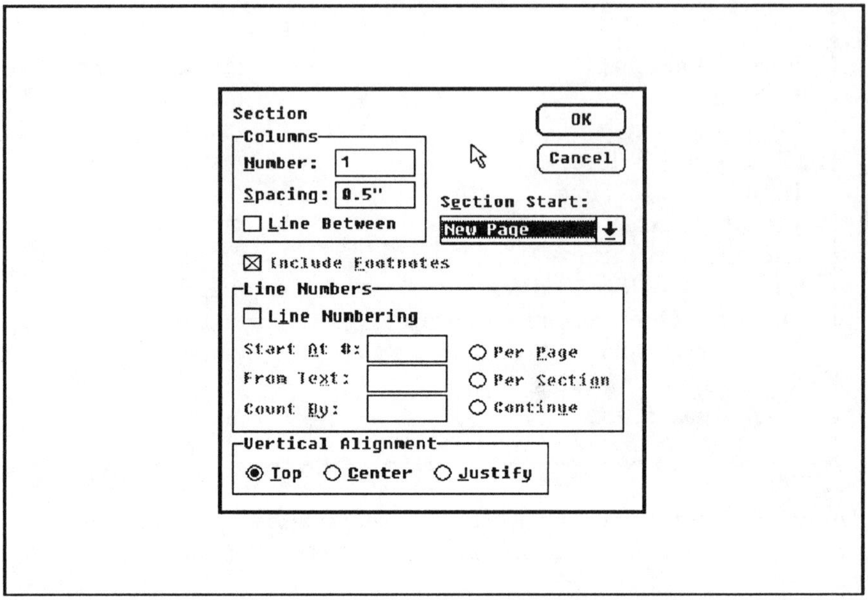

Format Section dialog box

within them, is usually the most time-consuming part of the document layout process used by desktop publishing programs. Unlike frames, Word for Windows sections cannot be interrupted and then continued later on an inside page of a document. Word for Windows requires that all of the text you block off be included in a section run continuously, on one or more pages, to its conclusion. After the section has concluded, you may format another section. Sequential Word for Windows sections can be set much more quickly, and require much less design planning, than desktop publishing frames.

Multicolumn Heads

Sectional formatting is a feature that most Word 4.0 and 5.0 users have probably wished for at various times. In these non-Windows versions of Word, you could only spread a single running head over multicolumned text, such as the masthead of a newspaper over front page articles. However, you cannot extend a head over multicolumned articles below a masthead with Word 4.0 or 5.0 or, in general, with any other word processing software. Word for Windows, however, allows you to create a masthead as a header over the first page as well as further sectional subheads over multicolumned sections of text below the masthead. Sections can also be different numbers of columns wide. Therefore, like articles in a newspaper frame, one Word for Windows section can be one column wide right next to another that is two columns wide. Each of these two sections can have its own headline stretching above it. These desktop publishing-like features of Word for Windows are discussed in depth in Chapter 10, "Desktop Publishing with Word for Windows."

Automatic Line Numbering

Another feature in Word for Windows' sectional formatting that was not available in versions 4.0 and 5.0 of Word is the ability to automatically number lines of text. To do this in earlier versions, you had to exit Word's Text entry mode and enter the Word Outlining mode. Then you had to reformat your text for lines to be automatically numbered. The Word for Windows Line Numbers feature, however, automatically numbers lines and is much faster and simpler than its counterpart in Word 4.0 and 5.0. For additional information on this feature, see the "Line Numbers" section later in this chapter.

Layout

In most documents in which you use sectional formatting, you will have more than one section. The placement of multiple sections in a document, also known as the *layout,* will be discussed in Chapter

4. Before considering layout, it is important to first become familiar with the types of formatting available within a single section.

```
┌Columns───────────┐
│ Number: [1      ]│
│ Spacing: [0.5"  ]│
│ □ Line Between   │
└──────────────────┘
```

Columns

The Columns option set appears at the top of the Format Section dialog box shown in Figure 2-4. While the default is 1, the maximum number of columns you enter in the Number field is limited only by the total width of the page (how wide a piece of paper) your printer can support and by the requirement that each column is at least 0.5" wide. Try to keep column widths under 60 characters, however, since columns wider than this make it difficult for the reader to find the beginning of each new line in the column. For most body text (10-14 points), a 30-45 character wide column is optimal. (With a horizontal spacing, or pitch, of 10 characters per inch, this is 3" to 4.5" width per column.) Columns of this size make it easy for the reader to find the beginning of each new line.

The second option in the Columns option set is Spacing, or the amount of white space, between columns. The default is 0.5"; this works well with the standard 2 column page set in 12 point type, and 1" margins on all sides of the text.

The last option field, Line Between, determines whether a line will be placed between columns. A vertical line will be inserted between columns if this box is filled with an "X." Since this feature is a toggle switch, it is activated or deactivated with a mouse click, or by tabbing to the Line Between box and typing the letter l. Thin lines between columns, which aid the reader's eye in moving down the column, are commonly seen in newspapers and newsletters. The thickness of the actual line placed between columns cannot be varied.

Columns have many uses. As mentioned earlier, multi-columned text with multiple headers can give reports prepared with Word for Windows extra flair. You can also surround graphics with columns of text. These column effects are discussed in Chapter 10.

Include Footnotes

⊠ Include Footnotes

The Include Footnotes option inserts any footnotes entered in a section at the end of the section. The Include Footnotes option is ghosted in Figure 2-4 because no footnotes have been added to the current document. If footnotes are a part of the document, this option will be available. Since it is a toggle box, however, even if it is available, it must be marked with an "X" to be activated. If you do not activate this command, footnotes can be inserted at the bottom of the same page on which they have been referenced, or at the end of the document, which is the default. This topic is discussed in depth in the sections on footnotes in Chapter 6 and in Chapter 7.

```
┌Line Numbers──────────────────
│ ☐ Line Numbering
│
│ Start At #: [        ]    ○ Per Page
│ From Text:  [        ]    ○ Per Section
│ Count By:   [        ]    ○ Continue
```

Line Numbers

If you turn on the Line Numbering option in the Format Section dialog box, all lines in the section are numbered. The numbers appear in the column to the left of the left margin. The numbers by default will begin with 1 and progress to 2, 3, 4, and so on. As was noted earlier in this chapter, the Format Paragraph Line

Numbering option takes precedence over the Format Section Line Numbers option. Because of this, you can selectively turn off the line numbering on paragraphs within a section by highlighting the desired paragraph and turning off the Line Numbering option in the Format Paragraph dialog box. This is useful if there is necessary explanatory text in-between items of a list that you want numbered.

Word for Windows inserts the number of each line to the left of the text in each line of an entire section if you activate the Format Section Line Numbering option toggle box. You can do this with the left mouse button, or by tabbing down to the Line Numbering box and typing the letter **i**. These numbers will appear only during printing or during View Page or File Print Preview (see sections on printing and onscreen printing previews in Chapter 5).

The Start At option displays which number Word for Windows will begin with when numbering lines within a section; the default is 1. From Text refers to the distance to the left of the left text margin that the numbers will appear. In a standard 1" margin, the default position of line numbers will be 0.5" to the left of the text margin.

If you are using more than one column, line numbers will appear to the left of each line; this means that some numbers will fall in the space between the columns. The default position for the line numbers with multicolumnar text is 0.13" to the left of each column, but both of these distances can be changed by entering a different value in the From Text option field.

The Count By option allows you to number lines in multiples other than 1. If you set the Count By option field at 5 and the Start At field at 0, the lines will be numbered in multiples of 5: 0, 5, 10, 15, and so on.

The Per Page option starts the line numbering from 1 on each page rather than continuing the count from the previous page. Per Section starts the line numbering over at the beginning of each section. Finally, if you choose to activate the Continue option, you are indicating that the numbering should begin at the next number counting from the last number in a previously numbered section. This would be another way to number items in a list if there was an intervening passage, especially if it was a long passage. In this case, you would block off the lines in the first part of the list and format it as a section with the Line Numbering option on. Then you would block off the portion of the list appearing later in the document. This second section would also be formatted as a section with Line Numbering activated, but it would also have the Continue option on so the numbering would start where the first numbered section left off. Note that the Per Page and Continue options are ghosted in Figure 2-4 because there is no text assigned to a section to accept Line Numbering. The use of automatic line numbering is discussed in depth in Chapter 7, "Time Saving Organization: Outlines and Tables of Contents."

Vertical Alignment

┌─Vertical Alignment──────────────┐
│ ◉ Iop   ○ Center   ○ Justify │
└─────────────────────────────────┘

Vertical Alignment is another option many Word 4.0 and 5.0 users have probably needed at one time or another. The Top option brings all the text in a section upward on a page so it is flush with the top of the page. The Center option places the section of text in the middle of a page, equidistant from both the top and bottom. The Justify option adds equal amounts of space between all of the lines so that the top line of the text is aligned with the top margin, whereas the bottom line of the text is flush with the bottom margin of the page. The space added between the lines for vertical justification comes from the residual space that would have been below the text had it been top-aligned. These options override the Paragraph Spacing options. You can preview vertically aligned text before you print with the Print Preview command discussed in Chapter 5.

Section Start

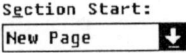

The Section Start option gives you control over where a section will be printed regardless of where it has been entered. The default for this option is New Page which automatically starts a section on a page of its own after a hard page break. The section start scroll-down box shown here shows all options that are available.

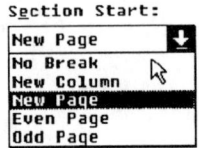

If you select No Break, the section will start printing without a break from the previous text. New Column starts a section printing in a new column after a hard column break. This option can be used only in a multicolumned document. Even Page starts the section printing on the next evenly numbered page, but does not limit printing to evenly numbered pages. Printing continues on both even- and odd-numbered pages until the section is finished. Similarly, Odd Page Section Start initiates printing on the next available odd page, but continues printing on both even and odd pages. Word for Windows therefore cannot print two different sections on separate facing pages. This means that you cannot have one section printing on the even-numbered pages while another section simultaneously prints on the odd-numbered facing pages. This would be like setting up frames on the even- and odd-numbered pages for different sections, and Word for

Windows has no frame function. As explained earlier, no matter what page sections start on (odd- or even-numbered), they must run to conclusion before another section can follow. However, you can use the Vertical Alignment and Line Between options discussed earlier in this section to ensure that several sections found on the same page are separated in a visually appealing way. Again, these effects are discussed in depth in Chapter 10.

Document Formatting

The Format Document dialog box shown in Figure 2-5 contains options that supersede all the other formatting options that have been discussed. Unlike the other Format dialog boxes, you do not need to highlight any text before you access the Format Document dialog box. Since you can only have the cursor in one document window at a time, you cannot format multiple documents with the Format Document dialog box. Features selected in this dialog box automatically apply to the whole document. The Format Document dialog box shown in Figure 2-5 will be referred to throughout the following discussion of Format Document commands.

Paper Size/ Tab Default

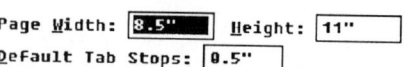

Paper size is set by the Page Width and Height options, which are set to the standard default of 8 1/2" by 11", as shown in Figure 2-5. Whether you will be able to enlarge the paper size beyond 8 1/2" by 11" depends on what kind of paper your printer can accept. Word for Windows will allow you to set up any size paper to print, but you may not be able to feed odd-sized paper into your printer.

Figure 2-5.

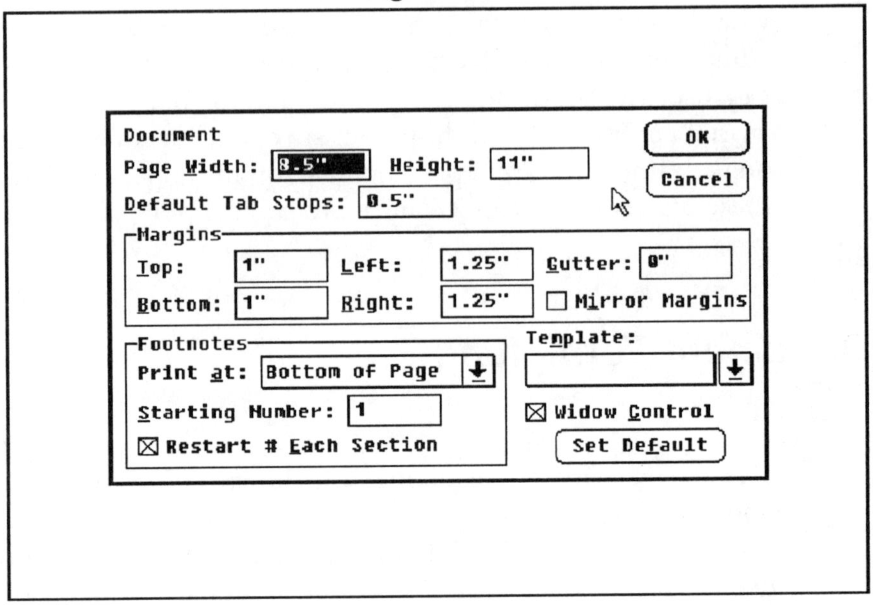

```
┌─────────────────────────────────────────────────────────────┐
│                                                               │
│   ┌───────────────────────────────────────────────────┐      │
│   │ Document                            ┌───────────┐   │      │
│   │ Page Width: [8.5"      ]  Height: [11"  ]  │   OK    │   │      │
│   │ Default Tab Stops: [0.5" ]          ┌───────────┐   │      │
│   │ ┌─Margins──────────────────────┐  ⟋  │  Cancel   │   │      │
│   │ │ Top:    [1"  ]  Left: [1.25"] Gutter: [0" ]      │   │      │
│   │ │ Bottom: [1"  ]  Right: [1.25"] □ Mirror Margins  │   │      │
│   │ ┌─Footnotes──────────────────┐  Template:           │      │
│   │ │ Print at: [Bottom of Page ↓]  [            ↓]    │   │      │
│   │ │ Starting Number: [1    ]    ⊠ Widow Control       │      │
│   │ │ ⊠ Restart # Each Section    (  Set Default  )     │      │
│   │ └──────────────────────────────────────────────┘  │      │
│   └───────────────────────────────────────────────────┘      │
│                                                               │
└─────────────────────────────────────────────────────────────┘
```

Format Document dialog box

The Default Tab Stops default is 0.5". For further information on setting tabs, see the ruler function discussion in Chapter 4.

Format Margins

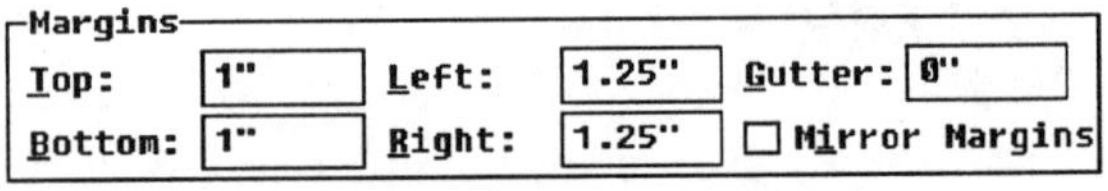

```
┌─Margins────────────────────────────────────┐
│ Top:    [1"  ]  Left: [1.25"] Gutter: [0" ]  │
│ Bottom: [1"  ]  Right: [1.25"] □ Mirror Margins│
└─────────────────────────────────────────────┘
```

As with Word versions 4.0 and 5.0, Word for Windows automatically sets the document margins to a default width of 1" at the top and bottom and 1.25" at either side. Since these are user-definable option fields, you can overtype those values.

The top margin is an important consideration when you have designated a large header since the header will not be printed unless it can clear the body text to be printed below it. For example, a 4-line, 12-point header that began at 0.5" from the top would not be printed if the body text is set to begin at 1" from the top, because for the header to print, it would have to overwrite the body text. Word for Windows will not print a header over body text but chooses instead to print the body text alone. To print both the overlapping header and the body text, you would have to set the body text so that it begins below the header.

The Mirror margin option is most commonly used to create mirrored sideheads. A *sidehead* is a margin at the outside of the page where highlights, page numbers, or section titles may appear. As shown in Figure 2-6, if a left (outside) margin of 2.5" and right (inside) margin of 1" were mirrored, the facing (right) page would have a right (outside) margin of 2.5" and an left (inside) margin of 1".

Gutters are empty columns at the right side of left pages and the left side of right pages; in other words, they occur on the inside of facing pages. Gutters are the space needed for pages to be bound together without covering any printed text. They are mirrored automatically and can be used together with mirrored text margins, as shown in Figure 2-6. The examples in Figure 2-6 demonstrate that you are not limited to using either gutters or mirrored margins. You can use both at once.

```
┌Footnotes──────────────────────┐
│ Print at: │Bottom of Page│ ↓│ │
│ Starting Number: │1        │  │
│ ⊠ Restart # Each Section       │
└────────────────────────────────┘
```

Footnotes

You can open the Footnotes option scroll-down box by clicking the left mouse button on the boxed down arrow to the right of the Print at option. You may also tab to the Print at option and use the

Figure 2-6.

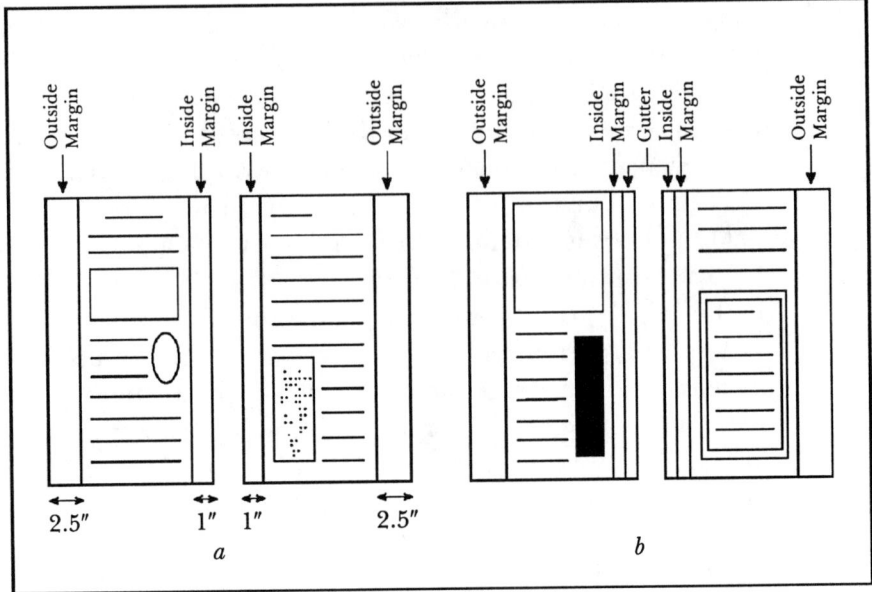

Document Margin options: (a) Facing pages, (b) Guttered facing pages

keypad UP ARROW and DOWN ARROW to view the available options one at a time. The default Footnotes option shown here is Bottom of Page.

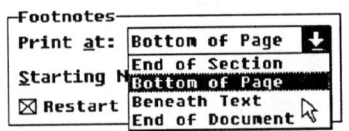

This means that if you add a footnote to a document and do not change the Format Document Footnotes option, this footnote will appear at the bottom of the page on which it is cited.

The Format Document Footnotes option can be overridden by the Format Section Include Footnotes option. For example, the default Document Footnotes setting, Bottom of Page, is active.

You, however, decide to change this setting to End of Document. Then you block off a few footnotes and activate the Format Section Include Footnotes. Those blocked-off footnotes would appear at the end of the section, not at the end of the document; any other footnotes outside of the one section formatted with the Include Footnotes option would still appear at the end of the document.

Another Print at option, Beneath Text, places all of the footnotes referenced on a page at the bottom of *that* page. The Bottom of Page option allows footnotes to be placed sequentially at the bottom of several contiguous pages. Footnotes formatted with the Beneath Text option can continue onto the next page as long as they begin on the page where they are originally referenced. If footnotes formatted with the Beneath Text option do continue onto the next page, they are placed underneath the maximum amount of body text that can fit on the page.

If you choose the End of Section option, the footnotes are printed at the end of the section, not the page, where they are referenced.

The End of Document option is used if you want the footnotes to appear on a separate page at the end of the document. To do this, you must end your document with a page break and an empty paragraph sign. Word for Windows will interpret the empty paragraph sign as the last entry and will set the footnotes below it. You could also place some text, for example the word "Footnotes," before this last paragraph marker. All of the various uses of footnotes are discussed in depth in Chapter 7.

Footnote Numbering System   The Starting Number option determines the numbering system for the footnotes. For example, if you are continuing a series of footnotes from an earlier document, enter the number of the footnote that continues the series of footnotes so that it follows the number of the last footnote in the previous document. Or, you can choose the Restart # Each Section option, which will group footnotes by section. If you decide to print footnotes numbered for each section at the end of the document, consider adding section headers to the footnotes. They will give your footnotes clear organization.

Template

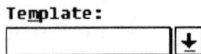

Word for Windows has a default template, NORMAL.DOT, which includes several paragraph styles. However, document templates can include styles, macros, glossaries, and boilerplate text. Saving so many features to a template is useful for creating standardized forms, letters, memos, and reports. Styles were explained earlier in this chapter in the section on paragraph styles. Macros are series of often repeated keystrokes and commands that you save so you can execute them later by pressing one keystroke combination. Glossaries are words, paragraphs, or passages, of text that you use repeatedly in a document and that are also saved to one keystroke combination. Boilerplate text is the part of a form that does not vary, like the "To:" and "From:" at the top of a memo. All of these features of templates are discussed in Chapter 4 and Chapter 6.

Templates can be used as the basis for a document, or can be merged into a document at any time. Templates are not available in versions 4.0 and 5.0 of Word. Note that no template has been assigned to the Word for Windows document when you first open the program as shown here.

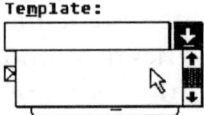

The default template NORMAL.DOT is not shown because no text has been entered. A Document Sampler exhibiting various templates is included in the Word for Windows tutorial.

Widow Control

☒ Widow Control

When the last line of a paragraph begins a new page, it is called a widow. The default setting for the Widow Control option is on (box has an "X" in it); therefore, no page will start with the last line of a paragraph from the previous page. When space is at a premium, or a document format calls for no widow control, this option can be turned off with a mouse click on the toggle box or by tabbing to the box and typing **c**.

Set Default

Set Default

If you click the left mouse button on Set Default, all of the currently selected Format Document options become permanent defaults. You might, for example, want to make 1" margins, double-spaced paragraphs, 0.5" indents, and the Footnotes End of Document option (normally off) the default. If you accidentally change your defaults and cannot remember the standard ones that were installed with Word for Windows, you can always recreate the original defaults. Simply exit Word for Windows and delete the WINWORD.INI and NORMAL.DOT files. The next time you start Word for Windows these files will be recreated with the default settings, and Word for Windows will load with its original default settings.

Summary

The formatting commands covered in this chapter have formed the core of Microsoft Word from its inception. The new section formatting options found in Word for Windows are the most striking additions to the formatting abilities already found in Word 4.0 and 5.0. However, it is the ability to quickly add fonts and graphics to Word for Windows documents that sets it off as a word publishing program. You have seen how fonts are added to Word for Windows documents. You will see how graphic images are inserted in a Word for Windows' document in the next chapter.

The entire Word for Windows Format menu has not been covered in this chapter. Tabs options and Styles and Define Styles options will be discussed in Chapter 4, "For the Record: Styles and Templates." The Position options for previewing the position of text and graphics are covered in Chapter 5, "Printing: Picture Perfect Output." Finally, the Format Tables dialog box is discussed in Chapter 3, "Cut and Paste: Adding Tables and Images."

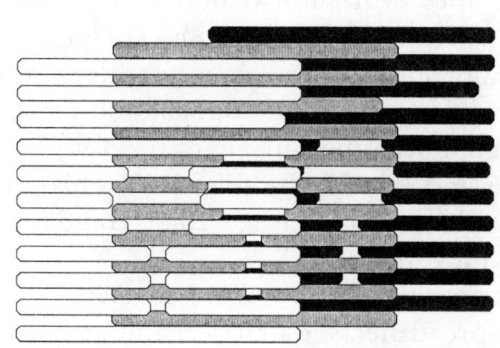

3

Cut and Paste: Adding Tables and Images

The Clipboard

Like Word 5.0, Word for Windows has excellent text and graphic image importation capabilities. Also, because Word for Windows runs under Microsoft Windows, importing text and graphic image files could not be easier. Word for Windows can import text as a table if you have separated cell entries by tabs or commas, and if each row ends with a carriage return (ENTER). The graphic images that can be imported into Word for Windows can range from simple line drawings to scanned photographs. For instance, you can add your company logo to the return address on your letterhead or you can scan a photo of yourself and place it into your resume. You can import either images or text for tables from both DOS applications and Windows applications. This process is discussed in depth in both Chapter 9, "Data Handling," and Chapter 11, "Fine Tuning Windows."

Text and image swapping between Word for Windows documents and Windows spreadsheets, databases, and graphic image programs (paint and draw programs) is particularly easy. Data swapping among Windows applications in general is accomplished by using a Windows tool called the *Clipboard*. Since it is easier to swap text and images among Windows applications (as compared to between Windows and non-Windows programs), you will learn how this is done first. You will then learn how to create your own tables within a Word for Windows document. Finally, you will learn how to import a graphic image into a Word for Windows document.

The Windows Clipboard enables you to take text and graphics from any Windows application and instantly paste it into Word for Windows. The Clipboard is similar in function to the Scrap in Word 4.0 and 5.0. Once you copy or cut (delete) a block of text or a graphic image to the Clipboard in any Windows application, you can paste (insert) that block anywhere else in the current program window or you can open another Windows program and paste the Clipboard contents into it. The Clipboard itself is a location in the computer's RAM (Random Access Memory) where a copied or cut block of text or image resides. Like the Scrap in Word 4.0 and 5.0, any time you copy something to the Clipboard, the new item writes over the previous item in the Clipboard, and when you turn off your computer whatever is in the Clipboard is lost (just like everything else stored in RAM while your PC is running).

The major difference between the Windows Clipboard and the Word 4.0 and 5.0 Scrap is that the Clipboard is active in all Windows applications, not just Word for Windows. The Word 4.0 and 5.0 Scrap is only useful for cutting and pasting within those two programs. The Clipboard is accessed in the Edit menu in all Windows applications. It contains the commands that you use to bring data into and out of the Clipboard, Edit Cut, Edit Copy and Edit Paste. (These commands will be discussed in depth later in this chapter.)

Linking Data

The Clipboard can be used to link a block of text or an image copied from outside of Word for Windows to a Word for Windows document. For example, a bar chart produced from data contained in an Excel spreadsheet could be copied to the Clipboard and then pasted in a Word for Windows document. If this paste is done with the Windows DDE (Dynamic Data Exchange) link function, whenever the data in a spreadsheet is changed, the linked chart in the Word for Windows document is dynamically (automatically) updated. In general, establishing a DDE link between data files in two Windows programs means that whenever the linked text or image is changed in the source, it is also changed in any programs into which it has been pasted. This would be especially helpful for generating reports based on spreadsheets or graphs, which change frequently. DDE linking of files is discussed in depth in Chapter 11.

Importing Data Using the Clipboard

Data files with text items that have been tabbed or separated by commas can be imported from outside Word for Windows and instantly pasted into a table in Word for Windows using the Clipboard. If the data has been generated in a non-Windows application, it can be added as a separate ASCII file and then converted into a table. When these types of data are imported into Word for Windows tables, tab or comma separations tell Word for Windows to place each entry into its own box in a table. The boxes that hold separate data entries in a table (or in a spreadsheet like Excel or Lotus) are called *cells*. When Word for Windows encounters a carriage return (ENTER) in these files, it starts a new row in the table.

Before you practice using the Clipboard or the ASCII import function, you need to learn how to create tables from within Word for Windows. You begin the process of creating a table with commands found in the Insert menu.

Creating a Table

The Insert menu is displayed either by pressing ALT-i or by clicking the left mouse button on the word "Insert" in the menu bar. You begin the creation of a table with the Insert Table command. Once the Insert menu is displayed, as shown on the next page,

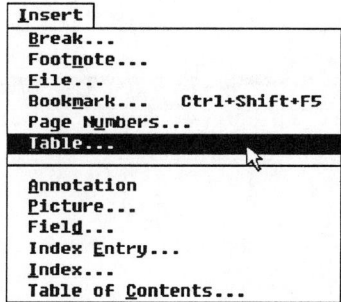

you can activate the Insert Table command by typing **t**, by clicking the left mouse button on the word "Table," or by moving the cursor through the Insert menu with the keypad DOWN ARROW and pressing ENTER when the cursor highlights the Insert Table command.

The Insert Table command activates the Insert Table dialog box shown here.

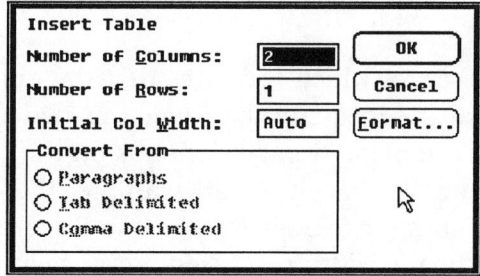

There are two ways to accept the default conditions shown in this dialog box. You can use the TAB key to move to the OK button, and then press ENTER. Or, you can click the left mouse button on the OK button. Accepting the default conditions produces a table with two columns in one row as shown in Figure 3-1. Note that in Figure 3-1, the default Number of Columns setting is 2 and the default Number of Rows setting is 1. The default Initial Col Width

Figure 3-1.

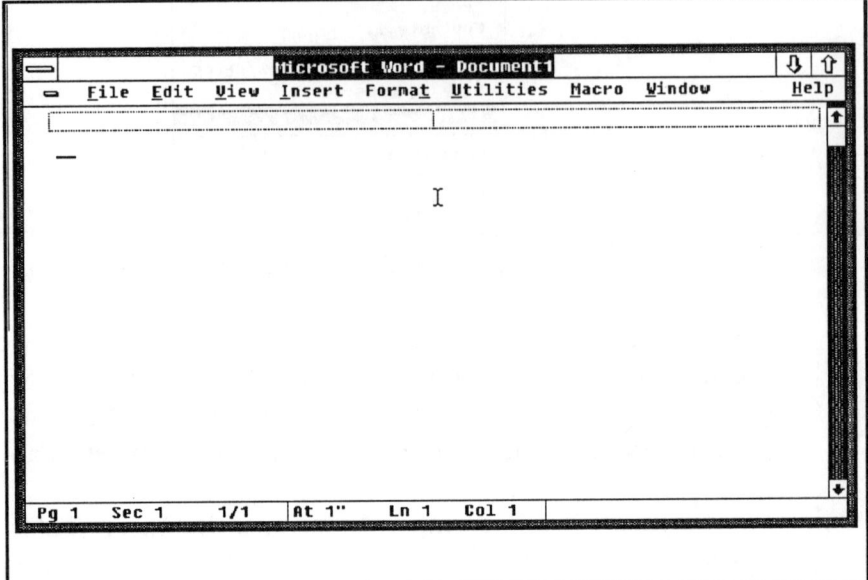

Two-column table, full page width

setting is Auto, which indicates that the entire width of the page will be divided equally between the two default columns. The width of the printed page depends on the width of the page and the size of the margins. For example, the default right and left margin settings are both 1.25" on an 8 1/2" wide page, giving you a printed page width of 6" (see the Format Document dialog box discussion in Chapter 2, "Formatting Text"). Therefore, the default width for each of the two columns will be 3".

The ghosted (unavailable) Convert From options will become active when you block off a portion of text to be inserted within a table before you invoke the Insert Table command. Entries separated by paragraphs (ENTER or carriage return), tabbed entries, and entries separated by commas can be assigned cells and converted to a table with this command. This set of options makes it easy for you to quickly convert a list to a table. You can also highlight all the data in a table and convert it to any of these formats (cell entries separated by paragraphs, tabs, or commas) with the Insert Table to Text option. These types of conversions are discussed later in this chapter in the "Incorporating Tabular Data into a Table" section.

If you decide you do not want to insert the table, you can delete the table with the Edit Undo Insert Table command in the Edit menu. This command is automatically added to the Edit menu immediately after you insert a table. However, the Edit Undo command only undoes the last command invoked. Therefore, if you want to delete a table after you have added text to the table or to another part of the document, you will have to use the Edit Table command. Note that the Edit Table command will be ghosted unless the cursor is on a table. (The Edit Table command is discussed in detail later in this chapter.)

The insertion of a table automatically leaves the text entry cursor in the upper left cell, cell number 1, of the table. Note that the status bar at the bottom of the Word for Windows screen in Figure 3-1 displays line, section, page number, and keyboard status information. In contrast, when you first open the Insert menu and highlight the Insert Table command, the status bar contains a help message explaining that the Insert Table command inserts a table.

You can move the text entry cursor from cell to cell by clicking the left mouse button. You can insert text, numerical data, or both into any cell of the table. If you type past the end of the line, the text will automatically wrap around at the end of the line, adding a new row within the cell but not a new cell. As you add one or more of these extra lines to a cell, the cell height of all cells in the row increases but the cell width stays constant.

In most cases, a single row, two-column, two-cell table will be inadequate and you will want to alter the default Insert Table settings. These options that apply to tables are chosen in the Format Table dialog box, which is accessed in the Format menu. Note that the Format Table command in the Format menu is ghosted until you insert a table with the Insert Table command. You can then choose Format table as shown here.

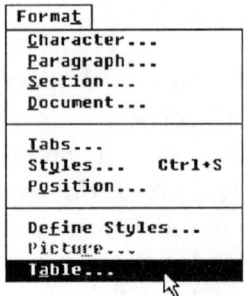

However, you can format a table before it is created with the Insert Table dialog box. By selecting the Format button in the Insert Table dialog box, you will display the same Format Table dialog box that appears if the Format Table command is selected in the Format menu. Once a table has been created, you can only change it with the Format Table dialog box via the Format Table command in the Format Menu (not Insert Table).

Format Table Options

The options in the Format Table dialog box, shown in Figure 3-2, allow you to precisely control the appearance of a table. In this example, the Width of Column option sets the horizontal width of column 1 because the text entry cursor was in column 1 (cell 1) when the dialog box was invoked. If you had moved the text entry cursor to column 2 (cell 2) before activating the Format Table dialog box, you would find Width of Column 2 listed instead. Since the default width of a page is 6", the default width of each cell in a two-column table is 3". Also, in this table, as shown in Figure 3-2, the default Space Between Cols is 0.11". The "Auto" shown for the Minimum Row Height is the same as the current line spacing setting in the Format Paragraph dialog box (12 points). However, since this is a text-entry field, you can either

Figure 3-2.

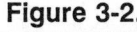

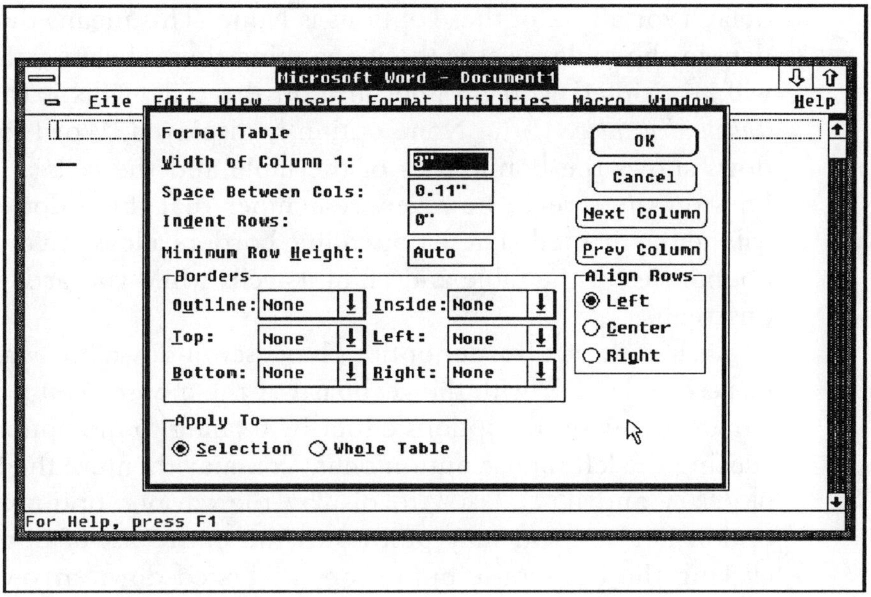

Format Table dialog box

decrease or increase the line spacing within the table by typing over the word "Auto" with a particular point, pica, inch, or centimeter setting.

The Next Column and Prev Column boxes move the text entry cursor within the table so you can format different columns without exiting from the Format Table dialog box. Since this table contains only two cells, choosing the Next Column option moves the text entry cursor to cell 2 without the need to leave the Format Table dialog box; simultaneously, the Width of Column 1 option changes to Width of Column 2. Selecting the Prev Column option would then move the text entry cursor back to cell 1.

Borders   If you want lines under, over, or around your table, you must choose the type of borders you want for the table. The set of six table border options appears in a box in the middle of the Format Table dialog box as shown in Figure 3-2. Note that the default for all six of these options is None. This means that if the data in the table is set without changing these defaults, the table will be printed with no lines around the cells. This is called an *unbounded table.* If the None option is displayed, Word for Windows shows the boundaries of the table and the cells as dotted lines on the screen; however, remember that these dotted lines will not be printed. These dotted line borders allow you to see the boundaries of the table and all of its cells while you are working onscreen.

Each of the six Border options has a scroll-down box which can be accessed either with the keyboard or the mouse. You move the cursor to any of the options either by tabbing to the option or by clicking the left mouse button on it. You may then use the keypad UP ARROW and DOWN ARROW to display the various options in the option field or you may pull down the entire list of options by clicking the left mouse button on the boxed down arrow at the right side of the scroll-down box as described in Chapter 1, "Up and Running," and Chapter 2, "Formatting Text." All five types of lines available with the table Border Outline options are shown in the following pull-down menu.

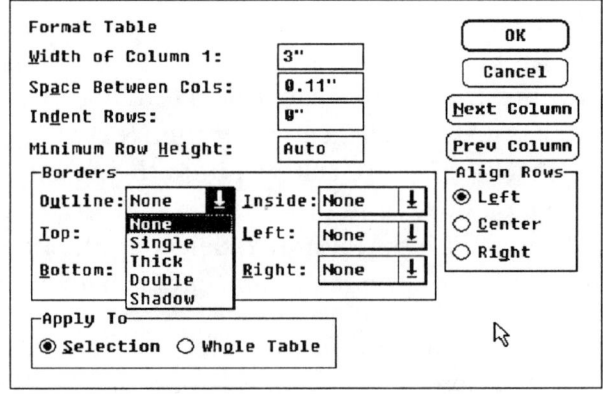

These are the same options that were available for boxing paragraphs in the Format Paragraph dialog box discussed in Chapter 2, "Formatting Text." All six Border option scroll-down boxes contain the same options as those contained in the Outline box, except that the Shadow option is available only in the Outline scroll-down box. The Inside scroll-down box controls the borders between cells within the table, whereas the Top, Bottom, Left, and Right options control the four sides, or outline, of whatever cells are highlighted when the dialog box is displayed. You can apply this formatting to all cells in the table by changing the Apply To option from Selection (the default) to Whole Table. When you change the Outline option, these four side wall options will change simultaneously as seen here.

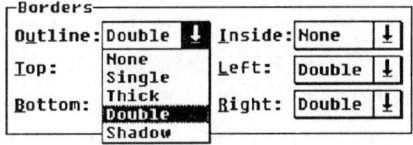

After you set the Outline option, you can change one or more of the four side walls with the Top, Bottom, Left, and Right options; however, if you change the Outline option again all four side wall options will show the same setting as the Outline option field. You can use the four side wall options to set up, for example, a thick line on the top and bottom of a table with thin lines between the cells and at the sides. In this way, you can highlight the presence of a table in the middle of a text-heavy document. You could also have a single thick line under the column headings alone. Varying the appearance of tables to suit document content and format is discussed in more detail in Chapter 10, "Desktop Publishing with Word for Windows."

Apply To Options   As mentioned in the discussion on borders, the next option set, Apply To, allows you to limit your formatting to one cell within a table, or to take the options selected for one cell and apply them to the whole table. The Selection option, which is the default, applies the options chosen in the Format Table dialog box to the cell on which the cursor is placed when the dialog box is activated. If you choose the Whole Table option, the options chosen in the Format Table dialog box will be applied to all cells in the table. You can also format more than one cell, or several selected columns of cells within the table, without formatting the entire table by blocking them off with the mouse before activating the Format Table menu; if the Selection option is active, you will be formatting only a subset of cells within the entire table.

Row Alignment   Finally, the Align Rows option aligns a row or all the rows of a table in relation to the margins of the page. This option allows you to treat the rows like paragraphs. The default sets all rows flush with the left margin of the page. You can, however, choose to have the row centered in the middle of the page or flush against the right margin of the page. You can designate the rows to be formatted before you invoke the Format Table dialog box by blocking off cells with the mouse. You can also choose to align the entire table (all rows) by choosing the Whole Table option in the Apply To option set (at the lower right corner of the Format Table dialog box). You do not need to block off all cells of a row to align an entire row; if the cursor is anywhere on the row before you invoke the Format Table dialog box, the entire row will be aligned.

Moving Around in Tables

Most often you will create tables with more than two cells. Working with larger tables requires you to move around within the table to enter data and format cells. You can move the cursor horizontally and vertically within tables with the TAB, UP ARROW, and DOWN ARROW keys. Word for Windows also has special mouse functions for tables. Whether you use the keyboard or mouse to move about in tables will depend upon what you want to do. In an empty table, for example, it is faster to use the TAB or UP ARROW and DOWN ARROW keys to move from cell to cell while you enter data than to reach for the mouse. While you are designing a table, or adding data to it, you may have to add or delete cells. You can do this most easily using the mouse with the Edit Table command, which is discussed in the section, "Deleting, Inserting, and Merging Cells," later in this chapter.

Using the Mouse

To learn to use the mouse within a table, you will first create a six-cell table. Begin by using the Insert Table command to display the Insert Table dialog box. Change the default setting for Number of Rows from 1 to 3, as shown here.

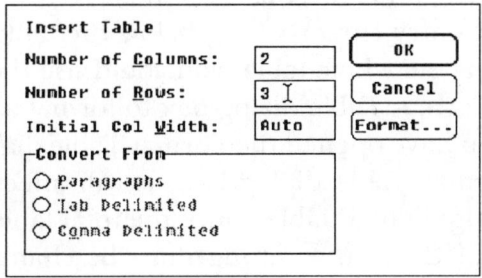

Then click the left mouse button on the OK button or press the ENTER key.

Next, change the default width of the table from 6" to 3" within the Format Table dialog box. Before you activate the Format Table dialog box, highlight the whole table so every cell in the table will be uniformly formatted. To do this, place the mouse arrow to the right of the first cell, in the upper left corner, as shown here.

Press the left mouse button and drag the mouse down and to the right until all six cells are highlighted, as shown here.

Make sure, however, that the cursor is within the table and not on the text entry cursor sitting below the table. (Even if you do not highlight the whole table, you could use the Whole Table option in the Format Table dialog box to format all the cells in the table after you have opened the Format Table dialog box.) Now activate the Format Table dialog box; it will affect formatting over the entire highlighted table. Since the total table width is to be 3", the Width of Column 1 setting must be changed from 3" to 1", as shown in Figure 3-3. This setting refers to the width of all highlighted columns in the table. The new 2" wide, six-cell table you just created is shown here.

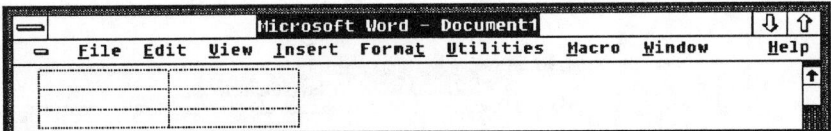

Note that when you place the mouse within each cell it becomes an I-beam (see Chapter 1, "Up and Running," for review of mouse configurations). Clicking the left mouse button on a cell moves the blinking text entry cursor to that cell. Using the I-beam mouse, move the cursor into each of the six cells of the table and add the text shown here to the table.

You are now ready to learn how to use the mouse within a table. As you have seen, when you place the mouse arrow outside the table to the left of a cell and click the left mouse button, the cell is highlighted. If you double-click (click the left mouse button twice), the entire row is highlighted.

Similarly, when you place the mouse arrow to the left of a cell within the table and click the left mouse button, the cell is highlighted, as seen in Figure 3-4b.

When you place the mouse arrow at the top of a column of cells, the arrow takes on a different appearance, as shown in Figure 3-4c.

Figure 3-3.

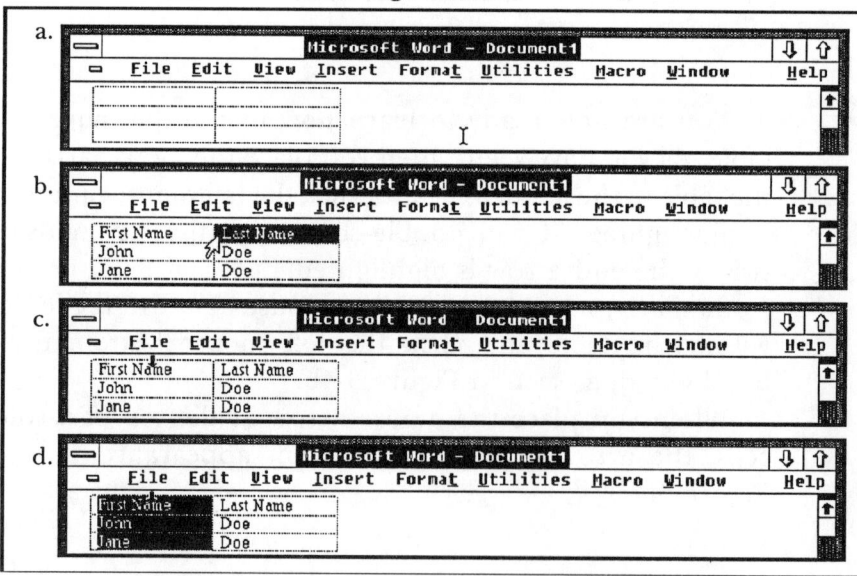

Changing cell width to 1" with Format Table dialog box

Figure 3-4.

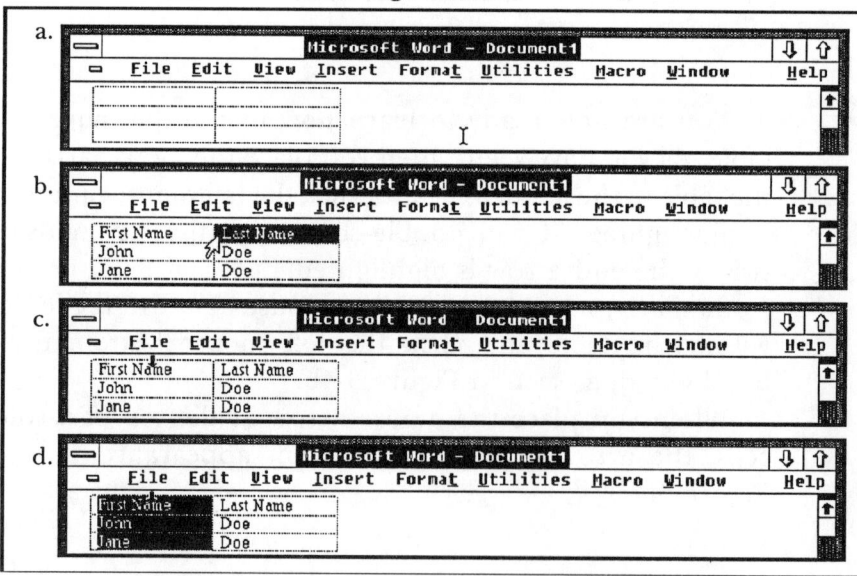

Using the mouse in a table

If you click the left mouse button at this time, the entire column is highlighted, as you can see in Figure 3-4d.

If you keep the left mouse button depressed and drag the mouse either to the left or the right, the highlight will extend to other columns.

Using the Keyboard

You can now try moving the cursor inside the table. Put the blinking cursor in the first cell by placing the I-beam mouse in the first cell and clicking the left mouse button. To move to the cell to the right using the keyboard, press the TAB key. Press the TAB key once again. As you can see, the TAB key moves you forward through the table (right to the end of a row, then down to the next row). Use SHIFT-TAB to move through the cells in the reverse direction. To move one space at a time within and between cells, use the RIGHT ARROW and LEFT ARROW keys. The keyboard commands for moving among cells are listed in Table 3-1.

You can also use the TAB key to add blank cells to the table. After you enter data in the last cell, press TAB. The cursor will move down and a new row with two open cells will be added. Now add three blank rows to the table by pressing TAB while the cursor is on the cell at the lower right corner. The first time you press TAB, you will create one new row with two cells. The next time you press TAB, the cursor will move to the right cell in this new row; the next time you press TAB, a second new row of two cells is created. Tabbing twice more creates the third row, as shown here.

Table 3-1.

Key	Action
TAB	Moves cursor right one cell to the end of the row and then down
SHIFT-TAB	Moves cursor left one cell to the beginning of the row and then up
ALT-HOME	Moves cursor to first cell in current row
ALT-END	Moves cursor to last cell in current row
ALT-PGUP	Moves cursor to top cell in current row
ALT-PGDN	Moves cursor to bottom cell in current row
ALT-(keypad)5	Selects the entire table
CTRL-SHIFT-ENTER	Inserts a paragraph above current row; this will split the table in two if you are not entering data in a cell in the table's first row

Keyboard commands for moving among cells

Deleting, Inserting, and Merging Cells

Now you will use the three empty rows in the table to practice deleting, inserting, and merging cells with the Edit Table command. In the column outside the table, place the mouse arrow to the left of the empty cell at the upper left (the fourth cell down). Keeping the left button depressed, drag the mouse arrow diagonally over the bottom half of the table so it appears as shown here.

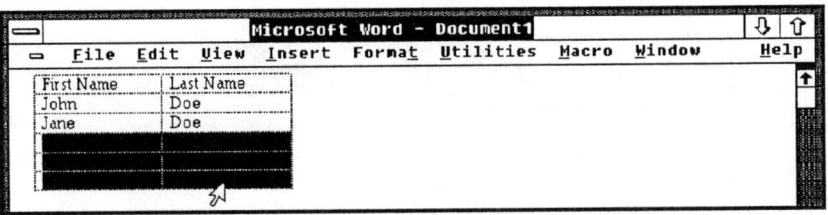

Release the left button and make sure the cursor remains within the table. Now activate the Edit Table dialog box as shown in Figure 3-5. Clicking the left mouse button on the Delete button in the Edit Table dialog box, as shown in Figure 3-6, will remove the three extraneous rows of cells. You cannot use the DEL or the BACKSPACE key to delete cells within a table so you should follow this procedure of highlighting the unwanted cells and then selecting the Delete option in the Edit Table dialog box. (You can use the DEL and BACKSPACE keys to delete cell entries, but not the cell itself.)

Now you will use the Edit Table dialog box to merge cells together within a table. First, highlight the remaining cells. Next, select the Edit Table dialog box and then select the Merge Cells option. The two columns of cells will merge into one as shown on the next page.

Figure 3-5.

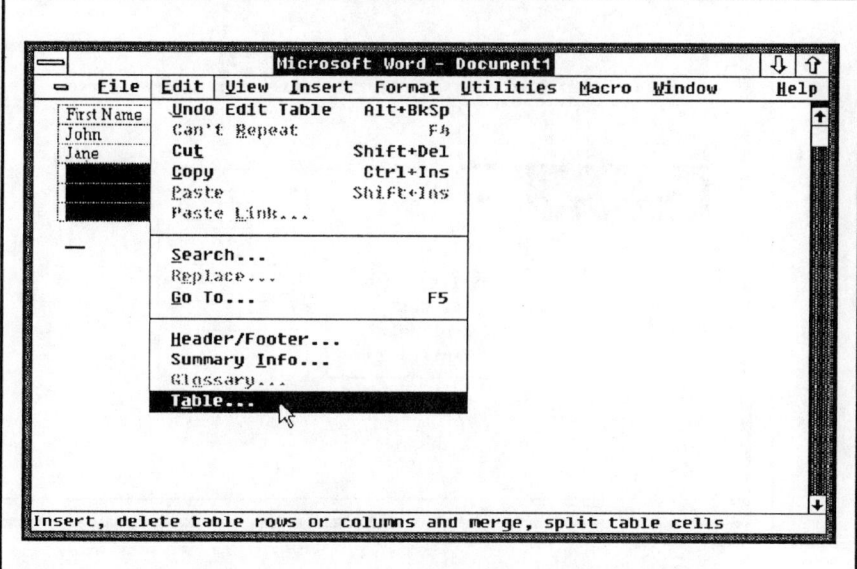

Edit Table command highlighted (note status bar at base of screen)

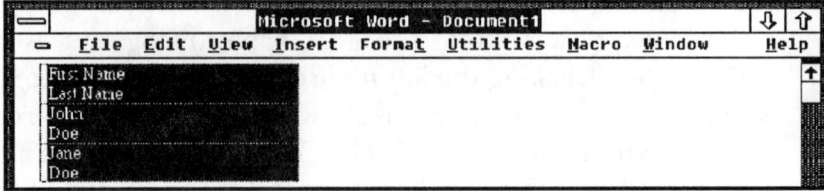

Notice that the second column's entries are on separate lines below those of the first column (in effect, the cells are now two lines deep). Each column's entry has been treated as a paragraph, forcing each to occupy a separate line. You can delete any unwanted text by dragging the I-beam mouse over it as shown on the next page, and pressing DEL.

Figure 3-6.

Deleting highlighted cells

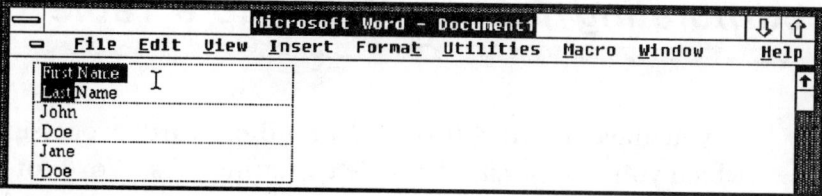

You can also delete the paragraph carriage returns (not seen onscreen) by inserting the blinking cursor at the beginning of the line after the carriage return and pressing BACKSPACE, as seen in Figure 3-7a. The new, cleaned-up, single column table looks like the one shown in Figure 3-7b. The next section discusses another means of creating tables, so delete the current practice table by highlighting the whole table and choosing the Delete option in the Edit Table dialog box.

Figure 3-7.

Finishing column merge with the Edit Table dialog box

Incorporating Tabular Data into a Table

If you have Word 4.0 or 5.0 or other word processing files in which you have created a table by setting tabs, Word for Windows can insert this data into a table. You can also create tables from text imported from other document files or from text you have typed into Word for Windows by placing tabs or commas between the entries that you want inserted into new cells. (Importing files from old versions of Word and other non-Windows word processing programs is discussed in Chapter 9. A new cell is created whenever a tab is encountered in the data and a new row is created after each carriage return (ENTER). (See the discussion in the section on the Clipboard earlier in this chapter to see how to import data with the Clipboard or from an ASCII file for conversion into a table.)

In the following example of converting tabbed text into a table, you will create a table by setting tabs in Word for Windows. You have probably used tabs in the past to set up tables. To begin formatting tabbed text, access the Format Tabs dialog box from the Format menu as shown here.

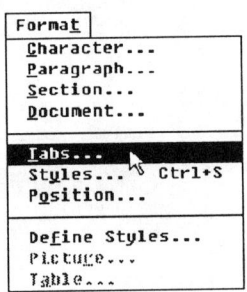

Note that the text entry cursor automatically appears in the Tab Position option field when the Format Tabs dialog box appears. Now you will type in 4 tabs, 1" apart, with the first tab starting 1"

in from the left margin. To do so, type **1** in the Tab Position option field and click the left mouse button on the Set button, as shown here.

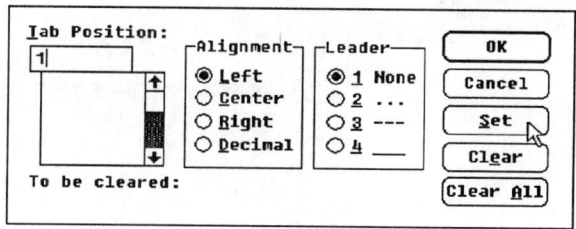

The Tab Position field now shows 1". Type **2** (as soon as you type **2**, the 1 will disappear), and click the left mouse button on the Set button. In the same way, set tabs at 3" and 4", until the Tab Position dialog box looks like that shown here.

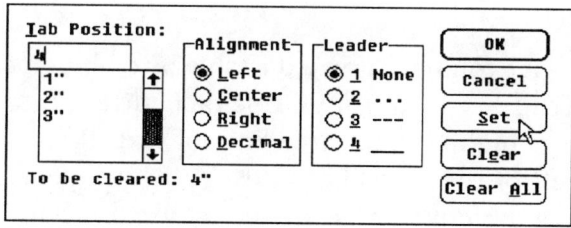

Click the mouse on the OK button when you are finished setting tabs. You will see a blank screen, but tabs will have been set.

Now type the following information, pressing the keys in parentheses as well:

Name (TAB)	**Score1** (TAB)	**Score2** (TAB)	**Score3** (ENTER)
John Doe (TAB)	**98** (TAB)	**78** (TAB)	**95** (ENTER)
Jane Doe (TAB)	**77** (TAB)	**95** (TAB)	**99** (ENTER)

Figure 3-8.

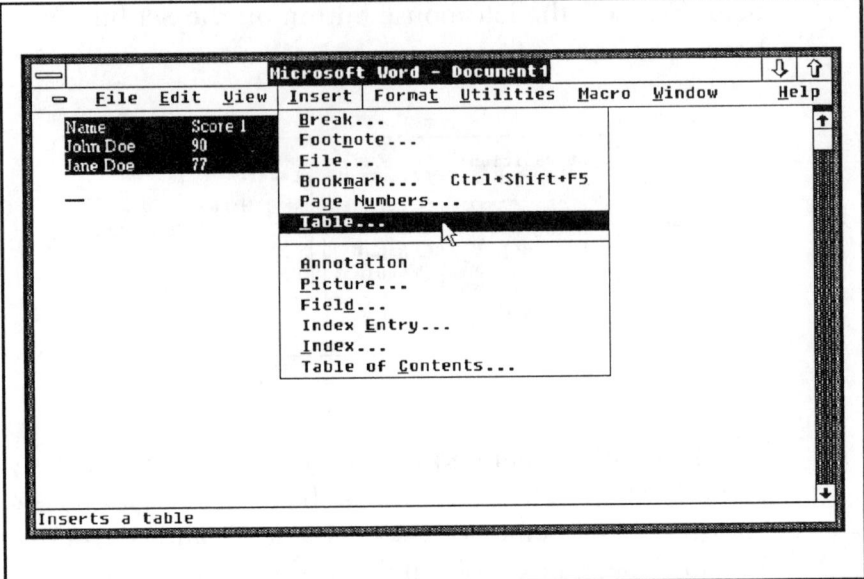

Insert Table command applied to highlighted tabbed text

Now that you have created a table by tabbing between entries, you are ready to incorporate this tabbed text into a table. First you need to highlight all three lines of text. Place the mouse arrow to the left of the first line of text. Click the left mouse button and, holding it depressed, drag the mouse down to the left of the third line of text. All three lines will now be highlighted as shown here.

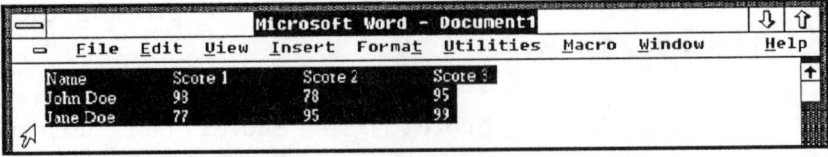

You are now ready to insert the block of text into a table. Activate the Insert Table dialog box from the Insert menu as shown in Figure 3-8. The parameters in this dialog box, as shown in Figure 3-9, reflect the text you have entered. The Tab Delimited button at the bottom of the Insert Table dialog box in Figure 3-9 is automatically bulleted when you open the Insert Table dialog box, signaling that you have used tabs to separate the entries it will place in cells of the new table. Note that the four tabs you had set have already been interpreted as four columns. Now, either use the TAB key to move the cursor over to the Format button and press ENTER, or click the left mouse button on the Format button.

The Format Table dialog box opens, just as it would if you had activated the Format Table command from the Format Menu. However, remember you are now pre-formatting a table from the Insert Table dialog box. For this new table, Word for Windows

Figure 3-9.

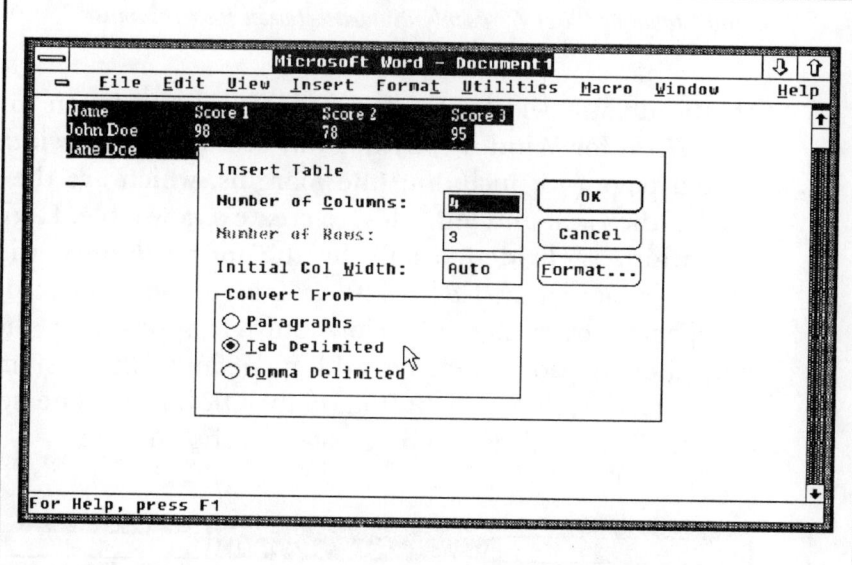

Insert Table dialog box with changed parameters

Figure 3-10.

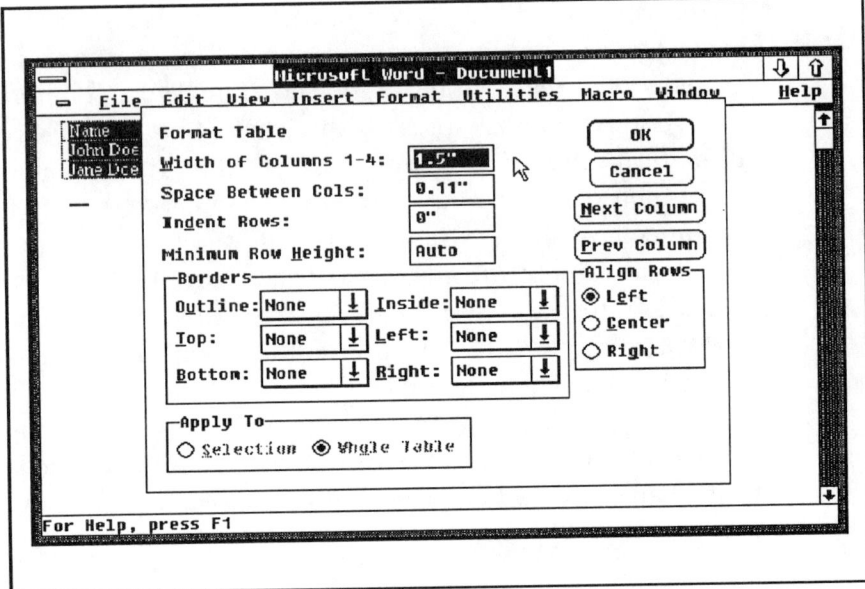

Default table width of 6" evenly divided between four columns

sets the default width of columns 1-4 to 1.5", shown in Figure 3-10. Word for Windows, by default, uses the entire width of the printed page (not including the margins, which are the default 1.25" at the right and left sides) to create a new table. Here the 6" page width is divided evenly by the four columns, with each column assigned a 1.5" width. Change the width to 1" by backspacing over the .5". Now only 1 appears in the field; remember you do not need to add the default " (inches) unit sign. Now, click the left mouse button on the OK button. The new table with its 1" cell widths will be created as shown here.

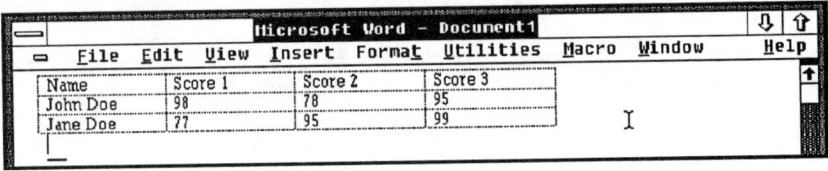

The 1" cell widths result in the text in the table appearing the same as it did with the 1" tabs used in the original table. The big difference is that now you can treat this data as a table. Each of the cells can be formatted, boxed, expanded upon, summed with other cells, or exported to another Windows application. The whole table can be boxed, shadowed, and otherwise formatted in the myriad ways discussed earlier in this chapter.

Before moving on to the next section, you can now delete the practice table by highlighting the whole table and choosing the Delete option in the Edit Table dialog box.

Importing an Image with the Clipboard

You are now familiar with the procedure to insert tables in Word for Windows documents. Inserting graphic images works in much the same way. A major difference is that although you can create the text to insert into a table within Word for Windows or import text from another application and then format it as a table, you cannot create graphic images within Word for Windows. All graphic images inserted into Word for Windows documents must come from an outside source.

The easiest way to import graphic images is by clipping out an image from another Windows program, either a paint or a draw program, and copying it to the Clipboard. You can then paste the image into a Word for Windows document. Note that all Windows graphics programs have the Edit Copy command, which lets you copy an image to the Clipboard. To see an example of this process, you will copy the SAILFOTO image displayed in Windows Paint in Figure 3-11 into the Clipboard and insert it in a Word for Windows document. Windows Paint is used here because it comes with Microsoft Windows. The SAILFOTO image is a Word for Windows sample image file that is copied to your hard disk as SAILFOTO.TIF when you install Word for Windows. It can be found in the WINWORD\WINWORD.CBT subdirectory.

Figure 3-11.

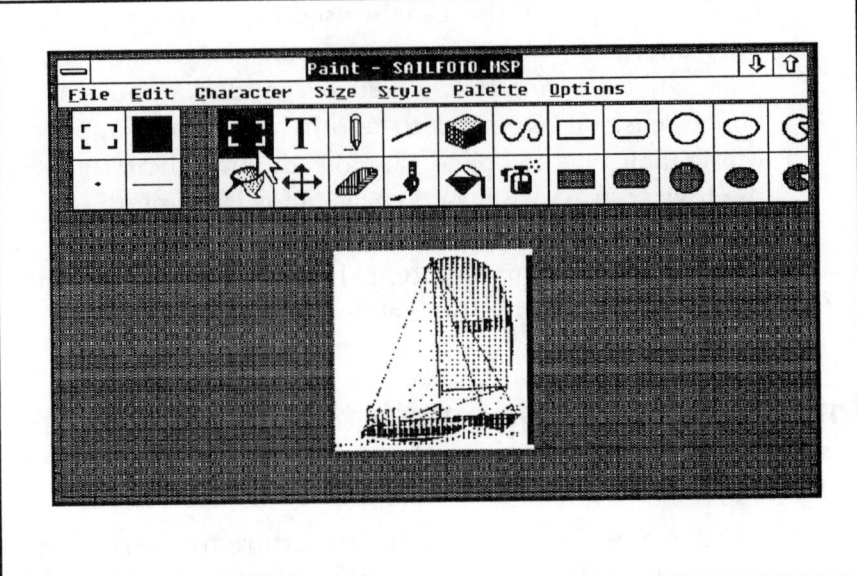

SAILFOTO image displayed in Microsoft Paint

Paint reads files with the extension *.MSP. SAILFOTO.TIF was converted to SAILFOTO.MSP with the conversion utility found with the non-Windows program Hijaak (see Appendix D, "Supporting Software and Hardware"). After it was converted from SAILFOTO.TIF to SAILFOTO.MSP, it could be read in Windows Paint. You do not have to use this image. You can import another image or create your own in Windows Paint to follow this exercise. You can also use another Windows paint package (like ClickArt) or a Windows draw package (like Designer) to display an image that you can then copy to the Clipboard. (The different uses of Windows paint and draw packages are discussed in depth in Chapter 10, Chapter 11, and Appendix D.) The kind of image you use is less important than learning to use the Clipboard to bring images into Word for Windows. Remember that access to the Clipboard is common to all Windows applications.

If you have the SAILFOTO.MSP file, or any other ∗.MSP graphic image file available on your hard disk, you display it in Windows Paint by choosing the image file's name in the Windows Paint File Open dialog box. If you do not have the SAIL-FOTO.MSP file available to you, substitute any ∗.MSP file for SAILFOTO in the following discussion on copying an image to the Clipboard.

Before the SAILFOTO image shown in Figure 3-11 can be copied to the Clipboard, all or part of it must be defined as an object. This is done with the Windows Paint Rectangle tool, often called a *Pick*. All Windows graphics programs will have some kind of Pick tool that lets you outline all or part of an image. Once you have defined the outlined area as an object with the Pick tool, you can copy it to the Clipboard, delete it, or resize it.

Now select all of the SAILFOTO image for inclusion in an object to be imported into a Word for Windows document. To do this, select the Pick tool by clicking the left mouse button on the box with four corners in the Windows Paint menu bar. The menu bar box with four corners will show in reverse video after you have selected it. Place the mouse arrow on the upper left corner of the SAILFOTO image (just inside the area of the screen taken up by the image), click the left mouse button, and drag the mouse diagonally over the image to just below the graphic's lower right corner. Next, release the left mouse button; this will select the image as a Windows object. (Do not release the left mouse button until you have moved it all the way to the lower right corner.) Whenever you release the mouse button, the area currently surrounded by the expanding dotted outline is selected as an object. If you do not want to keep the area surrounded by the Pick tool as an object, move the mouse off the graphic and click the left mouse button once; the dotted outline around the image will disappear. If you have surrounded the entire SAILFOTO image with the Pick tool, the SAILFOTO image should look like this onscreen.

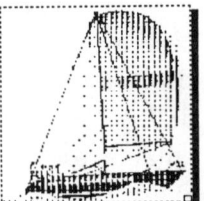

The image inside the dotted outline can now be treated as an object.

Activate the Edit Copy command, as shown in Figure 3-12, to copy the image to the Windows Clipboard. The Edit Copy command can be activated either by clicking the left mouse button

Figure 3-12.

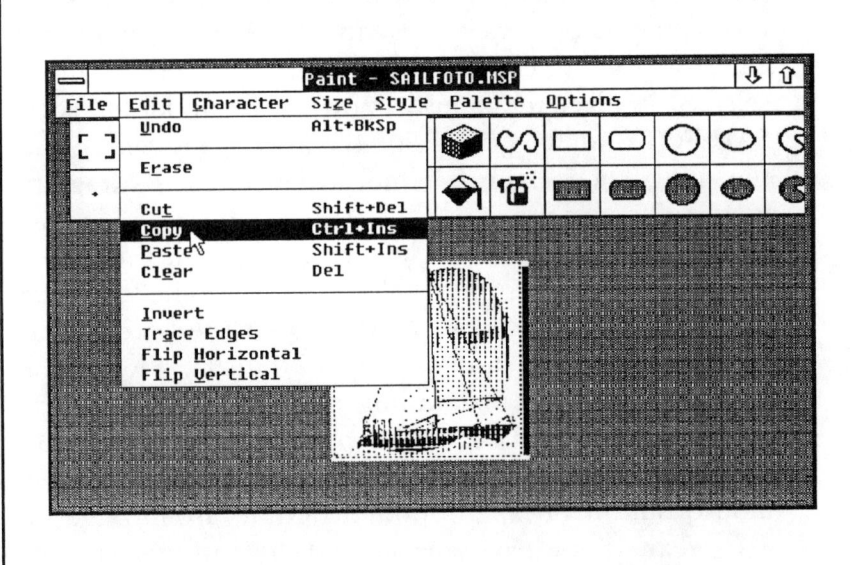

The Edit Copy command copies the image to the Windows Clipboard

on the word "Copy" in the Edit menu or by pressing CTRL-INS, which activates the command without displaying the Edit menu. If you use the Edit Cut command, shown just above the Edit Copy command in Figure 3-12, the outlined object is deleted from the screen to the Clipboard. You can activate the Edit Cut command by clicking the left mouse button on the word "Cut" in the Edit menu or by pressing SHIFT-DEL (this keystroke combination activates the command without displaying the Edit menu).

After you have closed Windows Paint or minimized it to an icon (these procedures were discussed in Chapter 1, "Up and Running"), you are ready to copy the image into a Word for Windows document. Open Word for Windows and pull down the Edit Paste command as shown here.

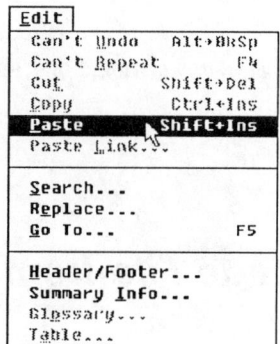

The Edit Paste command is activated either by clicking the left mouse button on the word "Paste" as shown above or by pressing SHIFT-INS. Activating the Edit Paste command inserts the SAILFOTO image onto the Word for Windows document page as shown in Figure 3-13.

Figure 3-13.

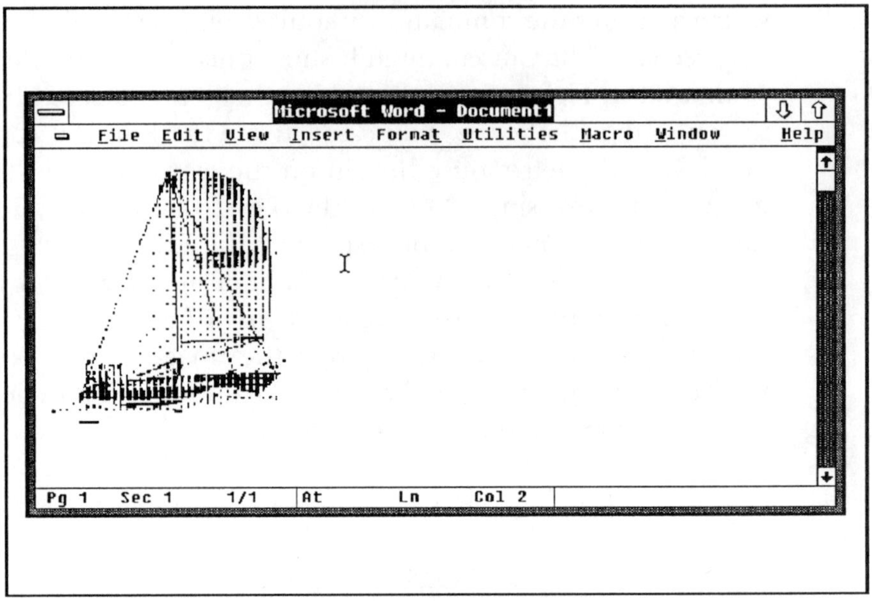

SAILFOTO image pasted into Word for Windows document

Inserting an Image File from Disk

Image files that you have saved to disk or purchased as clip art, especially those created in non-Windows applications, can also be inserted into a Word for Windows document. You do not need to use the Windows Clipboard with such image files. Activating the Insert Picture command, as shown here,

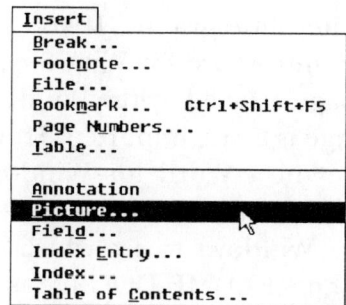

displays the Insert Picture dialog box shown here.

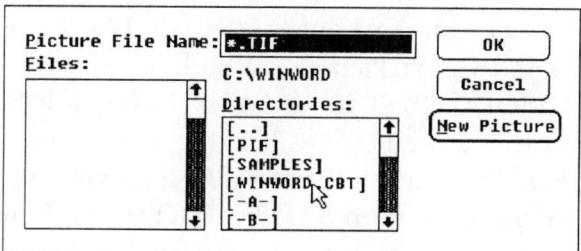

Notice that there are no image files ending with the *.TIF extension in the \WINWORD directory.

The default image file format that Word for Windows can import is *.TIF, which stands for TIFF (Tagged Image File Format). Many scanner programs create *.TIF files because this format includes grayscale information crucial to printing scanned black and white photographs. If you are using the Clipboard to import images into Word for Windows, it does not matter in what format the image is saved by the Windows graphics program from which the image is being imported. However, if you want to insert non-*.TIF files in a Word for Windows document without the Clipboard, you should check the README.DOC file that came with Word for Windows to see which graphic image formats are supported. The README.DOC file is discussed in Appendix C, "Setting Up Word for Windows." You can also convert an image file to a format that one of your Windows graphics programs can read and then copy the image to the Clipboard from that Windows graphics program. Conversion utilities are discussed in Appendix D, "Supporting Software and Hardware."

You have sample *.TIF files, including the SAILFOTO.TIF file, in the \WINWORD\WINWORD.CBT samples subdirectory which is created when you install Word for Windows. Again, access the Insert Picture dialog box from the Insert menu. The [WINWORD.CBT] subdirectory listing will be displayed in the Directories option set. Click the left mouse button on [WIN-WORD.CBT], and a list of *.TIF files will be displayed. Click the left mouse button on SAILFOTO.TIF, as shown here.

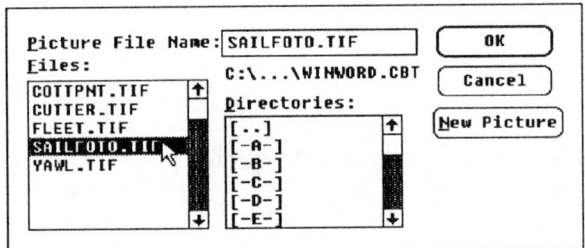

Then click the left mouse button on the OK button. The SAILFOTO image will be displayed in the Word for Windows document window as shown in Figure 3-14.

Figure 3-14.

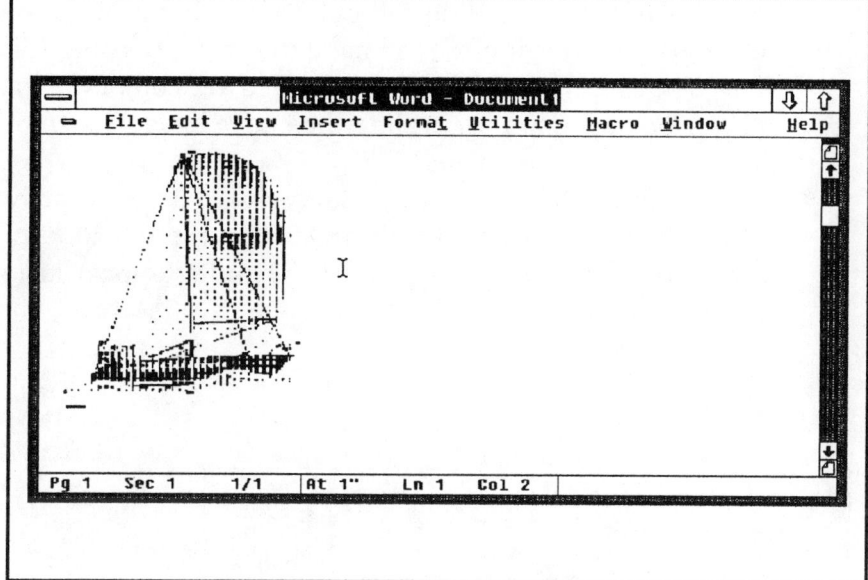

SAILFOTO image inserted into Word for Windows document

Cropping and Sizing Images

No matter how you incorporate an image into Word for Windows, whether with the Clipboard or with the Insert Picture command, you can always crop an image so that only the portion that complements the surrounding text is shown. To crop an image in Word for Windows, you treat it as a single object, no matter how many elements appear separately within the image. (You will not usually scale the image itself in Word for Windows. In most cases you will want to crop the borders of an image.) With Word for

Windows, you can outline a section of an image with a box. Portions of the image that fall outside the box will no longer be included. The portion of the image that you are using will be the same size as it was in the more extended version of the image. In other words, you are not scaling the entire image, but zooming in on a portion of the image.

To change the size of the image area, you must activate the Windows *sizing handles*. To do this, click the left mouse button anywhere on the image. Eight sizing handles appear around the image, as shown here.

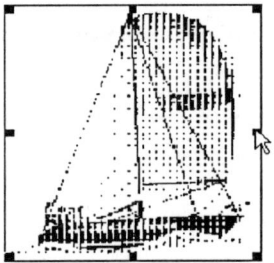

The sizing handles are the small black boxes, or nodes, around the edge of the boxed image. You can grab a handle with the mouse by placing the arrow over the handle and clicking the left mouse button. If you hold the mouse button down, you can drag the sizing handle inward or outward. The sizing handles at the corners will only move diagonally, the sizing handles on either side will only move horizontally, and the sizing handles on the top and bottom will only move vertically. In this way, you can visually size the space around the image so it fits flush with a column of text.

Figure 3-15.

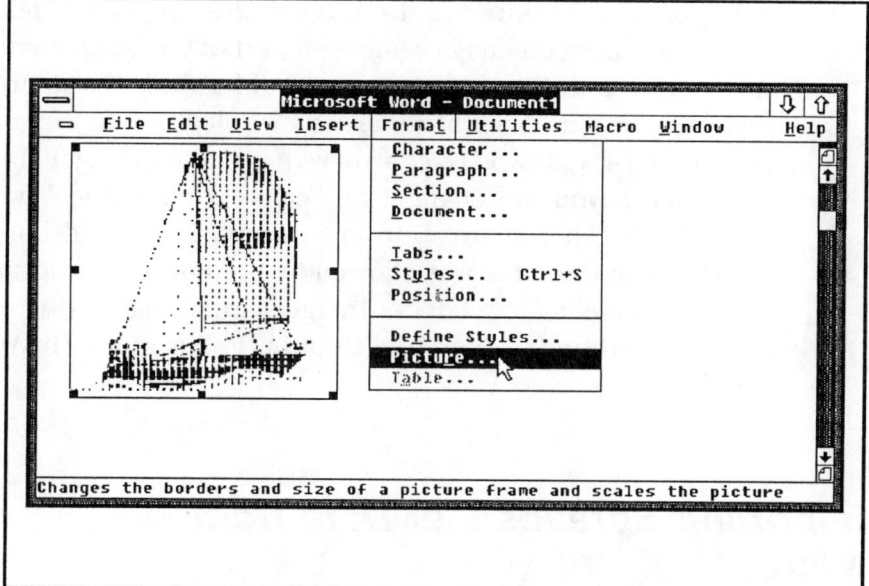

Format Picture command

If you want to be more precise, you can size the image itself with the Format Picture command, shown in Figure 3-15. Activating this command displays the Format Picture dialog box shown here.

Here you can see that the image is being shown at 100% of its original size.

The Format Picture dialog box also enables you to move the sizing handles by entering distances in the Crop From text entry fields. Cropping an image removes a part of the image that you do not want to use. For example, you could reduce the size of a box that contains an image of someone's whole body so that only the person's face is shown. To control reduction or enlargement of the image itself, you can change the Scaling Height and Width text entry fields. The Picture Border option lets you add borders to the image in the same way allowed by the Format Paragraph and Format Table dialog boxes. Image formatting is discussed in greater depth in Chapter 10, "Desktop Publishing with Word for Windows."

Importing Spreadsheet Data from Microsoft Excel

Many Word for Windows users will already be familiar with the Microsoft Windows spreadsheet program Excel. Excel, like Lotus 123, allows you to store data in tabular format, perform complex equations and statistics with the data, and generate graphic charts from the data. The data in the spreadsheet and the Excel charts generated from this data can be easily copied into Word for Windows via the Clipboard.

Data and/or charts from Excel (and from many other Windows applications) can also be linked between the source Excel spreadsheet or chart and the Word for Windows document. This linkage is called Dynamic Data Exchange (DDE), and it means that changes made to the spreadsheet or chart in Excel will be reflected in the Word for Windows document into which that information had been copied. DDE allows fast-changing spreadsheets like those containing stock quotes, experiments, or even students' grades (the following example) to automatically update

Figure 3-16.

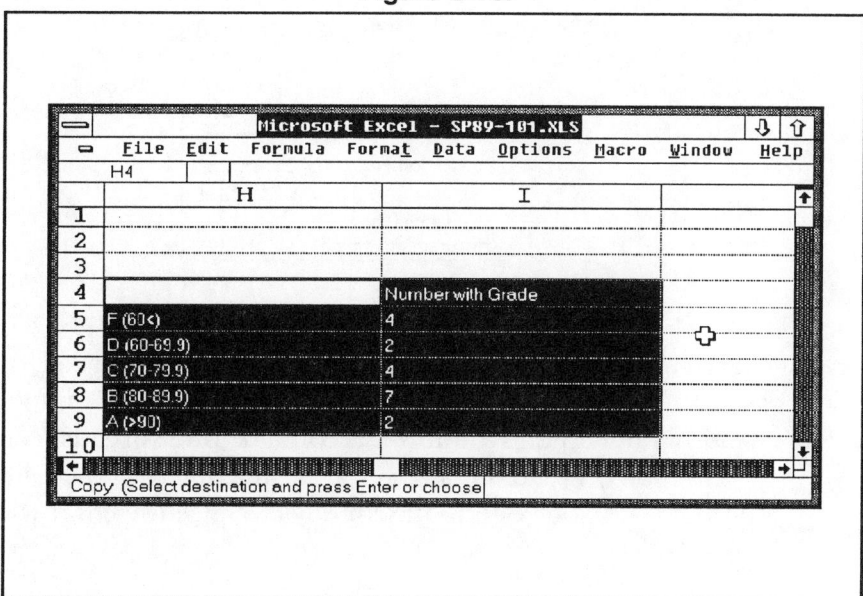

Highlighting data to include in Excel chart

a linked Word for Windows document. The importing of an Excel chart shown in the following example does not, however, involve a DDE paste link. See Chapter 11 for a full discussion of the DDE Paste Link command.

As can be seen from this example, you can load almost any spreadsheet into Excel. A sample Excel spreadsheet is shown in Figure 3-16. The mouse has been dragged diagonally over the two-column block to highlight the data, a college midterm grade distribution. Note that the mouse takes on a plus sign appearance in Excel.

A chart must be created in Excel before it can be pasted into a Word for Windows document. You can create a chart from any highlighted block of data by opening a new file with the File New command, as shown in Figure 3-17. When you activate this command, the File New dialog box appears from which you choose the Chart option button, as shown here.

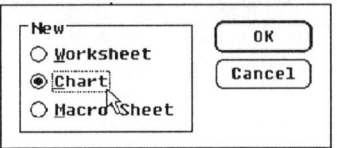

Next, click the left mouse button on the OK button. The bar graph chart shown in Figure 3-18 is immediately displayed over the original Excel worksheet (a worksheet is analogous to a Word for Windows document window—it contains one spreadsheet file).

The newly created chart can now be copied to the Clipboard, but first it must be defined as an object. Since the chart window is

Figure 3-17.

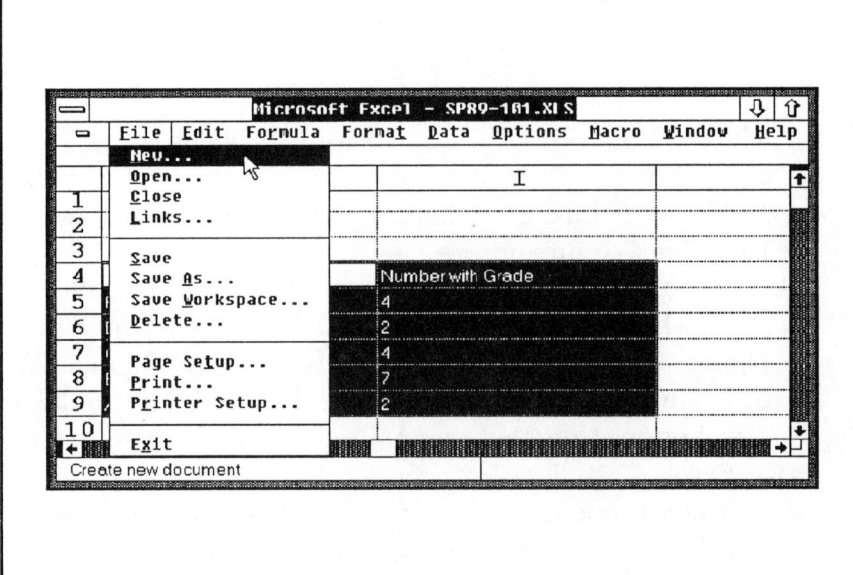

Open new file to create chart

Figure 3-18.

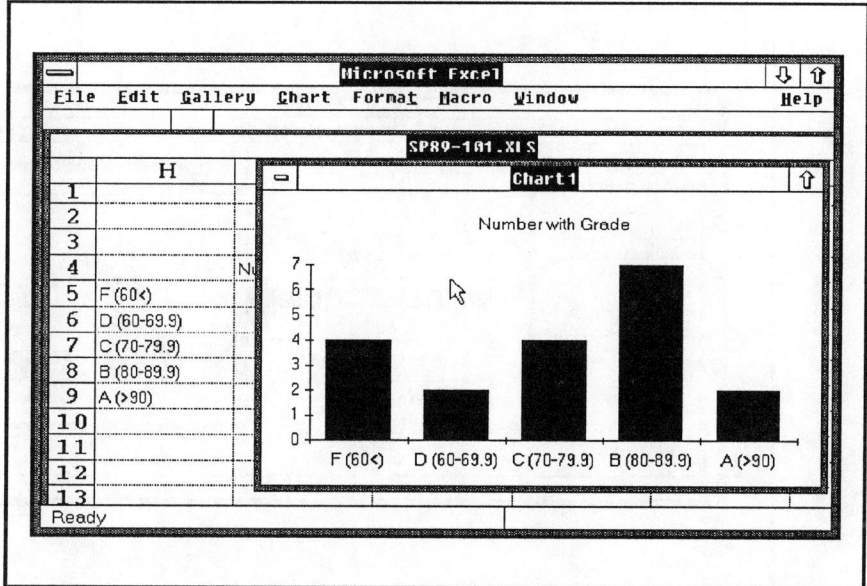

Newly created Excel chart can be copied to the Clipboard

the active window, you can activate the Chart Select Chart command as shown in Figure 3-19. The chart will now be surrounded by sizing handles indicating that it has been chosen as an object, as shown here.

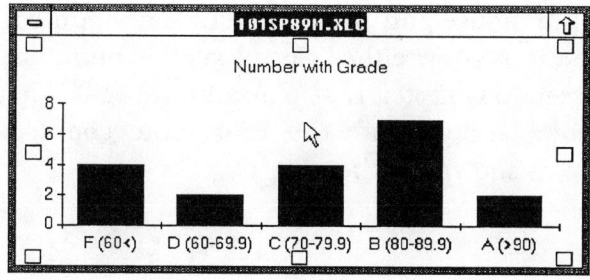

Figure 3-19.

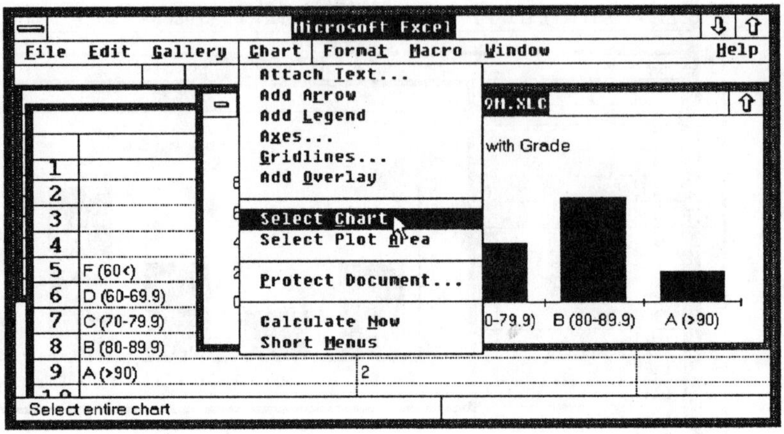

Activating Chart Select Chart command

You can now copy the chart to the Clipboard (you could also change its size by pulling on the handles as explained earlier in this chapter). The chart is copied to the Clipboard by activating the Edit Copy command with the mouse, as shown in Figure 3-20, or you can use the CTRL-INS keystroke combination which bypasses both the mouse and the display of the menu command.

You must now either close Excel or minimize it to an icon (as discussed in Chapter 1, "Up and Running"). Then open Word for Windows and activate the Edit Paste command by using the mouse as shown on the next page,

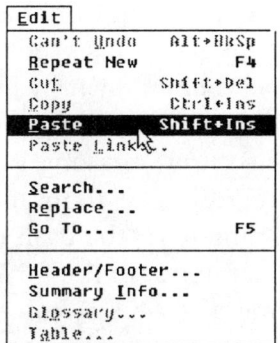

or by using the SHIFT-INS keys. Note that the Paste Link command is ghosted (unavailable). To link the chart to its source in Excel, you would have had to have chosen DDE linkage in Excel before

Figure 3-20.

Edit Copy command copies selected object, an Excel chart, to the Clipboard

you copied the chart to the Clipboard. (This process is discussed in Chapter 11.) The newly inserted chart is displayed in the Word for Windows document shown in Figure 3-21. This chart can be sized with the Format Picture command in the same way as was discussed in the section on sizing images.

The easy integration of fonts, graphics, and tables to create presentation documents is the basis of word publishing. However, there must be consistency in the format of documents that contain all of these elements. One way to create consistency is to use the same formatting, especially character and paragraph formatting, in the text around the tables and graphics that you add to your documents. The next chapter discusses styles and templates, which will help you to efficiently format your documents. Styles are records of character and paragraph formatting. Templates record styles and other elements of document organization that

Figure 3-21.

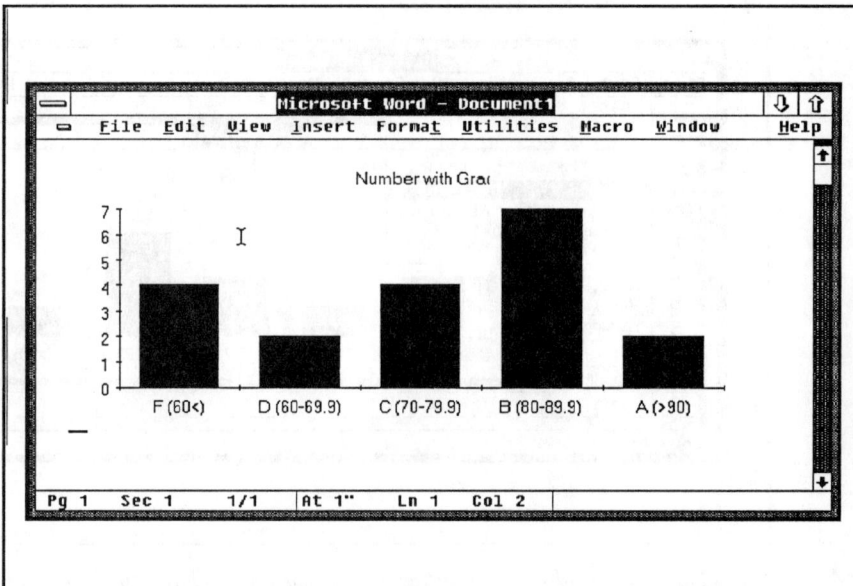

Excel chart inserted into Word for Windows document from the Clipboard

give you a skeleton each time you begin a similar type of document (for example, a letter, brochure, or report). The time you will save by using Word for Windows styles and templates along with the ease and speed of table and graphic image importing that you have learned about in this chapter together will increase the presentation quality of your work.

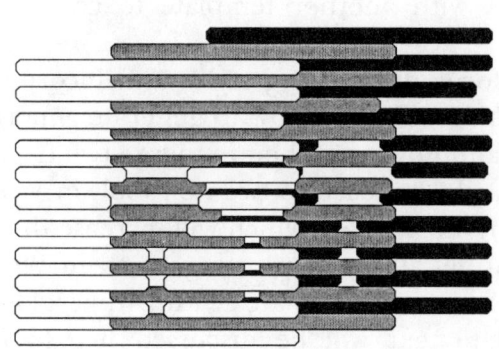

For the Record: Styles and Templates

Word for Windows offers you many ways to maximize your efforts by saving keystrokes. You can work more productively if you do not have to enter the same set of commands or block of text more than once. You can accomplish this goal by using glossaries, macros, and styles as part of a document template. Word 4.0 and 5.0 users will recognize the template as a new form of the stylesheet that includes glossaries and macros. Word for Windows adds another benefit to the document template; it allows you to save text in a template. Text that is part of a template is called *boilerplate text;* with it, you can set up standardized forms such as invoices, memos, reports, and so on. And like the Word 4.0 and 5.0 stylesheets, you can change a Word for Windows template at any time or merge it with another template to create a new template.

This chapter will focus on creating styles and incorporating them into templates. You will learn how to generate generic and specialized templates and how and when to merge two document templates. You will also be exposed to two new tools in Word for Windows, the ruler and the ribbon, which will increase the speed with which you can apply all the formatting saved in Word for Windows templates. Advanced template features like glossaries, macros, and boilerplate text will be discussed in Chapter 6, "Advanced Template Features."

Styles

Styles are the basic element of the document template. Styles contain character, paragraph, tab, and position formatting information. The most efficient way to use styles is to record the formatting information the *first* time you apply it to commonly used document parts such as titles, headlines, body text, and return addresses. Then the next time you need to format those parts of a document, you can quickly apply the style, either before you type the text or to a highlighted block of text you already typed. Applying a style to text saves you the time of displaying and configuring as many as four different menus.

You can apply styles to text either with the keyboard or the mouse. As with all other commands, the Format Style command can be accessed via the keyboard (CTRL-s) or the mouse. As mentioned earlier in this chapter, the ruler and the ribbon are two Word for Windows tools that speed the application of styles. (See the sections "The Ruler" and "The Ribbon" later in this chapter for more information.) These tools are designed to be used primarily with the mouse.

If you are doing work that does not require you to apply styles often, it is easiest to apply them with the Format Styles command. On the other hand, as you will see at the end of the chapter, if you are creating a template or applying styles frequently, you will probably want to use the ruler and the ribbon.

Creating Styles

Before you can apply styles to text with the Format Styles command, you must create some styles that are useful to you. In this section, you will see the Word for Windows default styles and learn how to create new styles.

The Format Define Styles Dialog Box

Invoking the Format Define Styles command causes Word for Windows to display the Format Define Styles dialog box. The Format Define Styles dialog box allows you to quickly set all of a style's formatting including the Character, Paragraph, Tabs, and Position Options.

Remember that when you call up a file in either Word 4.0 or 5.0, the program will beep if the file has not been attached to a stylesheet. Unlike its predecessors, Word for Windows automatically loads a document template, NORMAL.DOT, when you open the program. All templates end with the extension *.DOT. The

NORMAL.DOT default template automatically loads the following default styles: Normal (Body Text), Heading 1, Heading 2, and Heading 3.

You can invoke the default styles and change them with the Format Define Styles command that is accessed from the Format Define Styles dialog box shown in Figure 4-1. You can also invoke default styles from the Format Styles dialog box; however, as you will see, you cannot change the default styles or add new styles to a template without using the Format Define Styles dialog box. The Format Define Styles dialog box is accessed from the keyboard by pressing ALT-t and then **f**, or with a mouse by clicking the left mouse button first on the word "Format" in the menu bar and then on the words "Define Styles" in the Format menu as shown here.

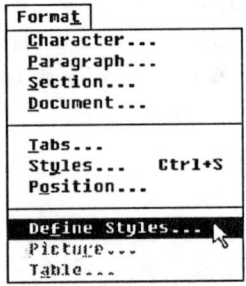

The Format Define Styles dialog box, as shown in Figure 4-1, is displayed when you choose the Format Define Styles command. You can see that no style has been chosen in the Define Style Name option field. You can choose one of the four default style entries in the Define Style Name scroll box or you can create your own style. Because Normal + is listed below the Define Style Name scroll box (the mouse arrow points to Normal + in Figure 4-1), any style you create will be based on the Normal style. A style based on another style begins with all of that base style's attributes and retains those defaults until you change and save

Figure 4-1.

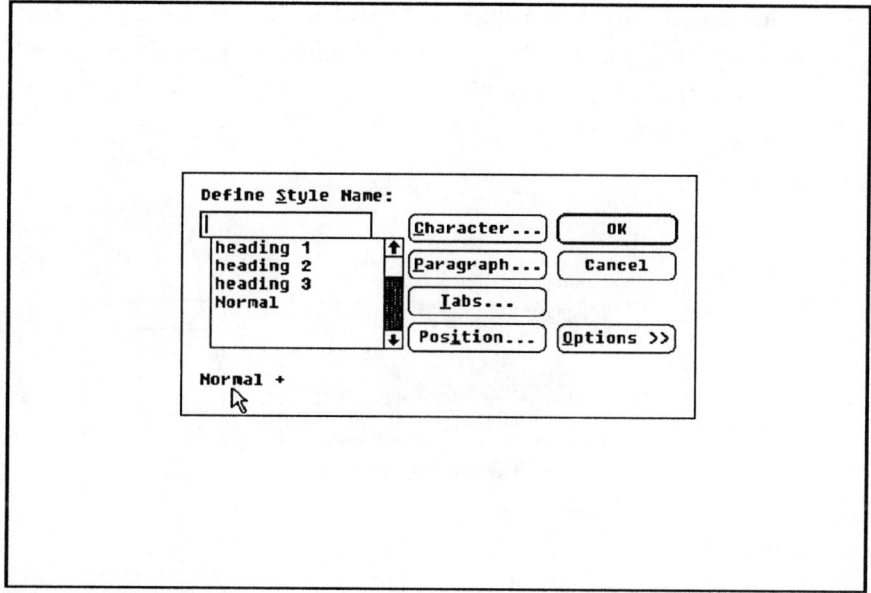

Format Define Styles dialog box

new style attributes. You save style attributes by activating the OK button or pressing ENTER. As you will see later, you can change the base style with the Options button at the lower right of the Format Define Styles dialog box. The four default styles, Normal, Heading 1, Heading 2, and Heading 3 can be altered, but they cannot be renamed or deleted.

The default, or Normal style, is intended to be the body text formatting style for whatever kind of document you are preparing. As you will see, you can use the Define Styles Options button to have the text switch back to the Normal style in the paragraph following any of the Heading styles. Activating this option allows you to select a Heading style for one paragraph, the paragraph containing the heading itself, and then, after you type the heading and press ENTER (ending the paragraph), the style will automatically revert back to that of the Normal style of the body text.

Before discussing these style options, this chapter will briefly survey the options associated with the default styles—Normal, and Headings 1, 2, and 3—as listed in the Define Style Name scroll box in Figure 4-1. The default Normal style for PostScript printers is shown here.

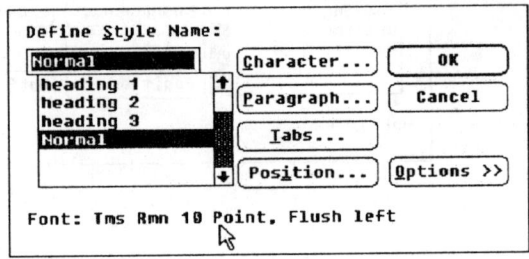

You can choose the default Normal style from the keyboard by pressing the DOWN ARROW or by clicking the left mouse button on the word "Normal" in the scroll box. The listing beneath the scroll box has now changed. Note that Normal +, listed below the scroll box, has been replaced with the text formatting associated with the Normal style. This indicates that you have chosen the Normal or body text style as a base style. (Remember, you create new styles from base styles in the Format Define Styles dialog box used here, and you apply styles from the Format Styles dialog box.)

The Normal style assigns character formatting of 10 point regular (not bold or italic) Times Roman font, and paragraph formatting of flush left and ragged right margins. No tabs have been set (the default is 0.5") and the default position of the text block from the margins (1.25" on the left and the right, 1" from the top and bottom) has not been changed. All of this formatting information is listed below the scroll box.

All of the options chosen for Heading 1, 2, and 3 styles are listed below the Define Styles scroll box, as shown in Figure 4-2. The purpose of the listing is to give you a quick look at the style.

Creating Your Own Styles

If you do not want to use the default styles, you can change them or create your own document template with entirely new styles (see "Creating Document Templates" later in this chapter). Remember, however, that if you create a new template and change the parameters of the default Normal style, you must still use the Normal style for your body text. You cannot delete the Normal

Figure 4-2.

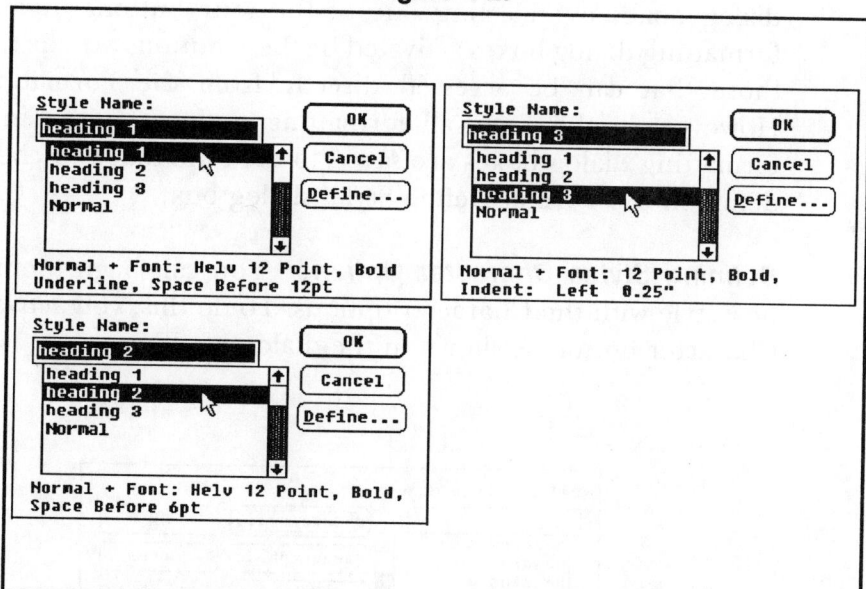

Heading 1, 2, and 3 styles

style, nor can you rename it. You can only change its parameters. As discussed later in this chapter, you can change the Normal style by accessing the Format Define Styles dialog box.

Styles consist of the four formatting categories, Character, Paragraph, Tabs, and Position, listed in the Format Define Styles dialog box. Each of these formatting categories is assigned a button in the Format Define Styles dialog box that further accesses the four dialog boxes corresponding to these four commands in the Format menu.

You may begin to format a new style by typing a name in the Define Style Name field (the cursor is automatically in this field when you open the Format Define Styles dialog box). Otherwise, you can modify one of the default styles after selecting it by clicking the left mouse button on its name in the scroll box or by pressing the DOWN ARROW until the desired style is highlighted. In either case, you would then open one of the four formatting dialog boxes by selecting one of the four buttons. Again, the formatting dialog boxes activated by these buttons are the same as those that can be accessed directly from the Format menu. However, in this case, all formatting options chosen in these formatting dialog boxes are saved to the style that you choose to define in the Format Define Styles dialog box.

Defining Styles Character Options   You can begin defining a new style with the Character options. To do this, you activate the Character button as shown in the dialog box here.

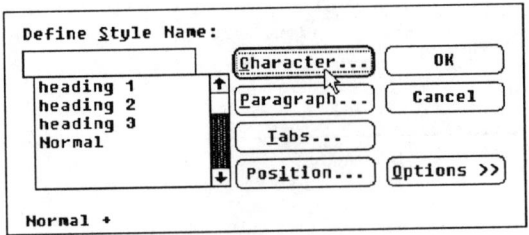

The Format Character dialog box that contains the Define Style Character options is then displayed as shown in Figure 4-3 (the Format Character dialog box is discussed in depth in Chapter 2, "Formatting Text"). You can access the Character button either by pressing the TAB key to move the cursor to the Character button and then pressing ENTER to select it or by clicking the left mouse button on the Character button. The options that you choose in the Format Character dialog box will be assigned to the style that you chose before you activated the Character button. Selecting the OK button when you have completed selecting Character options takes you back to the Format Define Styles dialog box. The character formatting that you have just chosen is now a part of the style that is still listed in the Define Style Name field.

Figure 4-3.

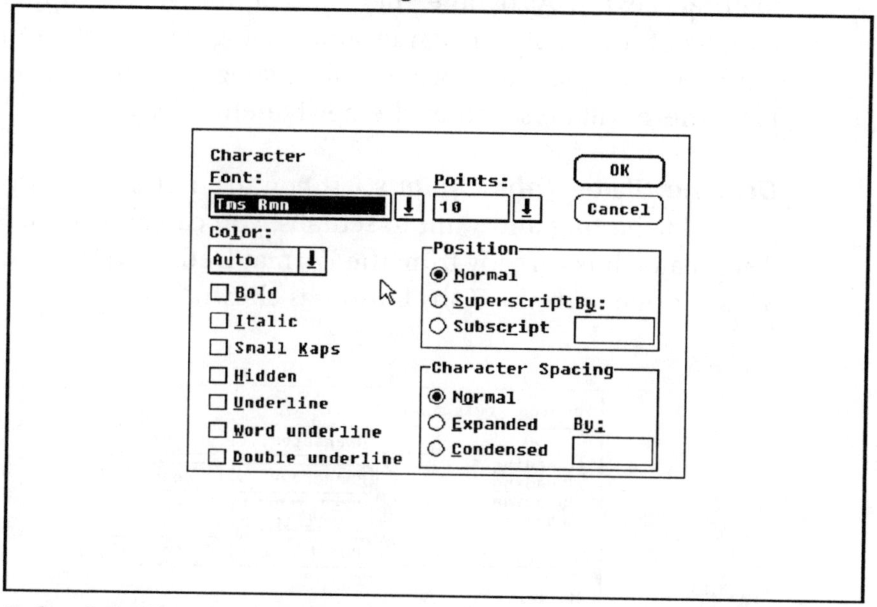

Define Style Character options

Defining Styles Paragraph Options   If you want to change the Paragraph options from those listed for the default style, select the Paragraph button as shown here.

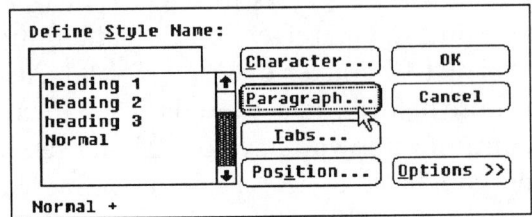

This activates the Format Paragraph dialog box that contains the Defines Style Paragraph options shown in Figure 4-4 (the Format Paragraph dialog box is discussed in depth in Chapter 2, "Formatting Text"). Also note the Tabs button in the upper right corner of the Format Paragraph dialog box. Activating this button will display the Format Tabs dialog box, and any changes made here will be saved to the newly defined style.

Defining Styles Tabs Options   If you are not setting any paragraph formatting and want to set tabs, you can access the Format Tabs dialog box directly from the Format Define Styles dialog box. This is done with the Tabs button as shown here.

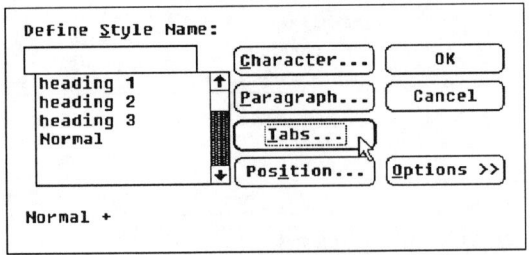

Figure 4-4.

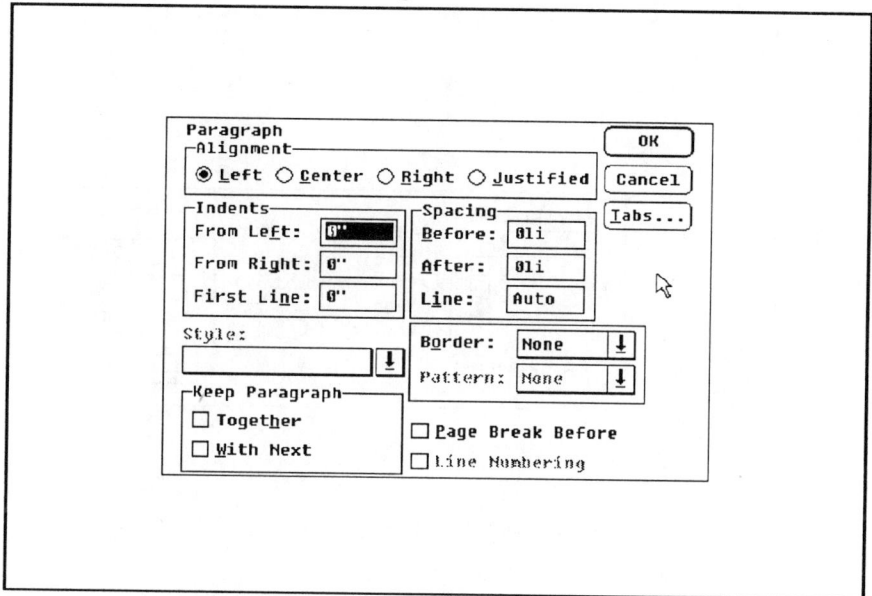

Define Style Paragraph options

You set tabs to be associated with the style in the Format Tabs dialog box that contains the Define Style Tabs options shown in Figure 4-5. The Format Tabs dialog box works the same way whether you access it from the Format Define Styles dialog box or from the Format menu. If you open the Format Tabs dialog box with the Format Tabs command, the tabs settings will be applied to the current paragraph. In this case, since you have opened the Format tabs dialog box via the Format Define Styles dialog box, all the tabs you set will be included in the style that you selected in the Format Define Styles dialog box.

Word for Windows allows you to set as many tabs as you like while the Format Tabs dialog box is displayed. You type tab settings in the Tab Position text entry field. The cursor is in this field when the Format Tabs dialog box is displayed. If you want to make only one entry, you can immediately press ENTER or click the left mouse button on the OK button. As with other format settings,

Figure 4-5.

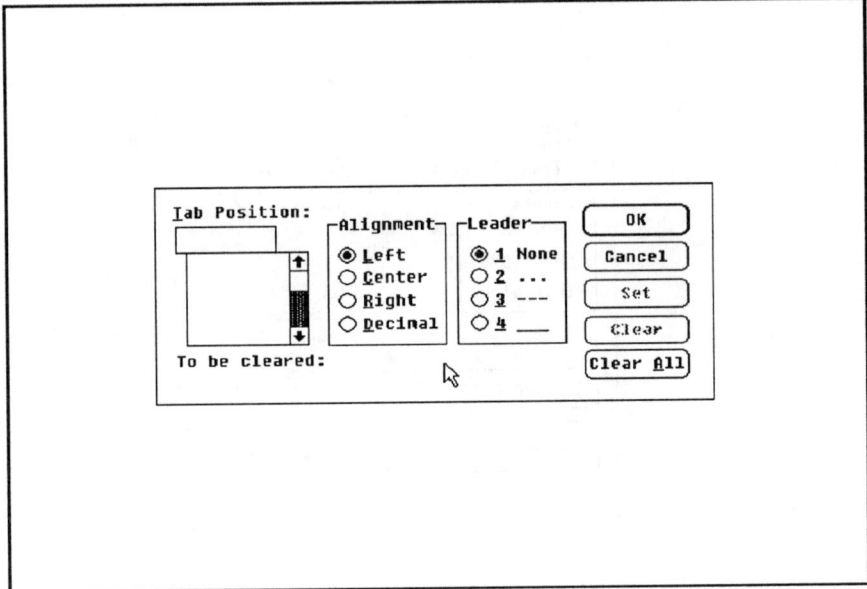

Define Style Tabs options

you need not enter the default unit of measurement, just the number (see Chapter 2, "Formatting Text," for a discussion of margin settings). If you want to set more than one tab with the keyboard, you must enter the position for the first tab in the Tab Position field. Then you must press the TAB key until the cursor is on the Set button. (Note that in Figure 4-5, the Set and Clear buttons are ghosted because no Tab Position field entry has been made. As soon as a number is entered into the Tab Position text entry field, these buttons become available.) Pressing ENTER now will accept the tab setting. At the same time, the cursor will reappear in the Tab Position field where you can type the location of the next tab. If you use the keyboard, you do not have to tab back to the Tab Position text entry field to enter another tab setting; the cursor automatically moves back to this field. To set tabs with the mouse, you click the left mouse button on the Set button after you type each tab entry in the Tab Position field. Remember that you do not have to enter the default unit sign, " (the inches symbol), after each tab entry; only the number is necessary, as shown here.

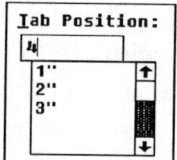

The Alignment option can be applied to one or more tabs that you are assigning to a style. You can choose the Alignment option either before or after you choose the Tab Position option, but it must always be selected before you activate the Set button. The Left, Center, and Right Alignment options will position text relative to the tab in the same way that these options work with the Format Paragraph dialog box (see Chapter 2).

The decimal tab setting places a decimal point at the location you set. After you press TAB, the cursor will be at the proper location where you set your decimal tab, but no decimal point will be present. To use a decimal tab, first type the numbers you want to appear to the left of the decimal point. Then type the decimal point (a period), followed by the numbers you want to appear to the right of the decimal point. The decimal point will move to the location at which you set the tab. In most cases, you will use a decimal tab for columns of numbers, especially to keep dollars that vary in amounts (ones, tens, hundreds, and so on) in a column to the left of the decimal point and cents in a column to the right. But you can also use a decimal tab for text. For example, you can use decimal tabs to vertically align a list of file names and their extensions at the period separating the file name and extension, as shown here.

```
WINDOWS.EXE
CONTROL.EXE
WINWORD.EXE
 NORMAL.DOT
 MYNAME.DOC
```

You can also set a leader to appear in the space that precedes a tabbed entry. As with the Tab Alignment option, the Leader option can be chosen either before or after the Tab Position option, but it must always be selected before you activate the Set button. Leaders set off each tabbed line's entry from the next. The Leader options include blank space, periods (. . .), hyphens (- - -), and an underline (_ _ _). Leaders are useful when you want to set up certain kinds of outlines or set off the second line of continued or repeated text. An example of this is a bibliography format in which the second mention of an author's name or a book (*ibid.*) is indicated with an underline leading to the date.

Defining Styles Position Options   The Format Position dialog box contains options that allow you to accurately position paragraphs on a page relative to several other page elements. The Format Position dialog box is displayed when you activate the Position button in the Format Define Styles dialog box. The Position button in the Format Define Styles dialog box, is shown here.

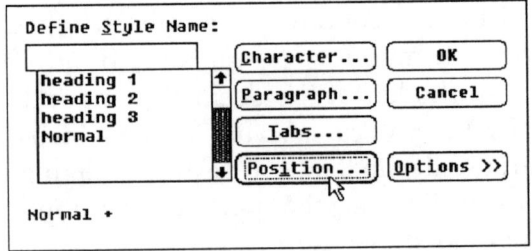

The Define Style Format Position dialog box that contains the Define Styles Position Option shown in Figure 4-6 works in the same way as the Format Position dialog box you access directly from the Format menu. (The Format Position command is discussed in depth in Chapter 5 and Chapter 10.) Remember that all option choices you make in the Format Position dialog box when accessed from the Format Define Styles dialog box will be assigned to the style selected in the Format Define Styles dialog box.

Pictures (images) and tables can also be positioned with the Format Position dialog box. They are positioned with the paragraph that contains them, even if this paragraph is just a carriage return with the chosen Format Paragraph options. Positioning pictures or tables *anchors* them to the text. You might want to anchor the position of a paragraph, table, or picture if it was going to appear in the same place on many pages or on every page. For

Figure 4-6.

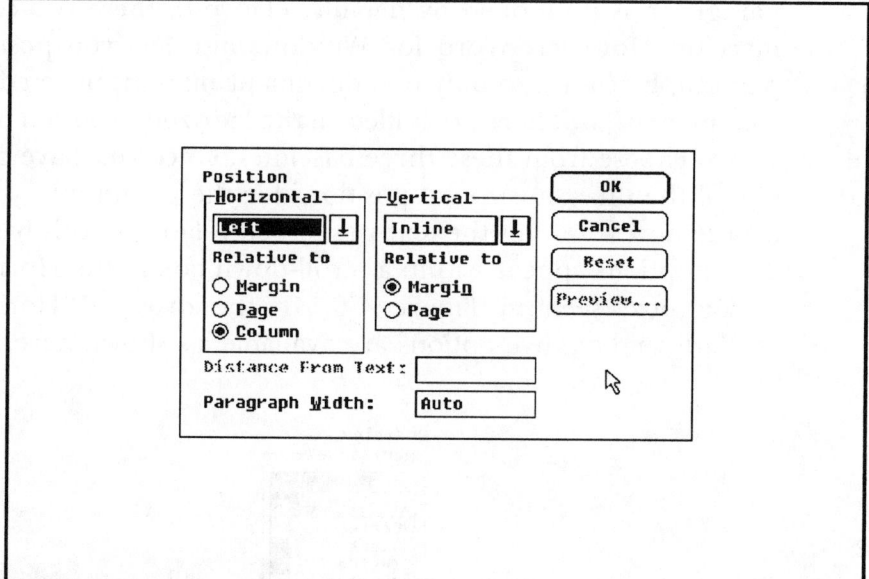

Define Style Position options

example, it might be useful to define in one style, the position of text or a graphic with the title and page number that appeared at the top of every even-numbered page and to define in another style an author's name and page number for the top of every odd-numbered page (see Chapter 10, "Desktop Publishing with Word for Windows").

The Format Position dialog box, as shown in Figure 4-6, has two option sets, Horizontal and Vertical. These option sets allow you to control both the vertical and the horizontal position of paragraphs, images, and tables. This discussion will focus on paragraphs, but these examples apply to images and tables as well.

On a page with one column and left-aligned or justified text, you assume that the horizontal position of a paragraph vis-a-vis the left edge of the paper will be the same as the left margin setting (as chosen in the Format Document dialog box—see Chapter 2). In this case, the paragraph's left margin begins at the document left margin, and the document left margin is the left column margin. The same can be said for the right margin. The paragraph is positioned by default relative to these two-column margins. However, Word for Windows also lets you position a paragraph relative to only one document margin, page edge, or column margin. There are bullets in the Horizontal option box for you to choose from these three baselines. Once you have chosen one of the three horizontal positions for the paragraph, you can choose how you want the text positioned relative to this baseline. These options appear within a scroll-down box in the Horizontal option box, seen in Figure 4-6. In the dropped Horizontal scroll-down box, five options are available, as shown here.

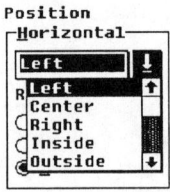

The default paragraph placement is Left. This means that the paragraph will be placed against the left side of the column. The Distance From Text option measures how much white space surrounds the column; in other words, how far away the nearest column of text is from the text in this column. This option is ghosted (unavailable) because the text has been placed flush against the left margin, and there can be no text to the left of it. If you choose any of the options other than the Left option, the Distance From Text field will display a default setting of 0.13". In this example, with the Column button chosen (it is covered by the dropped scroll-down box shown in Figure 4-6), the Center option would center the text in a paragraph within the column boundaries at least 0.13" away from text in another column. The Right option would place the same text against the right column at least 0.13" away from text in another column.

The Inside and Outside options are used to place text on facing pages. The Inside option places text flush against the left margin on odd-numbered pages and flush against the right margin on even-numbered pages. Remember that when you open a book, the left page is even numbered and the right page is odd numbered. The Inside option causes text to be positioned toward the binding of the book. As you may have guessed, the Outside option places text flush against the right margin on odd-numbered pages and flush against the left margin on even-numbered pages; this positions the text away from the binding of the book.

Whether or not you change the default horizontal position of one paragraph, or of a group of paragraphs, you can always set the vertical position of the paragraph on a page. As with the Horizontal options, you first set the vertical baseline to one of the two Vertical options: Relative to Margin (the top and bottom text margins set in the Format Document dialog box) or Relative to Page (the page edge). The text margin is the default vertical baseline. Next, you set the actual vertical position on the page by choosing options in the Vertical scroll-down box, as shown here.

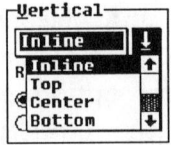

The default Inline setting, shown in the Vertical option box in Figure 4-6, lets the text fall in the natural flow of the document. The Top option would move the formatted paragraph to the top margin of the page on which it would fall if you had used the Inline option. The Center option would place the paragraph midway between the top and bottom margins. This is useful for one or more paragraphs that will be the only text on a page that does not continue from an earlier page or continue onto a later page. The Bottom option places the formatted text against the bottom margin on the page in which it would normally fall.

Note that the Distance From Text option remains ghosted; this is because with both the default Horizontal Left and Vertical Inline settings, nothing exists from which to distance the paragraph. In effect, the default settings are flush with the document margins of the page. However, all of the other settings would activate this option to a default setting of 0.13", which you can change by typing over the default.

The paragraph width can always be changed from the Auto option to any setting you prefer. The Auto setting fills the right and left margins with text; however, you can set the maximum line width to any measurement equal to or less than the width of the column. The Reset button is not available until you enter some settings. It then allows you to erase the settings that you have made and start over.

You cannot use the Preview button to see what the page will look like if you have set the Position options for a style. It will always be ghosted in the Format Position dialog box when it is accessed via the Position button in the Format Define Styles dialog box.

When you access the Format Position dialog box, the Preview button turns on the Print Preview mode (in which you can see the whole page). In the Print Preview mode, you can drag individual paragraphs around the page with the mouse. (Click the left mouse button on the paragraph or object to be moved, and, holding the button down, move the mouse until the object is properly positioned.) Alternatively, you can move a paragraph with the arrow keys. (The object must be selected before you enter Print Preview mode; then press the proper arrow keys to move it up or down or to the right or left.) Moving paragraphs and other objects in the Print Preview mode is discussed in depth in Chapter 5, "Printing: Picture Perfect Output."

Defining Styles Options   Activating the Options button in the Format Define Styles dialog box, as shown here,

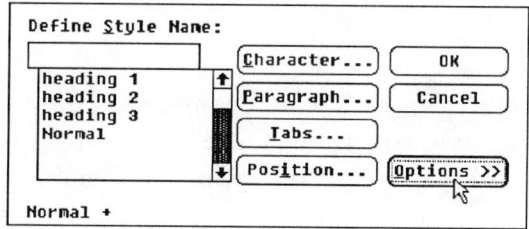

extends the dialog box to display additional Define Styles options, as shown in Figure 4-7. Note that once the Define Styles options are displayed, the Options button is ghosted (it does not toggle).

When you display the Define Styles options, the cursor is on the Based On text entry field as shown in Figure 4-7. The Based On option determines what the default parameters will be when you create new styles. Word for Windows sets up the Normal style, used primarily for body text, as the default. For example, if you want to add new Heading styles based on previously entered

Figure 4-7.

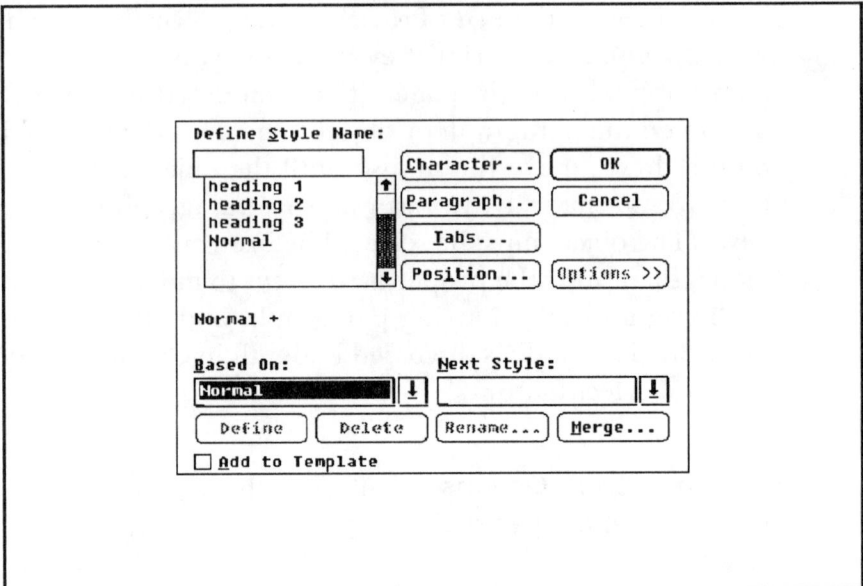

Define Style options

Heading styles, you can change the Based On option to the Heading style you want. Once you do this, the Character, Paragraph, Tabs, and Position options will all reflect the new Based On setting.

You can choose other styles in the Based On text entry field with the keyboard by pressing the DOWN ARROW until the desired style is displayed in the Based On text entry field. You can do the same task with the mouse by dropping the scroll-down box (click the left mouse button on the boxed arrow to the right of the Based On text entry field) as shown here,

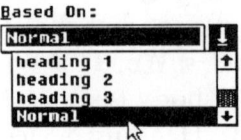

and then click the left mouse button on the desired style.

To the right of the Based On scroll-down box is the Next Style scroll-down box. This Define Styles option allows you to specify what style will follow the one currently being defined. If a style is entered in this field, it is automatically used in the text following a paragraph to which the style being defined is applied. This is useful when you are defining a Heading style, which is usually used on only one line, that is then followed by the body text style (in this case, Normal). You make choices with either the keyboard or the mouse in this scroll-down box in the same way as in the Based On scroll-down box. The available choices are shown here.

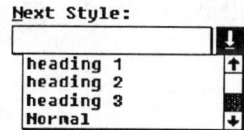

The Define, Delete, and Rename buttons shown here,

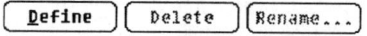

are located below the Next Style scroll-down box. These buttons apply to the style listed in the Define Style Name text entry field at the top of the Format Define Styles dialog box (see Figure 4-7). Since there is no style listed in the Define Style Name text entry field—that is, no style has been selected in that text entry field—these buttons are ghosted. (Remember, you cannot delete or rename any of the default styles.)

When you finish selecting options for a style and you want to define a different style, activate the Define button to clear the Define Style Name text entry field. The style that was being defined is automatically saved (if it is a new style, its name will now appear in the Define Style Name box), and the cursor moves to the Define Style Name text entry field so you can enter a new style name to define. You may select styles you have created from the Define Style Name box and delete or rename them with the Delete or Rename buttons.

Activating the Merge button displays the Define Styles Merge dialog box shown in Figure 4-8. The Define Styles Merge dialog box lists Word for Windows files and templates (files with *.DOT extension) from which you can merge the associated styles into the current document. If a style in the template or document that you are merging into the current template or document has the same name as a style in the current template or document, the current style's options will be copied over (superseded) by the imported

Figure 4-8.

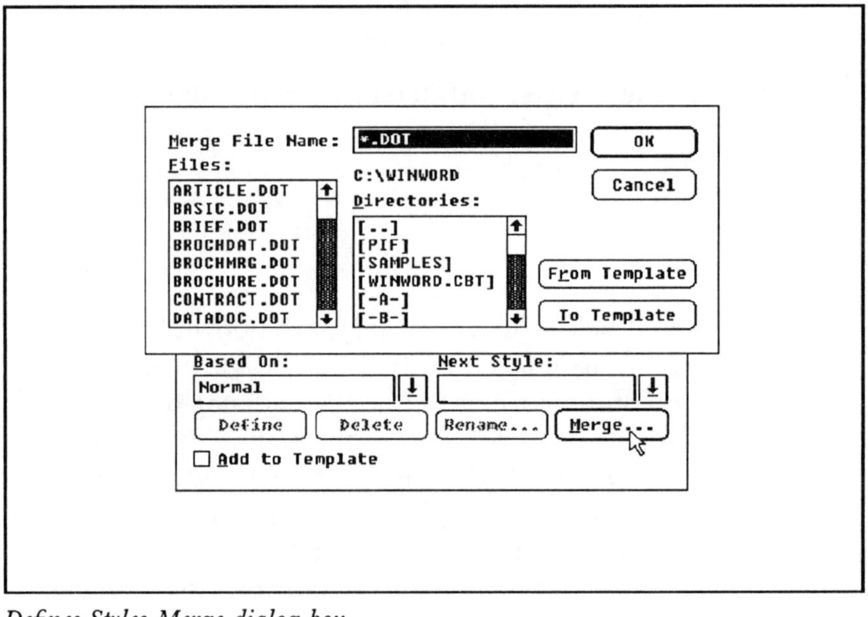

Defines Styles Merge dialog box

styles. If you have not yet activated the Define button to save the style you are creating in the Format Define Style dialog box, Word for Windows will ask if you want to save the style before it imports the new styles.

The styles are merged from the document or template listed in the Merge File Name text entry field when you activate the OK button. The Define Styles Merge dialog box only incorporates another template's styles into the current template, never vice versa. The From Template button merges styles from the current document's template with styles created in the current document (those styles you created with the Format Define Styles dialog box after you loaded the document template). The To Template button merges styles from the active document to its template. When you choose the OK button, Word for Windows reminds you that the like-named styles being merged *into* the active document or template will take precedence.

When you change templates in this fashion, you do not alter all other documents based on the changed template unless you reopen them and merge the changed styles. When you finish working in the Define Styles Merge dialog box, you are returned to the Format Define Styles dialog box. It will be useful for you to merge styles into templates when you are working on series of documents in which the styles evolve from document to document, such as memoranda or reports. In such a case, you will want the newest styles to be available in a single template from which you can begin the next document. Document template design and applications are discussed in Chapter 6.

Below the Merge button, you will notice the last Options option, the Add to Template toggle box, shown at the bottom of Figure 4-8. The default for this option is off (the toggle box is empty). Styles created in the Format Define Styles dialog box are not automatically saved to the current document's template, only to the document itself. Activating the Add to Template toggle box will cause all styles defined to be automatically saved to the document template. You can activate this option (the box will fill with an X) by clicking the left mouse button on the toggle box or by tabbing to the toggle box and entering **A**.

Templates

The bottom line is that templates save you keystrokes. They do so by saving the formatting information in styles, glossaries, macros, and boilerplate text. As you have seen, styles contain the character, paragraph, tab, and position formatting information for headers, body text, and other frequently used formats. As with Word 4.0 and 5.0, glossaries are passages of text saved to one or a few keystrokes. Macros are usually series of commands saved to a single keystroke. Boilerplate text is text that does not vary from document to document; examples such as memos and invoices contain text that sets off the areas for messages or data entry. Incorporating macros, glossaries, and boilerplate text into document templates is discussed in Chapter 6, "Advanced Template Features."

Why Create Document Templates?

A document template is a skeleton from which you can begin a new document. You open the generalized document template before you begin typing text. In this way, you can use all of the template's recorded formatting to speed the process of creating, formatting, and layout of a particular document's text. However, to save time by using a document template, you need to have created one. Word for Windows comes with a few sample document templates, but in most cases you will need to create your own. You create a document template by saving formatting information (especially styles, glossaries, macros, and boilerplate text) the first time you apply it to a document. The actual text of the document is not saved to the template unless you designate it as boilerplate text.

There are many different types of documents that will benefit from your saving formatting information to a document template. The first requirement is that you will be creating similar documents in the future. Memos, letters, reports, invoices, brochures, and forms of all kinds fall in this category. If several people produce these types of documents at one location, such as in a business office, each document template should be standardized so all of the office's communications are consistent. The standardization and consistency that document templates offer allow the recipients of the documents, once they become familiar with the format, to quickly find the key portions of the communication.

You may not be able to use document templates to save time if you create many unique documents. Another possibility is that you work with some documents that have very little formatting. Many authors are required to submit their manuscripts in pure ASCII text with the carriage return (ENTER key) being the only formatting allowed. If this is the case, a special document template (changing the default NORMAL.DOT document template) would be undesirable because you will not add to, change, or use any of its contained styles.

Creating Document Templates

Word for Windows allows you to save your formatting to a template at any time. You can create a document template while you are composing a new document. You can also enter all of the formatting information found in a document template before you enter any of the document's particular text and save the template by itself. And, of course, you can save all of the relevant formatting information to a document template after you have created a document. All of these cases differ minimally. It does not matter when you save the information recorded by a document template because Word for Windows lets you do this at any time.

Word for Windows does not automatically save to a template the styles, glossaries, macros and boilerplate text you create while working on a document. If you want Word for Windows to do this automatically, you must activate the Add to Template toggle box at the lower left corner of the Define Styles Options dialog box (see Figure 4-7). If you activate the Add to Template toggle box, but have not merged in a previously created document template or opened a new document template (discussed below), your formatting will be saved to the default (NORMAL.DOT) document template. If you do not activate the Add to Template option, Word for Windows will save some features, like styles, with the original document, and others, like glossaries and macros, to separate and unrelated files. This means that all this formatting information will be available to you only while you are working in the original document.

As mentioned, you can create a template any time during the preparation of a document. To do this, you activate the File New command. The File New dialog box, shown here,

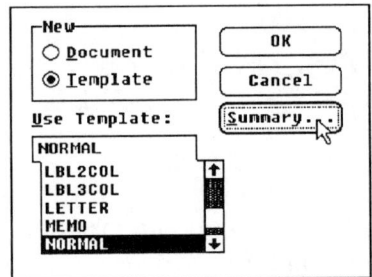

will be displayed. The word "Document" will be bulleted in the New box. You can change the bulleted option from Document to Template with the keyboard by entering **t** (note underlined t in Template) or by clicking the left mouse button on the Template bullet. Note that the current Use Template field entry contains the Normal template. This indicates that the Normal template will be the base template for your new template.

 NOTE   This does not mean your new template will be named "Normal." You name the new template when you open the File Save As dialog box discussed later in this section.

You can change the base template to any of the prepared Word for Windows templates or to one of your own.

The Use Template box, as seen before, contains Word for Windows templates that have formatting for two-column labels, three-column labels, a standard letter, and a memo. Several other templates come with Word for Windows; however, many of them are samples for the tutorial and are likely to be of little use to you as base templates. Most of the prepared Word for Windows templates are quite sophisticated and contain styles, macros, glossaries, and boilerplate text (the latter three topics are covered in depth in Chapter 6.

If you have already begun creating a new document, your base document template will be NORMAL.DOT. You should not create a new template after you have started entering text and formatting; doing so at this point would create a blank new document window without the information you want to save to the template. Instead, you can merge in a new document template with the Define Styles Merge dialog box (see the "Defining Styles Options" section earlier in this chapter); the conglomerate NORMAL.DOT and merged document template will become the base document template.

In either of these cases, you will need to name your new document template. To do this, you use the File Save As command to bring up the File Save As dialog box shown here.

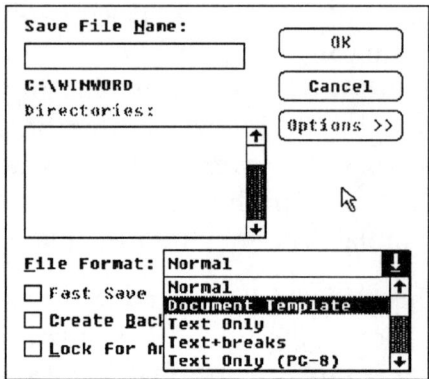

Note that in the File Format scroll-down box, in the lower portion of File Save As dialog box, Document Template is the highlighted option. Also note that the OK button is ghosted; this is because there is no name for the new template in the Save File Name field. The OK button becomes available after you enter the path with the new document template name (for example, C:\WINWORD\ TEMPLATE.DOT). Use the WINWORD directory as your path for document templates; you will find templates more easily if you keep them all in one directory.

Remember, even if you have opened a new document template, you must name it in the File Save As dialog box and activate the Add to Template toggle box at the lower left corner of the Define Styles Options dialog box to have your new document template recorded. Thereafter, using the File Save All command will save the text and formatting you are entering into the current document file and will at the same time save information relevant to the document template to the document template you just named in the File Save As dialog box.

Whether you are naming a new template or saving previously entered information to a template, once you save to a base template or newly named template and activate either the OK button or the Summary button, the Template Summary dialog

Figure 4-9.

```
┌────────────────────────────────────────────────────────────────┐
│  ═    ┌────────────────Microsoft Word - Template1──────────┐ ⇩ ⇧│
│  ☐  File  Edit  View  Insert  Format  Utilities  Macro  Window  Help│
│  ─    File Name: Template1              ┌──────────┐         │
│       Directory:                        │    OK    │         │
│       Title:    ┌──────────────────┐    └──────────┘         │
│       Subject:  └──────────────────┘    ┌──────────┐         │
│                 ┌──────────────────┐    │  Cancel  │         │
│       Author:   │ David Dean       │    └──────────┘         │
│       Keywords: ┌──────────────────┐    │Statistics...│      │
│       Comments: └──────────────────┘ ↑             ↖         │
│                 ┌──────────────────┐ │                       │
│                 │                  │ │                       │
│                 └──────────────────┘ ↓                       │
│ For Help, press F1                                          ↓│
└────────────────────────────────────────────────────────────────┘
```

Template Summary dialog box

box is displayed, as shown in Figure 4-9. The Template Summary dialog box allows you to save information about the template for future reference. (This is the same Summary dialog box you see when you save a document.) The directory where the template is stored is listed, but you cannot change it (type over it) in the Template Summary dialog box; this must be done in the File Save As dialog box. You can, but do not have to, give the template file a title in the Title text entry field. Because the title can be more than eight characters long (up to 255 characters), it is easier to remember the title than the document template filename which cannot exceed the DOS eight-character limit. You can also enter up to 255 characters in the Subject and Keywords fields. The Subject field can contain notes on the applicability of the document template. You can use Keywords to locate the document template file later with the File Find command. Note that these text entry fields are not wide enough to display 255 characters. If you type past the right end of the text entry field, the cursor follows what you are typing. To re-expose the beginning of the line, or any part of the line, use the RIGHT ARROW and LEFT ARROW keys or the HOME and END keys.

The Comments field also accepts up to 255 characters. It acts like a scroll box, letting you quickly scan all other notes or remarks on the document template. The Author field should contain your name automatically. The author's name is set when you install Word for Windows. Your default name can, however, be changed in the Utilities Customize dialog box or by overtyping the Author entry in the Template Summary dialog box.

You can see a synopsis of the Template Summary dialog box as well as other information on the template file by activating the Statistics button on the right side of the Template Summary dialog box shown in Figure 4-9. This displays the Template Statistics dialog box as shown in Figure 4-10.

Once again, you cannot change the Directory entry. In fact, none of the Template Statistics dialog box entries can be changed; they are merely information on when, where, and how the template file was created and printed. There is a "None" listing next to Template because no base template was chosen before going into this dialog box.

The Title Entry is the same as the title that you enter in the Template Summary dialog box. The rest of the information is quite explicit. The Created field for the date and time tell you when you opened the File New menu. The Last Saved field displays when you last saved the template file (that is, if you had already saved the template before you opened the Template Statistics dialog box). The Last Saved By field shows whose name was in the Utilities Customize dialog box the last time the file was opened. This would be different than the author name in the Template Summary dialog box if the last time the file was opened, the name in the Author field was different than the first time the file was saved. It would also be different if someone else worked

Figure 4-10.

```
File Name: Template1                              ┌────────┐
Directory:                                        │  OK    │
Template:   None                                  └────────┘
Title:                                            ┌────────┐
Created:           5/15/89 9:36 PM                │ Update │
Last saved:                                       └────────┘
Last saved by:
Revision number:    1
Total editing time: 0 Minutes                              ▷
Last printed:
As of last update:
# of pages:         1
# of words:         0
# of characters: 0
```

Template Statistics dialog box

on the file in his or her copy of Word for Windows and then gave the file back to you. The Revision Number field shows you how many times the template file has been changed and saved. The Total Editing Time field shows you how much time has been spent working on the template. The Last Printed field shows you when the template file was most recently printed. The three As of Last Update fields list the number of pages, words, and characters as of the last time the template file was saved.

Once you have created and saved a new template, it will appear in the Template field shown here,

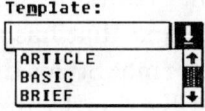

which is located at the bottom right of the Format Document dialog box.

The scroll-down box is dropped down by clicking the left mouse button on the boxed arrow to the right of the Template text entry field. You can also go through the list of available templates with the DOWN ARROW key, without dropping the scroll-down box.

Using Templates

Once you have created and saved a template, the next step is to use it. Word for Windows lets you apply the components of a template, such as styles, macros, and glossaries, from the Format menu. You can use these features much as you do with Word 4.0 and 5.0. However, Word for Windows also supplies you with two other onscreen tools, the ruler and ribbon, that you can use to quickly apply the styles incorporated in a document template.

Format Styles

The Format Styles command applies styles to text you are about to type or have already added to a document. You apply a style to the cursor if you want the style assigned to text you are about to type. If you apply a style to the cursor, all text typed thereafter will utilize the applied style until you move the cursor to a block of text in the document that contains different formatting. You can also highlight a block of text that has already been typed and apply a style to it with the Format Styles dialog box. As mentioned earlier, styles are recorded by the document template. By using procedures covered in the previous section, you can load or create a document template. The document template supplies you with a list of styles.

Applying styles is straightforward. You simply highlight the text you want formatted and choose the style name in the Format Styles dialog box or from the ruler. (The ruler is discussed later in this chapter.)

To display the Format Styles dialog box, you must activate the Format Styles command as shown here.

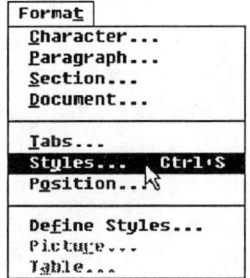

To apply a style with the keyboard, press the UP ARROW or DOWN ARROW keys until the style you want appears in the Style Name field. Then tab to the OK button and the style will be applied. To use the mouse, click the left mouse button on the desired style name; then click the left mouse button on the OK button.

The CTRL-s keystroke combination appears to the right of the Format Styles command (in the Format menu). Pressing CTRL-s is a fast way to assign styles to highlighted blocks of text. When you press CTRL-s, Word for Windows displays the query "Which Style?" in the status bar at the bottom of the Word for Windows screen. The Which Style? query is followed by a blinking cursor where you must type the style name that you want to apply. If you cannot remember the name of the style you want, press CTRL-s again and Word for Windows will display the entire Format Styles dialog box as shown here.

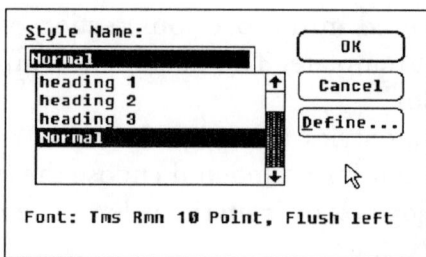

You are not limited to the styles in the Format Styles dialog box. If you activate the Define button, the Format Define Styles dialog box is displayed and you can construct and add a new style to the list. Similarly, if you have added formatting to a paragraph with the Format Character, Format Paragraph, Format Tabs, or Format Position dialog box, you can always save this formatting to a new style name with the Format Styles dialog box. In all cases, whatever the source of your formatting, you would activate the Format Define Styles dialog box, type the name of the new style, and either click the left mouse button on the OK button or press ENTER.

Using the Style Name Area

The Style Name Area is a portion of the Word for Windows Document Window in which you can view styles that have been assigned to text. By default the Style Name Area is inactive. When it is active, the Style Name Area is a bar at the left of the Document Window that lists the styles assigned to each passage of text. The Style Name Area is only useful if you are adding, or have already added, styles to a document. As an example application of the Style Name Area, open the REPORT.DOC sample file that comes with Word for Windows. Then, activate the View Preferences command. This brings up the View Preferences dialog box, shown here.

```
┌──────────────────────────────────────────────────────────────┐
│ Preferences                                       ┌─────────┐  │
│ ☐ Tabs          ☒ Display as Printed              │   OK    │  │
│ ☐ Spaces        ☒ Pictures                        └─────────┘  │
│ ☐ Paragraph Marks ☐ Text Boundaries               ┌─────────┐  │
│ ☐ Optional Hyphens ☐ Horizontal Scroll Bar        │ Cancel  │  │
│ ☐ Hidden Text   ☒ Vertical Scroll Bar             └─────────┘  │
│                 ☒ Table Gridlines                              │
│ ☐ Show All *    Style Area Width: [0.5"]                       │
└──────────────────────────────────────────────────────────────┘
```

As shown here, change the default 0" Style Area Width text entry field value to 0.5". Then either press ENTER or activate the OK button. Figure 4-11 shows the styles assigned to REPORT.DOC listed in a 0.5" Style Name Area to the left of the document.

The Ruler

The ruler allows you to quickly set most paragraph and many document formats. You can also use the ruler to add styles to a document. The ruler is displayed by activating the View Ruler command shown here.

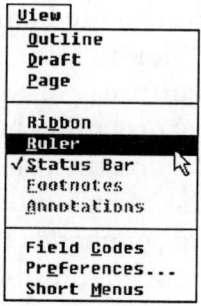

```
┌─────────────────┐
│ View            │
├─────────────────┤
│ Outline         │
│ Draft           │
│ Page            │
│                 │
│ Ribbon          │
│ ███Ruler███     │
│ √Status Bar     │
│ Footnotes       │
│ Annotations     │
│                 │
│ Field Codes     │
│ Preferences...  │
│ Short Menus     │
└─────────────────┘
```

Figure 4-11.

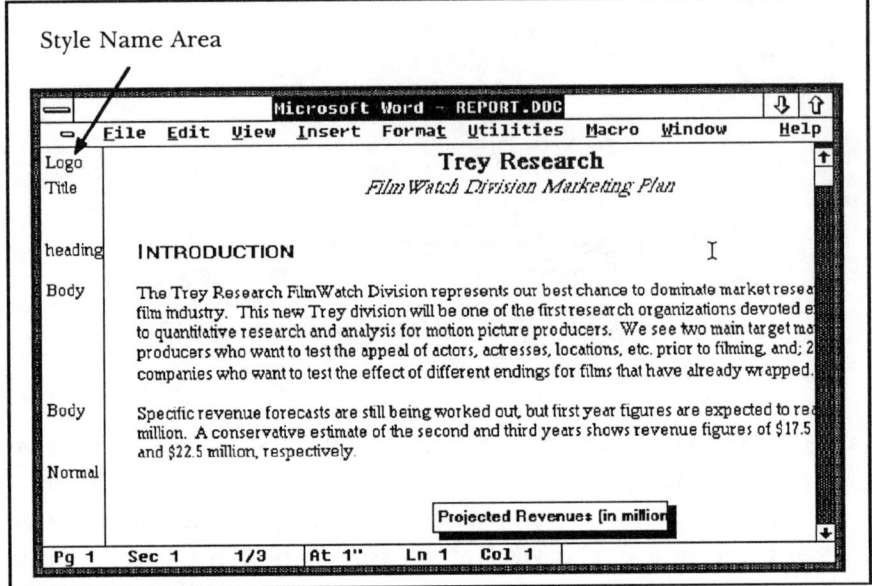

The Style Name Area

Note that when you choose the View Ruler command, the status bar mentions that this command toggles the ruler on and off. Once the ruler is displayed, you turn it off by activating the View Ruler command again. The key combination that displays the ruler is CTRL-SHIFT-F10.

As shown in Figure 4-12, the ruler has both a measurement bar set in inches—this is what gives the ruler its name—and a Style scroll-down box you can use in the same way as the Format Styles dialog box. In addition to setting styles, you can use the ruler to set four other major areas of formatting: paragraphs, columns, margins, and tabs. Formatting buttons appear to the right of the Style scroll-down box on the ruler. They are listed and defined in Table 4-1. All of the ruler buttons in Table 4-1, except the View icon, are formatting commands that were discussed in Chapter 2.

The ruler's Style scroll-down box can be dropped in the usual manner, as shown on the next page.

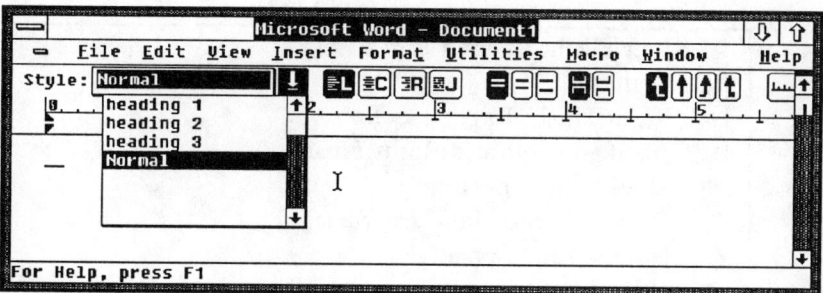

It displays all the available styles, which you can also select in the usual manner. Note that the buttons that show as reverse video (highlighted black) are included in the currently selected Normal style. Therefore, the Normal style includes flush left, single spaced, and default 0.5" right tabs.

Figure 4-12.

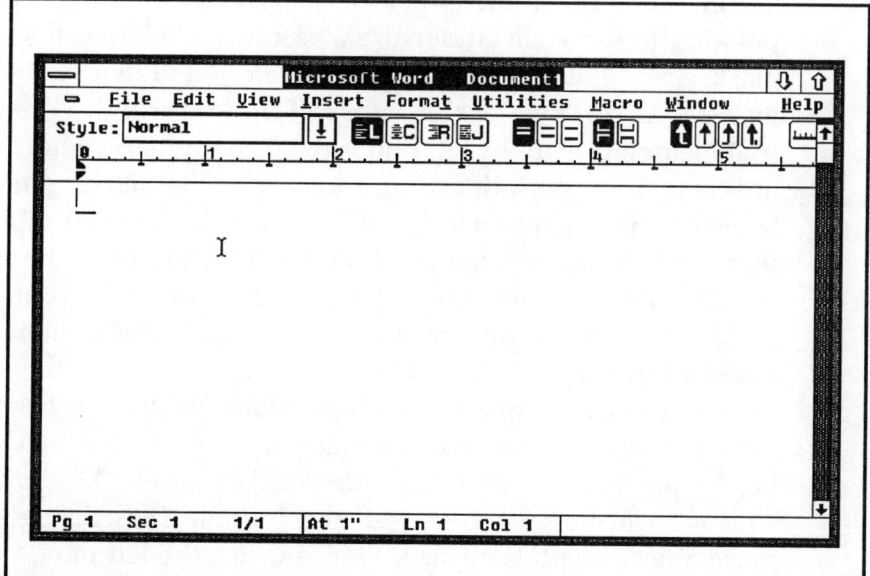

The Ruler

Table 4-1.

▣L	Left Flush, Ragged Right
▣C	Centered
▣R	Right Flush, Ragged Left
▣J	Justified (Left and Right Flush)
▤	Single-Line Spacing
▤	One-and-One-Half-Line Spacing
▤	Double-Line Spacing
▤	No Lines Before Paragraph
▤	One Line (Blank) Before Paragraph
▯	Tab with Text to Left
▯	Tab with Text Centered
▯	Tab with Text to Right
▯	Decimal Tab
▭	View Mode Icon

Ruler Buttons

On the measurement bar of the ruler, the upper triangle pointing to the right under the 0" setting is the first line indent marker, and the lower triangle is the left indent (left text margin) marker. As you type to the right (off the screen), you see a solid triangle pointing to the left under the 6" hash mark. That triangle indicates the right indent (right margin). The tabs are indicated by inverted "T"s under every 0.5" hash mark. A right tab means that after tabbing to a tab mark, all text typed flows to the right of the tab. The tab and line indent markers can all be moved by clicking the left mouse button on them and dragging them to the desired position.

A hard (not one of the default 0.5" tabs) left tab has been set in the ruler at 0.5" from the left margin. (Any tab that you set is a hard tab, whereas, by default, the TAB key enters 0.5" soft tabs.) This tab can be set either with the Format Tabs dialog box or more quickly, with the ruler. You can click the left mouse button once on the Left Tab button, highlighted at the right of the ruler shown on the next page,

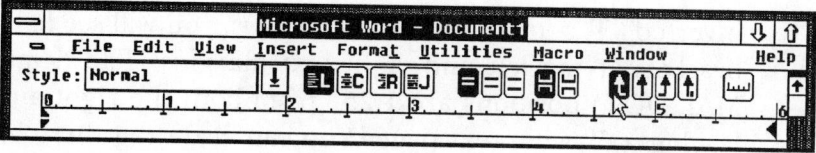

(see Table 4-1 for listing of Left Tab icon), and the mouse arrow picks up the tab. Then click the left mouse button at the 0.5" marker and a left tab will be inserted. If you want to move this tab (and all of the text positioned with the tab) later, you simply click the left mouse button on the Left Tab marker as shown here.

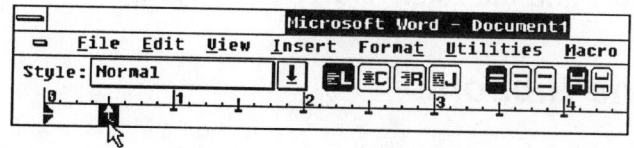

You can then drag the tab in either direction; it has been dragged to the right 0.5" to the 1" marker in the ruler shown here.

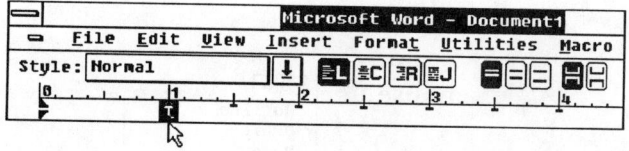

All the way to the right of the ruler is the View Mode icon. The current ruler view—the Paragraph view—is the one you will use most often. If you click the left mouse button on the View icon, the ruler changes to Margin view. In Margin view, instead of seeing inverted "T"s (tabs) and indent arrows, you will see left and right brackets at the left and right text margins. The default (NOR-MAL.DOT) positions are 1.25" from both the right and the left, leaving a 6" wide text page. You can also drag these brackets to new locations.

If the cursor is on a table, clicking the left mouse button on the View icon will put the ruler into Column view. In Column view, there will be solid left and right arrow indents and normal (not inverted) "T"s representing column boundaries under the ruler at the beginning of each column. These indents and column boundaries can also be dragged with the mouse. If you click the left mouse button on the View icon again, the ruler changes from Column view to Margin view; click the left mouse button once more and the ruler returns to Paragraph view.

The Ribbon

Just as the ruler is the fastest way to format paragraph options, the ribbon is the quickest way to format character options. Also, as with the ruler's Format Paragraph options, the ribbon's Format Character options can be saved to a new style in the Format Define Styles dialog box.

The ribbon is activated in the same way as the ruler. You use the View Ribbon command shown here.

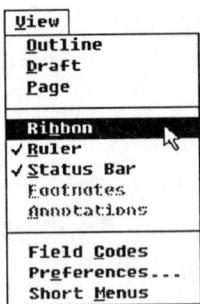

Both the Ribbon and Ruler commands in the View menu act as toggles. The ribbon can also be activated from the keyboard by pressing ALT-v and then **b**.

If you activate the ribbon after the ruler has been selected, both are displayed on the screen at once, as shown here.

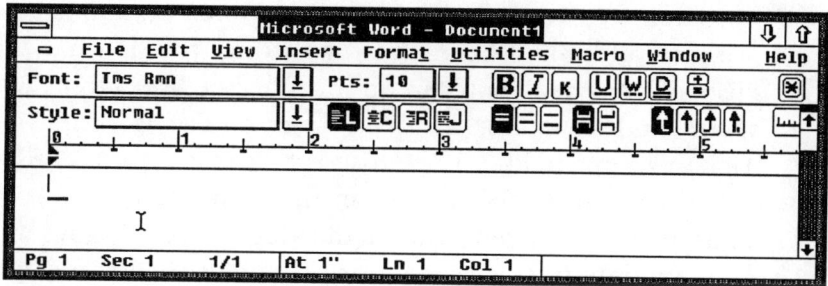

The ribbon contains both a Font and a Pts (point size) scroll-down box and several character formatting buttons identified in Table 4-2. All of these character formatting features are discussed in Chapter 2.

Table 4-2.

B	Bold
I	Italic
K	Small Kaps
U	Underlining of Whole Line
W	Word Underlining
D	Double Underlining
⊕	Superscript/Subscript
⊠	Show Special Marks

Ribbon Buttons

The last formatting button is the Special Marks button. When it is activated (highlighted), it causes the following symbols to be displayed on screen: the paragraph sign at the end of paragraphs, a dot for each blank character space, a square for the line break at the end of a text line. You can also use the Show All toggle box in the View Preferences dialog box to show these symbols. This is very much like the Options Visible command in Word 4.0 and 5.0.

Since the Normal style includes Times Roman 10 point text with no additional character formatting, that is what the ribbon displays. As usual, you can go through the list of fonts with the UP ARROW and DOWN ARROW; when your choice is displayed in the ribbon's Font field, you choose it by pressing ENTER. As with any other scroll-down box, you can move the cursor up to the Font text-entry field from text in the document window with a key combination, in this case by pressing CTRL-f. As you can with any other scroll-down box, you can drop this scroll-down box by clicking the left mouse button on the boxed down arrow at the right, as shown here.

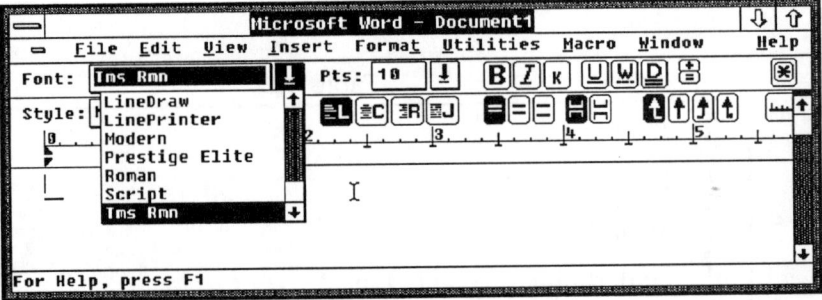

The scroll-down box now shows all the fonts currently installed for Word for Windows. Clicking the left mouse button on any of the font names in the dropped scroll-down box automatically selects that font. This is faster than pressing the OK button when you select fonts in the Format Character dialog box.

The point size listings for each font appear to the right of the Font text entry field. You can move the cursor to the Pts text entry field on the ribbon from text in the document window with the CTRL-p keystroke combination. You can go through the available point sizes with the keyboard in the same manner as with the Font options just discussed or you can use the mouse in the same manner as with the Font options. As shown here,

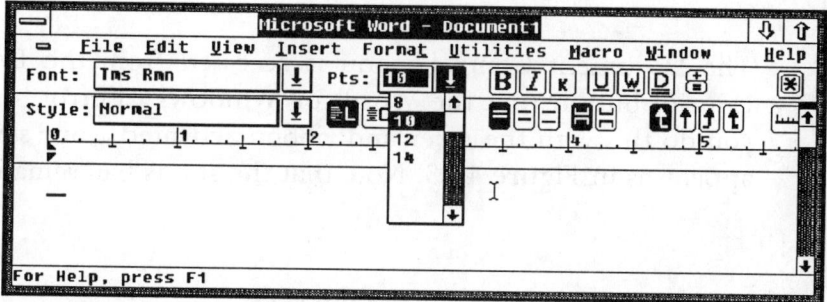

the Pts text entry field shows that the currently available point sizes for Times Roman are 8, 10, 12, and 14.

The Ruler and Ribbon with Multiple Document Windows

The ruler and ribbon can be used when several document windows are open. When there are multiple document windows open, each can have its own ruler, but they all share one ribbon.

When you open Word for Windows, the document window is usually maximized so you cannot see its borders, just the scroll bar at the right. You can display the document window borders in the

Document1 window. This is done by activating the Restore Command in the Document Control menu, as shown here.

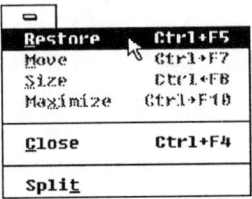

The Document Control menu is accessed from the Document Control button (not the Word for Windows Control button). If you do this with the ruler and ribbon activated, your screen will appear as in Figure 4-13. Note that the status bar remains at the

Figure 4-13.

![Document1 Window with borders]

Document1 Window with borders

bottom, the Document1 title is now in the document window itself, and all four document window borders are visible inside the Word for Windows program borders. Remember that you can size the document window by clicking the left mouse button on any of its borders and then holding the mouse button down and dragging the border to a new location. Also notice that the ruler has moved inside the Document1 window while the ribbon remained below the menu bar.

You can open a second document window with the File New command. The two document windows can be sized until they are edge to edge as shown in Figure 4-14 (or you can activate the Window Arrange Command). The ribbon and the menu bar are only active in the window in which the cursor is found. Since each document window has its own ruler, each document window's ruler is active only when the cursor is in that document window.

Figure 4-14.

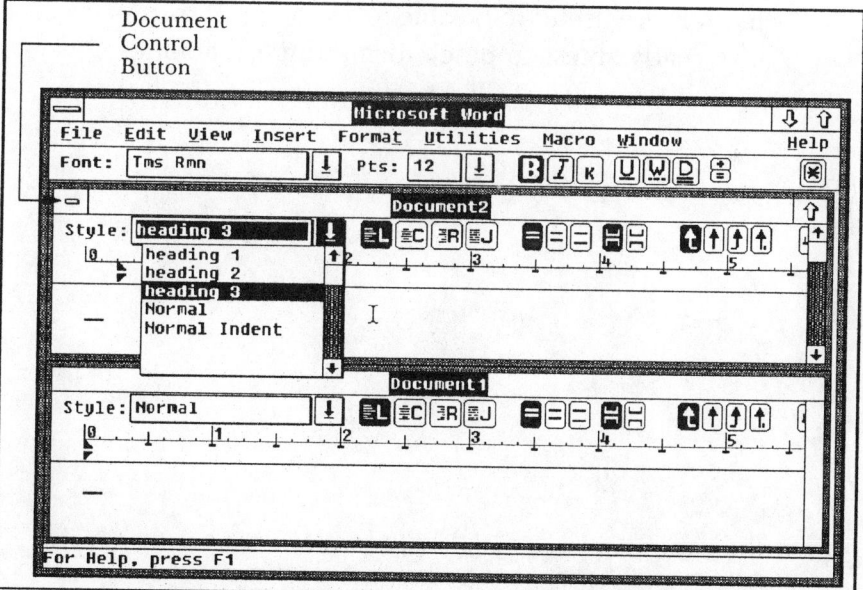

Document Control Button appears in active document window; both windows have a Ruler but share same Ribbon

Now if you begin work in the Document2 window, and you change the style from Normal to Heading 3, the ribbon would reflect these changes. This is shown in Figure 4-13. The Normal style is 10 point, Times Roman regular font, whereas the ribbon reflects the Heading 3 style: 12 point, Bold, Times Roman font being selected in the Document2 window.

The ruler and the ribbon allow you to quickly format text, especially when you apply styles. The only disadvantage to using them together is that they take up a great deal of document window space. These are tools you will use when you are creating styles, templates, or new kinds of documents. You will also want to use the ruler and the ribbon when you are creating documents that have complicated layouts; document layout is discussed in depth in Chapter 10, "Desktop Publishing with Word for Windows." Working with the ribbon and the ruler will help you learn many of the features of Word for Windows. If you are using a highly structured template, such as a business form letter or a legal brief in which all the formatting is preset, you will probably find it more useful to be able to see more of the document than to have ready access to quick formatting capabilities.

CHAPTER

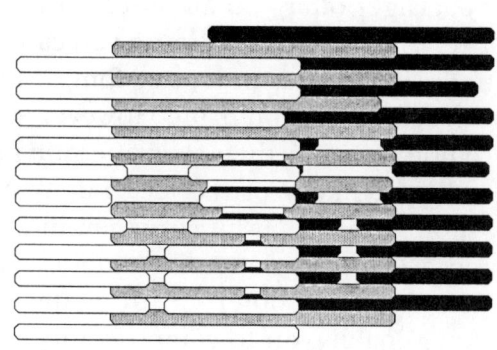

5

Printing:
Picture Perfect
Output

All word processing, word publishing, and desktop publishing applications are designed to help you get to the final step—printing. Printing itself is not the goal, instead, printing the *final* copy should be the last step in the production of a document.

Onscreen editing lets you avoid printing drafts of a document merely to proof typos. This is the original advantage word processing had over the typewriter. However, with most word processing software you need to print many proofs of your documents in order to mix different point size fonts. You have to print out word-processed documents with multiple point size fonts because you cannot see the different size fonts on the screen with those applications.

Desktop publishing packages offer you an onscreen representation of the printed page; this saves time because you can see the position of text formatted with various point size fonts, as well as graphic images, on the screen before you print. However, desktop publishing packages are notorious for their slow operating speed.

Word publishing packages, like WordPerfect 5.0, Word 5.0, and Word for Windows, offer you at least two screen modes—an editing screen mode and a Print Preview screen mode. In addition, Word for Windows offers three other screen modes. Its five screen modes, called *views,* enable you to compose and proof all aspects of your documents with no loss in operating speed. You can also be quite creative in producing documents (see Chapter 10, "Desktop Publishing with Word for Windows").

Word publishing packages, however, are more limited in their layout capabilities than desktop publishing programs. Desktop publishing packages allow word-processed or data base files to be imported and placed in frames that open on one page and continue on any page thereafter. Word publishing packages can import files from other sources, but the files must run from start to finish where they are inserted in the document. Word publishing packages also do not offer text kerning. However, the price you pay for these layout features in desktop publishing packages is editing power and program operation speed.

The five Word for Windows views are designed to help you complete all of your daily information processing work as quickly as possible. Word for Windows opens with the document window in the Normal Editing View. For most of your daily work, you will type text, create tables, and place graphics in the document window in its Normal Editing View. When you are ready to proof the appearance of an entire page in a Word for Windows document, the Print Preview screen helps you get to the point of actually printing out your final copy.

The first section of this chapter, "Word for Windows Views," covers tools like the Normal Editing View and Print Preview. In the next main section, "Printer Installation and Setup," you will learn how to install and set up a printer; printer setup is a Windows function, but it can be done from within Word for Windows. In the final main section, "Word for Windows Print Commands," you will learn how to use the Print commands found in the Word for Windows File menu. This last section includes information on the installation of soft fonts (fonts you purchase on a disk) into a printer driver (other font related issues are discussed in Appendix E). The last section of this chapter also introduces the Print Merge function. The last topic discussed is the File Print command itself. All of the features discussed in this chapter are tools that will speed you to the final stage in the production of any document—activating the File Print command.

Word for Windows Views

The five screens that Word for Windows offers are: Normal Editing View, Print Preview, Page View, Draft View, and Outline View. The first four are discussed in this chapter. Outline View is discussed in Chapter 7, "Time Saving Organization: Outlines and Tables of Contents."

The four views discussed here are tools that help you get to the final stage of working with a document—printing. Word for Windows Normal Editing View and Page View let you see a close up of your document, including its fonts, graphics, and tables. Print Preview lets you zoom out to see and adjust the layout of whole pages. Draft View is useful for inputting text in a hurry; it turns off the font display on the screen and inserts empty boxes where graphics have been inserted. You can switch between the five screen views at any time.

Normal Editing View

All of the figures shown in this book so far are from the Normal Editing View of the Word for Windows document window. You have already seen an important feature of the Normal Editing View, that it displays multiple screen fonts and graphic images. Not all word publishing programs can display fonts and graphics in their text screen modes. Word for Windows Normal Editing View comes very close to what the printed page will look like in most of your work. However, if you add complex formatting in Word for Windows, you will need to use the other views to proof your pages before you print.

Because Word for Windows runs under the Windows graphical user interface, it can display a rendition of the printed page in the default document window's Normal Editing View, Page View, as well as in Print Preview. Moreover, it is the Windows graphical user interface that gives all of these views their WYSIWYG (What You See Is What You Get) appearance. That is, Windows graphical user interface supplies all Windows programs with the ability to display more than one screen font. (Screen fonts are screen representations of the printer fonts that will be used to print your final copy.) These screen fonts can be virtually any point size.

DOS, on the other hand, is primarily a text-based user interface. The DOS-based document screens in Word 4.0 and 5.0 use the 256 ASCII (American Standard Code for Information Interchange) characters in the IBM PC character set (character sets are discussed in Appendix E, "Font Character Sets and Sources"). DOS applications like Word 4.0 and 5.0 are limited to displaying a single character set (font) on the screen at only one size. This means that no matter how many printer fonts you have (including different point sizes in bold, italics, and bold italics), you cannot see how they affect the appearance of your document, except in your mind's eye, until you print the document.

Windows does not use the IBM PC character set and is not limited to a single screen font. The Windows graphical user interface supplies all Windows applications with multiple screen fonts and the ability to display graphic images. With multiple screen fonts, you can easily see the interaction between, for example, 10-point Times Roman text and a 24-point Helvetica heading while you are working in the Word for Windows document window.

Windows applications use a special set of 256 characters called the Windows/ANSI (American National Standards Institute) character set. The Windows/ANSI character set is shown in Appendix E. You can install screen fonts in Windows for as many printer fonts as you wish (see Chapter 11, "Fine Tuning Windows"). Once you have installed a screen font in Windows, all other Windows applications, not just Word for Windows, can display this screen font.

Seeing screen fonts and graphics in the default Normal Editing View of the document window speeds up the production process of the document. You can immediately see how different fonts mix as headings, texts, and subtexts (such as inline quotes and footnotes). You can also see how a graphic image or table interplays with the fonts you have chosen. One drawback to the Normal Editing View is that you can see only about one-half of a printed page on the screen at a time. You can, however, see the whole page, or even two whole pages, in Word for Windows Print Preview.

Print Preview

Print Preview, commonly found in word publishing programs, has greatly added to the capabilities of these packages. The following comparison of word processing, desktop publishing, and word publishing features highlights this point.

Print Preview Advantage   Word processing packages usually have very fast text editing tools. Most word processors let you input text, cut and paste blocks of text, search and replace character strings, and spell-check text at breakneck speed. It is difficult, however, to add multiple fonts and graphics to word processing packages. When multiple fonts are used, the document often prints with the large fonts overwriting either each other or the smaller fonts. Moreover, without precise positioning tools, graphic images often overwrite the text. The major limitation of adding fonts and graphics in word processing packages is that you cannot see what the page will look like before you print. Usually you see codes representing the font and graphic image formatting on the screen, but these codes are not printed. Eventually, after going through draft after draft, you may be able to get everything to look just right.

At the other extreme, with desktop publishing packages, you can set up complex page layouts involving multiple fonts, tables, and graphics. You can also link multiple document files to create camera-ready book or journal copy. Desktop publishing programs, however, offer only rudimentary text editing tools, and most do not have a search-and-replace function or a spelling checker. Therefore, realistically, text for desktop publishing packages must first be prepared in a word processing or word publishing application. Finally, in most cases, the advanced page layout features of desktop publishing programs ensure that they will operate very slowly.

Word publishing programs let you quickly type, edit, cut and paste, search and replace, and spell-check text. In addition, they enable you to add fonts and graphics to a document and see them onscreen in a high speed, "real time" (graphic and font displays are immediate), graphical user interface. Word publishing programs also offer basic page layout functions that let you position and demarcate text, tables, and graphics. However, the word publishing feature that most speeds you to printing your final copy is the Print Preview screen mode.

The Print Preview screen lets you see how fonts of different sizes and styles (regular, bold, italic, and bold italic) interact on the page. Print Preview also lets you check and manipulate the positioning of blocks of text vis-a-vis graphic images. All of this is done quickly, onscreen, and *before you print.*

Using Print Preview With Word for Windows, the first things
you do to prepare a document involve entering, editing, and
formatting text and graphics in the Normal Editing View of the
document window. When you are satisfied with the content of
your document, you can view the full page results in Print
Preview. Print Preview is accessed with the File Print Preview
command.

Figure 5-1 shows one of the Word for Windows sample
documents in the Print Preview mode. Print Preview has its own
menu bar with five buttons. Also, since the status bar is unavailable
at the bottom of the screen, the total number of pages and the
page number of the displayed page (or pages) is listed to the right
of the Print Preview buttons. The total number of pages and the
pages shown will be the same if a two-page document is shown
with the Two Pages button active; in that case, the listing would be
"Page 1" if there is only one page displayed. If there are more
than two pages in the document, the total number of pages will be

Figure 5-1.

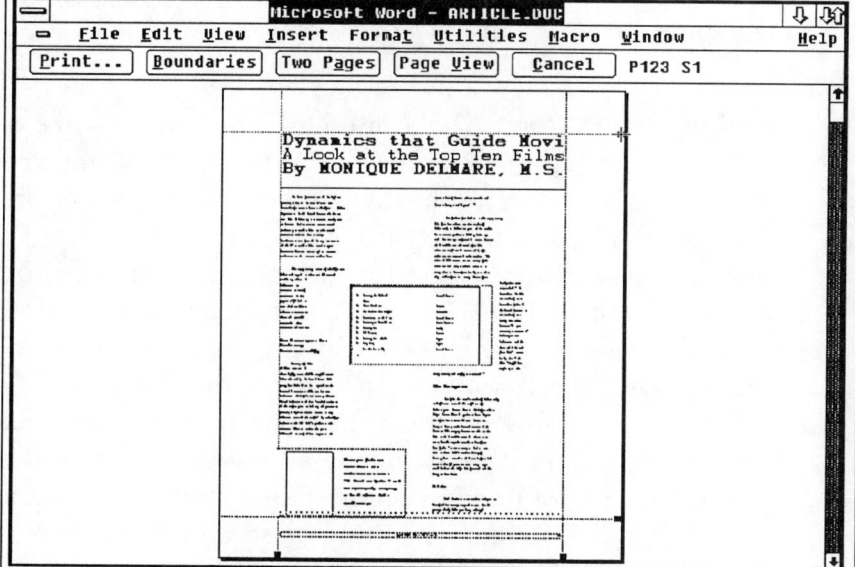

Print Preview with Boundaries button active

listed first (from left to right) as "Pages 1-X" (with X being the last page). However, if there are only three pages in the document (as in Figure 5-1), the total number of pages will be listed as "P123," and the pages shown will also be listed after an "S", for example "S1-2."

Unlike the Normal Editing View of the document window, Print Preview has only a vertical scroll bar at the right side of the screen. This means that you cannot scroll horizontally on a page in Print Preview, only vertically. Also, when you click the left mouse button on the boxed up or down arrow in the scroll bar, Print Preview will scroll up or down one page at a time. A discussion of the five Print Preview buttons, as seen from left to right in Figure 5-1, follows.

Print Button   The Print button is probably the last button you will use in the Print Preview screen. This button accesses the File Print dialog box. This dialog box is discussed in the "Print" section at the end of this chapter. The Print button can be activated either by clicking the left mouse button on it or by pressing ALT-p (note the underlined "P" in the word "Print").

Boundaries Button   The Boundaries button acts like a toggle switch. Activating the Boundaries button causes Print Preview to display all page margins, headers, footers, page breaks, and other positioned objects. *Objects* are parts of a Word for Windows document that can be treated separately from the body text of the document. In its Print Preview mode, Word for Windows takes borders (page margins and page breaks) and treats them as dotted line objects. The Boundaries are active in Figure 5-1. The four dotted lines represent the top, bottom, right, and left page margins. All other objects (headers, footers, tables, and graphic images) are surrounded by a dotted line rectangle or square box. Selecting the Boundaries button a second time turns off the boundaries display.

A black square at one end of the dotted line represents a page margin or a page break. This black square is called a *node*. When you move the mouse over a node, it changes from the arrow shape into a *cross-bar*. Note that the mouse, which is on the page's top margin node, is a cross-bar in Figure 5-1. If you are familiar with draw packages (such as Micrografx Designer, Computer Support Corporation Arts and Letters, Adobe Illustrator, and so on), you will know that nodes are the anchored portions of an object. To unanchor an object, you place the mouse on the node so that it becomes a cross-bar and click the left mouse button. You can then drag an unanchored object, such as the top margin line in Figure 5-1; top and bottom margins can be dragged vertically up and down a page. In this example, the margin line is treated as an object.

Microsoft defines objects in a different way in Word for Windows than do most draw programs. Word for Windows treats text, images, tables, and margins as objects if their positions on the page have been defined. Microsoft calls these objects *absolute positioned objects,* or APOs. Normally, text and graphics do not have an absolute position on the page. This means that when you make insertions somewhere in the middle of a document, any text and associated graphics that follow the insertion can move down toward the new end of the document. Graphic images, tables, and page margins set on a page (using the Format Position or Format Document commands) *do* have fixed positions.

You can make a character, a paragraph, a section, or even a whole document into an APO. After you do this, you will be able to move the APO block of text around the screen in Print Preview as you would graphic images, tables, or page margins. To make a block of text an APO, while in the Normal Editing View, highlight the part of the document that you want to remain fixed at its current location on the page. Then activate the Format Position dialog box. Now change any of the default values by as little as 0.01" in the Format Position dialog box. This fixes the position of the highlighted text block, and it becomes an APO. You can access the Print Preview directly from the Format Position dialog box to see how the new position of the APO text affects the appearance of the entire page. Activating the Print Preview Boundaries button will show you that the block of text is an APO object; it will appear inside a dotted-line box. You will also be able to change the position of the new text block object by dragging it with the mouse, just as you would any other APO, such as a graphic image or a table.

As mentioned, page margins or page breaks are treated as line objects when you have the Boundaries button active. If you keep the mouse button depressed on any margin's node, you can move the mouse and drag the dotted line representing the margin either vertically (top, bottom, and page margins) or horizontally (left and right margins). In this way, you can change the page margins and page breaks. The new page margin position(s) will be reflected in the Format Document dialog box after you exit the Print Preview.

Word for Windows treats headers, footers, charts, tables, and APO blocks of text differently than margins. They are objects, but they are surrounded by a dotted-line box, with no nodes. Whenever the mouse is anywhere over the dotted-line box, it becomes a cross-bar. You can click the left mouse button anywhere on the box and drag the box in any direction (not just vertically or horizontally) to a new location on the page.

Two Pages Button   Activating the Two Pages button changes the Print Preview display from one to two pages. Figure 5-2 shows an example of the two page Print Preview. Note that the Boundaries button is off in this figure. The Print Preview vertical scroll bar works the same way in two-page mode as it did in one-page mode. Note that the page number listing to the right of the Print Preview buttons now lists both of the displayed pages' numbers.

Page View and Cancel Buttons   The next button, Page View, gives you the most precise representation of what your document will look like when it comes out of your printer. In Print Preview, pages are compacted to give you a sense of the overall layout. When you activate the Page View button, you leave Print Preview and go to the close-up (25 lines of 12-point type) Page View

Figure 5-2.

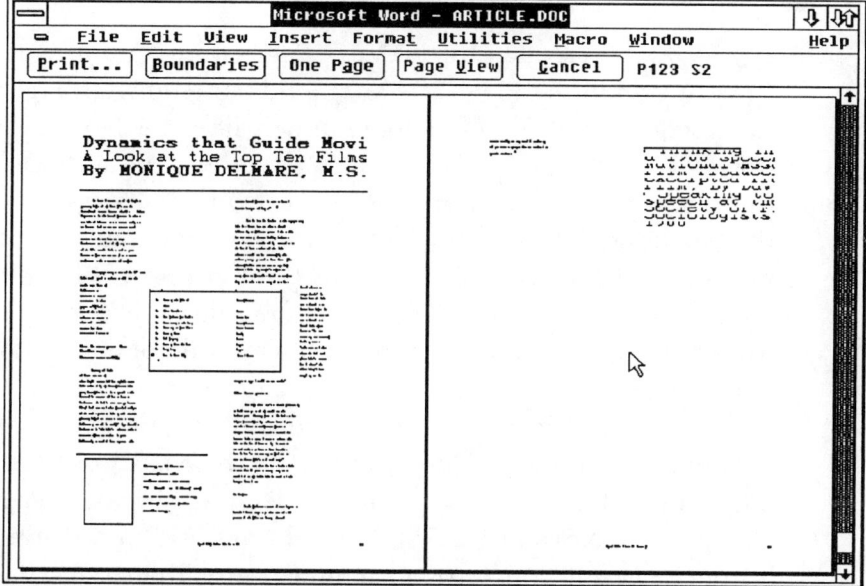

Print Preview with Two Pages button active

screen. Page View lets you see precisely how the layout changes
you made when you moved objects around the screen (using the
Boundaries button) affect each page's readability. Therefore, Page
View works symbiotically with Print Preview; that is why this
button is included in the Print Preview menu bar.

Page View can be accessed either from the Print Preview menu
bar or with the Page command in the View menu. The View Page
command is a toggle command. When it is active, a check mark
appears beside the command. The features of Page View are
discussed in the "Page View" section.

The Print Preview Cancel button, like the Cancel button in all
Word for Windows dialog boxes, exits Print Preview and returns
you to the previous document window. The Print Preview Page
View and Cancel buttons differ from the Boundaries and Two
Pages buttons. Once you activate the Page View or Cancel button,
you must reactivate the File Print Preview command to return to
the Print Preview.

Page View

Page View is activated by the View Page command or by the Page View button in the Print Preview menu bar (shown in Figure 5-2). At first glance Page View looks much like the Normal Editing View — you type and edit text in exactly the same way. Do not let this mislead you since Page View gives you a full size view (unlike the compacted Print Preview) of a document that is as close as possible to what will be printed by your printer. But unless you have a very large monitor (large monitors are discussed in Appendix B, "Peripheral Interests"), you will not be able to see an entire page (from top to bottom) in Page View.

Unlike the Normal Editing View, Page View lets you see headers, footnotes, and line numbers in the exact positions on the page in which they will be printed. Each page break in Page View changes the Normal Editing View dotted line to a distinct page border. Also, if you have formatted more than one column to snake around a graphic image or a table, these columns now appear in their exact relation to the image or table.

Snaking columns are used to frame a graphic image or a table instead of placing the graphic or table on the page with nothing on either side (snaking columns are discussed in Chapter 10, "Desktop Publishing with Word for Windows"). As an example, compare the Normal Editing View and Page View of a document that contains columns formatted to snake around a table. Figure 5-3 shows the Normal Editing View of a page with only one of the two columns that are formatted to snake around a table that is below the text; Figure 5-4 shows the Page View of the same page with the same columns placed around the table. Columns that are formatted to snake around a graphic image or a table in the Normal Editing View are not shown side by side. Rather, as with Word 4.0 and 5.0, only one column is shown on the page. A page like the one shown in Figures 5-3 and 5-4 would be very difficult to set up entirely in the Normal Editing View. However, there is no reason to even attempt this since you can use both the Print Preview and the Page View screens.

Figure 5-3.

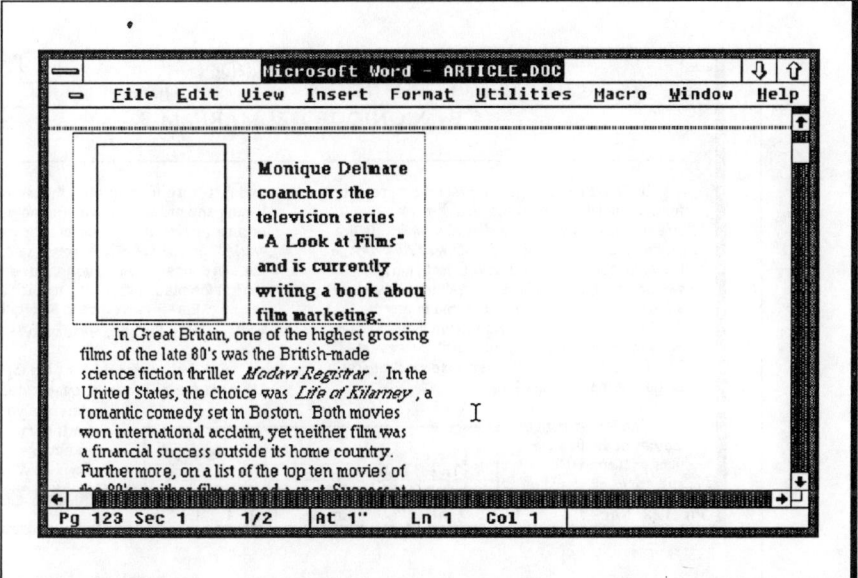

Normal Editing View with snaking columns

Page View gives you the truest WYSIWYG screen that Word for Windows' five views offer. Keep in mind, however, that documents laden with multiple fonts and graphic images will slow down all Word for Windows operations in both the Page View and the Normal Editing View.

Draft View

Of the five Word for Windows screen modes, Draft View is at the opposite end of the spectrum from Page View. Whereas Page View helps you concentrate on details, Draft View is useful for quick onscreen reading and editing of a document.

If a document contains more than 50 pages and has multiple fonts and graphics, both text entry (the speed at which characters are displayed on the screen as you are typing) and scrolling through a document may slow down. You can speed up text entry

Figure 5-4.

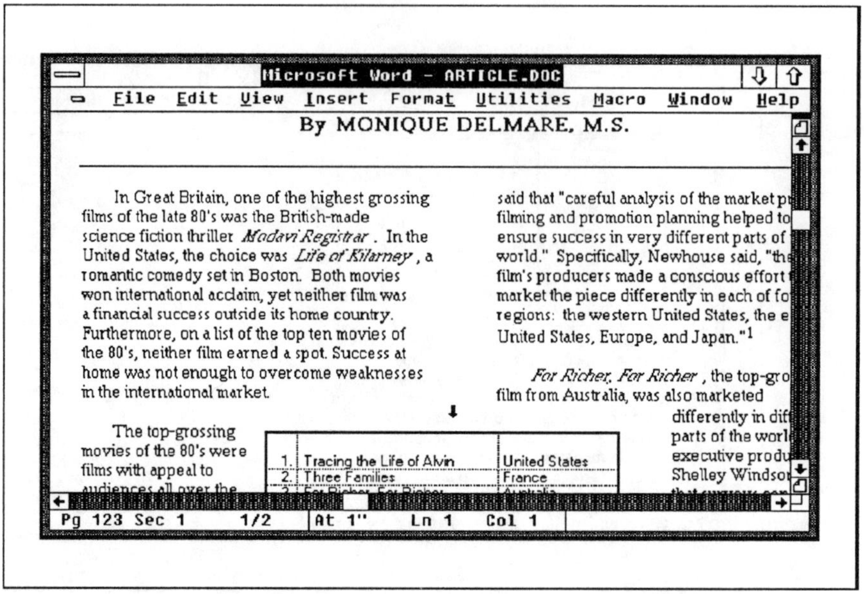

Page View with snaking columns

and scrolling by turning off the display of screen fonts and graphic images with the View Draft command. The View Draft command activates Draft View. Like the View Page command (which activates Page View), View Draft is a toggle command. When it is active, there will be a check mark beside it in the View menu.

When the View Draft command is active, only a single screen font will be displayed. As an example, look at the Word for Windows sample file shown in Figures 5-5 and 5-6; they show the same document in both the Normal Editing View and Draft View. The Draft View in Figure 5-6 is reminiscent of the text-entry screen, especially the uniform screen font, used in both Word 4.0 and 5.0. All text is displayed in the single screen font. Also, in Draft View graphic images are seen as empty boxes that mark their positions. Boxed paragraphs and tables remain boxed in Draft View.

Despite the lack of graphic image and screen font display, all Word for Windows commands are functional in Draft View. For example, you can still use the Format Character dialog box to add

Figure 5-5.

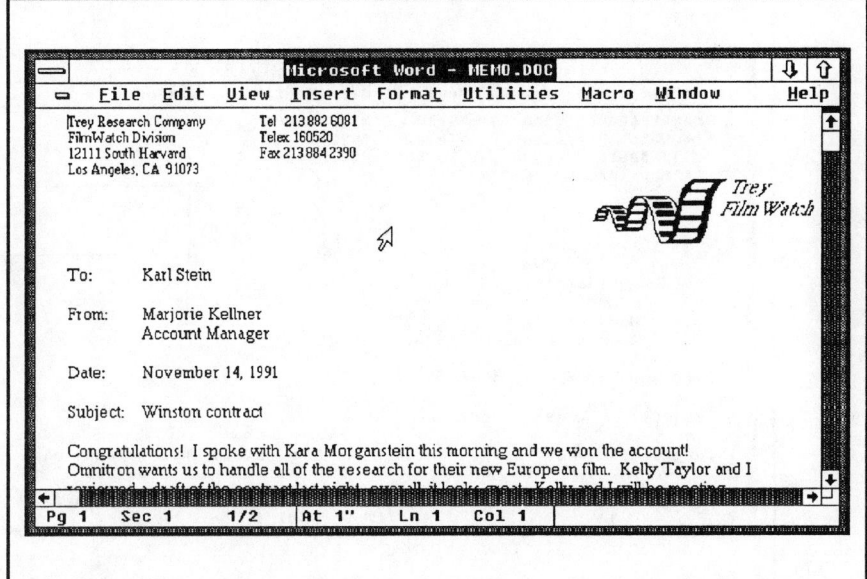

Normal Editing View displays fonts and graphics

font formatting to blocks of text even though you will not see the font on the screen. You can also use the Insert Picture command to insert graphic images in the Draft View mode, but remember that these images will be displayed as boxes.

The fact that these functions are still available misses the point of using Draft View. If your monitor's display slows down, Draft View will help you enter, scan, and edit your ideas onscreen as quickly as you can type. You can always temporarily switch off Draft View in the View menu to see what the screen fonts or graphic images will look like when you print the document.

Printer Installation and Setup

When you installed Windows, you selected at least one printer driver (see Appendix C, "Setting up Word for Windows"). The

Figure 5-6.

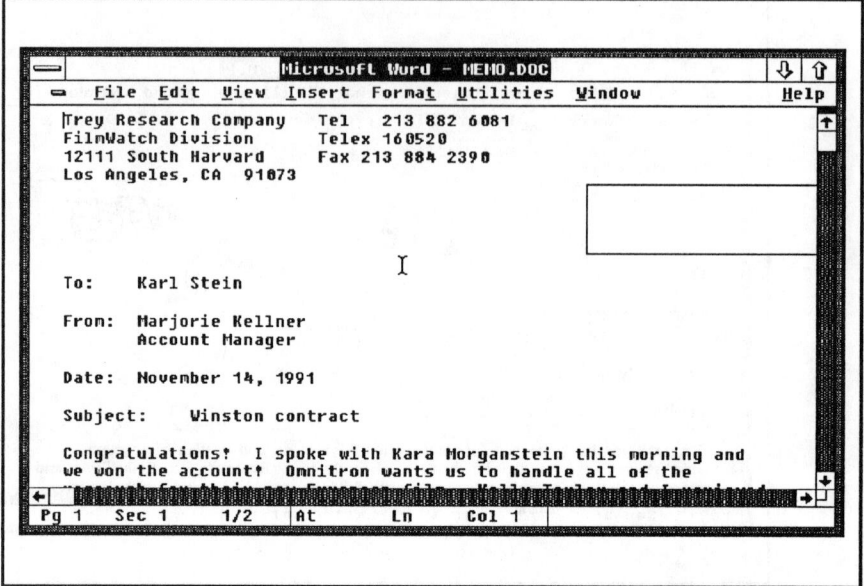

Draft View displays one screen font and graphics as boxes

installation program automatically copied the correct printer driver(s) to your hard disk. To install additional printers you do not need to, nor would you want to, reinstall the entire Windows program. You can simply add the printer drivers to Windows (not Word for Windows) with the Windows Control Panel program. The Control Panel program is found in the MS-DOS Executive (see Chapter 1, "Up and Running" for a discussion of the MS-DOS Executive).

After you have installed a Windows printer driver, you must set up the printer before you can print with Word for Windows or any other Windows application. The Printer Setup command is available from both the Windows Control Panel and the Word for Windows File menu. The Printer Setup command activates a printer driver and the printer port it will use (a printer port is the plug for the printer cable on your computer; it is discussed in the

"Selecting Ports" section later in this chapter). Only one printer driver and one printer port can be set up, that is, be active at any one time.

If you always use the same printer driver, you only need to set up the printer once. When you execute the File Printer Setup command, Windows writes the printer setup instructions for the active printer driver into the WIN.INI (Windows Initialization) file. Each time you open Windows, it remembers the most recently set up printer and reads its printer instructions, as well as any others in WIN.INI; the WIN.INI file serves as the Windows AUTOEXEC.BAT file. If you use several printers, you need to use the Printer Setup command each time you switch printers. You can only have one printer active at a time.

Installing More Than One Printer Driver

If you have only one printer hooked up to any particular computer, you probably do not need to install more than one printer driver. Even if the printer you use at work is different from the one you use at home, Windows adds printer formatting information when you are ready to print, not when you construct a file. Therefore, you can produce a file at home or at work and print it later at either location.

You may, however, want to install several printer drivers if your laser or dot matrix printer is capable of emulating other printers (for example, Epson FX, Diablo 630, HPGL, and IBM Graphics printer emulations are supported by many printers). Each emulation requires a different printer driver. Also, many laser printers and high resolution phototypesetting machines support both the PostScript (Apple LaserWriter) and PCL (LaserJet) Windows printer drivers. PostScript and PCL are usually referred to as *page description languages* (they are discussed in Appendix B,

"Peripheral Interests") because they contain information on using fonts and graphic images to construct a page before the printer begins to print. Usually you select printer emulations or page description languages by pressing buttons or moving switches on your printer. Whenever you change the printer emulation or page description language on your printer, you need to set up the corresponding Windows printer driver.

Printing to a File

There are printer drivers that print to a file. Printing to a file with Windows or DOS applications creates a file that includes the document plus printing instructions. One kind of printer driver that prints to a file is used to produce presentation graphics (usually color slides with text, charts, and sometimes prepared graphics like clip art). Currently, the most popular file format for presentation graphics is called SCODAL; all SCODAL files end with the extension *.SCD. A SCODAL file contains a high resolution screen capture that is saved to a file. Screen captures are a snapshot of what is seen on the screen; whenever you decide to print to a file, the SCODAL driver makes a screen capture and saves it to a file. The SCODAL file is then sent on disk or through a modem to a service bureau that usually sends back a slide produced with a matrix camera. Word for Windows does not come with a SCODAL printer driver. However, you could use a SCODAL printer driver from another Windows program, like Micrografx Designer or Corel Draw (see Appendix D, "Supporting Software and Hardware" for information on Designer) with Word for Windows. The only problem with printing Word for Windows screen captures to a file is the need to crop the Word for Windows interface (the title bar, menu bar, and scroll bars) off the page, leaving just the desired text, graphics, tables, and so on, in the area from which the slide is produced. Of course, if your lecture topic was Word for Windows, you might want the interface to remain.

Using the Control Panel

As mentioned in the "Printer Installation and Setup" section, you do not have to completely reinstall Windows to add new printer drivers. You can add printer drivers through the Windows MS-DOS Executive Control Panel program.

To open the MS-DOS Executive, you can either open Windows (without opening Word for Windows) or minimize your Word for Windows screen to an icon (see Chapter 1, "Up and Running," for a discussion of accessing the MS-DOS Executive) and maximize the MS-DOS Executive icon. Within the MS-DOS Executive, you will see a list of file names. You must switch to the Windows directory before you can open the Control Panel program. If you are not already in the Windows directory, the quickest way to do this is to press the BACKSPACE key until you get to the root directory. Then move the cursor with the UP ARROW or the DOWN ARROW until the Windows directory is highlighted; then press ENTER. Once you are in the Windows directory, the quickest way to activate the Control Panel dialog box is to click the left mouse button twice (double-click) on the Control Panel's file name, CONTROL.EXE.

You can also use the keyboard and either move the cursor down to the CONTROL.EXE file name with the DOWN ARROW, or type **c** until the highlight moves over CONTROL.EXE. You can then activate the program by pressing ENTER.

The Control Panel dialog box is unlike any of the Word for Windows dialog boxes in that it has its own menu bar as shown here.

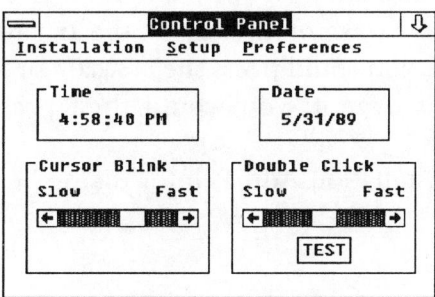

Note that it displays the current time and date. The Control Panel also lets you change the speed at which a Windows application text entry cursor will blink as well as how fast you have to double-click the left mouse button on a file name to activate a program.

Adding New Printer Drivers   After you have installed Windows, you add new printer drivers with the Installation menu in the Control Panel dialog box. You can display the Installation menu by clicking the left mouse button on the word "Installation" in the Control Panel dialog box menu bar or by pressing ALT-i.

The Installation menu's first command is Add New Printer, as seen here.

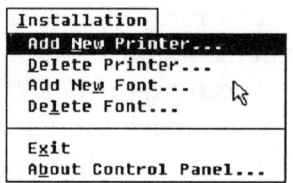

This command ends with ellipses (three dots), signifying that there is an Installation Add New Printer dialog box to follow. You can activate the Add New Printer command in the Installation menu either by clicking the left mouse button on the Add New Printer command or by pressing **n** for the underlined letter, "N". If the cursor was not already on the Installation Add New Printer command, you could press the UP ARROW or DOWN ARROW key until the cursor was over it; you would then press ENTER to activate the command.

The Installation Add Printer dialog box, shown here,

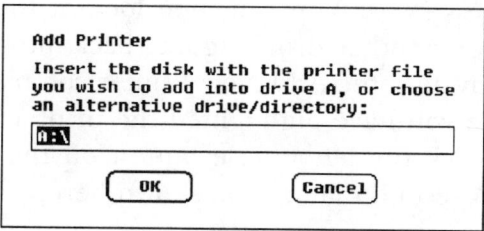

asks you to put the disk with the desired printer driver(s) in Drive A:. This disk may be one of the Windows printer disks or a new Windows printer driver you get on a separate disk from your printer's manufacturer, software publishers, or any other source.

If you have a set of disks and are not sure which has the desired printer driver on it, try them all. There is no penalty for guessing. Place one in drive A: and press ENTER or click the left mouse button on the OK button. When you press ENTER, the Control Panel program begins to look through the disk for printer driver files. Once the Control Panel program has found them all, it lists them in the Available Printers dialog box shown here.

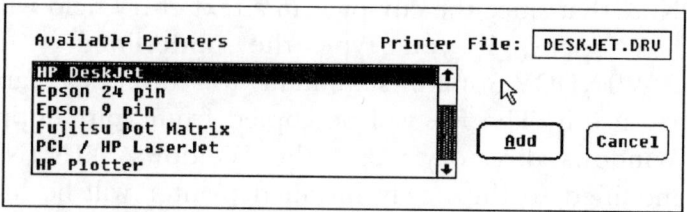

You can use the scroll bar at the left of the listing or the UP ARROW and DOWN ARROW to go through the disk contents until you find the desired printer driver. If this is the wrong disk, either click the left mouse button on the Cancel button or tab to the Cancel button and press ENTER. You can then look at the printer drivers contained on another disk by going back into the Installation menu and activating the Add New Printer command.

Once you have highlighted the printer driver that you want, either click the left mouse button on the Add button or press ENTER. A second dialog box, shown here,

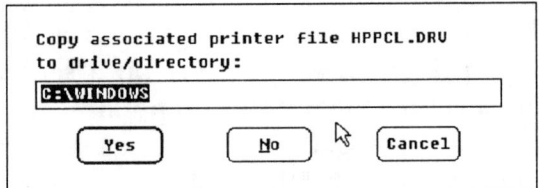

will appear overlaying the Available Printers dialog box. It asks if you want the chosen printer driver copied to your Windows directory. Respond in the affirmative by clicking the left mouse button on the Yes button or by tabbing to it and pressing ENTER. Note that since the cursor is in a text entry field when this dialog box opens, if you type the underlined **y** for Yes, the C:\WINDOWS path statement will disappear and a "y" will replace it. The file will be copied from your floppy disk to the Windows directory. Also, the Windows WIN.INI file will be modified so the newly installed printer will be listed as one of those available in the Printer Setup menu.

Selecting Ports   After you have installed a new printer driver, you must tell Windows which port on your computer you are using to plug in the printer cable that is connected to the newly installed printer. You do this by using the Setup menu of the Control Panel.

Displaying the Setup menu, as seen here,

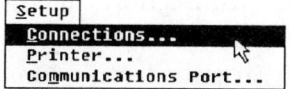

shows the Connections command. Activating that command displays the Setup Connections dialog box shown in Figure 5-7. In the Setup Connections dialog box, you see that two printer drivers have been installed, one for the PCL (LaserJet) PDL (page description language) and another for the PostScript PDL.

The first time you open the Setup Connections dialog box, all the printer drivers you have installed in the Installation Add New Printer dialog box will be listed as attached to None (no printer port). Before selecting a port for each printer driver, you must first select one of the printer drivers in the Printer scroll box at the

Figure 5-7.

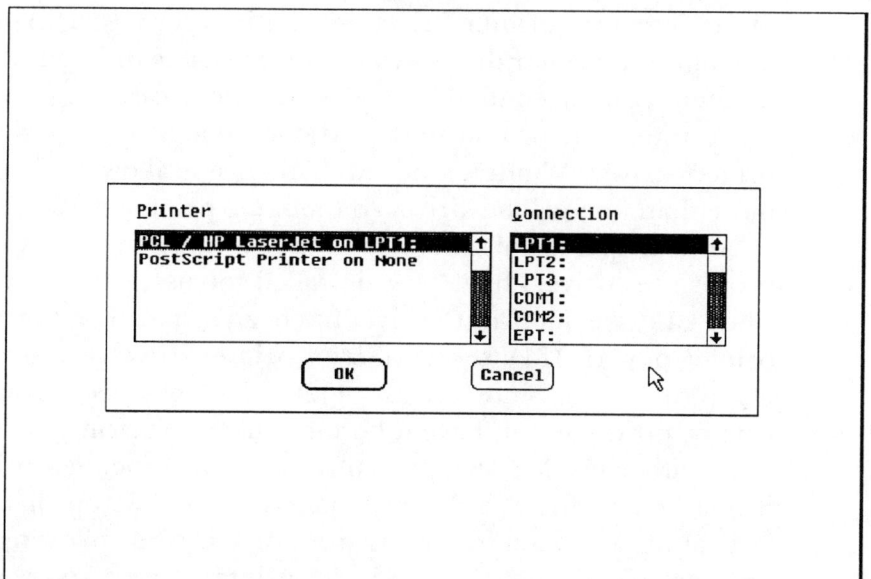

Setup Connections dialog box

left of the Setup Connections dialog box in Figure 5-7. To do this with the mouse, you may need to move the scroll bar to display the printer driver you want from a long list; then click the left mouse button on the printer driver's name to select it. To use the keyboard to select a printer driver, press the UP ARROW or DOWN ARROW to move the highlight to the desired printer driver. Now you can select a printer port with the mouse by first clicking the left mouse button on the printer port of your choice; again, if the port you want is not displayed in the Connection option scroll box, you may need to click the left mouse button on the scroll bar to the right to bring it into view. To choose a port with the keyboard after choosing a printer driver, press TAB once, then press the UP ARROW or DOWN ARROW to move the highlight onto the desired port. Finally, to activate your Connection choice (printer driver plus port), you either click the left mouse button on the OK button or press ENTER.

Many laser printers are capable of providing more than one PDL or more than one printer emulation mode (see "Installing More Than One Printer Driver" earlier in this chapter). You must use different printer drivers when you are using different PDLs or different printer emulation modes. In either case, you are using one printer, one printer port, and one cable with more than one printer driver. Windows, however, does not allow you to assign more than one printer driver to the same printer port and cable.

An example of this situation is shown in Figure 5-7, in which two printer drivers have been installed for use with one printer. The PCL/LaserJet printer driver has been installed on the parallel printer port (LPT1); the PostScript printer driver is installed on None (no port). Since the LaserJet driver has been assigned a printer port, you can have it become the active printer driver by using either the MS-DOS Executive Control Panel Setup Printer dialog box or the Word for Windows Printer Setup dialog box (activating a printer driver is discussed in the following three sections). To activate the PostScript printer driver, you would go back to the MS-DOS Executive Control Panel Setup Connections dialog box and assign the LaserJet driver to the None port. Do not click the left mouse button on OK or press ENTER after doing this since this would leave no printer driver to set up. Then select the PostScript driver and assign the LPT1 port to it. Either click the left mouse button on OK or press ENTER. You must reassign the printer ports in this fashion each time you want to change PDLs (or printer driver emulations) for one printer. One unusual exception is if you are using two cables and two ports, such as COM1 (serial port) for PCL/LaserJet and LPT1 for PostScript.

After you install one or more printer drivers and assign them to printer ports, you must select the printer driver which is to be active first. Only one printer driver can be active in Windows at any one time.

Activating an Installed Printer   You can activate a printer driver from either the MS-DOS Executive or from Word for Windows. You can also change the printer driver's default options (paper size, paper orientation, and so on) within either program.

To activate a printer driver in the MS-DOS Executive, you choose the Printer command in the Control Panel Setup menu as shown here.

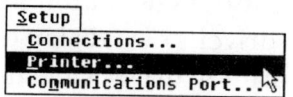

This displays the Setup Printer dialog box shown in Figure 5-8. The highlighted printer driver in the Default Printer scroll box is the currently active printer. You can select a printer driver in the Default Printer scroll box either by clicking the left mouse button on it (if it is not displayed in the scroll box, you may need to use

Figure 5-8.

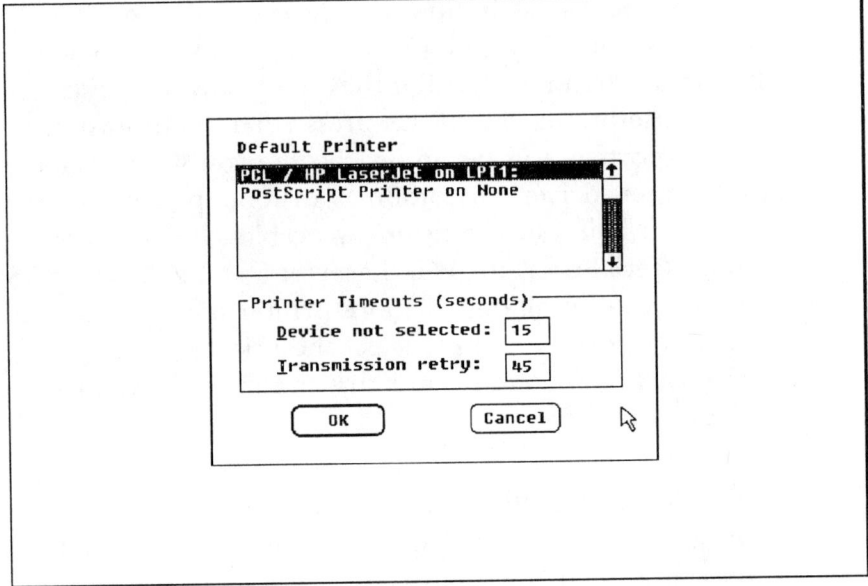

Setup Printer dialog box

the scroll bar to the right) or moving the highlight to it with the UP ARROW or DOWN ARROW. To activate the printer driver, either click the left mouse button on the OK button, press ENTER, or press TAB three times to highlight the OK button and press ENTER.

The printer driver's own dialog box will now be displayed. You can change a printer driver's default options (paper size, paper orientation, and so on) in this dialog box. You will, however, only need to change the defaults of the printer driver's option box when you are using a Windows program like Word for Windows. In most cases, you would click the left mouse button on the OK button or press TAB until the OK button is highlighted and then press ENTER to accept the default options. A situation in which you might want to change the defaults in a printer driver option box is given in the next section, "Printer Setup."

Word for Windows Print Commands

There are several Print commands in the Word for Windows File menu. One of the commands, File Print Preview, was fully discussed in the "Print Preview" section of this chapter. The other File menu Print commands are surveyed in this section. You begin where you left off in the last section, with the task of activating a printer driver. Remember, you can set up (activate) an installed printer driver in Word for Windows, but you cannot install new printer drivers nor can you assign printer drivers different printer ports from within Word for Windows. This must be done in the MS-DOS Executive Control Panel dialog box with the Setup Connections command discussed in the section on selecting ports.

Printer Setup

As with the MS-DOS Executive, you can activate a printer driver from within Word for Windows. You do this with the Printer Setup command in the File menu. First, you select the File Printer Setup command. The Word for Windows File Printer Setup dialog box, shown here,

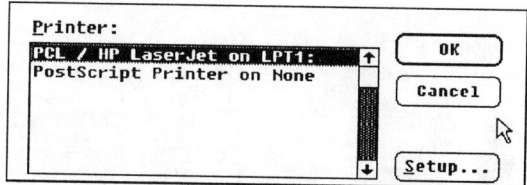

lists all the available printer drivers (those previously installed in the MS-DOS Executive Control Panel dialog box).

If you select a printer driver and activate the OK button, the printer driver will be automatically activated with all of its default options. If, however, you select a printer driver and activate the Setup button, the highlighted printer driver's dialog box (in this case, the LaserJet printer) will be displayed, as shown in Figure 5-9. The Printer Driver dialog box is also automatically displayed from Windows Control Panel Setup Printer dialog box, as previously mentioned in "Activating an Installed Printer."

The Printer Driver dialog box is different for each printer driver. The types of options you choose in these dialog boxes will, however, be similar. As an example, look at Figure 5-9, which shows the Hewlett Packard LaserJet printer. Beginning at the top, you can choose the number of uncollated copies; the default here is 1. This means that if you print several copies of a document, but leave the number of uncollated copies at 1, each complete copy of the document will be collated. This option also lets you type in any number of copies that will print out uncollated. With more than one uncollated copy, the specified number of uncollated copies of

Figure 5-9.

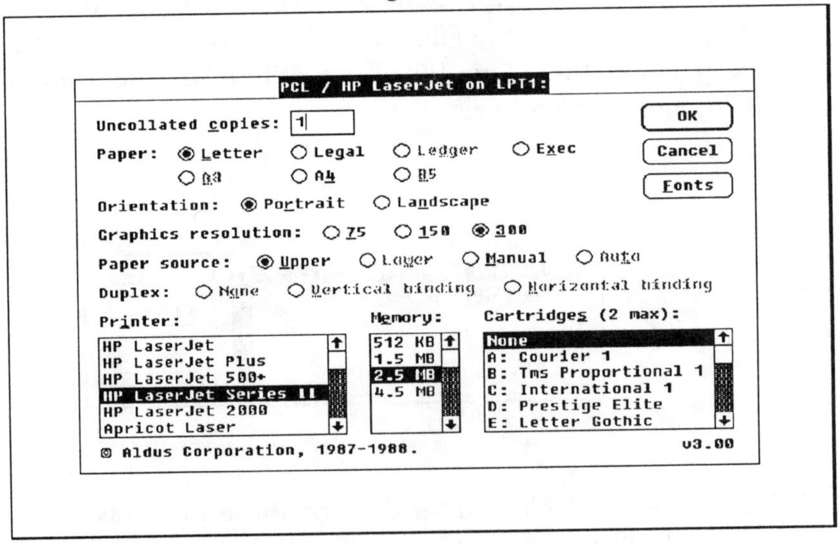

LaserJet Printer Driver dialog box

page 1 print out together, then all copies of page 2, and so on.

Next, you can choose the default paper size (usually 8 1/2" x 11" unless you are manually feeding envelopes or labels). You can then choose the orientation of the printing—Portrait or Landscape. Portrait is the standard; Landscape prints the page sideways, across an 11" width. In most cases, you must have landscape fonts available to use this option.

The next option set lets you choose which paper source, that is, tray, to use. You can choose Manual (you feed odd-sized paper by hand through the paper feed in the back of the LaserJet) or Auto (from the paper tray). The Duplex (double-sided) printing option set is next, available only with the LaserJet IID.

At the bottom left, you select the printer model from among the HP LaserJet family of printers or compatibles. Then, you tell Word for Windows how much memory you have installed in the printer. Next, you tell Word for Windows which font cartridge, if any, you have plugged into your LaserJet; the LaserJet printer offers many varied choices. (There is a full discussion of font issues in Appendix E.)

If you have purchased soft fonts (fonts that come on a floppy disk, not a cartridge), you can add them to the LaserJet printer driver now. To do so, activate the Fonts button shown below the Cancel button at the upper right of Figure 5-9. The Soft Font Installer dialog box will be displayed as shown in Figure 5-10. Any soft fonts that have previously been installed are listed in the scroll box on the left. In this case, no soft fonts have been installed. To add fonts from a disk, activate the Add Fonts button. The Add Fonts dialog box, shown here,

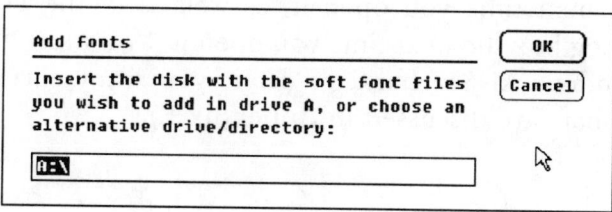

Figure 5-10.

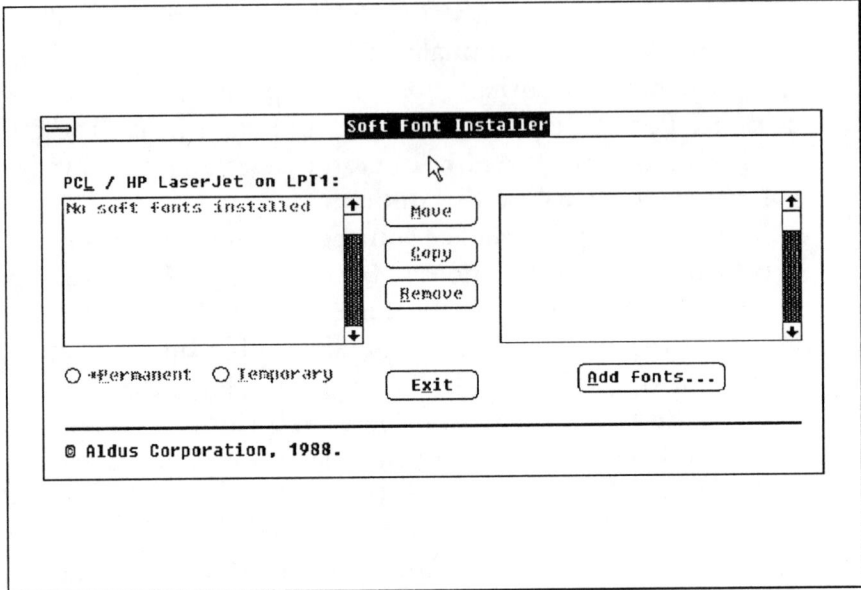

Windows Soft Font Installer dialog box

then overlays the Soft Font Installer dialog box. The Add Fonts dialog box asks you to tell it where to find the soft font files. By default, the Add Fonts dialog box will look in Drive A drive for the soft font files. You can overtype the A:\ path if you want the fonts copied from another drive or from a subdirectory on your hard disk.

In the LaserJet example, all of the fonts will be copied to a Windows subdirectory, C:\WINDOWS\PCLFONTS. The list of these fonts will then appear in the Soft Font Installer dialog box the next time you open it, as well as in the Format Character dialog box the next time you open it. You must use fonts with the Windows/ANSI character set if you want correct output (font formats are discussed in Appendix E).

Since the same Printer Driver dialog box is displayed from the MS-DOS Executive Control Panel program's Setup Printer dialog box, you install fonts from the MS-DOS Executive in the same manner as you install them from within Word for Windows.

Print Merge

The Print Merge command is in the File menu. Word for Windows File Print Merge command is used in much the same way as in Word 4.0 and 5.0. You either keep a list of records in a data base or output them from another data base application like Ashton Tate's dBASE or Borland's Paradox. Information from individual records in a data base output list can be output in the proper format to be a Word for Windows data document. This data document is then read and inserted, record by record, into a main document which is usually a form letter or a label page. If you have only a small list of records, it will be just as easy to keep track of it in a Word for Windows data document (setting up records in Word for Windows is discussed in Chapter 6 and Chapter 9), rather than using an intervening data base program.

The major difference between the Word for Windows print merge and that of Word 4.0 and 5.0 is the added power of Word for Windows fields. You use Word for Windows fields to position the insertion points for your records within form letter and label main documents. The new Word for Windows fields such as NEXTIF and SKIPIF allow you to set up more complex form letters, labels, and other documents than is possible with Word 4.0 or 5.0. The File Print Merge command and Word for Windows fields are both discussed in Chapter 6. There is further discussion of the File Print Merge command in Chapter 9.

Print

The Print command is accessed in the File menu, as shown here.

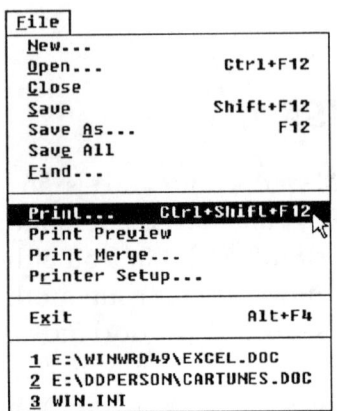

Note that you can use the mouse to activate the CTRL-SHIFT-F12 keyboard macro to activate this command. Activating the File Print command displays the File Print dialog box shown in Figure 5-11. There are three option sets in this dialog box: Print, Copies, and Pages. You can access additional Print options by clicking the left mouse button on the Options button. When all of the options are configured to your liking, press the OK button and your printer should begin printing.

Print Option Set   Figure 5-11 shows the default File Print dialog box with the Print scroll-down box and its Document listing ghosted. The Print scroll-down box is ghosted because no text or graphics were entered into the Word for Windows document window before the File Print dialog box was displayed. However, the default Document listing would not be ghosted if some text, a graphic image, or a combination of text and graphics was present in the Word for Windows document window.

Figure 5-11.

```
PCL / HP LaserJet on LPT1:

Print: Document            ↧      (    OK    )

Copies: 1                         ( Cancel  )
┌Pages────────────────
  ⊙ All                          ( Options >> )
  ○ Selection
  ○ From: [    ]   To: [    ]
```

File Print dialog box

Word for Windows lets you print features associated with a document. These features are displayed when the Print scroll-down box is dropped.

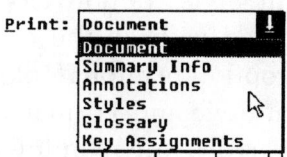

These features are discussed in the following sections.

Summary Information The feature listed in the Print scroll-down box after Document is Summary Info. If you choose this option, a document summary information sheet, which is like the summary information in Word 4.0 and 5.0, is printed. The document summary can be accessed and edited from within the Word for Windows document window with the Edit Summary Info command (discussed in Chapter 1, "Up and Running"). The document summary contains information and statistics on the document, including the file name, author, title, creation date, last revision date, time spent working on it, and total number of pages.

Annotations   The Print Annotations option lets you print only the annotations from a document and look at them all at once. Annotations can be added to Word for Windows documents by people other than the author. First, the author must "lock" the original document so another reader's annotations can be overlayed on the document without affecting the original text. These annotations can then be viewed in an *annotation pane* (the document window is divided into two panes, one with the original text and one with the associated annotations).

You may prefer to print the annotations and look at .them along with the document on the screen. You will be able to see more of the document on your screen if you look at a printed copy of the annotations instead of the annotation pane. The use of annotations is discussed in Chapter 8.

Styles   The Print Styles option lets you print a listing of the formatting associated with all the current document template's styles. The Styles option printout looks much like the style listings within the Format Style and Format Define Style dialog boxes.

If a group of Word for Windows users are using a single template, it would be useful for each member to have this printout. Since the printout only lists the style name, the stylesheet creator could add details on the proper context in which each style is to be used. The use of styles and templates are discussed in Chapter 4 and Chapter 6.

Glossary   The Print Glossary option prints a listing of all the glossaries assigned to the current document template. As in Word

4.0 and 5.0, glossaries are frequently used portions of text, like your address or the title of a manuscript. Word for Windows has an additional glossary feature not included in Word 4.0 or 5.0; it lets you include graphic images along with text in a glossary entry. You can assign a highlighted block of text, a graphic image, or text with graphics, to a character string from 1 to 31 characters long. When you type this character string and press F3, the glossary will be inserted into the document.

You can edit glossaries, one at a time, with the Edit Glossary dialog box; however, you cannot see the whole listing of a very long glossary in this dialog box, so it may be useful to print a glossary listing. Also, if you name a lot of glossaries to short character strings, it is useful to print them so you can see which glossaries you are currently using and which can be overwritten or deleted. Glossaries are discussed in depth in Chapter 6.

Key Assignments   The Print Key Assignments option lets you print all of the ALT and CTRL-key key assignments attached to the current document template. These include not only the default ALT, CTRL, and SHIFT-key keystroke combinations that help you use the Word for Windows menus and commands, but also keystroke combinations that you create with the Macro menu commands.

Word for Windows lets you see both the defaults and any of your own key assignments in a small scroll box in the Macro Assign to Key dialog box. (The Macro Assign to Key dialog box and macros in general are discussed in Chapter 6, "Advanced Template Features.") However, as with the annotation and glossary listings, it may be easier to see all of your key assignments on one or two sheets of paper than in the Macro Assign to Key dialog box. You may also want to keep this list posted near your computer, making it easier for you to learn and remember both your own and the Word for Windows key assignments.

Copies   When you display the File Print dialog box as shown in the following illustration , the Copies text entry field is highlighted by default.

```
┌─────────────────────────────────────────────┐
│  PostScript Printer on LPT1:                  │
│  ─────────────────────────────────────────   │
│  Print: │Document        │ ↓│ ┌   OK    ┐    │
│  Copies:│1              │     └─────────┘    │
│  ┌Pages─────────────────┐   ┌Options >>┐     │
│  │ ⊙ All                │   └──────────┘     │
│  │ ○ Selection          │                    │
│  │ ○ From  │      │  To:│         │          │
│  └──────────────────────┘                    │
│  ┌─────────────────────────┐                 │
│  □ Reverse Print Order                        │
│  □ Draft         Paper Feed:│Bin 1  │↓│      │
│  □ Update Fields                              │
│  ┌Include──────────────────────────────────┐ │
│  │ □ Summary Info      □ Hidden Text        │ │
│  │ □ Annotations       □ Field Codes        │ │
│  └──────────────────────────────────────────┘ │
└─────────────────────────────────────────────┘
```

This is because Microsoft determined that, statistically, it is the option you are most likely to reset. By highlighting it, you can quickly type the number of copies you want printed, or accept the default one copy and start printing right away. The number of copies can apply to a portion of a highlighted block of text on a page (a selection—see the next section, "Pages"), a few pages from the document, an entire document, or to any of the other Print options (Summary, Annotations, Styles, Glossary, or Key Assignments).

Pages   As with Word 4.0 and 5.0, you can print a highlighted block of text, called a selection (in Word for Windows and Word 4.0 and 5.0), or a set of pages by using the From and To fields, or an entire Document by using the default All option. The default All option tells Word for Windows to print the entire document. The Pages All option applies to any of the Print option set options: Document, Summary Info, Annotations, Styles, Glossary, or Key Assignments.

If you are not printing a document, the Selection option will be ghosted (unavailable). If you choose Selection, you must have highlight a block of text before you open the File Print dialog box. The Selection option is ghosted in Figure 5-11 because no text has been highlighted.

The From and To fields let you list pages within a document that you want printed. This is useful, for example, when you want to make changes on one page of a long document after you printed the entire document. You can make the changes on that page (or pages) on the screen and then print it (them) out. If you only want one page, you type the same number in both the From and the To fields.

Print Options Button When you activate the Options button in the File Print dialog box shown in Figure 5-11, the dialog box displays additional options as shown in Figure 5-12.

Reverse Print Order The Reverse Print Order option is useful if you have a laser printer, such as the original LaserJet, that prints pages face up. The original LaserJet prints pages in order, but since they come out of the printer face up, the top page is the last page, not the first. If you print pages in reverse order on this printer, the first page will be on top of the stack.

Draft The Draft option prints a document as it appears onscreen in Draft View (see "Draft View" earlier in this chapter). No character formatting or graphics are printed; only the printer's default font (usually Courier with a laser printer) is used, and empty boxes are inserted in place of graphics.

Update Fields The Update Fields option tells Word for Windows to print all of the fields in a document. The default File Print command does not print Field codes. Field codes are contextual codes you insert in a document such as a print merge document.

Figure 5-12.

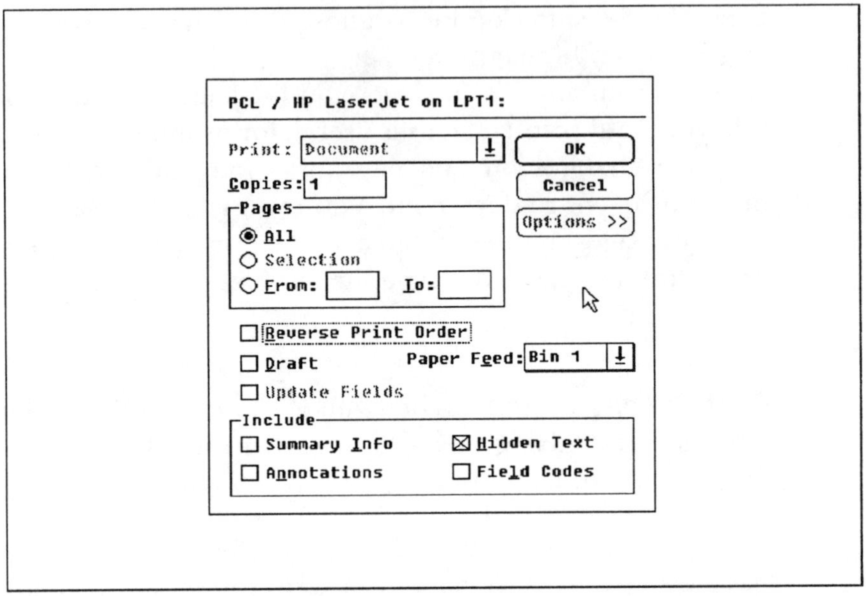

File Print dialog box with all options displayed

For example, these Field codes are used for the part of a print merge data base record that is to be inserted into a print merge document, such as a name or an address. Other Field codes insert information from the Word for Windows document summary (see the discussion of the Edit Summary Info command in Chapter 1) such as the date or the file name. Field codes are discussed in Chapter 6.

Paper Feed This is important only if you have more than one paper tray or paper feed for your printer. The LaserJet Series II printer has both a paper tray and a manual feed. If the LaserJet Series II was installed, the Paper Feed scroll-down box would offer Bin 1 and manual. The LaserJet Series IID printer has two paper trays and a manual feed, so the Paper Feed scroll-down box would offer you Bin 1, Bin 2, and manual. Usually, you will also have to select the active paper tray (if you have more than one) or manual feed on your printer and in the Printer Driver dialog box. The Printer Driver dialog box is accessed from either the Word for Windows File Printer Setup dialog box Setup button or the Windows MS-DOS Executive Control Panel Setup Printer dialog box. (Choosing a paper tray, or paper feed, is also discussed in the "Printer Setup" section of this chapter.)

Include Option Set The Include options are available only when you are printing a document; at that time, the Print option field should list Document. You can tell Word for Windows to add any of four toggle box options in the Include field to the printed document. If you add the summary information sheet, it will be printed out after the document has printed. (Summary information is discussed in Chapter 1, "Up and Running" and in the "Summary Information" section in this chapter.) The annotations, hidden text, and Field codes can be printed within the document.

Annotations and hidden text are discussed in Chapter 8, and Field codes are discussed in Chapter 6. Annotations are also discussed in the "Annotations" section and Field codes in the "Update Fields" section in this chapter.

Printing Once you have set all of the File Print dialog box options, you can begin printing by activating the OK button seen at the upper right of Figure 5-11. Word for Windows should tell you that it has begun formatting the document. Then Word for Windows should display a message that it is sending the document to the Windows print spooler. You can inactivate the Windows print spooler if you are short on memory; this is discussed in Chapter 11, "Fine Tuning Windows."

There is one common error message you may get while printing. Word for Windows may not print the document and instead tell you "Device Uninstalled." This probably means that you have not installed or set up a printer properly, or that your printer is not ready to print. In most cases, this is because the printer is off or the printer cable is not secured to the printer or to the printer port on your computer.

Printing is generally trouble free. This chapter has discussed most of the many Word for Windows onscreen proofing tools. These tools allow you to save printing drafts to proof their appearance. Microsoft has gone to great pains to allow you to construct the appearance of your documents entirely onscreen. Printing should be the grand finale of this time-saving document production process.

CHAPTER

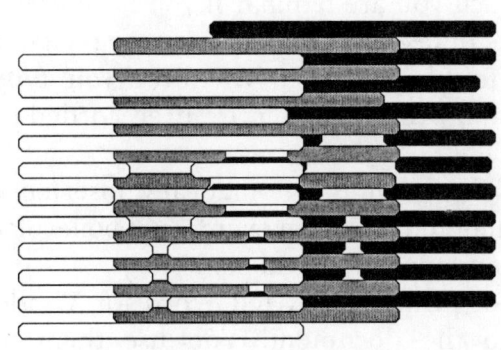

6

Advanced Template Features: Glossaries, Boilerplate Text, Fields, and Macros

The Word for Windows document template was introduced in Chapter 4, "For the Record: Styles and Templates." That chapter compared the document template to the stylesheets in Word 4.0 and 5.0. Recall that the stylesheet is a record of character and paragraph formatting styles that you can apply to text in documents you create. (Styles are discussed in Chapter 4.) Word for

Windows document templates are much more powerful than stylesheets; they record not only styles but also glossaries, boilerplate text, fields, and macros.

Glossaries, with which you are familiar if you have used Word 4.0 and 5.0, are blocks of text, text with images, or images alone, that you save to a few keystrokes. Whenever you type that glossary's keystrokes and press F3, the entire prerecorded block is inserted.

Boilerplate text is text that is automatically inserted into a document by a document template. An example of boilerplate text is the heading in a memo or letterhead stationery.

Fields codes are not printed; they tell Word for Windows to insert something into the document. You use them to add contextual information, such as the date or author found in the document summary, to a document template.

The page numbering format of Word 4.0 and 5.0 is a field. And, as in Word 4.0 and 5.0, some of the Word for Windows fields are contextual. Word for Windows fields such as IF, NEXTIF, and SKIPIF carry out an operation based on information you provide.

You use Word for Windows macros to save yourself from reentering commands and repeating other frequently used actions. The macros you create in Word for Windows are potentially more powerful than those you create with Word 4.0 and 5.0. In fact, the Word for Windows macro programming language is similar to BASIC. You do not, however, need to know BASIC to create Word for Windows macros.

You will be able to learn the BASIC-like commands in the Word for Windows macro language quickly since many are similar to DOS commands. Also, you can learn the Word for Windows macro language by looking at the structure of either the default macros or short macros that you create. With the Word for Windows Macro Record command, you create macros by recording actions you use while working in a document; these actions are automatically converted to the Word for Windows macro language. You can edit the macro language record of a macro later with the Macro Edit command, but until you are familiar with the Word for Windows macro language, it may be easier for you to recreate rather than edit the macro.

By using Word for Windows fields and the macro language, you can design highly interactive macros. An interactive macro asks you questions and makes decisions based on your answers. In this chapter, you will look at an example of an interactive macro that sorts through a data document, record by record, choosing which individuals you want to include in a hypothetical form letter mailing. After asking you which records to include, the macro creates a temporary data document that can be read by a form letter in a print merge operation (also called mail merge). By implementing this macro, you will also learn how to set up print merge data documents, fields, and other macros. Designing form letters in order to run a print merge is discussed in Chapter 9. First, however, you will learn the basics of glossaries, boilerplate text, fields, and macros.

Glossaries

Glossaries are blocks of text, text with images, or images alone that are saved to a glossary name. (If you have used Word 4.0 and 5.0, you are familiar with this feature.) The next time you want to insert this information in the same or another document, you need only type the glossary name and press the glossary key, F3.

Creating Glossaries

You create glossary entries in the Edit Glossary dialog box. First, however, you must create a block of data to save to a new glossary name. This block of data can be a block of alphanumeric text, text with one or more images, or one or more images and no text. Be sure that you add any character or paragraph formatting to the text that you want associated with the glossary entry; it will be saved by the glossary and inserted with the glossary text. Once you have created the block that is to be saved as a glossary, you highlight it. As an example, enter the text, **And the dish ran away with the spoon**. Highlight it and then open the Edit Glossary dialog box. The Glossary command is found in the Edit menu, shown here.

If you have not highlighted a block of text, one or more graphic images, or a combination of the two before you open the Edit menu, the Glossary command will be ghosted.

When you select the Edit Glossary command, the Edit Glossary dialog box will be displayed, as shown in Figure 6-1. Note that the Glossary Name text entry field is empty, and there are no entries in the Glossary Name scroll box below it. To name a glossary, you can use any character string up to 31 characters long. Type **Hey Diddle Diddle** for this entry. As soon as you begin to type, the Define button, previously ghosted, not only becomes available, but is highlighted.

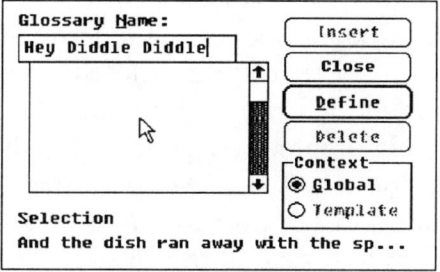

If you make a mistake typing the glossary name, you can back-space and retype it. You cannot use the arrow keys and overtype the glossary name because text entry fields are always in the Insert mode, not the Overtype mode. When the glossary name is correct, either press ENTER or click the left mouse button on the Define button. The Hey Diddle Diddle glossary is now recorded.

Figure 6-1.

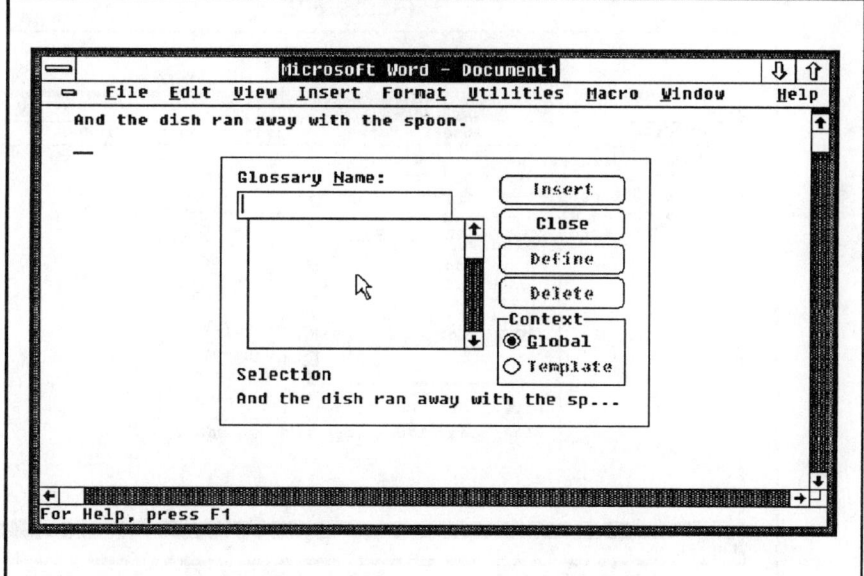

Edit Glossary dialog box

The next time you open the Edit Glossary dialog box, the name will appear in the Glossary Name scroll box. If you want to delete a glossary entry that appears in the Glossary Name scroll box, either click the left mouse button on it or press the DOWN ARROW until it is highlighted. In either case, the Delete button will be available. You can then either click the left mouse button on the Delete button or tab over to it and press ENTER.

The text entry field of the Glossary Name scroll box is only 19 characters wide and the Glossary Name scroll box itself is only 18 characters wide. Since glossary names can be up to 31 characters in length, you will not be able to see all of a long glossary name in the scroll box. However, you can always highlight a long glossary name and read it by pressing the RIGHT ARROW key to scroll to the right.

In Figure 6-2, a glossary named Little Miss Muffet has been selected in the scroll box; notice that after you make a selection in

Figure 6-2.

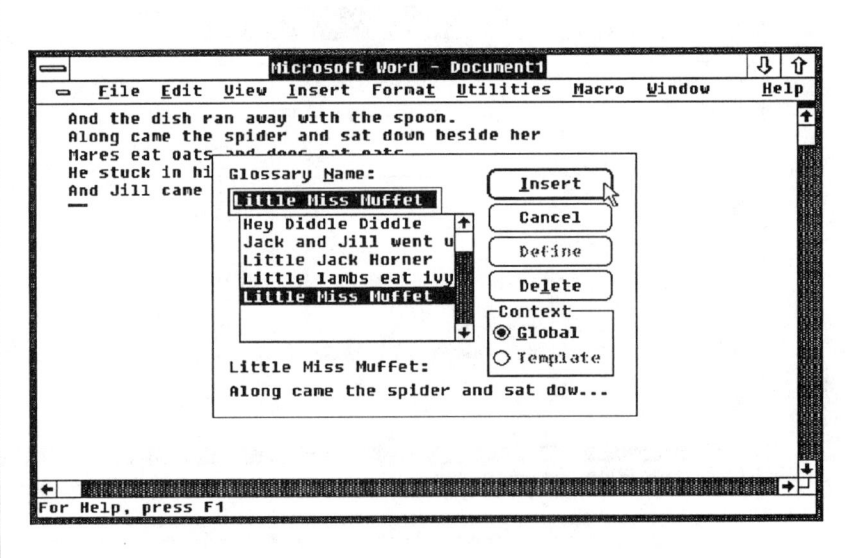

Inserting glossaries

the Glossary Name scroll box, the previously ghosted Insert and Delete buttons are available. The Insert button inserts the text associated with the glossary in the document at the present cursor location. The Delete button deletes the glossary from the glossary list in the Glossary Name scroll box. Also note in Figure 6-2 that the beginning of the text associated with a glossary appears at the bottom of the Edit Glossary dialog box.

You can print a listing of both the glossary names and their associated text and graphics by choosing the Glossary option in the Print field of the File Print dialog box (this is discussed in Chapter 5, "Printing: Picture Perfect Output").

There is one other set of options in the Edit Glossary dialog box—the Global and Template Context buttons, which are not ghosted. The Global button is activated by default to signal that the glossary will be available in all documents using any template. In effect, a global glossary becomes a default glossary. If you are working in a document with the NORMAL.DOT document template active, all glossaries will be global (the Template button is made unavailable). On the other hand, if you are building a document template and open it instead of a document, the Template button will be available when you name a glossary. If you are working from a document template other than the default NORMAL.DOT, you can select the Template button; that will deactivate the Global button. Glossaries are saved either globally or to a single document template.

To save your file as a document template, use the File Save All command. If the NORMAL.DOT document template is the active document template, you will be given the option to save the glossaries, macros, boilerplate text, and styles you have created to a new document template. Or, if you are using the NORMAL.DOT document template, Word for Windows will ask if you want to save your glossary entries globally when you exit the program. If you are using another document template, Word for Windows will ask if you want to save your glossary entries to that document template when you exit the program.

Boilerplate Text

Boilerplate text makes Word for Windows a more powerful and a greater time saver than Word 4.0 and 5.0. In Word 4.0 and 5.0, glossaries preserve text and formatting for you to insert anywhere in a document, but inserting several glossaries and formatting their positions on the page is much less convenient than having the text displayed automatically.

Boilerplate text, on the other hand, is displayed with its original formatting whenever you open a previously created document template. A common use of boilerplate text is in the creation of stationery and memo letterhead. The boilerplate text for a memo might look like that shown in Table 6-1. You can also use boilerplate text to standardize different versions of reports, brochures, advertisements, and manuals.

Boilerplate text is actually any text you include in a document template. In other words, whenever you save a document template, the text it contains becomes boilerplate text.

Table 6-1.

From the Desk of Cathy Jones Software City 1124 Central Avenue Bayou City, LA 70099 (504) 899-8881, ext. 232

To: Date:
Re:

Sample Memo Boilerplate Text

For example, you could create a document template from scratch using the text in Table 6-1; you can also substitute the appropriate text for your own application. Once you have finished typing and formatting the memo letterhead, open the File Save As dialog box.

If there are boilerplate text, macros, or glossaries in a default document template or in one that you have previously created, choose it as a base template in the File Format scroll-down box as shown here,

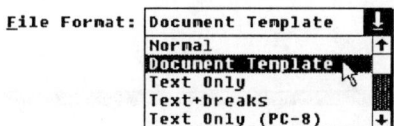

or, choose the default document template NORMAL.DOT. Remember, the base template brings along all of its styles, glossaries, macros, and boilerplate text.

After you have decided on a base document template, the new document template must be named; this can be done before you save. You can also wait until you close Word for Windows, and then save the new document template. Whenever you save the new document template, you will have to enter a name in the Save File Name text entry field, shown here,

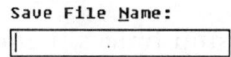

at the upper left of the File Save As dialog box. When you enter a name in this field, the OK button becomes available.

If you are creating a document template from a reopened document or from one that is already underway, be careful about the document's text. Remember that the next time you open the document template, all of the text will be brought up as boiler-plate text. Therefore, if you are in the middle of working on a document that you want to become a document template, first save the document as a document. Then be sure to delete all of the context-specific text that you do not not want for future applications as a document template. As a rule of thumb, any text you save as boilerplate text should be useful in the same way as the memo letterhead is in the earlier example.

Fields

Fields are *codes,* such as your name, the page number, the date, or a mail merge entry, that you can position anywhere in your document. On your screen, fields are set off from text by symbols that look like braces (the uppercase on the BRACKET keys), but are seen by Word for Windows as field *characters,* as shown here.

The actual fields and braces themselves are not printed, nor are they normally displayed onscreen. In the default Normal Editing View you will see the results of field codes at the location where the field codes have been inserted. The same is true when you print. For example, if the field code inserts the date, today's date will appear at the location where the field was inserted. When fields are used in a document template, they are saved in the same way that boilerplate text is saved. Fields are new to Word for Windows; they do not occur in Word 4.0 and 5.0.

Fields are useful for inserting in a document information such as text, images, the date, the time, and any information in the document summary (the document summary can be accessed and edited with the Summary Info command in the Edit menu). Fields can also be used to create tables of contents, indices (see Chapter 7), and bookmarks (see Chapter 8). Table 6-2 lists the Word for Windows field codes. Although all of the features in the table have not yet been covered, you will want to refer back to Table 6-2 when you read about them. In general, the more you know about Word for Windows, the more you will be able to use fields.

Inserting Fields

You can insert field codes into a document in two ways. Either use the Field command found in the Insert menu, shown here,

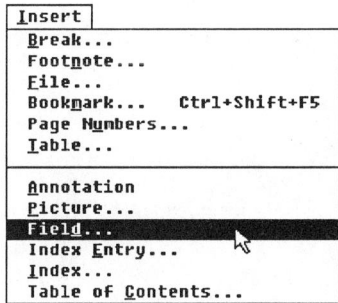

or type the field codes at the desired location within a document.

Table 6-2.

Field Code	Result
ASK	Requests bookmark text; cannot be used in footnotes, headers, footers, annotations, or macros[@]
AUTHOR	Inserts author's name
AUTONUM	Outline numbering using Arabic numbers (example: 1)[*]
AUTONUMLGL	Outline numbering using legal numbers (example: 1.1.1)[*]
AUTONUMOUT	Outline numbering using outline format (example: I. A. 1. a. i.)[*]
BOOKMARK	Contents of bookmark printed where bookmark name is listed in a field (use Ref Bookmark if bookmark name is the same as a print merge field type)
COMMENTS	Inserts Comments section in document summary.
CREATEDATE	Inserts original document creation date (not date last saved) from document summary
DATA	Identifies source (data document) of records to be used in print merge; cannot be used in footnotes, headers, footers, annotations, or data documents[@]
DATE	Inserts the date when field was inserted into document or when all fields were last updated. The Update Field key is F9.
DDE	Contents of field are paste linked from another application and are updated from information added to source file by Update Field (F9)

Word for Windows Field Codes (Adapted with permission from the documentation for Microsoft Word for Windows, Microsoft Corporation, 1990.)

Table 6-2.

Field Code	Result
DDEAUTO	Same as DDE but is automatically updated when change is made to source file
EDITTIME	Inserts the number of minutes that you have spent editing document since its creation from document summary
EQ	Starts a formula (EQ stands for expression) with = sign; see formulas for other formula codes*
FILENAME	Inserts file name from document summary
FILLIN	Prompts you for contents to be typed; \d option tells Word for Windows to use text following it if you type nothing and press ENTER
GLOSSARY	Inserts current glossary listing for glossary name that follows
GOTOBUTTON	Can be used with bookmark and DoFieldClick macro to display bookmark's name in a box that, if double-clicked on, will move cursor to bookmark's text*IF; can be used in normal step-by-step fashion in Conditional field
IMPORT	Can be used to import a document or image from another subdirectory for placement in document (if used below reference, saves hard disk space by not copying referred to file into document); \c option allows document format conversion from non-Word for Windows document
INDEX	Collects and displays Index Entry (XE) fields or outline headings to create an index; \b option collects entries only from pages marked by specific bookmark; \e "-" option will separate an index entry from its page numbers by specified character in quotes (example: Chapter 8, pages 3,5, and 9 reads 8-3,5,9); \g "-" option specifies

Word for Windows Field Codes (continued)

Table 6-2.

Field Code	Result
	that character in quotes is a range separator (example: 17-22); \h option "-A-" shows separation marks for index headings (example: -A-,-B-); \l ";" option shows how to separate numbers (example: 17;22;27); \p "x-z" option shows part of index that should be used (example only x-z); \r option separates topics from subtopics by colons, subtopics are separated by semicolons (example: Topic: subtopic 5, 12; subtopic 7, 29); \s "chapter" \d "-" option specifies second word is a sequence name and symbol (up to 3 characters) separates sequence from index listings (example 8-3 refers to Chapter 8, page 3)
INFO	Inserts this information from document summary
KEYWORDS	Inserts this information from document summary
LASTSAVEDBY	Inserts this information from document summary
MACROBUTTON	Displays Macro name so that if you double click on it, macro is executed[*]
MERGEREC	Inserts the number of the current print merge record; the number is updated with each copy of the print merge printed
NEXT	Prints next record in data document[@]
NEXTIF	Specifies conditions under which to print next record in a data document (example: {NEXTIF area code = 212})[@]
NUMCHARS	Inserts the number of characters listed in the document summary the last time you printed or opened the document summary
NUMPAGES	Inserts the number of pages listed in the document summary the last time you printed or opened the document summary

Word for Windows Field Codes (continued)

Table 6-2.

Field Code	Result
NUMWORDS	Inserts the number of words listed in the document summary the last time you printed or opened the document summary
PAGE	Inserts the number of the page on which the field appears
PAGEREF	Inserts the page number of a bookmark for cross-reference purposes
PRINT	Sends characters without translating them into printer control characters (called "printer literals") allowing you to print any font's entire character set; \p option defines printer literals as PostScript instructions*
PRINTDATE	Inserts the date the document was last printed from the document summary
QUOTE	Inserts following text into document
RD	Referenced Document code used to generate table of contents or index in very large document stored in multiple files@#
REF	Reference to a bookmark to be linked and pasted within a document; if found in a footnote, header, footer, or annotation, the bookmark contents come from the document, not the header or footer
REVNUM	Inserts number of times the document has been revised from document summary
SAVEDATE	Inserts the date the document was last saved from the document summary
SEQ	Inserts a number in a sequence for numbering tables, figures, illustrations, sections, subheadings, headings, titles, and so on
SET	Defines name of a bookmark with text following SET in quotes@
SKIPIF	Combines IF and the opposite of NEXT to be used in creating print merge document

Word for Windows Field Codes (continued)

Table 6-2.

Field Code	Result
STYLEREF	Inserts the text of the nearest paragraph with the style name that follows
SUBJECT	Inserts the subject from the document summary
TC	Text that follows used in creating table of contents; \f option indicates the letter following it as a table ID for the list you want this entry collected into; \l identifies the letter following it as the level number for this table of contents entry[#]
TEMPLATE	Inserts the name of the document's template from the document summary
TIME	Inserts the time Update Fields (F9) was last activated
TITLE	Inserts the title from the document summary
TOC	Collects labeled entries into a table of contents; \b option makes table of contents for portion of document covered by bookmark listed afterwards; \f option makes table of contents from TC fields entries only; \o option makes table of contents from outline; \s option identifies following word as a SEQ field; \s "SEQ" \d ":" option identifies characters (up to 3) to be used to separate a SEQ number from a page number
XE	Provides text and page number for an index entry; \r option identifies the following entry as the range of pages for a bookmark; \t option will print text following it instead of page number; \b option bolds page number in index entry; \i option italicizes page number in an index entry[#]

[*] Fields not affected by the Update Field key (F9)
[#] Fields not affected by the Toggle Field Codes key (SHIFT-F9)
[@] Fields without visible results

Word for Windows Field Codes (continued)

Using the Insert Field Dialog Box

To use the Insert Field command, make sure a file is open and place the cursor at the desired location within the document. Click the left mouse button on the Insert Field command, or press ALT-i, d to display the Insert Field dialog box shown in Figure 6-3. The Insert Field dialog box opens with the cursor on the Insert Field Type scroll box.

Insert Field Type Scroll Box The Insert Field Type scroll box lists all of the field codes. Note that they are listed by name, not by the abbreviated field codes as in Table 6-2; the whole field code name will be inserted inside the field characters. In Figure 6-3, for example, the AUTONUM field type is named "Auto No.," whereas the field code AUTONUM is actually used.

Figure 6-3.

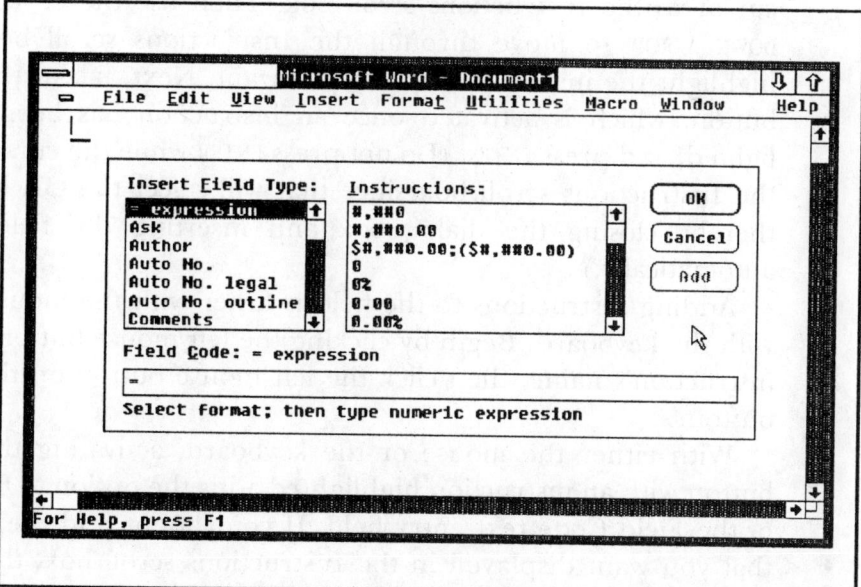

Insert Field dialog box

Instructions Scroll Box   To the right of the Insert Field Type scroll box is the Instructions scroll box. This box contains optional formatting that you can insert in a field. As an example, the Instructions scroll box in Figure 6-3 lists options for formatting the answer to a formula. The first listing, #,##0, formats numeric answers with a comma after every 3 digits, such as 2,353. The third listing formats the answer so it begins with a dollar sign, has a comma every 3 digits before the decimal point, and has only 2 digits after the decimal point (cents); for example, $2,353.00.

Field Code Scroll Box   The actual field code that will be inserted in the document is given in the Field Code text entry field, below the Insert Field Type scroll box. In Figure 6-3, the field code name, = expression, is shown. Below the field code name are the actual codes that will be inserted in the field characters. In the example so far, only the = sign (meaning "start an expression") is listed. You can add instruction options to this text entry field.

If you are using the keyboard, press TAB once to move the cursor to the Instructions scroll box. Then use the UP ARROW or DOWN ARROW to move through the Instructions scroll box and highlight the instruction option you want. Next, tab to the Add button, which is activated once an instruction has been highlighted, and press ENTER. (Do not press ENTER while the cursor is in the Instructions scroll box since that will select the OK button, thereby closing the dialog box and inserting the field code automatically.)

Adding instructions to the field is faster with the mouse than with the keyboard. Begin by clicking the left mouse button on an instruction's name; then click the left mouse button on the Add button.

With either the mouse or the keyboard, activating the Add button with an instruction highlighted adds the option to the end of the Field Code text entry field. If you cannot find the option that you want displayed in the Instructions scroll box, this may mean that the option set is longer than the list space available in the Instructions scroll box. In that case, more options can be exposed either with the mouse or the keyboard. To use the mouse to expose the end of long Instructions option sets, click the left mouse button on the boxed down arrow of the scroll bar at the right of the Instructions scroll box. Then highlight the desired option by clicking the left mouse button on it. To use the keyboard, you press the UP ARROW and DOWN ARROW until the highlight moves onto the desired option. Note also that once an option is added, the OK button will be highlighted and the Add button will be ghosted.

Using either the keyboard or the mouse inserts the instruction into the Field Code text entry field after the field code itself; options are always preceded by a backslash. Note also that formatting options are opened and closed by double quotes. For example, if you click the left mouse button on the first Instructions option in Figure 6-3, this option is inserted in the Field Code text entry field as follows:

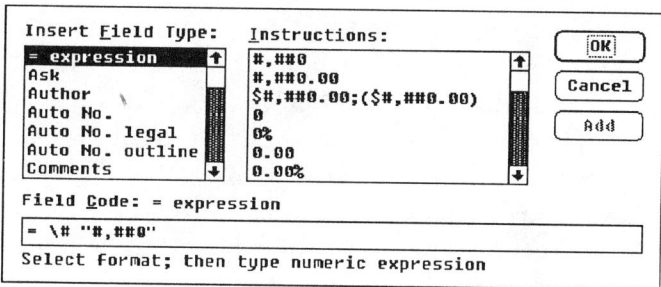

As with other examples, recall that a comma was added between numbers of each magnitude and a dollar sign was placed before a field result that represented a dollar amount. Each inserted option begins with the \# marker as well.

The \# tells Word for Windows that a *Numeric Picture* formatting option is about to follow. (Other types of field code options are discussed in the "Formatting Options" section in this chapter.) A Numeric Picture formatting option tells Word for Windows how to round off and in what format to present the numeric result of a field.

In the example, there is no formula in the field after the = sign and before the numeric picture formatting instructions. You can, however, either tab to the Field Code text entry field or place the mouse on it (the mouse assumes the I-beam text-entry shape on this field) and enter a formula. The characters and syntax you can use in a formula are discussed in Chapter 9.

Formatting Options   Different sets of formatting options are available for some of the field codes. The formatting options appear in the Instructions scroll box when a field code with which they can be used is highlighted in the Insert Field Type scroll box. These options format the results of the entire field that is entered in the Field Code text entry field. You can survey the instruction sets by pressing the UP ARROW or DOWN ARROW while the cursor is in the Insert Field Type scroll box. Note that if a field code does not have any associated options, the Instructions scroll box is ghosted when that field code is highlighted.

There are three basic kinds of instruction sets. Each shows different symbols preceded by a backslash when the symbols are inserted into a field. You have already seen an example of the first type of instruction option, the Numeric Picture instruction option. Numeric Picture options are preceded by the \# characters. These options specify the format for a number that the field will cause to be inserted in the document. This formatting information can include decimal point placement or the inclusion of $ or % signs. All of the Numeric Picture field formatting options are listed in Table 6-3.

Table 6-3.

Field Code	Resulting Format
Decimal Point	".": Used to set the number of numerals to be displayed in the result to the right or the left of the decimal point
Full Variant	"—x—": Displays a positive sign if the result is positive and a negative sign if the result is negative. The two Full Variant signs (—) on either side of the result (use zeros or numeral signs instead of x) are em dashes not minus signs.
Negative sign	"-": Displays a negative sign if the result is negative
Number Sign	"#": Unlike zeros, Number Sign format options do not call for the addition of zeros if there are fewer digits in the result than in the format picture.
Positive sign	"+ +": Displays a positive sign if the result is positive
Thousands Separator	",": Adds a comma if the numeral result is of large enough magnitude (also works with millions, billions, and so on)
Zero	"0": If the result has fewer digits on either side of the decimal point, zeros will be added. If there are additional digits to the left of the decimal point beyond the zeros, these numbers will be added. If there are additional numbers to the right of the decimal point beyond the zeros, these numbers will be rounded off.

Numeric Picture Field Formats (Numeric Picture Options Follow \\#) (Adapted with permission from the documentation for Microsoft Word for Windows, Microsoft Corporation, 1990.)

The options in the second type of instruction set, the General Format options are preceded by the * characters. These options apply to both numbers and text. An example of a text application is the Document Title field code and the Caps option. If the

Author field code was chosen in the Insert Field Type scroll box in the Insert Field dialog box and you then typed * **caps** following it in the Field Code text entry field and pressed ENTER, your name would be taken from the document summary and displayed in initial caps. An example of the general formatting options that apply to numbers is the Roman option. Adding this formatting causes the result to be displayed in Roman numerals. The General Field options are listed in Table 6-4.

The options in the third type of instruction set, the Date-Time Picture field formats, are preceded by the \@ characters. These options apply to your personal computer's calendar and clock outputs. An example of the Date-Time formatting options is the MMM option which causes the month to be displayed by its three-letter abbreviation (JAN, FEB, to DEC). The Date-Time Picture instruction options are listed in Table 6-5.

Inserting Field Codes Manually

To insert field codes and formatting options manually by typing them into a document (bypassing the Insert Field dialog box), you must create field characters in a document. To do so, type CTRL-F9; two field characters, which look like braces ({ } are the uppercase characters on the right and left bracket keys), appear around the cursor. The field characters are not printed; they merely signify to Word for Windows that they contain a field.

After displaying the field characters, you type one or more field codes between them. With some fields, you can also add a field *option*. Field options specify the format for the information that the field codes will insert in the document. To include them, skip one space after the field code, type \ (backslash) followed by one of the three types of options (**#**, *****, or **@**). Then type each option.

Table 6-4.

Field Code	Resulting Format
ALPHABETIC	Changes field results to alphabetic characters
ARABIC	Changes numbers in field results to Arabic cardinal form (example: 1 2 3)
CAPS	Changes all words in field results to initial caps
CARDTEXT	Changes field results to cardinal text form (example: {=* CARDTEXT 1+2} results in three being printed)
CHARFORMAT	Inserts new character format of first character in a field to all following characters
DOLLARTEXT	Changes field results to dollar amount, then adds a fractional representation of cents (example: "{=* DOLLARTEXT 6 + 3.1} Dollars" results in Nine and 10/100 Dollars being printed)
FIRSTCAP	Changes first word in field results to initial caps
HEX	Changes field results to hex form (example: {=* HEX 16 + 31} results in 2F being printed)
LOWER	Changes field results to lower case
MERGEFORMAT	Inserts formatting of the previous result, word for word, to the new result
ORDINAL	Changes numbers in field results to Arabic ordinal form (example: 1st 2nd 3rd)
ORDTEXT	Changes field results to ordinal text form (example: {=* ORDTEXT 1+2} results in third being printed)
ROMAN	Changes numbers in field results to roman numerals (example: I II III)
UPPER	Changes field results to uppercase

General Format Options (General Format Options Follow *) (Adapted with permission from the documentation for Microsoft Word for Windows, Microsoft Corporation, 1990.)

For example, to manually insert your name using the Caps option (initial letters capitalized), press CTRL-F9 and type the following: **{Author * Caps}**.

Table 6-5.

Field Code	Resulting Format
Am/Pm	AM/PM indicates a.m. and p.m. should be displayed in uppercase (example: 1a.m. = 1AM)
	am/pm indicates a.m. and p.m. should be displayed in lowercase (example 1a.m. = 1am)
	A/P indicates a.m. and p.m. should be indicated by uppercase A and P (example 1a.m. = 1A)
	a/p indicates a.m. and p.m. should be indicated by lowercase a and p (example: 1a.m. = 1a)
Day	D indicates day as one or two digits (example: first day of month is 1)
	DD indicates day as two digits, inserting 0 before days 1-9 (example: 1st day of month is 01)
	DDD indicates three letter abbreviation of day of the week (example: Monday is Mon)
	DDDD indicates unabbreviated spelling of day of the week (example: Monday)
Hours	h indicates using the 12-hour time scale without a zero before 1-9a.m. or p.m. (example: 1p.m. = 1)
	hh indicates using the 12-hour time scale; zero is to be added before 1-9a.m. or p.m. (example: 1pm = 01)
	H indicates using the 24 hour time scale without a zero before 1-9a.m. (example: 1a.m. = 1)
	HH indicates using the 24 hour time scale; zero is to be added before 1-9a.m. (example: 1a.m. = 01)
Literal Texts	'x' indicates that text inside single quotes (x) should be printed literally

Date-Time Picture Field Formats (Date-Time Field Options Follow \@) (Adapted with permission from the documentation for Microsoft Word for Windows, Microsoft Corporation, 1990.)

Table 6-5.

Field Code	Resulting Format
Minutes	m indicates no zero is to be added before minutes 1-9 (example: minute 1 = 1) mm indicates zero is to be added before minutes 1-9 (example: minute 1 = 01) Note: lowercase m must be added to distinguish minutes from month
Month	M indicates month as one or two digits (example: January is 1) MM indicates month as two digits, inserting 0 before January through September (example: January is 01) MMM indicates month as three letter abbreviation (example: January is Jan) MMMM indicates month as full name (example: January) Note: uppercase M must be used to distinguish Month from Minutes
Year	YY indicates last two digits of year (example: 1990 = 90) YYYY indicates unabbreviated date is to be used (example: 1990)

Date-Time Picture Field Formats (Date-Time Field Options Follow \@) (continued)

Then highlight the whole field and press F9, the Update Fields key (discussed in "Keeping Fields Up to Date" later in this chapter). You will see the hourglass appear showing you that Word for Windows is looking in the document summary for your name (the author's name). Then, leaving the field highlighted, press SHIFT-F9 to replace the field codes with the field results. SHIFT-F9 is the Field Codes toggle key; it is discussed in "Using the Field Codes Toggle Key" in this chapter.

You can include literal text to be printed with the option if you surround it with single quotes (see Literal Texts in Table 6-5). Field options are discussed in the section "Formatting Options."

You can also insert fields within fields; this is called nesting and it is discussed in "Nesting Field Codes" later in this chapter.

Using the Field Codes Toggle Key

When you insert a field code with the Insert Fields dialog box and the View Fields command off, you will not see the field code itself; rather you will see the result of the field code. You can, however, display field codes in order to edit them or add options to format their results.

To display a single field code that has been inserted in your document with the Insert Fields dialog box, simply highlight the field's result and press the Field Codes toggle key, SHIFT-F9. Highlighting a field code and pressing SHIFT-F9 alternately hides and displays the field code and the result of this field. In addition, you can toggle the display of field codes and their results on and off throughout the entire document with the Field Codes command in the Edit menu.

Keeping Fields Up to Date

If you are using fields from the Edit Summary Info dialog box, such as the Date Last Saved, Date Last Printed, or Number of Words, which change as you work, the field code will tell Word for Windows to print the information that was present when you opened the document. In fact, many of the document summary field values change as you work, so you would want to update these fields just before you print. For example, the number of words and characters in a document changes as you work.

However, if you inserted these field codes before the current work session, the fields will contain the information found in the document summary when you opened Word for Windows. If you inserted the fields in the current work session, the results of these field codes will exhibit the values true at the time of insertion.

The same is also true if you used the DDE field to paste link an image or a chart from another application (DDE Paste Link is discussed in Chapter 11, "Fine Tuning Windows"). If you added data to the source of the image or chart since you opened your Word for Windows document, the image or chart will not be updated.

You can insert the most current information into almost all field codes in a document with the Field Update key, F9. Not all fields are updatable. Those that are not appear with an asterisk in Table 6-2. All fields that are updatable are automatically updated when you activate the Field Update key. You can lock an updatable field with the \! Lock Formatting option. This is discussed in the "Locking Fields" section later in this chapter.

Nesting Field Codes

Inserting fields within fields is called nesting. One example of nesting fields is formulas, which will be discussed in Chapter 9. In a formula you might want to insert the numeric result of one field within another formula field. You nest fields in two ways. You can either insert an existing field within a new field or insert a new field within an existing field. Each field within a field is considered to be nested one level.

To nest an existing field within a new field, first highlight the existing field. Then insert a field with either the Insert Field dialog box or manually with the keyboard (CTRL-F9); the highlighted field would then be subsumed, or nested, inside the newly added field. The newly nested field would not change. It would also retain its right and left field characters. The presence of field characters within field characters would tip you off that this was a nested field.

If you want to insert a field within an existing field, place the cursor at the location inside the existing field where you want to insert the new field. Then insert the new field either with the Insert Field command or manually with the CTRL-F9 keystroke combination.

You can also nest documents within documents or images within documents with the Include field code. If you use the Include field code to insert a document inside another document, and then include a document or an image within the included document, you will have created a nested Include field. You can nest entries up to 20 levels; in other words, 19 insertions within insertions is the limit.

Locking Fields

If you have nested field codes within other field codes, the result of the entire field is partially dependent on the nested field code. For example, if you are using the result of one formula as data for another formula, the result of the initial formula will in part determine the result of the second formula. If you want the nested field code to become a constant after you insert it, add the \! option to it. This will lock the nested field code's value or text even if you press the Update Field key (F9). Unless they are locked, nested entries are normally updated before the fields that contain them when you press F9.

Macros

You may already be familiar with the power of macros. Macros are present in Word 4.0 and 5.0, as well as in Lotus 1-2-3, Excel 2.1, and a host of other applications. In addition, programs such as SuperKey and ProKey are devoted to bringing macros to all applications. Even if you are not familiar with these applications, you *are* familiar with the ALT-*key*, CTRL-*key*, and SHIFT-*key* combinations mentioned so far in this book; they are all macros. Basically, macros are a sequence of actions that have been saved to a single key or keystroke combination. The actions you perform in Word for Windows include highlighting blocks of text, choosing menu commands, selecting options in dialog boxes, pressing keyboard command keys, and typing text. All of these actions can be saved to a macro key or keystroke combination.

Keep in mind that when you save a macro to a single key, you are in effect redefining that key. You must therefore be sure you do not need that key's default function. Word for Windows will remind you if you are choosing a keystroke combination for a new macro that has already been assigned, and asks you if you want to reassign it. You do not have to save macros to ALT-*key*, CTRL-*key*, or SHIFT-*key* combinations. You can choose keys other than ALT, CTRL, and SHIFT to use in keystroke combinations. However, you should keep in mind the risk of accidentally setting off a macro by typing whatever keystroke combination you choose.

Word for Windows macros are mostly used for frequently performed tasks. These tasks include standard operations that normally involve more than one keystroke, such as displaying the File Open dialog box with a list of files in a specific directory on your hard disk, displaying Print Preview with the Boundaries button active, or printing without changing any of the default options.

You can also design macros that accomplish different tasks depending upon specific information that you supply. Macros that act upon information you input are termed *interactive*. For example, you can write a macro that asks you which document file subdirectory to use before displaying the File Open dialog box. You will implement an interactive macro in "Creating an Interactive Print Merge Macro" later in this chapter. Word for Windows has a BASIC-like macro language that enables you to write simple or complex interactive macros; this macro language is discussed later in this chapter under "Macro Editor."

Auto Macros

Word for Windows comes with several Auto macros. The Auto New macro automatically updates fields in a document template. You could, for example, configure it to update the Date field and the Time field when you load a letter or memo document template (remember, these fields will be the same as when you last saved the template unless you update them). The AutoOpen macro runs after you open a document from the File Open or File Find dialog box or from the list of most recently opened documents at the bottom of the File menu.

Another Auto macro, the AutoExec macro, runs when you open Word for Windows. You can program this macro to automatically open the most recently opened document when you open Word for Windows. To do this, type the following line and save it to the macro named AutoExec (see the "Macro Edit" section later in this chapter):

if filename$ ( ) = "" then fileopen filename$ (1)

and press ENTER.

This command accomplishes the same result as the Word/l option of Word 4.0 and 5.0. And, like these programs, you can load a document from the DOS prompt. For example, if the document you wanted to load was MEMO.DOC, you would open Word for Windows from the C:\ prompt with the command:

C:\> WIN WINWORD MEMO

and press ENTER.

If MEMO.DOC was not the most recently opened file, it would still be loaded, overriding the AutoExec macro. You could also override the AutoExec macro by opening Word for Windows at the C:\ prompt with the /M option:

WIN WINWORD /M

and press ENTER.

The AutoClose macro runs when you close a document window, and the AutoExit macro runs when you close Word for Windows.

These examples show that Word for Windows lets you add new commands to existing macros and assign commands to different keys on the keyboard. In addition, Word for Windows lets you add a macro to a menu and activate it there. Moreover, as has been mentioned, macros can be saved either to a single document template or globally so they are available from all document templates. The rest of this chapter will cover macros in greater detail. You will first learn how to create macros.

Macro Recorder

You begin to construct a macro while you are working on a document. When you know the action you are about to perform will be useful to you later, initiate the Macro Record command. The Macro Record command, shown here,

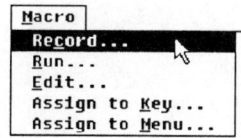

is in the Macro menu. The Macro Record command opens the Macro Record dialog box shown in Figure 6-4. When the dialog box opens, the cursor is in the Record Macro Name text entry field, which has a default macro name, Macro1. Enter the name of the new macro in the Record Macro Name text entry field by overtyping Macro1. When you start to type the name, the default macro name will disappear and the OK button will become available (it is ghosted when you open the dialog box). Do not leave any spaces between the letters. Next you can type a short explanation of what the macro will do in the Description text entry field below the Context option set. The description can be up to 256 characters long, but try to keep it succinct so you get the gist of it without having to scroll across this text entry field.

The Context option set, below the Record Macro Name text entry field, is set on Global by default. The Template option

Figure 6-4.

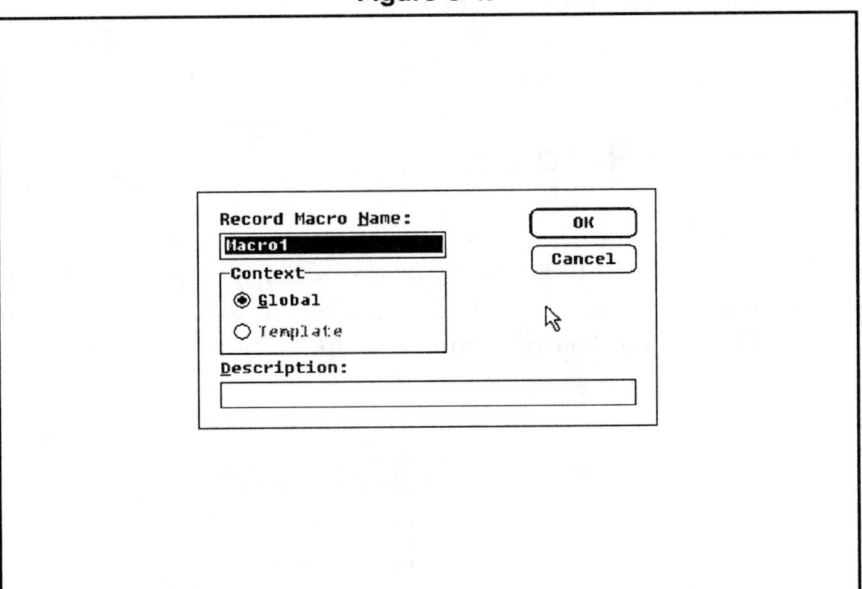

Macro Record dialog box

is ghosted here because no template has been chosen nor is one being created. The active template is the default NORMAL.DOT, and macros saved to it are, in effect, global.

To begin entering the information that is to be saved by the macro, either press ENTER or click the left mouse button on the OK button. This tells Word for Windows to save all keystrokes and mouse actions that you enter until you activate the Stop Recorder command (ALT-m, c). While you are recording keystrokes, the Macro Recorder is active. For example, you can make a macro that will automatically activate Print Preview with the Boundaries button active. To do this, activate the Macro Record command. Type **PrintPreviewBoundary** (no spaces) in the Record Macro Name text entry field. Next, type **Print Preview w/Boundaries Active** in the Description text entry field. Then activate the OK button. The Macro Record dialog box is now active; all commands executed will be saved to the PrintPreviewBoundary macro until you deactivate the Macro Recorder. Now activate the File Print Preview command. Next, activate the Boundaries button. Finally, activate the Macro Stop Recorder command. This macro is now available for use in all of your Word for Windows documents. Deleting the macro is discussed in "Macro Edit Command" later in this chapter.

The Macro Record dialog box shown in Figure 6-4 can also be displayed by pressing ALT-m, then c. Note that when you press ALT-m while the Macro Recorder is activated, the Macro menu no longer contains a Macro Record command. Instead, there is a Stop Recorder command with the "c" underlined. You use the same ALT-m, c keystroke combination that is used to start the Macro Recorder to stop it. In this way, the Macro Record command works as a toggle switch.

Macro Run Command

The Macro Run command is in the Macro menu. It causes the Macro Run dialog box, shown here,

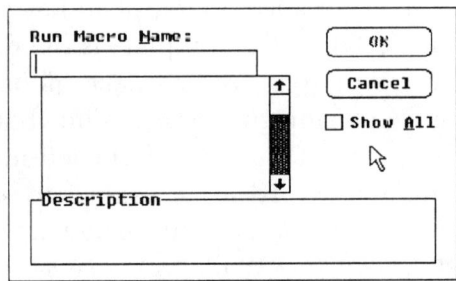

to be displayed. The Macro Run dialog box lets you select any of the macros you have created or any of the Word for Windows default macros. If you have not created any macros, none will be listed in the Run Macro Name text entry field or the Run Macro Name scroll box the first time you open this dialog box.

To list all of the default Word for Windows macros, activate the Show All toggle box below the Cancel button. The Run Macro Description box shows you a description of the macro that is highlighted in the Run Macro Name field. Note that you can see three lines in each macro's description in the Macro Run dialog box Description field, whereas you can only see one in the Macro Record dialog box Description field where you originally typed the description.

Once you have highlighted a macro in the Run Macro Name field, the OK button is also activated (it is no longer ghosted). To run the highlighted macro, you can either click the left mouse button on the OK button or press ENTER.

Assign to Key

The Macro menu has an Assign to Key command that activates the Macro Assign to Key dialog box shown in Figure 6-5. All of the Word for Windows macros, both the default macros and the ones

Figure 6-5.

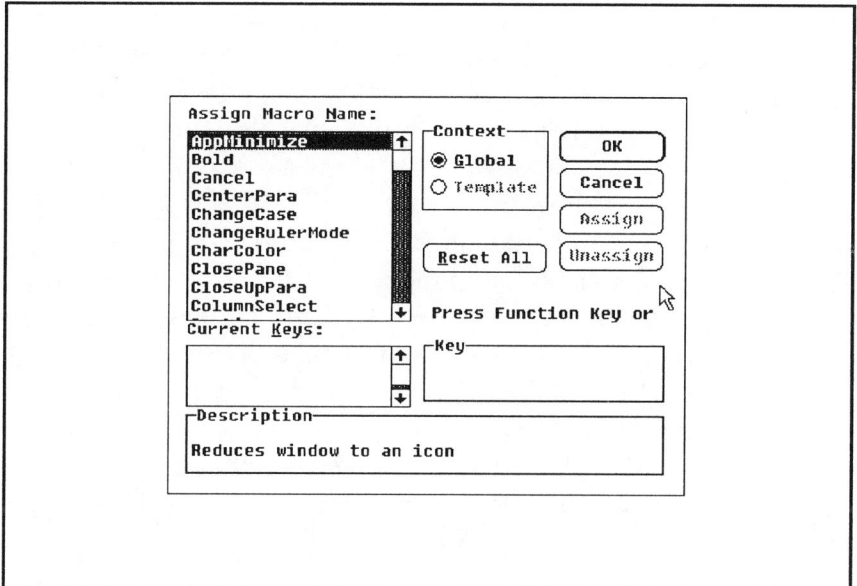

Macro Assign to Key dialog box

you create, are listed in the Assign Macro Name scroll box. Some of these macros are internal to Word for Windows and therefore are not assigned to any key or keystroke combination. For example, the first macro listed, AppMinimize, has no listing in the Current Keys scroll box. A synopsis of what each macro does is displayed in the Description box at the bottom of the Macro Assign to Key dialog box as each macro is highlighted in the Assign Macro Name scroll box.

When you highlight a macro such as Bold which has a key or keystroke combination assignment, the keystroke(s) will be listed in the Current Keys scroll box. If you then highlight the CTRL-B macro that appears in the Current Keys scroll box and activate the Unassign button, the CTRL-B macro disappears. You can now type a different keystroke combination in the Current Keys scroll box; the Key text box will then list any current setting that the keystroke combination has associated with it. Once you have a setting that you would rather use than CTRL-B, you can activate the Assign button. The Bold macro will be assigned to this new macro. If you change your mind and want to go back to the previous macro key assignment, you can activate the Unassign or Close button any time before you press ENTER or click the left mouse button on the OK button.

If you change default macros and decide you want to go back to the original key assignments, you do not have to reinstall Word for Windows. Look up the default macro key assignments in the Word for Windows documentation and reassign the keys to match the default condition. You can also print out the default macro key assignments before you make any changes with the File Print Command's Macro option (see Chapter 5, "Printing: Picture Perfect Output," for a discussion of the File Print dialog box).

Assign to Menu

If you find that you frequently use several of your macros and think it would be easier to access them from a menu rather than via the keyboard, you can assign a macro that you have created to one of the Word for Windows menus. This is done with the Assign to Menu command in the Macro menu. The Macro Assign to Menu command activates the Macro Assign to Menu dialog box.

The Macro Assign to Menu dialog box is shown in Figure 6-6. The Assign Macro Name scroll box lists all the current macros. The Menu scroll box lists all of Word for Windows menus. The Description text entry field describes the highlighted macro. The Menu Text scroll box lists all the commands currently assigned to the highlighted menu. The Context box lets you set where the menu will be changed.

When you first open the Macro Assign to Menu dialog box, the Template option is ghosted because the NORMAL.DOT template is active and any changes you make will be global. When you

Figure 6-6.

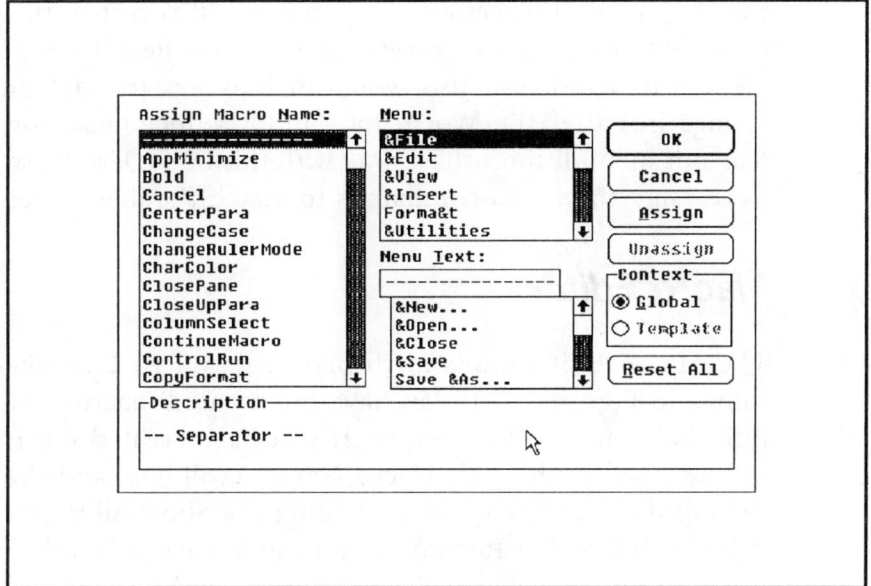

Macro Assign to Menu dialog box

highlight a macro in the Assign Macro Name scroll box, it appears in the Menu Text text entry field. Use the Reassign button to place commands that are already assigned to a menu into different menus. If you make a mistake assigning a command to a menu, use the Unassign button to take the command back out of the menu. The Separator option, which is the first listing by default, is not a command. When it is placed between commands in a menu, it causes a horizontal line to be drawn across the menu at this location to indicate a new category of commands within the menu. You can activate the Cancel or Unassign button if you want to delete the changes made in the Macro Assign to Menu dialog box. Otherwise, the changes you make are recorded when you press ENTER or click the left mouse button on the OK button.

If you change the default menu listings and decide you want to go back to the original assignments, you do not have to reinstall

Word for Windows. You can delete the WINWORD.INI file from
the WINWORD directory. The menus will revert to the default
condition, along with everything else, the next time you load
Word for Windows. Also, you can look up the default menu
listings in either the Word for Windows documentation or the
tear-out menu listings that come with this book. Use these listings
to reassign the menu commands to match the default condition.

Macro Editor

The Macro Edit command displays the Macro Edit dialog box
shown in Figure 6-7. If you have not created macros, the Macro
Edit dialog box will be empty. If you have created macros, they
will be listed in the Edit Macro Name scroll box, and the cursor
will highlight the first one. Activating the Show All toggle box (it
is found below the Rename button in Figure 6-7) will cause all

Figure 6-7.

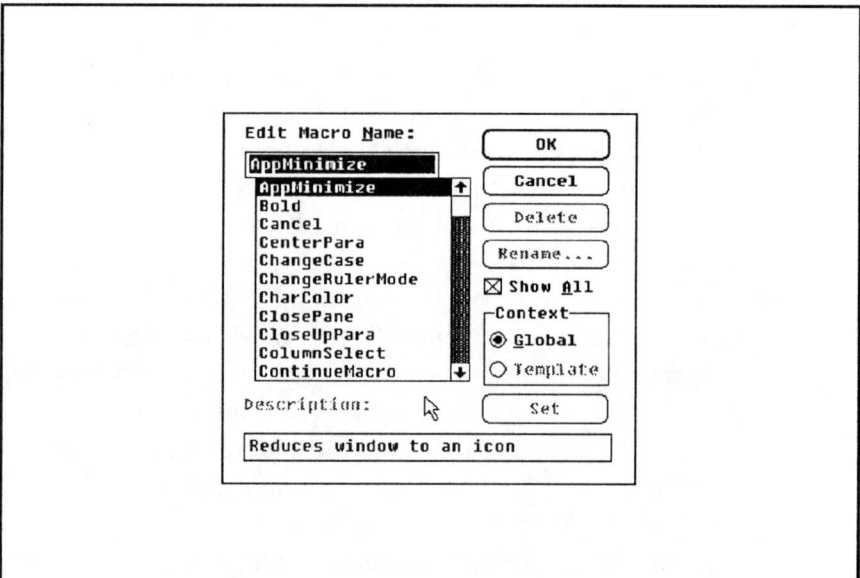

Macro Edit dialog box

of the default macros to be displayed in the Edit Macro Name field, as seen in Figure 6-7. The description of each macro appears in the Description field.

The Delete button deletes a macro. The Rename button becomes available when a macro you have created is highlighted. Activating the Rename button after highlighting Macro1 (a non-default Macro) displays the Rename dialog box as shown in Figure 6-8. Here you can type over the macro's original name and save a new name by clicking the left mouse button on the OK button or by pressing ENTER. The Set button adds a new description of a macro if you type over the original listing.

You will not be able to choose the Template Context option in the Macro Edit dialog box unless you have loaded a document template other than NORMAL.DOT. This is because any changes made to this default document template are considered global.

When you are finished selecting a macro to edit in the Macro Edit dialog box, you can bring up the Word for Windows Macro

Figure 6-8.

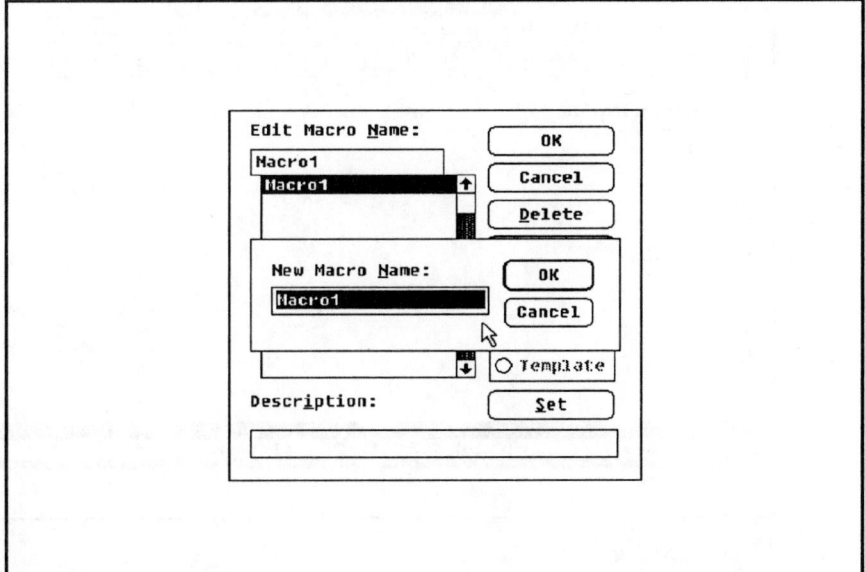

Renaming Macro1

Editor, shown in Figure 6-9, in one of these ways. You can press ENTER, click the left mouse button on the OK button, or double-click (click the left mouse button twice rapidly) on a macro name listed in the Macro Edit Name scroll box.

The Macro Editor has five Macro Edit buttons in a button bar under the Word for Windows menu bar. The name of the current macro is listed at the end of the Macro Editor button bar. The Start button runs the macro. In this case, Word for Windows would be minimized to an icon. If you highlight a line of the macro, the Step button will run the instructions in that one line. When you run one line of the macro, the Start button converts to a Continue button. Activating the Continue button runs the rest of the macro. The Step SUBS button runs a single line from a macro and then stops; if the macro is one you created, however, the Step SUBS button runs it in its entirety in a single step. The Trace

Figure 6-9.

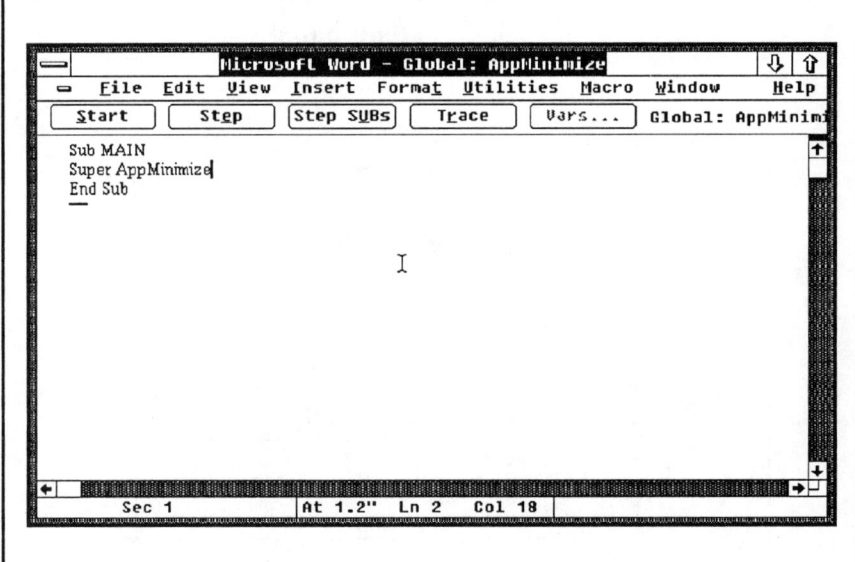

Macro Edit buttons

button runs each line of the macro, highlighting each line as the macro is carried out. The Vars button brings up a dialog box showing the variables used by the macro. If there are no variables used, as in this case, the Vars button is ghosted.

If you had edited a macro (or created a new one, as you will do in the "Creating an Interactive Print Merge Macro" section), like the AutoExec Macro addition suggested in this chapter's "Macros" section, the Macro Edit screen would be displayed with the command Sub MAIN on the first line, a blinking cursor waiting for you to enter Word for Windows macro language commands on the second line, and End Sub on the third line. To install the AutoExec macro listed in the "Macros" section, type

if filename$ ( ) = "" then fileopen filename$ (1)

on the blank second line. Then you would activate the Start button to run the macro and save your entry.

In Figure 6-9, the AppMinimize macro starts with the command line Sub MAIN. All Word for Windows macros start with this command because the Word for Windows macros actually perform as subroutines of the Word for Windows program. Thus, when you create a macro, you are actually adding a subroutine to the code that makes up the Word for Windows program. The Word for Windows macro language is, in fact, a subset of the BASIC computer language. Its commands are listed in the Technical Reference Guide that comes with Word for Windows. In Figure 6-9, the Super command tells Word for Windows to ignore the current layer and drop down to the next layer, where it finds that the AppMinimize command collapses Windows programs into icons. The End Sub command closes the macro.

Now, to get a feeling for the power that is available to you with the Word for Windows macro language, go through the following example, "Creating an Interactive Print Merge Macro."

Creating an Interactive Print Merge Macro

In this example, you will implement an interactive Word for Windows macro that sorts the names and addresses you enter into a Print Merge data base and puts the ones you want to use for a particular mailing into a temporary data document. Before you begin, there are some terms with which you should be familiar. Word 4.0, 5.0, and Word for Windows all refer to a print merge data base as a data document. A data document contains records that are inserted into a *print merge document*. Print merge documents are usually form letters or mailing labels. Chapter 9 gives some examples of print merge documents.

The first task in using the interactive print merge macro is to create a data document, a data base of names and addresses for the macro to sort.

Word for Windows Data Documents

Creating a print merge data document is not new to Word for Windows; Word 4.0 and 5.0 both have Print Merge commands. What is new in Word for Windows is the added flexibility in the data document structure. The common data document format in all versions of Word has each entry within records separated by a comma (comma-delimited fields) and each complete record separated by a carriage return (ENTER). Word for Windows gives you more of a choice by also letting you enter data in tab-delimited or table format.

The addition of the table format is a major advance in Word for Windows over Word 4.0 and 5.0. Using column and row format makes data entry and editing much easier than they are with a comma- or tab-delimited structure.

One problem with the Word 4.0 and 5.0 comma-delimited data document structure is that you cannot see if there are enough or too few entries in each record. Even if there is no data for a particular entry in a record, you must still enter a comma. That is because Word 4.0 and 5.0 count the commas in order to know how to use each entry. It is very difficult to count the number of commas in each record. It is also difficult to gauge the placement of commas in each record to see if they match the format of the data document set out in the first record. If you are missing an entry, such as the phone number for one record, you must still enter a comma to signify the position of that field. If you forget to do so, the Word 4.0 or 5.0 print merge will often fail entirely. And if you have used the Word 4.0 or 5.0 print merge, you know that it is difficult to see where you have forgotten or misplaced one comma in a large data document.

Entering records into rows and columns in a Word for Windows table is much easier than counting commas. There is another advantage to using the table format for a data document in Word for Windows. If you do not have an entry in one cell in a record, Word for Windows does not crash during the print merge because you have forgotten a comma. It recognizes an empty cell as a complete, not missing, entry.

Another advantage of the Word for Windows flexible data document structure is that you can always convert any one of the three formats into either of the other two (see Chapter 3, "Cut and Paste: Adding Tables and Images" for a discussion of converting comma- and tab-delimited data entries into tables and vice versa). The conversion feature also allows you to import Word 4.0 and 5.0 comma-delimited data documents into Word for Windows data documents and convert them to table format. In Chapter 9 you will learn how to import data from Windows and non-Windows data base programs into a Word for Windows data document.

The first record in a Word for Windows data document always contains a list of bookmark names such as Lastname, Firstname, Business, Address, City, State, Zip, and Phone. This first record is not printed by the print merge document; Word for Windows considers the record following it to be data record number 1. Thus, record number 1 might be "Smith, David, PC Systems, 19 Java St., Brooklyn, NY, 11222, (718) 322-9979 <ENTER>." Each additional record would be input in the same way. The bookmark names in the first record are included in the fields that will be used in a print merge document such as a form letter or a mailing label template.

Create an eight-column, six-row table, leaving the last row blank. You can use the sample data in Table 6-6 if you wish, or make up your own. Save the table as DATA.DOC. Recall that you create a table with the Insert Table command. Remember also that you can move forward between cells and add new rows with

Table 6-6.

LastName	FirstName	Business	Address	City
Smith	David	PC Systems	19 Java St.	Brooklyn
Granger	Debby	Computer World	84 Great Jones St.	Brooklyn
McGillicutty	Lucy	Software City	117 West 23 St.	New York
Forsberg	Daniel	Deep Rom	155 Central Park W.	New York

Sample Print Merge DATA.DOC

the TAB key. (For more details on table construction, see Chapter 3, "Cut and Paste: Adding Tables and Images.") If you create your own data, be sure the first column contains the criterion on which you want to sort the data document; last name is the most common criterion.

Interactive Print Merge Macro

You will now implement an interactive macro that will be used with the data document, DATA.DOC, that you just created. The macro will list each record and ask you if you want to include it in a new, temporary data document. The temporary data document in no way affects your permanent data document. Rather, it lets you select individuals in your data document whom you want to include in a form letter mailing or for whom you want to create mailing labels. You list the name of the temporary data document in your print merge document, create the form letters or labels you need with the print merge document, and then discard the temporary data document by quitting Word for Windows without saving it. This macro will sort through any Word for Windows data document that is in table format. (However, it will not work with either a comma- or tab-delimited data document.) The process of having a print merge document use temporary and other types of data documents in Word for Windows is discussed in Chapter 9.

After you enter the data in Table 6-6, or your own data, and save it as DATA.DOC (see the "Word for Windows Data Documents" section), your Word for Windows screen should look like that seen in Figure 6-10. Note that there is a blank row at the bottom of the table. The interactive Print Merge macro that you are about to construct will automatically ignore both blank rows and any records that begin with an empty cell.

Figure 6-10.

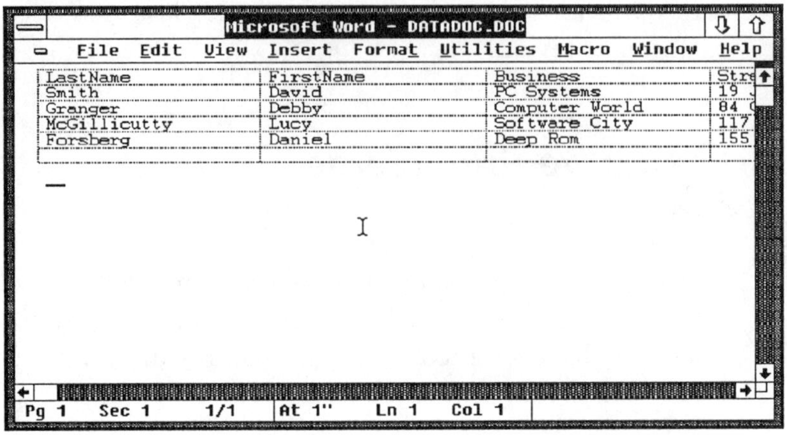

Data document table

You can now begin to create the macro. First, activate the Macro Edit command (see "Macro Editor" earlier in this chapter). Name the macro you are about to create "FormLetter," as shown in Figure 6-11; then activate the OK button.

Once you have activated the OK button in the Macro Edit dialog box, you see the features shown in Figure 6-12. The Macro Edit menu bar will appear on the screen. The document listed at the top of the screen will be Global: FormLetter. This indicates that you are working on a global macro that will be named FormLetter. (The macro could have been attached to a particular document template if you had opened one before you created DATA.DOC. In the example, only NORMAL.DOT is available, but remember you can save this macro later to a specific document template and delete it from the list of global macros in the Macro Edit dialog box.) The FormLetter macro name is listed to

Figure 6-11.

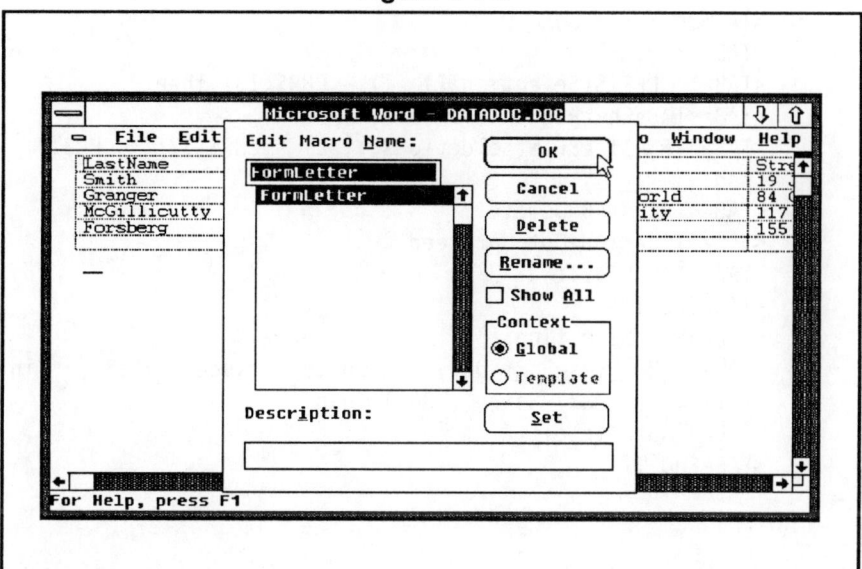

Opening Macro Edit over data document

the right of the Vars button in the Macro Edit menu bar. Finally, two commands, with an open line in between, appear in the document window. These two commands, Sub MAIN and End Sub, tell you that Word for Windows will treat your macro as a subprogram.

The cursor is at the end of the line listing Sub MAIN. Make sure that you press ENTER at the end of each line. Also, make sure that you type a zero, not the letter "O," when you see a lone 0. Your screen should look like Figure 6-13.

```
Sub MAIN
FileNew .Template = FileName$()
While CmpBookmarks("\sel", "\endofdoc")
<TAB>LineDown 1
<TAB>On Error Goto bye
```

```
<TAB>NextCell
<TAB>On Error Goto 0
<TAB>PrevCell
<TAB>If LEFT$(Selection$(), 1) = CHR$(13) Then
<TAB><TAB>CharRight 1, 1
<TAB><TAB>If LEFT$(Selection$(), 2) = CHR$(13) + CHR$(7)
Then
<TAB><TAB><TAB>Deleteit
<TAB><TAB><TAB>Goto proceed
<TAB><TAB>End If
<TAB>End If
<TAB>A$ = Selection$()
<TAB>If Not (MsgBox("Do you wish to include " + a$ + " in your
mailing?", "Mail Merge", 36)) Then
<TAB><TAB>Deleteit
<TAB>End If
```

Figure 6-12.

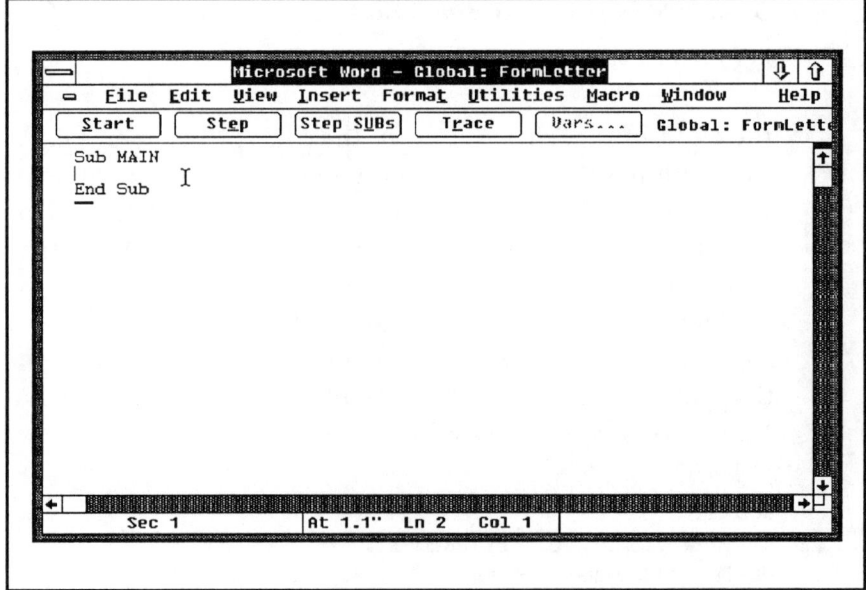

Begin entering FormLetter macro on open second line

```
proceed:
Wend
bye: Print "Macro Completed"
End Sub

Sub Deleteit
<TAB><TAB>EndOfRow 1
<TAB><TAB>EditTable 0, .Delete
<TAB><TAB>LineUp 1
End Sub
```

(Permission granted by Michel Girard, Microsoft Corporation, for use of this macro.)

Double check your entry to make sure that it is exactly the same as the preceding listing.

Although the BASIC commands in this macro may look foreboding, this macro is not complicated. The first line, after the obligatory Sub MAIN line, tells Word for Windows that it will be

Figure 6-13.

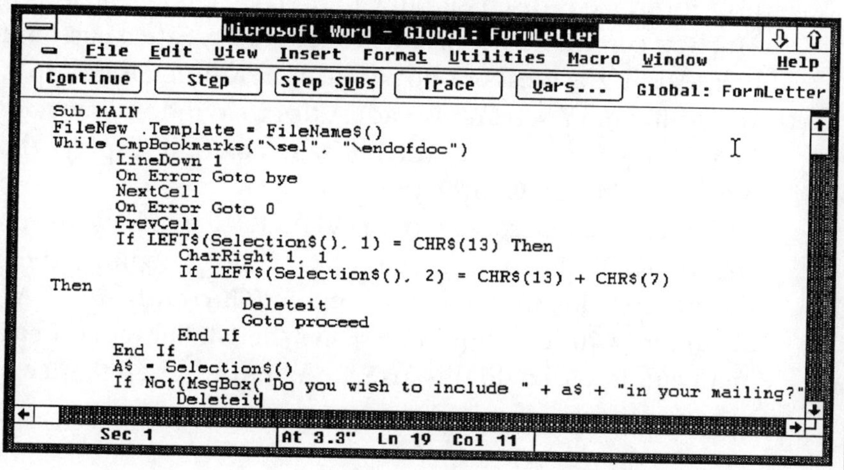

Interactive Print Merge macro in Macro Edit

creating a new file. (This new file will be the temporary data document you create after you have sorted through each record to decide which ones to keep.) The second line tells Word for Windows that it will be looking at the first bookmark name in the print merge data document. The next 16 lines, ending with the last End If, are devoted to deleting records that begin with an empty cell. The key lines here are the two that begin "If LEFT$(Selection$( ),". These lines are asking if the first cell is empty. If it is, the entire row is deleted. If it is not empty, the Macro displays a message box (MsgBox) querying you: "Do you wish to include" the row named by the first cell (A$) "in your mailing." The last five lines, the Deleteit subroutine, delete a line with an empty first cell or one you told the macro you do not want to keep. When you have gone through all the records in your data document, you will see the message "Macro Completed" and a new data document will have been created containing only the records you want to include.

Part of the power of the Word for Windows macro language comes from the Windows graphical user interface (the graphical user interface is discussed in Chapter 1, "Up and Running"). The MsgBox command in this macro lets you create a custom message box. Adding a message box to a nongraphic DOS application is very difficult. You can also add titles to Windows message boxes. Mail Merge is the title of the message box that displays the closing message, "Macro Completed."

To test the macro with the DATA.DOC, you have to reopen the DATA.DOC document window while keeping the Global: FormLetter document window open. (Currently, the DATA.DOC document window should be *under* the Global: FormLetter document window.) To do this, use the Window Arrange All command, as shown here.

The Window Arrange All command displays all open documents in equal-sized document windows.

Your screen should look like that in Figure 6-14. You will be able to see all of the data entries in DATA.DOC. Note the empty record at the end of DATA.DOC. You will also see that the Macro Edit menu bar is still active at the top of the screen. You will now use it to test your macro.

To test the macro, DATA.DOC must be the active document. The Edit Macro screen will use whichever document window is active. In Figure 6-14, the left mouse button is being clicked on the DATA.DOC document title bar; this activates the DATA. DOC document window. Note that only one window has a document Control button at a time. In Figure 6-14, the DATA.DOC window has the Control button; there is no Control button in the Global: FormLetter document window. If the Global: Form-

Figure 6-14.

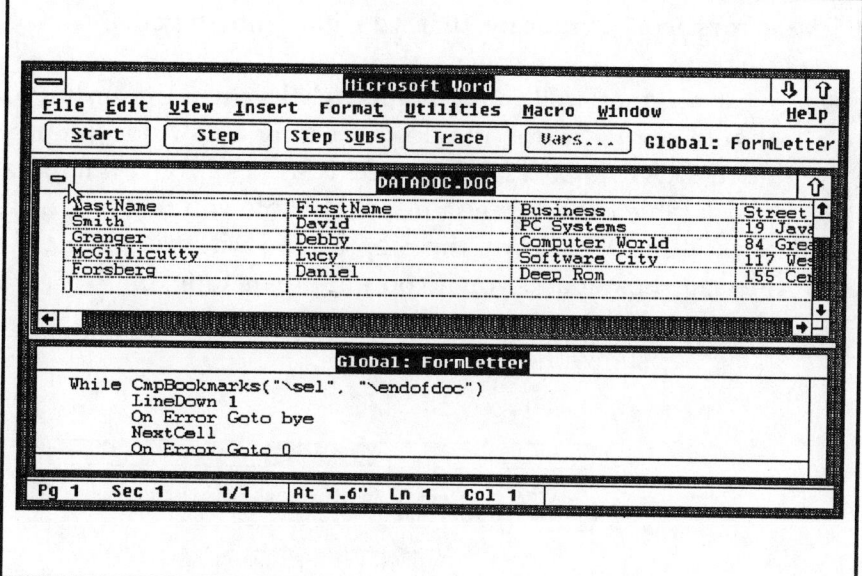

Activating DATA.DOC document window

Letter document window has the Control button, click the left mouse button on the DATA.DOC window's title bar and the Control button will shift.

As mentioned in the "Macro Editor" section, the Step button of the Macro Edit menu bar will check your macro line by line to see if it is functioning correctly. You can activate the Step button as shown here.

Continue clicking the left mouse button on the Step button. You will see each line highlighted as it is read and acted on by Word for Windows each time you press the Step button. If there is any problem with a line of the macro, you will get an error message. If you get an error message stating that you have a path error or the current document is not valid for the operation, you have probably not made DATA.DOC the active document. Other errors would indicate that you have not typed the macro text correctly.

If all goes well, after several clicks on the Step button, you should see Word for Windows creating a new document window titled DOCUMENT2.DOC. DOCUMENT2.DOC will initially display a table exactly the same as the table you had in DATA.DOC. Several more clicks on the Step button will bring you to the first message box; it asks you if you want to include Smith (or whatever the first LastName was that you entered in your DATA.DOC table), as shown here.

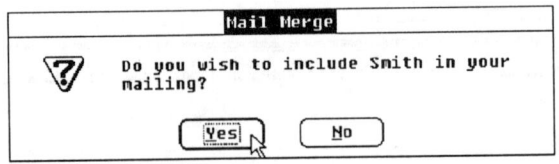

If you continue clicking the left mouse button on the Step button, you will be queried about all the records in your DATA.DOC. If you answer No, you will see the record being deleted. Finally, the macro will detect the empty row at the bottom of the table and will automatically delete it. Then you will get the message "Macro Completed."

DOCUMENT2.DOC is your new temporary data document to be used in a print merge operation. If you had chosen to keep all four records in Table 6-6, DOCUMENT2.DOC would look like Figure 6-15.

You can now use the File Open command to display another document window with a print merge document. You would insert DOCUMENT2.DOC in a field that tells Word for Windows it is to be used as the data document. Then you would activate the File Print Merge command. Once you had printed all of the form

Figure 6-15.

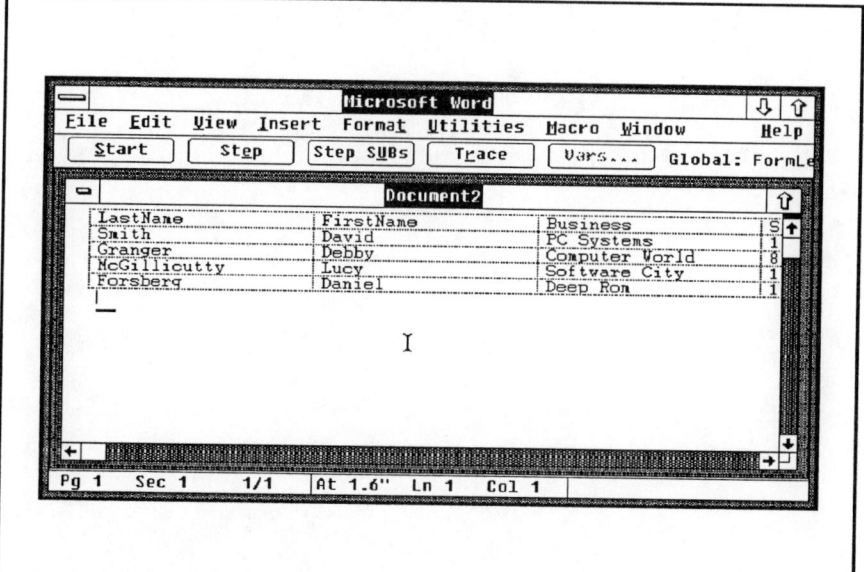

Temporary data document, Document2, created by interactive Print Merge macro

letters or labels you wanted, you could close Word for Windows and opt not to save DOCUMENT2.DOC. The use of both temporary and permanent data documents, as well as data documents created with the assistance of both Windows and non-Windows data bases, will be discussed in Chapter 9.

As with styles and templates (discussed in Chapter 4), glossaries, boilerplate text, fields, and macros offer you a great deal of power in recording formatting, text, and other actions you perform while using Word for Windows. As you continue reading, you will see that you can use these features to train Word for Windows to aid you in almost all your information processing projects.

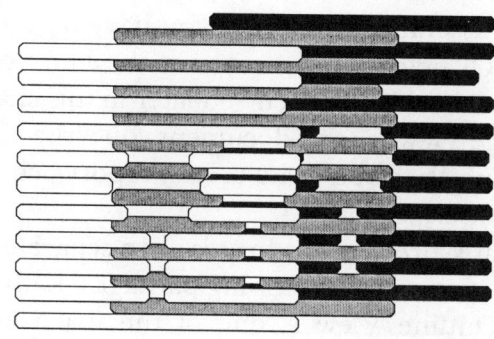

7

Time Saving Organization: Outlines and Tables of Contents

The outline and table of contents features of Word for Windows will enhance the organization of your documents and make it easier for readers to quickly comprehend your writing. The major benefit of these features in Word for Windows is that they are interlinked. Word for Windows provides you with the Outline

View to speed outline creation. You then use the document's outline to produce a table of contents. Further, when you create an outline, Word for Windows automatically formats the heads with the proper heading style. Word for Windows can also create a table of contents by assembling text that you have tagged with Table of Contents (TC) fields. (There are times when you will prefer to use this method, which is discussed later in this chapter.) You can use the Outline View for any document you write and will find it especially helpful when you write essays, reports, chapters, books, and other manuscripts.

The Outline View in Word for Windows is not a separate mode of operation, as it is in most word processing packages. Rather, the Word for Windows Outline View is one of the five views, or screens, through which you can work on a single document. The other four views, the Normal Editing View, Print Preview, Page View, and Draft View, were introduced in Chapter 5, "Printing: Picture Perfect Output." You can move between all five views quickly by using the appropriate Word for Windows keyboard macros.

With the Outline View, you enter text and quickly assign it a level of importance in the outline. Heads are indented in 1/2" increments according to their levels of importance. The Outline View has several tools that help you assign head levels. Also, you can collapse subheads and body text under higher-level heads. Collapsing subheads and body text under a head is useful since it lets you see and move just the heads until you are satisfied with the material's flow and organization.

You can also have Word for Windows number the heads, subheads, and body text in the Outline View. There are two ways to number heads. The Edit Renumber command will assign standard outline, legal, or sequential numbers to each head. Alternatively, you can have Word for Windows number each line within a section with the Format Section Line Numbering option. The Line Numbering option places the numbers in the left margin. A lawyer may want to format the whole document as one section in order to refer to each line by its number. You could also save time by formatting a small list as a section and turning on the Line Numbering option; Word for Windows would then automatically number each item.

Outline Processing

The Word for Windows Outline View is a powerful composition tool. That power comes from the ability of Word for Windows to collapse subheads, subtext, and notes under heads at a level that you specify. For example, you can display only level 1, 2, and 3 heads; all lower-level heads (level 4 and down) and body text under level 3 would be collapsed (not displayed) under the displayed heads. Heads that contain collapsed subheads and body text are displayed with an indented, dotted underline.

When you move heads containing collapsed subheads and body text, the invisible collapsed subheads and body text move with them. Later, when you are ready to write and switch to the Normal Editing View, the previously hidden subheads and body text are displayed again.

The Outline View also gives you access to the heading styles. When you change the level of a head within the Outline View with either the Outline View buttons or with the mouse, the appropriate style is automatically applied to the head. In other words, Word for Windows Outline View links head level and head style. The Heading 1 style is automatically assigned to a level 1 head; the Heading 2 style is automatically applied to a level 2 head, and so on. Body text is automatically assigned the Normal style.

As with the other four views, you can move in and out of the Outline View without converting the document to a different format. Because of this, you can use the Word for Windows

Outline View at any stage of document composition. This added flexibility lets you juggle the topics to be discussed in a document before you begin writing and reorganize them at any later stage.

Outline View Buttons

The Word for Windows Outline View is activated from the keyboard with the ALT-V, O macro or with the mouse by clicking the left mouse button on the Outline command in the View menu, as shown here.

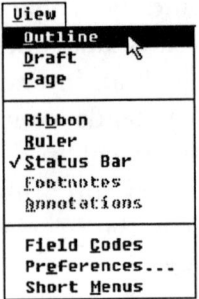

The Outline View has a set of Outline buttons as seen in Figure 7-1. From left to right, there are five arrow buttons followed by a plus sign and minus sign, and then Show level buttons. Most of the buttons are used to assign or reassign different level heads. Recall that Word for Windows comes with the default Heading 1-3 styles (styles are discussed in Chapter 4, "For the Record: Styles and Templates"). However, Word for Windows will automatically add heading styles as you create lower-level heads in the Outline View.

Figure 7-1.

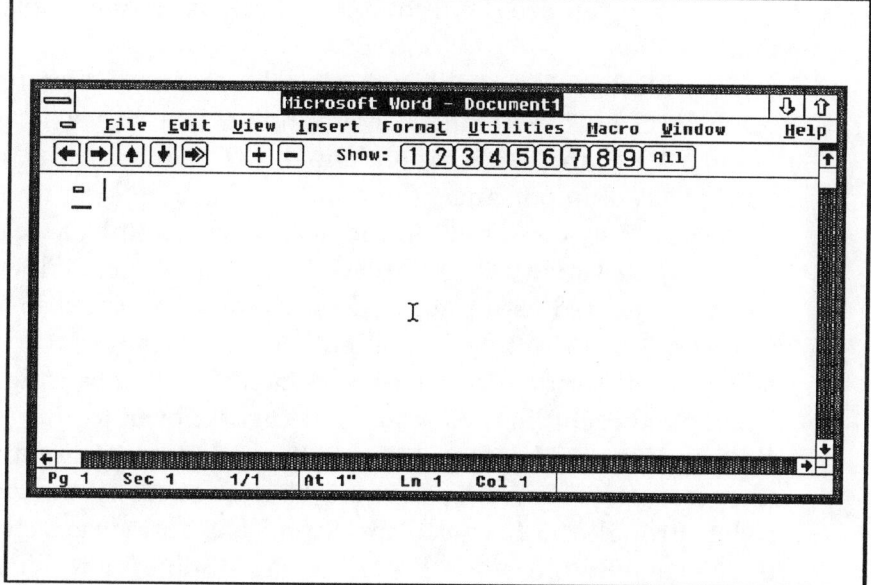

Outline View and its buttons

You can also create your own heading styles for Heading 4 and higher; and, since the Heading 1-3 styles already exist, you can change these styles to fit your particular needs.

Once you change the default heading styles, you should create a new document template rather than saving the new styles to the global NORMAL.DOT document template. Remember that these heading styles will not only be used to create an outline, they will also be used in the document in the Normal Editing View. Other than the heading styles, any other styles that you want to add to the document template are only of use to you in the Normal Editing View where you create your document. Of course, all styles are displayed in the Format Styles dialog box, but only the heading styles will be automatically assigned to text set at the same head level in the Outline View. Also, remember that you cannot rename or delete the default heading styles. You would not want to rename or delete these default heading styles in any case because you can use them to quickly organize a document in the Outline View.

The Outline View will automatically format a first through ninth level head with the corresponding heading style. In the Outline View, the heads are indented by 1/2" increments to show their levels of importance; these indents have nothing to do with the heading style assigned to the head. For example, a head with the Heading 1 style will be displayed flush left. A second level head will be formatted with the Heading 2 style and tabbed in 1/2". A third level head will be formatted with the Heading 3 style and tabbed in 1", and so on. The incremental 1/2" tabs assigned to heads in the Outline View are not carried over to the Normal Editing View of the document; they are for visual organization purposes only. Any tabs that may be assigned by the heading styles through the Format Paragraph Tabs options are shown in the Normal Editing View, but not in the Outline View. Figure 7-2 shows heads formatted from levels 1 to 5. Note that all heads other than the lowest-level head are preceded by large plus signs and that the lowest-level head is preceded by a large minus sign. The plus sign indicates that a head is not the lowest-level head in a section, whereas the large minus sign indicates that the head is at the lowest level of any head in that section. If there are several heads at this level, they are all preceded by large minus signs. Body text at that level is preceded by a minus sign half the width of the minus sign preceding the lowest-level head; the half-width minus sign indicates that the body text is at the lowest possible level. The incremental 1/2" indentations of lower-level heads disappear when you return to the Normal Editing View.

As an introduction to the Outline View buttons, type the text seen in Figure 7-2. Place the cursor anywhere on the second through fifth level heads and click the left mouse button on the right arrow Outline View button. By using this button, you should be able to indent the heads so they look the same as Figure 7-2. If you overshoot the heading level, you can raise the head's level by

Figure 7-2.

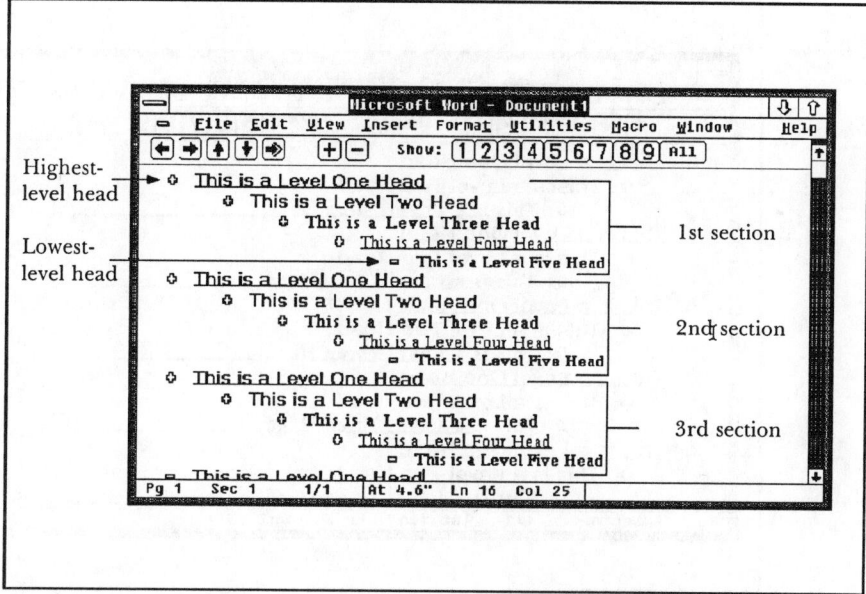

Different level headings in Outline View

clicking the left mouse button on the left arrow Outline View button. Now experiment with the outline View up arrow button and down arrow button; place the cursor anywhere on a head and click the left mouse button on one of these buttons to move the head up or down past other heads. Click the left mouse button on different Show buttons; these buttons will let you display only the heads you want to see. This abbreviated view of your outline makes it easier to rearrange the highest-level, and most important, heads.

As an example of the Show buttons, Figure 7-3 contains the same heads as in Figure 7-2; however, the Show level 3 button has been activated. Note that only head levels 1 to 3 are displayed in Figure 7-3. All heads (and body text) below level 3 are collapsed into the higher-level heads. The level 3 heads that contain collapsed subheads and text exhibit an indented, dotted under-

Figure 7-3.

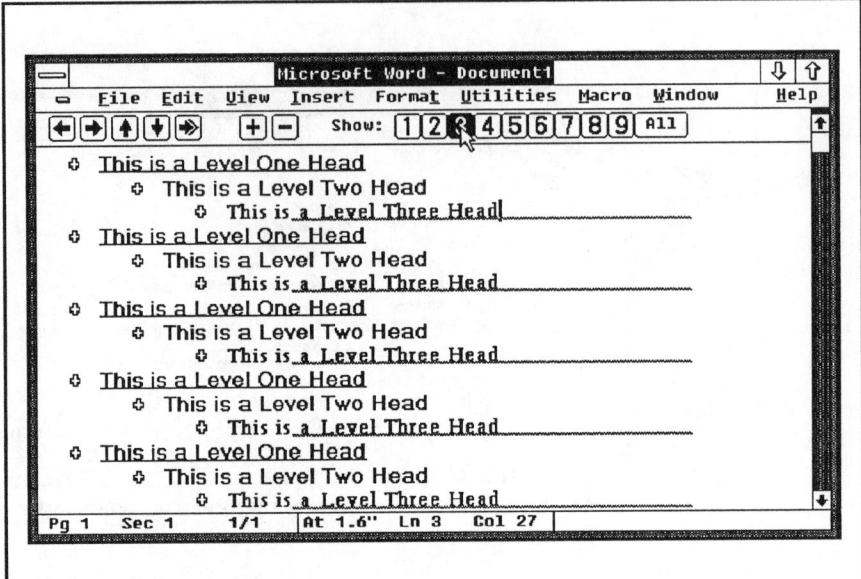

Show Heads to level 3 only

line that represents the collapsed text. If you move heads that have an indented, dotted underline, the collapsed subheads and body text move with them. You can redisplay the collapsed subheads and body text by activating the Show All button after you have finished moving and reorganizing your heads and text.

As mentioned, you only need to have the cursor on a head to change its level, move it up or down in the outline, or to collapse subheads and body text; the head does not have to be highlighted. Word for Windows does, however, allow you to perform all the outlining operations on highlighted groups of heads. Unlike the outline features in Word 4.0 and 5.0, you can highlight multiple heads in Word for Windows. All of the heads and paragraphs of body text that are highlighted in the Outline View will be moved or reformatted as paragraphs by the Outline buttons.

Promote Button

The Promote button elevates the level of a head. For example, if the cursor was on a head formatted with the Heading 2 style and you click the left mouse button on the Promote button, the head would be elevated to level 1. It would also assume the Heading 1 formatting.

You can also activate the Promote button from the keyboard by entering the ALT-SHIFT-LEFT ARROW macro. All of the Outline View button macros are listed in Table 7-1.

Demote Button

The Demote button will lower the head by one level. For example, if you have the cursor on a level 2 head, the Demote button will

Table 7-1.

Keyboard Macro	Outline View Button
ALT-SHIFT-LEFT ARROW	Promote Heading
ALT-SHIFT-RIGHT ARROW	Demote Heading
ALT-SHIFT-KEYPAD 5	Demote Heading to Text
ALT-SHIFT-UP ARROW	Move Heading Up on Page
ALT-SHIFT-DOWN ARROW	Move Heading Down on Page
ALT-SHIFT-PLUS	Expand Body Text
ALT-SHIFT-MINUS	Collapse Body Text
ALT-SHIFT-F	Show Only First Line of Body Text

Outline View Button Macros (Adapted with permission from the documentation for Microsoft Word for Windows, Microsoft Corporation, 1990.)

lower it to a level 3 head. The Demote button can be activated by clicking the left mouse button on it or with the ALT-SHIFT-RIGHT ARROW macro.

Vertical Move Up Button

The Vertical Move Up button moves all the heads, subheads, and body text highlighted by the cursor above the paragraph that immediately precedes the highlighted section. All heads and text under a level 1 head are considered to be part of a single section. If the paragraph preceding the highlighted section is a hidden paragraph, Word for Windows will move the highlighted section above the nearest preceding non-hidden paragraph. You can activate the Vertical Move Up button by clicking the left mouse button on it or with the ALT-SHIFT-UP ARROW macro.

Vertical Move Down Button

The Vertical Move Down button moves all of the highlighted heads, subheads, and body text down one line. You can activate the Vertical Move Down button with the mouse by clicking the left mouse button on it or with the ALT-SHIFT-DOWN ARROW macro.

Demote to Body Text Button

The Demote to Body Text button lowers the level of any heads that the cursor is on to body text. It also adds the body text style, which is the Normal style in the NORMAL.DOT default document template, to the demoted text. You can activate the Demote to Body Text button by clicking the left mouse button on it or with the ALT-SHIFT-KEYPAD 5 macro (NormalStyle).

Figure 7-4a shows the text from Figure 7-2 with a head subset highlighted. Figure 7-4b shows what happens to that highlighted block when you activate the Demote to Body Text button; all the highlighted heads are converted to body text and assigned the Normal style. Note that since the body text is below a level 5 head (Heading 5 style), it is automatically associated with that head, and the level 5 head is no longer the lowest-level category in its section. This is evidenced by the conversion of the minus sign in front of the level 5 head in Figure 7-4a to a plus sign in Figure 7-4b. The

Figure 7-4.

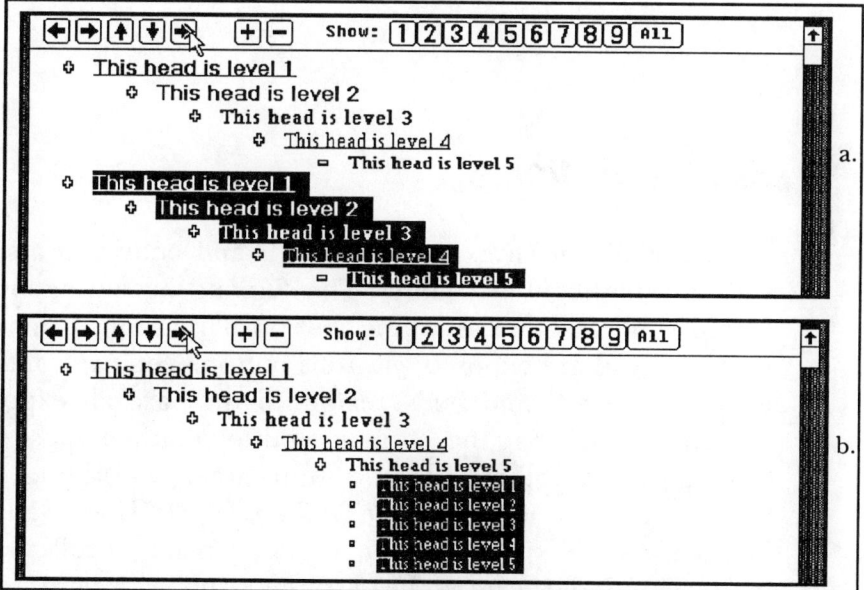

Highlighted heads and heads demoted to body text

conversion takes place when body text is added below the level 5 head that had previously been the lowest-level entry in the section. The half-width minus sign in front of the body text indicates that it is now the lowest-level entry under the level 1 head that starts this section.

The association of heads and body text is new to Word for Windows; versions 4.0 and 5.0 of Word did not associate body text with particular heads. In the earlier versions of Word, heads and underlying body text must be moved and reformatted as separate items; you cannot highlight more than one head or one paragraph of body text at a time. Each head and body text paragraph is treated as a separate item in the outline mode of these earlier versions of Word. In Word for Windows, however, you can highlight, move, or reformat multiple heads and body text paragraphs.

Expand Button   ⊞

The Expand button exposes subheads and body text associated with any highlighted head(s). The Expand button exposes collapsed subheads one at a time, but all paragraphs of body text under a head are exposed with this button. You can continue to expose subheads and body text until they are all exposed by continuously clicking the left mouse button on the Expose button. You can activate the Expand button either by clicking the left mouse button on it or with the ALT-SHIFT-PLUS SIGN macro.

To use the Expand button, you first need to collapse some body text underneath a head. When subheads and text are collapsed into a head, that head has a dotted underline indented 1/2" that may continue past the end of the line.

Collapse Button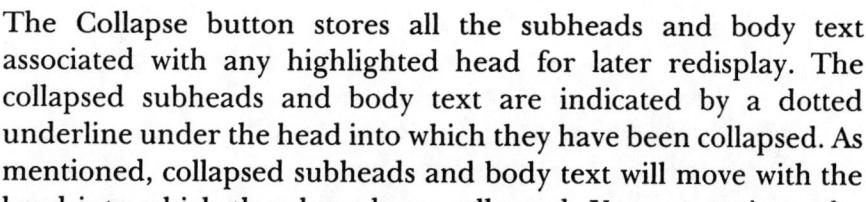

The Collapse button stores all the subheads and body text associated with any highlighted head for later redisplay. The collapsed subheads and body text are indicated by a dotted underline under the head into which they have been collapsed. As mentioned, collapsed subheads and body text will move with the head into which they have been collapsed. You can activate the Collapse button either by clicking the left mouse button on it or with the ALT-SHIFT-MINUS SIGN macro.

The Collapse button also acts on one paragraph at a time. If you have the cursor on a head and press the Collapse button, the lowest-level subhead or body text under that head will be collapsed. For example, in the outline in Figure 7-2, if the cursor was at a level 1 head and you clicked the left mouse button on the Collapse button once, the level 5 head would be collapsed. The level 4 head would have an indented, dotted underline signifying the collapsed level 5 subhead, as shown here.

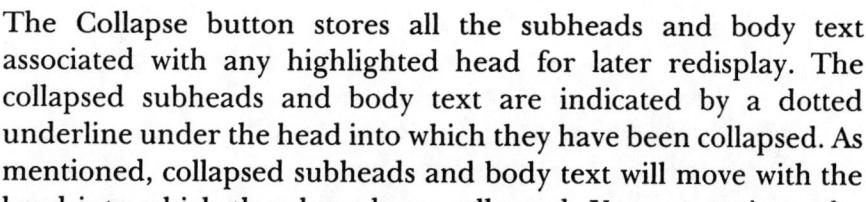

If you clicked the left mouse button once more on the Collapse button, the level 4 head would be collapsed, and the level 3 head would display the indented, dotted underline.

Show Buttons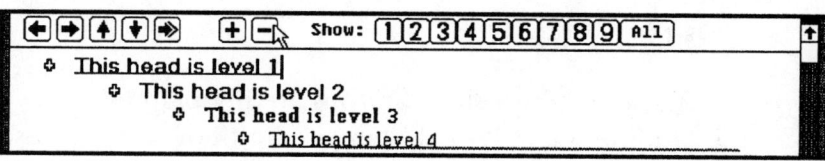

The Show buttons determine the level of heads displayed in the Outline View. If, for example, you click the left mouse button on the Show 1 button, only the level 1 heads are shown. All of the subheads and body text in the document are collapsed into these heads. This does not mean that the collapsed text no longer exists. Its presence is indicated by indented, dotted lines under the displayed heads. When you move a head that has collapsed subheads and body text, either with the Vertical Move buttons or manually (discussed in "Moving Heads Manually" in this chapter), the invisible collapsed subheads and text are automatically brought with it. You can redisplay the collapsed subheads and text at any time with the Expand button.

The default condition is Show All; however, when you activate the Outline View, the All button is not highlighted, as shown here.

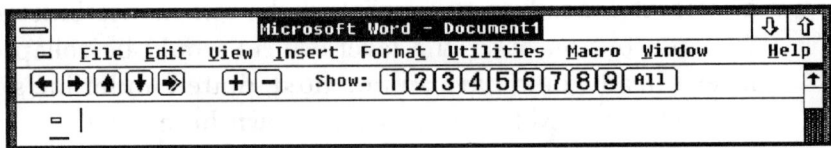

In fact, none of the Show buttons are highlighted when you open the Outline View. You highlight the Show buttons as they are needed. For example, you activate the All button, displaying the whole document, after you select the Show 1 button to see only first level heads.

The Show buttons are useful for reorganizing heads that are over a lot of subheads and body text. Since subheads and body text create space between the major heads, you cannot always see the major heads whose positions you want to change. It can be difficult to see all of the major heads in just one 25-line Word for Windows document window. By collapsing the subheads and body text, you will be able to see all the major heads in one document window without scrolling.

The Show buttons are also useful if you are creating an outline with many heads. If you want to rearrange heads and their associated subheads and body text, you can collapse the subheads into the heads and use the Vertical Move buttons. Alternatively, you can manually move heads and their collapsed contents together (as discussed in "Moving Heads Manually" in this chapter).

Outline View Tools

When you begin a document in the Outline View, you can work with section heads, which represent topics or ideas, unhampered by subheads and body text. The Outline View is designed to allow you to quickly change the order in which you present ideas in a document. Spending time choosing and organizing heads before you begin writing will make your presentation clearer and more logical.

Of course, no matter how much time you spend on an outline, you will often decide later that you need to reorganize a document. Remember, the heading structure you choose before you begin writing is not written in stone. Word for Windows lets you go into Outline View at any time and reorganize the order in which the heads appear. The Show buttons (discussed earlier in "Show Buttons") are especially helpful for collapsing subheads and body text so you can reorganize documents that contain a lot of heads, subheads, and body text.

When you begin a document as an outline, you work with ideas one by one. The Outline View buttons — Promote/Demote, Vertical Move, and Expand/Collapse — move, format, expand, and collapse heads one at a time, and are therefore most useful when you begin a document as an outline. However, other outline tools are available such as manual head movement (done with a mouse), head numbering, alphanumeric sorting of heads, and the addition of footnotes to outlines. These tools work with highlighted blocks of multiple heads; therefore, they are useful when you use the Outline View with a document that you have begun writing, but want to reorganize. These multihead tools are discussed in the next few sections.

Moving Heads Manually

The manual movement of heads changes their levels or their positions in the outline. It is the fastest way to revise an outline. When you are creating an outline, you are usually dealing with heads one at a time, and you have no intervening passages of text between them. The Promote, Demote, Vertical Move Up, and Vertical Move Down buttons move highlighted heads one line at a time. Often, it is faster to move highlighted blocks of heads and body text manually.

To move heads or body text manually, place the mouse over the outline symbol (either the plus sign or the minus sign) to the left of the head or body text. Then click the left mouse button on the outline symbol and drag it to a new location. When you move the mouse over the plus sign or minus sign, it becomes a four-sided arrow, shown here.

This looks like the Word for Windows sizing arrow (the sizing arrow was discussed in Chapter 1, "Up and Running").

For example, if you type the text in Figure 7-2, you can manually change the level of any head. To do this, hold the left mouse button down on the plus sign and press it; the head becomes highlighted. As you drag the plus sign to the right or the

Figure 7-5.

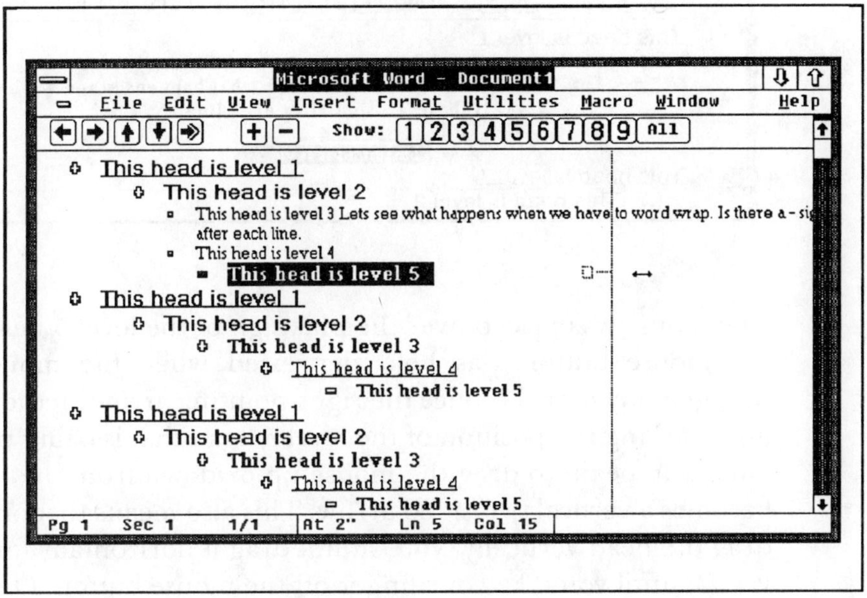

Changing head level with the mouse

left, you will see a vertical dotted line and box appear. The vertical
line shows you the new level of the head were you to release the
left mouse button. The box is where the plus sign will be placed if
you let go of the left mouse button.

An example of manually moving a head is shown in Figure 7-5.
The vertical dotted line and box show where the head will be
placed if you release the mouse; the cursor is six levels below (to
the right of) the original head.

You can also move heads to different parts of the outline by
dragging them vertically. When you drag a head either up or
down, you will see a horizontal dotted line and an arrow on the
line indicating where the head is currently placed.

An example using the text in Figure 7-5 is shown here.

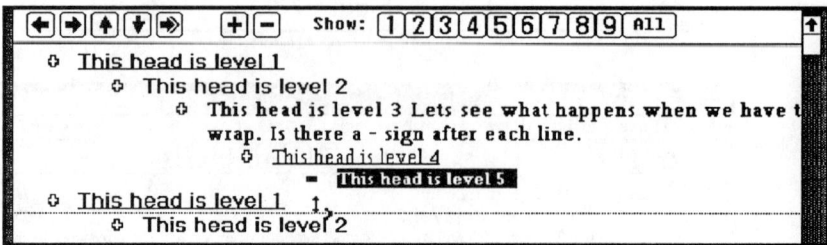

The mouse was placed over the plus sign of the level 5 head. The left mouse button was held depressed while the mouse was dragged downward (notice the right-pointing arrow on the dotted line marking the position of the level 5 head that is being placed). Once you begin to drag the mouse up or down from the head, it becomes a vertical two-sided arrow. This also means that once you drag the head vertically, you cannot drag it horizontally (and vice versa), until you take your finger off the mouse button. Once you have released the mouse button, you can click the left mouse button on the head again and drag it in the other direction. This separation between vertical and horizontal repositioning of heads works in the same way as the vertical and horizontal repositioning of the windows borders with the sizing arrow. Once you commit to movement in one direction, you cannot move in the other direction until you release the mouse.

Numbering Heads

The Outline View lets you automatically assign numbers to headings. If you later change the positions or the levels of heads or body text in the Outline View, Word for Windows can automatically renumber them.

The Utilities Renumber command can automatically number heads and body text that may or may not have been already numbered. Since only non-collapsed heads, subheads, and body text are numbered, you use the Show button to collapse the levels that you do not want numbered. When you reexpand the document, the previously collapsed heads, subheads, and body text will not be numbered.

You begin numbering an outline by activating the Utilities Renumber command, shown here.

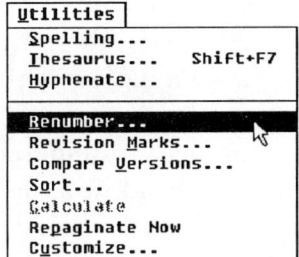

This activates the Utilities Renumber dialog box shown here.

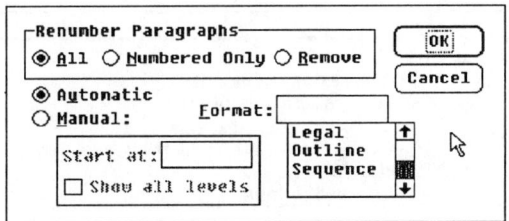

The Renumber Paragraphs option set offers three choices: to renumber or number all paragraphs for the first time, to renumber only those paragraphs that are already numbered, or to remove the numbering. The Utilities Renumber dialog box only applies to paragraphs. Remember, all heads and subheads are treated as paragraphs by Word for Windows. Numbering individual lines is discussed later in this chapter in "Line Numbering."

There are four formats available for outline numbering. These are shown in Figure 7-6 using the text from Figure 7-2. Figure

7-6a shows the Outline format. This is useful for organizing and presenting outlines of ideas. Figure 7-6b shows the Legal head numbering format. It is used in legal documents, along with line numbering, to control and locate legal language precisely. Figure 7-6c shows the Sequence head numbering format. This format is most useful for general tables of contents assembled from a Word for Windows outline (discussed in "Generating a Table of Contents").

You can choose to make the renumbering automatic or manual. If you choose automatic, every time you move a head it will be automatically assigned a new number. Whenever you add a new head, all of the currently numbered heads with levels that are affected by the new head will be automatically renumbered. However, the newly inserted head itself will not be assigned a

Figure 7-6.

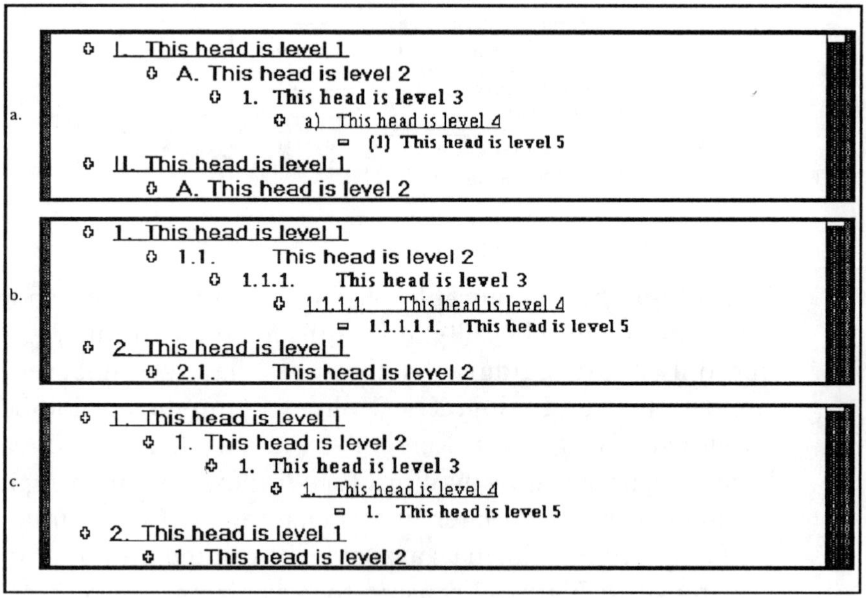

Outline numbering formats

number. For example, if you have created a list of heads numbered 1 through 6 and you insert a new head after number 3, all the heads following the newly inserted head will change: 4 will become 5 and so on. The new number 3 head will not be numbered. To add a number to an inserted head, you must execute the Utilities Renumber command after you insert a head. The automatic renumbering feature only affects heads within a section and will not renumber heads that fall in a different section. If you use the manual option, you must activate the Utilities Renumber command to renumber all the document heads, subheads, and body text paragraphs. Use the manual option if you want to retain your original numbering scheme.

The fourth numbering format, Learn, is not shown in Figure 7-6. It is only available when you choose the manual numbering option. When the Learn format is activated, Word for Windows will look at the the numbering format of the first section of heads and use it to renumber all the other heads. (Remember, a section of heads is all heads from a level 1 head to the lowest-level head or body text entry before the next level 1 head.) Therefore, you only need to type a format for the first entry. Then you activate the Utilites Renumber command. As a sample of a Learn format, a numbering format with alternating periods and right parentheses, similar but not the same as the Outline numbering format, is shown here.

```
 ✧  l. This head is level 1
      ✧  A) This head is level 2
           ✧  1. This head is level 3
                ✧  a) This head is level 4
                     ▭  i. This head is level 5
```

Note that you can use roman and arabic numerals, as well as upper- and lowercase letters. There must be a punctuation mark after each numbering format sample; it can be a period, comma, quotation mark, colon, semicolon, question mark, exclamation point, or parentheses. If you do not end each numbering format with some form of punctuation, Word for Windows will ignore that line when it tries to learn your format.

After you create the sample numbering format, activate the Utilities Renumber command. Activate the Manual button; notice that the Numbering Paragraph option switches from All to Numbered Only. If you want Word for Windows to learn your format from the first entry and apply it to the rest of the entries, make sure you switch the Numbering Paragraph option back to All before you press ENTER. If you do not do this, and the first entry is the only entry with a numbering format, nothing will happen. If you tell Word for Windows to number all of the heads, you will see a moving "percent done" listing at the bottom while Word for Windows numbers the heads; when it reaches "100% done" the heads will be displayed with the new format.

Also, when you choose the Manual option, the Start At and Show All options become available (they are ghosted in the Utilities Renumber dialog box). In the Start At field, you specify what number the numbering function should begin with. This is useful if the paragraphs in the current document are not the first in a sequence, such as any chapter in a book after the first.

The Show All Levels toggle box lets you list the highest-level head number with all of its lower-level subheads and body text.

The example shown here

```
 ♦  I.  This head is level 1
        ♦  A. This head is level 2
              ♦  1.  This head is level 3
                    ♦  a)  This head is level 4
                          ▫  (1) This head is level 5
```

shows the normal listing in Outline format. Activate the Manual button, type **1** in the Start At field, and activate the Show All Levels field, as shown here.

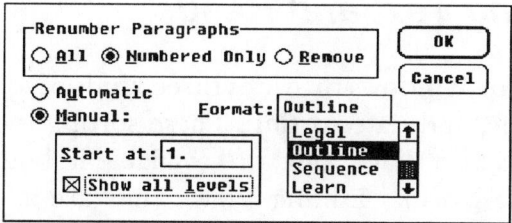

The roman numeral I will appear in front of all heads in the first section, not only the highest-level head. Similarly, the A in front of the level 2 head now appears in front of the level 3 through 5 heads in the first section, and so on. The same can be said for the second section, except all of these heads begin with the roman numeral II, and so on, as shown here.

```
⊕  I.   This head is level 1
      ⊕  I.A.        This head is level 2
           ⊕  I.A.1.       This head is level 3
                ⊕  I.A.1.a)    This head is level 4
                     ⊟  I.A.1.a.1)  This head is level 5
```

This type of formatting can be applied to a highlighted block or to the whole document. If you highlight a block of heads before you open the Utilities Renumber dialog box, the formatting will be applied to that block only. If you do not highlight a block of heads, the numbering will apply to all the visible (uncollapsed) heads.

The Utilities Renumber command is also available in the Normal Editing View. In that view, you can use it to apply numbers to a Document in the same way; however, because the Normal Editing View does not have a Show button, you cannot apply numbers only to certain level heads.

The numbers added by the Utilities Renumber command can be used to create a numbering system for a table of contents (discussed in this chapter in "Generating a Table of Contents"). The Sequence numbering format is useful for referring to sections and pages of a document.

Sorting Text and Heads

Word for Windows provides three kinds of sorting: alphanumeric, numeric, and date sorting. These sorting tools, which are in the Utilities Sort dialog box, are available in both the Outline View and the Normal Editing View. They are all useful in arranging topics into a logical sequence.

Alphanumeric, Numeric, and Date Sorting

The Utilities Sort dialog box is displayed when you activate the Utilities Sort command shown here.

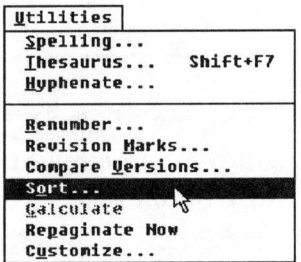

It provides options for sorting text in alphanumeric, numeric, or date order. You can apply these options to text in the Outline View or in the Normal Editing View. Also, you can apply them to the whole document or to a highlighted block (which must be highlighted before you open the dialog box).

The Utilities Sort dialog box, shown here,

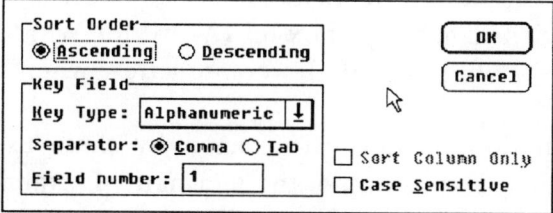

has two option sets—Sort Order and Key Field—and two toggle boxes—Sort Column Only (ghosted in default) and Case Sensitive.

The Sort Order options, Ascending and Descending, determine the order in which a sort is performed. Items in an ascending alphanumeric sort are listed from the beginning of the alphabet to the end and from low to high numbers. Items in an ascending numeric sort are listed from lowest to highest. Those in an ascending date sort are listed from past to present. The Descending option sorts in the opposite order.

The three Sort options are found in a scroll box, as in the Key Fields option set shown here.

All three types of sorts ignore accents, diacritical marks, spaces, and tabs.

The default sort listing is the Alphanumeric option. Normally, the alphanumeric sort does not discriminate between upper- and lowercase letters. When you choose that option, however, the Case Sensitive toggle box becomes available (it is ghosted when you choose either Date or Numeric), giving you the choice of whether uppercase and lowercase are factors in the sort. When active, the Case Sensitive toggle box tells Word for Windows that uppercase letters should precede lowercase letters when sorting on any one letter.

International letters are sorted by their uses in the English alphabet. For example, the German "β" stands for a double "s" and is sorted as "ss." The alphanumeric sort handles numerals in the same way as the numeric sort.

Figure 7-7 shows text from a billing statement that has been entered in the Outline View. Running an alphanumeric sort on this text produces the list seen in Figure 7-8. Note that within each alphabetical group (Balance, Billings, and Payments) the entries are then further sorted numerically. In this case, the numbers that

Figure 7-7.

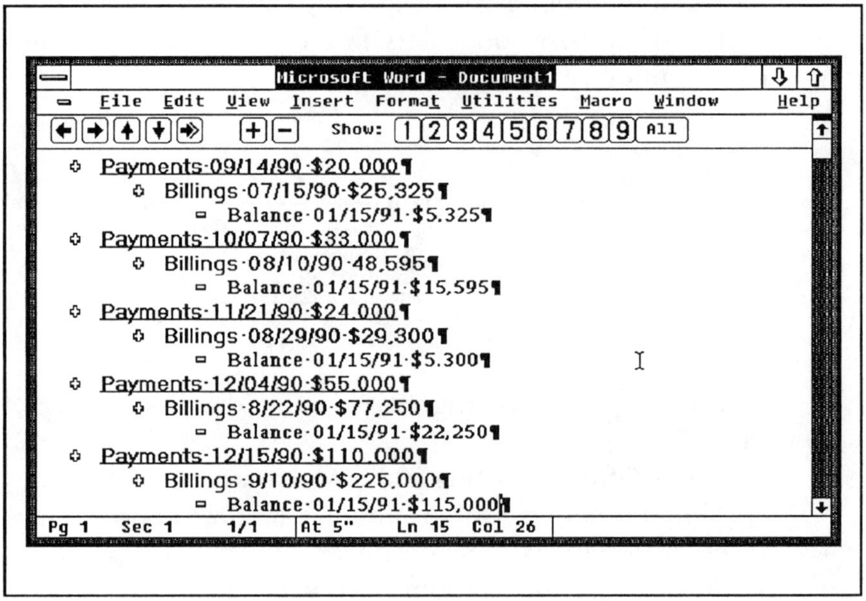

Unsorted outline

Figure 7-8.

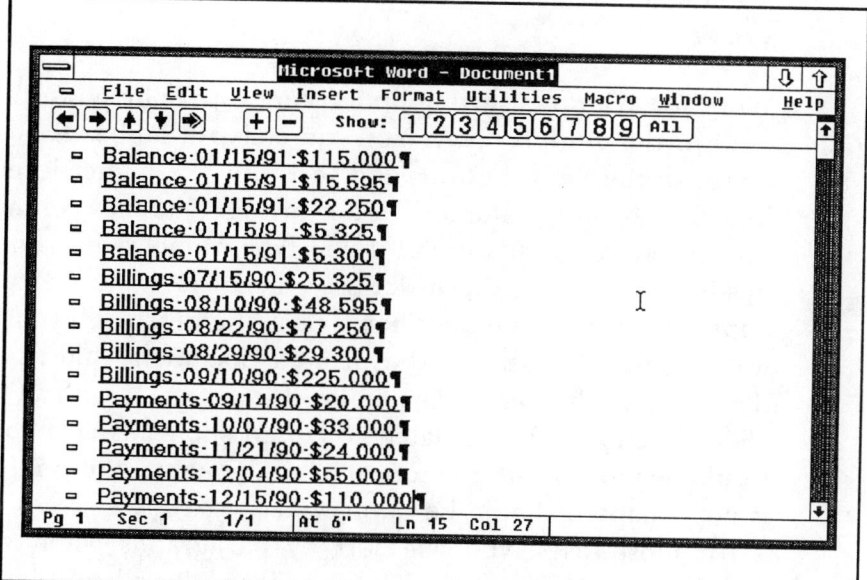

Alphanumeric sort of outline

have been sorted are the dates, but this was not a date sort. Note that the months that were single digits had zeros in front of them; this made the numeric sort on the dates accurate.

The Numeric Sort option does a digit by digit, not numeral by numeral, comparison. Therefore a 9 would precede a 10 because 9 is greater than 1. In a numeral by numeral comparison 10 would precede 9, and 100 would precede 99, because the first digits are compared; in both cases, 1 and 9 are the first digits, and 1 is less than 9.

Date sorting ignores all other characters and numbers. The dates must be listed in one of the formats that Word for Windows recognizes in order to run this sort. See Chapter 6 for correct date formats.

Sorting in the Outline View

Word for Windows sorting options are especially powerful when used in the Outline View. You can collapse subheads and body text with the Show buttons and sort only the higher-level heads into alphabetical or numeric order or by a date they contain. The numeric order sort is useful if you type numbers in front of the heads to represent the order in which you want the topics to appear. You could number heads using hidden text if you did not want them to appear in the printed document (hidden text is discussed in Chapter 8, "Group Productions"). As with all Outline View functions, all associated collapsed subheads and body text would be moved with the sorted heads. Each paragraph item that is not collapsed should be numbered.

In most cases, you will sort by paragraphs when you are creating an outline in the Outline View. (Recall that heads are treated by Word for Windows as paragraphs.) But Word for Windows also lets you sort by columns or fields, which can be useful after you have begun writing a document and want to organize the material in a multicolumn document or table with the Outline View.

To do this, the highlighted block or document must be in a multicolumn format when you open the Utilities sort. The default is a one-column document; you select more than one column by typing a number of 2 or greater in the Columns Number option of the Format Section dialog box. Otherwise, the Sort Column Only toggle box will be ghosted; it must be activated before you can sort by columns or fields. You choose either the Comma or the Tab separator button to sort by columns. Fields are separated by commas in a print merge data document (see Chapter 6 for a discussion of data documents). Cells in a table can be converted to comma- or tab-delimited format, sorted, then converted back into a table. If you are using a print merge data document, you have to tell Word for Windows which field to sort on. For example, you may have Name, Address, City, State, or Phone as fields. If you were to choose the City field, you would type **3** in the field Number text entry box. Similarly, if you are sorting columnar data, the number entered in the Field Number text entry box would indicate the column in which the sorted entry is found. The Microsoft Word for Windows documentation refers to the column or field that you choose to sort on as a Sort Key and the comma or tab delimitation of the fields or commas as Sort Separators.

Adding Footnotes

You may need to insert footnotes when you are working in the Outline View. You use footnotes because you want to make sure the topic referred to by the footnote is covered, but you do not want this information to interupt the flow of the document. To create a footnote, you must deactivate the View Outline command by clicking the left mouse button on it; this brings you back into the Normal Editing View. Although you must enter footnotes in the Normal Editing View, you can quickly switch back to the Outline View with the View Outline command. Footnotes are displayed, and can be collapsed, in the Outline View.

To create a footnote in the Normal Editing View, activate the Insert Footnote command, shown here.

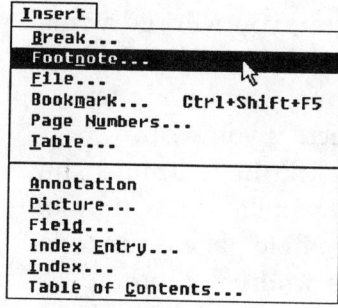

This command brings up the Insert Footnote dialog box shown here.

```
┌─────────────────────────────────────────────────────────────┐
│                                                               │
│            ☒ A̲uto-numbered Reference         ┌──────────┐    │
│                        or                     │    OK    │    │
│            F̲ootnote Reference Mark: │          └──────────┘    │
│                                               ┌──────────┐    │
│                                               │  Cancel  │    │
│         ┌Footnote Separators────────────────  └──────────┘    │
│         │ (S̲eparator...) (C̲ont. Separator...) (Cont. N̲otice...) │
│         └──────────────────────────────────────────────────   │
└─────────────────────────────────────────────────────────────┘
```

By default, Word for Windows will automatically number footnotes for you. You can turn this option off by clicking the left mouse button on the Auto-numbered Reference toggle box. If you do so, you will need to add your own reference mark in the Footnote Reference Mark text entry field. You can use any and as many characters as you wish in this field. Try, however, to limit the entry to one or two characters so they do not break up the flow of the document by their presence. Word for Windows automatically makes whatever footnote reference mark you use (the default numbers or reference mark you type) a superscript. You can manually remove the superscript from the reference mark with the Format Character dialog box.

You will usually have some sort of separation between footnotes and body text. Separators were referred to in "Footnotes" in Chapter 2, "Formatting Text." You choose a footnote separator by clicking the left mouse button on one of the options in the Footnote Separators field. If you click the left mouse button on the Separator button, you will see a small pane at the bottom of the screen with the default 2" line that Word for Windows uses to separate footnotes from body text. You can delete this line and type any characters you wish.

When you click the left mouse button on the Cont. Separator button, a small pane at the bottom of the screen with a default 6" line across the whole page is displayed. This continue separator is used on pages where a footnote has been carried over from a previous page. You can delete this line and use any characters that you wish for the continue separator.

The Cont. Notice button also opens a small pane at the bottom of the document window. The continue notice is the message that will appear at the bottom of a footnote that continues onto another page. There will be no entry in it because the default is no notice. You can type in any message. Usually you do not need a continue message because the reader can see that the footnote is unfinished.

Once you have entered a reference mark and any separator information, activate the OK button either by tabbing over to it and pressing ENTER or by clicking the left mouse button on it. This will cause the reference mark to be inserted into the document at the point where the cursor was last placed. A footnote pane will open at the bottom of the page.

The footnote pane is shown in Figure 7-9. It will contain all footnotes in the document, whether they are to appear on the

Figure 7-9.

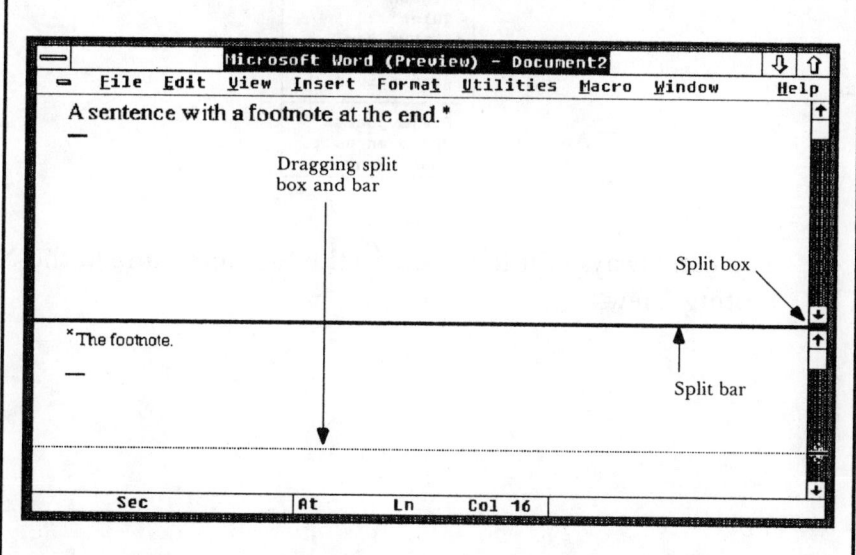

Closing footnote pane

page they are referenced or at the end of the document. .The cursor will be blinking in the footnote pane in the space after the superscripted reference mark, ready for you to type the footnote. When you are finished typing the footnote, you can close the footnote pane by placing the mouse between the scroll bar for the footnote pane and the scroll bar for the rest of the document window. When you click the left mouse button on that area, called the *split box,* and drag the left mouse button down, a dotted line appears, as shown in Figure 7-9. If you let go of the left mouse button before reaching the bottom of the document window, the top of the footnote pane, called the *split bar,* will appear. If you bring the split bar all the way to the bottom of the document window, the footnote pane closes completely.

You can always redisplay the footnote pane with the View Footnotes command, shown here.

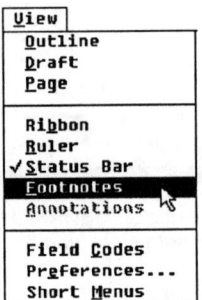

You can always edit footnotes in the footnote pane in the Normal Editing View.

You can place footnotes on the same page, at the end of a section, or at the end of a document. The placement of footnotes within a document is discussed in Chapter 2.

Line Numbering

Line numbering is especially important in legal documents, where the text on each line is referred to by its number. Line numbering can also be used to quickly add numbers to a list of items. Line numbering can only be added in the Normal Editing View, Page View, and Draft View; not the Outline View. You will not see line numbering in the Outline View. You can only see line numbering in Print Preview or when you actually print a document. However, line numbering can be used in any of these views to number heads, subheads, and body text that you entered in the Outline View.

Line numbering is a section feature (for a discussion of sections see "Format Section" in Chapter 2). When you format the first section in a document to contain line numbering, the whole document will be assigned line numbering no matter what part of the document you highlight before opening the Format Section dialog box. To block off a section for line numbering, place the cursor at the beginning of the block and activate the Insert Break dialog box. Choose the Continuous button and then the OK button. You will see a double dotted line appear at the point where the cursor was placed; this is the section break. Then place the cursor at the end of the block and activate the Insert Break dialog box. Again, select the Continuous button, and then the OK button. Another double dotted line appears indicating another section break. Now highlight the text between both section breaks. Activate the Line Numbering toggle box in the Format Section dialog box, shown here.

```
┌──────────────────────────────────────────────────┐
│  Section                        ┌──────────┐      │
│  ┌Columns───────────┐           │    OK    │      │
│  │ Number: │1    │               └──────────┘      │
│  │                                ┌──────────┐      │
│  │ Spacing:│0.5" │                │  Cancel  │      │
│  │ ☐ Line Between │     Section Start:           │
│  └─────────────────┘     ┌─────────────────┐      │
│                          │New Page       │↓│       │
│  ☒ Include Footnotes     └─────────────────┘      │
│  ┌Line Numbers──────────────────────────────┐     │
│  │ ☒ Line Numbering                          │     │
│  │                                           │     │
│  │ Start At #: │1    │    ⦿ Per Page         │     │
│  │ From Text:  │Auto │    ○ Per Section       │     │
│  │ Count By:   │1    │    ○ Continue          │     │
│  └───────────────────────────────────────────┘     │
│  ┌Vertical Alignment─────────────────────────┐     │
│  │ ⦿ Top  ○ Center  ○ Justify                │     │
│  └───────────────────────────────────────────┘     │
└──────────────────────────────────────────────────┘
```

By default, the Line Numbering toggle box is off and the Line Numbers option set is ghosted. When you activate the toggle box, the Line Numbers option set becomes activated. The Start At option lets you specify at what number the line numbering should begin. The From Text field specifies how far the line numbers should be to the left of each line. The Auto default entry is 0.25". If you use the Auto default spacing with multiple columns, there must be at least 0.38" between each column. Figure 7-10 shows that line numbers must be at least 0.13" from any column of text; 0.13" plus 0.25" is 0.38".

The Count By field determines the intervals in which the line numbers will run; they do not have to run sequentially, such as 1,2,3, and so on. You can specify that lines increase in multiples of

Figure 7-10.

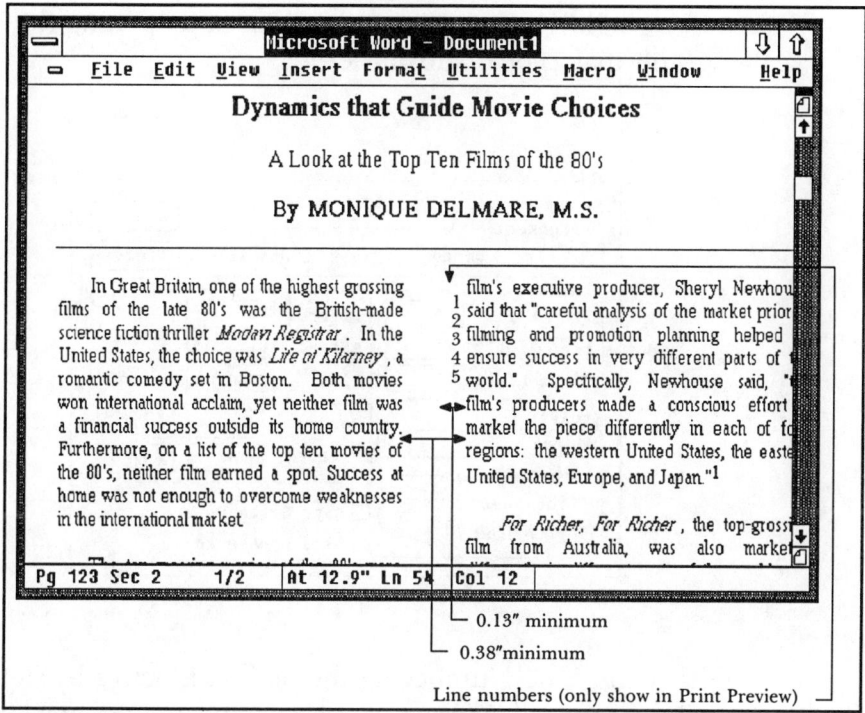

Column widths

any number that you like. For example, if you typed **5** in the Count By field, the line numbers would read 5, 10, 15, 20, and so on.

The Per Page and Per Section options tell Word for Windows where to begin the line numbering each time. The default is every page, which means the first line on every page will be assigned a 1. If you choose the Per Section option, the count would continue throughout a section. The Continue option picks up the numbering count from the previous section in which you used line numbering.

After you apply line numbering to a section, the renumbering becomes automatic. That is, whenever you insert a new line in a section, it will be assigned the proper number and all subsequent lines will be renumbered.

You can turn off the line numbering in paragraphs within a section by highlighting those paragraphs and opening the Format Paragraph dialog box, shown here.

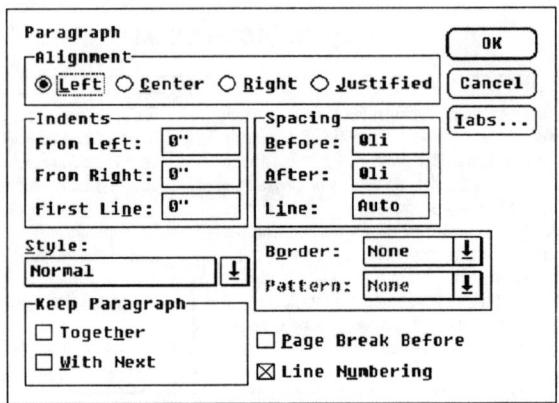

Note that the Line Numbering toggle box is active by default. If you click the left mouse button on this toggle box, thereby inactivating it, the line numbering will skip the highlighted paragraphs. Lines that are skipped are omitted from the numbering sequence; the line numbers continue on the next line in the section that is formatted to include line numbering.

Another way to skip a passage between line numbered sections is to add a section break with the Insert Break command before you type the paragraph(s) you want to insert. You would lose the line numbering in the part of the section that followed the insert. You could turn line numbering back on by choosing the Continue option in the Format Section Line Numbers option set. The previously formatted line numbers would reappear in the section following the insert. Turning off line numbering in an insert with the Format Paragraph dialog box is a much easier way to preserve the line numbering around an insert.

Generating a Table of Contents

Word for Windows lets you create a table of contents in either the Outline View or the Normal Editing View. To create a table of contents in the Outline View, first you choose the heads you want, and then you activate the Insert Table of Contents command. To create a table of contents in the Normal Editing View, you can also activate the Insert Table of Contents command or you can use fields to indicate the items to be included in the table of contents. In either case, Word for Windows automatically assembles a table of contents.

Creating a Table of Contents in the Outline View

Before you generate a table of contents, you must choose the heads you want to appear in it. Make sure each head has the level that corresponds to its importance in the table of contents. You can use the Show buttons to limit the table of contents to only the higher-level heads, or use the Show All button to include all heads.

To generate a table of contents in the Outline View, place the cursor in the document where you want the table of contents to appear. Then, choose the Table of Contents command in the Insert Menu, as shown here.

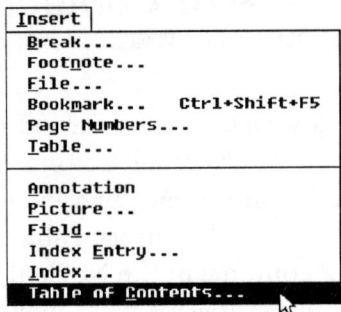

This will cause the Insert Table of Contents dialog box to be displayed, as shown here.

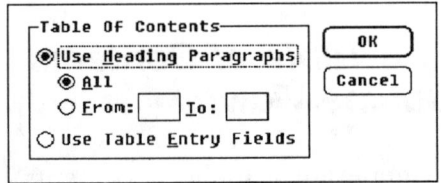

By default, the Use Heading Paragraphs and All buttons are active. Clicking the left mouse button on the OK button at this point will create a table of contents using all heads.

You do not have to use all the heads in a table of contents. You can list the levels of heads you want in the From and To fields in the Insert Table of Contents dialog box or you can collapse the heads you do not want included by using the Show buttons. In

Figure 7-11, the text from Figure 7-2 was used to generate a table of contents with level 1 and 2 heads. Note in Figure 7-11 that the Show 2 button was activated before the Insert Table of Contents command, limiting the displayed heads to levels 1 and 2.

Each line of text in a table of contents has a row of dots ending in a page number. This dotted line is a spacing mechanism; it is not printed. Only the page numbers are printed.

Changing the Table of Contents Format with the Replace Command You can choose both the text and the format of a table of contents. To change the text, such as from all level 1 heads to level 1 and level 2 heads, you can use either the From and To fields in the Insert Table of Contents dialog box, or you can activate the appropriate Show button before you open the Insert Table of Contents dialog box. To change the format of a table of

Figure 7-11.

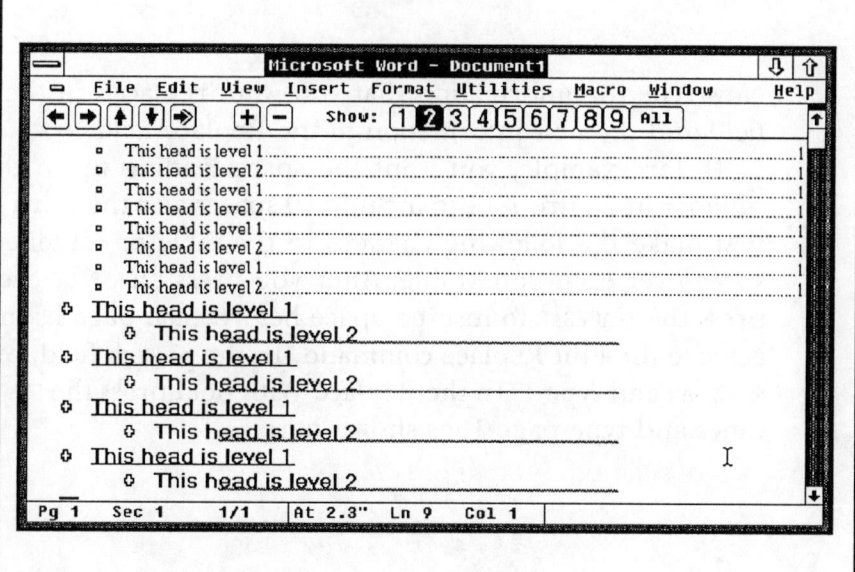

Table of contents based on level 1 and level 2 heads

contents, you can use the Edit Replace command or fields to create the table of contents.

Unlike most processing and publishing packages, search and replace is not a single function in Word for Windows. The Edit Search command feature can find a character string anywhere in a document. However, like the earlier versions of Word, the Word for Windows Edit Search command is linked to the Edit Replace command. If you have previously made an entry in the Edit Search dialog box, it will appear in the Search field of the Edit Replace dialog box, shown here.

```
┌─────────────────────────────────────────────────────────────┐
│  Search For:                                   ┌──────────┐  │
│  ┌─────────────────────────────────────────┐   │    OK    │  │
│  └─────────────────────────────────────────┘   └──────────┘  │
│  Replace With:                                 ┌──────────┐  │
│  ┌─────────────────────────────────────────┐   │  Cancel  │  │
│  └─────────────────────────────────────────┘   └──────────┘  │
│                                                               │
│  ☐ Whole Word                                                 │
│  ☐ Match Upper/Lowercase            ☒ Confirm Changes         │
└─────────────────────────────────────────────────────────────┘
```

Now type the information that you want replaced in the Search field and the new information in the Replace field.

If, for example, you want the space leading up to the page number in Figure 7-11 to include 10 spaces and the word "page," first make the following changes to the table of contents. Backspace over each dotted line. After you press BACKSPACE each time, press the SPACEBAR to insert a space before each page listing. Now activate the Edit Replace command. In the Search field, press the SPACEBAR and type **1**. In the Replace With field press the SPACEBAR 10 times and type **page 1,** as shown here.

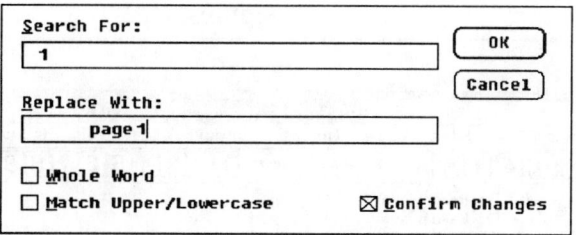

Next, click the left mouse button on the OK button. Word for Windows will now search for the character string you typed in the Search field. When it finds the first occurrence, it will highlight the passage and prompt you with the following message box:

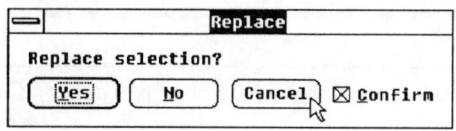

If the passage is one that you want replaced with the text in the Replace field, click the left mouse button on the OK button. If you do not want the passage replaced and you wish to continue searching, click the left mouse button on the No button. After you have replaced the last occurrence of the Search character string, click the left mouse button on the Cancel button; the replacement process will stop.

When you are finished replacing the dotted lines with 10 spaces and the word "page," your table of contents will look like the one in Figure 7-12. The Edit Search and Edit Replace commands are discussed in depth in Chapter 8, "Group Productions."

Figure 7-12.

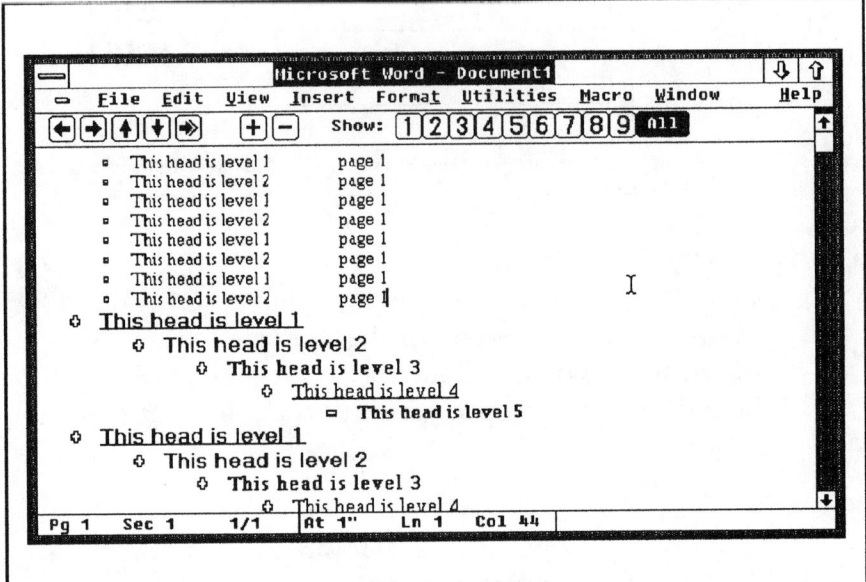

Use of Edit Replace command to change Table of Contents format

You can also Search and Replace formatted text or just formatting. Type the formatting codes shown in Table 7-2 before selected text or alone to delete or change the formatting within a document. Formatting characters are normally hidden, but they can be displayed by pressing CTRL-SHIFT-*.

Creating a Table of Contents in the Normal Editing View

The quickest way to create a table of contents is to use the Insert Table of Contents command. You can use this command in both the Outline View and the Normal Editing View. This method, however, does not give you much control over the format of the table of contents. If you create a Table of Contents field (TOC) in

Table 7-2.

Formatting	Code to Type in Edit Search or Replace Field
Any ASCII characters*	CTRL-xxx (xxx = Windows/ANSI code)
Bold	CTRL-b
Caret	CTRL-^
Column Break	CTRL-14
Double Underline	CTRL-d
Footnote Reference Mark	CTRL-5
Graphic Image	CTRL-l
Hidden Text	CTRL-h
Italic	CTRL-i
Line Break	CTRL-n
Nonbreaking Hyphen	CTRL-^
Nonbreaking Space	CTRL-s
Optional Hyphen	CTRL-hyphen
Page or Section Break	CTRL-d
Paragraph	CTRL-p
Question Mark	CTRL-?
Small Caps	CTRL-k
Strikethrough	CTRL-z
Tab	CTRL-t
Underline	CTRL-u
White Space	CTRL-s
Word Underline	CTRL-w

*See Windows/ANSI character set in Appendix E, "Font Character Sets and Sources

Codes for Search or Replace of formatting (Adapted with permission from the documentation for Microsoft Word for Windows, Microsoft Corporation, 1990.)

the Normal Editing View, you have more control over the text and format.

In "Creating a Table of Contents in the Outline View," earlier in this chapter, you used the Insert Table of Contents command to include text that had been formatted with heading styles. You can also use this command to incorporate text that has been assigned the TC field into a table of contents.

If you want more control over the text and format in a table of contents than you have with the Insert Table of Contents command, you can use very specific TC and TOC fields. You insert the TOC field at the location where you want the table of contents. You specify the format of each listing in the table of contents with TC field options and you specify the text and format of the table of contents with TOC field options.

Using the TC Fields   There are two ways to make entries for a table of contents. The use of the heading styles was discussed in the previous section entitled "Creating a Table of Contents in the Outline View." You can also specify entries while you type a document by adding table of contents listings in separate TC fields (fields are discussed in Chapter 6, "Advanced Template Features: Glossaries, Boilerplate Text, Fields, and Macros").

To begin labeling text to be included in a table of contents, activate the Insert Field command immediately after typing the text (do not add a space). Click the left mouse button on the Insert Fields command or press ALT-i, d. Then choose the TC field in the Insert Field Type scroll box. TC appears in the Field Code text entry field.

As an example, suppose you had just typed the introduction head in your document. Without pressing the SPACEBAR after you type **Introduction**, activate the Insert Field command. You could now create a TC field like the one shown here.

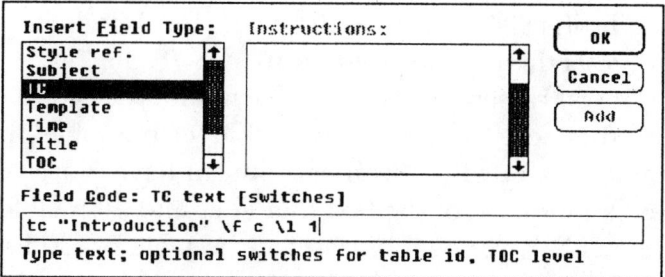

To do so, place the cursor in the Field Code text entry field and enter a space after the TC field code and type **Introduction**. The text in quotes is a head that will be included in the table of contents. Next you add another space and a backslash (\) to signal that field options are to follow, as shown. The first option is **f** for format, after which you add a space and the letter **c** to represent a table of contents entry. Then type another space, type **** (backslash), a lowercase **l**, space, and a number indicating the level the text should take in the table of contents. In the example, Introduction has been assigned level 1; remember, level 1 heads automatically assume a Heading 1 style.

Using TC Fields for Other Table of . . . Listings   You can also make TC entries for a table of . . . listings other than a table of contents. To do this, you add letters other than **c** after the \f format option. For example, you can create other tables of . . . listings within one document such as a table of authorities, a table of figures, a table of graphs (or charts), a table of illustrations, a table of photos, and so on, by coding each TC field with the proper \f option. The letter you add will depend on what kind of table of . . . listings you were creating and the letter that codes for each particular table of . . . listings. In fact, you can make up any system of coding for the format options that you desire. Whatever letter scheme you use, make sure that you use it consistently with each type of table of . . . listings. The same letter that you enter in the TC field will be used by the TOC field to create each table of

. . . listings. The Microsoft Word for Windows documentation suggests the notation system used in Table 7-3.

If you can create TC fields each time you type a head, subhead, or other text that you want included in a table of contents or in another table of . . . listings, you can have more control over the text and format of the text that goes into each table of . . . listings. Remember, you will not create the table of . . . listings until you finish the document. At that time you will insert a TOC field for each table of . . . listings.

Using TC Field Entries with the Insert Table of Contents Command

There are two methods by which you can create a table of contents or any other table of . . . listings with TC fields in the Normal Editing View. First, you can use the Insert Table of Contents command. After you have made all your TC field entries, you activate the Insert Table of Contents command (see "Creating a

Table 7-3.

Field Type	Option
Authorities	\ a
Contents	\ c (Word for Windows default)
Figures	\ f
Graphs or Charts	\ g
Illustrations	\ i
Photos	\ p
Tables	\ t

Field Options for Tables of . . . (TC) Listings (Adapted with permission from the documentation for Microsoft Word for Windows, Microsoft Corporation, 1990.)

Table of Contents in the Outline View") at the desired location in the document. The Insert Table of Contents dialog box is then displayed, as shown here.

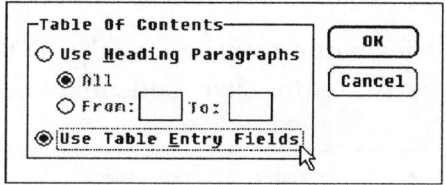

Activate the Use Table Entry Fields button, as shown. Notice that the From and To fields are ghosted in this dialog box; they are not available when you use fields. Therefore, you must use all the TC fields with this command. When you click the left mouse button on the OK button, Word for Windows will use all the TC fields that have been formatted with the selected heading styles.

Remember that you can assign heading styles to the listings in the TC fields with the \l option; see "Using the TC Fields." These heading styles will be used to format the text that is inserted in the table of contents, but you have no control over the format of the rest of the text and the page numbers that will be inserted in the table of contents. You must use the Table of Contents field (TOC) if you want to change the default table of contents format after the table of contents is created.

Using TC Field Entries with the TOC Field

To create a table of contents using the TC fields, first you must have made all your TC field insertions (see "Using the TC Fields"). First, place the cursor at the location in the document where you want the table of contents to appear. Then activate the Insert Field command. This causes the Insert Field dialog box to be displayed. Choose the TOC field in the Insert Field dialog box. The increased control that you have over the format of the table of contents is achieved by adding options to the field in this dialog box.

To add formatting options to the TOC field, you must first move the cursor to the Field Code text entry field, as shown here.

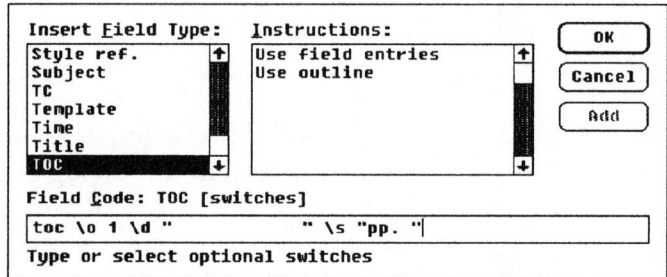

The \o option in this example is used to specify that only the level 1 heads should be used to create the table of contents. (The introduction head would have to have been formatted with the Heading 1 style before the TOC field was inserted.) The \d option is used to indicate that spaces inside the quotes should separate the head and the page number. Finally, the \s option indicates a prefix for the page numbers. The first listing in the table of contents created by this TOC field will look like the following:

Introduction   pp. 1

The complete set of TOC field options is listed in Table 7-4. Note the Sequence (\s) field option in Table 7-4. This is used to create a table of . . . listing from sequence numbers rather than TC fields.

If you insert a Sequence field (SEQ) for a non-table of contents listing, a sequence number will be inserted at the location of the Sequence field. For example, you might insert a field at the location of every figure caption in a document like the following:

Figure {SEQ Figure}: A Doll.

Then Word for Windows will insert a running sequence number at the same spot when you print. If this sample Sequence field was the first inserted, the text as printed would read:

Figure 1: A Doll.

To be consistent, you must type all your figure captions in the same way. If you put a \s Figure option in the TOC field, Word for Windows will create a table of . . . listings for all the {SEQ Figure} fields. This is just one example of the increased flexibility you gain by creating a table of . . . listings from TC fields with the TOC field.

Table 7-4.

Field Type	Option
Make TOC only from bookmark	\b
Add characters in quotes as separators between sequence numbers and page numbers	\d "characters"
Use only TC fields with this format marker	\f
Use only TC fields with these outline heading levels	\o
Use number or character in SEQ field specific to each table of . . . listing	\s

Field Options for Tables of . . . (TC) Listings (Adapted with permission from the documentation for Microsoft Word for Windows, Microsoft Corporation, 1990.)

You now know how powerful Word for Windows Outline View is in organizing a document, as well as in assembling tables of contents listings. It is also clear that you gain a great deal of flexibility in creating tables of . . . listings by using TC and TOC fields. You should be able to use the links between all these tools to make your document creation more efficient than ever before.

PART

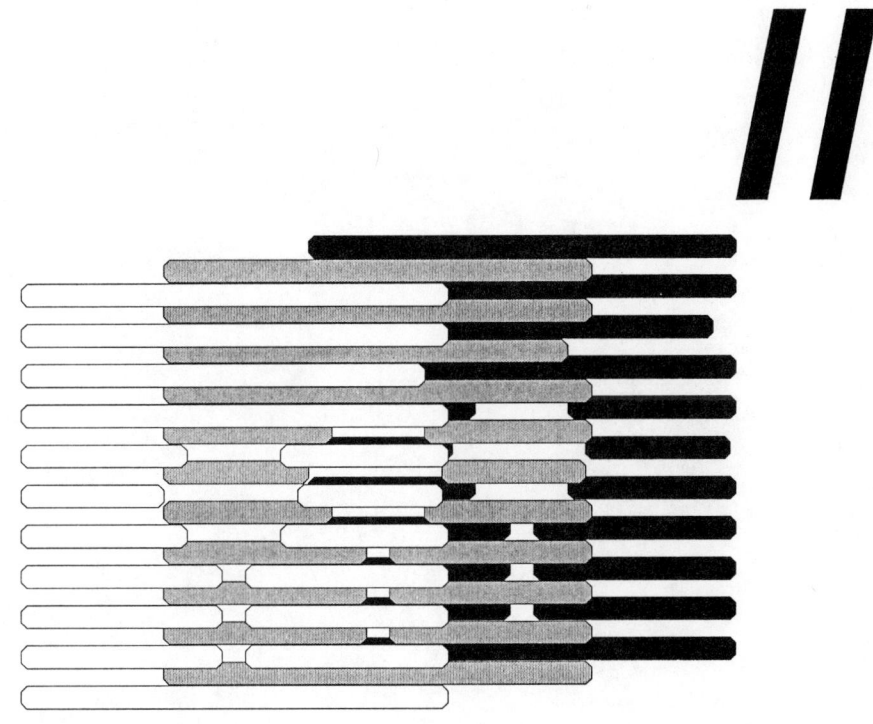

II

Added Power of Word
for Windows

CHAPTER

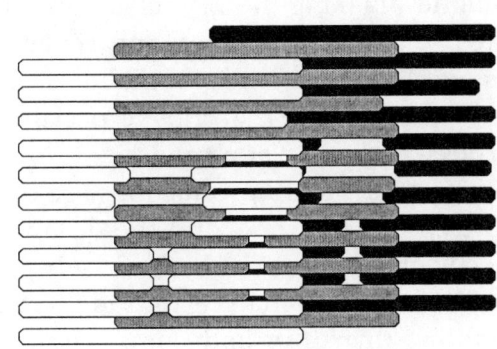

8

Group Productions

A major advantage of word publishing in comparison to desktop publishing software is the speed at which it lets you get work done. That work speed is even more important when you are part of a group trying to get a report, a presentation, or a legal contract into shape. Desktop publishing programs can add finishing font and graphic flourish to such documents, but are not designed for the production process — that is, putting projects through numerous drafts, edits, and revisions.

Word processing packages are also limited with regard to group produced documents. First, they are primarily aimed at single users. This is why most word processing packages lack the capacity to accept annotations and compare a revision with the original version of a document. Second, word processors slow down the production of group projects because they lack font and graphic handling capabilities, making the results flat and lifeless. Word for Windows gives you both annotation and version comparison tools as well as excellent font and graphic tools. Both of these increase the productivity of work groups, especially those with more than one project underway at a time.

In many office environments, group productions are done on a network. Although the cost of networks and the distance they traverse limit their effectiveness, networks have already become the most effective tool for coordinating intradepartmental projects. Word for Windows thrives in both local area network (LAN) and wide area network (WAN) environments. Word for Windows protects files that all users need access to, while allowing multiple users simultaneous access to the same document. Whenever it is available, the OS/2 version of Word for Windows will add further communications and memory management flexibility.

This chapter discusses all the nuts and bolts of group production in an office environment. Creating documents for annotation, version comparison, and exchange on a network are the major topics. The focus will be on a project in which the author sends out a document for comments (perhaps on a network), incorporates those comments, and then compares the differences between the original version and the revised version.

Annotations

The annotation pane is one of Word for Windows most important tools for a multiauthor document. After finishing the first draft of a document, the writer *locks* the document. In a locked document, no edits can be made to the original text; many reviewers or editors can, however, read the document and make comments, or annotations, in the Word for Windows annotation pane. The annotation pane works the same way as the split document window pane (see Chapter 1) and the footnote pane (see Chapter 7). After the reviewers have surveyed the document, the author can review their comments and make changes to the original document.

There are two ways to compare the original document with the version into which the author has incorporated other people's comments. The most powerful way is to use the Utilities Compare command. Another way is to open a second document window and view both versions simultaneously.

Preparing a Document for Annotation

When you are preparing a document that will be annotated, keep in mind three major considerations. First, ask yourself if you want to call any parts of the document to the reviewer's attention. If so, you can easily do this with bookmarks.

Second, let the reader know how many characters, words, and pages the document currently contains and any limits of each. These parameters may influence the scope and depth of comments the reviewer makes.

Finally, keep in mind the commands that are available and unavailable to the reviewer of a locked document. All these considerations should be addressed before you lock a document that is to be annotated.

Inserting Bookmarks

Bookmarks are used to call attention to passages in documents being prepared for annotation. Depending on how you name the bookmark, it can be addressed to one or more specific reviewers.

The bookmark name can also refer to a particular topic or passage. Reviewers use the Edit Go To command (see "Using the Edit Go To Command" later in the chapter) to see the names of Bookmarks.

To insert a bookmark, highlight a block of text and activate the Insert Bookmark command, shown here.

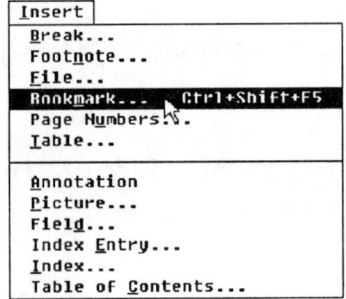

Note that you can also use the CTRL-SHIFT-F5 macro to activate this command. If you use the CTRL-SHIFT-F5 macro, a prompt will appear in the status bar where you can type the bookmark name; then press ENTER. Use the mouse to display the Insert Bookmark dialog box and type the name of the bookmark in the Bookmark Name text entry field shown here.

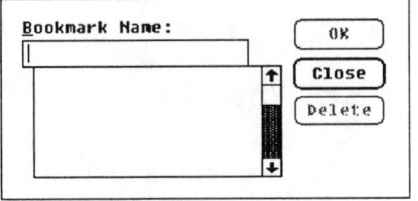

As soon as you begin typing, the OK and Delete buttons will become available. You can type up to 20 characters in the Bookmark Name field. The name must begin with a letter, although it can have numbers and punctuation marks (hyphen, underline, question mark, etc.), other than a period after the first letter. You cannot insert spaces in the Bookmark Name field.

After you add a bookmark, it is displayed in the Bookmark Name scroll box. Remember, you can name bookmarks to call attention to particular reviewers, or to particular topics that will be covered in the passage, or both. For example, in the Bookmark Name scroll box shown here,

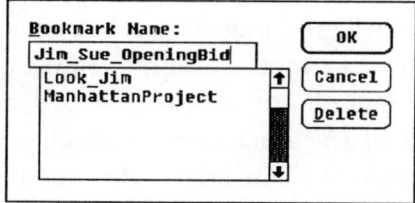

the Look_Jim bookmark (the underline mark is used here instead of a space, which cannot be used in a bookmark) calls Jim's attention to a passage of text. The ManhattanProject bookmark calls all reviewers' attention to the passage on the Manhattan Project. The Jim_Sue_OpeningBid Bookmark calls Jim's and Sue's attention to a passage on the opening bid. In this way, bookmarks save reviewers' time by focusing their attention on the areas and topics for which you most need feedback.

An important point to keep in mind when using bookmarks is that the reader must know that there are bookmarks in the locked document. You can, for example, include a cover note telling the reviewer to look at the bookmark listing in the Go To scroll box in the Edit Go To dialog box. In fact, you may want to ask a very busy reviewer to give you specific feedback only on the passages assigned to a limited set of bookmarks.

Using Character, Word, and Page Counts

For many projects, it is important to know the character, word, and page counts. For example, many types of legal documents require line numbering (see Chapter 7 for a discussion of line numbering) in order to limit the number of, and to refer to, lines and pages. Many granting agencies and journals impose word limits. Character counts are often useful for calculating costs involved in sending documents via electronic mail. These counts also let you and the reviewers know how close the document is to a character, word, or page limit.

Word for Windows offers an easy way to supply reviewers with character, word, and page count information. That information is found in the document summary statistics, shown in Figure 8-1.

You can include the character, word, and page count information shown in the document summary in a cover letter with a locked document. You access the document summary with the Edit Summary Info command. This command displays the Edit Document Summary dialog box. Activating the Statistics button in this dialog box displays the document summary statistics.

In the example shown in Figure 8-1, note that the character and word counts are 0. That is what you might see if you had created a document but did not save it. The character, word, and page counts will be automatically updated each time you save a document.

Instead of leaving the document summary, you can also activate the Update button in the Document Summary Statistics dialog box. The character, word, and page counts will be automatically updated. You can then include this latest information in a cover letter to the reviewers.

You can also automatically insert the character, word, and page counts in the document, either as hidden text (seen on the

Figure 8-1.

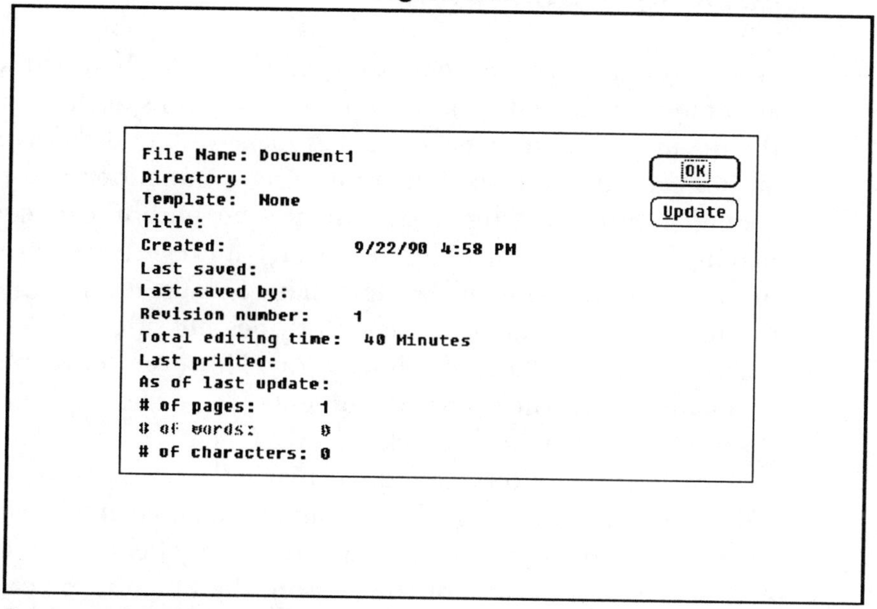

```
File Name: Document1                              ┌────────┐
Directory:                                        │  :OK:  │
Template:  None                                   └────────┘
Title:                                            ┌────────┐
Created:              9/22/90 4:58 PM             │ Update │
Last saved:                                       └────────┘
Last saved by:
Revision number:   1
Total editing time:  40 Minutes
Last printed:
As of last update:
# of pages:        1
# of words:        0
# of characters: 0
```

Document Summary Statistics

screen but not printed), or as a printed part of the document. This is done by inserting the Numchars (character count), Numwords (word count), or Numpages (page count) fields in your document. These fields will have the latest character, word, and page numbers as long as you either save the document or press the Update Fields key (F9) before you lock the document for annotation. If you want the result of these fields to be hidden text (displayed, but not printed), then you must first make sure the View Field Codes command is inactive. Then highlight the character, word, and page counts and use the Format Character dialog box to format them as hidden text. You will also need to tell your reviewers in a cover letter to activate the Hidden Text toggle box in the View Preferences dialog box.

Locking a Document

When you are ready to send your document to the reviewers for annotation, you first lock it. Only a document's author can lock the document; moreover, once it is locked, only the document's author can unlock it (see "Incorporating Annotations" later in the chapter). After locking a document, the author can continue making changes to it. The reviewers, however, are limited to inserting annotations in the document because they cannot edit the text at all. Locking a document does not affect the author's ability to edit the document in any way. However, authors cannot annotate any of their own documents, regardless of whether a document is locked or unlocked.

Word for Windows can discern whether a reviewer or the author has opened a locked document because each user will have a different name in the Your Name text entry field in the Utilities Customize dialog box. For this reason, the file must be called up by another reviewer, using a separately installed copy of Word for Windows or on another terminal or node in a network, for the annotation features to work. You cannot create and lock a document and then ask the reviewer to use your computer to annotate the document, unless you change the name in the Your Name field in the Utilites Customize dialog box.

To lock a document, activate the File Save As command, click the left mouse button on the Options button, and select the Lock for Annotations toggle box, as shown here.

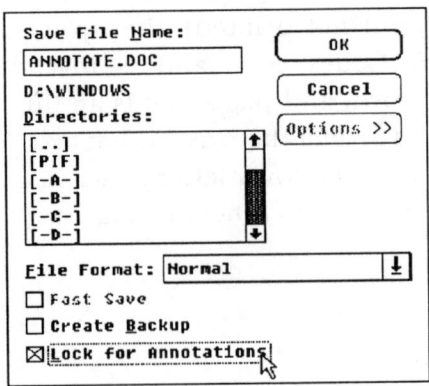

Then activate the OK button. The document will now be saved as a locked document.

Unavailable Features in Locked Documents

Many commands and actions will be unavailable in both the document window and the annotation pane when you open a locked document with a copy of Word for Windows that has a Utilities Customize Your Name field different from that of the locked document's author. (Recall that the annotation pane is displayed with the View Annotation command.)

When you lock a document, it is important for the author of the document to remember which features reviewers will not be able to access. For example, a reviewer will not be able to change the document's styles or use any of the Format commands in the document window. Table 8-1 lists the unavailable features.

The reviewers will, however, be able to check the styles with the ruler. If there is any reason why the reviewer might comment on the styles, make a copy of the styles information. To do this, either print the styles information on paper using the Print Styles option in the File Print dialog box or print this information to a file (for a discussion of printing, see Chapter 5, "Printing: Picture Perfect Output").

Entering Annotations

Once you have a locked document ready for review, send the file to the reviewers via E-Mail (electronic mail) or on a floppy disk. If

Table 8-1.

Part I	
Menu	**Document Window Command**
File	Save As Lock option
Edit	Undo, Repeat, Cut, Paste, Paste Link, Replace, Summary Info, Header/Footer, Glossaries, Table
View	Outline, Page, Annotations
Format	All commands
Utilities	Customize
Macro	Template option ghosted with both Assign to Menu and Assign to Key, all default formatting macros
View	Both Ribbon and Ruler can be used only to view settings, not to format
Part II	
Menu	**Annotation Pane Command**
File	Save As Lock option
Edit	Summary Info, Header/Footer, Glossaries, Table
View	Outline, Page, Footnote
Format	Section, Document, Styles, Position, Define Styles
Utilities	Repaginate Now, Revision Marks, Compare Versions, Calculate
Macro	Template option ghosted with both Assign to Menu and Assign to Key

Actions Unavailable with a Locked Document (Adapted with permission from the documentation for Microsoft Word for Windows, Microsoft Corporation, 1990.)

you are working on a network, you can probably leave the file in your folder as long as the reviewers can access it.

You open a locked document the same way you open any other document, with the File Open command. You can then read the document on the screen or print it. When you come to a passage you want to annotate (comment on), put the cursor either at the beginning, anywhere within, or after the passage. Then activate the Insert Annotation command shown here.

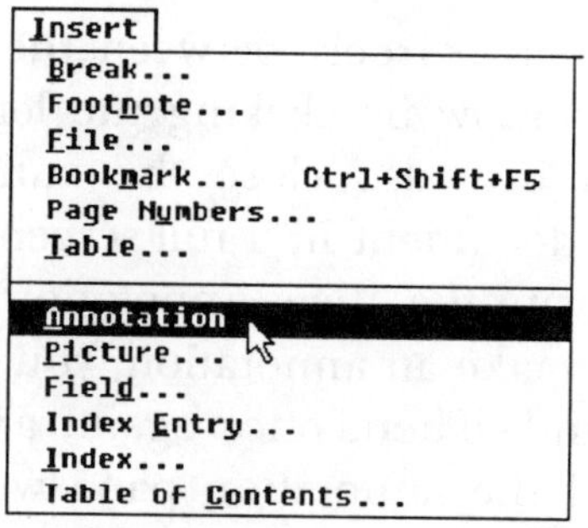

```
┌─────────────┐
│ Insert      │
├─────────────────────────────────────────┐
│ Break...                                 │
│ Footnote...                              │
│ File...                                  │
│ Bookmark...    Ctrl+Shift+F5             │
│ Page Numbers...                          │
│ Table...                                 │
│                                          │
│ ▓Annotation▓                             │
│ Picture...   ⊳                           │
│ Field...                                 │
│ Index Entry...                           │
│ Index...                                 │
│ Table of Contents...                     │
└──────────────────────────────────────────┘
```

This command automatically inserts your initials into the locked document at the location of the cursor. Word for Windows also keeps track of how many annotation marks you make and inserts that number after your initials. This annotation mark—your initials and the number—is displayed onscreen but will not print; it is in hidden text. At the same time that Word for Windows inserts an annotation mark, an annotation pane, like that seen in Figure 8-2, opens at the bottom of the screen.

Figure 8-2.

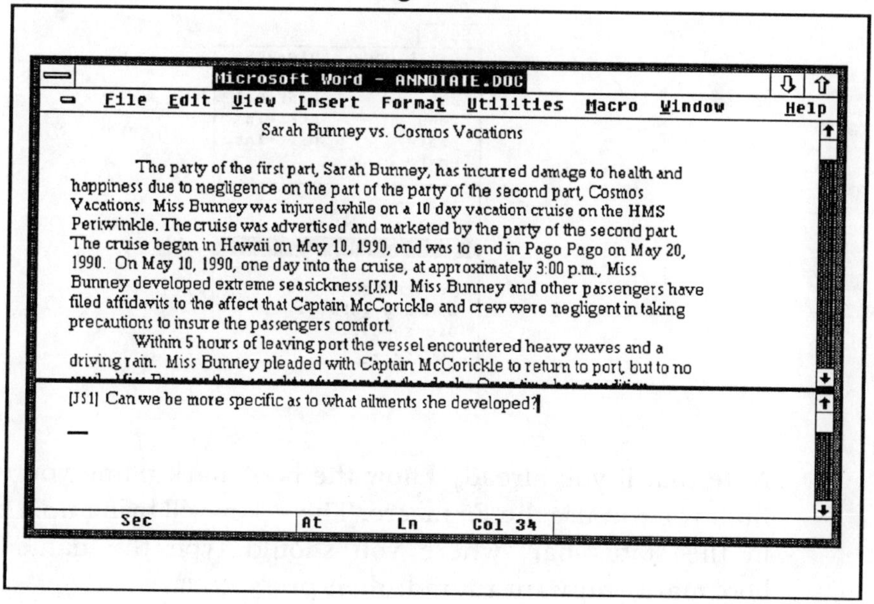

Inserting an annotation

You can move freely between the annotation pane and the document window by clicking the left mouse button on either screen. You can also close the annotation pane to continue reading the document in a full-screen Normal Editing View. To do this, activate the View Annotation command. The next time you want to make an annotation, you activate the Insert Annotation command. Then, once again, an annotation mark will be inserted and the annotation pane will open. Figure 8-3 shows what the annotation pane looks like with several annotations.

Locating Bookmarks

To find bookmarks, use the Edit Go To command, shown here.

Note that if you already know the bookmark name you want to find, you can use the F5 macro. The F5 key will bring up a prompt in the status bar, where you should type the name of the bookmark you want to find; then press ENTER.

If you activate the Edit Go To command with the mouse, the Edit Go To dialog box, seen here,

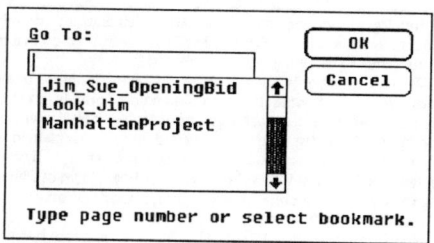

is then displayed. You can choose bookmarks either by clicking the left mouse button on their names in the Go To scroll box or by using the UP ARROW and DOWN ARROW. After choosing a bookmark, either press ENTER or click the left mouse button on the OK button. Word for Windows will automatically scan the document and place the cursor on the location where the bookmark was inserted.

Incorporating Annotations

When you receive a locked document from a reviewer, you must decide how to incorporate the reviewer's comments. When you open the file, you do not need to unlock the document. All commands will be available as long as you open the file when Word for Windows has your name in the Your Name text entry box in the Utilities Customize dialog box.

The first step in incorporating annotations is to view them. Activating the View Annotations command will open the annotation pane in the lower half of the document window, as seen in Figure 8-3. Because the annotation pane takes up a large portion

Figure 8-3.

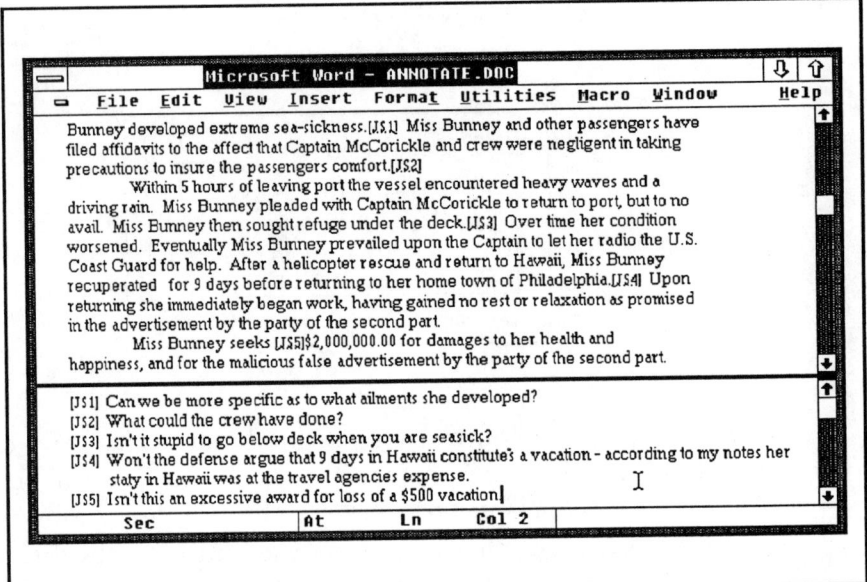

Annotation pane with five annotations

of the Word for Windows screen, you may have difficulty seeing all the annotations. Therefore it is a good idea to print a copy of the annotations by using the Print Annotations option in the File Print dialog box (for a discussion of printing annotations, see Chapter 5).

After printing the annotations, open the annotation pane with the View Annotations command. Now you can begin deciding which annotations to incorporate. To delete an annotation, place the cursor on the hidden text of the annotation mark and delete it. Note that when you click the left mouse button anywhere on the annotation mark, the whole mark is highlighted. When you delete an annotation mark, the associated annotation in the annotation pane will also disappear.

To insert all or part of an annotation into the document, first highlight what you want to insert, as shown in the example in Figure 8-4. Next press F2, the Move key; you will see the status bar display:

```
Move to where?
```

as in Figure 8-4. This key copies the highlighted text to memory so you can paste it in the document window.

Next press F6, the Next Pane key. Notice that the mouse in the annotation pane changes from an I-beam to an arrow shape. When you move the mouse over the document window, it reverts to the I-beam shape. This is because the Next Pane key (F6) changes the active window from the annotation pane to the document window. (Another way to move the mouse between the annotation pane and the document window is to click the mouse once anywhere in the document window.)

After you press F6 and have the I-beam-shaped mouse in the document window, place the cursor at the spot where you want to insert the highlighted annotation. Then press ENTER. The annotation will appear in the document window, as in Figure 8-5. You can go through all the annotations in this way.

Using the Edit Go To Command

The Edit Go To command enables you to move to any annotation very quickly. Then, if you have a printout of your annotations and know which ones you want to incorporate, you can quickly insert them.

If you are at the beginning of the document and want to go to the first annotation, type **a** in the Go To field of the Edit Go To dialog box and press ENTER. The cursor will go to the first annotation. To go to the next annotation in the document from any other point in the document, you also type **a** in this field and press ENTER. To go to a particular annotation, type **a#** (a and the

Figure 8-4.

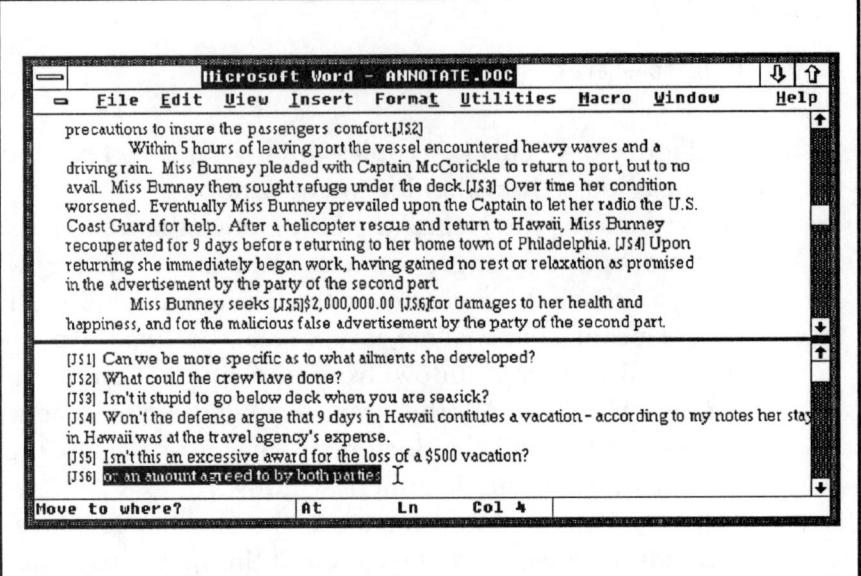

Moving an annotation into a document

Figure 8-5.

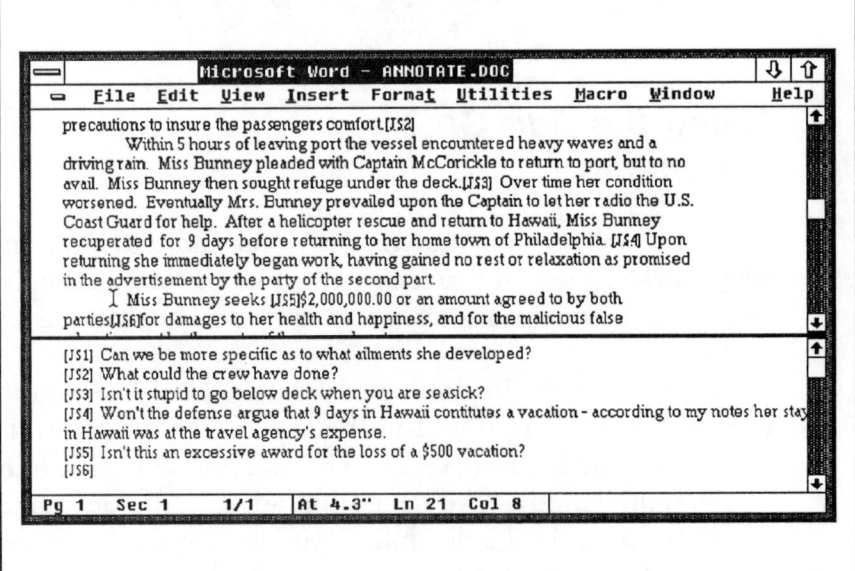

Annotation inserted into document

annotation number) in the Go To field. For example, to go to the fourth annotation from any location in the document, type **a4** in the Go To field.

If you type **a+#** in the Go To field, the cursor moves that many annotations past its present location. For example, a+3 would move the cursor 3 annotations forward. Similarly, typing **a−#** moves the cursor that many annotations back towards the beginning of the document.

Another use of the Go To field is to identify annotations by their sections and page locations. The variable for section is s; the variable for page is p. You cannot use the a+ or a− statements with the s or p variables. You can, however, combine the a and p, a and s, or a, p, and s variables in any combination and in any order you wish. (You can determine the a and p variables by counting annotations on the screen; however, it will take you less time to count the annotations on a printed copy of the document that includes just the annotations. Once you know the number and page of the annotation from the printed copy, you can use the a and p variables in the Go To field of the Edit Go To dialog box to find the annotation onscreen. See the section on the Print Annotation option in Chapter 5, "Printing: Picture Perfect Output." You can only determine the section number by counting the sections on the screen.) Keep in mind that the original document must have section formatting for you to use the s variable. Here are some examples:

Go To Field Entry	Cursor Jumps To
$a3$	3rd annotation
$a3s2$	3rd annotation
$s2a3$	2nd section
$a4p5$	4th annotation
$p5a4$	5th page

a2s3p4	2nd annotation
s3a2p4	3rd section
p4s3a2	4th page
p4a2s3	

Comparing Revised and Original Documents

After you incorporate annotations into a document, you might want to compare the rewrite with the original document. There are three ways to do this: with multiple document windows, with the Compare Versions command, and with the Revision Marks command. These three methods give you varying degrees of control over finding changes made in the original document during the revision process. With all three processes, make sure you save the rewritten document to a file name other than that of the original document. This will preserve the original document for comparison with the rewrite.

Using Multiple Document Windows

If the document is short, the most efficient way to compare the original and revised versions is to use two document windows. First open the original document with the File Open command. Then open the second, annotated document. The newly opened file fills the entire document window, even though the original document is still open. You can display both document windows simultaneously (half-screen views) by activating the Window Arrange All command, shown here.

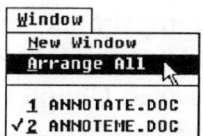

Word for Windows will arrange all the currently open document windows into equally sized document windows within the program window. Figure 8-6 shows an example with the original

Figure 8-6.

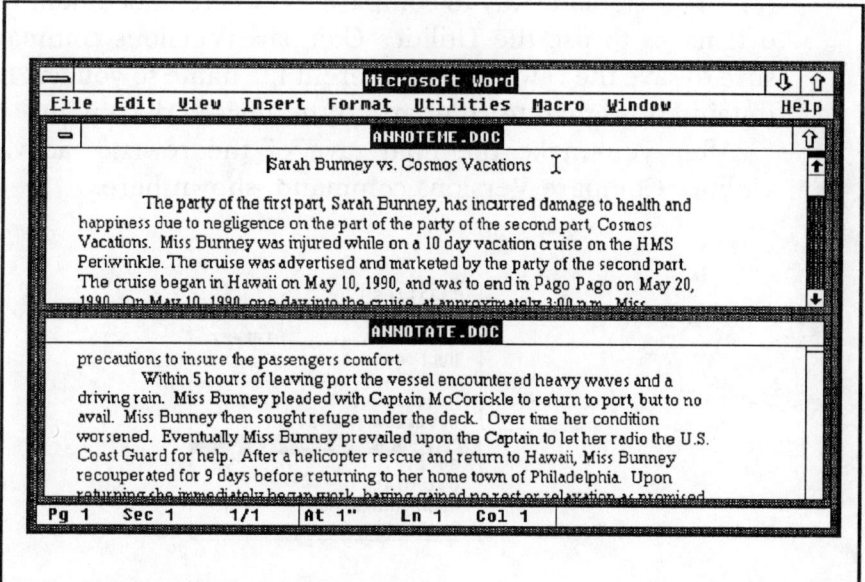

Setting up document windows for comparison

document, ANNOTEME.DOC, in the second (top) document window.

Note that only the active document window has a Document Control Menu button. You can make the other document window active by clicking the left mouse button on the inactive window's title bar, or by clicking the left mouse button on the text in the inactive document window. You can also change the size of the document windows (see Chapter 1, "Up and Running"). With both document windows displayed, you can compare texts.

Using the Utilities Compare Versions Command

A more systematic way to compare a rewritten document with the original is to use the Utilities Compare Versions command. Be sure to save the rewrite to a different file name so you will have an untainted original to compare to the revised document.

After you make the final save of the rewrite, activate the Utilities Compare Versions command, shown here.

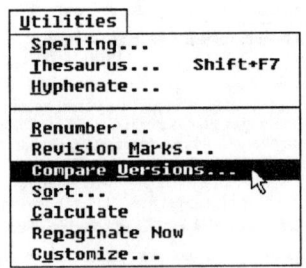

It displays the Utilities Compare Versions dialog box, shown in Figure 8-7. Choose the original, unannotated document to com-

Figure 8-7.

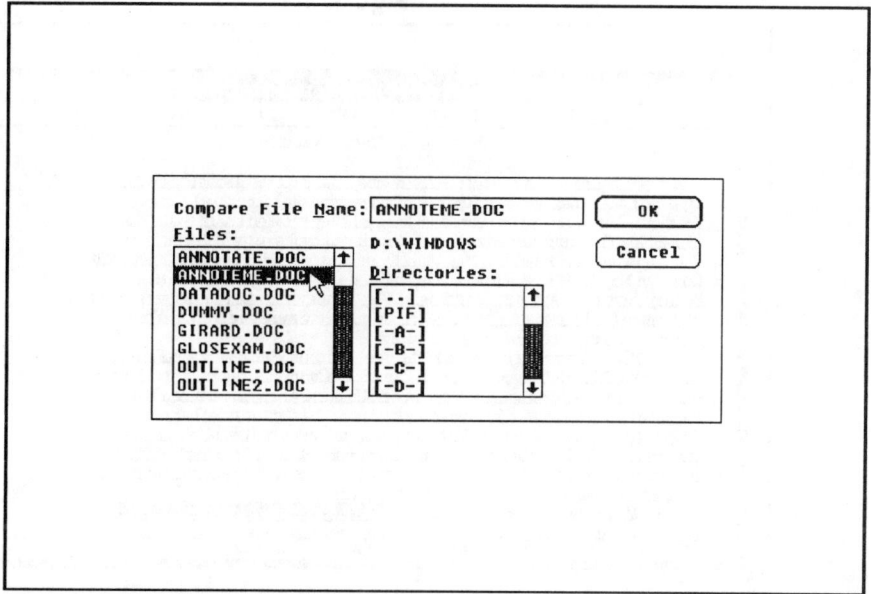

Utilities Compare Versions dialog box

pare with the version that contains the incorporated annotations. You can change the current directory by quickly clicking the left mouse button twice (double-clicking) on the listings in the Directories scroll box. Then select files in that directory by double-clicking the left mouse button on a file in the Files scroll box; immediately the selected file will be compared to the file currently open. (If you only click the left mouse button once on the file name in the Files scroll box, you can either press ENTER or click the left mouse button on the OK button to begin the comparison.)

Material that has been altered will be underlined and have a *change bar* (a line running along the outside margin, which is the left margin of an even-numbered page or the right of an odd-numbered page). Figure 8-8 shows the result of a default comparison between the edited ANNOTATE.DOC and the original ANNOTEME.DOC. Paragraphs that have been moved, but not rewritten, will not have a change bar in the left margin.

Figure 8-8.

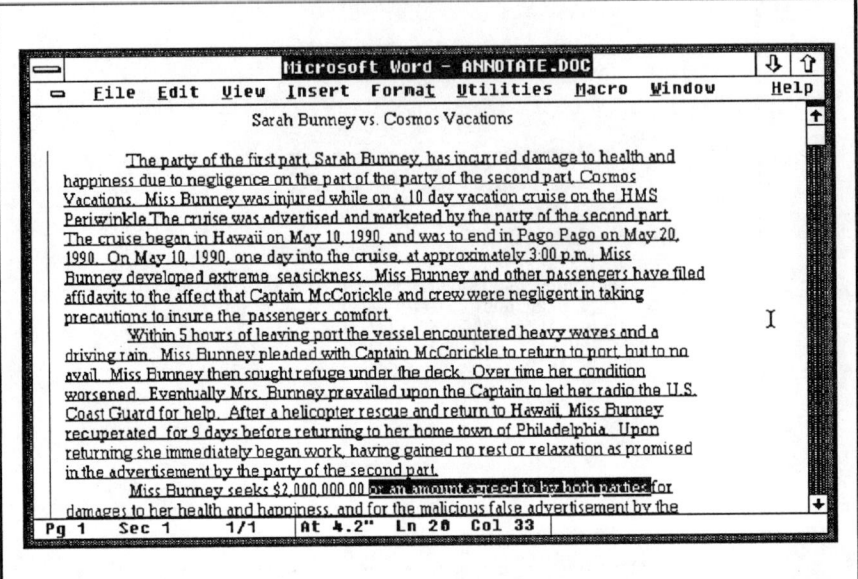

Revision marking after running Utilities Compare Versions command

Deleted text will be shown with a strike-through, referred to as redlining (no text was deleted, only additions were made in ANNOTATE.DOC). You should save the document resulting from the Utilities Compare Versions command to a new file name, so as not to confuse it with the original or rewritten documents.

Using the Utilities Revision Marks Command

The previous section showed the method of comparing documents with the Utilities Compare Versions command, which is the default. There are other methods for marking documents with the Utilities Revision Marks command so that the report produced by the Utilities Compare Versions command will highlight differences between documents in different ways.

The Utilities Revision Marks command, shown here,

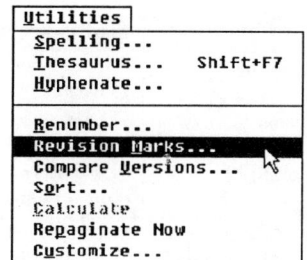

allows you to change the default Utilities Compare Versions command method of marking a rewritten document. The default Utilities Revision Marks settings are listed in the Utilities Revision Marks dialog box shown in Figure 8-9.

Note that when you display the Utilities Revision Marks dialog box, the Mark Revisions toggle box is highlighted, but not active (there is no "x" in the toggle box). This is because the Mark Revisions toggle box is off by default. This means that none of the options in the Utilities Revision Marks dialog box are used by default with the Utilities Compare Versions command. Therefore, to activate the settings in the Revision Bars and Mark New Text With option sets, you must first activate the Mark Revisions toggle box.

If only the Mark Revisions toggle box was activated, and the Outside Revision Bars and Underline Mark New Text With options were selected, the Utilities Compare Versions command would produce a report in the same format as in Figure 8-8. The revision bar detects changes made to the text within a paragraph; therefore, it displays a revision bar in the left or right margin of paragraphs. No revision bar is displayed next to moved, but

Figure 8-9.

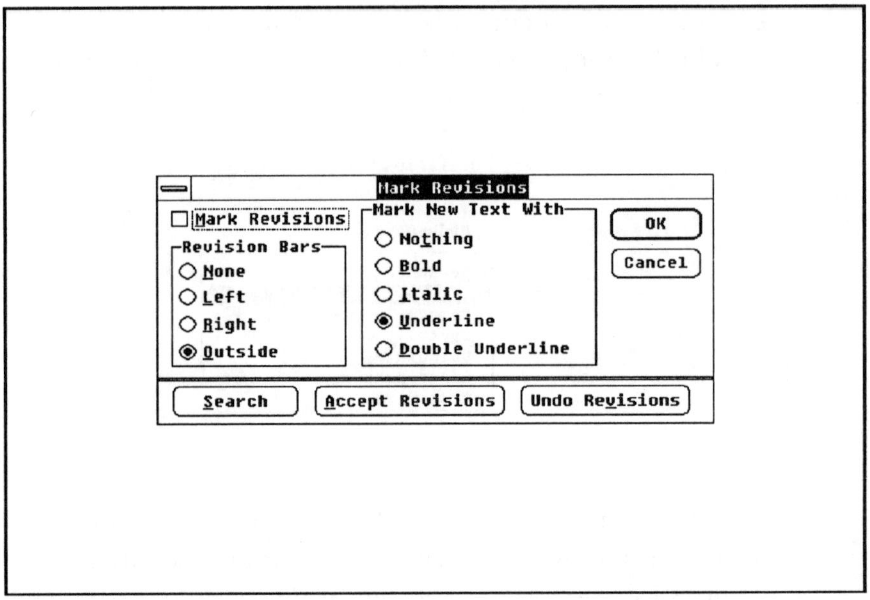

Utilities Revision Marks dialog box

unedited, paragraphs. If you choose the Left or Right option in the Revision Bars option set, the revision bar will always appear in that margin. A Utilities Compare Versions command run with the None Revision Bars option would produce no revision bar.

If you choose the Bold, Italic, or Double Underline option in the Mark New Text With option set, any text that was inserted in the revised document would appear in bold, italic, or double underline character format.

The Mark Revisions Search button will highlight revised or deleted text associated with the first revision mark. The Accept Revisions button removes change bars and strike-throughs from any paragraph under the cursor or a highlight. The Undo Revisions button removes any edited text with strike-throughs in any paragraph under the cursor or a highlight. You can use these buttons to accept or reject changes that you made to a document during the incorporation of annotations (see "Incorporating Annotations" earlier in this chapter).

Word for Windows on a Network

As long as you have read and write access to all Word for Windows files, the program runs no differently on a network than on a single-user workstation. The advantage to running Word for Windows on either a LAN (local area network) or a WAN (wide area network) is that you can share data files with your colleagues via the file server.

If you install Word for Windows on a LAN or a WAN, each PC must have read and write access to the WINWORD.INI file. This file tells Word for Windows what your view preferences are. Word for Windows will not open if it cannot both read and write to this file.

If your network manager has standardized the default document template, you may not have access to NORMAL.DOT. In this case, you would not be able to make any global changes. This is because global changes must be saved to NORMAL.DOT. You will be able to open and use the NORMAL.DOT document template as a base document template for other document templates that you create, but you could not change it (make a global change). You could, however, make your own document templates based on NORMAL.DOT and save them to a local hard disk partition or a network server partition to which you have read and write access.

You now know how powerful Word for Windows is in helping groups produce documents. The structured use of Word for Windows document locking, annotation, and revision marking commands should help you delegate different parts of group projects. The most obvious applications are in the legal and academic professions and in businesses; however the possibilities are limitless.

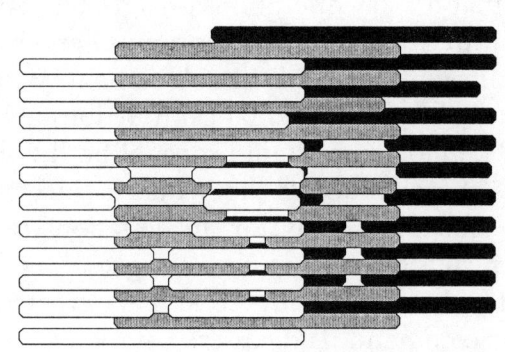

9

Data Handling: Formulas, Equations, Indexing, and File Importation

This chapter covers three types of data handling you can do with Word for Windows: formulas and equations, indexing, and file importation. All three applications require text or numbers to be formatted in specific ways. Thus, a goal of this chapter is to familiarize you with the various data formats used by Word for Windows.

Formulas are fields that display operations on variables you list. *Equations* are fields that perform operations on numbers that you list or on numeric results of other fields in a document. Word for Windows has a large number of mathematical functions available for use in equations. The most important aspect of both Formula and Equation fields is their syntax; if the syntax is incorrect, a formula will be expressed incorrectly, or an equation (in most cases) will not have a result, only an error message.

Index entries are fields that begin with XE and are created with the Insert Index Entry command. Indices are compiled from XE fields with the Insert Index command or the Index field (INDEX). As with formulas and equations, Index field syntax is important. There are two types of indices discussed in this chapter. The first is the standard topical index and the other is an index used to create a glossary. Note that the term *glossary* is used in two new ways in this chapter. The first type of glossary discussed here is the traditional one containing definitions of technical terms. The second use of glossary, the Word for Windows Spike Glossary, discussed under "Spike Glossaries," is an adjunct to the clipboard. A third type of glossary, Word for Windows Glossaries, is also discussed in Chapter 6. With a topical index, the page numbers for the topics are critical. For a glossary, you make index entries and compile an index, but then add definitions of the indexed terms. Most glossaries do not have page number listings.

Word for Windows has powerful data importation capabilities that enable you to access output files created in other word processing, spreadsheet, and database programs. In all of these cases, the format of the data in the output file is critical to Word for Windows' ability to read and import the file. One of the most important Word for Windows applications that uses imported data is the Print Merge function. This chapter presents two Print

Merge applications: form letters (also called mail merge) and address labels.

Formulas and Equations

Formulas and equations are related Word for Windows fields. Formulas use Word for Windows powerful text formatting capabilities to express mathematical relationships between variables. Equations use Word for Windows powerful mathematical capabilities to perform calculations using data that has been entered or pasted into a Word for Windows document. Formulas use the EQ field; equations use the Expression field ($=$). As with other fields, you can add options to Formula and Equation fields. By using options, you can insert text into a formula or an answer into an equation.

To print formulas, you need a laser printer that uses either the PostScript or PCL (LaserJet or compatible) page description language (see Appendix B, "Peripheral Interests"). Since only the results of equations are printed, you do not need the graphic capabilities of a laser printer.

Using Formulas

Formula fields let you present variables and operations in unsolved equations. You can use the Insert Field dialog box to tell Word for Windows what variables and which mathematical symbols to use. Word for Windows then creates the formula and displays it onscreen. Word for Windows creates graphical characters like square root signs and exponents to fit the formula as you

have described it. Because Word for Windows is creating graphical characters that are not supported by Windows dot matrix
printer drivers, you must print your document on a laser printer.

When the View Field Codes command is on in the Normal
Editing View, you can see the components you entered in the EQ
field in the format you entered them. When the View Field Codes
is off, you see the result of the EQ field. To work with formulas, it
is therefore best to split the document window into two panes. In
one pane, turn the View Field Codes command on; in the other,
leave the View Field Codes command off.

To create two panes, choose the Document Control button
menu Split command, as shown here.

Restore	Ctrl+F5
Move	Ctrl+F7
Size	Ctrl+F8
Maximize	Ctrl+F10
Close	Ctrl+F4
Split	

The split bar will appear in the middle of the document window,
as shown in Figure 9-1. Keep the split bar in the middle of the
document window, and press the left mouse button. The split
bar's position will be set. The bottom pane will be active; press F6
to make the top pane active. (Another way to change an active
window pane is to click the mouse once within a pane.) Then
activate the View Field Codes command. Leave the View Field
Codes command inactive in the lower pane.

You are now ready to begin creating a formula. In the top
window, where the View Field Codes button is active, you will see
the Formula Field Codes. In the bottom window, you will see the
result of those Formula Field Codes.

Figure 9-1.

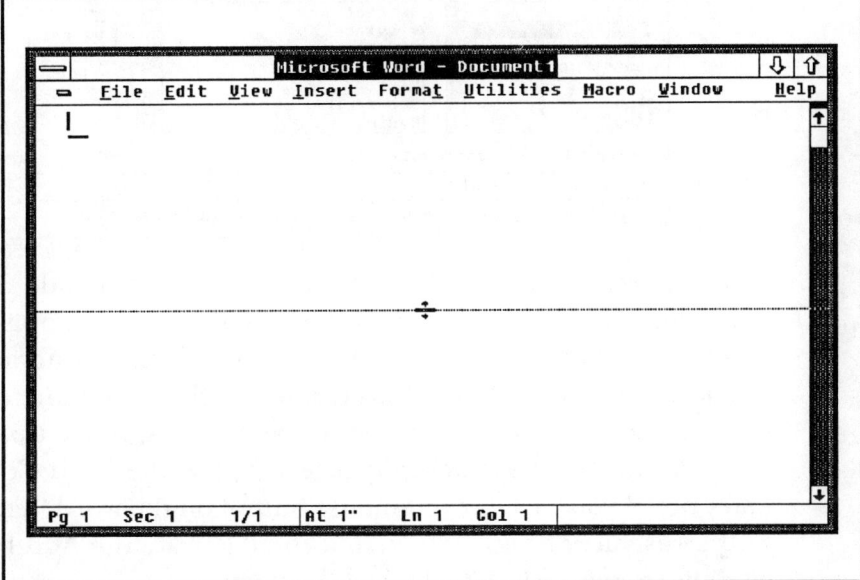

Split screen

As an example you will create the quadratic formula, shown here.

$$x = \frac{-b \pm \sqrt{b^2 - 4ac}}{2a}$$

In the top pane, begin creating the formula by activating the Insert Field command. Scroll down the Insert Field Type scroll box in the Insert Field dialog box to Formulas. EQ will then appear in the Field Code text entry box. Begin typing the quadratic formula one space after the EQ field, as shown here.

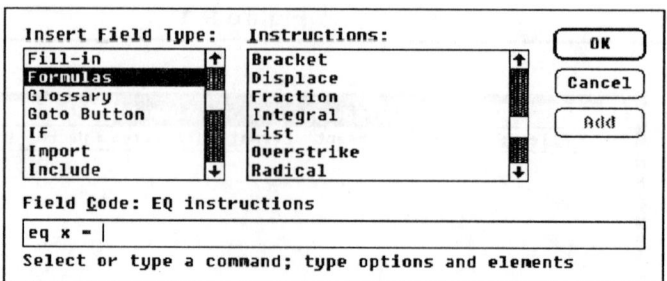

Since the rest of the quadratic formula is a fraction, add another space, and type \ (backslash) followed by **F**. The F option signifies that the text before the comma (but after F) is the numerator of a fraction and the text after the comma is the denominator. The entire fraction must be enclosed in parentheses. (Note that Word for Windows will automatically insert \F(,) in the Field Code text entry box if you click the left mouse button on the word "Fraction" in the Instructions scroll box, and then activate the Add button.) Therefore, type **−b +/−** before the comma.

The next part of the equation is a square root. Type **\R** so Word for Windows knows to put a radical (square root sign) over the variables that follow it. After you type the \R option, type the variables that go under the radical, **b2 −4ac**, within parentheses. (Note: You cannot insert an \R option and parentheses by clicking the left mouse button on the word "Radical" in the Instructions box; this is because Word for Windows will place the \R option outside the fraction parentheses.)

Do not worry about the 2 being an exponent. Finally, type a comma followed by the denominator, **2a**, and the closing right parentheses. The entire formula should look like this:

```
            Fraction option
                   |
                          ┌─ Comma separating numerator and denominator
Field Code: EQ instructions
┌──────────────────────────────────────────────┐
│ eq x = \F(-b +/- \R(b2-4ac),2a)│             │
└──────────────────────────────────────────────┘
            Radical option
```

Click the left mouse button on the OK button to insert the formula. With the cursor in the top pane, position the 2 over the

Figure 9-2.

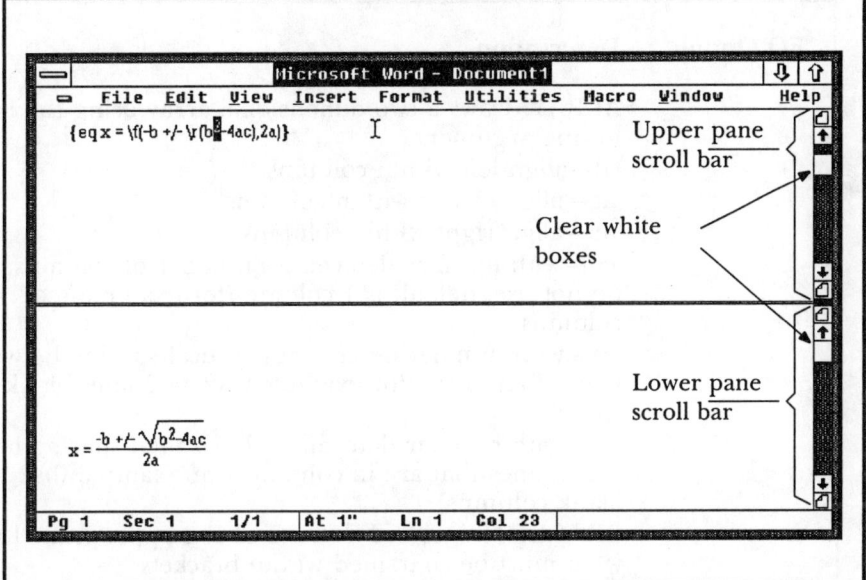

Formula creation

variable b, yet under the radical as a superscript (representing a squared exponent). To do so, highlight it and use the Format Character dialog box. The result is shown in Figure 9-2, where the upper pane has the View Field Codes command active and the lower pane does not. Note in the bottom pane of Figure 9-2 that since the 2 is superscripted, the radical extends upwards over it. Because these types of variable graphic math characters (such as a radical) are not supported by Windows dot matrix printer drivers, Word for Windows can only print formulas on laser printers.

 NOTE You must make sure that both panes exhibit the same part of the document. Check to see that the clear white boxes on both pane scroll bars, shown in Figure 9-2, are even. Otherwise, you will not be able to view both the Field Codes and the formula.

There are many other options available for Formula (EQ) fields. They are listed in Table 9-1.

Table 9-1.

FQ Option	Description
\A	ARRAY draws a two-dimensional array using the following arguments: \al—align left within columns \ac—align center within columns \ar—align right within columns \co—with number determines number of columns, if do not use, default is 1 column (for example \co2 = 2 columns) \vs—with number determines vertical spacing between lines of an array (for example \vs2 = 2 lines blank space) \hs—with number determines horizontal spacing between lines that are in columns (for example \hs2 = 2 blank columns)
\B	BRACKETS inserted that are of size appropriate to what must be contained within brackets
\D	DISPLACE works with following options to precisely control where next horizontal character is placed: \fo—with number determines number of blank spaces in front of previous entry (for example \fo2 = 2 blanks) \ba—with number determines number of blank spaces previous entry (for example \ba2 = 2 blanks) \li—draw a line from end of previous character to next character
\F	FRACTION numerator typed before comma, denominator typed after comma; both within parentheses
\I	INTEGRAL created with the following variables: \su—changes integral symbol to capital Sigma (summation) \in—in-line integral with limits to the right, not above and below \fc—fixed height symbol \vc—variable height symbol

Formula (EQ) Options (Adapted with permission from the documentation for Microsoft Word for Windows, Microsoft Corporation, 1990.)

Table 9-1.

FQ Option	Description
\L	LIST created from characters in parentheses, separated by commas
\O	OVERSTRIKE will overprint the character following this option over the character preceding it, works with: \al—aligns left edges of two characters \ar—aligns right edges of two characters \ac—aligns center of two characters
\R	RADICAL places over following characters
\S	SUPERSCRIPTS or SUBSCRIPTS following characters depending on: \up—plus number of points up (for example \up3 is 3 points superscripted, default is 2) \do—plus number of points down (for example \do3 is 3 points subscripted, default is 2)
\X	BOX around following characters, or draw borders with: \to—top border only \bo—bottom border only \le—left border only \ri—right border only

Formula (EQ) Options (continued)

Using Equations

An Equation field enables you to do actual calculations that use data you type or paste into that field. You use the Expression Field Code (=) to begin all Equation fields. These fields must also contain data or references to data as well as at least one mathematical operation. Unlike formulas, only the result, not the expression, is printed from an equation.

You can type or paste data directly into an equation. Or, if the data appears elsewhere in the document, you can highlight each number and assign it to a bookmark name (see Chapter 8, "Group

Productions" for a discussion of assigning bookmark names). You can then insert the bookmark name into an Equation field.

No matter where the data comes from, equations offer you many powerful math functions and logical operators. Table 9-2 lists the math functions available for equations; Table 9-3 lists the logical operators used to make conditional statements about equations.

Table 9-2.

Description	Function Performed
+	Addition
/	Division
=	Equals
>	Greater than
> =	Greater than or equal to
<	Less than
< =	Less than or equal to
* .	Multiplication
< >	Not equal to
%	Percentage
^	Powers and roots
[R#C#]	Specifies a cell by row and column when insert numbers for # signs
Bookmark[R#C#]	Specifies a cell by row and column that is associated with this bookmark name when insert numbers for # signs
Bookmark[R#C#:R#C#]	Specifies a range of cells by row and column that are associated with this bookmark name when insert numbers for # signs
–	Subtraction

Equation (=) Functions (Adapted with permission from the documentation for Microsoft Word for Windows, Microsoft Corporation, 1990.)

Table 9-3.

Operation (Parentheses may contain numbers or equations, X means single variable only, X, Y, and Z means 2 or 3 variables or co-ordinates allowed)

ABS( )	MOD(X,Y)
AND(X,Y)	NEXTIF( )
AVERAGE( )	NOT(X)
COUNT( )	OR(X,Y)
DEFINED(X)	PRODUCT( )
FALSE	ROUND(X,Y)
IF(X,Y,Z)	SIGN(X)
INT(X)	SKIPIF( )
MAX( )	SUM( )
MIN( )	TRUE

Equation (=) Operators (Adapted with permission from the documentation for Microsoft Word for Windows, Microsoft Corporation, 1990.)

As an example of an Equation field, use variables in cells within a table that are assigned bookmark names. Remember, you can also type these numbers directly into the equation. However, if the table is the result of a DDE Paste Link, you would want the DDE link to keep the values in each cell equivalent to the current entries in the source Excel spreadsheet (or other Windows spread-sheet or database file).

To begin, create a table with six rows and six columns with cells 0.75" in width (for a discussion of creating tables, see Chapter 3, "Cut and Paste: Adding Tables and Images"). Enter the following cell entries in the table.

1990 Regional Sales

Region	1st Qtr	2nd Qtr	3rd Qtr	4th Qtr	Yr Total
North	3045.87	2977.76	3357.98	3859.65	13241.26
East	1587.22	1071.88	1289.76	1499.89	5448.75
West	2798.44	2688.76	2802.54	3232.84	11522.58
South	2054.89	1987.09	2298.98	2798.78	9139.74

Now highlight the North region's yearly total. Make sure you use the I-beam mouse to highlight only the numbers, 13241.26, not the entire space inside the cell. Then activate the Insert Bookmark command. Type **NorthSales** in the Bookmark Name text entry box as shown in Figure 9-3. To accept the bookmark name, either click the left mouse button on the OK button or press ENTER. Then highlight each of the other yearly total entries and name them in the same way, as shown here.

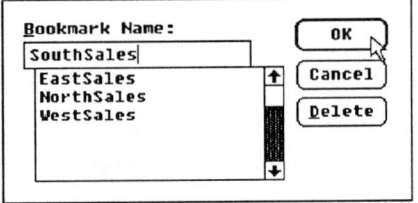

Now type the following text below the table:

Average Regional Yearly Sales for 1990:

Next activate the Insert Field dialog box. The Equation Field Code is highlighted by default so you can start entering the field in the Field Code text entry box. Since you want an average for all regions, use the AVERAGE equation operation. Type **Average** in the Field Code text entry box, followed by a left parenthesis without a space. Next type the names of all four bookmarks to be

Figure 9-3.

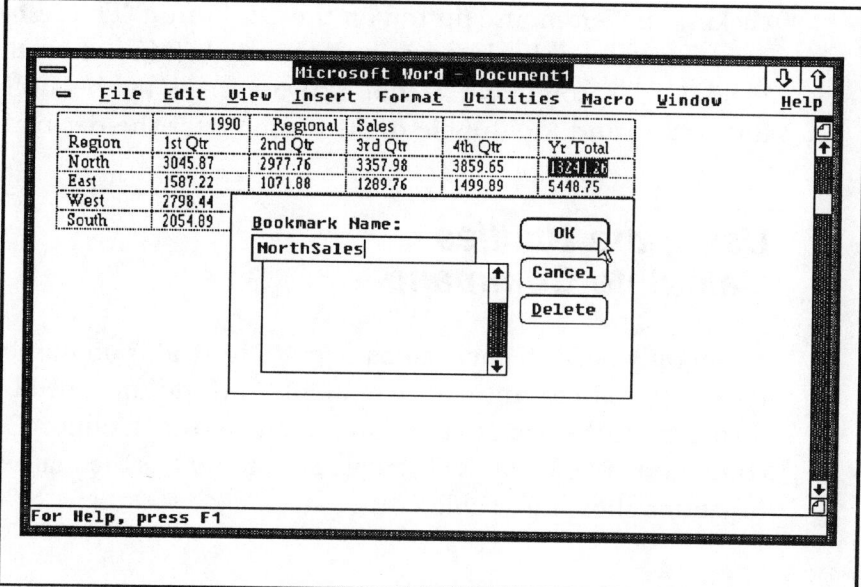

Assigning data to a bookmark

averaged, separated by commas and no spaces. End the equation with a right parenthesis. Next, insert the dollar formatting option by typing a space and clicking the left mouse button on the $#,##0.00;($#,##0.00) Instructions option. To add this option to the field, click the left mouse button on the Add button. The Insert Field dialog box should now look like this:

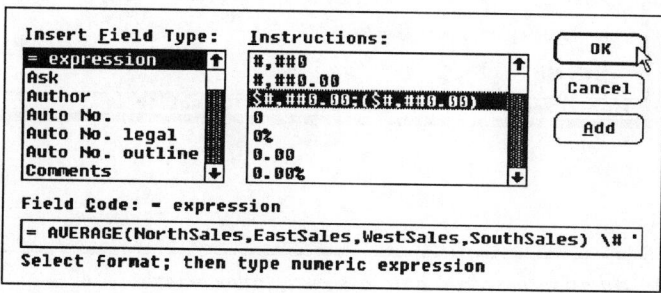

Insert the field in your document either by pressing ENTER or by clicking the left mouse button on the OK button. The result of the equation will be displayed as in Figure 9-4. (Make sure the View Field Codes command is not activated.) Note the dollar sign formatting and the double digits (cents) after the decimal point.

Using the Utilities Calculate Command

If you only need to perform basic math functions on numbers you typed or pasted into a document and do not need special formatting, the fastest method to use is the Utilities Calculate command. The Utilities Calculate command has the mathematical functions shown in Table 9-4.

Figure 9-4.

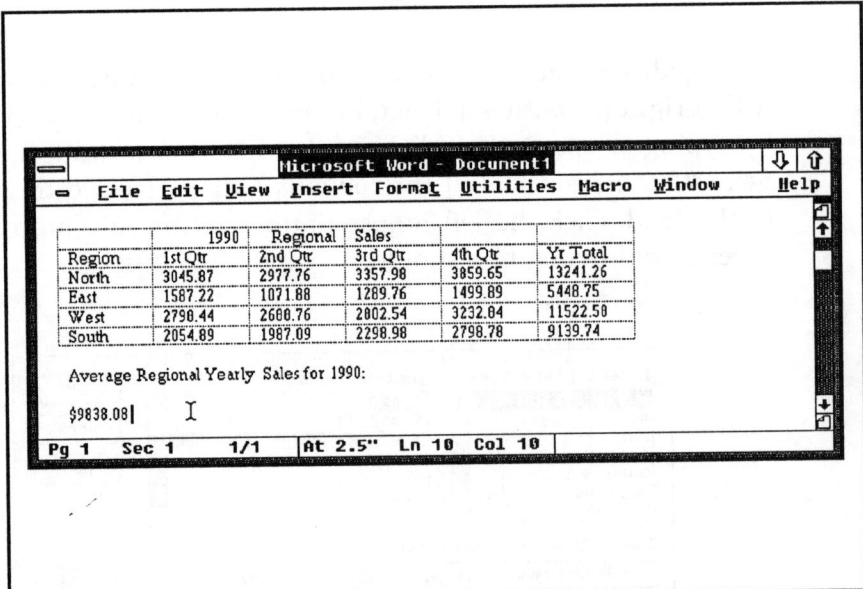

An equation based on data assigned to bookmarks

The Utilities Calculate command solves simple equations and puts the answers in the Windows Clipboard. It also displays the answer in the status bar. You can then use the Edit Paste command to place the answer in the document wherever you need it.

As an example, use the table you input for the equation example (see Figure 9-2). Erase the North region's yearly total entry. To calculate the yearly total with the Utilities Calculate command, highlight all of the North region's entries as shown here.

	1990	Regional	Sales		
Region	1st Qtr	2nd Qtr	3rd Qtr	4th Qtr	Yr Total
North	3045.37	2977.76	3357.98	3859.65	
East	1587.22	1071.88	1289.76	1499.89	5448.75
West	2798.44	2688.76	2802.54	3232.84	11522.58
South	2054.89	1987.09	2298.98	2798.78	9139.74

Then activate the Utilities Calculate command shown here.

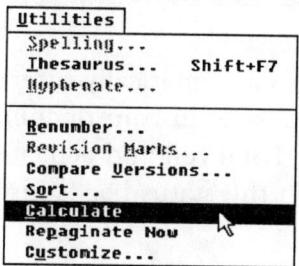

Since there are no function symbols, such as * for multiplication or / for division, in the highlighted block, the numbers will be added. To multiply the numbers, you would insert an asterisk in front of

Table 9-4.

Symbol	Operation
+	Add (default, if no function selected, will add)
/	Divide
*	Multiply
%	Percent (multiplies denominator by 100, then divides result into numerator)
^	Power (if exponent greater than 1) or Root if exponent (between 0 and 1)
—	Subtract

Utilities Calculate Functions (Adapted with permission from the documentation for Microsoft Word for Windows, Microsoft Corporation, 1990.)

the second through fourth quarter entries before highlighting them. To perform any of the other operations shown in Table 9-4, you would insert their function symbols.

After activating the Utilities Calculate command, the answer is displayed in the status bar as shown here.

```
The result of computation is: 13241.26
```

The answer is also automatically inserted into the Clipboard.

To insert the answer in your document, place the cursor in the empty North Yr Total cell and activate the Edit Paste command. The value seen in the status bar is inserted in the table.

Indices and Glossaries

You create an index or glossary in much the same way you create a table of contents (see Chapter 7, "Time Saving Organization: Outlines and Tables of Contents"). But instead of creating TC fields, you create Index Entry fields with the XE field. In addition, just as you compiled TC fields into a Table of Contents field using the TOC field, index entries are assembled into an index using the Index field (INDEX).

Word for Windows provides you with an Insert Index Entry command and dialog box so you do not have to scroll through the Insert Field dialog box of the Insert Field Type scroll box for the XE field. There is also a timesaving Insert Index command.

Indices and glossaries are compiled similarly. For both you make index entries and then use the Insert Index command to compile those entries. With indices you use the page number information assembled by the Index field; with glossaries you insert definitions next to the compiled terms.

You can compile an index or glossary at any time during the document creation process. You can create entries as you type a document or after you finish it.

Creating Index Entries

To create an index or glossary as you type a document, activate the Insert Index Entry command immediately after you type the word or words you want in the index. The Insert Index Entry dialog box appears when you activate the Insert Index Entry command, as shown here.

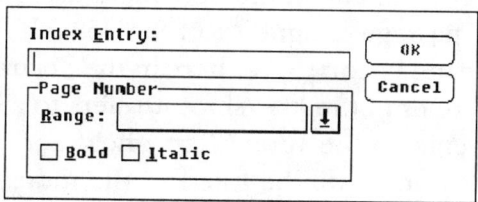

The Insert Index Entry dialog box opens with the cursor in the Index Entry field. If you have highlighted text that the Index

Entry is to refer to before opening the Insert Index Entry dialog box, this text will be displayed in the Index Entry field. Do not add spaces between the Index Entry field and the Index Entry itself; a space could lead to the index entry being referenced to the wrong page. A problem may arise if the space separating the item referenced in the XE field and the field itself was to fall on the next page after the document is paginated. If this happened, the index would refer the item to the wrong page. A page break cannot be inserted between the item referenced and the XE field unless you insert a space.

Note the Page Number options. You can use the Range field to assign an index entry to a range of pages. These pages are referred to by a bookmark name. Keep in mind, however, that before you can have an index entry refer to a bookmark name, you must first insert the bookmark.

To insert a bookmark, highlight all the pages to which the bookmark is to refer. Then activate the Insert Bookmark command and assign these highlighted pages a bookmark name. This bookmark name will be available in the Page Number Range scroll-down box the next time you activate the Index Entry command. (Bookmarks are also discussed in Chapter 8, "Group Productions.")

You can also use bookmarks to cross reference index entries. To do this, you assign the same bookmark to several index entries, which do not have to be on or near the same page as the text referred to by the bookmark. You can also have a topic not mentioned by name in the document listed in an index and refer it to the passage assigned to a bookmark. In this case, you can insert the index entry anywhere in the document. (The location of this field does not matter since it refers to a bookmark.) You type the reference in the Index Entry field and assign it a bookmark. This index entry will be listed in the index and will refer to the pages assigned to the bookmark, even though it is not derived from text entered in the document.

Another option in the Insert Index Entry Page Numbers option set is the use of bold or italic formatting of page numbers.

You would activate these toggle boxes, which are under the Range text entry field, to specify that you want bold or italic formatting for either the range of page numbers or, if there is no bookmark specified, for the single page listing.

You would format an index entry in bold or italic depending on the index format you are using. Often a bold index entry signifies that this listing is the document's most important and complete listing. An italic index entry often signifies that this index entry is a table, figure, or illustration.

To create a sample index, type the following text, ending each line with a page break (CTRL-ENTER).

E.	**This is index entry**	**1**	CTRL-ENTER
D.	**This is index entry**	**2**	CTRL-ENTER
C.	**This is index entry**	**3**	CTRL-ENTER
B.	**This is index entry**	**4**	CTRL-ENTER
A.	**This is index entry**	**5**	CTRL-ENTER

Now highlight entry E on the first page, and activate the Insert Index Entry command as shown here.

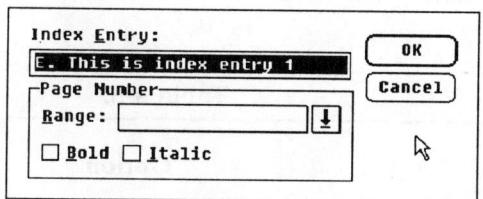

Note that the highlighted text is automatically inserted in the Index Entry text entry field. Next, accept the index entry either by pressing ENTER or clicking the left mouse button on the OK button. Repeat this procedure for the other four index entries. You will then create an index with these Index Entry fields by using the Insert Index command.

Each time you activate the OK button in the Insert Index Entry dialog box, Word for Windows automatically inserts an XE field that contains the information you have highlighted before activating the Insert Index Entry command. To see the XE field in the Normal Editing View, you must have the View Field Codes command active. When this command is active, the information you typed in the Index Entry field will be enclosed in quotes following the XE Field Code. If you have entered a Range bookmark, you will also see a \r option followed by a bookmark name. Table 9-5 lists all the options available for index entries.

To create a glossary, you would make index entries and insert an index in the same way. The only difference is that you may want to delete the page listings and replace them with definitions.

Using the Insert Index Command

Once you finish creating all of your index entries, you are ready to create an index or a glossary. You will create an index using the index entries you entered in "Creating Index Entries."

Table 9-5.

Field Type	Option
Print Index Entry in Bold Type	b
Print Index Entry in Italic Type	i
Range (Bookmark Name)	"Bookmark"
Print Text, not page number	"Text"

Index Entry (XE) Field Options (Adapted with permission from the documentation for Microsoft Word for Windows, Microsoft Corporation, 1990.)

Begin by placing the cursor at the end of the document, one line after the line A (press ENTER to create a blank line after line A). (Remember, you can insert the index or glossary at any location in the document.) Activate the Insert Index command; you will see the Insert Index dialog box, shown here.

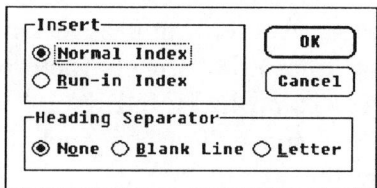

To create the index, either press ENTER or click the left mouse button on the OK button. The index will look like the one in Figure 9-5. In Figure 9-5, each index entry is followed by a comma and the page number on which the index entry appears. This is the default format for an index. Note that the index is compiled in alphabetical order, so that the last listing which began with A is listed first in the index.

Now consider the other index formatting options in the Insert Index dialog box. In all cases, index entries will be listed in alphabetical order. The Normal Index button produces an index like that seen in Figure 9-5. The Run-in Index button Insert option lists all the index entries on a single line (no carriage return between index entries). As you saw in the example, the default None Heading Separator option inserts no heading separator between index entries that begin with different letters. The Letter button will cause Word for Windows to add A-Z letter headings above the appropriate index entries. The Blank Line option adds a blank line between the index entries assigned to each letter of the alphabet.

You can also specify options to control the format of an index. These formatting options cannot be added to an Index field in the Insert Index dialog box. You must add them after the Index Field Code in the Field Code text entry box of the Insert Field dialog box. Most of the Index formatting options are the same as in the Table of Contents (TOC) field (see Chapter 6, "Advanced Template Features: Glossaries, Boilerplate Text, Fields, and Macros"). For example, if you want to separate the index entry from its page number listing by something other than the default comma and a space, type **\c** followed by the characters or spaces you want inside of quotes. For example, {INDEX \ c " "} would create an index with one blank space between each index entry and its page number listing.

You can also create an index from one more bookmark with the \b option; if you use more than one bookmark, separate them by commas. Bookmarks are useful if you need to create different index listings within a single document. An example would be a

Figure 9-5.

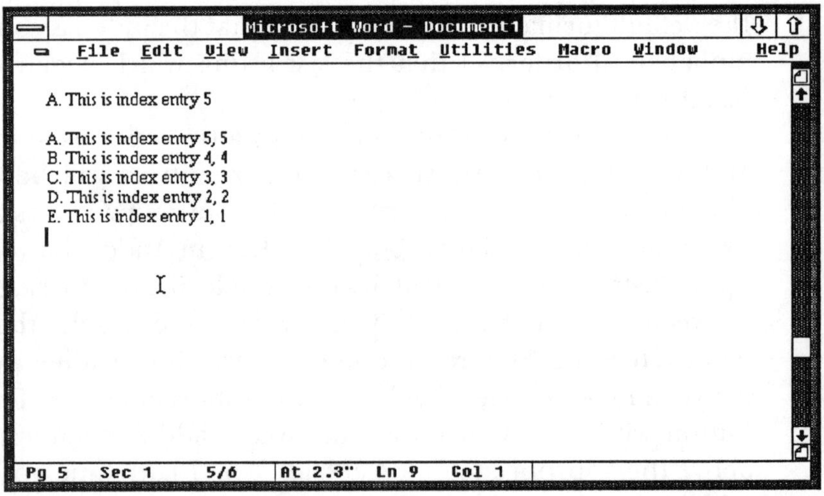

Sample index entries

Table 9-6.

Field Type	Option
Use Only This Bookmark	\b "Bookmark"
Text Between Index Entry and Page No.	\c "Text"
Separator Between Sequence Numbers and Page Numbers (usually ";")	
Used with \s	\d "Text"
Text Between Range Numbers	\g
Page Number Separator (usually ";")	\l
For Specified Letters	\p
Run-in Style Entries	\r
Prefix Page Numbers with Sequence Numbers	\s

Index (INDEX) Field Options (Adapted with permission from the documentation for Microsoft Word for Windows, Microsoft Corporation, 1990.)

document with both an index and a glossary (remember you use the Insert Index Entry command to create both index entries and glossary entries).

All the index options are listed in Table 9-6. You can add these options to the Index field for an index that has already been created after activating the View Field Codes command.

If you alter any of the index entries with the View Field Codes command after you have created the index, remember to press the field Update Key (F9). If you do not press F9, the index will not be updated if you print before saving the file. Also, if you are using key words, consider adding the most important index or glossary words as key words in the document summary.

Long Documents

If you want to create a table of contents or an index from more than one document, you must create a long document. A *long* document is a separate document file that you open with the File New command, just as you would open any other document. The long document can consist of as little as some RD (Reference Document) fields telling Word for Windows which documents to use in compiling summary tables of contents and indices. When you insert a Table of Contents (TOC) or Index field into the long document, the table of contents and indices from all of the referenced documents will be compiled into one table of contents and one index listing. You can also compile other Table of . . . Listings from the referenced documents as long as you use the proper options in the TOC field. You also assemble glossaries in the same way that you create indices. The long document is useful for books or any multidocument project.

The first step in creating a long document is to create the tables of contents and indices in the individual documents that you will reference. The next step is to open a new document with the File New command; this will be the long document. Then, using the Insert Field dialog box, create separate Reference Document (RD) fields for each document. Finally, also using the Insert Field command, insert a Table of Contents (TOC) field and an Index field after the RD fields. An example of the fields in a long document is shown in Figure 9-6.

Note that if a long document index or a single document index has more than 4000 entries, you will need to break it up into parts that contain less than 4000 listings. To do this, add the letter entries after the \p option. The example, shown here,

{INDEX \p A-L}

{INDEX \p M-Z}

divides an index in two parts based on the alphabet: A to L and M to Z index entries.

Spike Glossaries

If there are any other parts of the original document that you want to include in the long document, you can transfer them with a *spike glossary*. The spike is similar to the Edit Copy command. It saves text and graphics to the Clipboard, which can then be pasted into another document. The difference is that each block you copy to the Clipboard with the Edit Copy command replaces the previous entry. The spike glossary, on the other hand, accumulates entries in the Clipboard in the order they are copied. In other words, the Clipboard accepts items sequentially, whereas the Word for Windows spike glossary lets you accumulate items.

To use the spike, open a document window for each document referenced in the long document. Then highlight the text and graphics you want to cut and paste, block by block. After each

Figure 9-6.

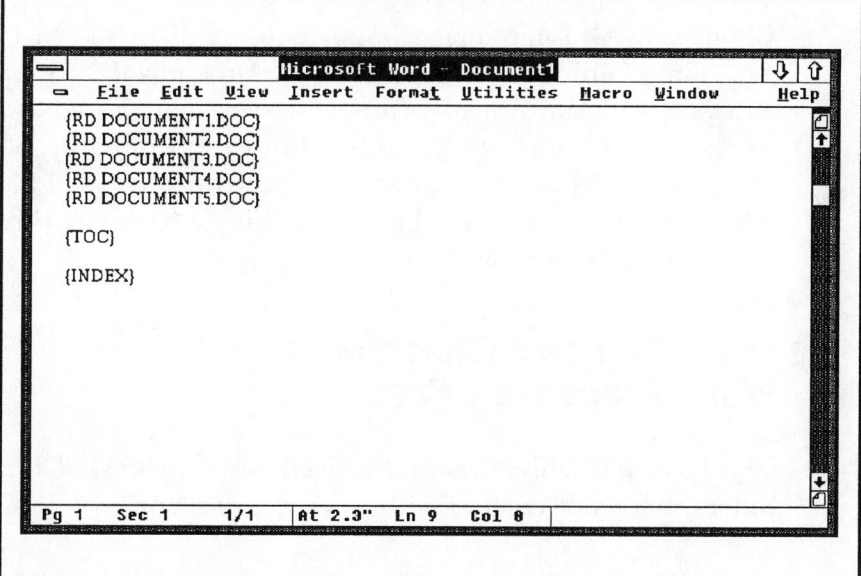

Example of fields in a long document

block is highlighted, press CTRL-F3 and the information will be copied to the spike. Then go to the next block of information, highlight it, and copy it to the spike (CTRL-F3). Make sure you copy the information you want from each of the source documents in the order you want it inserted in the long document. When you have all the information in the spike, place the cursor in the long document, and press CTRL-SHIFT-F3. All contents of the spike will be pasted into the long document at the cursor's location; the first item you copied to the spike will be at the top and the last item at the bottom.

File Importation

There are three kinds of files you are most likely to import into Word for Windows. They are word processed, database, and graphic image files. Importing graphic images into Word for Windows is straightforward because you can use the Windows Clipboard. (Graphic image importation is discussed in Chapter 11, "Fine Tuning Windows," and in Appendix D, "Supporting Software and Hardware.") Importing word processed and database files into Word for Windows, however, can be problematic. Often you need to find a way to accept word processed files from a colleague or to import database records for use in a print merge (mail merge) operation.

Importing and Exporting Word Processed Files

You have probably already received word processed files from others that were created with a word processor you do not use.

When you attempted to display these files in your own word processor, you were probably greeted by a host of nonstandard text such as smiling faces, hearts, and musical notes. These nonstandard characters are the control characters that your colleague's word processor uses to format documents.

Word processed files are filled with control characters that supply all kinds of text and paragraph formatting. The fact that these control characters are different for each word processing program can make importing and exporting word processed files difficult. If you attempt to display documents created in programs other than Word for Windows without first converting them, you will be greeted by the usual array of smiling face, heart, and musical note control characters. You can strip the control characters from the file by having your colleague save the file as ASCII (that is, alphanumeric characters with no formatting). If you do this, however, you will lose the valuable time that was spent formatting the document in the first place. An alternative is to convert one word processor's format into another. With some file formats, you can use Word for Windows to do the conversion. With others, you will need to use supporting file conversion software (see Appendix D).

Importing Non-Word for Windows Files   To convert files from one format into another, Word for Windows provides import filters. *Import filters* are subprograms in individual Windows Dynamic Link Libraries (DLL) that convert another program's formatting into the Word for Windows formatting. You use these filters when you want to open a file that is not in Word for Windows format.

The first step in converting a file to Word for Windows format is to save the file and note in what format it was saved. You need

to know what software was used, the version of that software, and
the file extension (∗.EXT) used (Word for Windows looks for
∗.DOC files by default). The next step is to copy that file to your
hard disk and attempt to display it with the File Open command.

For example, suppose there is a Word 4.0 format file, called
WINWORD.DOC, in the WINWORD directory. Since that file
uses the same extension (∗.DOC) as Word for Windows, the Open
File dialog box, shown here,

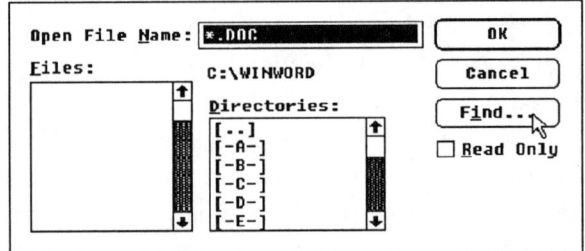

should detect WINWORD.DOC. Note, however, that the File
Open dialog box shown here has no files listed. That is because no
matter what extension the import file has, no non-Word for
Windows files will ever be listed in the Open File dialog box. Also
note that if you tried to import files that ended with a different
extension, you would need to overtype the ∗.DOC with the proper
extension. Moreover, if the file you want to import is in a different
directory, you can also type the path before the extension. Thus,
if you had a WordStar directory named WS on your hard disk,
you would type **C:\WS\∗.WS**.

The next step is to activate the Find button. When you do so,
the Open File Find dialog box, shown here,

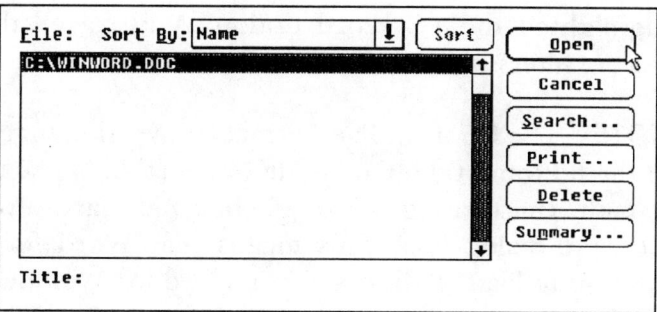

will be displayed. The File scroll box lists all files with the path and extension that you typed in the Open File Name text entry box. Highlight the file you wish to import, as in the example. Then activate the Open button. The Open File Convert dialog box is displayed, as shown here,

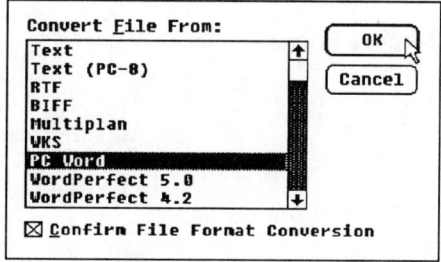

All the Word for Windows import filters are listed in the Convert File From scroll box. Often Word for Windows will detect which word processing format is used in the import file. In the example, Word for Windows detected that the import file was in DOS Word (Word 4.0 or 5.0) format and automatically highlighted the PC Word option. A list of all the import and export filters is shown in Table 9-7.

NOTE   The Confirm File Format Conversion toggle box appears at the bottom of the Open File Convert dialog box. It is active by default. Inactivating this toggle box will inactivate the Open File Convert dialog box. This means that Word for Windows will attempt to load all files as either Word for Windows or Text Only (ASCII) format. The Open File Convert dialog box is dropped when you inactivate the Confirm File Format Conversion toggle box because a statement CONVERSIONS = NO is added to your Windows WIN.INI files (see Chapter 1 and Chapter 11, "Fine Tuning Windows," for a discussion of the WIN.INI file). You must manually change the NO to YES in the WIN.INI with Word for Windows or another word processor in order to reactivate the Open File Convert dialog box.

Table 9-7.

Import and Export Formats	Versions
ASCII	Any (Text Only)
*.BIFF	All (Microsoft Excel, no export capability)
DCA/RTF	All (DisplayWrite)
DOS Word	All
Microsoft Works	All
Multimate	3.3, 3.6, Advantage
Multiplan	All (Document and *.BIFF)
RTF	Macintosh Word, other text and image files stored in ASCII
Windows Write	All
WordPerfect	4.1, 4.2, 5.0, 5.1
WordStar	3.3, 3.4, 4.0

Import and Export Filters (Adapted with permission from the documentation for Microsoft Word for Windows, Microsoft Corporation, 1990.)

In the example, after you choose the PC Word option, Word for Windows searches for a stylesheet, as seen in the Open File Style Sheet dialog box, shown here.

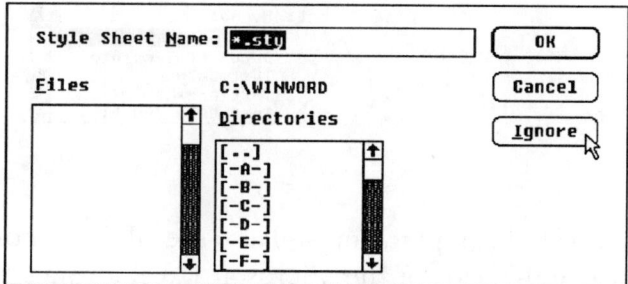

If a stylesheet was attached to a PC Word format document, it would be listed in the Files scroll box. Since there is no stylesheet in this example, just activate the Ignore button; and then the WINWORD.DOC file is converted and opened. As it is working, Word for Windows shows you the progress of the conversion by percent of the document converted in the status bar.

Exporting Word for Windows Files   You can also save Word for Windows documents in all the same document formats that you can import, except the *.BIFF (Binary Information File Format) that Excel uses. Once you have saved a Word for Windows file in one of these non-Word for Windows formats, you can export it to the application that uses that format. This means that if you are working with a colleague who uses one of the file formats listed in Table 9-7, you will be able to import that colleague's files for editing as well as export files for her or him to work on.

To export a Word for Windows file, you will need to save it in a non-Word for Windows format with the File Save As command. To do this, first activate the File Save As command. Next, activate the Options button in the displayed File Save As dialog box. You will see the File Format scroll-down box at the lower right. If you drop this scroll-down box, as shown here,

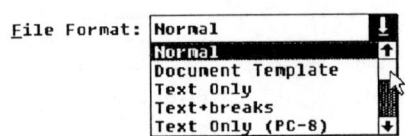

and scroll through it, you will also see all the export formats listed in Table 9-7, except the Microsoft Excel format, *.BIFF. Normal, the default, is the Word for Windows file format. You can click the left mouse button on any of the file formats in this scroll-down box. Then activate the OK button and the file will be saved in that format. If you need to work on the file in Word for Windows, you might want to save the non-Word for Windows file to a different name. That way you can avoid having to convert the file the next time you open it in Word for Windows.

If the file format you want is not listed in the File Save As dialog box File Format scroll-down box, this conversion filter has not been installed in your WIN.INI file. You must install the conversion filter as a DLL (Dynamic Link Library) in your WIN.INI file and it should then be listed in this scroll-down box. Installing conversion filters as DLLs is discussed in Chapter 11.

Electronic Mail Transfer of Word for Windows Document or Document Template Files   Another use for the non-Word for Windows file format is to convert files so they can be sent to colleagues by electronic mail. Electronic mail, or E-Mail services such as MCI Mail, CompuServe, GEnie, and so on, usually require that you send ASCII files.

If you wanted to send a Word for Windows file by E-Mail to a colleague who also had Word for Windows, and you wanted to preserve the formatting in that file, you could save it in RTF format. Remember that Word for Windows has an import file filter (conversion) for *.RTF files in the Open File Convert dialog box. RTF format contains only ASCII characters, but unlike a Text Only ASCII file, it preserves all formatting and graphic images contained in a Word for Windows document. This way your colleague can begin working on the *.RTF file sent by E-Mail right away. If you send a Text Only ASCII file, the recipient will have to recreate all of the formatting you originally had in the document.

Importing Database and Spreadsheet Files

In many cases, when you import files from a database or spreadsheet program, you will want to use that data as a Word for Windows data document. (See Chapter 6 for a discussion of Word for Windows data document structure.) Data documents contain records that are used to print form letters or address labels with the File Print Merge command (see "Print Merge Form Letters" and "Print Merge Address Labels" later in this chapter).

The only spreadsheet file format that you can import directly is that of Microsoft Excel, BIFF. But it is much easier to use the Windows Clipboard to import only the data you want from an Excel spreadsheet, or from any other Windows application. (The only Windows database available at this writing is Superbase 2, as listed in Appendix D). You can also DDE Paste Link (the DDE Paste Link command is discussed in Chapter 11) the data that you want to use in the Word for Windows data document so it is automatically updated whenever a change is made in the source database such as Excel or Superbase 2. However, if you have data in a DOS spreadsheet such as Lotus 1-2-3 or a DOS database such as dBASE IV, Paradox, or Rbase, you need to output the data that you want into an ASCII file.

Data documents are discussed in detail in Chapter 6 but they will be described here briefly. When you save a file that is to become a Word for Windows data document in a DOS spreadsheet or database, it must have a header record at the top before all the data record listings. The header record is a list of field names for the fields in each data record. You will use these field names in the print merge form letter or address label main document (the document into which the data records are merged; see "Print Merge Form Letters" and "Print Merge Address Labels" in this chapter). Only the fields you will use in the data document are to be included in the header and data records in the output file; do not include all the fields that are in the original database or spreadsheet from which the file has been saved, unless data representing all these fields is included in every record in the file to be imported. The fields in both the header and the data fields should be separated either by commas or tabs; do not insert spaces after the commas. End each record with a carriage return (paragraph sign). Finally, be sure to save the data document as an ASCII file; otherwise, Word for Windows will be unable to read it.

You need not convert ASCII data document files in order to import them; Word for Windows assumes data document files will be in either Word for Windows or ASCII format. Once you load an ASCII data document file that was output from a non-Word for Windows program, Word for Windows will, by default, save the file in Word for Windows format. If you want to preserve the output file in its ASCII format, you can either activate the Read-Only toggle box in the File Open dialog box or you can specify Text Only in the File Format field in the File Save As dialog box.

Print Merge Form Letters

To perform a print merge (also called mail merge), you must first create a data document either by inputting data in a Word for Windows document or by outputting data from a database or spreadsheet in the proper format as described in the previous section "Importing Database and Spreadsheet Files." (The section "Creating an Interactive Print Merge Macro" in Chapter 6 presents a useful macro that allows you to choose the records from a large database that are to be included in a data document for a specific print merge operation.) Once you have a data document, you are ready to construct a main document into which the records contained in the data document will be merged.

As an example, use the File Open command to load first DATA.DOC and then FRMLTR.DOC, both of which come with Word for Windows as sample files. As suggested by their file names, DATA.DOC is a sample data document and the file FRMLTR.DOC is a sample form letter. Both are intended to be used in a print merge operation. You should find both of these files in the LIBRARY subdirectory of the WINWORD directory or on the original Word for Windows disks. Because you have opened FRMLTR.DOC second, its document window completely covers the DATA.DOC document window. This is fine for now. Next, activate the View Field Codes command to see the fields in FRMLTR.DOC that should be listed in the header record (record number 1) of the DATA.DOC. Then display both documents on the screen by activating the Window Arrange All command. The screen should look like Figure 9-7. You may need to scroll the top window (FRMLTR.DOC) down to expose the fields displayed in Figure 9-7 (note that each document window has its own scroll bar).

The fields in FRMLTR.DOC are all that are necessary for a successful print merge. Note in Figure 9-7 that the fields that will be printed are placed under a data field that lists the data document's file name (DATA.DOC). The Data field tells Word for Windows which Data Document to use to insert the fields (name, address, and so on) that will be printed below it. You can create both the Data field and the printed fields with the Insert Field command, or manually type the field name inside field characters (to display field characters, press CTRL-F9). A data field should begin with the word Data, followed by a space, then the name of the data document. As noted, in the example, the data document's file name is DATA.DOC.

After you have inserted the Data field, you can insert fields referred to in the header line of the data document anywhere you like. In the example, the complete address appears before "Dear {ref title} {lastname},". This shows that you can use the fields as

Figure 9-7.

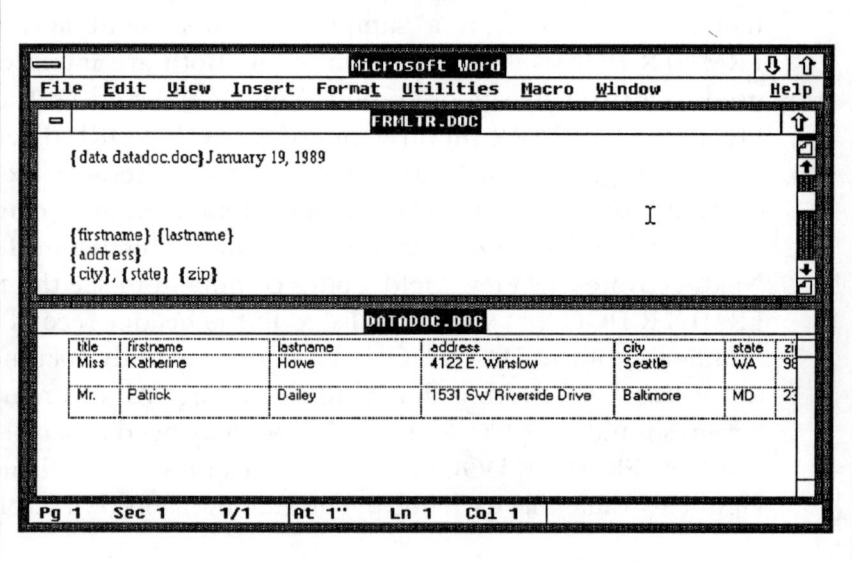

Both documents displayed on screen

often as you like in the main document. Also, you do not have to use all the fields listed in the data document header line. You may also want to insert a Date field at the top of a main document. After you have printed all your form letters, you can delete the text that is particular to this letter and save the general text, Date fields, and Data Document fields as boilerplate text in a document template.

To print your form letters from the main document using the data document, make sure the main document window is the active document window (its document window title bar should have a Control button and the data document window title bar will not). Then activate the File Print Merge command. The File Print Merge dialog box is displayed, as shown here.

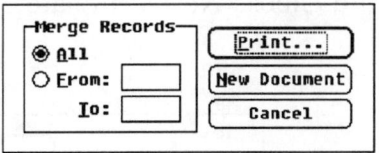

If you want to use all the records in the data document, either press ENTER or click the left mouse button on the Print button. If you do not want to use all the data records, list the numbers of the ones you do want to use in the From and To fields (the header record does not count). When you activate the Print button in the File Print Merge dialog box, the File Print dialog box is displayed, as shown here.

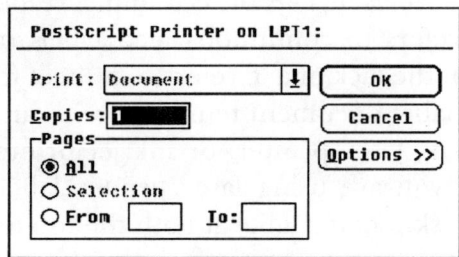

Activating the OK button will start Word for Windows printing the form letters with the data records you have specified.

Print Merge Address Labels

Word for Windows comes with three document templates that enable you to format and print data records onto standard size (1" by 2 5/8") labels. You can test these address label formats with the same DATA.DOC that was used in "Print Merge Form Letters." If you have just finished the "Print Merge Form Letters" example, close the FRMLTR.DOC document window. Activate the File New command and choose New Template option, as shown here.

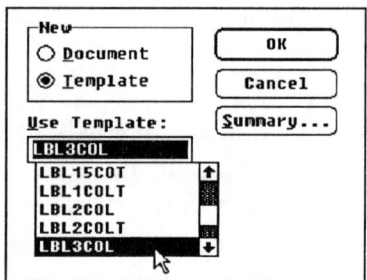

The choices are LBL 1, 2, and 3 COL document templates, which will place labels in 1, 2, or 3 columns, respectively, on a page. A T ending refers to continuous feed labels (usually for dot matrix printers); the lack of a T refers to a sheet feeder. You can use any of these label document templates with any printer (daisy wheel, dot matrix, laser printer, or ink jet printer) supported by Windows. If you are using laser printer labels, Word for Windows knows to skip half a label at both the top and bottom of the page.

For the example, choose the LBL3COL.DOT document template. Then activate the Windows Arrange All command to display both the LBL3COL.DOT document template and the DATA.DOC data document.

Next, activate the View Field Codes in that document window. You will see that the header fields have been set up in the main document template as cells within a table as seen in Figure 9-8. Now you are ready to print three-column labels by activating the File Print Merge command as in "Print Merge Form Letters."

If the fields you chose to use in your header line in the data document are different from those in the prepared address label document templates, you can overtype them with the fields you would like to use.

Figure 9-8.

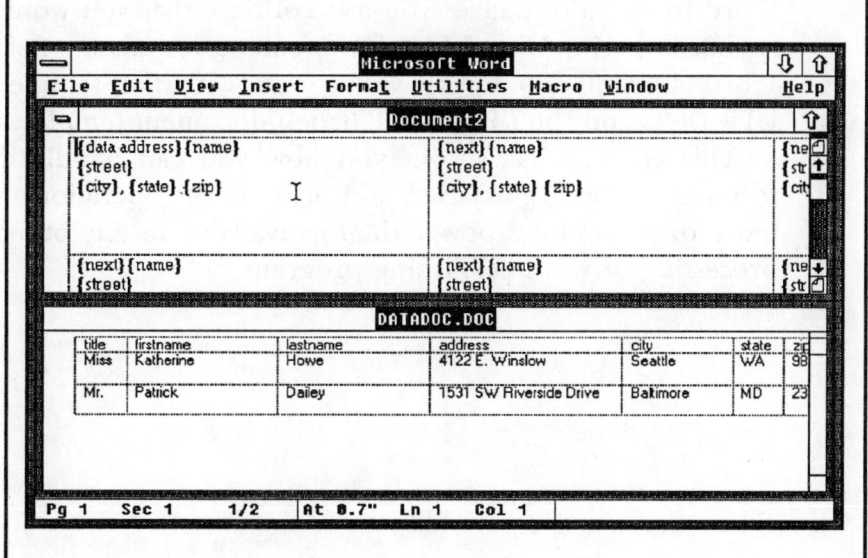

Header fields set up as cells within tables

Missing Fields

Often you do not have every field for all data records in a data document that you want to use in a main document for a form letter or a label document template. If you have some data records that are missing a field entry, such as an affiliation or a business name, you can insert the following field directly after the field that may be missing in each label:

{IF {FIELDNAME} = " ""{FIELDNAME}ENTER "}

In this example, FIELDNAME is the field that may be missing in some data records. The above field will also insure that there is no blank line printed on the label when the FIELDNAME field is missing. If you want a blank line where a data field is missing, insert the following field:

{IF {FIELDNAME} = " "" {FIELDNAME}}

Word for Windows saves you a lot of time that you would have spent composing IF and ENDIF statements for missing fields with Word 4.0 and 5.0 by providing you with the sample FRM-LTR.DOC and the LBL*.DOT (label) document templates.

This chapter has shown you how you can handle data in formulas, indices, glossaries, and print merge operations. This is more data handling power than is available in any other word processing or word publishing program.

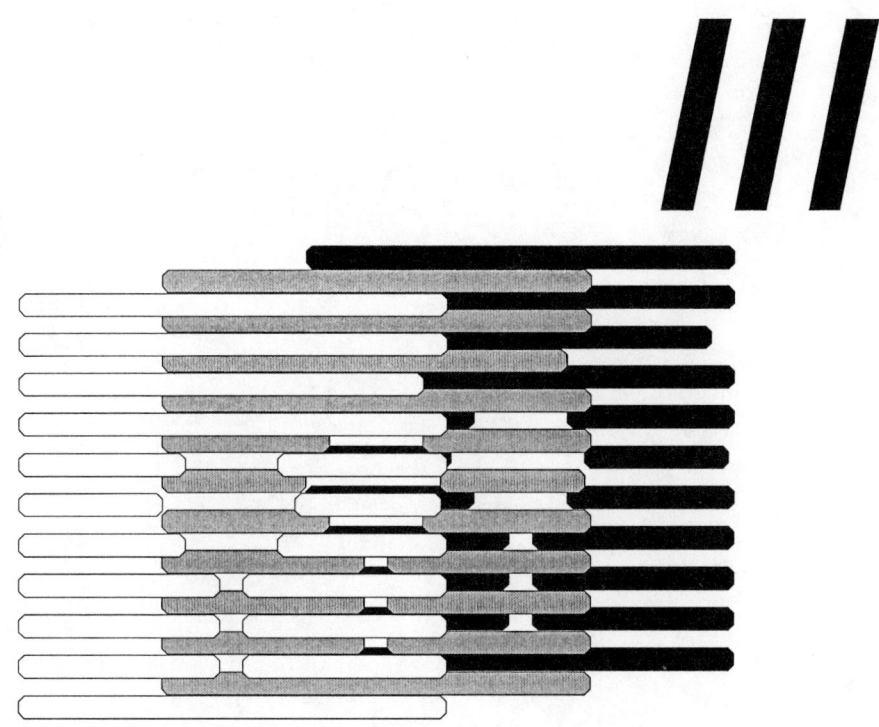

Making the Most of Word for Windows

CHAPTER

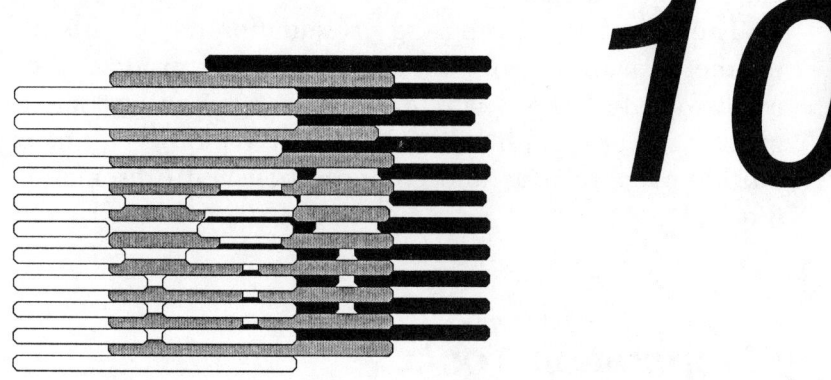

10

Desktop Publishing with Word for Windows

This chapter presents tools, such as the spell checker, thesaurus, typographic settings, and column settings, that can help you with the finishing touches that go into preparing presentation documents; such as newsletters, brochures, and reports. Keep in mind that Word for Windows, like all word publishing software, is not intended to replace desktop publishing software. Rather, Word for Windows is a powerful complement to programs such as Aldus PageMaker and Xerox Ventura Publisher. For an in-depth review of the differences between word processing, word publishing, and desktop publishing, refer to Chapter 1, "Up and Running," and Chapter 2, "Formatting Text."

The first step in preparing presentation documents is to work up the final draft, your *copy*. Copy is fully proofed text that is ready to be formatted with fonts, set in columns, and laid out with graphic images and headers. Word for Windows will help you to quickly prepare copy and compose polished presentation documents.

Copy Preparation Tools

Almost any document you write will be read by someone else. Word for Windows copy preparation tools—that is, its Utilities Spelling, Utilities Thesaurus, and Utilities Hyphenate commands—will help you prepare documents for others. These tools will also help you prepare text for importation into desktop publishing programs like PageMaker and Ventura Publisher. Since it is not easy to edit text in either of these packages, you want to make sure that your copy is letter-perfect while it is still in Word for Windows.

Using the Utilities Spelling Command

Unlike Word 4.0 and 5.0, where spell checking is an adjunct to the major program, the Word for Windows spelling checker is completely integrated into the document creation process. In Word 4.0 and 5.0, when you invoke the Library Spell command, the document you are working on is automatically saved. Then you leave Word and the Microlytic spell checking program goes to work on the text. When you are finished with the spell checker, Word 4.0 or 5.0 and the corrected document are reopened.

The Word for Windows spell checker is activated from within the program by the Utilities menu Spelling command. The Utilities Spelling command is available (not ghosted) in the Normal Editing View, Draft View, and Page View, but not in the Outline View or Print Preview. The Utilities Spelling command is in the menus that appear when you select either Menu or Full Menu commands. The Word for Windows spell checker has been optimized for speed; however, there are some measures you can take to make it run as fast as possible (see "Optimizing the Spell Checker" later in this section).

The Utilities Spelling command is accessed through the Utilities menu, seen here.

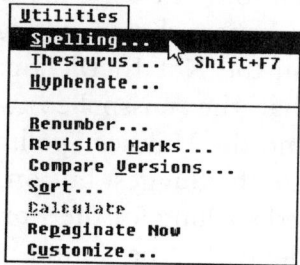

The Utilities Spelling command causes the first of two spell checker dialog boxes to appear. The first Utilities Spelling dialog box, shown here,

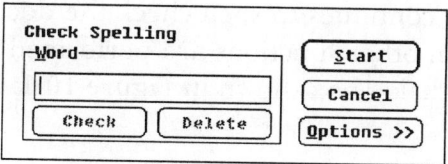

lets you check the spelling of a single word or a highlighted passage. To check the spelling of a single word, either highlight the word before activating the Utilities Spelling command or type the word in the Check Spelling text entry box. In either case, note that the Check and Delete buttons will become available when there is an entry in the Check Spelling text entry box. Either press ENTER or activate the Start button to have the spell checker look up this single word.

To check all or part of a document, do not highlight a word or type one into the Check Word text entry box. Instead, press ENTER or activate the the Start button when the first Utilities Spelling dialog box appears. Word for Windows will then begin spell checking all text in the document that is positioned after the current location of the cursor. If the cursor is not at the top of the document, Word for Windows will ask if you want to check the whole document or only the portion following the cursor.

The Start button activates the second of the two Utilities Spelling dialog boxes, shown in Figure 10-1. Each misspelled word is listed in the Not In Dictionary text entry box. Note in Figure 10-1 that the misspelled word is highlighted in the document behind the Utilities Spelling dialog box.

If you activate the Suggest button, as has been done in Figure 10-1, a suggested spelling for the word appears in the Change To field (unless none can be found in the Word for Windows dictionary). Other suggested spellings from the Word for Windows dictionary are listed in the Suggestions scroll box. If you double-click on any of these words, that word moves to the Change To field. If none of the suggested spellings is acceptable, type your own spelling in the Change To field. In either case, then activate the Change button. Word for Windows corrects the word and then continues to spell check the document.

Several other functions are performed by the second Utilities Spelling dialog box shown in Figure 10-1. Not only does the spell

Figure 10-1.

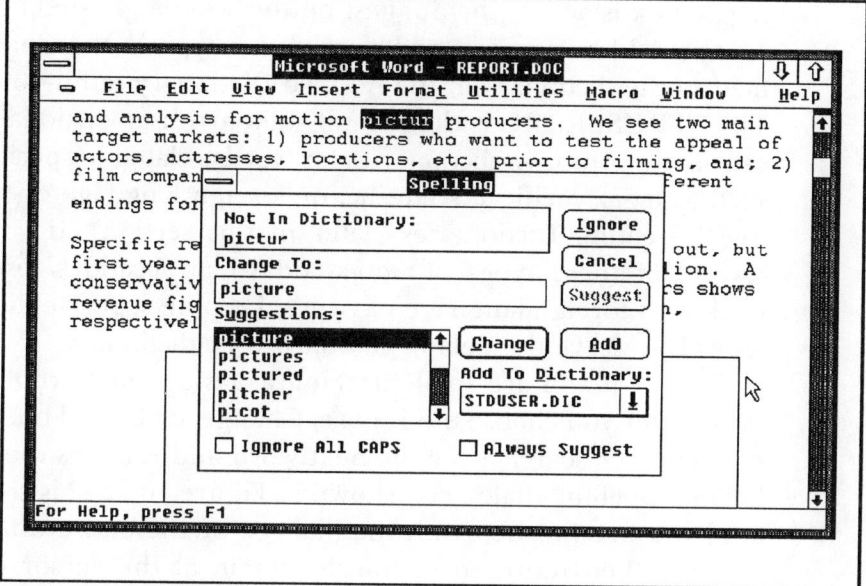

Spell checking

checker highlight misspellings, it also detects words that you have typed twice, such as "that that" or "is is." Activating the Change button will remove one of the repeated words.

The spell checker will also detect words typed in all caps or words with initial caps after the first word of a sentence; in other words, the only word the spell checker expects to contain an uppercase letter is the first word of a sentence. The spell checker detects these words to give you the chance to change the uppercase letters back to lowercase. In this book, commands are typed using initial caps and keyboard keys are typed using all small caps. If you were spell checking this book, you would not want the spell checker to detect an uppercase letter after the first letter of a sentence as an error. You can tell Word for Windows to ignore these words by activating the Ignore All Caps toggle box.

Another option is to have Word for Windows display a list of words in the Suggestions scroll box without you telling it to do so.

Just activate the Always Suggest toggle box. Note that when this toggle box is active, the Suggest button will be ghosted.

The Add button will add a word you type in the Change To field to the dictionary in the Add To Dictionary scroll-down box. The STDUSER.DIC is the default standard user dictionary. You can create your own dictionaries for words related to special tasks, such as legal, medical, scientific, or foreign language documents (see "Creating Dictionaries" later in this section). If you have several of these types of non-standard applications, especially work with foreign language passages, keeping separate dictionaries will preserve the default standard user dictionary.

Finally, if you are spell checking a passage or a whole document, after you choose the Ignore, Change, or Cancel button, the spell checker searches for the next word and reopens the second Utilities Spelling dialog box shown in Figure 10-1. This continues until you are finished with the passage or the entire document. You are then returned to the document at the cursor location where you activated the Utilities Spelling command. If you are spell checking only a single word, after you choose one of these three buttons, you are returned to the document at that word's location.

Spell Checking One Word   You can also spell check a single word with the F7 spelling key. First highlight the word and then press the F7 spelling key. The second Utilities Spelling dialog box, seen in Figure 10-1 (and mentioned in "Using the Spelling Command"), will appear if the spell checker does not recognize the word or if it is misspelled.

Creating Dictionaries   When you run the spelling checker, many names, places, and jargon words are tagged as misspelled. As with the earlier versions of Word, you can add these and other words to either the standard dictionary or to a special purpose dictionary you create.

To start collecting specialized terms in a new dictionary, activate the Utilities Spelling dialog box Options button. The options are displayed, as shown here.

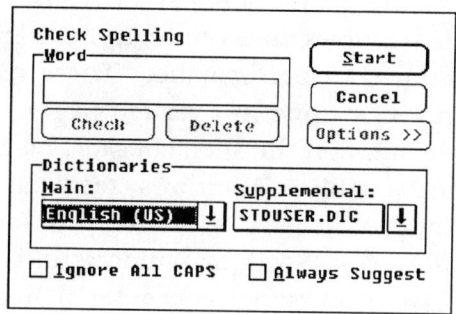

Put the cursor in the Supplemental text entry field and type over the STDUSER.DIC listing. You must add the *.DIC extension to your dictionary title; Word for Windows only recognizes dictionaries with the *.DIC extension. Then, when you activate the Start button, Word for Windows will ask if you want to create a new dictionary. Activate the Yes button; you will now have a new dictionary that includes all the words in the standard user dictionary, plus those you add to it via the second Utilities Spelling dialog box.

Whenever you want to use the new dictionary, you can select it in the first Utilities Spelling dialog box from the Options Supplemental scroll-down box. An even easier way to use the new dictionary is to select it from the Add To Dictionary scroll-down box in the second Utilities Spelling dialog box.

Note that the Ignore All Caps and Always Suggest toggle boxes are available after the option button is activated in the first Utilities Spelling dialog box and in the second Utilities Spelling dialog box. They work in the same way in both dialog boxes. If you activate either the Ignore All Caps or Always Suggest toggle box, or both, each toggle box will be displayed as active every time you use the Utilities Spelling command until you deactivate that option.

Optimizing the Spell Checker   Because the spell checker runs under the Windows environment, there are a few things you can do to optimize its performance. These considerations are most important for documents over ten pages.

Before you open the spell checker, make sure that you have a disk cache available to Windows (see Chapter 11 for a discussion of the Windows Smart Drive cache program). If you are working on a network, run Word for Windows and save your document on the local (your personal computer's) hard disk. Turn off any network connections and unload any memory resident programs (often called TSR programs—Terminate and Stay Ready). Before you activate the Utilities Spelling command, make sure the MS-DOS Executive is minimized. Also, make sure the document you are spell checking is the only one open. Turn off the Background Pagination command in the Utilities Customize menu and the Style Name Area toggle box in the View Preferences dialog box ("set it back to the default 0"). Also turn off the View Status Bar, View Ruler, and View Ribbon commands. Turn on the View Draft command. All of these actions will either speed access to the spell checker's dictionary or free memory used to investigate each word's spelling.

Using the Utilities Thesaurus Command

A thesaurus—although technically not a copy proofing tool—can help you find words to lessen repetition and make your document more interesting and effective.

The Library Thesaurus command in Word 4.0 and 5.0 offers a box with a list of nouns, verbs, and adjectives that are synonyms of a chosen word. Any of these synonyms can be substituted for the selected word. The Word for Windows Utilities Thesaurus command works in a similar way, but it also has a sizable expansion of interactive capabilities.

To use the Utilities Thesaurus command, first highlight the word for which you need a synonym. Then activate the Utilities Thesaurus command, shown here,

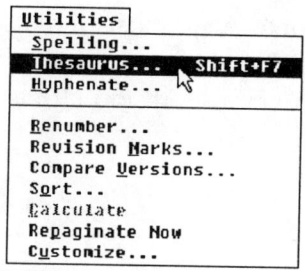

or use the Thesaurus macro, SHIFT-F7. You will then see the Utilities Thesaurus dialog box, as shown in Figure 10-2.

Note that the search word, "picture," is highlighted in the text above the dialog box in Figure 10-2. Within the Utilities Thesaurus dialog box, "picture" has been automatically inserted in the Look Up field text entry box. The first listing in the Synonyms scroll box is the word that Word for Windows assumes is most closely associated with the word you have selected. The Verb display box lists the full definition for the first listing in the Definitions scroll box below it. If you click the left mouse button on another listing in the Definitions scroll box, its full listing will appear in the Verb display box (the listings scroll off to the right of the Definitions scroll box). In this case, all the definitions are of verbs; but with other words in the Synonyms scroll box there could be noun or adjective listings. The Verb display box changes to a noun or adjective display box depending on which definition has been highlighted.

Changing the definition will usually change the list of synonyms. If you see a synonym you prefer to the Look Up word, double-click the left mouse button on it. It will then replace the word listed in the Look Up text entry field. Then activate the Replace button, as shown in Figure 10-2, to have this word inserted in the place of the original Look Up word.

If you wish, you can get a list of synonyms for any of the words in the Synonyms scroll-down box. Just click the left mouse button twice on the word. A new list of synonyms, which is likely to be very different from the prior list, will appear in the Synonyms scroll box. For example, if you choose "vision" in Figure 10-2, it

Figure 10-2.

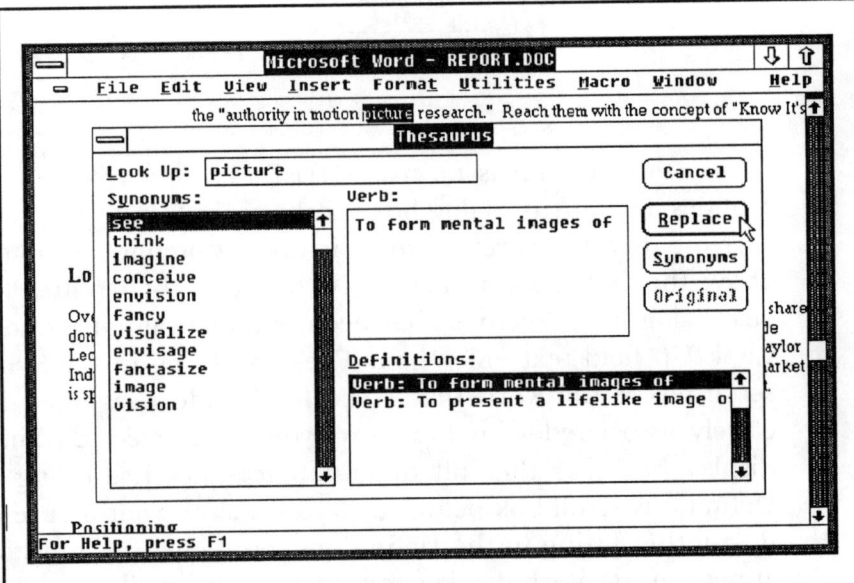

Utilities Thesaurus dialog box

brings "dream" to the top of the Synonyms list, as shown here.

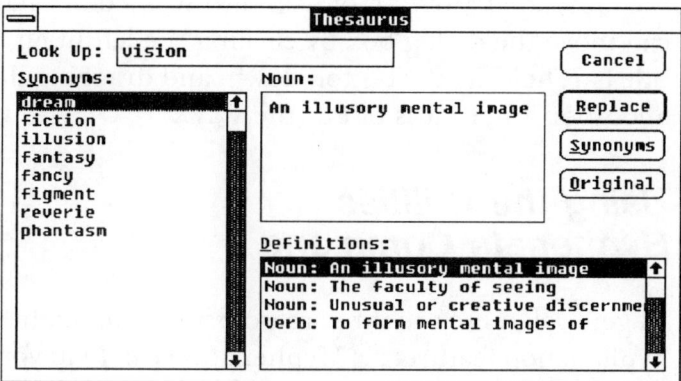

You can get back to your original word—in this case,"picture"—
by clicking the left mouse button on the Original button, which is
no longer ghosted.

If the word in the Look Up text entry box does not give you a
synonym you can use, type another word in this field and activate
the Synonyms button. Again, to insert the word in the Look Up
text entry field in your text, activate the Replace button.

If the Utilities Thesaurus scroll box is covering up part of the
passage that you are trying to edit, you can move the box. Notice
that this dialog box has a title bar with a Control button. The
Control button menu, shown here,

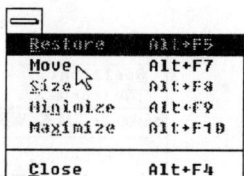

has only two commands available, Restore and Move. Since you cannot minimize this dialog box, Restore closes the Control menu. To move the box, you can use the Move command, which displays the four-sided Move arrow (this is discussed in Chapter 1). Or you can move the dialog box by clicking the left mouse button on the title bar, holding the button down, and dragging the dialog box to a location where it is out of the way.

Using the Utilities Hyphenate Command

In general, there are three reasons why you might want to use the hyphenation feature. (1) Hyphenation can help you squeeze more text into a limited number of lines and pages. (2) Hyphenation can lessen the raggedness of ragged right columns. (3) Hyphenation can lessen the amount of interword space in justified text (refer to Chapter 2, "Formatting Text," for a discussion of column formatting).

Word for Windows offers you several hyphenation tools not available in Word 4.0 and 5.0. In fact, the hyphenation features of Word for Windows are as powerful as those in many desktop publishing programs. Because of that and because the Word for Windows Utilities Hyphenate command operates much more quickly than the hyphenation tools in desktop publishing programs, you can add hyphenation to copy before you import the copy into a desktop publishing program.

The Utilities Hyphenate command is activated in the Utilities menu, as shown here.

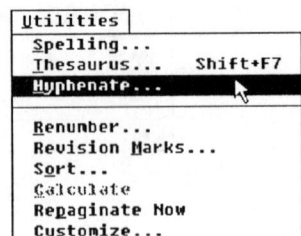

The Utilities Hyphenate command displays the Utilities Hyphenate dialog box, shown here.

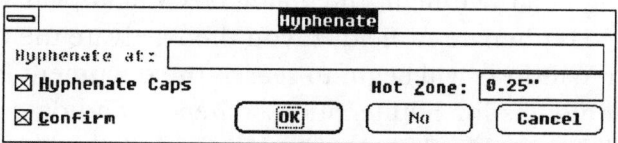

If you activate this command when the cursor is not on a word that can be hyphenated, such as the top of a document, the Hyphenate At text entry field will be empty and ghosted. The Hyphenate Caps toggle box is active by default. This option ensures that words typed in all uppercase letters will be considered for hyphenation. The Confirm toggle box is also active by default; it allows you to accept or reject each word to be hyphenated with the OK or No button. If the Confirm button is inactive, either a highlighted word or all words (if no word is highlighted) will be hyphenated. The Cancel button ends the hyphenation process.

The Hot Zone text entry field is a powerful new feature in Word for Windows. The 0.25" default value represents an amount of space at the end of each line between the last character and the right margin. If at least this much blank space exists after the last word in a line with a ragged right margin, the first word on the next line is hyphenated. Similarly, if 0.25" of blank space is available for additional space between words before a line is justified, the first word on the next line is hyphenated. In a justified line, space that would appear at the end of the line (if the words had a single space between them) is equally apportioned between the words as interword space. Thus, a large Hot Zone entry will lead to few words being hyphenated; a small Hot Zone entry will lead to many words being hyphenated. The column width will also have a large influence on the the effect of the hot zone. The narrower the column, the greater the chance words will be hyphenated because fewer whole words will be able to fit on a line, and vice versa. The default 0.25" is a moderate Hot Zone setting for the standard 6" column width.

If you activate the Utilities Hyphenate command at the beginning of a document, the dialog box will appear without a word in the Hyphenate At field. If you then activate the OK button, Word for Windows will begin to search the document for words that are candidates for hyphenation. When a candidate word is found, it will be displayed in the Hyphenate At field, broken into syllables, with the best hyphenation location highlighted.

An example using the word "several" in the REPORT.DOC sample document is shown in Figure 10-3. Note that the high-

Figure 10-3.

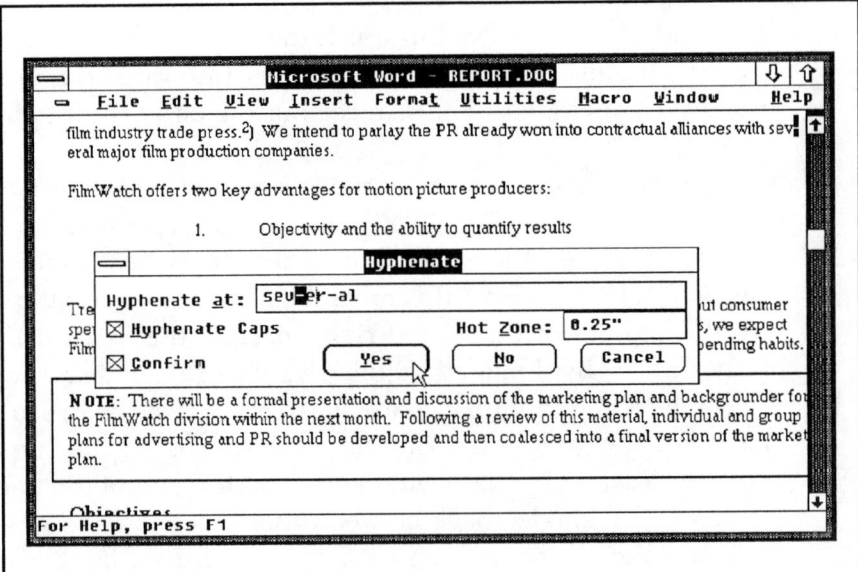

Utilities Hyphenate dialog box

lighted syllable break is shown as it would appear in the document. If you activate the Yes button, the word will be hyphenated as suggested.

Note the dotted vertical line between "e" and "r" in the word "several" in the Hyphenate At field. This shows where the right column margin would pass through the unhyphenated word if it were placed at the end of the line. Since the second syllable break between the "r" and the "a" comes after this line break, it is not a plausible choice. If you try to choose a hyphenation point after the line break by clicking the left mouse button on a hyphen that appears after the line break in the Hyphenation At field, the word will not be hyphenated in the document. However, if you make changes to the document such that the hyphen you chose went to the other side of the line break, Word for Windows would use this hyphenation point.

Inserting Hyphens Manually   In addition to using Word for Windows Utilities Hyphenate feature, you can insert hyphens manually. There are three kinds of hyphens—regular, optional, and nonbreaking—each of which is used in a different situation.

The regular hyphen is one you type, using the - (dash key) between syllables (for example, between two syllables in a long word that comes at the end of a line), or between associated words. Words or syllables joined by regular hyphens will always be separated at the end of a line (the first part including the hyphen will fall at the end of the line and the second part will begin the next line) if the regular hyphen falls within the hot zone (see "Using the Hyphenate Command"). If a word with a regular hyphen falls at the end of a line, but the hyphen is not in the hot zone, both parts of the word will remain together at the end of the line.

Optional hyphens are the same as those inserted at the end of a line by the Utilities Hyphenate command. They are used for words that cannot fit entirely at the end of a line. They help you make a ragged right margin less ragged or reduce the interword space in justified text. If insertions or deletions made after inserting an optional hyphen move the word away from the end of the line, the optional hyphen is dropped. To insert an optional hyphen, you type CTRL– (CTRL-DASH).

Nonbreaking hyphens, or dashes, have several uses. They can be used to connect two words that, when seen apart, connote something different than when their meanings are joined. For example, without the hyphen between "pass-through," referring to an opening connecting the kitchen and dining area in a restaurant, the reader may not be able to mentally connect the words "pass" and "through" as a noun in a sentence. Nonbreaking hyphens can also be used to connect standard prefixes to words such as "half-baked" and "co-worker." A final example of the use of a nonbreaking hyphen is as a minus sign in a mathematical equation. To insert a nonbreaking hyphen you press CTRL-SHIFT- (CTRL-SHIFT-DASH).

Images

The ability to import graphic images into Word for Windows documents gives you several dimensions beyond text in which to express your ideas. There are basically two kinds of graphic images—bitmap images, which are created in paint packages, and object images, which are created in draw packages. A major concern when working with images is the conversion of one image format to another. Conversion of image formats is discussed in Appendix D, "Supporting Software and Hardware."

Word for Windows does not contain any tools for creating images; for that, you will need to use supporting software. This software is discussed in Appendix D. The uses of these image producing programs are discussed here.

Paint: Bitmap Images

Bitmap images, which are created in paint programs, are sets of dots that form an image that can be printed by your dot matrix or laser printer. These images are called bitmaps because the dots are positioned along horizontal lines from the top to the bottom of a page. Each dot position on each line is coded in the file sent to the printer as a bit. Bits are a binary 0 or 1 code; a 1 codes for on—telling the printer to print the dot in this position—and a 0 off listing leaves the position blank. The pattern of 1s and 0s determining where dots will be printed is called a bitmap. These dots are often called pixels. Pixel editing is the process of erasing or adding dots to a bitmap image.

Scanned images, which are usually taken from manual drawings, professionally prepared clip art, book illustrations, or photographs, are, by definition, bitmap images. Some paint applications offer "intelligent scaling" of bitmap images. This is an attempt to resize (make smaller or larger), while retaining the pattern of dots that makes up a bitmap image. For the most part, scaling bitmap images is more work than it is worth. For example, the amount of pixel editing required after intelligently scaling a scanned image of a photograph often leaves it unrecognizable. Thus, if you are scanning images to be used as bitmap files in a Word for Windows document, you should try to make the original scanned image the size you want it to be in your document.

Another source of images that can be scanned is professionally prepared clip art. Most makers of presentation graphics software also offer catalogs of clip art, and there are several suppliers who specialize in clip art (see Appendix D). Many clip art images can be used in reports or advertisements. A computer graphic that is part of the clip art library sold by T/Maker is shown here.

Clip art can come to you on paper or on disk. Clip art is usually less expensive when purchased on paper; this is because you do the work of scanning it and cleaning it up. Many clip art libraries, however, come entirely on disk. Often the clip art on disk is not in a bitmap image format (such as *.TIF or *.PCX); rather it is in the form of a scalable object file (such as PostScript *.EPS). (See PostScript in "Draw: Object Oriented Art" later in this chapter.)

Black and white photographs can often be scanned with acceptable results. The quality of the image depends on both the resolution of your scanner (since laser printers print at 300 dpi [dots per inch], most scanners also scan at 300 dpi) and the number of shades of grey that it can detect (the three common levels are 16, 64, and 256 levels of grey). The more shades of grey your scanner has, the more contrast it will pick up; greater grey scale tonality makes the interiors, borders, and backgrounds of objects show up more clearly. With many paint packages you can also experiment with pixel patterns, called *dithering elements;* you can experiment with different dithering patterns until you find one that gives you the maximum contrast for a particular photograph.

It is rare that you would want to use an entire black and white photograph. Most often you will want to clip out pieces of the image. These pieces of black and white photographs can be cleaned up and labeled with text in a paint package before they are inserted in a Word for Windows document. Figure 10-4 shows a photograph of a mechanical part that has been scanned, cleaned up, and labeled. This process can also be done with photographs of people and scenery.

Figure 10-4.

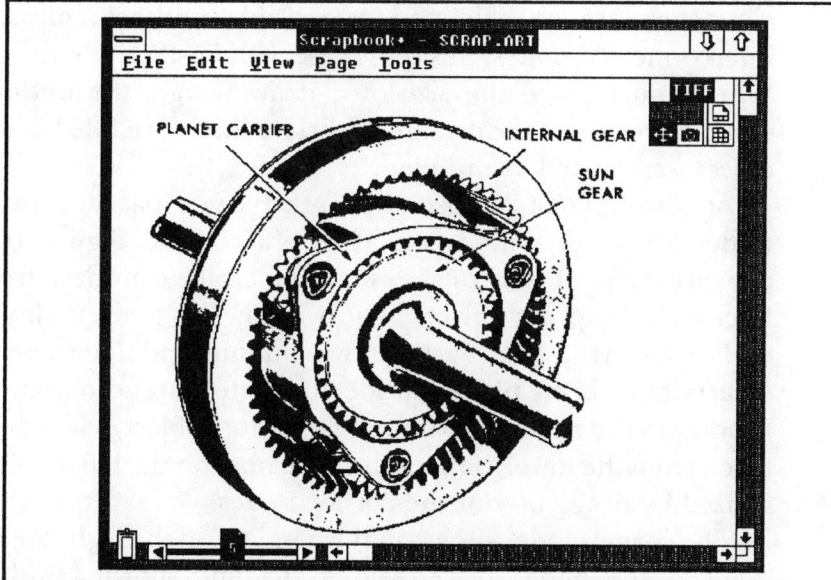

Image taken from a scanned black and white photograph

Draw: Object Oriented Art

Object images are collections of geometric outlines, such as circles, ovals, and squares. These geometric outlines are created in draw packages. They can then be scaled up and down in size within the draw package before being inserted in a Word for Windows document. Simple geometric line art, such as a corporate logo, is the easiest kind of image to create in a draw package.

In a draw package, the geometric outlines making up the edge of an object are connected at nodes. Nodes connect areas where the curvature of the line making up the edge changes. The shape of a curved line between two nodes is determined by a mathematical equation. For example, the curves in PostScript (*.EPS) object images are defined as equations referred to as Bezier splines. The equations allow the image to be scaled without changing its appearance. You can add text to these images as long as the characters are also defined as scalable outlines consisting of interconnected nodes; this is the case with PostScript font outlines. When you change the size of a draw image, the outlines are stretched mathematically, and interiors that were filled before the object was resized are refilled.

An example of a PostScript-based draw package that runs under Microsoft Windows is Micrografx Draw. Figure 10-5 is a clip art map of Wisconsin, with all of its counties, from the Micrografx clip art library. The window on the left shows that each county is an object with its own outline, and that these county objects have been placed inside the state outline object. In the window to the right, the Milwaukee County object, which has been taken from the lower right of the state map on the left, copied, and resized by dragging out the corner nodes.

The corner nodes shown in the window on the right are not the same as the nodes placed along the line showing Milwaukee County itself. These corner nodes are placed in the same position around the image box for every object. You can always click the left mouse button on one of these nodes and resize the object within the box. If you drag one of the corner nodes diagonally (in or out) the object is resized proportionately. If you drag one of the middle, top, or bottom nodes sideways, up, or down, the object will be oblong; for example, if you drag the middle nodes on either side outward, the object will appear flattened.

Another important application for draw packages is to convert bitmap images into scalable images. Many draw packages will import bitmap images and convert them directly to scalable images. This is not usually desirable because the curved edges (those that are not vertical or horizontal) of bitmap images tend to have jagged, or stepped, bitmap patterns. These edges are straight in an image created in a draw program, and they remain

Figure 10-5.

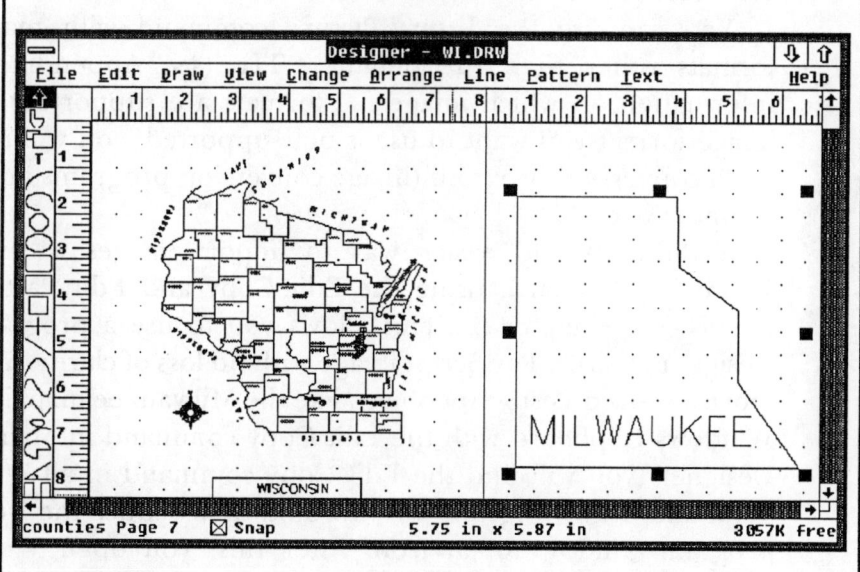

Draw objects

straight when the image is resized. The newest draw packages offer "auto-trace" functions that automatically convert the jagged edge around a bitmap object to a scalable outline (see Appendix D). This process works especially well with scanned line art that is intended to be geometrically symmetrical, and less well with scanned photographs, because the important details, especially light and dark shading, are usually not geometrical.

Importing Images into Word for Windows

The importation of image files is discussed in Chapter 3. However, now that you know more about the preparation of images, you may want to import images from programs other than Windows Paint.

You can use the Insert Picture command with many file formats other than the default *.TIF (see Appendix C for information on which image file formats are supported). If the image format you want to use is not supported, you will need to use a conversion program (image conversion programs are listed in Appendix D).

A different and easier way to import images is with the Windows Clipboard, using the Edit Copy and Edit Paste commands (see Chapter 3). This allows you to use a program like Designer to size a PostScript image with no loss of clarity. You can move a resized PostScript object, like the Milwaukee map, into the Windows Clipboard with the Edit Copy command in Micrografx Designer (you will find the Edit Copy command in all Windows paint and draw programs). You would then reduce the Designer program window to an icon. After this, you open Word for

Windows and use the Edit Paste command to place the image into a Word for Windows document.

Desktop Publishing Preformatting

The text brought into desktop publishing programs like Page-Maker and Ventura Publisher is prepared with word processing software. To prepare that text, Word for Windows offers several advantages over most word processing packages. First, it is easier to proof copy before bringing it into a desktop publishing environment (see "Copy Preparation Tools"). Second, it is faster to format copy by adding styles (see Chapter 4, "For the Record: Styles and Templates"), columns (see "Columns"), special marks (see "Special Marks"), and characters (see "Setting Type") with Word for Windows than it is in PageMaker or Ventura Publisher.

The final production runs of many desktop-published documents are done on laser printers. A laser printer is capable of 300 dpi (dots per inch) resolution, which creates jagged edges on characters that are perceptible to most people. You may want to have your master copies printed at a desktop publishing service bureau that offers typeset quality output on paper or film that can be printed from your disk for between $1 and $25 per page, depending on the time it takes to print the pages. The increased resolution on the master copy, usually between 1200 and 2540 dpi, is often worth the extra cost (see "Typeset Quality Printing and Service Bureaus"). In most cases, a laser printer output is adequate as a master copy for documents that will be reproduced by xerographic or camera-ready (offset printing) methods.

Word for Windows can also be used to prepare page proofs. These page proofs allow you to see how the typeset version will look, and others can then make their editorial changes on these proofs. However, it is not practical to consider publishing a journal or a book with Word for Windows and a laser printer alone. All but the most expensive laser printers produce text at a resolution that is too low (300 dpi versus 2540 dpi for books) and are too slow (8 pages per minute [ppm] versus 100 and more ppm for publishing systems) to use for these publishing purposes.

Special Marks

The desktop publishing revolution is predicated on the ability to output proofs on a laser printer at 300 dpi resolution that mirror the higher-resolution (1200-2540 dpi) output master draft that can be printed at greater expense on professional paper and film typesetters. Less complex documents, such as reports and simple brochures, can be prepared with Word for Windows and given to a desktop publishing service bureau directly. More complex documents, such as manuals and books, need to be laid out in desktop publishing software like PageMaker or Ventura Publisher. These files can then be submitted to a desktop publishing service bureau.

Aside from placing graphic images on a page, word publishing and desktop publishing software give you the ability to use the same fonts used by high resolution typesetters. It is this uniformity of fonts that allows you to print proofs of a document on a laser printer that will have the same placement of words on a line and columns of text in relation to graphic images as the master copy you receive from a desktop publishing service bureau.

The reason that font formats are so important is that if the character widths are at all different between the fonts used on your laser printer and those used by the desktop publishing service bureau's typesetter, your output will not match theirs (hundredths of an inch make a huge difference here). If this happens, you can expect the typeset copy to have lines of text overwriting both each other and graphic images and you can also expect misaligned columns. Generally, if the service bureau's fonts are too narrow, you will have more text on each line in your proof than on the typeset copy. If the service bureau's fonts are too wide, you will not have enough words on each line of typeset copy.

The need for character width compatibility between your printer's fonts and your desktop publishing service bureau's fonts extends to the spaces between characters and text that you display on your screen but do not print (such as hidden text). To keep track of these spaces and nonprinting characters, Word for Windows lets you display special marks. Special marks are not shown by default. To display them, you activate the View Preferences command. The special marks are listed as toggle box options on the left side of the View Preferences dialog box, shown here.

```
┌──────────────────────────────────────────────────────┐
│ Preferences                              ┌──────────┐  │
│ ☐ Iabs          ☒ Display as Printed     │    OK    │  │
│ ☐ Spaces        ☒ Pictures               └──────────┘  │
│ ☐ Paragraph Marks ☐ Text Boundaries      ┌──────────┐  │
│ ☐ Optional Hyphens ☐ Horizontal Scroll Bar│  Cancel  │ │
│ ☐ Hidden Text   ☒ Vertical Scroll Bar    └──────────┘  │
│                 ☒ Table Gridlines                      │
│ ☒ Show All  ▪   Style Area Width: 0"                   │
└──────────────────────────────────────────────────────┘
```

Special marks can be displayed for tabs, spaces, ends of paragraphs (carriage returns), optional hyphens (regular and nonbreaking hyphens are always displayed), and hidden text. You can display special marks individually by activating the Preferences toggle boxes or you can display them all with the Show All toggle box at the bottom left of the View Preferences dialog box. You can also activate the Show All option with the CTRL-SHIFT-8 macro.

Table 10-1.

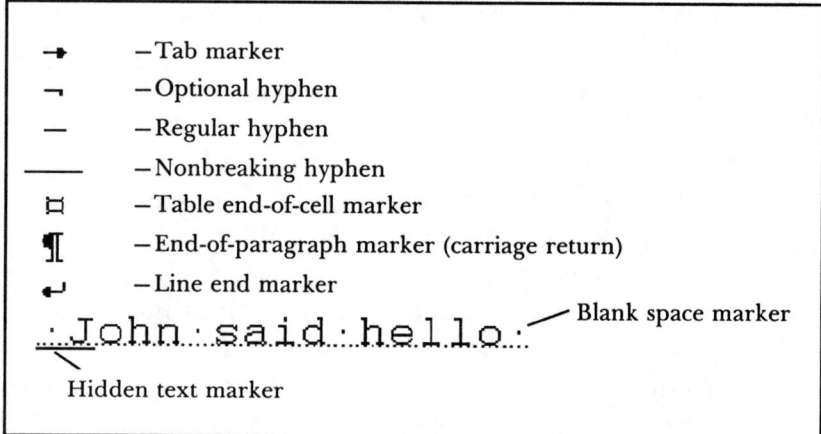

Special Marks.

The screen characters used to represent the special marks are listed in Table 10-1. The Table end-of-cell and line end markers are displayed when you activate either the Paragraph Marks or Show All toggle box in the View Preferences dialog box.

Typeset Quality Printing and Service Bureaus

If you produce a presentation document such as a brochure or company report with Word for Windows, you may want to have an original printed at 1200 or 2540 dpi on high quality paper or film. Typeset paper output can be reproduced by photocopy or offset printing techniques. Offset printing is of much higher quality than photocopying; and, with a large run, you will be surprised how little the difference in price can be. Desktop publishing service bureaus usually accept a document file only for reproduction by traditional phototypesetting methods.

You can have a master copy of your presentation document prepared at a desktop publishing service bureau. Look in the yellow pages under desktop publishing bureaus or copy services (see Appendix F, "Journals, Books, and User Groups"). Some copy services can do desktop publishing jobs. Often, however, copy professionals will be much less expensive than a desktop publishing service bureau for photocopying and offset reproduction services.

When you telephone, find out the following information. First, ask what file formats the service bureau accepts. Most desktop publishing service bureaus accept only PostScript files. If you do not have a PostScript laser printer, you will still be able to proof your Document onscreen with Page View; you would then print the document to a file with the Windows PostScript printer driver. This limits you to PostScript fonts both onscreen and for your printer. If you have an HP LaserJet or compatible printer, you may want to look into the multiple ways of printing PostScript output on your printer (see Appendix D). If the desktop publishing service bureau accepts Word for Windows files, the next question becomes imperative.

Ask your desktop publishing service bureau what fonts you must use to proof your Word for Windows files on your non-PostScript laser printer. Sometimes the service bureau will provide you with laser printer or dot matrix fonts that are width compatible with their own. Many service bureaus can accept non-PostScript files that contain Bitstream fonts.

Next ask how the bureau handles photographs. If the bureau cannot handle photos directly, you or the service bureau would have to scan the images, edit them, and insert them in your Word for Windows document as graphic images. Your results will usually be much crisper if the photos are stripped in after the document is printed. You cannot, however, strip in glossy black and white photos. You will have to have them screened (create a halftone picture, like that in a newspaper, from your original glossy photo) at the service bureau or a reproduction service. Screening usually costs about $5 for a 4" x 6" photo.

Finally, ask the service bureau how you should deliver your document. Often service bureaus accept documents (PostScript and other formats as well) and image files by modem. The service bureau will usually provide you with modem software that logs you into its own bulletin board. If you have photos that must be stripped into the final document, you will have to send these separately.

If the service bureau can satisfy all of your document production and reproduction needs, then, within reason, cost becomes a less important consideration. It is often easy to find a bureau that will do part of a job for less money. But usually the least expensive service bureaus cut costs by reducing the number of services that they offer; this means they will not be able to meet all the specifications of the job. Usually price varies not only with the resolution of the output (1200 or 2540 dpi) and the medium (paper or film), but also by how soon you want the result back.

Layout Tools

Word for Windows provides you with many commands to help you prepare presentation documents. Whether or not the copy goes into a desktop publishing program or to a service bureau, you will find these commands useful.

The commands used in preparing presentation documents can be roughly broken down into two categories: those related to type (or fonts) and those related to page layout (setting up columns, margins, images, tables, and so on, on a page).

Before you can use the Word for Windows type commands to the fullest, you will need to understand the basic concepts of typography (see "Setting Type"). Similarly, to use the Word for Windows page layout commands, you must have an idea what you want the page to look like (see "Page Layout").

Setting Type

When formatting a presentation document with multiple type-faces, the width of each character, as well as the amount of blank space around each character and word and between each line, are important considerations. Word for Windows gives you several Format Character commands to control space within and between words. There are also several Format Paragraph options to control the space between lines. These options were introduced in Chapter 2, "Formatting Text." The discussions under "Leading" and "Letterspacing" will give you a better idea of how to use these Word for Windows options.

Leading

The spacing between lines of type is generally called *leading* (pronounced ledding); another word for it is *linespacing*. The Format Paragraph dialog box, shown in Figure 10-6, uses the word "Spacing" for the option set that controls the vertical space, or leading, between lines of type in a document. To review briefly, the Spacing Line option controls the amount of space between lines within a paragraph. The Spacing Before and After options control the amount of blank space that is inserted before and after a paragraph (see Chapter 2 for a complete discussion).

Figure 10-7 illustrates how to measure linespacing. Linespacing depends upon the baseline of the text. The baseline is the imaginary line on which all the letters in a line sit (letters with descenders like "g" or "y" go below the baseline). The linespace of one line is thus the space between its baseline and the baseline of the text above it. The units used to measure linespacing are points and picas. There are 72 points to an inch and there are 6 picas to an inch. Therefore, there are 12 points to a pica. In the Utilities Customize menu, you can choose the unit of measure to be points, picas, inches, or centimeters. These units of measure will apply to vertical leading measurements as well as to the horizontal letter-spacing measurements (see "Letterspacing"). As an example, the typesetting phrase "10 on 12" refers to 10 points of text on 12 points of leading. In this case, the leading is set at 12 points.

Word for Windows lets you adjust the leading of a document very precisely. Learning how to choose proper leading, however, is a process of experimentation with your documents. At first, see what works for others. Later, your own experience will dictate what looks good. For now, here are some guidelines.

When using the common body text point sizes (that is, between 10 and 14 points), leave two points of space, about 20%, blank space between lines. In fact, two points of space is the Word for

Figure 10-6.

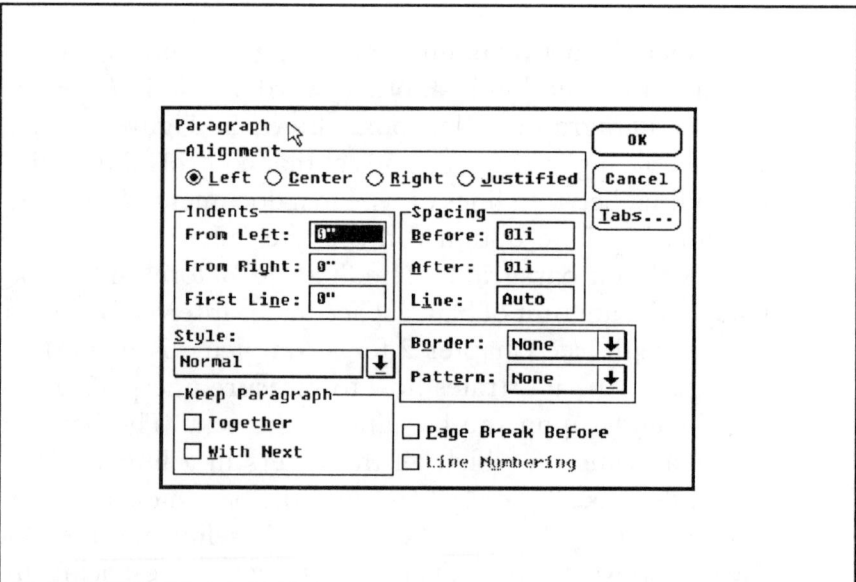

Format Paragraph dialog box

Windows default setting for all point sizes. At 10 points, the additional 2 points to determine leading is exactly 20% additional space. Unless you specify otherwise, Word for Windows automatically adjusts the leading to two points greater than the largest point size used in a line of text. If you use 24-point type, the Line option field will read Auto, but you will have 26 points of leading. Because you want 20% leading in most cases, this will be insufficient leading. Without the minimally necessary 28.8 points (calculated 24-point text + 20% of 24 [4.8] blank interline space = 28.8), the descenders of one line will cut off the tops of letters on the line below.

You can change the default by typing another leading over Auto in the Format Paragraph Line option. For example, if you use 26-point type, the 2-point Auto leading will be too little. You

Figure 10-7.

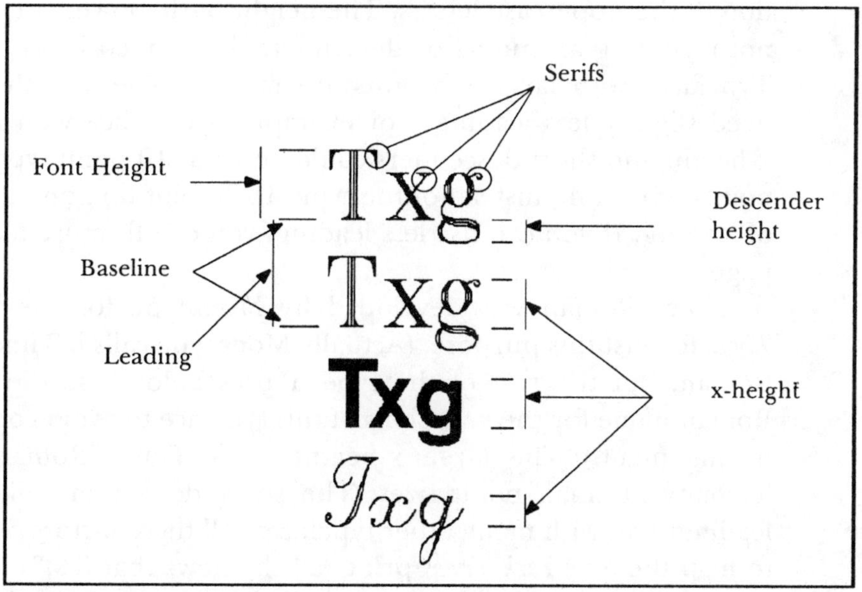

Linespacing elements (typefaces from top to bottom: Z-Soft Roman, Helvetica, and Script)

should type at least **28.8** over Auto. But remember, if you use too much leading, readers will have a hard time when they shift their gaze to the left from the end of each line to the beginning of the next line. If you use too little leading, the tops of the characters will overwrite the bottoms of the characters in the line above them. You will avoid these problems if you stick to the 20% rule, but the appearance may not be optimal, especially with larger point sizes. Remember you can always manually adjust the leading for optimal effect.

A few typographic factors should be considered when choosing the optimal amount of leading. The design of the typeface is important. In Figure 10-7, notice that the descender on the lowercase Helvetica "g" does not go far below the text baseline. Therefore, you do not need much leading with this typeface. Some typefaces have long descenders and thus require more leading.

In Figure 10-7, the lowercase Roman letters are tall in proportion to the uppercase letters. The height of the lowercase letters, not including ascenders or descenders, is referred to as *x-height*. Typefaces with large x-heights are more legible and therefore need slightly less leading. For example, a typeface with a large x-height and short descenders could be set as 10-point type on 11 points of leading instead of the typical 10-point text on 12 points of leading. If you can use less leading, you can fit more text on a page.

Times Roman was developed by Monotype for the *London Times* for just this purpose. (Actually Monotype calls it Times New Roman, but the rest of the type houses boldly use the Times Roman name for their versions of this typeface to avoid copyright infringement.) The large x-height gives Times Roman clear legibility at small point sizes. The short descenders allow less leading than with many other typefaces. All these factors combine to help the *New York Times* print "all the news that fits."

Another typographic factor is whether or not a typeface has *serifs*. Serifs are the flourishes at the end of different strokes making up a character. Serifs play a critical role in the legibility of most body text. The serifs of Times Roman type add legibility by directing the eye to the right along a line of type. Helvetica, which has no serifs, is a *sanserif* typeface. Serifs, by directing your eye to the right, also prevent your eye from dropping too far down at the end of a line. If your eye drops down at the end of a line, it is difficult to find the beginning of the next line. This is why sanserif typefaces generally work better as headings than as body text.

Letterspacing

A font is a complete character set of one typeface at a single point size. All font character sets include the upper- and lowercase letters, numbers, punctuation, a few symbols, and foreign language characters (Windows uses the Windows/ANSI character set; the different character sets are listed in Appendix E). For each point size of a typeface, there is a standard character box. The height of this box is the point size for the entire font. The width depends on the pitch of the font. Pitch is measured in cpi (characters per inch). The most famous font pitches are the typewriter fonts, Pica and Elite. Pica is 10 cpi and Elite is 12 cpi.

In typewritten text, each character has the same amount of space. In other words, each character has the same character box width. An "i" is given the same amount of space as an "m." The pitch in such fonts is called *monospace*. Monospaced fonts are useful in setting up columns, especially in tables. However, you can also set tabs or cell borders in Word for Windows and have aligned columns.

Unlike typewriters, computer-driven printers are not limited to monospaced fonts. When fonts are designed for dot matrix, laser, and professional typesetting printers, the width of each character box is adjusted to the actual width of the character. The justification and kerning features of desktop publishing programs take this adjustment to its fullest.

Kerning is the minimization of space between characters within words. For example, an "a" can be tucked in under a "T", and the joined cross bars on adjacent "t"s and "f"s are termed ligatures. Word for Windows does not have a kerning option.

Justification is the maximization of space between words on each line. The Format Paragraph Justification option assumes that you want flush right and left margins. If you set up a line of words with single character spaces between each word (flush left), there will be space left over between the last word and the absolute right column margin. The justification of text is a process that takes this left over space and divides it evenly between all of the words in a line of text. Increasing the interword space makes words, as units, more recognizable to the reader; this also makes the text faster to read.

Word for Windows also offers three Format Character dialog box Character Spacing options to help you control letterspacing. These options are Normal, Expanded, and Condensed, as shown in Figure 10-8. The Normal button tells Word for Windows to use the letterspacing defined in the font. The Expanded option tells Word for Windows to add the amount of horizontal width in the Character Spacing By field to the right side of each character box. The Condensed option tells Word for Windows to subtract the amount of space in the By field from the right side of each character box. The default By field value will be 3 points; you can enter settings between 0 and 63.5 points in 0.5 point increments.

One use of the Character Spacing Expanded option is to stretch a title across a masthead. Or, you can stretch your name across the top of your personal stationary. The most important use for the Character Spacing Condensed option is to squeeze more words on a page. It can also be useful with sanserif typefaces like Helvetica and Futura. These faces can be condensed to fit long headings on one or two lines. If it is longer than two lines, a heading, especially a subheading, starts to look like a passage of text or a quote.

Type houses usually offer special condensed or expanded versions of typefaces. Condensed typefaces have shortened characters, box widths, and intercharacter spaces built in. Expanded typefaces are adjusted in the opposite direction. These typefaces will be somewhat more legible than when you adjust normal-spaced fonts with Word for Windows Character Spacing options. However, you may not want to spend the extra money for these typefaces considering their limited applications.

Setting Off Text

In addition to using different typefaces, point sizes, and linespacing to set off headings from body text, you can use variations of style. Variations on the regular style of a font that help the reader

Figure 10-8.

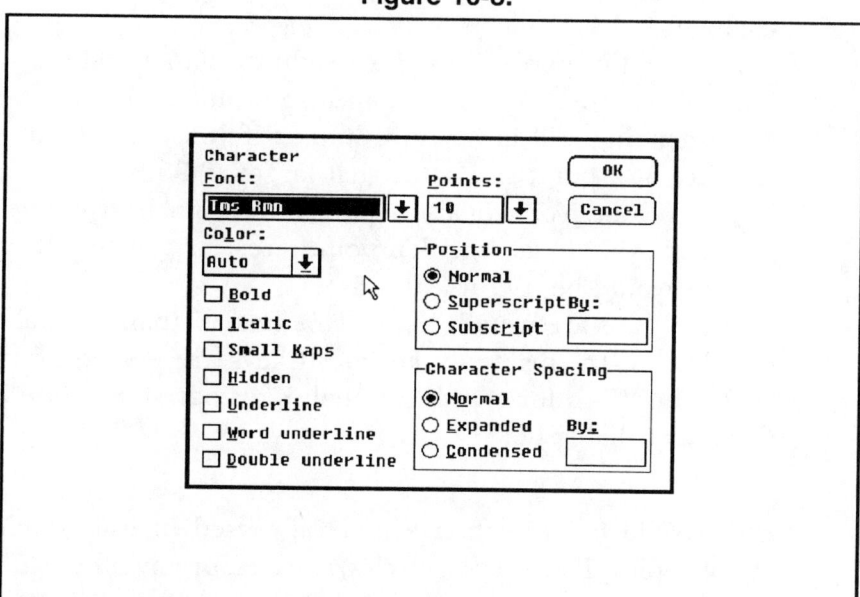

Format Character dialog box

discern a header from body text include bold, italic, bold italic, and intial caps. There are also elements and passages within the body text that need to be set off from the main discussion, such as lists, quotes, parentheticals, and repeated clauses. Word for Windows provides you with tools such as bullets, em and en dashes, and tab stop leaders to set off portions of body text.

Case   Word for Windows gives you a number of ways to quickly change the case of passages to help them connote their positions (such as title, header, technical term, and so on) in the document. The quickest way to type all uppercase letters is to activate the CAPS LOCK key. You can also convert highlighted lowercase text to all caps with the Case key, SHIFT-F3. Pressing the Case key again toggles the text back to lowercase. There is no quick way to format text as initial caps. You can also format a highlighted passage or word with the Small Kaps option with the Format Character command.

Using all uppercase text for headings is an attention grabber, but it also tends to deflate the message contained in the heading. Your heading will have more impact if you use a bold sanserif typeface at a point size somewhat larger (20-50%) than the serif body text font. You can also set off short passages from the rest of the text by indents, smaller point sizes, or italics. All of these devices would be useful with quotes.

Small caps are usually about 10% smaller than normal upper-case letters. In this book, keyboard keys are presented in small caps. The Word for Windows Small Kaps option is in the Format Character dialog box.

Bulleted Lists   Bullets are generally used in lists to highlight major topics. They can be circles, squares, or any other shape that calls attention to a point. Bulleted lists are useful in advertisements, newsletters, and summary pages. The bulleted list shown here,

☐ News Flash: Word for Windows Bullets Lists

☐ Call Attention To Major Topics

☐ Highlight Each Point

uses open square bullets. Sometimes these squares can also be used as check boxes on forms.

To set up a bulleted list, first pick a font that has a bullet symbol in it. Use the Font scroll-down box in the Format Character dialog box. If you have a PostScript printer, you can pick the Symbol font shown here.

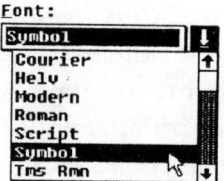

If your bulleted items are one line or less, you do not have to worry about paragraph formatting. If they are more than one line long, format the paragraph indents so all lines after the first are indented at least 1/4" more than the first. The Format Paragraph Indents options should be set as shown here.

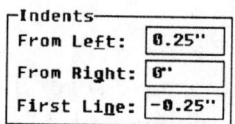

You can get very fancy with bullets. The Zapf and other Dingbat typefaces are complete symbol character sets, many of which can be used for bullets. They are available for PostScript as well as LaserJet and compatible laser printers (see Appendix E, "Font Character Sets and Sources" for a list of these characters). All of these characters call attention to major points in different ways.

You do not enter these symbols by typing characters on the keyboard. Instead, you must first activate the NUMLOCK key. Then, while holding down the ALT key, type the number sequence assigned to the character you want on the numeric keypad (each font should come with a table of the numeric assignments for each character). The character should appear onscreen when you take your finger off the ALT key.

Outdents and Tab Stops   Some lists are easier to read if you indent every line after the first. This is referred to as *outdenting* the first line. To outdent, you type a negative first line indent in the Format Paragraph Indents option set. Usually the left indent will be the same value as the first line indent except it will be positive. One example of an outdented list is a bibliography.

To create an outdented list, set up the Format Paragraph Indents with a 0.5" outdent as shown here.

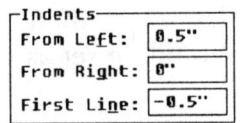

Bibliographies often have several papers by the same author. In these cases, some bibliography formats have a tab stop leader. A tab stop leader is a tab filled in with periods, hyphens, or an underline. To create one, choose a leader type in the Leader option set in the Format Tabs dialog box. The following example shows a 0.5" tab to match the outdent. The Underline Leader option is activated.

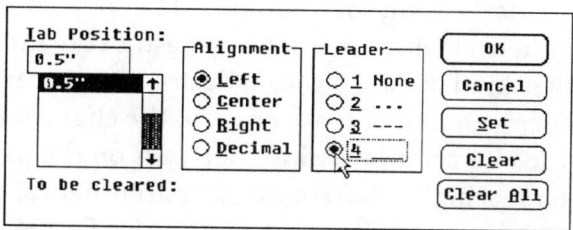

You can also choose leaders from the ribbon (see Chapter 4, "For the Record: Styles and Templates"). If you pressed TAB every time an author's name was repeated, the bibliography would look like the one in Figure 10-9.

Dashes and Parenthetical Phrases   Often it is useful to high-light a parenthetical phrase rather than to bury it. The phrase may add to the meaning of the sentence and should not break up

Figure 10-9.

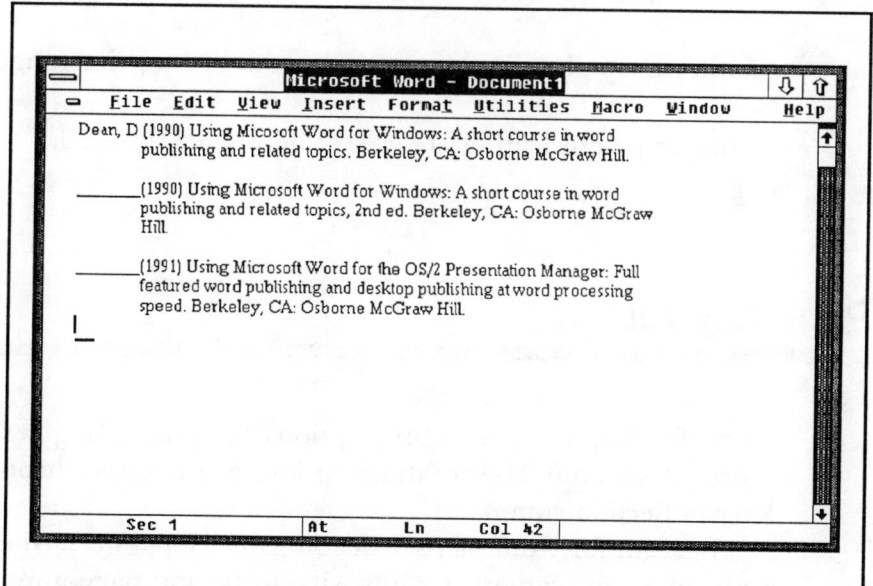

Outdents and Tab Stop with leader

the reader's train of thought. The best way to set off such parenthetical phrases is with a dash. You can use an em dash. Another kind of dash—the en dash—is also available in most fonts.

An em is a unit of space equal to the character box width. Recall that the character box width depends on the pitch of the font (see "Letterspacing"). Surround a parenthetical phrase with em dashes when you want to highlight it. To type an em dash, you activate the NUMLOCK, hold down the ALT key, and type **0150**. An example using em dashes is the following sentence: All headings can be made to stand out most clearly in bold type—sanserif typefaces benefit the most—much more so than in all caps.

En dashes are used between the numbers in a range. An en dash is one-half character box wide. To type an en dash, you activate the NUMLOCK, hold down the ALT key, and type **0151**.

An index listing a range of pages for a topic is an example of where an en dash is appropriate.

Word processing 17-25, 39-44, 267

Another example using an en dash would be a price range.

Italian patent leather shoes cost between $100-150.

Page Layout

Word for Windows has more options for positioning text than Word 4.0 and 5.0. Most of these options are accessed through the Format Section command.

You can, for example, set headings for separate sections and set headers and footers, usually with a title and page numbering, on every page in the top or bottom margins. Separate sections can also have multiple columns, which can be designed to surround graphic images. All of the section options are discussed in Chapter 2.

The section features also allow you to set up complex title pages and column arrangements. These topics, as well as headers and footers, are covered in the remainder of this chapter.

Title Pages

A title page is usually formatted differently from the rest of a document. It lists the title, author, and date, and does not have a printed page number. The title page is, however, counted in the page numbering of the document.

The text on a title page is generally in a horizontally centered paragraph format and has a vertically centered position on the page from top to bottom. To construct a title page, first type the text. You can use the following text as an example:

Word for Windows: < 14-point Helvetica >
Word Publishing in the Windows Environment. < 14-point Helvetica >
By: David Dean < 12-point Times Roman bold >
Submitted to: Osborne/McGraw-Hill < 12-point Helvetica bold >
June 16, 1990 < 12-point Helvetica bold >

Now highlight all of the text and use the Format Paragraph command to center it horizontally. The fastest way to do this is to use the ALT-t, p macro to bring up the Format Paragraph dialog box. Then select the Alignment Center option either with the mouse or by pressing ALT-c. Finally, activate the OK button.

To center the text vertically on the page, insert a Next Page break with the Section Break command. The fastest way to do this is to place the cursor on the space after the last character on the title page (in the example, 0) and press ALT-i, b, which will bring up the Insert Break dialog box. Press ALT-n to choose the Section Next Page break, as shown here.

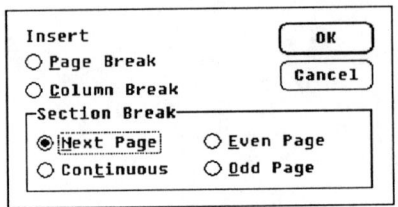

Then press ENTER. Now open the Format Section dialog box and activate the Vertical Alignment Center button, as shown here.

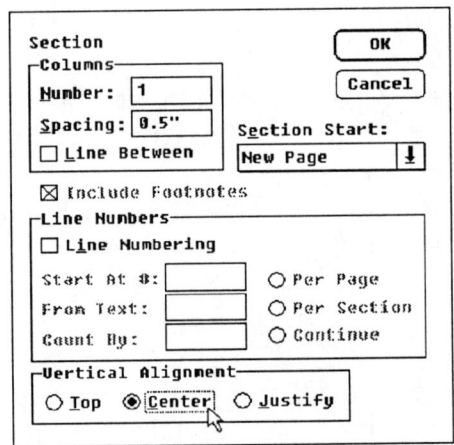

The text should be centered on the page as shown in Figure 10-10.

Figure 10-10.

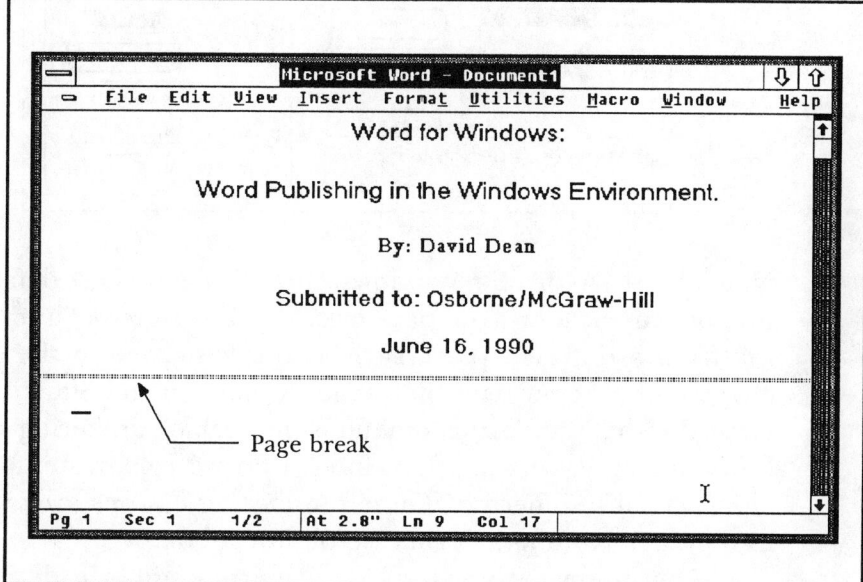

Title page

Since you have a title page in this document, you will want to set up a page header (a footer would be done in the same way) that does not print on the first page. To do this, you use the Word for Windows header/footer pane.

Headers and Footers

Next, you will add a running head to your document. First, open the header/footer pane with the Edit Header/Footer command. Click the left mouse button on the Options button and select Different First Page, then Header. The Edit Header/Footer dialog box will look like the following:

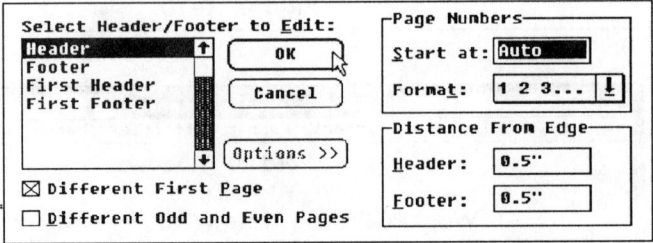

Note that the Word for Windows Auto Page Numbers default will number the header from page one. If you wish to begin numbering from a different page, such as the first page in the second chapter of a book, type that page number in the Start At field. Note also that the Format default is the arabic numbering system; but you can also use upper- and lowercase roman numerals or alphabetical numbering. These numbering options are available in the Page Numbers Format scroll-down box.

Other options include the Distance From Edge Header option. It is set to 0.5" from the top of the page by default. This would place the header in the middle of a 1" top page margin. Note that when you activate the Different First Page toggle box, First Header and First Footer options appear in the Select Header/Footer To Edit scroll box. This allows you to have a different header and footer on the first page of your document. The Different Odd And Even Pages toggle box lets you have different headers on right and left pages, like those discussed in Chapter 2, "Formatting Text."

Now activate the OK button in the Edit Header/Footer dialog box; this will accept the default to begin creating a header. The header/footer pane is displayed. This pane has a split line and box much like the footnote and annotation panes (see Chapter 8, "Group Productions"). The split line separates the document window from the header/footer pane; the split box is the bar between the document Window scroll bar and the Header/Footer Pane scroll bar. If you click the left mouse button on the split box, you can drag the split line up and down. In fact, you can close the header/footer pane by dragging it all the way down; you can always reopen the header/footer pane with the Edit Header/Footer command. Within the header/footer pane are three icons that you can use to insert fields into the header. As an example of a header, type the following text in the header/footer pane: **- Dean: Word for Windows - Page.** Now highlight this text and use the Format Paragraph command to center the header. Next, put the cursor at the beginning of this line and click the left mouse button on the date icon (it is the middle icon of the three). A date field will be inserted, and the date will become visible. Now, type a space that will separate the date from the first dash. Now place the cursor at the end of the line after: "Page." Click the left mouse button on the left icon—page number. Then type another period to close off the page number. The completed page header is shown in Figure 10-11. (Note that the right icon is the time icon.)

Figure 10-11.

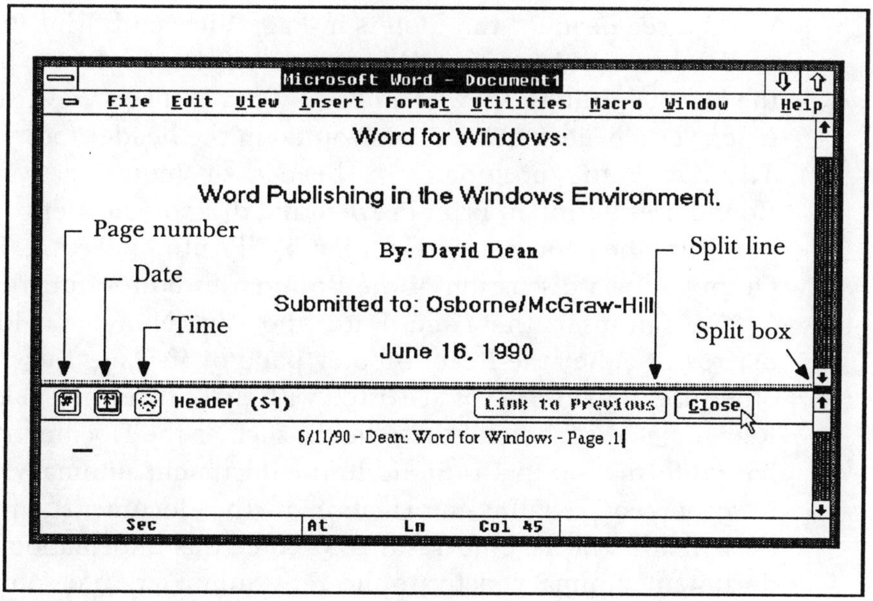

Header/Footer pane

Table 10-2.

Field	Macro
Author's Name	CTRL-F9, **author**, ENTER
Chapter-Page Number	CTRL-F9, **seq 1 \c**, RIGHT ARROW, HYPHEN, SHIFT-F10, **p** (example: Chapter 1, Page 1: 1-1)
Date	SHIFT-F10, **d**
Document File Name	CTRL-F9, **filename**, ENTER
Page Number	SHIFT-F10, **p**
Time	SHIFT-F10, **t**
Title of Document	CTRL-F9, **title**, ENTER

Edit Header/Footer Pane Field Macros (Adapted with permission from the documentation for Microsoft Word for Windows, Microsoft Corporation, 1990.)

Activate the close button in the edit header/footer pane to close the pane. You will not see the header in the Normal Editing View; you can see headers and footers in Page View and Print Preview.

You can edit headers and footers in the header/footer pane in the Normal Editing View or in Page View. In Page View, you can type over a header or footer as you do in the header/footer pane. To change the position of a header or footer, activate the Boundaries button in Print Preview and drag the header or footer box with the mouse (see Chapter 5, "Printing: Picture Perfect Output," for a discussion of the Boundaries button functions).

You can insert the Time, Date, and Page Number fields with macros in either the header/footer pane or in Page View. A few other useful field macros are listed with these three in Table 10-2. Remember that some of these fields, such as the Document Title, have information that is found in the document summary. If you have not entered this information in the document summary, these fields will have no result. To enter this information in the document summary, activate the Edit Summary Info command.

You should see headers and footers on your printed document. If they do not print, make sure none of the body text is formatted in the margin where the header and footer are set to print. For example, if the top margin of the document is set for 0.25" and the header is set to print at 0.5" from the top edge of the page, Word for Windows will not print the header. The top margin setting must be greater than the header setting.

Columns

Word for Windows can print three types of columns: side-by-side, snaking, and tabular. Examples of all three types are shown in Figure 10-12. In Word for Windows, side-by-side columns are positioned next to each other and are unbroken by graphic

Figure 10-12.

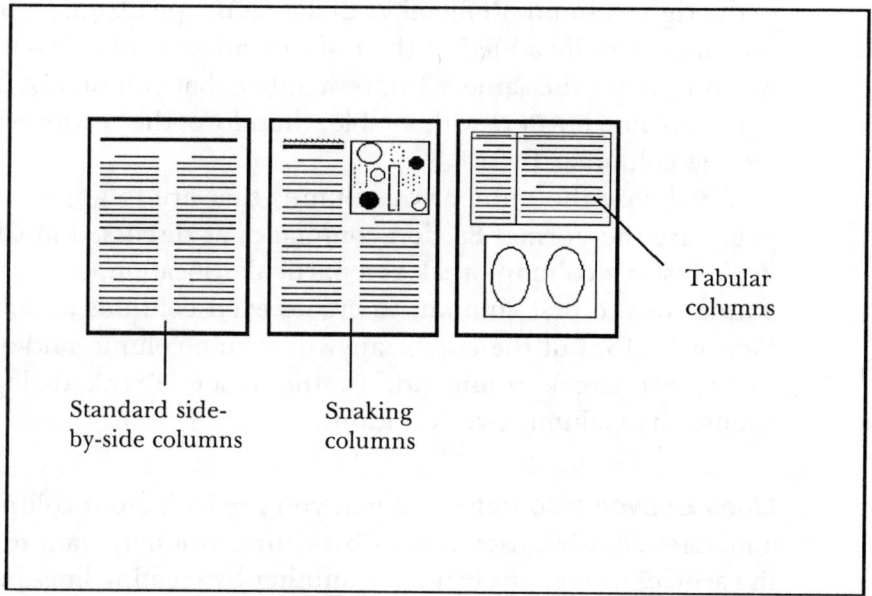

Standard side-by-side columns

Snaking columns

Tabular columns

Three types of column formatting

images. Snaking columns flow around a graphic image. Tabular columns are created as part of Word for Windows tables.

If you are not using graphic images, Word for Windows sets side-by-side columns. You can create them with the Format Section command or the Insert Break command. You may have to insert and delete continuous section breaks a few times until the bottoms of side-by-side columns match up.

If there is a graphic image on a page, Word for Windows will automatically snake text around it. This ensures that the text will not print over the image. In the Normal Editing View, you will see the text as a single column above and below the graphic. In Page View or Print Preview, you will see text snake around the graphic.

If there is a graphic image on a page, and you want side-by-side columns, you can create tabular columns using Word for Windows Table options. Tabular side-by-side columns are also useful if you must align paragraphs in the two columns; one example is a script with stage directions in the left column and spoken parts in the right column. Remember that as you type text in a cell, lines are automatically added to the cell—creating a column— but the width remains the same. Also, remember that you do not have to print any line borders with a table; therefore, the reader will only see the columnar text.

To choose the number of columns that are to appear on the page, use the Format Section command, as discussed in Chapter 2. To insert a column break at a particular location, such as at the bottom of the first column, to create even columns as shown in Figure 10-13, put the cursor anywhere in a column and activate the Insert Break command. In the Insert Break dialog box, choose the Column Break button.

Lines Between Columns   When you are laying out columns for a newsletter, advertisement, or brochure, you may want to set off the articles or sections from one another by creating lines between them. Horizontal or vertical line separations, as well as boxed

Figure 10-13.

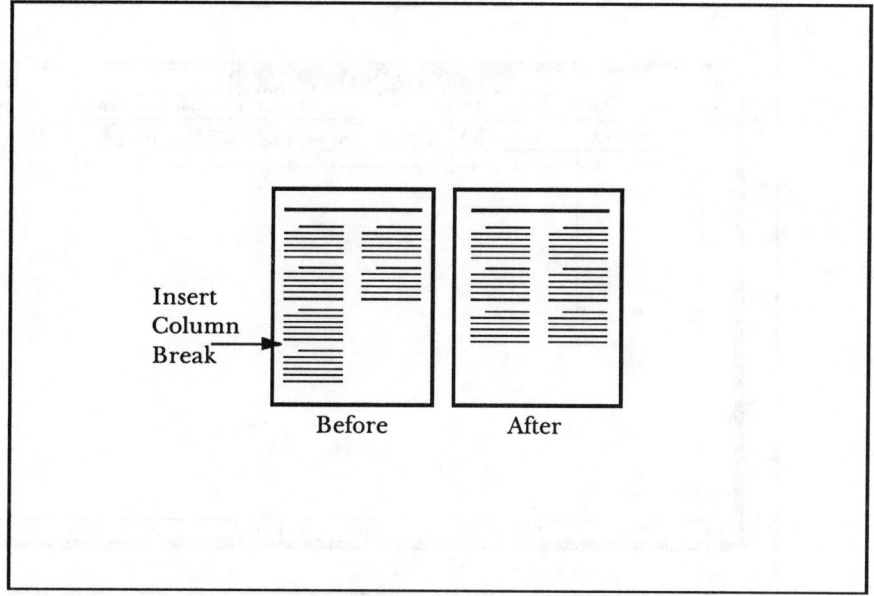

Insert
Column
Break

Before   After

Balancing columns: before and after inserting a Column Break

insets, make it easier for the reader to scan all the articles or sections for those of particular interest.

Like Word 4.0 and 5.0, Word for Windows can draw lines on the sides, above, and below columns (borders). You can also draw boxes around one or more paragraphs to create an inset. Adding boxes and borders to text is discussed in Chapter 2.

Images and Snaking Columns   Whether or not you are able to create images on your computer, you can hold a space open for later insertion of a graphic or photograph. To measure the image box size exactly, first activate the ruler with the View Ruler command. Then open a space for the graphic or picture with the Insert Picture dialog box by choosing the New Picture button. Click the left mouse button on any node of the new picture box

Figure 10-14.

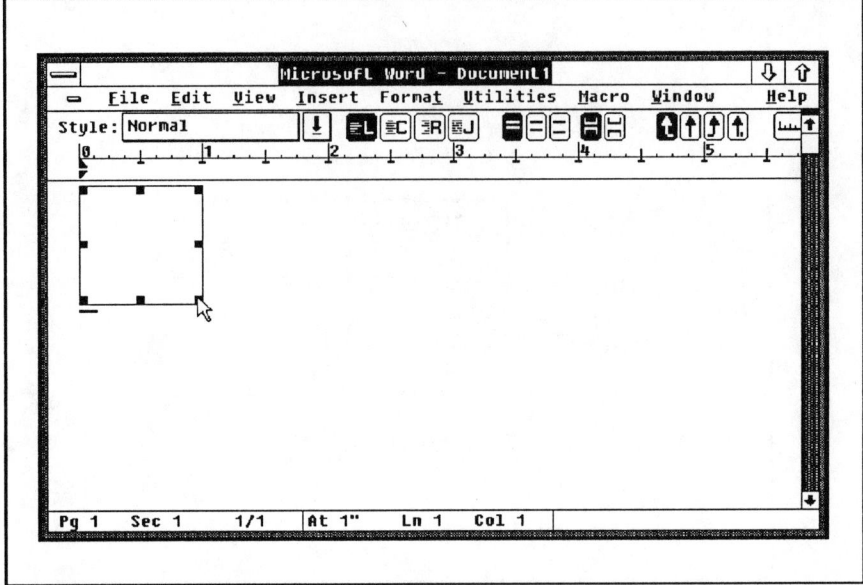

Sizing a Blank Image box

and drag it to fill the area your picture will take up, as shown in
Figure 10-14. When you add text, it will snake around the area
saved for the picture.

You have learned about many Word for Windows commands
that will help you prepare presentation documents in this chapter.
However, this chapter has in no way exhausted the possible uses
of Word for Windows commands to prepare these documents. It
should also be clear what kinds of documents are most amenable
to Word for Windows. If you stick to advertisements, reports,
brochures, and simple newsletters, you will increase your productivity. For complex documents like newspapers, manuals, and
books, you are better off using Word for Windows as a means of
preparing and proofing copy for insertion into a desktop publishing program. In this regard, Word for Windows is also probably
the best tool available.

CHAPTER

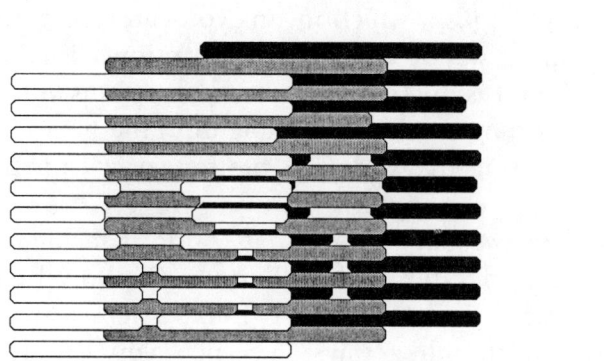

11

Fine Tuning Windows

This chapter discusses several applications of the Windows GUI (Graphical User Interface) that you can use with Word for Windows. You have already seen three examples of how applications operate under Windows. In Chapter 1, "Up and Running," you became familiar with the general Windows interface, including its screen elements, the MS-DOS Executive, and the Control Panel. In Chapter 3, "Cut and Paste: Adding Tables and Images," you used the Windows Clipboard to paste an Excel chart into a Word for Windows document. In Chapter 5, "Printing: Picture Perfect Output," you learned about installing printer and screen fonts into Windows printer drivers using the MS-DOS Executive Control Panel program.

Most of these features of Windows are listed in the WIN.INI file that is read when you open Windows. The WIN.INI lists options that you choose when you install Windows. WIN.INI is a text file written in English, which means you can edit it in Word for Windows. Since Windows checks the options listed in the WIN.INI file when it is opened, any new instructions you add to the WIN.INI file do not become available until the next time you load Windows. Editing the WIN.INI file for special purposes is covered in detail in this chapter.

Next, there are two major ways that windows facilitates data exchange among applications: the Windows Clipboard and the DDE (Dynamic Data Exchange) Paste Link. These features are discussed, along with other ways in which you can use and customize Windows to meet your needs.

Also discussed are printing and data recovery. Under Windows, you can print to a file rather than to the printer. This feature is useful when you need an alternative format file, such as for graphic images, that is not printed on paper. Data recovery works like it did in Word 4.0 and 5.0. Word for Windows automatically creates *.TMP files. These *.TMP files store your keystrokes until you save the file you are working on. You can use these files to recover data if your computer unexpectedly crashes.

Editing WIN.INI

The WIN.INI file is the equivalent of Windows AUTOEXEC.BAT file. Whenever you open Windows, the settings in the WIN.INI file determine which programs and features of those programs are available.

The WIN.INI file is created when you install Windows and select options. It is changed when you install or delete printers and fonts using the Control Panel program, CONTROL.EXE (see Chapter 1). The WIN.INI file is written in ASCII text and therefore contains no formatting. This means you can change the WIN.INI file in Word for Windows.

Use the File Open command to display the WIN.INI file. First, check to see that the directory listing in the File Open dialog box is your Windows subdirectory, as shown here.

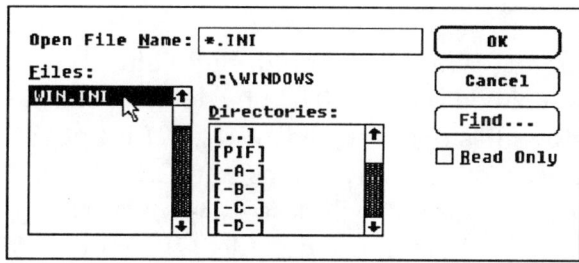

If the Windows directory is not listed, use the Directories scroll box to select it. If you are on the wrong disk drive (such as Drive A or B) or hard disk partition (such as partition C, D, E, or F), click the left mouse button on the partition that includes the Windows subdirectory. Then click the left mouse button twice on the Windows directory listing in the Directories scroll box. Once you are in the Windows directory, note that the File Open dialog box Open File Name text entry field displays *.DOC as a default file extension. Type **ini** over this extension and press ENTER. Next, click the left mouse button twice on the WIN.INI file listing in the Files scroll box. Word for Windows will display the Open File Convert dialog box, shown here:

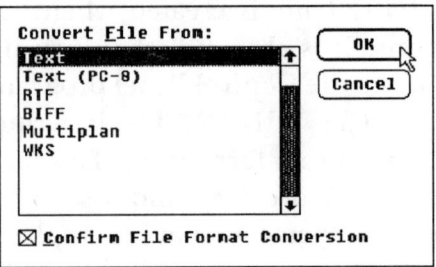

Word for Windows should highlight the Text option in the Convert File From scroll box by default. This means that Word for Windows has detected that WIN.INI is an ASCII text file. (For a discussion of file conversions, see Chapter 9.) Do not worry that Word for Windows will destroy your WIN.INI file by converting it to a non-ASCII, formatted file. Like Word 4.0 and 5.0, Word for Windows always saves a file in ASCII that was imported as ASCII text. Activate the OK button to display WIN.INI.

Word for Windows will save WIN.INI as a Text Only ASCII file. To check that it did, activate the Options button in the File Save As dialog box. You will see the following File Format field when you activate the Options button.

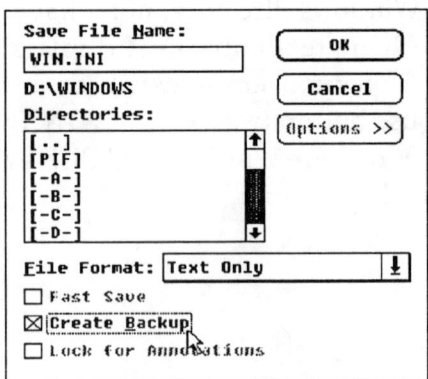

Word for Windows automatically chose the Text Only option when you imported the file as text in the File Open dialog box.

Since you will edit your WIN.INI, and may make errors, activate the Create Backup toggle box. This tells Word for Windows to make a backup file, WIN.BAK in this case, when you activate the OK button. Word for Windows will do this each time you use the File Save command. Since you only want a backup of the unedited WIN.INI, reopen the File Save As dialog box, click the left mouse button on the Options button, and inactivate the Create Backup toggle box. This will preserve the original WIN.INI as WIN.BAK, should you need to copy it to WIN.INI later.

WIN.INI Sections

The WIN.INI file consists of sections and comments. Sections contain options for each program that runs under Windows, including the MS-DOS Executive. Each section has the name of its corresponding program. Comments tell you what the options mean and how to adjust them.

Figure 11-1 shows the top of the WIN.INI file. The first statement tells you that lines preceded by a semicolon (;) are comments. The WIN.INI file contains comments. You can add your own comment lines, as long as they begin with a semicolon. The first section in Figure 11-1 is the Windows/MS-DOS Executive section. It is headed by its section name corresponding to the program name in brackets: [windows].

The Windows section lists the settings you chose when you ran the setup program. These include use of the Windows spooler (spooler=yes is on) and the mouse button settings (including MouseThreshold—how close the mouse has to be to a screen element to activate it—and SwapMouseButtons=yes is for a left-handed person). One useful aspect of the WIN.INI file format is that you can change some of its settings. To do so, use the Control Panel program in the MS-DOS Executive. Settings you

Figure 11-1.

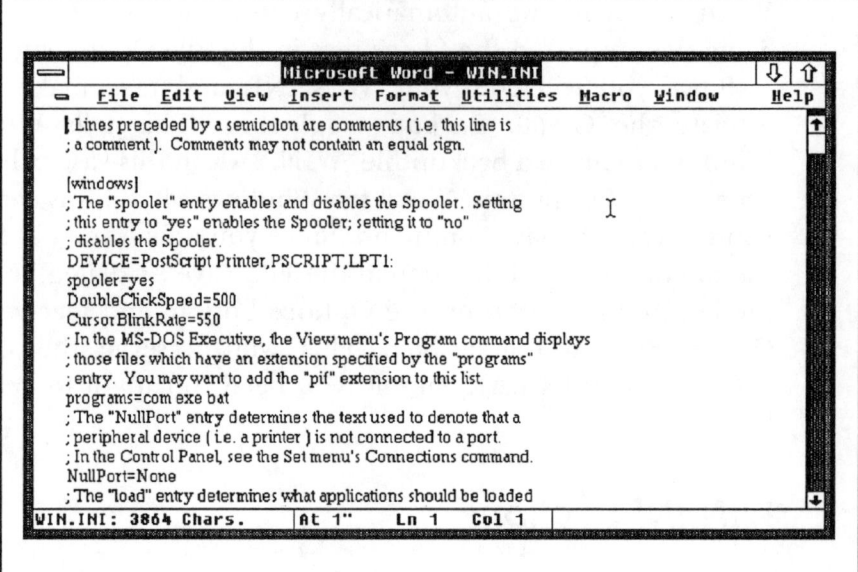

The WIN.INI file

Figure 11-2.

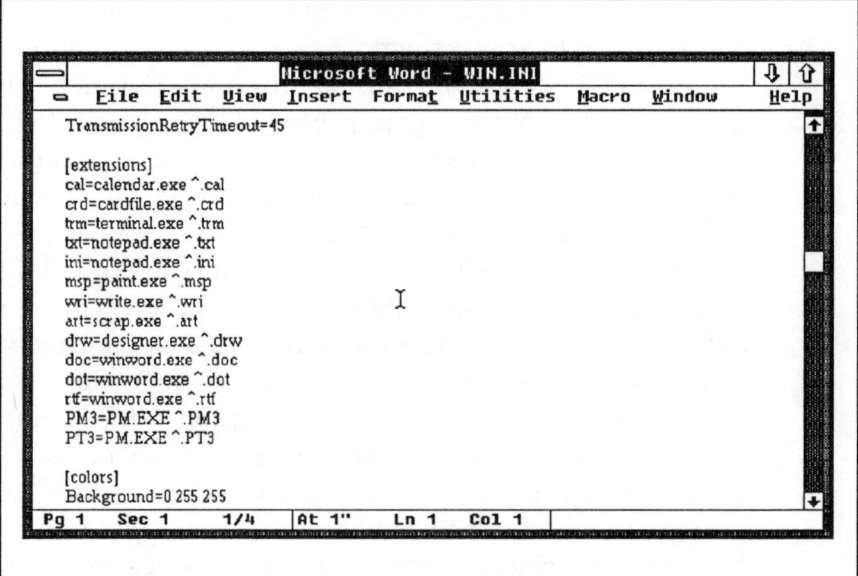

WIN.INI [extensions] and [colors] sections

can change include the double-click speed (DoubleClickSpeed —how fast the click speed has to be to activate a program), the speed at which the cursor blinks (CursorBlinkRate), how many times your computer attempts to send a file to the printer before displaying a print error message (TransmissionRetryTimeout), and the default printer, its printer driver, and which printer port to use (in the example, PostScript Printer = PSCRIPT,LPTI:). You can also adjust colors with the Control Panel Program. If you have a color monitor, you can change the colors that Windows displays in the Control Panel Preferences Screen Colors dialog box.

Following the [windows] section is the [extensions] section, as shown in Figure 11-2. The [extensions] section lists the file name extensions that should be displayed by the File Open dialog box of each installed Windows program. This is for your convenience.

Several other sections control aspects of Windows. Figure 11-3

Figure 11-3.

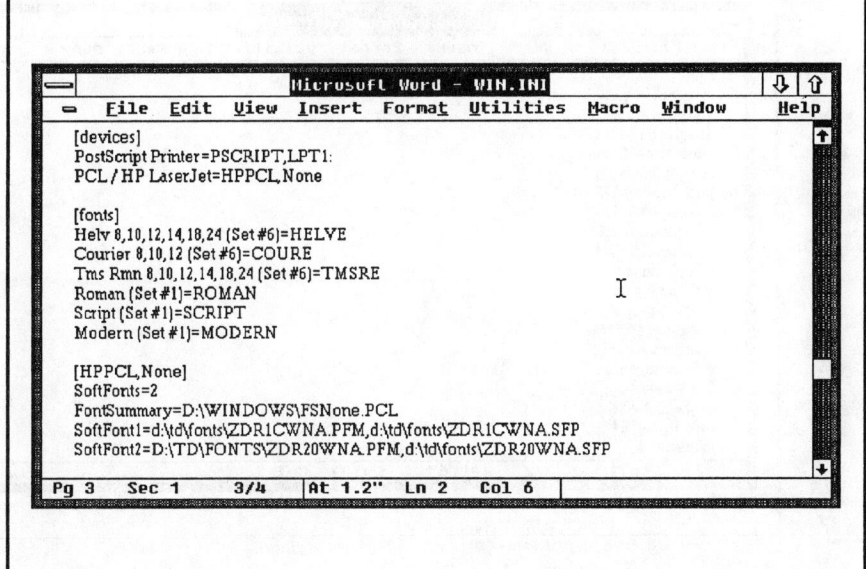

WIN.INI [devices], [fonts], and printer driver sections

shows these sections. The [devices] section lists the two printer drivers (PostScript and PCL/HP LaserJet). Other devices could include a scanner, a modem, or a video input. The [fonts] section lists the screen and printer fonts available to Windows. The [HPPCL,None] section is a LaserJet printer driver section listing available fonts.

Another section that configures Windows is the [pif] section. It lists the amount of memory programs should be limited to while running under Windows. It is important to know that information if you are running more than one application under Windows. Figure 11-4 lists DOS programs you access from the MS-DOS Executive (note the familiar diskcopy and format). The trade-off

Figure 11-4.

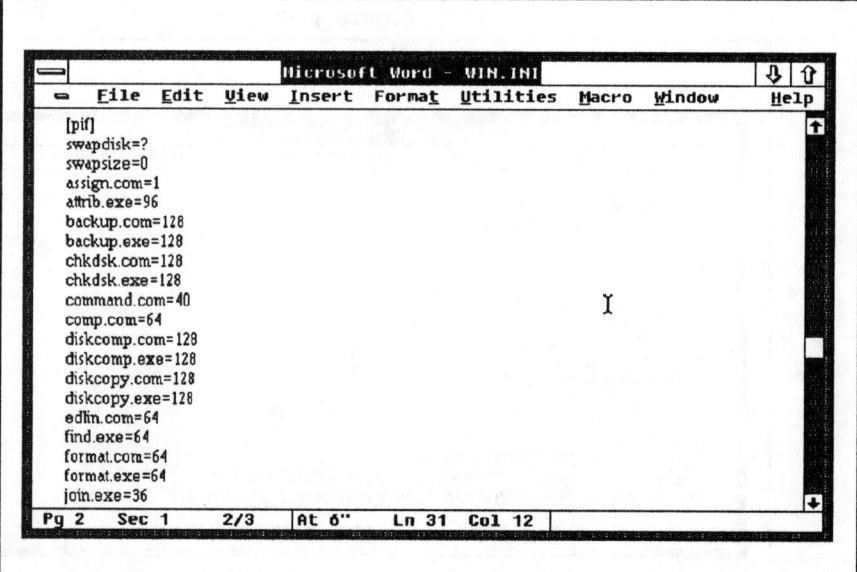

WIN.INI [pif] section

here is that often if you give a program access to more memory, it will run more quickly. However, if you give it too much memory, you will not be able to run any more programs under Windows.

The last type of section in the WIN.INI file lists a program and its default settings. Figure 11-5 shows four different program sections. The settings in each section are options that the program needs to have set when it is loaded. The [wingrab] section is a screen capture program from SymSoft. The display=8 setting refers to the eight Windows default colors displayed in the VGA mode. The [Microsoft Word] section shows that the conversions are turned on (see Chapter 9 for a discussion of how to turn off the conversion programs).

Changing or adding options in Windows is as simple as deleting or inserting text. The following sections discuss changes

Figure 11-5.

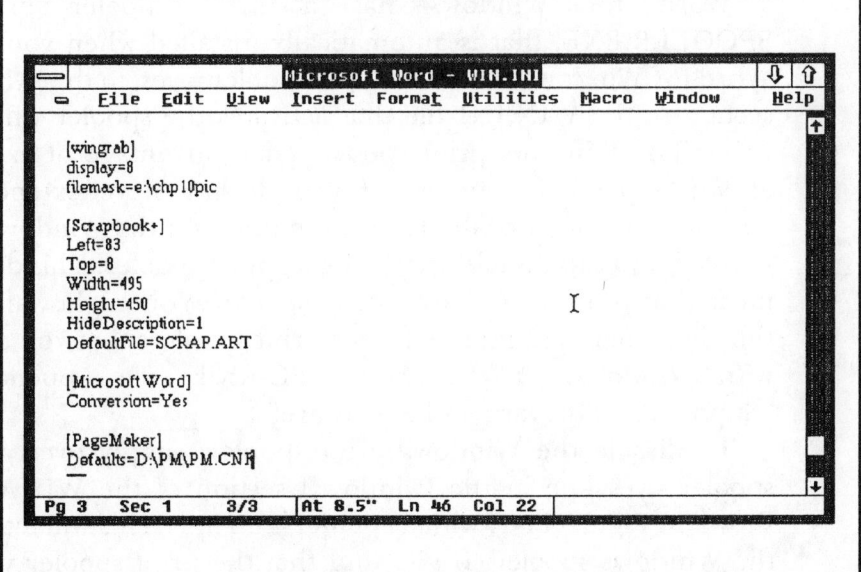

WIN.INI Windows program sections

you can make to the WIN.INI file that might improve the operation of Word for Windows. There are many more options you can adjust to fine-tune the operation of Windows and other programs that run under it. For other ideas on the WIN.INI file, see the Microsoft Windows User's Guide, or any of a number of other helpful books listed in Appendix F, "Journals, Books, and User Groups."

Windows Print Spooler

A print spooler takes files as they are sent to the printer and stores them in RAM until the printer is ready to print them. Without a print spooler, you must wait until your printer is done printing before you can use the program from which you are printing. A print spooler can hold a 10-page document in 15K of RAM and feed it to the printer at a rate the printer can handle, and you can continue working.

Word for Windows has a print spooler program, SPOOLER.EXE, that is automatically installed when you set up Word for Windows. There is a line, spooler=yes, in the [windows] section of the WIN.INI file that activates the spooler when you print. The Windows print spooler takes advantage of extended and/or expanded memory. If you do not have extended or expanded memory or do not want to use it for the Windows print spooler, you can disable the Windows print spooler. This does not mean that you will not have a print spooler. You might want to do this since there are more efficient print spoolers that you can use with Windows, such as Super PC-Kwik (see Appendix D, "Supporting Software and Hardware").

To disable the Windows print spooler, simply overtype the spooler=yes line in the [windows] section of the WIN.INI, as shown in Figure 11-1, with a **spooler=no** line. This will inactivate the Windows spooler. If you find that the print spooler you are using does not improve the functioning of Windows in the way you had hoped, you do not have to reinstall Windows to reactivate the print spooler. As long as you have not deleted the SPOOLER .EXE program from your Windows directory, all you need to do to reactivate the spooler is overtype the spooler = no line in the [windows] section with a **spooler = yes** line.

Windows SMARTDrive Disk Cache

Windows and Word for Windows will run most quickly if their active program files can be completely loaded into RAM. The Windows SMARTDrive disk cache program will attempt to load all of the active Windows program and data files into RAM (Random Access Memory). However, it can only use extended or expanded memory that you list as available when you install Windows. If you tell the Windows setup program that you have no extended or expanded memory, SMARTDrive will not be installed. Even if you have extended or expanded memory in your computer, depending on what kind of software you use other than Windows, you may opt not to make any extended or expanded memory available to Windows. To make an informed choice, it is therefore essential that you understand how RAM is allocated in your computer.

Your computer's CPU (Central Processing Unit) chip (8086, 80286, or 80386) can find programs many times more quickly in RAM than from your hard disk; this is true no matter how fast your hard disk is. There are three kinds of RAM that Windows can take advantage of to help you run Word for Windows more quickly. They are conventional, extended, and expanded memory.

Conventional memory, consisting of the first 640K of RAM, is the limit of program memory available to the original IBM personal computer that was introduced in 1981. The original PC reserved this first 640K of RAM for software out of the total 1024K bytes of available RAM. The RAM between 640K and 1024K was termed extended memory. At that time, 1981, there was no way for software to access extended memory. Extended memory, the memory between 640K and 1024K, was reserved for the installation of the monitor, keyboard, add-on boards, and other aspects of the PC's operating system and hardware. Currently there are many ways to use the extended memory between 640K and 1024K, as well as extended memory that lies beyond the first 1024K. Because extended memory is now used by disk caching, print spooling, and other types of programs, many manufacturers allow you to install extended memory either on the motherboard of your computer or as add-in memory expansion boards.

On a computer with an 8086 or 80286 CPU, you can install a RAM expansion board that gives you extended memory or LIM-EMS (Lotus-Intel-Microsoft Expanded Memory Specification) expanded memory. LIM-EMS expanded memory was introduced in 1984 mainly as a repository for loading data files that your software must constantly access, such as documents, spreadsheet files, data bases, or laser printer fonts. Expanded memory is also used by memory management programs to swap programs in and out of conventional memory. If the swapped program is put on hold when it is taken from conventional memory and put into expanded memory, the operation is called task switching. If the swapped program continues to run in expanded memory, the operation is called multitasking. Only task switching is possible on 8086 or 80286 based computers, whereas computers based on the 80386 chip are capable of true multitasking. This is why Windows/286 is a task switching program, while Windows/386 is a true multitasking program.

In 8086, 80286, and 80386 based computers, you can make both extended and expanded memory additions. Extended memory is mainly intended to hold active program and data files, and therefore speeds your software's internal and data access operations. Expanded memory is mainly intended to swap program and data files in and out of conventional RAM and therefore allows you to either task switch or multitask between applications. Computers with an 80386 CPU are much more flexible than their predecessors because they do not require special extended or expanded memory boards. You can set up the RAM over 1024K as either extended or expanded memory with memory managing software (not hardware boards as with the 8086 or 80286) like the Windows/386 SMARTDrive, Qualitas' 386-to-the-Max, or Quarterdeck's QEMM (see Appendix D, "Supporting Software and Hardware").

When you set up any version of Windows, you are asked if you have any extended or expanded memory. If you say you do, the program will attempt to run MEMSET. MEMSET will install both the SMARTDrive disk cache program and the HIMEM.SYS memory management program. You cannot configure HIMEM.SYS and SMARTDrive's use of your RAM. By default, SMARTDrive attempts to use the second 1024K of RAM as extended memory for Windows program files alone. This makes Windows run very quickly but also may be an inefficient use of your RAM and hard disk space. A possible conflict with hard disk space arises when MEMSET installs SMARTDrive and HIMEM.SYS. This is because Windows may attempt to swap information to your hard disk when it detects your extended or expanded memory is full. Swapping information to disk makes it possible for you to task switch with Windows/286 or multitask with Windows/386, but it is also very slow (it is faster to work with one application at a time). There is also the possibility that you will run out of room on your hard disk if too much is swapped to it. If this happens, when you go to save a file, you will be told you are out of hard disk space and must save to a floppy.

In many cases, it is better to use a more programmable memory management, disk caching, and print spooling strategy. If you want to use other software to supply these functions, make sure you first install Windows. If the Windows setup program detects an alien memory manager, it will not continue until you uninstall the offending software. If you first install Windows, then the disk caching and print spooling software, Windows will function normally.

The following example shows how Windows attempts to use your hard disk space as well as RAM memory. DESQview 386 and QEMM memory management software, as well as the Super PC-Kwik disk caching and print spooling program, were installed on an 80386 PC after Windows was installed. Using DESQview 386, each application window is assigned a portion of 2000K (2MB) of available expanded memory. The Microsoft Windows application DESQview window has been assigned 530K of conventional memory and 2000K of expanded memory. The MS-DOS Executive File About dialog box, as follows, shows that there is 746K of hard disk space, 174K of conventional memory, and 1344K of expanded memory available to Windows.

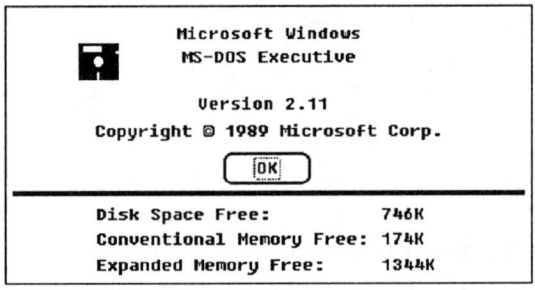

After opening Word for Windows from the MS-DOS Executive, the Word for Windows Help About dialog box, as follows, lists 48K of conventional memory available, 1547K of expanded memory free, and *no* available disk space.

```
                    Microsoft Word

                    Version 1.0

          Copyright © 1989 Microsoft Corporation.

                      ┌─────┐
                      │ OK  │
                      └─────┘
    ─────────────────────────────────────────

          Conventional Memory:  48 KB Free
             Expanded Memory:  1547 KB Free
          Math Co-processor:  Present
                  Disk Space:  0 KB Free
```

This does not mean that there is no room on the hard disk; the MS-DOS Executive File About dialog box had already shown that there was space available to save files. The reason that Word for Windows does not detect any hard disk space is that Windows was told that there was no available extended or expanded memory when Windows was installed. After Word for Windows is opened, Windows attempts to reserve some of the available hard disk space for storing already opened programs and data. That is, if you open a program other than Word for Windows, Windows would attempt to copy or swap Word for Windows and its associated data files to the hard disk. When you reactivated Word for Windows, it would read the program and data files back into RAM. In this case, you would ignore the Word for Windows Help About dialog box reading of hard disk space; either DESQview or the Super PC-Kwik disk cache that was set up would intercept any Windows attempt to copy Word for Windows to the hard disk. Instead, Word for Windows and its data files would either be copied to extended memory or swapped to expanded memory.

Another benefit of running non-Windows memory management software to set up Windows and Word for Windows is that you can use the same software to allocate RAM for your DOS applications. Windows/286 and Windows/386 offer you a means to run DOS applications from Windows, but the memory management capabilities are often more limiting than with DOS based task switching and multitasking environments like

DESQview (see Appendix D, "Supporting Software and Hardware"). However, it may be more advantageous for you to use Windows/386 to multitask if you have a 80386 based computer and run only Windows applications.

Windows Dynamic Link Libraries: Format Conversions

One of the most important features of the Windows environment is that all programs running under Windows can potentially share several Windows tools. The most prominent of these tools are in the Word for Windows Edit menu. They are the Edit Copy and Paste commands, which give you access to the Windows Clipboard (see Chapter 3, "Cut and Paste: Adding Tables and Images," for a discussion of the Clipboard). Another important tool is Windows DDE (Dynamic Data Exchange) capability which allows you to link data that has been cut and pasted into various Windows applications to the source file. For example, in Word for Windows the Edit Dynamic Data Exchange Paste Link function lets you link tables, charts, graphs, and note files to a source data file in another Windows application such as Excel, Superbase 2, or Pack Rat. This capability is useful in cases in which the original data is constantly changing and you want the pasted table, chart, or graph to reflect the most current data (see "DDE Paste Link").

Microsoft has built the Clipboard and DDE into Windows. In addition, Microsoft has left open the possibility for other developers to design tools that can potentially be used in all Windows applications. These universal tools are programs assigned to libraries called DLLs (Dynamic Link Libraries). Unlike the DOS LINK command that can link only one or more non-program files to a *.EXE (executable) program file each time you run the LINK command (a static link), DLL files may be linked to executable files at any time (a dynamic link). Also, several

Windows programs can access one or more DLLs simultaneously. This saves you a lot of RAM and hard disk space.

A future example of a DLL that will impact Word for Windows as well as almost all other Windows applications involves the Windows screen and printer fonts. Currently, the Windows screen and printer fonts are installed as separate files. In the future, however, typeface outlines will be scaled to the size you choose on the fly for both screen display (screen fonts) and printing (printer fonts). These typeface outlines will reside as files on your hard disk; the actual screen and printer fonts used by Windows applications will be generated from these outlines by a Windows DLL.

Now that Apple and Microsoft have announced the Royal screen and printer font scaling standard, Microsoft will most likely make this font format available to typeface vendors as a DLL. Once vendors have designed screen and printer typeface outlines that can be scaled by the Royal DLL, users will be able to install both the Royal DLL and each vendor's typeface outlines in Windows via the Control Panel or by adding a Royal section in the WIN.INI file. Adobe also plans to implement its unified screen/printer font scaling mechanism, referred to as Type Manager on the Apple Macintosh, for Windows on the PC. Other typeface vendors who use different font scaling programs, such as PCL (LaserJet), will also have to write a DLL to generate screen and printer fonts from their current typeface outlines.

Installing Word for Windows Conversion Utilities Windows DLLs can also be intended for access by a single program. For example, you can install the Word for Windows conversion utilities, which let you use the File Save As command to save a file to a non-Word for Windows file format without first importing a file in that format.

There are nine Word for Windows conversion DLLs. They are all automatically installed when you use the File Open command to load a non-Word for Windows file, but remain unavailable until you do so. This means if you do not have a file to import in a non-Word for Windows format, Word for Windows will not automatically install the conversion DLLs; that is, they will not be available when you try to use them in the File Save As dialog box. Note that if the conversion DLLs have not previously been installed by the File Open command, when you try to save a file in a non-Word for Windows format in the File Save As dialog box, you will not find the file format listed in the Options File Format scroll-down box, as shown here:

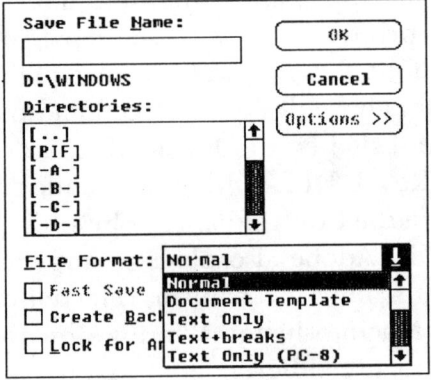

To install all nine Word for Windows conversion programs, add the following lines to the Microsoft Word section of your WIN.INI file:

```
[Microsoft Word]
Conversion=Yes
CONV1="PC Word" E:\WINWORD\CONV-WRD.DLL ^.DOC
CONV2="WordPerfect 5.0" E:\WINWORD\CONV-WP5.DLL ^.DOC
CONV3="WordPerfect 4.2" E:\WINWORD\CONV-WP.DLL ^.DOC
CONV4="WordPerfect 4.1" E:\WINWORD\CONV-WP.DLL ^.DOC
CONV5="WordStar 5.5" E:\WINWORD\CONV-WS.DLL ^.DOC
```

```
CONV6="WordStar 5.0" E:\WINWORD\CONV-WS.DLL ^.DOC
CONV7="WordStar 4.0" E:\WINWORD\CONV-WS.DLL ^.DOC
CONV8="WordStar 3.45" E:\WINWORD\CONV-WS.DLL ^.DOC
CONV9="WordStar 3.3" E:\WINWORD\CONV-WS.DLL ^.DOC
```

Note that the conversion program files end with the extension
*.DLL, signifying a Dynamic Link Library. Also, the ^.DOC
extension following the conversion file name tells Word for
Windows the extension of the Word 4.0 and 5.0 format.

Since the WIN.INI file, including the section you just added, is
read only when you open Windows, close Windows and reopen it.
The File Format scroll-down box in the Save As dialog box should
now include the additional file formats shown here:

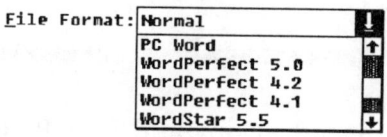

Installing Screen Fonts

The current version of Windows uses separate files for printer and
screen fonts. Installing printer fonts into Word for Windows was
discussed under "Printer Setup" in Chapter 5.

When you buy printer fonts to use with Windows, you will
usually be given screen fonts and installation software that automatically installs both printer and screen fonts. If you have only
printer font files, and they are in the HP LaserJet font format, you
can use SoftCraft's WYSIfonts program (see Appendix D) to
generate screen fonts. Otherwise, if you only install printer fonts,

Windows will automatically display a default screen font that most closely matches the printer font you installed. Any serif printer font installed without a corresponding screen font will probably cause Word for Windows to display a Times Roman-like font called Tms Rmn. Any sanserif printer font installed without a screen font will probably cause Windows to display a Helvetica-like font, called Helv. The spacing of text on your display may appear to be off if you do not have screen fonts for all of your printer fonts. For example, justified text may not line up at the right margin. However, you will always see the correct number of characters on each line. You can view the list of installed screen fonts in the [FONTS] section of Window's WIN.INI file in Word for Windows.

DDE Paste Link

You have used the Edit Copy and Edit Paste commands, which access the Clipboard, for various tasks within Word for Windows (see Chapter 1). The Clipboard in Word for Windows functions much like the Scrap in Word 4.0 and 5.0. However, the Clipboard can also bring data in from other Windows applications.

The Clipboard acts as a cut and paste tool. However, if an application takes advantage of the DDE (Dynamic Data Exchange) protocol, data passed between applications with the Edit Paste Link command is automatically linked to its source. There are two ways to link this pasted data to its source, with a regular link or an Auto Update link. The only difference between these two types of DDE Paste Links is that with a regular link, you press the Update Fields key, F9, to have Word for Windows check the source file to see if any changes have been made. With the Auto Update link, any linked files in Word for Windows or other Windows applications will be automatically updated when you change or add to the source file.

To get data in other Windows applications, minimize Word for

Windows to an icon. Then open the other application, such as Excel, Superbase 2, or Pack Rat. As an example, open Excel and enter the following data into a spreadsheet:

1990 Regional Sales

Region	1st Qtr	2nd Qtr	3rd Qtr	4th Qtr	Yr Total
North	3045.87	2977.76	3357.98	3859.65	13241.26
East	1587.22	1071.88	1289.76	1499.89	5448.75
West	2798.44	2688.76	2802.54	3232.84	11522.58
South	2054.89	1987.09	2298.98	2798.78	9139.74

Note that this is the same data used in "Using Equations" in Chapter 9. Your Excel spreadsheet should look like Figure 11-6. Next, highlight the data and activate the Edit Copy command as shown in Figure 11-7. The highlighted block is now copied to the Clipboard.

Figure 11-6.

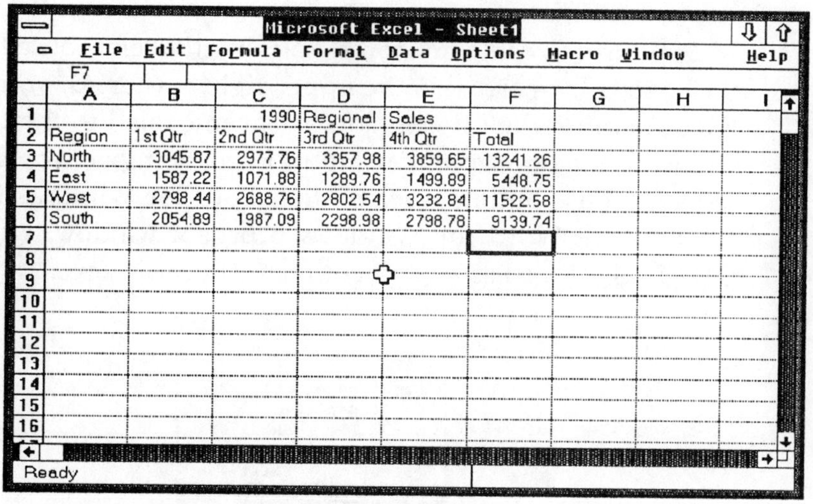

Excel spreadsheet

Figure 11-7.

Edit Copy command selected

Minimize Excel to an icon by clicking the left mouse button on the boxed down arrow in the upper right corner. Or you can close Excel, because the information has been copied to the Clipboard and is no longer dependent upon Excel being active. Next, click the left mouse button twice on the Word for Windows icon.

Once the Word for Windows program window is displayed, activate the Edit Paste Link command, shown here:

Note that the Edit Undo, Edit Repeat, Edit Cut, and Edit Copy commands are ghosted. This is because nothing has been added to the document. The Edit Paste and Edit Paste Link commands are not ghosted because the Clipboard contains the cells you just copied from Excel.

You will see the Edit Paste Link dialog box, shown here:

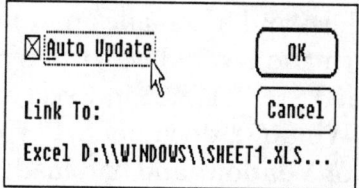

If you want to make a regular link for the Excel table in the Clipboard and its source file, just activate the OK button. You will then have to use the Update Fields key, F9, to check the Excel source file for new additions that would change the pasted-in table. Even with a regular link, however, the table pasted into Word for Windows would be updated each time the file was loaded.

To create an Auto Update Link, activate the Auto Update toggle box, as shown in the previous illustration, and then activate the OK button. The Auto Update toggle box is inactive by default.

After activating the OK button, with or without the Auto Update option, the Excel table is pasted into the Word for Windows document window, as shown in Figure 11-8.

Any time you change an entry in the table in its Excel source file, SHEET1.XLS, the corresponding cell will be updated in the Word for Windows table. Moreover, if you create an Auto Update Link, each time you open that Word for Windows document, you will get a message asking if you want to update those Auto Update Links, as shown here:

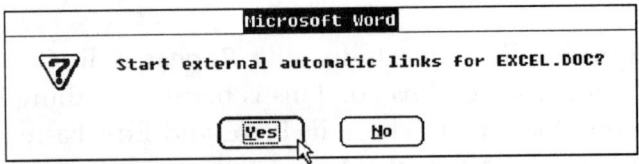

The reverse is not true. If you change a cell's contents in a table pasted with a link in a Word for Windows document, the source file in Excel is not changed. If you made changes to the table in Word for Windows and had made an Auto Update Link, the Excel source file information would be written over your changes either when you opened SHEET.XLS in Excel or when you next opened the Word for Windows document. If you made changes to the table in Word for Windows and had made a regular paste link, the

Figure 11-8.

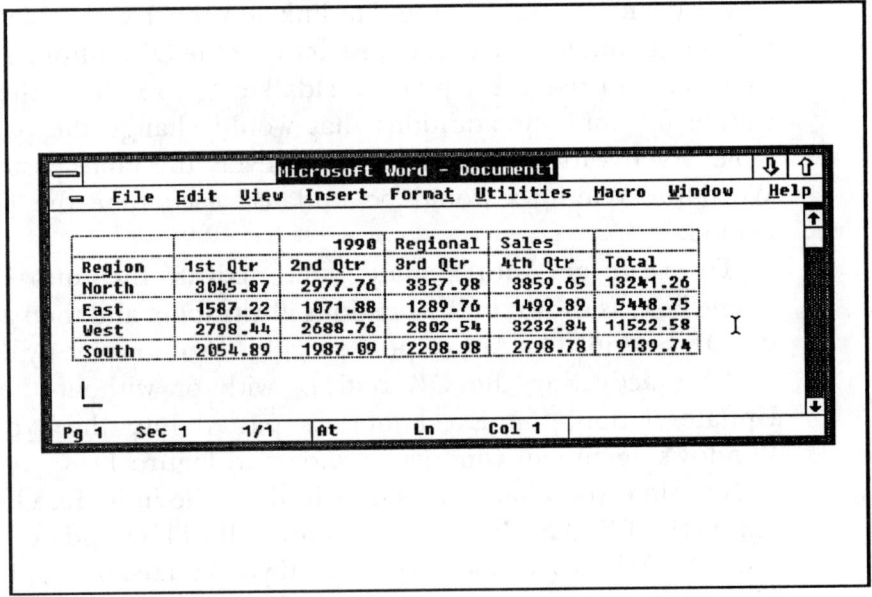

Excel table pasted into Word for Windows document

changes you made to the table in the Word for Windows document would be overwritten with the Excel source file information whenever you activated the Update Fields key, F9.

You can also paste link Excel charts (see "Importing Spreadsheet Data from Microsoft Excel" in Chapter 3 for a discussion of copying an Excel chart to the Clipboard) and graphs, as well as portions of Superbase 2 text, numeric, or graphic image data bases, into Word for Windows documents. Another interesting DDE link is between notes kept in Pack Rat, a PIM (Personal Information Manager), and Word for Windows. Most other Windows applications that do not now have a DDE Paste Link option should be developing it for release sometime soon.

Printing to a File

Many graphic design packages that run under Windows, such as Micrografx Designer, Arts and Letters, and some CAD (Computer Aided Design) packages cannot use the generic Windows printer drivers. Most require a PostScript laser printer or Hewlett Packard plotter. Also, these packages save images to a special image format. Since you cannot load a file from a graphics package that prints to your printer, you have to convert the file to the format you need. The most efficient way to convert files is to first print to a file rather than to a printer. Then load the file into a program that specializes in file conversion, such as Inset System's HiJaak.

The first step in printing to a file is to insert a line into the [ports] section of your WIN.INI file such as the last line of the following:

```
[ports]
; A line with [filename].PRN followed by an equal sign causes
; [filename] to appear in the Control Panel's Connections dialog.
; A printer connected to [filename] directs its output into this file.
LPT1:=
LPT2:=
LPT3:=
COM1:=9600,n,8,1
COM2:=9600,n,8,1
EPT:=
OUTPUT.PRN=
```

Next use the MS-DOS Executive Control Panel program Setup Connections command to install the OUTPUT.PRN port with the printer driver used by your graphics package. Go into the graphics package, load the file you want to print, and activate the Print command. Instead of sending the file to the printer, Windows will create a file named OUTPUT.PRN. You can now close the graphics application.

The next step is to rename the OUTPUT.PRN so it has the extension of the file format that the graphics package uses; for example, a Micrografx Designer file would be renamed to OUT-PUT.DRW. You can now use a file conversion program to convert your graphic image to a format that is compatible with your printer. The new file will be, for example, OUTPUT.PCX if converted to ZSoft's PC Paintbrush, or OUTPUT.PCL if converted to generic LaserJet format. T/Maker's Scrapbook+is a useful Windows graphic image management program. Inset System's HiJaak is one of the most comprehensive graphic image conversion programs, although it is a DOS application (it does not run under Windows). Both of these programs are listed in Appendix D.

What Happens When Windows Freezes?

While you are working on a document, Word for Windows keeps track of your work in a *.TMP file. When you save (or autosave) your document, the *.TMP file is incorporated into the document and is deleted by Word for Windows. Normally this process is transparent to you.

Unfortunately, things do not always work as smoothly as you would like, and once in a while you may experience a "freeze" (the keyboard and the mouse stop functioning and the only option is to reboot) while running Word for Windows. When your computer freezes without you closing Word for Windows or if you accidentally power-off or reboot, a *.TMP file will be left on your hard disk. You can use this *.TMP file to try to recover some or all of your lost work. If you do not need to recover data from this file, however, do not try to use Word for Windows with this file on your hard disk. As with Word 4.0 and 5.0, these *.TMP files can accidentally be incorporated into documents. You may have a document garbled or ruined by a loose *.TMP file. As good hard disk maintenance, frequently delete all Word for Windows *.TMP and other unnecessary files, especially before you back up your hard disk.

To recover data from a *.TMP file, first rename that file to any file name ending with the extension *.TXT. You can use the MS-DOS Executive File Rename command or the DOS RENAME command to do this. Then open the *.TXT file in Word for Windows. If Word for Windows asks if this file is an ASCII text format file, activate the OK button. You will probably see some control characters (non-text, such as smiley faces, hearts, and music notes). Delete all the control characters and copy the useful blocks of text into the file you were working on before your PC froze.

This concludes the explanatory portion of this book. In summary, Chapters 1 to 11 described all of the Word for Windows features, and provided information to help you get around in the Windows environment. This book is by no means exhaustive of the possible applications of Word for Windows, interactions between Word for Windows and other Windows applications, or the Windows environment itself.

The basic purpose of this book is to help you get to the stage where you can complete all of your pressing document processing work. It would also be rewarding if this book whetted your appetite to explore further applications of Word for Windows, especially those involving use of fonts, graphic images, or data imported from other Windows applications. The appendixes that follow are sources for further information on Word for Windows as well as useful supporting hardware and software.

IV

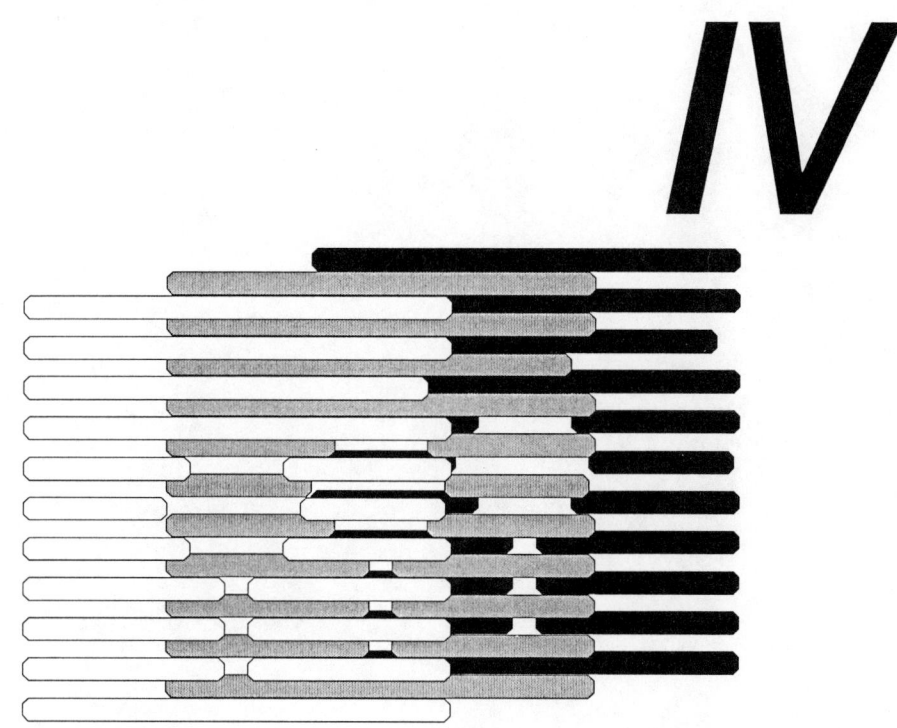

Appendixes

APPENDIX

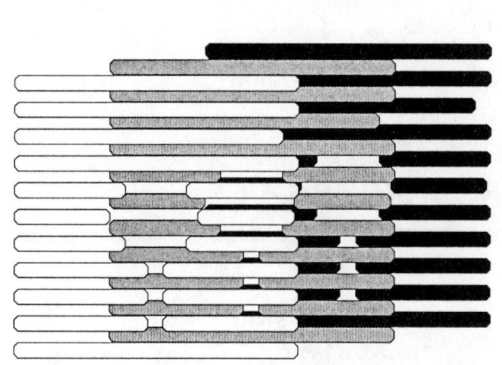

How Much PC Do I Need?

The minimum configuration with which you can run Windows and Word for Windows consists of an IBM PC or compatible PC with an Intel 80286 microprocessor (called the "286"), 640K (kilobytes) of RAM (Random Access Memory), a 20MB hard disk, one floppy disk drive, and a monochrome graphics ("Hercules" graphics) card and monitor. This equipment should cost you about $1100. And, of course, this does not include the decision you will have to make about a printer.

From this basic equipment, there are several directions that you can take to increase the comfort, processing power, and speed of your PC. The issues relevant to your choice of equipment are discussed in this appendix. Considerations relevant to your choice of peripherals, such as monitors, printers, keyboards, mice, and modems, are discussed in Appendix B. Other hardware interests are discussed in Appendix D.

System CPU: 80286 or 80386?

Currently, four CPU (Central Processing Unit) chips are put in IBM and compatible PCs. The original PC, introduced in 1981, used the Intel 8086 chip, which is an 8-bit chip. This means that data flows in and out of the CPU chip in bytes (a byte is like a word to the CPU chip), which each consist of 8 bits. The data stream between your hard disk and the CPU, the monitor and your CPU, the keyboard and your CPU, and the printer and your CPU, is referred to as the *bus*. The number of bits per byte moving through the bus is termed the bus width; therefore, 8086 based PCs have an 8-bit bus width.

Bus width determines how fast data can move in and out of your CPU. So does the clock speed of the computer. The clock speed determines the number of times per second data is sent in and out of the CPU. The original PC ran at a speed of 4.77MHz (Megahertz = million data processing cycles/second), although current 8086 chips can operate at twice this speed, 10MHz. The current version of Windows runs too slowly on these machines to be an acceptable environment for Word for Windows.

The original IBM AT, introduced in 1983, used the Intel 80286 chip, called the "286." The 286 is a 16-bit chip. Therefore, because of the 16-bit bus, if a 286 based PC operates at 10MHz, it actually handles 4 times as much data as the original IBM PC (2 × 8-bit bus width and 2 × 4.77MHz clock speed = 4 times total speed). Currently, many vendors offer 286 PCs running at 20MHz, 8 times faster data handling than the original IBM PC.

Intel introduced the 80386 chip, better known as the "386," in 1986. The 386 is a 32-bit chip, and the most common versions run at 20MHz; the 386 has 16 times the data processing power of the original IBM PC (4 × 8-bit bus width and 4 × 4.77MHz clock speed = 16 times total speed). The new 33MHz 386 chip appears to be the baseline chip of the 1990s. 50MHz is likely to be the top speed this chip will ever attain (40 times the processing power of the original IBM PC). The 386 addresses memory above the first 640K more freely than its two predecessors. This makes it capable of true multitasking (processing data in more than one application simultaneously). Purchasing a 386 PC is probably the most important way you can speed the operation of Word for Windows. The baseline cost for a system box with an IBM-compatible 386 CPU (no monitor, no hard disk, no printer, usually 1MB RAM) is about $2000.

IBM no longer makes either the PC or the AT. However, IBM's PS/2 Models 50 and 60 have a 286 chip. The Models 70 and 80 have 386 chips with an option to upgrade to an 80486 chip. The PS/2 Models 70 and 80 both have a 32-bit bus called MicroChannel Architecture, or MCA. MCA is the major innovation of the PS/2 line of computers. There are hundreds of other manufacturers of 386 PCs, but most of these have a 32-bit bus to a memory card and a 16-bit bus throughout the rest of the PC. A few companies have licensed IBM's MCA, and are offering MCA 386 and 486 PCs. MCA allows software written to take advantage of a 32-bit PC to run at its fullest potential. The MCA also allows for *bus-mastering boards*. Busmaster boards can have their own CPU that will work alongside of the CPU on the motherboard. IBM has a busmaster board that controls the hard disk and floppy drives so you can format disks and copy files without slowing down the main CPU.

The "Gang of Nine," a group of nine companies led by Compaq, have decided to expand the 16-bit bus in the IBM PC, XT (the PC with a hard disk), and AT for 386 and 486 based PCs, rather than use MCA. (Note that the PC and XT have only 8-bit buses; the AT has both 8- and 16-bit bus capability, which is an expansion on the PC and XT bus.) The PC, XT, and AT 16-bit bus is called the Industry Standard Architecture, or ISA. The new expanded bus is called the Extended Industry Standard Architecture, or EISA. The advantage of EISA for IBM's competitors is two-fold. First, they do not have to pay IBM royalties for MCA. Second, cards that are currently in PC, XT, and AT level machines can be installed in EISA PCs, but not in MCA PCs. The Gang of Nine hopes that these PC owners will not want to buy new cards for MCA machines and that potential EISA PC purchasers will find the EISA bus competitive with or better than the MCA bus. The whole affair has been called "bus wars."

Software

To run Word for Windows, you should have Windows version 2.11 or higher (Word for Windows comes with a run-time version of Windows, but it has severe limits—see Appendix C), and you must have DOS. Your PC's CPU (its bus type does not matter here) will determine which version of Windows you can use. There are two versions of Windows 2.11, Windows/286 and Windows/386. Windows/286 runs on 286 PCs, but can also be used on a 386. Windows/386 requires a 386 PC. You can open up more than one program window in Windows/286, but only the window that is in the foreground (active) will be in operation (the others are temporarily frozen). Windows/386 is a true multitasking environment because applications can run in the background.

You can run Windows as long as you boot your PC from DOS version 2.0 or higher. The most widely used version of DOS is 3.30. Each computer vendor licenses a version of MS-DOS (Microsoft DOS), and may call it by the vendor's own name, such as IBM PC-DOS. However, the version number is supplied by Microsoft.

If you are considering the latest version of DOS, 4.01, you may want to do a little research on the pitfalls and benefits of this new release. DOS 4.01 lets you format your entire hard disk as a single partition, allowing you to conveniently address all of it as drive C. All versions of DOS before 4.00 require you to divide your hard disk into 32MB partitions. A 32MB partition limit is not a bad idea when you consider the operation of your programs. While they operate, programs loaded into RAM often search the hard disk for subprogram or data files. The larger the partition searched, the longer the search time. Also, many articles have been written about problems with the way DOS 4.00 and 4.01 address expanded memory. Windows greatly benefits from unhindered access to both expanded and extended memory (see Chapter 11, "Fine Tuning Windows").

Random Access Memory

You can install Windows and Word for Windows on a PC with only the base 640K of RAM (Random Access Memory). As discussed in Chapter 11, Windows will attempt to swap program and data files to your hard disk if it runs out of RAM. Swapping programs to disk will greatly slow down the operation of Word for Windows and any other Windows applications you run alongside it.

Adding extended and expanded memory will greatly speed up the operation of Word for Windows. Of course there is a point of diminishing returns. Between 1 and 4MB of DRAM (Dynamic RAM), sometimes more, can usually be added to the motherboard (the board on the bottom of your PC system box with the 286 or 386 chip on it). Windows will use this memory to make Word for Windows run faster. However, if you are running only Word for Windows on a 286 or 386 PC, 1MB will be sufficient. If you run programs other than Windows, such as Excel, going to 2 or 3MB of RAM will improve your PC's performance substantially. Memory expansion options are discussed in Chapter 11.

Floppy and Hard Disk Drives

You must have at least one floppy and one hard disk drive to install Word for Windows. If you do not create huge documents daily, it is easiest to back up your work onto floppy disks as well. Other backup options include magnetic tape, read/write CD disks, and specialized media like Bernouli boxes.

Four types of floppy disk drives are currently widely used with PCs. You are likely to receive any one of these types of floppy disks from colleagues or software manufacturers. Among the four types of floppy disk drives, there are two sizes of floppy disks, 5.25" and 3.5". Each of these comes in double (DD) and high (HD) density formats. The 5.25" DD disks hold 360K, 5.25" HD disks hold 1.2MB, 3.5" DD hold 720K, and 3.5" HD disks hold 1.44MB.

You can buy floppy drives that support only the DD disk format in either size. The HD floppy drives for both sizes can read and write either DD or HD. Unfortunately, because of its design, the HD 5.25" floppy drive does not always accurately write to DD 5.25" floppies. But HD 5.25" floppy drives read DD 5.25" floppies accurately. Because of this write problem you should try, if possible, to install high density 3.5 and 5.25" disk drives and a 5.25" low density disk drive in your PC. If you write to DD 5.25" floppies infrequently, just the two high density drives will be adequate. If you occasionally copy files to 5.25" DD disks on a 5.25" HD disk drive, you can use the DOS COMP (COMPare files) command to check that the files are exactly the same on both the floppy and your hard disk. If they are not, copy them again until no compare errors occur.

Both Word 4.0 and 5.0 offer you the option to run on a dual floppy drive system with no hard disk. Running Windows and Word for Windows requires that you have at least a 20MB hard disk. If you have been using a dual floppy drive PC, expect an improvement in operating speed in the neighborhood of 10-100 times when you first begin to use a hard disk. The degree of improvement that you see, the difference between 10 and 100 times, depends on the type of hard disk you purchase.

You can purchase a 20MB hard disk with 65 msec (millisecond) access time (the average amount of time it takes to find a file on the drive), such as the Seagate ST-225, and a controller card, such as the Western Digital WD-1000 series, for about $275. This is the disk drive made for the mass market and has a high failure rate, although the reliability of these drives has gotten better in the last few years. Larger hard disks, beginning with 40MB drives, require faster access speeds because any search for a file is over a larger area. Some of the large hard disk drives have access times less than 5 msec. Because of the need to operate accurately at high speeds, the larger hard disk drives are usually better built and are more reliable than 20MB drives. Generally, the faster a drive runs, the more expensive it is.

When choosing the size of your hard disk, remember that most of the hard disk will be used to hold your software, not data. DOS, Windows, and Word for Windows will use approximately 5MB. Add in the other software you use and leave yourself at least another 30-50% space for growth. Check to make sure that your PC has an extra hard disk drive bay for an additional hard disk in case your current drive becomes filled.

The ST-225 hard disk is sold with an MFM type controller card. For the larger hard disk drives, 40MB and up, you have several other types of controller cards to choose from. The fastest is the SCSI (called "scuzzy"); you will also see ESDI and ST406/506 cards advertised. SCSI is the most expensive, then ESDI, and last the ST406/506. All of these are dependable controller cards. Another type of controller card, RLL, writes 50% faster to a hard disk, thus increasing the amount of data it can hold by 50%. These drives have a reputation for corrupting data. While the reputation of RLL has gotten better over the last year, it is a good idea to avoid these drives until they are given a clean bill of health.

APPENDIX

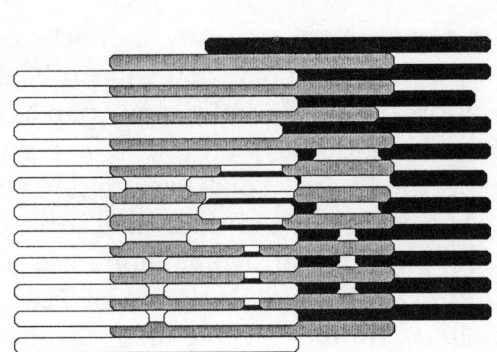

B

Peripheral Interests

All of the devices that are attached to your PC via cables, such as monitors, printers, keyboards, mice, and modems, are referred to as peripherals. Modems can also operate entirely from within your PC's system box, but are still considered peripheral instruments. You should consider all of these items as basic equipment for the document processing workstation where you will use Word for Windows.

Monitors

There are primarily two categories of monitors, monochrome and color. Within the monochrome category, you will probably find only three types of monitors, plain, Hercules, and "paper white." A plain monochrome monitor displays only text, not graphics, and therefore cannot be used with Word for Windows or any Windows application. The Hercules graphics card, or compatibles, can be attached to regular monochrome monitors, allowing them to display text and graphics at a resolution of 720 vertical lines by 348 horizontal lines. An inexpensive monochrome monitor and Hercules controller card cost about $150 for the pair. Hercules equipped monitors are acceptable for Windows; however, the program interface is more intuitive in color. Paper white monitors are usually oversize (16" to 30") and offer high resolution (1200 x 1200 or better). They are used primarily on systems devoted to CAD (Computer Aided Design) or desktop publishing.

Color monitors come primarily in four standards. From lowest to highest resolution, they are CGA (Color Graphics Adapter), EGA (Enhanced Graphics Adapter), VGA (Video Graphics Array), and the IBM 8514 specification. Currently, VGA is the most popular color monitor standard. Its 640 x 480 resolution is the minimum you should use with Word for Windows because text looks fuzzy at lower resolutions. VGA monitor and controller card combinations range from $500 to $1000. The higher priced models are brighter, have switches allowing you to show multiple resolutions (CGA, EGA, and VGA), and sometimes have a flat screen (no distortion at the edges), such as those from Zenith; all of these features tend to reduce eyestrain. The IBM 8514 standard has 1024 x 768 resolution, which will make the text in Word for Windows look noticeably clearer. 8514 monitors and controller cards require special Windows or DOS drivers which are not available for most applications. If you do not have drivers for a particular application, an 8514 usually defaults to VGA.

You should also consider a glare/radiation screen to cover your monitor. You may see the reflections of objects in your monitor's screen if you work near a window or light source. This can be very distracting. Many dealers sell glare shields for all sizes of monitors for between $25 and $100; make sure you get the right size for your monitor. Radiation shielding is a controversial issue. Investigative studies have found that working on a PC or computer terminal over 20 hours per week is associated with high rates of miscarriage and acne. The long-term effects are as yet unknown. These tests did not determine if the source of the radiation was the front of the monitor, the screen, or if it could be the sides or back of the monitor. Glare shields that are also leaded to protect against radiation cost between $100 and $200. Some monochrome and color monitors come with glare shields; however, few of these are leaded to protect against radiation.

Printers

In spite of the thousands of printer models available, there are primarily three types of printers to choose from, dot matrix, ink-jet, and laser printers. A fourth variety, daisy wheel printers (such as the Xerox Diablo 630), are often supported by Windows, but they can only print text in the font found on a daisy wheel and cannot print graphics.

Dot matrix printers come in primarily two varieties, 9- and 24-pin. The actual print head of a dot matrix printer consists of wire pins that form a block of 9 or 24. These pins push a printer ribbon against paper, forming a pattern of dots that you recognize as text or graphics. The 24-pin printers are more expensive than 9-pin models because they produce higher resolution copy. Dot matrix printers are also priced on the basis of speed. Often they offer one or more very high speed draft modes of up to 500 cps (characters per second), which print text and graphics at low resolution copy (fuzzy); fast draft printing is useful for proofing. These same dot matrix printers usually offer a slower NLQ (Near Letter Quality—only typewriters, daisy wheel, inkjet, and laser printers print non-fuzzy letter-quality copy) 40-80 cps mode; 24-pin dot matrix NLQ copy is useful for many presentation purposes. An inexpensive 9-pin dot matrix printer, such as the Epson Fx286 costs about $200 mail order; an inexpensive 24-pin dot matrix printer, such as the ALPS Allegro, costs about $350 mail order.

Inkjet printers started out as small portable printers which required special thermal paper. A recent resurgence in this type of printer has been led by the HP DeskJet. The DeskJet produces up to 2 ppm (pages per minute) of text and graphics on regular paper, at a laser printer resolution of 300 x 300 dpi (dots per inch). Many software products are available, such as Laser Twin (Metro Software, Tuscon, AZ), that allow you to download fonts to DeskJet printers. The *street price* (mail order) of the DeskJet is about $550.

The Hewlett Packard LaserJet began the laser printer boom in 1984. Like most laser printers, it is built around the Canon SX printer engine. This engine produces a maximum of 8 ppm of graphics and text at a resolution of 300 x 300 dpi. In the best of all worlds, everyone would have 15 ppm (page per minute) laser printers that offered both PostScript and LaserJet compatibility. Unfortunately, this type of printer costs well over $7000. Even the slower laser printers with true PostScript capability list for over $3500. The high cost for PostScript laser printers is due to the PostScript language interpreter on the printer's controller board; it is licensed at a high cost from Adobe Systems. The PostScript PDL (Page Description Language) allows you to use PostScript scalable font outlines and print scalable PostScript graphic images. While graphic images are generally less flexible on the LaserJet and compatibles, several font vendors offer scalable fonts for the LaserJet (see Appendix E). The street price of the 8 ppm HP LaserJet Series II (the current standard) is about $1600. The new HP LaserJet IIP prints at a maximum 4 ppm clip, but otherwise is a real laser printer with the Canon engine. Its street price is about $1000.

Keyboards

Most PC buyers purchase their keyboard from the same vendor that supplies their PC; however, you usually have the option to buy a keyboard from another vendor. There are several features you should consider when looking at keyboards.

The first is the tactile feel of the keyboard. IBM keyboards have an audible click response to typing. The audible click lets you know, without looking at the monitor or keyboard (touch typing), that you have activated the key. The audible click is produced by springs within the keys. At the other extreme is a mushy keyboard that gives no feedback when you press a key; these keyboards, however, allow you to type more quickly. Many manufacturers offer a mushy keyboard with an optional audible click that is produced by your PC's speaker.

Another important feature of a keyboard is its layout. The current IBM keyboard has the function keys, F1-F12, in a line above the main alphabetic keys. Older models had the function keys to the left of the alphabetic keys. With the function keys to the left, it is very easy to press the left ALT, SHIFT, and CTRL keys with your thumb and simultaneously hit a function key. This gives you 36 easy to reach keystrokes for macros that you define yourself. Northgate (Minneapolis, MN) specializes in making these types of keyboards.

The position of the keys is another layout feature you should consider. Most current keyboards offer a second set of arrow keys separate from the numeric keypad. This feature is aimed at non-mouse users, such as Lotus 1-2-3 spreadsheet users. Therefore, separate arrow keys are not critical for Word for Windows.

You should also consider the keys themselves. Can you replace them if they are damaged? Make sure that you have extra-wide ENTER, CTRL, BACKSPACE, BACKSLASH (\), and ALT keys. You need to be able to reach and find these keys with your little fingers. Since they are not in the main alphabetic set, you must reach further for them than the smaller alphanumeric keys in the middle of the keyboard. Make sure that the f and j keys are *ribbed*. The rib is usually a small raised ridge at the bottom of these two keys which tells your two index fingers that they have found the home row. Often the 5 key in the numeric keypad is ribbed or has a raised dot in the center. This bump is for calculator touch typing on the keypad and is not important for most Word for Windows applications.

Other than IBM, Northgate and Keytronics (Spokane, WA), make very high quality keyboards. An average keyboard from these vendors will cost about $100.

Mice

A mouse is critical to Windows and Word for Windows. The most popular mouse is the Microsoft mouse; however, there are many other brands to choose from. If you choose one of these mice, make sure it is compatible with Microsoft Windows.

Most mice are fairly equivalent in function. A few require that a controller card be placed in a slot in your computer's motherboard to supply an interface. The majority, however, use a serial port and a software driver that is loaded from your CONFIG.SYS or AUTOEXEC.BAT file. The majority of mice have two buttons, not three. Most Windows applications use only the left mouse button.

Also consider purchasing a mouse pad. Usually, a mouse pad is a 6" by 6" piece of textured fabric on foam rubber that goes between the mouse and your desk. The poor friction between a desk and the mouse trackball (underneath most mice) make you push the mouse a lot further across your desk than you would with a mouse pad. A mouse pad costs about $5, although many software companies give them away free as promotions.

Microsoft's newest mouse should revolutionize the mouse market. Most mice have a trackball that is placed near the back of the mouse. The new Microsoft mouse has the ball near the front, under the buttons. This increases the distance from your wrist to the ball, allowing the mouse to move much further across the screen using less wrist action. The arrow image of most mice is displayed at 200 ppi (pixels per inch). The new Microsoft mouse is displayed at 400 ppi. This makes pointing at commands in menus and highlighting text in Word for Windows much more accurate and, therefore, quicker. Microsoft compatible mice sell for as little as $30; the street price of the Microsoft mouse is about $110.

Modems

Word for Windows documents can be sent over the telephone by various E-Mail (electronic mail) programs in unformatted ASCII, RTF, or as a formatted *.DOC file (see Chapter 9 for a discussion on sending Word for Windows via E-Mail). MCI Mail is one of the largest networks and is particularly proficient at sending all of these formats. You can also use MCI Mail to send an unformatted document to a FAX machine. To take advantage of E-Mail, you need a modem.

If you have a free slot on the motherboard in your PC, you can get an internal modem. If you have no more free slots, you can attach an external modem via a serial port and RS232C serial cable. Internal modems cost about $50 less than external modems. While you can hear both an internal and external modem dial your phone, external modems also have panels of between one and eight flashing lights that tell you whether or not the modem is actively transmitting or receiving data. Seeing these lights can be a big help when you are not sure if your communication software is working properly.

Make sure that whatever modem you purchase, it is Hayes (Norcross, GA) Smartmodem compatible. The Smartmodem language is used by almost all communications software. Although it is uncommon, if there are any problems with a particular manufacturer's implementation of the Hayes architecture, you will eventually have problems with your communcations.

Modems are usually priced on the basis of how fast they send documents. The faster you transmit documents, the less you have to spend on long distance charges (although MCI Mail uses a toll-free 800 access number). The common speeds are 300, 1200, 2400, and 9600 bps (bits per second, also referred to as baud rate). Currently the standard PC modem is 2400 bps, with the 9600 bps modems costing more than twice as much. An inexpensive Hayes compatible 2400 bps modem costs about $150-200.

APPENDIX

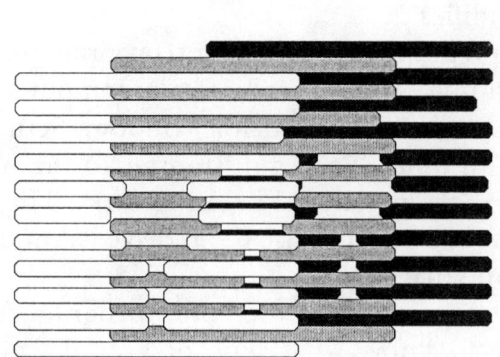

C

Setting Up Word for Windows

Since Word for Windows is a Windows application, it needs to be run within the Microsoft Windows environment. If you do not own Microsoft Windows, Word for Windows will install a *run-time* version of Windows. If you choose this option, you will find that the run-time version of Windows is automatically loaded when you open Word for Windows. You cannot run any Windows applications, other than Word for Windows, if you install the run-time version of Windows. With Windows versions 2.03-2.11, you can either load Windows before Word for Windows or both simultaneously (discussed later in this appendix). If you have Windows 2.03-2.11, install it before Word for Windows; the Word for Windows Setup program detects Windows during the installation process and modifies it.

To install Word for Windows, run the Setup program that is on the Setup disk. Depending on the speed of your computer, hard disk, and floppy disk drive, the Word for Windows Setup program will take about an hour. To begin, transfer to the A drive from your hard disk by typing **A:** and pressing ENTER. Then type **Setup** and press ENTER. (You can also use the B drive if A and B are different types of floppy drives.)

The first screen welcomes you to the Setup program. Before you begin, you need to know what type of graphics adapter (usually Hercules monochrome or VGA color), keyboard, mouse, printer, and printer port (printer cable is plugged into this) you are using. However, this is not all the information you will need to run the Setup program, especially if you have not already installed Windows. It is also important that you know what text is in your AUTOEXEC.BAT and CONFIG.SYS files. If you do not know this, exit the Setup program. To do this, exit the opening screen by pressing ENTER. Figure C-1 shows the second Setup screen that presents you with three options. Choose the Exit Setup option with the DOWN ARROW key and press ENTER. Go to your root directory, C:\, and type **type autoexec.bat** and press ENTER. The contents of your AUTOEXEC.BAT file will be written on the screen. You can print this information by turning on your printer and pressing SHIFT-PRTSC (Shift-Print Screen). Next, display and print the CONFIG.SYS file in the same way. Then, restart the Setup program.

After reopening the initial Setup screen, press ENTER to go to the second Setup screen. Choose the View the README File option. The README.DOC file contains information about Word for Windows that became available too late to be included in the documentation published by Microsoft. Use the PGDN and PGUP keys to scroll through the README.DOC file page by page. Press ESC when you want to go back to the Setup menu. Remember, if your

Figure C-1.

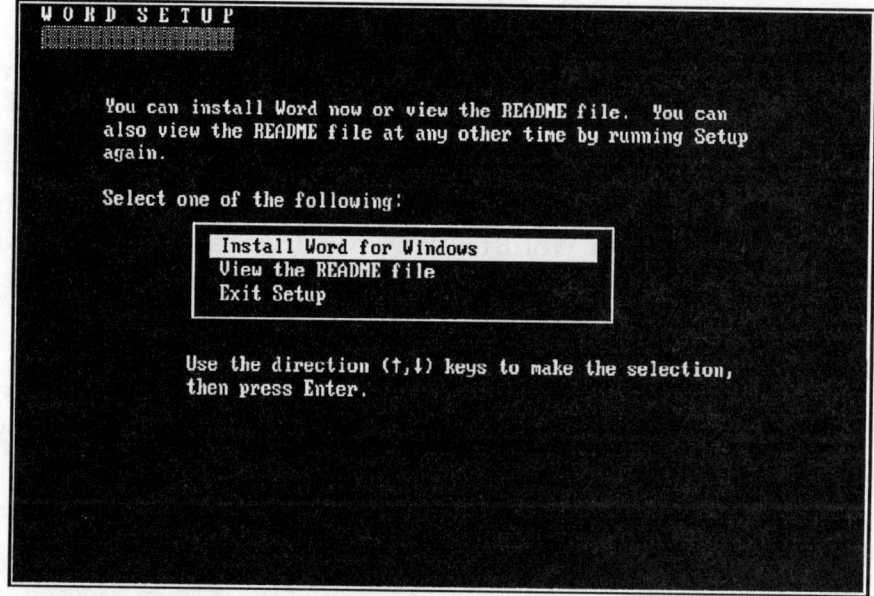

View the README.DOC file first

printer is on, you can print any of the README.DOC file's screens by pressing SHIFT-PRTSC; you can also print the whole file from Word for Windows once it is installed.

When you are finished with the README.DOC file, choose the Install Word for Windows option and press ENTER. The next screen will remind you that if you do not have Windows installed, you need to know what graphics adapter (such as monochrome graphics, EGA, or VGA), mouse, printer, and printer port you are using. Also note at the lower right of the screen that you can exit the Setup program at any time hereafter with the CTRL-x keystroke combination. Press ENTER to continue.

On the next screen, you will see a list of hard disk partitions. Use the DOWN ARROW to choose the one where you want Word for Windows installed. Word for Windows does not have to be installed on the same hard disk partition as Windows. Press ENTER when your choice is highlighted.

The next screen allows you to change your mind or continue. The first option, Exit Setup, closes the Setup program. The second option, Install Word on Another Hard Disk, takes you back to the previous screen so you can choose a different hard disk partition on which to install Word for Windows. The last option, Continue with Word for Windows Installation, takes you to the first installation screen where you begin to configure Word for Windows as you install it, shown in Figure C-2 . Press ENTER after you have made your choice.

If you choose the Continue with Word for Windows Installation option, you will be asked to type the path where you want to install Word for Windows. Figure C-2 shows that the default is in

Figure C-2.

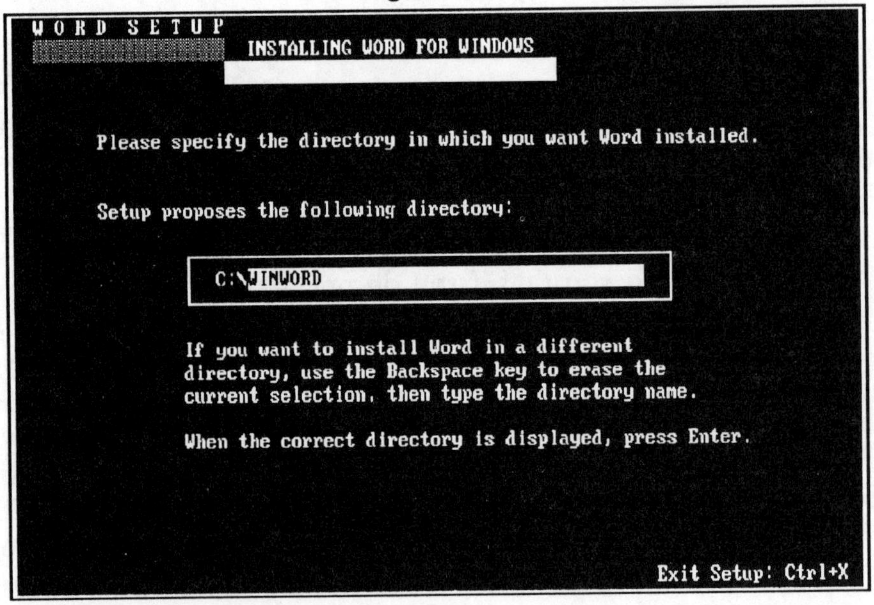

```
W O R D   S E T U P
▓▓▓▓▓▓▓▓▓▓▓▓▓    INSTALLING WORD FOR WINDOWS


      Please specify the directory in which you want Word installed.


      Setup proposes the following directory:


          C:\WINWORD


      If you want to install Word in a different
      directory, use the Backspace key to erase the
      current selection, then type the directory name.

      When the correct directory is displayed, press Enter.




                                              Exit Setup: Ctrl+X
```

Default Word for Windows subdirectory

a directory named WINWORD on the hard disk partition you previously chose. You can backspace over WINWORD and type a directory name of your choice. Press ENTER when you are finished typing or to accept the default.

After choosing a subdirectory, you are asked to insert the Word for Windows Program disk. The program files, including WINWORD.EXE (the main program file), will be listed on the screen as they are copied to your hard disk. After the program disk has been copied, the Setup program will ask you to put your Conversions 1 disk in drive A, and to press ENTER. Several more program files will be copied from this disk; the entire process may take several minutes.

The next screen to appear will ask if you want to install the Word for Windows conversion programs. The Setup program mentions that these installation programs are used to import non-Word for Windows documents into Word for Windows. However, not mentioned is that these same conversion programs are used to export Word for Windows files to these non-Word for Windows formats. This latter process allows you to share documents you create in Word for Windows with colleagues who do not use Word for Windows (for a discussion of importing and exporting files with these conversions, see Chapter 11).

There are two options from which to choose in regards to the conversion programs, Install Conversions and Do Not Install Conversions. If you decide to install the conversion programs, you will see the screen that asks you to select the conversion programs you want to use. Move the cursor down over the word processing file formats you expect to import documents from or export Word for Windows documents to; then press ENTER. This selects the highlighted conversion program and returns you to the previous screen that allows you to either select another conversion program or install the one you have selected. Each time you select another conversion filter, your previous selection will have an asterisk to the left of it. Figure C-3 shows what the conversion program selection screen will look like when all are selected. PC Word represents Word 4.0 and 5.0. Not shown in Figure C-3 is the MultiMate conversion program that is chosen by pressing the PGDN key and ENTER.

You should choose only the conversion programs that you anticipate using. If you do not find any that will be of use, select the No Conversion option seen in Figure C-3. This option allows you to exit the conversion installation process without making any choices. You can always add more conversion programs later by running the Setup program again. You will conserve hard disk space by installing only those conversion programs you need.

The conversion programs are activated the first time by using the File Open command for a non-Word for Windows document or by modifying the WIN.INI file as shown in Chapter 11.

Figure C-3.

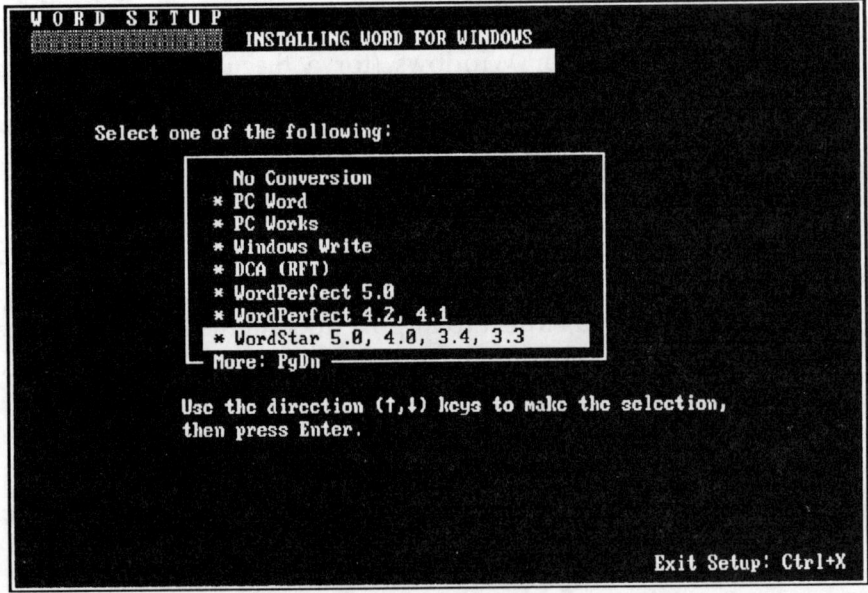

Conversion program selection

After the conversion programs have been copied from the conversion disks, a screen will appear informing you that Word for Windows will now install graphic filters that enable you to open graphic image files created with other programs. You can directly import files in any of the offered image formats with the Word for Windows Insert Picture command. The supported image formats include: Lotus 1-2-3's *.PIC, Micrografx Designer's *.DRW, and the scanner grey-scale format *.TIF. Noticably missing is the ZSoft *.PCX format. However, you can convert a *.PCX file to one of the supported formats with programs like HiJaak (see Appendix D, "Supporting Software and Hardware"). You can also cut and paste graphic images directly from other Windows applications using the Clipboard (see Chapter 3, "Cut and Paste: Adding Tables and Images").

As with the conversion programs, select the graphic filters one by one. To conserve hard disk space, choose only the graphic image formats that correspond to applications you use. Figure C-4 depicts the selection of all the graphic filters except the Windows Metafile format. Use the DOWN ARROW key to expose and select the Windows Metafile Format option. Once you are finished selecting image formats, highlight the Install Graphic Filters option and press ENTER to begin copying the graphic filter files. As with the conversion program installation, you can select the No Graphics Filters option if none of the listed filters match applications you have or if you decide not to install any graphic image filters at this time. Remember, you can run the Setup program later to install graphic filters if you find you need them.

The tutorial lessons are the next set of files that you can opt to install. If you choose to install the tutorial files, you will be asked to put both Tutorial disks into drive A so these files can be copied to your hard disk. You will be asked to insert the Help and Proofing Tools disks as well. Remember, you can install the tutorial later if you decide not to install it now.

After copying the tutorial, help, and proofing files to your hard disk, the Setup program searches your hard disk for Windows. Figure C-5 shows the message from the Setup program that is

Figure C-4.

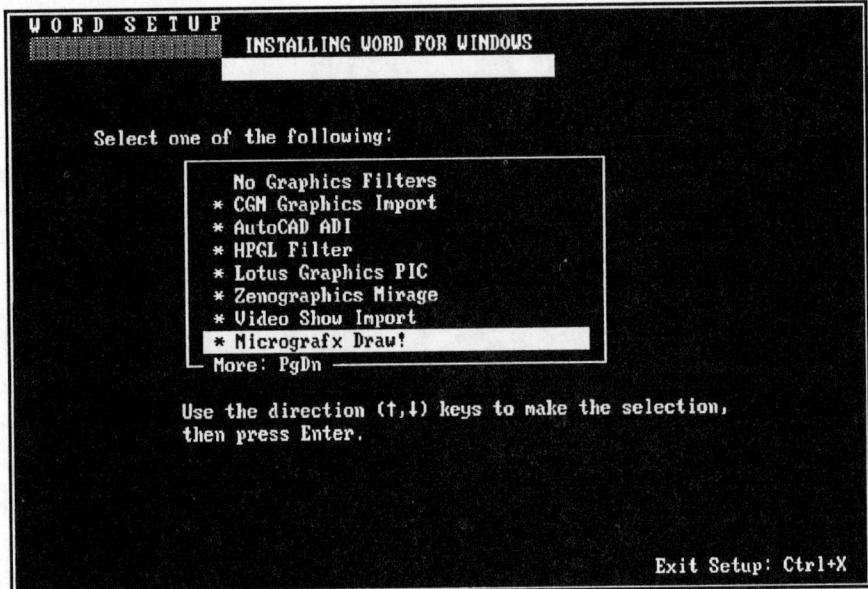

Graphic image import filters

displayed if Windows 2.03-2.11 has already been installed on your hard disk (note that in this case Windows is on the D partition). It gives you the option of installing a run-time version of Windows 2.11 to be used only with Word for Windows. You should not install the run-time version of Windows if you have already installed Windows 2.03-2.11. You cannot run other Windows applications, including the MS-DOS Executive (see Chapter 1), from a run-time version of Windows. The run-time version of Windows is of use only to Word for Windows users who have not yet purchased (or do not plan to purchase) Windows. If you choose to install the run-time version of Windows 2.11, the installation program will copy files from the Build, Displays, and Fonts disks to your hard disk.

If you already have Windows installed, and do not opt to install a run-time version of Windows, you will be asked to insert one or

Figure C-5.

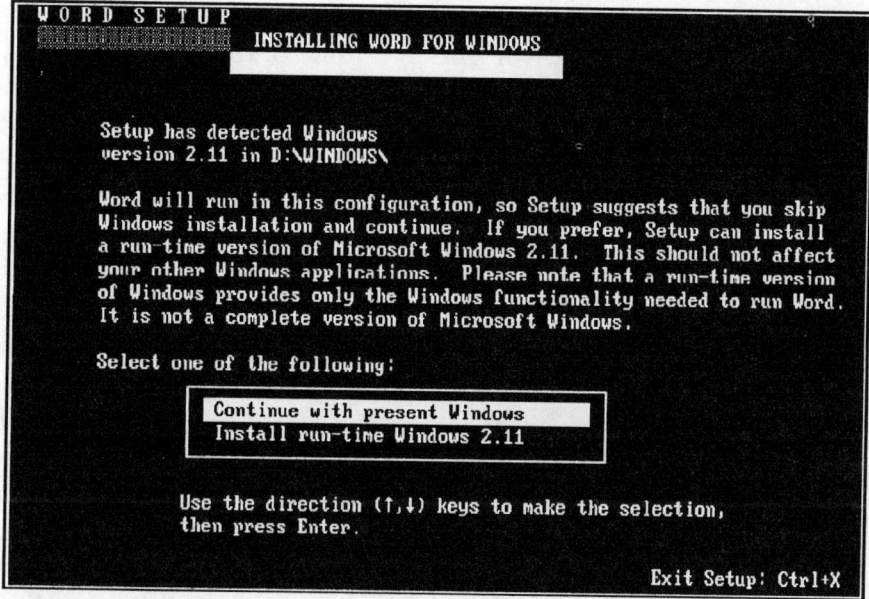

Option to install run-time version of Windows

both of the two Utilities disks. This is because the Setup program has read the list of printers that you installed in Windows and will install complementary or updated printer drivers in Word for Windows. All Windows printer drivers are *.DRV files. For example, HPPCL.DRV is the printer driver for the HP LaserJet, which uses the PCL (Printer Controller Language) PDL (Page Description Language) to format pages as they are sent to the printer from Window's print spooler; PSCRIPT.DRV is the printer driver for laser printers using the PostScript PDL.

The next screen to be displayed will offer you the Install Printer Drivers option that you may want to add to your Windows program or to the run-time version of Windows. If you have already installed Windows, you will probably not want to add any printer drivers. If you are installing the run-time version of Windows, you will need to select your printer either from the list of printer drivers shown in Figure C-6 or from the others that appear when you use the DOWN ARROW key. As before, you can select the No Printer Driver option if none of the listed drivers apply to your printer. However, before making the decision that none of the listed printer drivers apply to your printer, look through your printer's manual and the Word for Windows Printer Guide (a pamphlet that comes with Word for Windows). You may find that your printer can emulate one of the listed printer drivers.

If you still cannot find a selection that will support your printer, you can call Microsoft Technical Support at (206) 454-2030. If your printer has been available for less than a year, you may find out that Microsoft has just developed or is working on a new printer driver. If your printer has been available for more than a year, you should ask the printer manufacturer where to get a Windows driver. Note that when you install a printer driver for

Figure C-6.

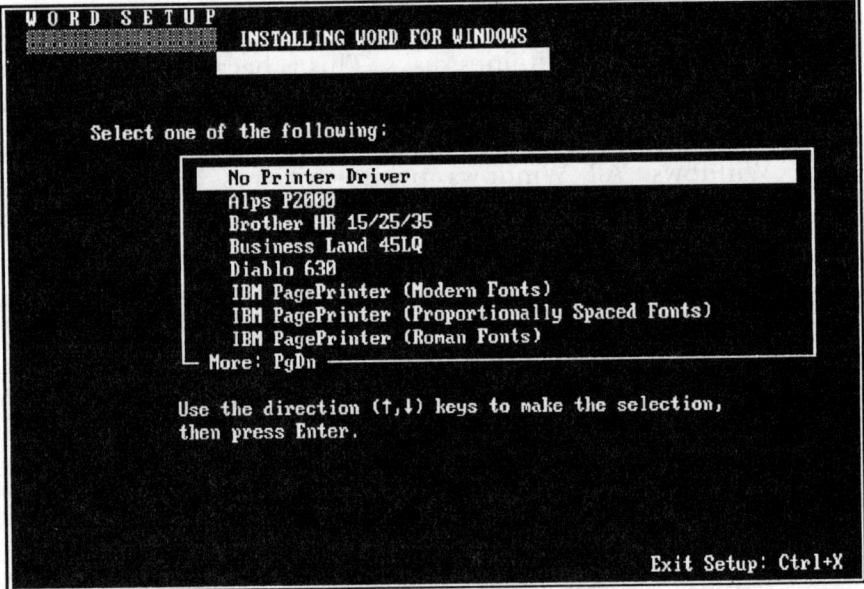

Printer driver choices

Word for Windows, it is available to all Windows applications; the reverse is also true. This means that a general Windows driver for your printer that comes from your printer manufacturer or any software vendor other than Microsoft will work with Word for Windows. If you have installed Windows, you do not need to run the Setup program to install printer drivers at a later date; the MS-DOS Executive Control Panel program can be used to install printer drivers (see Chapter 1).

If you have a laser printer such as a LaserJet (or compatible) or a PostScript printer, you will be asked if you want to install any *soft fonts* for display in Windows or your printer. Soft fonts are fonts that you purchase on disk and are either displayed on the screen in Windows (screen fonts) to let you see what your document will look like before printing or are downloaded to the printer (printer fonts) when a document formatted with these fonts is printed (see Appendix E). You do not need to run the Setup program to install soft fonts at a later date. If you choose not to install any soft fonts with an HP LaserJet or compatible, the Setup program will still copy the Symbol screen and printer font to your hard disk so that you will be able to see these symbols in Windows and print them. You can use the MS-DOS Executive Control Panel program to add screen and printer fonts at a later date (see Chapter 1).

Next, Word for Windows will check the AUTOEXEC.BAT file in your root directory. Depending on the state of this file, no message will be displayed or you might see one of two messages. You will see no message if the Setup program detects that the PATH statement in your AUTOEXEC.BAT file does not list Word for Windows, it will be added automatically to the end of the PATH statement. (If you do not have a PATH statement in your AUTOEXEC.BAT file, the Setup program will automatically create one that lists only the WINWORD (Word for Windows) subdirectory.) In this case, you will not see any indication from the Setup program that this has occurred. If the Setup program detects that you do not have an AUTOEXEC.BAT file, it will ask which subdirectory contains your AUTOEXEC.BAT file. Press

ENTER if you do not have an AUTOEXEC.BAT file, or type in the correct subdirectory. (Your AUTOEXEC.BAT file must be in the root directory for it to be used during booting.) If you do not have an AUTOEXEC.BAT file, the Setup program will create one that has a PATH statement listing only the WINWORD directory. If you have an AUTOEXEC.BAT file in another directory, either a PATH statement will be added or the existing one will be amended with the WINWORD directory. If the Setup program detects a PATH statement in your AUTOEXEC.BAT file that is greater than 127 characters (the DOS limit for a PATH statement), the Setup program offers to write the overlength PATH statement to a file, ADDPATH.NEW, or leave your AUTOEXEC-.BAT as is. You can use the ADDPATH.NEW file to decide how to modify your AUTOEXEC.BAT to include the WINWORD subdirectory. Word for Windows will not run unless the Windows and WINWORD subdirectories are included in the PATH statement. Finally, if you have installed a run-time version of Windows, you will be asked if you want to run the MEMSET program. This program installs the SMARTDrive program that gives Windows access to RAM that you have in excess of 640K. If you have no more memory in your PC, do not run MEMSET. If you do not want to allow the run-time version of Windows to access this memory, do not run MEMSET. If you have already installed Windows on your PC, you should not be asked to run MEMSET. If you think that you did not install the run-time version of Windows, but were asked to run MEMSET, choose not to run MEMSET. Then make sure that the next, and final, screen tells you that you are running Word for Windows from a full featured Windows, not from a run-time version of Windows.

The final screen of the Setup program tells you how to open Word for Windows. Figure C-7 is the final screen if you run the Setup program after installing Windows 2.03-2.11. Note that the Setup program leaves you in the WINWORD directory, where the Word for Windows program files are located. If you have installed

Figure C-7.

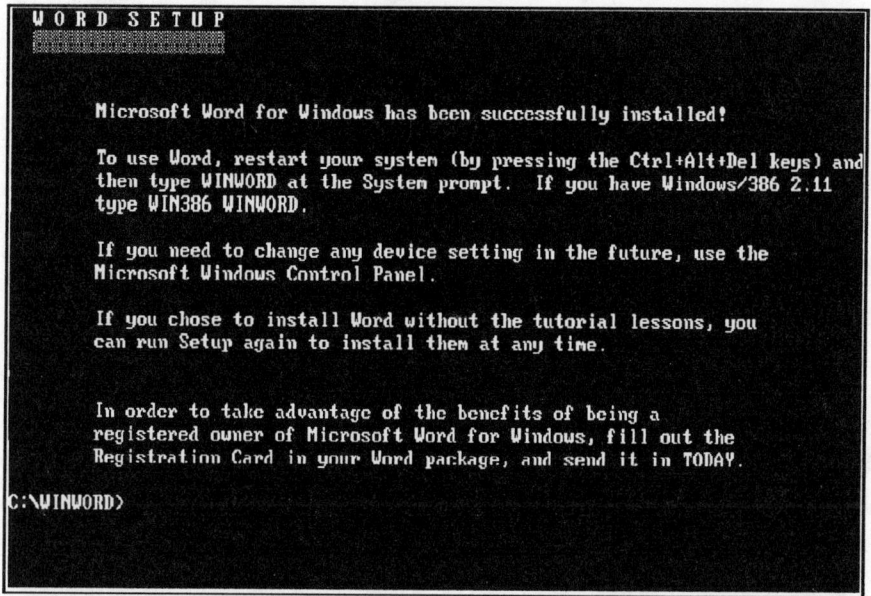

Notification of successful installation

Windows/286 version 2.11 before running the Setup program, you can open Word for Windows now from any subdirectory by typing **WIN WINWORD** and pressing ENTER.

APPENDIX

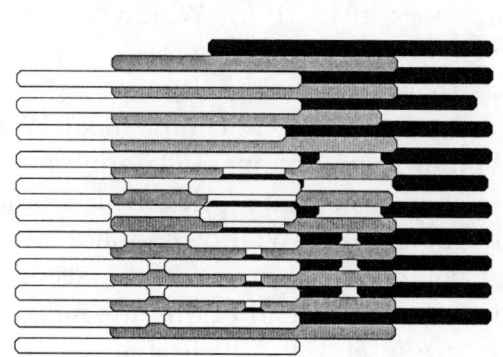

D

Supporting Software and Hardware

Word for Windows is not an island unto itself. One of the major attractions of Word for Windows is the Windows environment itself. The exchange of data, images, and charts is facilitated by the DDE (Dynamic Data Exchange) protocol discussed in Chapter 11. There is also the Windows Clipboard, discussed in Chapter 3, which lets you exchange data, text, and images between Windows applications.

533

The many Windows applications that provide you with memory management, file management, utility, paint, draw, presentation graphics, spreadsheet, and database programs, can all play a part in supporting your work in Word for Windows. Since DOS has been around six years longer than Windows, there are still more DOS applications than Windows applications. Many DOS applications supply functions that nicely complement Word for Windows and other Windows applications. DOS applications are also covered under the above listed categories. Unless otherwise noted, all of the listed programs are Windows applications.

Hardware options, beyond the common peripherals discussed in Appendix B, are discussed at the end of this appendix. These hardware components are useful for dedicated graphic and document production, especially like the production discussed in Chapter 10.

Memory and File Management

Bridge/286* and *Bridge/386   These two programs enhance the PIF editor of both Windows/286 and Windows/386. The PIF editor lets you run non-Windows applications from within Windows.

Softbridge Microsystems Corporation
125 Cambridge Park Drive
Cambridge, MA 02140
(617) 576-2257

Command Post   Command Post provides file management for Windows, enhancing the MS-DOS Executive (see Chapter 1). It includes a screen dimmer, menu creation, and window arranging.

Wilson WindowWare
3377 59th Street Southwest
Seattle, WA 98116
(206) 937-9335

DESQview   DESQview is a DOS application. It comes with QEMM, a memory manager for 80386 based PCs. QEMM and DESQview give you more control over the use of your extended and expanded memory than do Windows versions 2.03-2.11. DESQview lets you task-switch (open more than one program at once) between Windows and non-Windows programs on an 8086 or 80286 PC. On an 80386 PC, it allows true multitasking between Windows and non-Windows applications.

Quarterdeck Office Systems
150 Pico Boulevard
Santa Monica, CA 90405
(213) 392-9851

hDC Windows Express, hDC Color, and hDC Windows Manager

These utilities let you create an icon driven menu of your Windows applications. They also let you add more colors for display on a VGA monitor in Windows. They give you more utility programs than MS-DOS Executive.

hDC Computer Corporation
15379 Northeast 90th Street
Redmond, WA 98052-3522
(206) 885-5550

New Wave   New Wave lets you create an icon driven menu of your Windows applications. It also lets you change menus, create dialog boxes, and personalize all of your Windows applications.

Hewlett-Packard Company
19310 Pruneridge Avenue
Cupertino, CA 95014
(800) 752-0900/(800) 523-2121

PubTech File Organizer   This package beefs up the file management capabilities of the MS-DOS Executive.

Publishing Technologies
7719 Wood Hollow Drive, Suite 260
Austin, TX 78731
(800) PUBTECH/(512) 346-2835

PC MOS   PC MOS lets you task-switch between Windows and non-Windows programs on an 80286 PC or multitask on an 80386 PC.

The Software Link
3577 Parkway Lane
Norcross, GA 30092
(800) 451-LINK/(404) 263-6474

Prompt!   Prompt! is a hard disk manager. It shows the hard disk tree structure.

Access Softek
3204 Adeline Street
Berkeley, CA 94703
(415) 654-0116

Simple Win   Simple Win lets you create icon driven menus for your Windows applications. It includes a file manager to complement the MS-DOS Executive.

Matesys Corp. N.A.
WTIG Incorporated N.A.
2001 L Street Northwest, Suite 801
Washington, DC 20036
(202) 785-0770

Super PC-Kwik   Super PC-Kwik is a DOS program that adds print spooling and disk caching capabilities to 8086, 80286, and 80386 PCs. It is very efficient at using extended and expanded memory for these purposes. To use Super PC-Kwik with Word for Windows, opt not to install SMARTDrive and disable the Windows print spooler (see Chapter 11).

Multisoft Corporation
15100 Southwest Koll Parkway, Suite L
Beaverton, OR 97006
(503) 644-5644

The Desktop Set   This package adds extra utilities and file management capabilities to the MS-DOS Executive.

Okna Corporation
P.O. Box 522
Lyndhurst, NJ 07071
(201) 460-0677

386MAX   386MAX is a memory manager very similar to Quarterdeck's QEMM; it is not specifically aimed at working with DESQview and may give you additional flexibility to configure your extended or expanded memory if you choose not to use DESQview.

Qualitas Incorporated
8314 Thoreau Drive
Bethesda, MD 20817
(301) 469-8848

Utilities

APE   APE (A Programmable Emulator) provides an environment in which you may create terminal emulation screens for users who interact with mainframe computers.

HI-Q International Inc.
1142 Pelican Bay Drive
Daytona Beach, FL 32119
(904) 756-8988

Crosstalk for Windows   This is the Windows version of the leading communications program for DOS. It supports DDE and aids retrieval of E-Mail from CompuServe, MCI Mail, and so on.

Crosstalk Communications
Digital Communications Associates, Inc.
1000 Holcomb, GA 30076-2575
(404) 442-4000

Da Vinci eMAIL   Da Vinci eMAIL is designed to handle LAN E-Mail under Windows. It can use DDE to exchange and update messages across a local area network.

>   Da Vinci Systems Corporation
>   P.O. Box 5427
>   Raleigh, NC 27650
>   (919) 781-5924

DynaComm   DynaComm is a communications program that supports DDE and provides most modem protocols and mainframe terminal emulations.

>   Future Soft Engineering, Incorporated
>   1001 South Dairy Ashford, Suite 203
>   Houston, TX 77077
>   (713) 496-1090

FAXit for Windows   This utiliy will intercept a document as it is printed and FAX it. It works in tandem with FAX boards such as the Intel Connection CoProcessor.

>   Alien Computing
>   37919 50th Street East
>   Palmdale, CA 93550
>   (805) 947-1310

HiJaak/InSet   These two DOS programs include screen capture and complete image format conversion, including PostScript and FAX.

>   Inset Systems Incorporated
>   71 Commerce Road
>   Brookfield, CT 06804
>   (203) 775-5866

HotShot Graphics   HotShot Graphics is primarily a screen capture program. It uses CTRL-ALT to save screens to a file. HotShot can also convert its native file format to several commonly used formats.

SymSoft Incorp.
P.O. Box 4477
Mountain View, CA 94040
(415) 941-1552

Polaris Pack Rat   Pack Rat is a PIM (Personal Information Manager). You can cut and paste Pack Rat address lists, your schedule, notes, and so on, into Word for Windows documents with DDE linking.

Polaris Software
613 West Valley Parkway, Suite 323
Escondido, CA 92025
(619) 743-7800

Software Bridge   Software Bridge is a DOS application. It is the leading word processor document conversion program. It maintains all formatting (character, paragraph, headers, footnotes, and so on) during conversion.

Systems Compatibility
401 North Wabash, Suite 600
Chicago, IL 60611

Paint, Draw, and Presentation Graphics Packages

Adobe Streamline and Adobe Illustrator You can autotrace scanned images and clip art with Streamline. Illustrator is one of the premier presentation graphics packages. Both are from the maker of PostScript.

Adobe Systems Incorporated
1585 Charleston Road
P.O. Box 7900
Mountain View, CA 94039-7900
(415) 962-0911
Arts & Letters

Arts & Letters Arts & Letters is a full featured presentation graphics package that includes a large clip art library and has slide making tools.

Computer Support Corporation
15926 Midway Road
Dallas, TX 75244
(214) 661-8960

Designer, Draw Plus, Graph Plus These applications allow you to produce state of the art presentation graphics from the company that is leading Windows and OS/2 application development. Each includes a large clip art library.

Micrografx, Incorporated
1820 North Greenville Avenue
Richardson, TX 75801
(800) 272-3729/(214) 234-1769

Draw!   Draw! is the hottest new kid on the presentation graphics block. It has excellent font handling capabilities.

> Corel Systems Corporation
> Corel Building
> 1600 Carling Avenue
> Ottawa, Ontario, Canada K1Z 7M4
> (613) 728-8200

Opus I   Opus I integrates images, tables, charts, and maps. It includes a file manager that stores information about data records and images created in Opus I.

> Roykore Software, Incorporated
> 749 Brunswick Street
> San Francisco, CA 94112
> (415) 333-7833

Picture Publisher   Picture Publisher lets you do grey scale editing (halftone) of black and white scanned photos. It provides many tools for editing and manipulating grey scale photos.

> Astral Development Corporation
> Londonderry Square, Suite 112
> Londonderry, NH 03053
> (603) 432-6800

Pixie   Pixie is a presentation graphics application supported by most desktop publishing service bureaus.

> Zenographics
> 19752 MacArthur Boulevard, Suite 250
> Irvine, CA 92715-9976
> (714) 851-2266

Scrapbook + There is a large library of clip art for use with Scrapbook + available from T/Maker. It imports and exports images produced by DOS applications.

T/Maker Company
1973 Landings Drive
Mountain View, CA 94043
(415) 962-0195

SnapShot SnapShot is an application for grey scale editing and autotracing of scanned images from the makers of PageMaker.

Aldus Corporation
411 First Avenue South
Seattle, WA 98104
(800) 333-2538/(206) 622-5500

Xerox Presents and Formbase Presents is a presentation graphics package for slides and charts, using clip art and multiple fonts. Formbase creates forms for businesses, as well as for databases that can store text and graphic images.

Xerox Corporation
P.O. Box 660512
Dallas, TX 75266-0512
(800) 822-8221/(214) 436-2616

Spreadsheets

Microsoft Excel Excel is Microsoft's answer to Lotus 1-2-3. It supports DDE cut and paste of spreadsheets and charts to Word for Windows.

Microsoft Corporation
16011 Northeast 36th Way
Box 97017
Redmond, WA 98073-9717
(800) 426-9400/(206) 882-8080

Databases

Superbase 2   Superbase 2 lets you create databases of images or text. It supports DDE cut and paste to Word for Windows. You can create databases for mail merge, reports, phone numbers for communications programs, and clip art.

Precision Incorporated
8404 Sterling Street A
Irving, TX 75063
(214) 929-4888

Specialized Hardware Options

There are a myriad of ways to input data into your PC for use in Word for Windows. You can use a mouse to draw images in paint and draw programs, but this is not the only way to input images. You can also expand your printing options with additional hardware.

Two other ways of inputting images, other than with a mouse, have a lot of supporting hardware. The first is by hand, the second is by scanning. If you want to produce images by hand more precisely than with a regular mouse, you can use a trackball mouse, a light pen (to write on your screen), or a digitizing tablet (also to write on your screen). The second way to acquire images for use in Word for Windows is to use desktop scanners to import line art and black and white photographs. You can also receive scanned images and text via a FAX board that goes in a slot in your PC.

There are many hardware options to expand the capabilities of your laser printer, especially if it is the HP LaserJet Series II printer. Many add-in controller boards will either add PostScript to your LaserJet or make it print faster. Both of these types of controller boards bypass the printer controller board in your LaserJet.

Manual Input Devices

Trackball mice are really upside-down mice. The idea of the trackball mouse has never really caught on. You get the least leverage over a trackball mouse of any kind of mouse. Trackball mice are useful primarily in situations in which desk space is extremely small.

Light pens are very useful for inputting data to a screen that is best coded by hand. An example of this is saving a signature as a graphic image file to be appended to letters. A signature can be inaccurately drawn with a mouse in a draw or paint program. The other option is to scan the signature. The light pen offers the quickest means of putting handwritten information on disk.

By far the most popular alternate input device is the digitizing tablet. A digitizing tablet is a small table top, usually about 15" x 15", attached to an input device that looks like a mouse with a gun sight in the middle. To use a digitizing tablet, first tape the two-dimensional image (on paper or plastic sheet, such as a photograph, a map, or an x-ray) to be traced on the tablet. Then place the sight hole in the input device over the boundary of the image that is to be traced. Keep the input device's button depressed and drag the input device's sight along the boundary. This boundary will be drawn on screen as the input device is dragged. The Kurta digitizing tablet (about $1100) is the best seller.

Scanners

Desktop scanners have evolved from the FAX machine, which is itself a low resolution scanner connected to a telephone. Most desktop scanners import images at 300 dpi (dots per inch) resolution, whereas FAX machines record images at 200 dpi.

Desktop scanners are also more sensitive to tonality. Scanners that record images using 4 bits per pixel (4 pieces of information coding each pixel, or dot) are capable of eight different levels of grey scale (halftone) information. This is adequate for line art or OCR (Optical Character Reading, which puts scanned text into a word processor file), which is either dark black lines or white background. Scanners that code 6 bits per pixel are capable of 64 levels of grey. These scanners are the minimum for scanning shaded pencil or pen drawings and do a fair job on less complex black and white photographs, such as faces. Inexpensive 8-bit scanners cost between $1200 and $2000. The HP ScanJet now supports 64 levels of grey, but has a street price of only about $1500. Scanners recording 8 bits per pixel are becoming common and, depending on the software you use, can do superb jobs with black and white photographs.

When buying a scanner, you must decide whether you want a sheet fed or flatbed scanner. Sheet fed scanners are used to OCR piles of pages. OCR software (such as Omnipage) capable of reading multifont documents has come a long way recently. However, this software remains expensive, usually over $1000. Much less expensive OCR software, included with many scanner controller software packages, can read typewritten pages with very high accuracy. You need a flatbed scanner if you want to scan images directly from books. You can always photocopy an image and feed it into a sheet fed scanner, but photocopying the image loses much of the detail unless it is line art.

Be careful of how much software you purchase with a scanner. Many of the scanner manufacturers try to sell scanner software for almost as much as the scanner itself. You would probably do better to not buy any of the scanner manufacturer's software. Many of the paint, draw, and grey-scale editing packages that run under Windows control scanners directly, bringing the scanned image up inside the program itself. There is also a great deal of third-party OCR software available for less than $500.

Add-in Boards for LaserJet Printers

JetNet/4+1   This is a controller card that allows five PCs to share one LaserJet without conflicts.

Qubit Corporation
544 Weddell Drive, #2
Sunnyvale, CA 94089-2123

JLaserPlus   JLaserPlus is a controller board that adds dedicated printer memory and accepts downloaded fonts.

Tall Tree Systems
2585 East Bayshore Road
Palo Alto, CA 94303
(415) 493-1980

LC and LX Add-in Controller Boards   These boards come with large sets of fonts. They speed up your LaserJet printer to its maximum capacity. They also increase the resolution of your printing. LaserMaster controller boards also allow you to proof PostScript output on your LaserJet.

LaserMaster Corporation
7156 Shady Oak Road
Eden Prairy, MN 55344
(612) 944-6069

PostScript in a Cartridge, JetScript   PostScript in a Cartridge puts true PostScript, not emulation, in your HP LaserJet IID or IIP. The JetScript (made by QMS for HP) controller board gives true PostScript capabilities to the LaserJet Series II.

Hewlett-Packard Company
11311 Chinden Boulevard
Boise, ID 83714
(800) 752-0900/(208) 323-2551

PS Jet Plus   PS Jet Plus provides PostScript capabilities for LaserJet printers.

The Laser Connection, Incorporated
P.O. Box 850296
Mobile, AL 36689
(205) 633-4300

QuadLaser PS   QuadLaser PS is a controller board that provides PostScript to LaserJet printers.

Quadram Corporation
One Quad Way
Norcross, GA 30093
(404) 923-6666

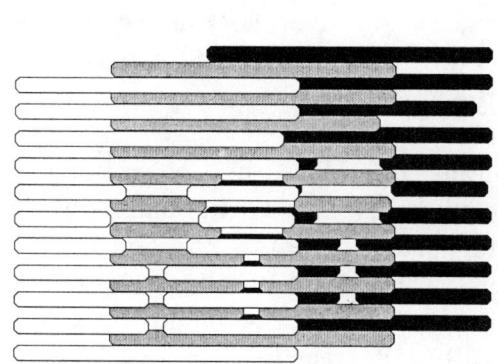

Font Character Sets and Sources

One of the major attractions of Word for Windows is the ease with which you can format documents with fonts. Fonts used in Word for Windows are installed in the [fonts] section in the WIN.INI file (see Chapter 11) via the Control Panel program.

A font is a set of characters, representing a particular typeface, assigned to different positions in the 256 position ASCII character table. All windows applications use the Windows/ANSI character set. You can get any of these characters to be displayed on the screen and then be printed, by first activating the NUMLOCK key; then hold down the ALT key and type the ASCII number code. For the characters on the alphanumeric part of the keyboard, this is unnecessary. It is necessary, however, for the foreign language characters and symbols in the Windows/ANSI character set. You will also need to know the ASCII character assignments for symbol fonts like Zapf Dingbats.

Tables E-1 through E-5 list the characters in the Windows/ANSI character set as well as the characters in other major ASCII character sets, including the entire Bitstream International character set. The IBM PC character set is used in most DOS applications. The HP Roman-8 character set is used in the fonts that come with HP LaserJet printers. The Ventura character set is used in that desktop publishing application.

This appendix ends with a listing of font sources and utilities useful for Microsoft Windows. Many of these utilities automatically install both screen and printer fonts in Windows, allowing you to avoid using the Control Panel program to install fonts one at a time.

Font Sources

Most of the fonts available for use in Windows are sold as software typeface outlines. Font cartridges are another major source of fonts. Both sources offer different benefits to the user.

A typeface outline vendor supplies a font generator that scales the outlines to a desired point size, thus creating a font. These fonts are then installed in Windows, usually with software supplied by the same vendor.

Table E-1.

Windows/ANSI (AN)

	0	1	2	3	4	5	6	7	8	9
00										
10										
20										
30				!	"	#	$	%	&	'
40	(	)	*	+	,	-	.	/	0	1
50	2	3	4	5	6	7	8	9	:	;
60	<	=	>	?	@	A	B	C	D	E
70	F	G	H	I	J	K	L	M	N	O
80	P	Q	R	S	T	U	V	W	X	Y
90	Z	[	\	]	^	_	`	a	b	c
100	d	e	f	g	h	i	j	k	l	m
110	n	o	p	q	r	s	t	u	v	w
120	x	y	z	{	|	}	~		fi	fl
130	ff	ffi	ffl				‘	’	“	”
140	,	„	†	‡	—	‘	’	■	™	£
150	ƒ	Ÿ	Œ	œ	Š	š	Ž	ž	Ł	ł
160		¡	¢	£	¤	¥	¦	§	¨	©
170	ª	«	¬		®	¯	°	±	²	³
180	´	µ	¶	·	¸	¹	º	»	¼	½
190	¾	¿	À	Á	Â	Ã	Ä	Å	Æ	Ç
200	È	É	Ê	Ë	Ì	Í	Î	Ï	Ð	Ñ
210	Ò	Ó	Ô	Õ	Ö	–	Ø	Ù	Ú	Û
220	Ü	Ý	Þ	ß	à	á	â	ã	ä	å
230	æ	ç	è	é	ê	ë	ì	í	î	ï
240	ð	ñ	ò	ó	ô	õ	ö	•	ø	ù
250	ú	û	ü	ý	þ	ÿ				

IBM PC (PC)

	0	1	2	3	4	5	6	7	8	9
00		☺	●	♥	♦	♣	♠	•	◘	○
10	◙	♂	♀	♪	♫	☼	►	◄	↕	‼
20	¶	§	▬	↨	↑	↓	→	←	∟	↔
30	▲	▼		!	"	#	$	%	&	'
40	(	)	*	+	,	-	.	/	0	1
50	2	3	4	5	6	7	8	9	:	;
60	<	=	>	?	@	A	B	C	D	E
70	F	G	H	I	J	K	L	M	N	O
80	P	Q	R	S	T	U	V	W	X	Y
90	Z	[	\	]	^	_	`	a	b	c
100	d	e	f	g	h	i	j	k	l	m
110	n	o	p	q	r	s	t	u	v	w
120	x	y	z	{	|	}	~	⌂	Ç	ü
130	é	â	ä	à	å	ç	ê	ë	è	ï
140	î	ì	Ä	Å	É	æ	Æ	ô	ö	ò
150	û	ù	ÿ	Ö	Ü	¢	£	¥	₧	ƒ
160	á	í	ó	ú	ñ	Ñ	ª	º	¿	⌐
170	¬	½	¼	¡	«	»	░	▒	▓	│
180	┤	╡	╢	╖	╕	╣	║	╗	╝	╜
190	╛	┐	└	┴	┬	├	─	┼	╞	╟
200	╚	╔	╩	╦	╠	═	╬	╧	╨	╤
210	╥	╙	╘	╒	╓	╫	╪	┘	┌	█
220	▄	▌	▐	▀	α	β	Γ	π	Σ	σ
230	µ	τ	Φ	θ	Ω	δ	∞	φ	ε	∩
240	≡	±	≥	≤	⌠	⌡	÷	≈	°	•
250	·	√	η	²	■					

Windows/ANSI and IBM PC Character Sets (Adapted with permission from the documentation for SoftCraft Font Selection Pack, SoftCraft, Inc.)

Table E-2.

HP Roman-8 (R8)

	0	1	2	3	4	5	6	7	8	9
00										
10										
20										
30				!	"	#	$	%	&	'
40	(	)	*	+	,	-	.	/	0	1
50	2	3	4	5	6	7	8	9	:	;
60	<	=	>	?	@	A	B	C	D	E
70	F	G	H	I	J	K	L	M	N	O
80	P	Q	R	S	T	U	V	W	X	Y
90	Z	[	\	]	^	_	`	a	b	c
100	d	e	f	g	h	i	j	k	l	m
110	n	o	p	q	r	s	t	u	v	w
120	x	y	z	{	|	}	~	▒		
130										
140										
150										
160		À	Â	È	Ê	Ë	Î	Ï	´	`
170	ˆ	¨	˜	Ù	Û	£	¯	Ý	ý	°
180	Ç	ç	Ñ	ñ	¡	¿	¤	£	¥	§
190	ƒ	¢	â	ê	ô	û	á	é	ó	ú
200	à	è	ò	ù	ä	ë	ö	ü	Å	î
210	Ø	Æ	å	í	ø	æ	Ä	ì	Ö	Ü
220	É	ï	ß	Ô	Á	Ã	ã	Ð	đ	Í
230	Ì	Ó	Ò	Õ	õ	Š	š	Ú	Ÿ	ÿ
240	Þ	þ	·	µ	¶	¾	—	¼	½	ª
250	º	«	■	»	±					

HP Roman Extension (RX)

	0	1	2	3	4	5	6	7	8	9
00										
10										
20										
30				À	Â	È	Ê	Ë	Î	Ï
40	´	`	ˆ	¨	˜	Ù	Û	¯		Ý
50	ý	°	Ç	ç	Ñ	ñ	¡	¿	¤	£
60	¥	§	ƒ	¢	â	ê	ô	û	á	é
70	ó	ú	à	è	ò	ù	ä	ë	ö	ü
80	Å	î	Ø	Æ	å	í	ø	æ	Ä	ì
90	Ö	Ü	É	ï	ß	Ô	Á	Ã	ã	Ð
100	đ	Í	Ì	Ó	Ò	Õ	õ	Š	š	Ú
110	Ÿ	ÿ	Þ	þ	·	µ	¶	¾	—	¼
120	½	ª	º	«	■	»	±			
130										
140										
150										
250										

HP Roman-8 and HP Roman Extension Character Sets (Adapted with permission from the documentation for SoftCraft Font Selection Pack, SoftCraft, Inc.)

Table E-3.

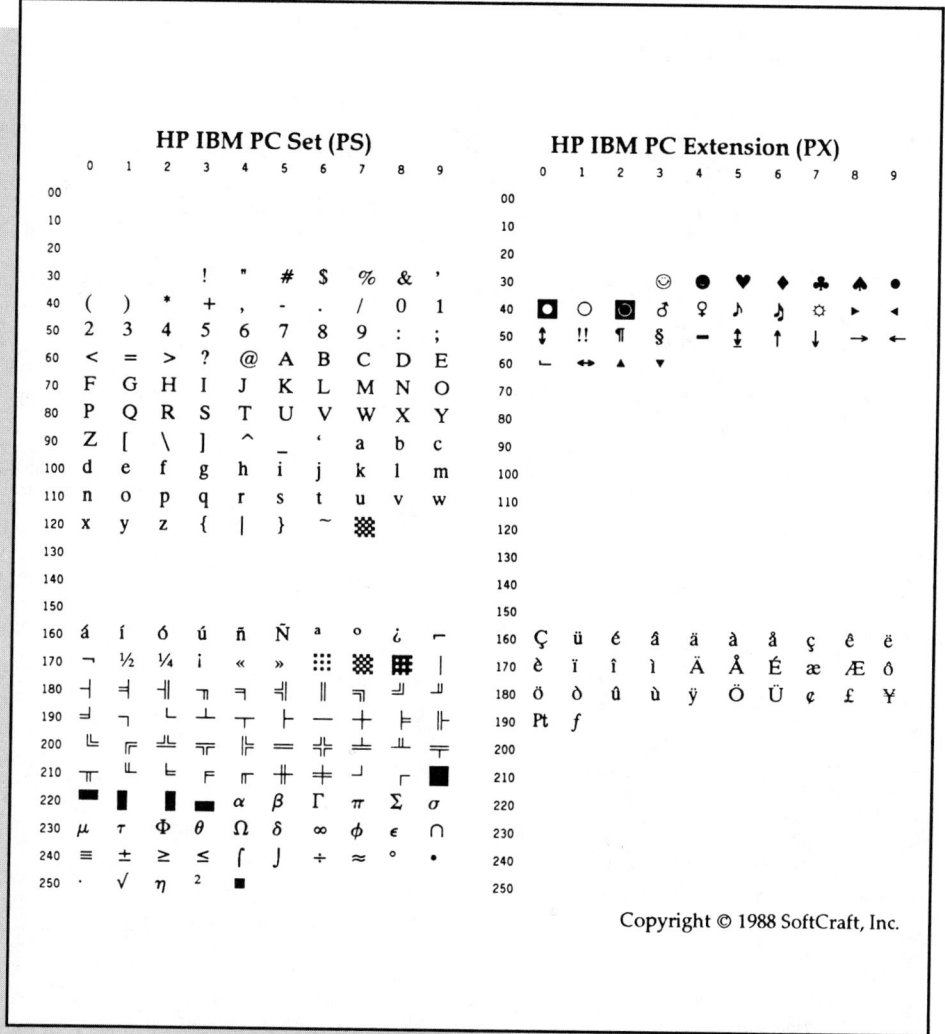

HP IBM PC and HP IBM PC Extension Character Sets (Adapted with permission from the documentation for SoftCraft Font Selection Pack, SoftCraft, Inc.)

Table E-4.

Ventura (SF)

	0	1	2	3	4	5	6	7	8	9
00										
10										
20										
30				!	"	#	$	%	&	'
40	(	)	*	+	,	-	.	/	0	1
50	2	3	4	5	6	7	8	9	:	;
60	<	=	>	?	@	A	B	C	D	E
70	F	G	H	I	J	K	L	M	N	O
80	P	Q	R	S	T	U	V	W	X	Y
90	Z	[	\	]	^	_	`	a	b	c
100	d	e	f	g	h	i	j	k	l	m
110	n	o	p	q	r	s	t	u	v	w
120	x	y	z	{	|	}	~			
130										
140										
150										
160	„	À	Â	È	Ê	Ë	Î	Ï	©	®
170	™	‹	›	Ù	Û		‰	"	"	°
180	Ç	ç	Ñ	ñ	¡	¿	¤	£	¥	§
190	ƒ	¢	â	ê	ô	û	á	é	ó	ú
200	à	è	ò	ù	ä	ë	ö	ü	Å	î
210	Ø	Æ	å	í	ø	æ	Ä	ì	Ö	Ü
220	É	ï	ß	Ô	Á	Ã	ã			Í
230	Ì	Ó	Ò	Õ	õ	Š	š	Ú	Ÿ	ÿ
240	Œ	œ	¶	†	‡	—	–			ª
250	°	«	•	»	Ž	…				

Ventura Code Correspondence

	0	1	2	3	4	5	6	7	8	9
160	192 „	182 À	200 Â	201 È	202 Ê	203 Ë	206 Î	207 Ï	189 ©	190 ®
170	191 ™	171 ‹	172 ›	213 Ù	215 Û		194 ‰	169 "	170 "	198 °
180	128 Ç	135 ç	165 Ñ	164 ñ	173 ¡	165 ¿	158 ¤	156 £	157 ¥	185 §
190	159 ƒ	155 ¢	131 â	136 ê	147 ô	150 û	160 á	130 é	162 ó	163 ú
200	133 à	138 è	149 ò	151 ù	132 ä	137 ë	148 ö	129 ü	143 Å	140 î
210	178 Ø	146 Æ	134 å	161 í	179 ø	145 æ	142 Ä	141 ì	153 Ö	154 Ü
220	144 É	139 ï	217 ß	210 Ô	199 Á	183 Ã	176 ã			205 Í
230	204 Ì	209 Ó	208 Ò	184 Õ	177 õ	211 Š	212 š	214 Ú	216 Ÿ	152 ÿ
240	181 Œ	180 œ	188 ¶	187 †	186 ‡	197 —	196 –			166 ª
250	167 °	174 «	195 •	175 »	218 Ž	193 …				

Ventura Character Set (Adapted with permission from the documentation for SoftCraft Font Selection Pack, SoftCraft, Inc.)

Table E-5.

	!	"	#	$	%	&	'	(	)	*	+	,	-	.	/
0032	0033	0034	0035	0036	0037	0038	0039	0040	0041	0042	0043	0044	0045	0046	0047
0	1	2	3	4	5	6	7	8	9	:	;	<	=	>	?
0048	0049	0050	0051	0052	0053	0054	0055	0056	0057	0058	0059	0060	0061	0062	0063
@	A	B	C	D	E	F	G	H	I	J	K	L	M	N	O
0064	0065	0066	0067	0068	0069	0070	0071	0072	0073	0074	0075	0076	0077	0078	0079
P	Q	R	S	T	U	V	W	X	Y	Z	[	\	]	^	_
0080	0081	0082	0083	0084	0085	0086	0087	0088	0089	0090	0091	0092	0093	0094	0095
`	a	b	c	d	e	f	g	h	i	j	k	l	m	n	o
0096	0097	0098	0099	0100	0101	0102	0103	0104	0105	0106	0107	0108	0109	0110	0111
p	q	r	s	t	u	v	w	x	y	z	{	|	}	~	fi
0112	0113	0114	0115	0116	0117	0118	0119	0120	0121	0122	0123	0124	0125	0126	0129
fl	£	¢	f	‰	/	·	'	"	"	,	„	†	‡	§	–
0130	0131	0132	0133	0134	0135	0136	0137	0138	0139	0140	0141	0142	0143	0144	0145
—	Å	Æ	Ø	Œ	å	æ	ø	œ	ß	ı	‹	›	«	»	¿
0146	0147	0148	0149	0150	0151	0152	0153	0154	0155	0156	0157	0158	0159	0160	0161
¡	´	`	`	^	^	¨	¨	ˉ	ˉ	ˇ	ˇ	˙	ˉ		
0162	0163	0164	0165	0166	0167	0168	0169	0170	0171	0172	0173	0174	0175	0177	0178
˘	˜	°	°	Ç	ç	⅛	¼	⅜	½	⅝	¾	⅞	⅓	⅔	¹
0179	0180	0181	0182	0183	0184	0185	0186	0187	0188	0189	0190	0191	0192	0193	0194
²	³	⁴	⁵	⁶	⁷	⁸	⁹	⁰	Đ	Ł	Ą	Ę	đ	ł	Ľ
0195	0196	0197	0198	0199	0200	0201	0202	0203	0225	0226	0227	0228	0229	0230	0231
J	ą	ę	ĿL	ʜ	·	'	˝	˙	ˍ	.	,	‚	‚	ˍ	
0232	0233	0234	0235	0236	0237	0238	0239	0240	0241	0242	0243	0244	0245	0246	0248

Bitstream International Character Set (Adapted with permission from the documentation for SoftCraft Font Selection Pack, SoftCraft, Inc.)

Table E-5.

- 0249	ń 0320	Ń 0321	ñ 0322	Ñ 0323	ň 0324	Ň 0325	ó 0326	Ó 0327	ò 0328	Ò 0329	ô 0330	Ô 0331	ŏ 0332	Ö 0333	õ 0334
Ō 0335	ú 0336	Ú 0337	ù 0338	Ù 0339	û 0340	Û 0341	ü 0342	Ü 0343	ū 0344	Ū 0345	ů 0346	Ů 0347	ÿ 0348	Ÿ 0349	ý 0350
Ý 0351	ɨ 0353	ɨ 0354	ɨ 0355	) 0362	(0363	‾ 0366	´ 0367	l' 0368	Ī 0369	ī 0370	Ï 0371	ï 0372	Î 0373	î 0374	Ì 0375
ì 0376	í 0377	í 0378	Ě 0379	ě 0380	Ë 0383	ë 0384	Ê 0385	ê 0386	È 0387	è 0388	É 0389	é 0390	Ā 0391	ā 0392	Ä 0393
ä 0394	Â 0395	â 0396	À 0397	à 0398	Á 0399	á 0400	'n 0404	' 0410	!! 0411	Pt 0414	— 0418	ų 0421	' 0422	… 0423	Þ 0424
þ 0425	ð 0426	¥ 0427	ij 0433	IJ 0434	¡ 0435	¤ 0436	¶ 0442	ffl 0446	ffi 0447	ff 0448	– 0449	× 0450	÷ 0451	± 0452	≡ 0453
≠ 0454	≈ 0455	≥ 0456	≤ 0457	↓ 0458	← 0459	→ 0460	↑ 0461	↕ 0462	↔ 0463	∈ 0464	∩ 0465	⌠ 0470	⌡ 0471	√ 0476	∞ 0478
▬ 0479	▬ 0480	█ 0481	█ 0482	■ 0484	¬ 0486	⌐ 0487	- 0488	+ 0489	Γ 0500	Δ 0501	Θ 0505	Σ 0515	Φ 0518	Ω 0521	α 0522
β 0523	δ 0526	ε 0527	η 0529	θ 0530	μ 0534	π 0538	σ 0540	τ 0542	φ 0544	♪ 0562	♫ 0563	© 0564	® 0565	™ 0566	■ 0567
□ 0568	' 0570	" 0571	° 0572	↕ 0573	· 0575	● 0576	● 0577	◘ 0579	► 0581	◄ 0582	▼ 0583	▲ 0584	♂ 0585	♀ 0586	♥ 0587
♣ 0588	♦ 0589	♠ 0590	– 0591	❙ 0592	▦ 0593	▨ 0594	▦ 0595	☼ 0598	☺ 0599	● 0600	ť 0605	Ţ 0606	ŷ 0607	Ŷ 0608	ź 0609
Ź 0610	ż 0611	Ž 0612	ż 0613	Ż 0614	ă 0619	Ă 0620	ć 0621	Ć 0622	č 0623	Č 0624	ď 0625	đ 0628	Đ 0629	ě 0630	Ē 0631

Bitstream International Character Set (Adapted with permission from the documentation for SoftCraft Font Selection Pack, SoftCraft, Inc.)(continued)

Table E-5.

Char	Code	Char	Code	Char	Code	Char	Code	Char	Code	Char	Code	Char	Code	Char	Code
g̊	0634	Ģ	0637	ɪ	0638	Ī	0639	i	0640	İ	0641	į	0642	Į	0643
ķ	0644	Ķ	0645	ĺ	0646	Ļ	0647	ī	0648	Ĺ	0649	ļ	0650	Ļ	0651
Ñ	0653	ņ	0654	Ņ	0655	ő	0656	Ő	0657	ŕ	0660	Ř	0661	ŗ	0662
Ŗ	0663	ś	0664	Ś	0665	š	0666	Š	0667	Š	0669	ş	0670	Ş	0671
ī	0674	Ť	0675	ţ	0676	Ţ	0677	ū	0678	Ū	0679	ű	0680	Ú	0681
ŵ	0682	Ŵ	0683	ẙ	0684	Ÿ	0685	ɸ	0693	∝	0695	¬	0797	/	1223
˙	1364	´	1365	`	1368	ˆ	1369	˜	1372	¨	1373	ˉ	1376	¨	1377
ˉ	1380	ˉ	1381	ˉ	1384	ˉ	1385	ˎ	1388	ˉ	1392	ˉ	1393	˜	1396
˘	1397	•	1400	•	1401	L·	1661	l·	1667	·	1743	ˆ	1744	·	1747
ˆ	1748	،	1751	،	1752	،	1753	ˍ	1756	·	1761	·	1766	·	1771
،	1776	•	1996	1	2022	2	2028	3	2034	4	2040	5	2046	6	2052
7	2058	8	2064	9	2070	0	2076	ă	2647	Ā	2653	D'	2776	ğ	2984
Ğ	2990	ñ	3396	ŕ	3580	Ř	3586	ş	3704	ş	3738	Ş	3744	=	4472
ˊ	4488	ˋ	4489	ˌ	4490	Fr	4524	∓	4736	~	4744	⌐	4903	●	5042
│	5085	ℓ	5147	■	5196	°	5243	•	5244	∟	5249	ε	5262	☉	5371
⊛	5372	○	5403	◎	5408	∎	5410	⌂	5418	─	5421	⌐	5422	⌐	5423
└	5424	┼	5427	┬	5428	┴	5429	├	5430	┤	5431	│	5432	=	5434
⌐	5435	⌐	5436	⌐	5437	⌐	5438	┼	5441	┬	5442	┴	5443	├	5444
┤	5445	‖	5446	├	5461	┤	5462	┴	5463	┬	5464	┼	5465	├	5466
┤	5467	┤	5468	a	5510	e	5514	i	5518	l	5521	m	5522	n	5523
o	5524	r	5527	s	5528	t	5529	┴	5536	┬	5537	┐	5538	┐	5539
┘	5540	┘	5541	⌐	5542	└	5543	⌐	5544	└	5545	\	5548	∏	5554
	5594		5595		5596	☺	6458										

Copyright © 1988 SoftCraft, Inc.

Bitstream International Character Set (Adapted with permission from the documentation for SoftCraft Font Selection Pack, SoftCraft, Inc.) (continued)

Along with the font scaling and installation utilities sold with typeface outlines, there are numerous font editors and special effects packages. Font editors can be used to redraw particular characters in a font, or to add new characters to a font. Font editors are useful for creating special symbols, logos, and small images that will be repetitively used, like the characters in a font. You can also add graphic images to a font with many font editors.

Font special effect packages can add shadows, shaded backgrounds, or pattern backgrounds to the characters in a font. You can also bold, tilt, or even rotate the characters in a font with many special effects packages. Special effects fonts are useful for calling attention to headings in advertisements, brochures, and internal company reports.

You may also wish to consider LaserJet font cartridges. Documents formatted with font cartridge fonts print very quickly since there is no scaling of typeface outlines or downloading of fonts. Also, the fonts in font cartridges do not take up any room on your hard disk. Make sure there is a Windows installation program with a font cartridge before you buy it.

Word for Windows allows you to quickly apply all of these font variations. To become familiar with font management, editing, special effects, and the tasteful use of particular typefaces, read the font columns in desktop publishing magazines (see Appendix F).

Typeface Vendors

A-Z Series and ProCollection Font Cartridges   These are font cartridges used with Windows printer drivers in Word for Windows Setup program (see Appendix C) or through the Windows Control Panel program (see Chapter 1).

Hewlett-Packard Company
P.O. Box 10301
Palo Alto, CA 95303-0890
(800) 752-0900/(415) 857-1501

A-to-Z and Hardfont Font Cartridges   A-to-Z contains all fonts in separate font cartridges in HP's A through Z series. Hardfont cartridges mimic this series.

Everex
48431 Milmont Drive
Fremont, CA 94538
(800) 821-0806, ext. 2226/(415) 683-2226

AlphaJet and Maxi Font Cartridges   The AlphaJet series mimics the HP A-Z series of font cartridges. The Maxi series combines different sets of fonts from the HP A-Z series.

Anacom General Corporation
Computer Products Division
1335 South Claudina Street
Anaheim, CA 92805-6235
(714) 774-8080

Custom Font Cartridges   This is a large line of legal font cartridges. These custom font cartridges are made to order.

GNU Business Information Systems, Inc.
100 Hilltop Road
Ramsey, NJ 07446
(201) 825-1222
800-222-3571

Digi-Duit!   This is a typeface library of hundreds of faces for less than $500.

Digi-Fonts, Inc.
3000 Youngfield Street, Suite 285
Lakewood, CO 80215
(800) 242-5665/(303) 233-8113

FontMaker   FontMaker intercepts documents as they are sent to the printer. It then scales high quality typeface outlines on the fly to the sizes called for by the document.

Good Software Corporation
13601 Preston Road, Suite 500W
Dallas, TX 75240
(214) 239-6085

Fontware   Bitstream offers a very large library of typefaces of the highest quality. Fontware is the most widely used source of fonts in the PC arena.

Bitstream Inc.
Athenaeum House
215 First Street
Cambridge, MA 02142
(800) 522-3668/(617) 497-6222

Glyphix   SWFTE has two libraries of typefaces, the Business Series and the high quality Foundry Series. These typefaces are much less expensive than the competition.

SWFTE International, Ltd.
P.O. Box 219
Rockland, DE 19732
(800) 237-9383/(302) 429-8434

Interfont Font Cartridges   This company specializes in large font set font cartridges, and has a large line of ready made cartridges. Font cartridges are also made to order.

Intercon Associates, Inc.
One Cambridge Place
P.O. Box 18099
1850 Winston Road South
Rochester, NY 14618
(716) 244-1250

JetFont Superset and A-Z cartridges   The Superset font cartridge has 150 fonts.

Computer Peripherals, Inc.
667 Rancho Canejo Blvd.
Newbury Park, CA 91320
(800) 854-7600/(805) 499-5751

MEGAFONTS   Express Lane Data is a new company with many inexpensive typeface outlines.

Express Lane Data
2900 Wilcrest, Suite 425
Houston, TX 77042
(800) 645-2287/(713) 932-1635

MoreFonts   MicroLogic Software is a quickly growing font vendor with inexpensive, high quality typefaces.

MicroLogic Software
6400 Hollis Street, Suite 9
Emeryville, CA 94608
(415) 652-5464
(800) 888-9078

PostScript Fonts   To use PostScript fonts, you need a PostScript laser printer. There are many PostScript font vendors for the Apple Macintosh, but far fewer for the PC. The largest PostScript library for the PC is that of Adobe.

Adobe Systems Inc.
1585 Charleston Road, P.O. Box 7900
Mountain View, CA 94039-7900
(800) 344-8335/(415) 961-4400

Publisher's PowerPak   Publisher's PowerPak can generate fonts from typeface outlines on the fly as a document requiring those fonts is sent to the printer. Atech markets its own line of typeface outlines in addition to the high quality Monotype typeface outlines. The Monotype typeface outlines are less expensive than comparable products from Bitstream and HP/Compugraphic.

Atech Software
5962 La Place Court, Suite 245
Carlsbad, CA 92008
(619) 438-6883/FAX: (619) 438-6898

Super Cartridges I and II   These are easy to use font cartridges with large font sets.

IQ Engineering
P.O. Box 60955
Sunnyvale, CA 94086
(408) 734-1161

Turbo, Combination, and LaserJet Compatible Font Cartridges
Turbo font cartridges have font sets useful for legal and desktop publishing applications. The LaserJet Compatible series mimics the HP A-Z series. The Combination series combines various HP cartridges in the A-Z series.

UDP Data Products, Inc.
1309 Laurel Avenue
Manhattan Beach, CA 90266
(213) 782-9800

25 Cartridges in One, Headlines, Pacific Page, Plotter in a Cartridge, Z Cartridge, LaserJet Memory Upgrades This is a complete line of LaserJet font cartridges and memory upgrades. 25 Cartridges in One contains full HP A-Z font cartridges. Pacific Page is a PostScript emulator for the LaserJet.

Pacific Data Products
6404 Nancy Ridge Drive
San Diego, CA 92121
(619) 552-0880/FAX (619) 552-0889

Type Director Type Director runs under DOS, but it generates and installs screen printer fonts in Windows. HP/Compugraphic have introduced a large library of scalable typeface outlines. These typefaces are superbly designed.

Agfa Corporation
90 Industrial Way
Wilmington, MA 01887
(800) 873-FONT/(508) 658-5600

Hewlett-Packard Company
P.O. Box 10301
Palo Alto, CA 95303-0890
(800) 752-0900/(415) 857-1501

VS Font Packs VS Font Pack is the last of a breed. They are very high quality font packages.

VS Software
209 West 2nd Street
P.O. Box 6158
Little Rock, AR 72216
(501) 376-2083

Font Editing

MSD Edit   This application allows you to edit and install Windows printer and screen fonts.

Mephistopheles Systems
3629 Lankershim Blvd.
Hollywood, CA 90068
(818) 762-8150

Megafont   Megafont lets you convert scanned images into fonts. Scanning service is provided.

Advanced Vision Research
2201 Qume Drive
San Jose, CA 95133
(800) 54-IMAGE/(408) 434-1115

PC Metafont   PC Metafont has design font elements like serifs, bowls, strokes, descenders, and ascenders. It scales outlines into fonts.

Personal Tex, Inc.
12 Madrona Avenue
Mill Valley, CA 95133
(415) 388-8853

Profont Editing System Profont Editing System imports graphic images, including logos and signatures, for conversion to font format.

> FontCenter
> P.O. Box 6007
> Lynwood, WA 98036
> (206) 355-8529

Publisher's Type Foundry This is a two part font editor. You can import and pixel edit font characters or graphic images in the bitmap editor. The outline editor scales clean bitmap objects to the needed point sizes.

> Z-Soft Corporation
> 450 Franklin Road, #100
> Marietta, GA 30067
> (404) 428-0008

SoftCraft Font Editor This application imports most graphic image formats and converts image files into fonts. It includes many drawing tools and offers simultaneous zoomed and unzoomed views of characters.

> SoftCraft Inc.
> 16 North Carroll Street, #500
> Madison, WI 53703
> (800) 351-0500/(608) 257-3300

SLEd and FontGen V SLEd (Signature Logo Editor) offers 17 drawing tools. FontGen V offers a full view of a font character set and font special effects. FontGen V generates screen fonts for Windows and GEM applications.

VS Software
209 West 2nd Street
P.O. Box 6158
Little Rock, AR 72216
(501) 376-2083

Font Management

Font Solution Pack   Font Solution Pack is a complete font management package. Its font generator supports both Fontware (Bitstream) and Type Director (HP/Compugraphic) font outlines and Microsoft Word 5.0. It installs printer and screen fonts in Windows. It includes a font editor and special effects modules.

SoftCraft Inc.
16 North Carroll St., #500
Madison, WI 53703
(800) 351-0500/(608) 257-3300

FontSpace   FontSpace compresses font files by as much as 97%, saving hard disk space. It works on the fly and is transparent to the user.

Isogon Corporation
330 7th Avenue
New York, NY 10001
(212) 967-2424

MSDmanager and MSDprn   MSDware MSDmanager creates a printer driver with MSD fonts. MSDware MSDprn converts portrait to landscape.

Mephistopheles Systems
3629 Lankershim Blvd.
Hollywood, CA 90068
(818) 762-8150

Tool Kit   Tool Kit is a complete font manager. It creates a printer driver and works in conjunction with VS Font Packs.

VS Software
209 West 2nd Street
P.O. Box 6158
Little Rock, AR 72216
(501) 376-2083

Special Effects

Draw!, Headline, Newfont   Draw! is a full-featured presentation graphics package that evolved out of Headline. Headline adds special effects to PostScript fonts which require adjustment of the baseline, such as contort, slant, and rotate. Newfont adds special effects that require devices, such as outline and shadowing of characters.

Corel Systems Corporation
Corel Building
1600 Carling
Ottawa, Ontario K1Z 8R7
Canada
(613) 728-8200

Font Effects and Spinfont   Font Effects creates special effects such as shadows, outlines, pattern infills, slanting, and reverse video. Spinfont rotates font baselines to write around circles, arches, or diagonally across a page.

SoftCraft Inc.
16 North Carroll Street, #500
Madison, WI 53703
(800) 351-0500/(608) 257-3300

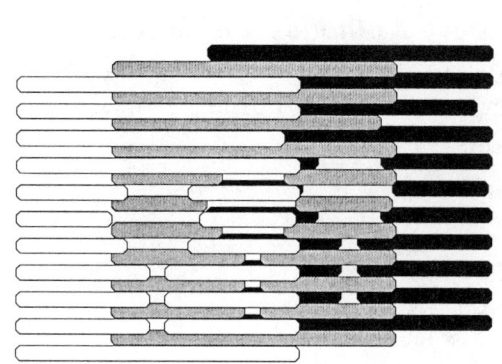

Journals,
Books, and
User Groups

Word publishing programs like Word for Windows aid your exploration of new applications of fonts and graphic images. You can also get ideas from journals, books, and colleagues in PC user groups. You will have to look up your own local PC user groups. However, some of the nationally known journals, books, and user groups that should aid your exploration are listed in this appendix, for your convenience.

Journals

Desktop Publishing, Bove & Rhodes' Inside Report   This is a very expensive, authoritative discussion of issues, hardware, and software. The husband and wife editorial team also writes for many other publications.

> Desktop Publishing
> 501 Second Street
> San Francisco, CA 94107
> (415) 546-7722

Electronic Designs   This is a how-to newsletter for desktop publishers. It covers complex topics like adding color, PostScript graphics, and using type. *Electronic Design* discusses PC issues, but is heavily Macintosh oriented.

> Dynamic Graphics, Incorporated
> 6000 North Forest Park Drive
> Peoria, IL 61614-3592
> (800) 255-8800

Electronic Publishing & Printing   This publication often offers free subscriptions. It covers all of the issues relevant to PC desktop publishers.

> *Electronic Publishing & Printing*
> Circulation Department
> 29 North Wacker Drive
> Chicago, IL 60606
> (312) 726-2802

InfoWorld *InfoWorld* is a comprehensive industry weekly out of San Francisco; it is free to qualified applicants (such as volume PC buyers). Stories foreshadow or report industry trends and events.

> *InfoWorld*
> P.O. Box 5994
> Pasadena, CA 91117
> (818) 577-7233

LaserJet Journal This is Hewlett-Packard's LaserJet newsletter. Keep up with the latest "approved" happenings with the LaserJet family of printers. No reportage or advertising of third party add-ons and support for LaserJet printers is included.

> *LaserJet Journal*
> 1945 Techny Road, #8
> Northbrook, IL 60062
> (800) 323-2686/(312) 498-0920

National Association of Desktop Publishers Journal This journal mainly features reprints from recent articles and books that show how to get different jobs done. The journal is one benefit of joining the association.

> National Association of Desktop Publishers
> 1260 Boylston Street
> Boston, MA 02215
> (617) 437-6472

PC Magazine *PC Magazine* is a bi-weekly covering the whole PC industry and is the number one source of information on PC software and hardware. One or more issues per year include roundups on all desktop publishing software, graphic image software, fonts, and Windows applications. If you only get one journal, get this one.

PC Magazine
P.O. Box 54093
Boulder, CO 80322
(800) 289-0429

PC Publishing   *PC Publishing* covers all PC desktop publishing issues. It is one of the industry's oldest desktop publishing magazines.

PC Publishing
950 Lee Street
Des Plaines, IL 60016
(312) 296-0770

PC Week   This is a comprehensive industry published weekly out of Boston. It is free to qualified applicants (such as volume PC buyers) and has stories that foreshadow or report industry trends and events.

PC Week
Customer Service Department
P.O. Box 5970
Cherry Hill, NJ 08034
(609) 428-5000

Personal Publishing   *Personal Publishing* covers all PC desktop publishing issues.

Personal Publishing
191 South Gary Avenue
Carol Stream, IL 60188
(800) 727-6937/(312) 462-2225

Publish!   *Publish!* covers all issues of desktop publishing and is one of the industry's oldest desktop publishing magazines. It was originally biased toward the high end Macintosh/PostScript way of doing things, but its coverage has become more balanced of late.

> *Publish!*
> Subscription Department
> 501 Second Street
> San Francisco, CA 94107
> (800) 222-2990/(415) 243-0600

Seybold Report on Desktop Publishing   This is a very expensive, authoritative discussion of issues, hardware, and software. The publishers are the sponsors of the bi-annual Seybold Conference on Desktop Publishing (fall in San Francisco; spring in Boston).

> Seybold Publications, Incorporated
> Box 644
> Media, PA 19063
> (215) 565-2480

U&lc (Upper and lowercase)   This is a free, stylish, oversized monthly journal published by ITC (International Typeface Corporation) devoted to typeface applications.

> *U&lc*
> Subscription Department
> 2 Hammarskjold Plaza
> New York, NY 10017
> (212) 371-0699

Word for Word   *Word for Word* is a monthly newsletter dedicated to Microsoft Word users. It covers the nitty gritty issues that help you get the job done. The Cobb group plans to begin publishing a Word for Windows newsletter by Spring 1990.

Word for Word
The Cobb Group
9420 Bunsen Parkway, Suite 300
Louisville, KY 40220
(800) 223-8720

Books

Desktop Publishing Bible (J. Stockford, ed.)   This book covers all aspects of desktop publishing on PC, Macintosh, and UNIX based systems.

Howard W. Sams & Co.
Indianapolis

Desktop Publishing Type & Graphics (D. McClelland, C. Danuloff)   This book covers the use of fonts for both PostScript and LaserJet users.

Harcourt, Brace, Jovanovich, Publishers
New York

Desktop Publishing with Style (D. Will-Harris)   This volume covers all issues related to assembling and implementing either a word publishing or desktop publishing workstation. It also covers document production techniques.

And Books
South Bend, IN

Editing Your Newsletter (M. Beach) This book covers all aspects of creating an effective newsletter via word publishing or desktop publishing means.

> Coast to Coast
> Portland, OR

LaserJet Companion (M.Crane, J. Pierce) *LaserJet Companion* covers all issues relevant to LaserJet owners.

> The Cobb Group
> Louisville, KY

LaserJet Unlimited (T. Nace, M. Gardner), Macintosh Font Book (E. Fenton), Inside PostScript (F. Braswell) *LaserJet Unlimited* covers all aspects of LaserJet printers. *Macintosh Font Book* covers font issues that are of interest to both PostScript and LaserJet users. *Inside PostScript* shows how to write programs to take maximum advantage of PostScript.

> Peachpit Press, Incorporated
> Berkeley, CA

Looking Good in Print, The Makeover Book (R. Parker) This is a pair of best selling books on design for word publishing and desktop publishing. They are the best guides to snazzing up documents for beginning users of Word for Windows.

> Ventana Press
> Chapel Hill, NC

The Hewlett-Packard LaserJet Printer Handbook This handbook covers all issues relevant to LaserJet owners.

Dow Jones/Irwin
New York

The LaserJet Handbook & Laser Printer Power Pack (S. Bennett, P. Randall)   This book covers all issues relevant to LaserJet owners and includes a disk.

Brady
New York

Typographic Design (R. Carter, B. Day, P. Meggs)   This book has lessons in the use of type.

Van Nostrand Reinhold
New York

Using Type Right (P. Brady) Ready-to-use Layouts for Desktop Design (D. Collier, K. Floyd)   *Using Type Right* has basic lessons in using type. *Ready-to-use Layouts for Desktop Design* includes lessons in how to lay out type and graphic images and has many examples.

North Light Books
Cincinnati

User Groups

Adobe Conference on CompuServe   Access CompuServe E-Mail network and type **GO ADOBE**

Bulletin Board: (800) 423-8011
Information: (800) 635-6225

Dallas/Association of Desktop Publishers   This is a local user group.

> Dallas/Association of Desktop Publishers
> c/o Debbie Dickson
> Responsive Computer Systems
> Plano, TX
> (214) 423-5944

LaserStuff   LaserStuff is a monthly journal and bulletin board provided by Orbit Enterprises (a private business). It is an excellent source of free fonts, shareware utilities, and general information on LaserJet printers.

> Orbit Enterprises, Incorporated
> P.O. Box 2875
> Glen Ellyn, IL 60138
> Phone: (708) 469-3405/Bulletin Board: (708) 469-4850

Microsoft   For information on all Microsoft products, including the latest on Word for Windows, access CompuServe and type **GO MSOFT**.

> Bulletin Board: (800) 423-8011/Information: (800) 635-6225

National Association of Desktop Publishers   This is a non-commercial, independent desktop publishing organization. Membership benefits include six times/year *ADP Forum* (newsletter), quarterly NADP journal, on-line RoundTable on GEnie E-Mail network, and discounts on books.

> National Association of Desktop Publishers
> P.O. Box 508
> Kenmore Station
> Boston, MA 02215
> (617) 437-6472

New York Personal Computer User's Group This local user group has many monthly SIG (Special Interest Groups) meetings and a monthly newsletter. Often these are major (national scope) product announcements or issue discussions at the monthly general meeting.

NYPC
40 Wall Street, Suite 2124
New York, NY 10005-1301
(212) 533-NYPC

New York Professional PostScript Users Group, Incorporated
This is a local user group.

NYPPUG
3058 Ann Street
Baldwin, NY 11510
(212) 222-1220

PC Publisher Bulletin Board
Bulletin Board: (713) 448-9267
The Desktop Publisher Bulletin Board
Bulletin Board: (415) 856-2771

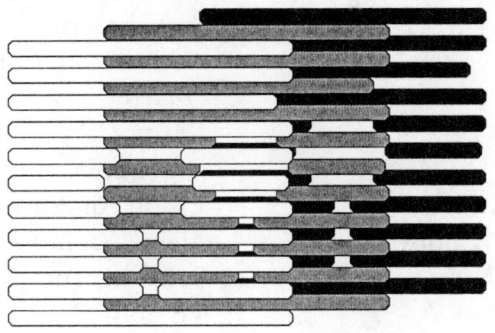

Trademarks

Adobe Illustrator®	Adobe Systems, Inc.
Adobe Streamliner™	Adobe Systems, Inc.
Adobe Type Manager™	Adobe Systems, Inc.
Allegro™	ALPS
AlphaJet™	Anacom General Corp.
APE™	HI-Q International Inc.
Bridge/286™	Softbridge Microsystems Corporation
Bridge/386™	Softbridge Microsystems Corporation
25 Cartridges in One™	Pacific Data Products
ClickArt® Series of Image Portfolios	T/Maker Company
Command Post™	Wilson WindowWare
CompuServe®	CompuServe, Inc.
Crosstalk® for Windows	Digital Communications Associates, Inc.

Custom Font® Cartridges	GNU Business Information Systems, Inc.
dBASE®	Ashton-Tate Corporation
DESQview® 386	Quarterdeck Office Systems
Diablo® 630	Xerox Corporation
Digi-Duit®	Digi-Fonts, Inc.
EPSON® FX™	Epson America, Inc.
FAXit™ for Windows	Alien™ Computing
Font Effects®	SoftCraft Inc.
FontGen V®	VS Software
FontMaker®	Good Software Corporation
FontSpace™	Isogon Corporation
GEnie™	General Electric Information Services
Glyphix™	SWFTE International, Ltd.
Headlines™	Pacific Data Products
hDC Color™	hDC Computer Corporation
hDC Windows Express™	hDC Computer Corporation
hDC Windows Manager™	hDC Computer Corporation
Hewlett-Packard®	Hewlett-Packard Company
HiJaak™	Inset Systems, Inc.
HotShot® Graphics	SymSoft Corp.
InSet®	Inset Systems, Inc.
Intel® 80286 microprocessor	Intel Corporation
Intel® 80386 microprocessor	Intel Corporation
Interfont™ Font Cartridges	Intercon Associates, Inc.
JetFont Superset®	Computer Peripherals, Inc.
JLaserPlus™	Tall Tree Systems
LaserJet™	Hewlett-Packard Company
LaserTwin™	Metro
LaserWriter®	Apple Computer, Inc.
Lotus® 1-2-3®	Lotus Development Corporation
Macintosh®	Apple Computer, Inc.
MCI® Mail™	MCI Communication Corporation
Mega-Font™	Advance Vision Research

Micrografx Designer™	Micrografx, Inc.
Micrografx Draw Plus™	Micrografx, Inc.
Micrografx Graph Plus™	Micrografx, Inc.
Microsoft® BASIC	Microsoft Corporation
Microsoft® Excel	Microsoft Corporation
Microsoft® OS/2	Microsoft Corporation
Microsoft® Windows	Microsoft Corporation
Microsoft® Word	Microsoft Corporation
Microsoft® Word for Windows	Microsoft Corporation
MoreFonts®	MicroLogic Software
MSD Edit™	Mephistopheles Systems
MSDmanager™	Mephistopheles Systems
MS-DOS®	Microsoft Corporation
MSDprn™	Mephistopheles Systems
New Wave™	Hewlett-Packard Company
OmniKey/PLUS™	Northgate
Opus I™	Roykore Software, Inc.
Pacific Page™	Pacific Data Products
PageMaker®	Aldus Corporation
Paradox®	Borland International, Inc.
PC Metafont™	Personal Tex, Inc.
PC MOS™	The Software Link
PC Paintbrush®	Z-Soft Corporation
Picture Publisher®	Astral Development Corporation
Pixie™	Zenographics
Polaris PackRat™	Polaris Software
Postscript®	Adobe Systems Incorporated
Presentation Manager™	International Business Machines, Inc.
Procollection™ Font Cartridges	Hewlett-Packard Company
Profont Editing System™	FontCenter
ProKey™	RoseSoft, Inc.
PS Jet® Plus	The Laser Connection, Inc.
PS/2®	International Business Machines, Inc.
Publisher's PowerPak™	Atech Softwarete

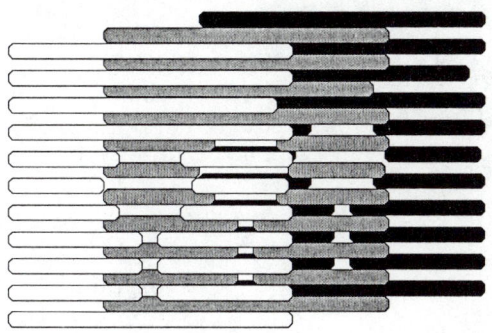

Index

A

Absolute Positioned Object
   (APO), 217-218
ADDPATH.NEW, 530
Address labels, 413, 418-420
Adobe
      Illustrator, 217
      Type Manager, 489
Aldus PageMaker, 423-424,
   445-450
ALT-key. *See* Keystroke
   combinations
Annotations, 242, 356-379. *See*
   View Annotations
      incorporating, 367-379

Annotations, *Continued*
      locking, 356, 362-363
      marking, 363, 368
      pane, 242, 356-357,
         363-374, 466
      printing, 242, 368
Apple, 8
      Macintosh, 489
ASCII, 120, 187, 212, 407, 410,
   412-414, 475-476, 517
      character set, 549-550
Ashton Tate dBASE, 414
Auto Update link, 494-497. *See
   also* Edit Paste Link
AUTOEXEC.BAT, 7, 225, 474,
   517, 520, 529-530
Autosave, 44-45

B

Backup devices, 508-509
Baseline position, 84
BASIC, 250, 277, 295
Bezier splines, 442
Bibliographies, 460-462
Bitmap images. *See* Paint
   software
Bitstream
      character set, 555-557
      fontware, 449
Blocking off text, 66, 74-75
Boilerplate text, 164, 186-189,
   250, 256-258, 417
Bold, 73, 77, 398, 458, 463
Bookmark, 37, 298, 366-367,
   390-392, 402-403
      page number ranges,
         398-400
Books, 574-576
Border control arrows, 25
Borland Paradox, 414
Bullets, 458-460
Bus, 504-506. *See also* CPU
      bus-mastering boards, 505

C

Cable, 518
CAD (Computer Aided Design),
   497-498
Calculations. *See* Equations, Math
   functions
Cells, 120
Change bar, 375-380
Character. *See* Format Character
Character sets, 455
Character spacing. *See*
   Letterspacing

Check boxes. *See* Dialog boxes,
   toggle boxes
Clip art, 148, 226, 439-440,
   442-444
Clipboard, 29-30, 36-37,
   117-120, 143-148, 160, 382,
   395, 405, 406, 444, 488,
   493-497
Collapsed heads and text,
   305-331
Color, 80-81
Columns, 104-105, 178-179,
   423-424, 445, 469-472
      lines between, 470-471
      side-by-side, 469-472
      snaking, 220, 469-472
      tabular, 469-472
Comma delimited, 118, 122-123,
   138-143, 290, 293, 330, 414
COMP, 508
Compound document, 5-6
CompuServe, 412
Computer Aided Design (CAD),
   497-498
Computer Support Corporation
   Arts & Letters, 217, 497-498
Conditional statements, 390-391
CONFIG.SYS, 517, 520
Control button, 10, 417, 433
Control characters, 407
Control menu, 10-11, 27-32, 206
      Minimize, 28
      Move, 28, 434
      Restore, 28, 31, 434
      Run, 29
      Split, 31-33, 357, 384
Control Panel (CONTROL.EXE),
   29-30, 224, 227-236, 247, 473,
   475, 479, 529
Conventional memory, 483-484
Conversions. *See* File importation
Copy, 25, 210, 424, 445-446, 450

Corel Draw!, 226
CPU (8086, 80286, 80386), 7, 483, 503-506
Cropping images, 151-154, 160, 226
    sizing handles, 152
CTRL-key. *See* Keystroke combinations

D

Daisy wheel printers, 418
Dashes. *See* Em dash, En dash
Database, 382, 391, 406, 413, 415, 544
Data document, 251, 290-302, 413-420
    header fields, 417
    missing fields, 420
Data recovery, 474, 498-500
Date, 467-468
DDE. *See* Microsoft Windows
Desktop publishing, 59, 101-102, 209-210, 213-214, 355, 423-424, 434, 445-450, 455
    service bureaus 445-472
Dialog boxes, 6, 16-17, 49-57, 67-73
    buttons, 55-57, 72
    option fields, 67-69
    scroll bar, 70
    scroll boxes, 51
    scroll-down boxes, 52-54, 69-71
    tabbing between options, 68-69
    text entry fields, 49-52, 68 (Illustration)
    toggle boxes, 55-57, 71-72
    user-definable option fields, 68, 73

Dictionaries, 426
    adding words, 427
    custom dictionaries, 428
Dingbats, 458-460
Disk cache, 430, 484-488. *See also* Microsoft Windows SMART-Drive, Multisys Super PC-Kwik
DLL. *See* Microsoft Windows
Document summary. *See* Edit Summary Info
Document template, 61, 160, 163-208, 242, 249, 280, 379, 419
    merge, 164
    Normal. *See* NORMAL.DOT
    summary, 191-193
Document window, 27 (Figure 1-9), 207, 369-374, 417
DOCUMENT1.DOC, 47
DOS, 9, 212, 506-507
Dot matrix printers, 384, 387, 418, 439, 455
Double clicking, 15, 24
Double underline, 77
Draft View. *See* View Draft
Dragging with mouse, 74, 434, 443
Draw software, 118, 144, 216, 438, 442-445, 541-543
Dynamic Data Exchange (DDE). *See* Microsoft Windows
Dynamic Link Libraries (DLL). *See* Microsoft Windows

E

Edit, 35-38, 119
    Copy, 36, 119, 143, 146-147, 405, 444-445, 488, 493-497
    Cut, 36, 119, 147

Edit, *continued*
  Glossary, 37, 251-255
  Go To, 37, 42, 358-359,
    366-372
  Header/Footer, 37, 462,
    465-469
  Paste, 25, 36, 119, 147,
    158, 444, 488
  Paste Link, 36, 155, 159,
    391, 413, 474, 488,
    494-497
  Renumber, 304
  Repeat, 35-36
  Replace, 37, 341-345
  Search, 36-37, 341-345
  Summary Info, 241-242,
    247, 274, 360-361, 403,
    468
  Table, 38, 134-137
  Undo, 35, 123
EISA. *See* Bus
Electronic Mail (E-Mail), 360,
  363, 412
Elite, 455
Em dash, 458, 461-462
En dash, 458, 461-462
Epson FX, 225, 514
Equations, 381-382, 389-395
Error message, 248
Expanded and extended
  memory, 483-488, 507
Expanded heads and text,
  305-331
Exponents, 383, 387
Exportation, *See* File exportation
Extend cursor key (F8), 23, 74
Extended Industry Standard
  Architecture (EISA). *See* Bus

F

Facing pages, 112 (Figure 2-7)

Field characters, 258-259, 270,
  416
Field update key (F9), 274-276,
  403
Fields, 250, 258-276
  average (AVERAGE), 392
  date (DATE), 467-468
  date-time picture options,
    270
  Equations (=), 383-384,
    387
  general options, 266,
    269-270
  Index (INDEX). *See* Insert
    Index
  locking, 275-276
  nesting, 275-276
  numeric picture options,
    268
  page number, 467-468
  reference documents (RD),
    404
  sequence, 350-352
  table of contents, 344-352,
    397, 402, 404
  time (TIME), 467-468
  view toggle key, 273-274
  XE. *See* Insert Index Entry
File, 16, 32-34, 224
  Close, 32
  Find, 191
  New, 32, 155, 187-189,
    207, 404, 418
  Open, 32, 145, 372,
    408-409, 415, 475, 479,
    524
  Print. *See* Printing
  Print Merge. *See* Printing,
    Print Merge
  Print Preview. *See* Printing,
    Print Preview
  Printer Setup, 235-239

File, *continued*
    Save, 33
    Save All, 34
    Save As, 33, 189-190, 362,
        411-412, 415. 489
File exportation, 411-412
File importation, 381, 406-415,
  488-491, 523
File management, 534-538
File name extensions
    *.BIFF, 411-412
    *.DIC, 429
    *.DLL, 490-491
    *.DOC, 407-408, 475, 491,
      517
    *.DOT, 184
    *.DRV, 527
    *.DRW, 498, 525
    *.EPS, 440, 442
    *.EXE, 488
    *.MSP, 444
    *.PCL, 498
    *.PCX, 440, 444, 498, 525
    *.PIC, 525
    *.RTF, 413
    *.SCD, 226
    *.STY, 411 (Illustration)
    *.TIF, 149-150, 440, 525
    *.TMP, 474, 498-500
    *.TXT, 498-500
    *.WS, 408
File server, 379
Floppy disk, 363, 508-509
Flush left. *See* Ragged right
Flush right. *See* Ragged left
Fonts, 78-80, 209, 213-214, 222,
  226, 237-239, 424, 446. *See also*
  Linespacing, Letterspacing
    baseline, 453 (Figure 10-7)
    cartridge, 237
    downloading, 484
    editing, 564-566

Fonts, *continued*
    installation, 529
    management, 566-567
    special effects, 567-568
    typeface outlines, 489
    vendors, 558-564
Footers. *See* Edit Header/Footer
Footnotes, 105, 111-114,
  331-335. *See also* Insert
  Footnote, View Footnotes
    pane, 333, 466
    reference mark, 331
    separator, 331
Foreign language characters, 455
Form letters. *See* Printing, Print
  Merge
Format, 42, 61-63, 75-116
    Character, 39, 53-57,
      73-74, 76-88, 196, 204,
      222, 361, 458
    Define Styles, 165-186, 242
    Document, 6, 109-116, 179
    Paragraph, 39, 88-109,
      172, 196, 453, 463
    Picture, 153-154, 160
    Position, 176-181, 196
    Section, 100-109, 462-465,
      470
    Styles, 194-196, 242
    Table, 200
    Tabs, 172-176, 200
Formulas, 381-389
Freezing. *See* Data recovery
Futura, 456

G

GEnie, 412
Ghosted commands, 67, 123
Glossaries, 163-164, 186-189,
  194, 242-243, 250-255, 382,
  396-405

Graphic images, 117-118,
212-214, 219, 226, 243, 406,
424, 438-445, 469-472
importation filters, 525
Graphical User Interface (GUI),
6-26, 212, 473
Gray scale, 150, 440
dithering, 441
Gutters, 111

H

Hard disk, 379, 430, 486-487,
503, 508-509, 522
controller cards, 509
Hayes Smartmodem, 518
Heads and text, expanded,
305-331
Headers, 424. *See also* Edit
Header/Footer
Help, 47-48
About, 486
Active Window, 48
Index, 47
Keyboard, 47-48
Helvetica, 454-456, 463, 492
Hidden text, 77, 82, 365, 447
HPGL, 225
HP LaserJet, 225, 236-239, 246,
449, 489, 514-515, 527, 529
add-in boards, 547-548
manual paper feed, 237,
246
HP Roman-8 character set, 550,
552
Hyphenation. *See* Utilities
Hyphenate
Hot zone, 435-437
nonbreaking, optional,
regular hyphens,
437-438, 447

I

IBM graphics, 225
IBM PC (including XT, AT,
PS/2), 7, 212, 483-488, 503-509
character set, 550-551
Icons
program 15, 18, 31, 147,
158, 288, 493
windows 7, 12, 14
Images. *See* Graphic images
Importing files. *See* File
importation
Indents, 90-91
Indices, 381, 396-404. *See also*
Insert Index, Insert Index
Entry, Fields
run-in index, 401
Initial Caps, 427, 458
Inkjet printers, 418, 514
Insert, 40-42, 120
Annotation, 42
Break, 41, 335-339, 464,
470
Bookmark, 41, 357-359,
392, 398
Field, 40, 42, 259-270, 276,
383-394, 404
File, 41
Footnote, 41, 331-335
Index (INDEX), 382,
396-404
Index Entry (XE), 42, 382,
396-404
Page Numbers, 41
Picture 148-151, 223, 444,
472, 525
Table, 41, 120-124,
138-143
Table of Contents, 42,
339-352

Inset, 472
Inset Systems HiJaak, 497-498
Installation printer, 223-226,
    228-234
Italic, 77, 398, 458

J

Journals, 570-574
Justification, 89-90, 434, 455-456

K

Keeping paragraphs together,
    93-94
Kerning, 85-86, 210, 455-456
Key words, 403
Keyboards, 515-516
Keystroke combinations, 10-11,
    62, 64-67, 243

L

LAN (Local Area Network), 356,
    379-380
Landscape, 237
Laser printers, 384, 418, 439,
    455
LaserJet. *See* HP LaserJet
Leading. *See* Linespacing
Legal numbering, 322
Letterspacing, 85-86, 455-457
    condensed, 85, 456-457
    expanded, 85, 456-457
Levels of gray. *See* Gray scale
Line art, 442
Line Numbering, 98-99,
    103-107, 304, 320-331,
    335-339
Linespacing, 84, 95, 451-455
LINK, 488

Local Area Network (LAN), 356,
    379-380
Logos, 442
Long Documents, 403-404
Lotus 1-2-3, 120, 414, 525
Lowercase, 466
LPT1. *See* Ports

M

Macros, 45-46, 163, 186-189,
    194, 250, 276-302
    AppMinimize, 283
    Assign to Key, 45, 243,
        282-284
    Assign to Menu, 46,
        284-286
    AutoClose, AutoExec,
        AutoNew, AutoOpen,
        278-279
    Edit, 45, 251, 286-302
    Record, 45, 250, 279-281
    Run, 281-282
    Stop Recorder, 45
Magazines. *See* Journals
Mail merge. *See* Printing, Print
    Merge
Main document, 414
    header fields, 414, 419
Math functions, 389-396
Math symbols, 383
Maximize, 12-14
MCI Mail, 412
Measure. *See* Units
Memory. *See also* RAM
    conventional, 483-484
    expanded and extended,
        483-488, 507
    management, 534-538
Memory resident programs, 430

Menu Bar, 9 (Figure 1-1), 16, 26-27
Microchannel Architecture (MCA). *See* Bus
Micrografx Designer, 217, 226, 444-445, 497-498, 525
Micrografx Draw, 442
Microlytic spell checker, 425
Microrim Rbase, 414
Microsoft Excel, 120, 154-161, 391-404, 412-414, 488, 492-497
Microsoft Technical Support Line, 528
Microsoft Windows
   disk space, 486-488
   Dynamic Data Exchange (DDE), 119, 154-155, 159, 391, 413, 474, 492
   Dynamic Link Libraries (DLL), 407-415, 488-491
   HIMEM.SYS, 485
   Import filters, 407-415
   MEMSET, 485, 530
   message box, 298
   MS-DOS Executive, 9-27, 29-30, 34, 227, 233, 235, 239, 247, 430, 473, 477, 486-487, 498
   Paint, 143, 145, 147
   run-time version, 519-531
   setup problems, 485
   SMARTDrive, 482-488, 530
   spooler, 477, 482-483
   swapping data to hard disk, 485-487, 507
Minimize, 12-14, 147, 158, 288, 493
Modem, 450, 517-518

Monitor, 503, 512-513, 520-521
   glare and radiation shields, 512-513
Monospace, 455
Mouse, 22-25, 50-51, 56, 65-67, 129-133, 217, 318-320, 477-479, 516-517
   manual input devices, 545-546
Multisoft Super PC-Kwik, 482, 486-487
Multitasking, 15, 484-488

N

Network, 356, 379-380, 430
New York Times, 455
Newsletters, 423
Next pane key (F6), 369, 384
Nodes, 152, 217, 442
NORMAL.DOT, 114-115, 165-166, 187-194, 202, 255, 257, 284, 287, 294, 307, 379
Normal editing view, 210-213, 215-216, 219, 221-222, 258, 304, 308, 326, 331, 335, 339, 344-352, 366, 384, 425, 470
Numbering heads, 320-331

O

Object images. *See* Draw software
OS/2, 8
Outdents, 90, 460-462. *See also* Tabs
Outline symbol, 318
Outline View. *See* View Outline
OUTPUT.PRN, 498. *See also* Printing to a file
Overtype (INS key), 39

P

Page break, 97-98, 399
Page Description Language
  (PDL), 225-226, 231-233
Page layout, 214
Page margins, 110-111
Page numbers, 265, 398, 462,
  467-468
      range, 398-399, 462. *See
      also* Bookmark
Page View. *See* View Page
Pagination, 398, 430
Paint software, 118, 438-441,
  443-444, 541-543
Panes, 31, 242, 384, 387, 464
Paper size, 68, 109-110, 237
Paragraph. *See* Format
  Paragraph
Paragraph borders and boxes,
  96-97, 222
Paragraphs, keeping together,
  93-94
Parenthetical phrases, 461-462
PARC Interface, 8
Paste. *See* Edit Paste
Paste Link. *See* Edit Paste Link
PATH, 7, 408, 529-530
PCL, 225, 231-233, 383, 489,
  527, 529
PDL, 225-226, 231-233
Photographs, 440-441, 444, 449,
  472
Pica, 455
Pictures. *See* Graphic images
Personal Information Manager
  (PIM), 497
Pixel editing, 439. *See also* Paint
  software
Points, 83
Polaris Pack Rat, 488, 492, 497

Portrait, 237
Ports
      LPT1, 232-233, 479
      COM1, 232-233
Positioning text, 176-181
PostScript, 78, 225, 232, 383,
  440, 449, 479, 489, 514-515,
  527, 529
Precision Software Superbase 2,
  413-414, 488, 492, 497
Presentation documents,
  423-424, 448
Presentation graphics, 226, 440,
  541-543
Printers, 513-515
Printing, 211, 240-248, 417-418
      Annotations, 242, 368
      Drafts, 245
      Field Codes, 247
      to a file, 497-498
      Glossaries, 242-243
      Key Assignments, 243
      Print Merge, 34, 239, 277,
      406, 413, 415-420
      Print Preview, 34, 181,
      210-219, 335, 425, 470
      Reverse Order, 245
      Spooler, 247
      Styles, 242
      Summary Info, 241-242,
      247
Program icons. *See* Icons
Proofs. *See* Copy

Q

Quadratic formula, 386
Qualitas 386-to-the-Max, 485
Quarterdeck DESQview 386,
  486-487
Quarterdeck QEMM, 485-486

R

Ragged left, 89, 434-438, 456
Ragged right, 89, 434-438, 456
RAM, 26, 118-119, 483-489, 507, 530. *See also* Expanded and extended memory, Conventional memory
Read only, 415
README.DOC, 520-521
Redlining, 375-380
Reference Documents (RD), 404
Regular link, 494-497. *See also* Edit Paste Link
RENAME, 499
Renumbering. *See* Utilities Renumber
Repeated words, 427
Replace. *See* Edit Replace
Restore, 12-14
Revision bar, 377-378
Revision marks, 372-380
Ribbon, 86, 164-165, 202-208
Royal, 489
Ruler, 165, 197-202, 205-208
    Column view, 202
    Margin view, 201
    Paragraph view, 202

S

Sanserif, 455-458, 462, 492
Scaling images, 439, 442-444
Scanning, 118, 150, 439-441, 444, 546-547
Screen colors, 479
Screen fonts, 212, 222, 473, 489, 491-492
Scroll bar, 25
Search. *See* Edit Search
Section. *See* Format Section, Insert Break

Section, *continued*
    break, 463-465
    vertical alignment, 464
Selection bar, 23
Serif, 454-455
Setting up Word for Windows, 519-531
SHEET1.XLS, 494-497
SHIFT-key. *See* Keystroke combinations
Show All, 204, 316, 340
Sidehead, 111
Sizing. *See* Scaling images
Slides (35 mm), 226
Small Caps (Small Kaps), 77, 81, 458
SoftCraft WYSIfonts, 491
Special marks, 204, 445-448. *See also* View Preferences
Speed Formatting
    character, 86-88
    paragraph, 100-101
Speed of operation, 425, 430
Spell checker. *See also* Utilities Spell Checker
    one word, 428
    optimizing, 430
    options, 429-430
Spell checker dictionaries. *See* Dictionaries
Spike glossary, 382, 405-406
SPOOLER.EXE, 482. *See also* Microsoft Windows, WIN.INI
Spreadsheet, 154-161, 382, 391, 413-415, 492-497, 543-544
Square root sign (radical), 383-387
Subscripts, 84
Summary Information. *See* Edit Summary Info
Superscripts, 84, 387
Status bar. *See* View Status Bar

STDUSER.DIC, 428-429
Strike-through, 376
Style name area, 196-197, 430
Styles, 91-93, 160, 163-187, 194, 242, 445. *See also* Format Styles, Format Define Styles
    character, 165-172
    defining, 165-186
    heading, 91-92, 167-172, 305-314, 339-351
    merging, 184-185, 189
    Next Style, 182-186
    Normal, 167-172, 181-183, 199
    paragraph, 172
    tabs, 172-176
Stylesheet, 411
Symbols, 459-460
Synonyms. *See* Utilities Thesaurus

T

Table, 220, 291
    add cells, 133
    deleting, inserting, merging cells, 134-137
    end-of-cell marker, 448
    end-of-line marker, 448
    mouse, 129-133
    moving between borders, 125-127
    moving between cells, 123-124, 128-129, 133-134, 140
    pasting (regular or DDE paste link), 494-497. *See also* Edit Paste
Table of contents, 339-352, 397
    entries (TC), 304, 344-352, 397

Table of contents, *continued*
    table of . . . listings, 347-351
Tables, 118, 120, 213-214, *See also* Format Table, Insert
Tabs, 109-110
    delimited 118, 122-123, 138-143, 290, 293, 330, 414
    setting, 172-176, 200-202
    stops, 460-462
Task switching, 484-488
Technical Support, 528
Text and heads, expanded, 305-331
Thesaurus. *See* Utilities Thesaurus
Time, 467-468
Times Roman, 454-455, 463, 492
Title bar, 9 (Figure 1-1), 12, 434
Title pages, 463-465
T/Maker ClickArt, 144, 440, 498
Typesetting. *See* Desktop publishing service bureaus
Typography, 423. *See also* Fonts

U

Units, 41, 90, 451-452
Underline, 77, 82
Update fields key, 274-276, 361
Uppercase, 427, 458, 466
User groups, 576-578
Utilities, 43-45
    calculate, 43, 394-396
    Compare Versions, 44, 357, 372-380
    Customize, 44, 192, 362-363, 451
    Hyphenate, 424, 434-438

Utilities, *continued*
    Renumber, 323-331
    Repaginate Now, 44
    Revision Marks, 44
    sort, 43, 326-331
    spell checker, 43, 423-430
    thesaurus, 43, 423-424,
       430-434
Utility software, 538-540

V

Ventura character set, 550, 554
Vertical positioning of sections,
  107-108
View, 35-37
    Annotations, 40, 363,
      366-374. *See* Annotations
    Draft, 35, 211, 221-223,
      335, 425, 430
    Field Codes, 40, 361, 384,
      387, 394, 419
    Footnotes, 40, 331-335
    Full Menus, 40, 64, 425
    Outline, 35, 211, 304-331,
      335, 339-352, 425
    Page, 35, 211-212,
      219-221, 425, 449, 470
    Preferences, 196-197, 204,
      430
    Ribbon, 35, 202-208, 430
    Ruler, 35, 197-202,
      205-208, 472
    Short Menus, 40, 64, 425
    Status Bar, 39, 123, 206,
      411, 430

W

Wide Area Network (WAN), 356,
  379-380
Widows, 115
Window, 46-47
    Arrange All, 46, 298-299,
      373
    New Window, 46
Window sizing arrow, 12, 15, 17
Windows/ANSI character set,
  213, 238, 549
WIN.INI, 225, 230, 410, 412,
  474-498, 524, 549
    comments, 477-491
    sections, 477-491
WINWORD.EXE, 21, 523
WINWORD.INI, 115, 379
Word processing, 59, 64, 209,
  213-214, 342, 355, 382,
  406-407, 424, 446
Word publishing, 5, 59, 64, 209,
  213-214, 342, 423-424
Word underline, 77
WordPerfect, 210
WYSIWYG, 38, 212, 221

X

XE. *See* Insert Index Entry
Xerox Diablo 630, 225, 513
Xerox Ventura Publisher,
  423-424, 445-450

Z

Zapf Dingbats, 458, 550
ZSoft, 525

The manuscript for this book was prepared and submitted to Osborne/McGraw-Hill in electronic form. The acquisitions editor for this project was Elizabeth Fisher and the technical reviewer was Harriet Serenkin.

Text design by Marcela Hancik, using Baskerville for text body and Swiss boldface for display.

Cover art by Bay Graphics Design, Inc. Color separation and cover supplier, Phoenix Color Corporation. Screens produced with HotShot, from SymSoft Corp. Book printed and bound by R.R. Donnelley & Sons Company, Crawfordsville, Indiana.

Word for Windows Default Menus

Word for Windows Control Menu
Restore	Alt+F5
Move	Alt+F7
Size	Alt+F8
Minimize	Alt+F9
Maximize	Alt+F10
Close	Alt+F4

Document Control Menu
Restore	Ctrl+F5
Move	Ctrl+F7
Size	Ctrl+F8
Maximize	Ctrl+F10
Close	Ctrl+F4
Split	

File
New...	
Open...	Ctrl+F12
Close	
Save	Shift+F12
Save As...	F12
Save All	
Find...	
Print...	Ctrl+Shift+F12
Print Preview	
Print Merge...	
Printer Setup...	
Exit	
1 C:\WINWORD\ARTICLE.DOC	
2 TABLE.DOC	
3 C:\WINWORD\DOCDOC.DOC	

Edit
Can't Undo	Alt+BkSp
Can't Repeat	F4
Cut	Shift+Del
Copy	Ctrl+Ins
Paste	Shift+Ins
Paste Link...	
Search...	
Replace...	
Go To...	F5
Header/Footer...	
Summary Info...	
Glossary...	
Table...	

View
Outline	
√Draft	
Page	
Ribbon	
Ruler	
√Status Bar	
Footnotes	
Annotations	
Field Codes	
Preferences...	
Short Menus	

Insert
Break...
Footnote...
File... Ctrl+Shift+F5
Bookmark...
Page Numbers...
Table...
Annotation
Picture...
Field...
Index Entry...
Index...
Table of Contents...

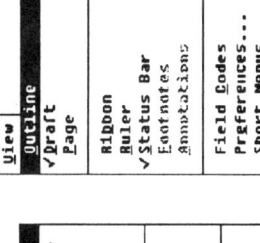

Format
Character...	
Paragraph...	
Section...	
Document...	
Tabs...	
Styles...	Ctrl+S
Position...	
Define Styles...	
Picture...	
Table...	

Utilities
Spelling...	Shift+F7
Thesaurus...	
Hyphenate...	
Renumber...	
Revision Marks...	
Compare Versions...	
Sort...	
Calculate	
Repaginate Now	
Customize...	

Macro
Record...
Run...
Edit...
Assign to Key...
Assign to Menu...

Window
New Window
Arrange All
√1 Document1

Help
Index
Keyboard
Active Window
Tutorial
Using Help
About...

Using Microsoft Word for Windows